A FRESH APPROACH TO OB

designed to teach students to think critically and develop their management skills with hands-on applications and exercises

1. **Critical-thinking approach equips** students with the mindset and skills needed to thrive in today's complex organizations.
2. Unique, continuing **case study narratives** inspired by real people and real events illustrate OB concepts and critical thinking in action, showing students why OB matters and how OB topics fit together.
3. Numerous **hands-on, experiential exercises, self-assessments, case studies, and online multimedia resources** appeal to a variety of learning styles and allow students to experience OB.

PRAISE FOR ORGANIZATIONAL BEHAVIOR: A CRITICAL-THINKING APPROACH

"**Organizational Behavior: A Critical-Thinking Approach** will clear your head of the cobwebs as you engage your brain skills in multiple critical-thinking exercises."

—JANICE S. GATES, WESTERN ILLINOIS UNIVERSITY

"This text provides a unique view of organizational behavior and how organizational behavior can be applied in modern organizational settings."

—JACKIE MAYFIELD, TEXAS A&M INTERNATIONAL UNIVERSITY

"I don't usually get excited about changing textbooks, but this book has real potential."

—HARRIET L. ROJAS, INDIANA WESLEYAN UNIVERSITY

CASE STUDY NARRATIVES

"I like the extended narratives running through the chapters. They provide solid real-life examples of how the theory plays out in practice. Stories are memorable and will help students remember and associate concepts."

—MARLA LOWENTHAL, UNIVERSITY OF SAN FRANCISCO

"This text is current and has all the theory and practical applications that we need to teach OB and prepare our students for the world of work. These extended narratives are very useful in linking together the concepts in adjacent chapters to real-world situations."

—WARREN MATTHEWS, LETOURNEAU UNIVERSITY

FRESH APPROACH TO OB

"Students enjoy stories and the narrative approach of this text is a refreshing change to often dry OB textbooks."

—TRACY H. PORTER, CLEVELAND STATE UNIVERSITY

"A unique approach to OB that emphasizes practical, hands-on information based on a solid theoretical foundation."

—SAMIRA B. HUSSEIN, JOHNSON COUNTY COMMUNITY COLLEGE

REACHES TODAY'S STUDENTS

"Carefully thought out, well researched, and invitingly pleasant to read."

—DANIEL S. MARRONE, FARMINGDALE STATE COLLEGE

"This is a very readable text suited for any graduate or undergraduate student. It contains real-life examples that make the concepts understandable and explainable."

—ROBERT D. GULBRO, FLORIDA INSTITUTE OF TECHNOLOGY

HELP YOUR STUDENTS THINK CRITICALLY...

THINKING CRITICALLY questions tied to Bloom's Taxonomy challenge students to achieve higher levels of learning.

THINKING CRITICALLY

1. Choose one of the perceptual distortions discussed (stereotypes, selective attention, halo effect, primary effect, recency effect, contrast effect, project, self-fulfilling prophecy, and impression management) and briefly describe a situation where your perception of another person was impacted by that distortion. **[Understand/ Apply]**
2. What do you think are the top three perceptual distortions that managers are most likely to be affected by when forming perceptions of their direct reports? Explain your answer. **[Apply/Analyze]**
3. What do you think are the top three perceptual distortions that employees are most likely to be affected by when forming perceptions of a new manager? Defend your answer. **[Apply/ Analyze]**

THINKING CRITICALLY ABOUT THE CASE OF LAURA PIERCE

Put yourself in Laura Pierce's position as a new employee at WTRT and apply the Five-Step Critical-Thinking Framework introduced in Chapter 1 in relation to diversity and individual differences within the theatre company.

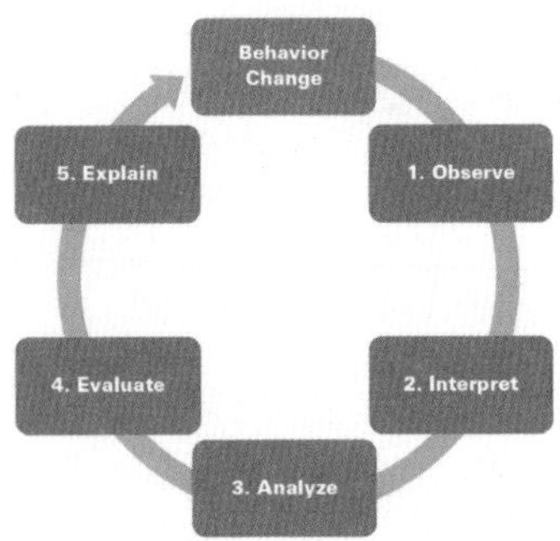

OBSERVE

What cultural and background differences do you observe among the existing staff (Abigail, Tony, Cheryl, and Joey) based on the chapter's descriptions of these characters and Laura's first-day interactions with them? How does Laura's culture and background compare to the others?

What individual differences do you observe among the existing staff and Laura? List at least 3 individual differences for each character.

INTERPRET

Based on the diversity and range of individual differences among the characters as well as the description of Laura's first day, what types of conflicts is Laura likely to encounter at WTRT? What conflicts is Laura likely to cause as she tries to do her job?

ANALYZE

Laura seems to have managed to keep an optimistic perspective on the challenges her new job will bring, but provide your own analysis of ways she may be able to forge positive relationships with her new boss and coworkers despite her differences with them.

EVALUATE

Evaluate which colleagues Laura should approach first as she begins her work at WTRT. What are three things she could do to learn more about her job and have a chance to interact with her colleagues? What potential problems could arise as Laura begins to reach out to her coworkers in order to learn more about the organization in which she is working?

EXPLAIN

Choose the first action you listed above and explain how you, as Laura, would approach accomplishing this task. If a problem arose, explain how you would attempt to handle it.

THINKING CRITICALLY ABOUT THE CASE requires students to apply the 5-step critical thinking framework to the chapter case narrative.

> "New twist on old subjects with a very strong emphasis on critical-thinking skills that are needed in today's work world."
>
> —HERBERT SHERMAN, LIU-BROOKLYN

EXPERIENTIAL EXERCISES provide hands-on activities that allow students to experience OB firsthand and develop their OB skills.

EXERCISE 5.3: YOUR MOTIVATION FOR SELECTING YOUR MAJOR

Objective:

This exercise will help you develop your ability to *explain* the basic motivation process, *compare* the different needs motivation theories, and *select* a needs motivation theory that is most useful in understanding situations.

Instructions:

This exercise will help you to apply chapter concepts for analyzing your decisions, and give you a foundation to make choices that are more likely to fulfill your expectations. In this exercise, you will be applying decision-making models and concepts that you have learned in this chapter to better analyze the process of selecting a major.

Step 1. Select a partner for the exercise. Ideally this person should be someone who you do not know well or work with on a regular basis. The person who has had a birthday most recently will take the role of the *teller* and the other person will be the *analyzer*. Both partners will have a chance to play each role. Introduce yourselves to each other, and tell each other your majors. (5 minutes)

Step 2. The *teller* should tell the process by which he or she chose a major. The *teller* should be as explicit as possible about this decision making process. It may be that the decision about a major was not a direct decision about a major—the person may have been following the advice of a parent or older sibling. If this is the case, then the decision to be analyzed is why the person chose to follow someone else's advice on major selection. (10 to 15 minutes)

The *analyzer* should restate the major selection in terms of chapter concepts. Specifically, select one of the chapter needs theories, and describe the *teller's* needs in terms of the theory. Once you and the *teller* agree on the needs, describe the selection process based on *the motivation process* model.

Step 3. Switch roles and repeat step 2. (10 to 15 minutes)

Step 4. Be prepared to report your analyses to the class. (10 to 20 minutes)

Reflection Questions:

1. How conscious and rational was your major selection?
2. Does your major selection meet the needs identified in this exercise?
3. After examining your major selection choice using chapter concepts, do you see any way to improve future decision processes to better meet your needs?
4. How could you apply this process to selecting a career or new job?

Exercise contributed by Milton R. Mayfield, Professor of Business, Texas A&M International University and Jaqueline R. Mayfield, Professor of Business, Texas A&M International University.

> "A new innovative approach to Organizational Behavior that challenges students to think critically by integrating the workplace into the classroom."
>
> —ANDREA E. SMITH-HUNTER, SIENA COLLEGE

OB IN THE REAL WORLD

boxes include real-life examples from seasoned business professionals who describe how they have used OB concepts to achieve organizational success.

STUART MEASE, *Director of Undergraduate Career Services, Virginia Tech.*

OB in the Real World

© Stuart Mease

As director of Undergraduate Career Services for the Pamplin College of Business at Virginia Tech for several years, Stuart Mease has been connecting employers with college students who are looking for jobs after graduation. He is proactive in his approach and welcomes metrics and accountability. He actively seeks to engage employers in new and innovative ways so they feel invested in the students at Virginia Tech. One of his most ...increase the diversity of the student ... employers' request. Stuart's team ...s with a two-page strategy document

thinking time will make something go away. I'm more comfortable dealing with the consequences than letting something sit there. If you make a bad decision, how do you make up for it? 'Fess up to it. Hey it's my fault I made a bad decision. If you make a good decision you want to be applauded for what you did. If you make a bad decision you have to be willing to step up and admit to doing a wrong.

Stuart also tells students that it's up to them to decide the nature of their ethics and values and to check them against the decisions they make. "For example," Stuart says,

> if the university system says that when you go out of town for two days you are allowed a $75 per diem, how you spend that money is up to you. However, let's say I go on business and every single one of my meals is paid for by an employer. To me, I don't feel comfortable taking the $75 because it was really meant to cover my expenses and I didn't have any. Sure, if I took that per diem someone can

SNAKES, SELF-EFFICACY, AND TASK PERFORMANCE

Too Much of a Good Thing?

Examining the Evidence

Some very interesting early classic studies examining the concept of self-efficacy focused on people with a fear of snakes.* Albert Bandura and his colleagues set up an experiment using both an experimental group and a control group, with a pre-test indicating that both groups had strong fear of snakes and low self-efficacy for approaching and handling them. The researchers then carried out an intervention with the experimental group. They explained that the snakes were not poisonous and would not bite, and they described how the snakes would react when the subjects handled them. They also informed the group that the snakes were not cold and slimy, but actually dry and scaly. The researchers then measured the fear and self-efficacy levels in both groups again. Both groups still had a high fear of snakes, but the experimental group had a much higher level of self-efficacy for approaching and handing the snakes. Consequently, when members of both groups were asked to approach and handle the snakes, those from the experimental group whose level of self-efficacy had increased were able to do so at a much higher rate than those with low self-efficacy.

Although hundreds of studies have shown similar positive effects for self-efficacy on task performance, some recent studies have called this relationship into question.# These studies suggest that high levels of self-efficacy within an individual could cause that person to become overconfident and to allocate fewer resources and less effort to the task at hand, thereby resulting in lower levels of task performance. For example, one study of students playing an analytical game showed a negative relationship between self-efficacy and performance.[42] Self-efficacy resulted in overconfidence and the increased likelihood of making a logical error in the game.

Critical Thinking Questions:

1. **Given the conflicting research evidence, how can self-efficacy affect individual task performance in the workplace?**
2. **What can managers do to try to enhance the positive effects of self-efficacy in their employees?**

SOURCES

*Bandura, Albert, and Nancy E. Adams. "Analysis of Self-Efficacy Theory of Behavioral Change." *Cognitive Therapy and Research* 1, no. 4 (December 1977): 287–310; Bandura, Albert, Linda Reese, and Nancy E. Adams. "Microanalysis of Action and Fear Arousal as a Function of Differential Levels of Perceived Self-Efficacy." *Journal of Personality and Social Psychology* 43, no. 1 (July 1982): 5–21.

#Vancouver, Jeffrey B., Charles M. Thompson, E. Casey Tischner, and Dan J. Putka. "Two Studies Examining the Negative Effect of Self-Efficacy on Performance." *Journal of Applied Psychology* 87, no. 3 (June 2002): 506–516.

EXAMINING THE EVIDENCE

boxes highlight a recent seminal OB study and discuss its application to the real world.

> "I really value the end of chapter material. You have pioneered some enhancements in that arena that will give this text competitive advantage. It offers a fresh take on some familiar material."
>
> —DAVID J. BIEMER,

> "This textbook is centered on student engagement by including features which enable the student to learn by using critical thinking skills."
>
> —MARIA D. VITALE,

THE BIG PICTURE

THE BIG PICTURE shows students how OB topics fit together and influence important outcomes like job satisfaction.

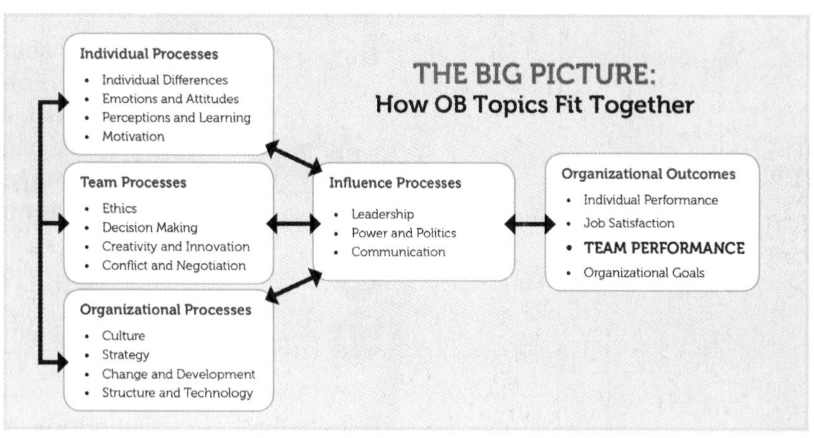

... AND BRING ORGANIZATIONAL BEHAVIOR CONCEPTS TO LIFE

THE EDGE EVERY STUDENT NEEDS

edge.sagepub.com/neckob

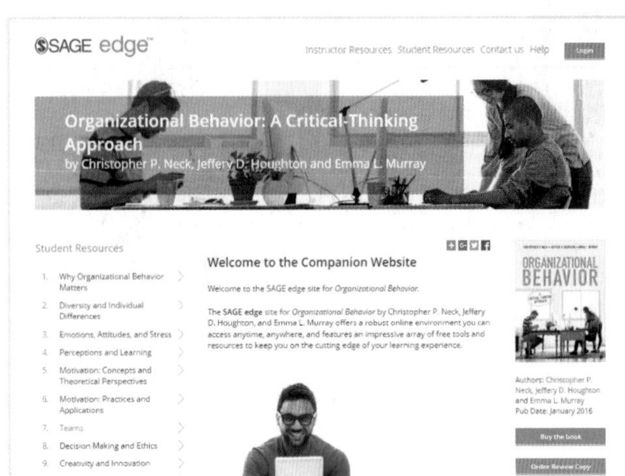

SAGE edge offers a robust online environment featuring an impressive array of tools and resources for review, study, and further exploration, keeping both instructors and students on the cutting edge of teaching and learning.

SAGE edge for Instructors supports teaching by making it easy to integrate quality content and create a rich learning environment for students.

SAGE EDGE FOR INSTRUCTORS

- Course cartridges for easy LMS integration, with over 1,000 quiz questions
- Test banks built on Bloom's taxonomy with over 1,700 questions tagged with AACSB standard, learning objective, difficulty level, answer location, and more
- PowerPoint® slides
- Lecture notes
- Experiential exercises
- Sample answers to questions in the text
- Case notes
- Ethical Dilemmas based on real-world scenarios
- Additional critical-thinking challenges, including suggested writing prompts and assignments
- Exclusive! Full-text SAGE journal articles
- Multimedia content that spans different learning styles
- Links to relevant articles on the web
- OB in the Movies: Suggested film clips that include analysis and critical-thinking questions
- Sample course syllabi

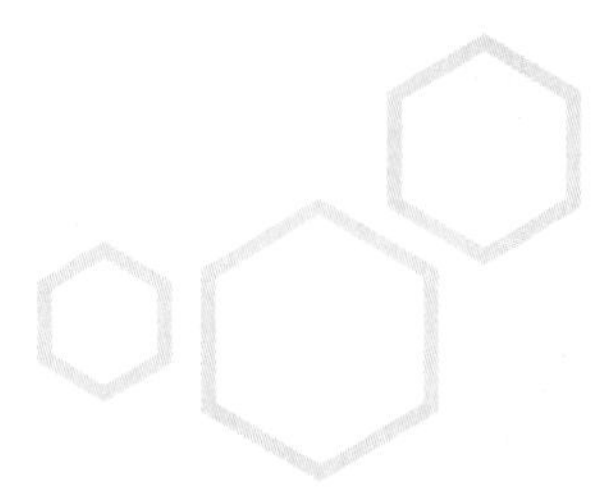

INTERACTIVE EBOOK

Organizational Behavior is also available as a dynamic Interactive eBook which can be packaged with the text or purchased separately.

Fully searchable, the Interactive eBook offers hyperlinks to videos, Web resources, audio content, and SAGE journal articles, all from the same pages found in the printed text. Users will also have immediate access to study tools such as highlighting, bookmarking, note-taking, and more.

 Video Links

 Web Links

 Audio Links

 Journal Links

Bundle the Interactive eBook at no extra cost to your students using ISBN: **978-1-5063-3798-2**

ORGANIZATIONAL BEHAVIOR

We dedicate Organizational Behavior: A Critical-Thinking Approach *to all of our students who have believed in us, inspired us, and encouraged us to try new ways of teaching.*

Chris Neck dedicates this book to his wife, Jennifer, and his children, Bryton and GiGe, for helping him realize what is truly important in life.

Jeff Houghton dedicates this book to his wife, Loree, and sons, Pierce and Sloan, and thanks them for all their support, encouragement, and love.

Emma Murray dedicates this book to her husband, Sam, and her children, Ava and Anya, for their unending love and support.

SAGE was founded in 1965 by Sara Miller McCune to support the dissemination of usable knowledge by publishing innovative and high-quality research and teaching content. Today, we publish over 900 journals, including those of more than 400 learned societies, more than 800 new books per year, and a growing range of library products including archives, data, case studies, reports, and video. SAGE remains majority-owned by our founder, and after Sara's lifetime will become owned by a charitable trust that secures our continued independence.

Los Angeles | London | New Delhi | Singapore | Washington DC

ORGANIZATIONAL BEHAVIOR

CHRISTOPHER P. NECK
Arizona State University, Tempe

JEFFERY D. HOUGHTON
West Virginia University

EMMA L. MURRAY

Los Angeles | London | New Delhi
Singapore | Washington DC

Los Angeles | London | New Delhi
Singapore | Washington DC

FOR INFORMATION:

SAGE Publications, Inc.
2455 Teller Road
Thousand Oaks, California 91320
E-mail: order@sagepub.com

SAGE Publications Ltd.
1 Oliver's Yard
55 City Road
London EC1Y 1SP
United Kingdom

SAGE Publications India Pvt. Ltd.
B 1/I 1 Mohan Cooperative Industrial Area
Mathura Road, New Delhi 110 044
India

SAGE Publications Asia-Pacific Pte. Ltd.
3 Church Street
#10-04 Samsung Hub
Singapore 049483

Acquisitions Editor: Maggie Stanley
Associate Editor: Abbie Rickard
eLearning Editor: Katie Bierach
Editorial Assistants: Neda Dallal, Nicole Mangona
Production Editor: David C. Felts
Copy Editor: Pam Suwinsky
Typesetter: C&M Digitals (P) Ltd.
Proofreaders: Eleni Georgiou, Alison Syring
Indexer: Molly Hall
Cover Designer: Gail Buschman
Marketing Manager: Ashlee Blunk

Printed in the United States of America

Names: Neck, Christopher P., author. | Houghton, Jeffery D., author. | Murray, Emma L., author.

Title: Organizational behavior : a critical-thinking approach / Christopher P. Neck, Jeffery D. Houghton, Emma L. Murray.

Description: Los Angeles : SAGE, [2017] | Includes bibliographical references and index.

Identifiers: LCCN 2015039717 | ISBN 9781506314402 (hardcover : alk. paper)

Subjects: LCSH: Organizational behavior.

Classification: LCC HD58.7 .N43 2017 | DDC 658.3—dc23 LC record available at http://lccn.loc.gov/2015039717

This book is printed on acid-free paper.

16 17 18 19 20 10 9 8 7 6 5 4 3 2 1

BRIEF CONTENTS

Part 5. Organizational Context

DETAILED CONTENTS

Part 4. Leadership and Influence Processes

Part 5. Organizational Context

PREFACE

Nikos Kazantzakis once wrote:

> Ideal teachers are those who use themselves as bridges over which they invite their students to cross; then having facilitated their crossing, joyfully collapse, encouraging them to create bridges of their own.

Our goal as an author team was to write an organizational behavior (OB) textbook that really engaged students—not one that involved memorizing its content for the sole purpose of passing exams and then quickly forgetting whatever they had learned. We wanted to write a textbook that students could use well after the semester was over to help them actively learn and think critically in order to understand how people behave as they pursue their career goals. In other words, we wanted to help students "build bridges" to their goals and dreams. We hope we have achieved our goal in *Organizational Behavior: A Critical-Thinking Approach* for students in organizational behavior classes across the world.

In our 21st-century business world, organizational behavior has taken on a new significance. In an environment in which competition is fiercer than ever, it is people who act as differentiators in the workplace. In every aspect of business, people are the cornerstone of success. This is why it is so important to understand human behavior.

The following quote from Curt Coffman and Gabriela Gonzalez-Molina in *Follow This Path: How the World's Greatest Organizations Drive Growth by Unleashing Human Potential* reinforces the importance of understanding human behavior in organizations:

> The success of your organization doesn't depend on your understanding of economics, or organizational development, or marketing. It depends, quite simply, on your understanding of human psychology: how each individual employee connects with your company and how each individual employee connects with your customers.

One of the earliest studies of organizational behavior was carried out at AT&T's Western Electric Hawthorne plant by Harvard's Elton Mayo in 1927. The principle findings of this study showed that when workers are given the opportunity to contribute their thinking and learning to workplace issues, their job performance improves. This finding is still relevant today. Studies in organizational behavior add to our understanding of the individuals working within all types of businesses, from corporate to entrepreneurial. *Organizational Behavior: A Critical-Thinking Approach* attempts to capture the body of knowledge that encompasses the organizational behavioral research into a book that is fun to read, captures the reader's attention, and imparts the organizational behavioral knowledge in a way that promotes critical thinking.

OUR VISION

Organizational Behavior: A Critical-Thinking Approach is a textbook for college-level undergraduate students seeking insight into individual behavior, group behavior, organizational structure, and organizational processes through the lens of critical thinking.

Organizational behavior courses are defined by the following trends: larger course sizes, the need for continually changing content to stay relevant, and instructors working to make vast online resources meaningful to the student experience. The cumulative effect of these trends on instructors is a much more demanding environment for teaching and learning. In a quickly changing business environment, many books need a complete rewrite to be fully up-to-date. Even better, though, this is a new book—written from today's perspective, with an eye to the near future. Our goal in writing this book is to bring to the classroom a fresh view of human behavior in organizations.

What Makes Our Book Unique

- *Critical-thinking approach.* Students learn to analyze behavior patterns and assess consequences to predictive paths. Managers make decisions that have delayed consequences on situations, with extraordinary complexity, yet predictable patterns of behavior. A student's ability to make decisions that result in expected and desirable consequences should be the sole objective of all organizational behavior textbooks.
- *Continuing case narratives.* Students are associative thinkers and continuously seek multiple data points to connect into a constellation of meaning. People retain knowledge through meaningful narratives, which means that stories that illustrate richly textured situations are better for learning than listing brands and public figures in the chapters.
- *Practical applications, self-assessments, experiential exercises,* and additional pedagogical features make OB come to life and encourage students to engage with OB concepts in meaningful ways.

A Critical-Thinking Approach

We believe that in today's business world, organizational behavior is more important than ever. Companies are looking for employees and managers who have strong organizational behavior skills. Critical thinking, problem solving, and creativity are valuable and essential commodities. Critical thinking is an essential skill; managers use critical thinking to understand, explain, predict, and influence behavior in the workplace.

Our text provides a comprehensive overview of OB theories and processes with a strong emphasis on critical-thinking applications in order to equip students with the information and skills they need to thrive in organizations today.

Why Critical Thinking Matters in OB

A critical thinker uses his or her intelligence, knowledge, and skills to question and carefully explore situations and to arrive at thoughtful conclusions based on evidence and reason. Someone thinking critically is able to get past biases and view situations from different perspectives to ultimately improve his or her understanding of the world.

Business leaders use critical thinking when making decisions, solving problems, gathering information, and asking questions. Time and again, research has shown the effectiveness of critical thinking in the workplace. In an article published in the journal *Current Directions in Psychological Science*, the authors report that cognitive ability tests, including critical-thinking tests "are among the strongest and most consistent predictors of performance across academic and work settings."[1]

In *Organizational Behavior: A Critical-Thinking Approach*, we use the components and core skills of critical thinking to teach the many facets of organizational behavior to students. Adding critical thinking to these behaviors further enhances students' abilities to strategically think as well as analyze and solve problems. By seeking first to understand the dynamics of human behavior, then sharing the knowledge learned, they will be able to build more successful relationships within their personal and professional lives.

How Our Book Incorporates Critical Thinking

A lot of OB books claim to help students to develop their critical-thinking skills. What makes our book different? Our book incorporates critical thinking on every page. Instead of passively reading through each chapter, the student is asked to pause, reflect, and engage more critically with the content.

- Chapter 1 explains the central role critical thinking plays in OB and introduces a five-step **critical-thinking framework** that students can apply to challenging scenarios, problems, decisions, and other issues.
- **Thinking Critically** questions tied to Bloom's Taxonomy appear throughout each chapter. Bracketed notations identify which domain(s) of Bloom's Taxonomy the question falls into: understand, apply, analyze, evaluate, and create. These questions don't necessarily have a right or wrong answer but rather are designed to challenge students to think critically and achieve higher levels of learning.
- **Examining the Evidence** boxes highlight a recent seminal OB study from high-quality OB journals and discusses its practical applications in the business world. Critical-thinking questions at the end of each box allow students to see how research in academe applies to real-life settings.
- **OB in the Real World** boxes feature real-world anecdotes, quotes, and examples from seasoned business professionals who share their knowledge and experience with students by describing how they used OB to positively influence outcomes and achieve organizational success. Critical-thinking questions help students see how OB concepts impact real people and organizations.

These critical-thinking elements are perfect for assignments or class discussions and lively debate.

Continuing Case Narratives

In order to support our balanced approach to research and practice, and our pedagogical commitment to critical thinking, *Organizational Behavior: A Critical-Thinking Approach* takes a new approach to the style of OB textbooks. We include all the concepts and key terms that are expected, but we do so in a context that aids instructors in showing how and why they are applied in real world situations, and in a style that ignites the imagination and sparks discussion.

Rather than a series of unrelated organizational snapshots that offer only a superficial understanding of OB content, we create rich, continuing case study narratives that illustrate the exciting and challenging complexities of the real world. Each of the main OB subdivisions is presented through business case narratives that span multiple chapters. These continuing case narratives serve two key purposes:

1. Provide fully imagined characters and relationships that reflect challenges and opportunities that managers encounter
2. Provide sufficiently rich contexts to practice critical-thinking skills in ways that mimic actual workplace dynamics. How do we ensure that these case narratives are consistent with top-tier research and the challenges that businesses are addressing in today's economy?

For Parts 2–5 of the book, we develop a case representing an industry and featuring several managers in an organization. These continuing cases are inspired by real people and real events but fictionalized for the learning process. Chapters include a Back to the Case recap that summarizes the events of the previous chapter's case narrative, making it easy for instructors to assign chapters out of order.

Following is a summary of each continuing case narrative in the text:

Chapters 2–4. The Case of Laura Pierce: Differences at the West Texas Regional Theatre

The narrative focuses on Laura Pierce, a newly employed marketing and development director at the financially struggling West Texas Regional Theatre (WTRT), and the challenges she faces in trying to overcome individual differences in order to help save the theatre. In Chapter 2, Laura meets her new colleagues and gets to know more about their different backgrounds and personalities. In Chapter 3, Laura introduces her ideas to drive business to WTRT but needs to navigate the attitude and behavior of the staff. In Chapter 4, Laura deals with the consequences of differing perceptions as she meets with the WTRT board members to discuss the theatre's financial decline.

Chapters 5–6. The Case of Katie O'Donnell: Motivating Staff at the Waterfront Grill

Katie O'Donnell is an MBA student who has been a server at the restaurant for the past two years and just accepted the job of assistant manager at the Waterfront Grill in upstate New York. She sees her promotion as an opportunity to identify and solve a number of problems she has experienced at the restaurant over the past two years. In Chapter 5, Katie focuses on addressing high turnover by suggesting different strategies to resolve problems and motivate staff at the Waterfront Grill. In Chapter 6, Katie starts to put some of these motivational concepts into practice with mixed results.

Chapters 7–10. The Case of Brian Stevens: Trouble at the Tractor Assembly Plant

HR Manager Brian Stevens has been working in a tractor-engine manufacturing plant in the Midwest. He recently received a promotion to plant manager at the company's tractor assembly plant and reports directly to the president of the company, Hans Wagner. Over the course of the narrative, Brian faces challenges across different teams and departments and is forced to make some tough decisions. In Chapter 7, Brian discovers one of the main problems in the tractor assembly plant: the team in the purchasing department is underperforming and he must work with the team to resolve the issue. In Chapter 8,

Brian faces an ethical dilemma when his boss, Hans Wagner, tries to convince Brian to accept his decision to make some unethical cost-cutting initiatives. In Chapter 9, Brian faces the challenge of creating innovative new machinery that will increase productivity. In Chapter 10, Brian must deal with some conflict when new competitors threaten the plant's new product and use some negotiation strategies in order to resolve the conflict.

Chapters 11–13. The Case of Langston Burrows: Leadership Challenges

Langston Burrows is a recent college graduate with a bachelor's degree in business administration who has been offered a place in the leadership development program (LDP) at a mid-sized regional bank. Langston sets out to determine his own leadership style. In Chapter 11, Langston begins a three-month rotational leadership position and gets to know the bank staff and experiment with different leadership styles. In Chapter 12, Langston learns about how different people wield power and influence and endures the unfair political behavior of a more senior colleague. In Chapter 13, Langston must overcome some communication barriers in order to find a new role within the bank.

Chapters 14–17. The Case of Yolande Turner: Pioneering Health Goes International

Pioneering Health is a small organization based outside Chicago and consisting of 300 people. Headed by founder and CEO Yolande Turner, a former pharmaceutical-product line manager, the company sells disease management strategies to other health care providers, associations, and corporations that offer health insurance. This OB Story follows Yolande as she takes the business international in an effort to break into new markets. Chapter 14 describes Pioneering Health and its organizational culture. In Chapter 15, Yolande and her senior team work out strategies to expand the business internationally, choosing Germany as a location. In Chapter 16, Yolande must implement some organizational changes and developments to improve the working relationships among staff members and overcome resistance to change. In Chapter 17, Yolande introduces a new organizational structure to meet the needs of the rapidly expanding Frankfurt office.

END-OF-CHAPTER FEATURES

In each chapter, we include traditional chapter review materials to help students check their comprehension and prepare for quizzes and exams.

- **In Review,** organized by learning objective, summarizes key chapter information
- **Thinking Critically About the Case** challenges students to apply the five-step critical-thinking framework to the fictionalized chapter case.
- **Short exercises and experiential exercises** are designed to help students build valuable experience and increase their skills through decision-oriented and hands-on exercises. Notes on the instructor resources site include tips on how to best use the exercises in class as well as suggestions for adapting these experiential exercises to use in online or large classes.
- **Self-assessments.** The assessments allow students to apply chapter content to their own lives and better understand their own behaviors, skills, and strengths.

- **Case studies** profile real-world companies and people and illustrate how OB concepts function in the real world, providing students with engaging case examples and opportunities to apply OB concepts to the case studies.
- **Self-Tests** allow students to quickly check their knowledge of key chapter ideas.

CONTENT AND ORGANIZATION

Each chapter is introduced by an OB model that provides students with a big picture overview of how all the chapters and parts fit together.

Chapter 1, "Why Organizational Behavior Matters," explains how and why OB has become significant in today's organizations and describes the value of critical thinking in making thoughtful, effective decisions.

Chapter 2, "Diversity and Individual Differences," explores the types of diversity and the importance of accepting and respecting individual personalities in order to create a harmonious workforce.

Chapter 3, "Emotions, Attitudes, and Stress," examines how emotions influence our behavior and the behavior of those around us in the workplace; common workplace attitudes and the relationship between attitudes and behaviors; and the different ways in which stress can affect behavior in the workplace.

Chapter 4, "Perception and Learning," describes the ways in which we interpret our environment; the factors that can influence and distort perception; and the different learning processes that shape our perceptions.

Chapter 5, "Motivation: Concepts and Theoretical Perspectives," introduces the theories of motivation and how they influence behavior in the workforce.

Chapter 6, "Motivation: Practices and Applications," outlines the practical ways and strategies used by organizations to encourage motivation and empower employees.

Chapter 7, "Teams," emphasizes the critical role of teams and teamwork in today's organizations; types of teams; and the components that make up an effective team.

Chapter 8, "Decision Making and Ethics," addresses the main types of decisions made in organizations; the factors that influence how these decisions are made; and the various approaches to ethical decision-making.

Chapter 9, "Creativity and Innovation," highlights the types of creativity and innovation processes; their importance to organizations; and how they affect organizational behavior.

Chapter 10, "Conflict and Negotiation," describes the impact of conflict on organizational behavior and the ways in which negotiation and bargaining can help resolve conflict.

Chapter 11, "Leadership Perspectives," explains the different types of leaders through theories and perspectives and discusses cultural and gender issues in leadership.

Chapter 12, "Influence, Power, Politics," discusses power and politics in the context of leadership, and describes the tactics and outcomes of different influence tactics.

Chapter 13, "Effective Communication," provides an overview of the basic model of communication; the types of communication channels; and key barriers to effective communication.

Chapter 14, "Organizational Culture," explores the facets of organizational culture and how culture is shaped and molded in organizations.

Chapter 15, "Organizational Strategy," describes the importance of effective strategies in order to achieve organizational goals and explores strategies in the context of globalization and across cultures.

Chapter 16, "Organizational Change and Development," explains the change process; the reasons behind resistance to change; and how organizational development is used to cope with internal and external changes.

Chapter 17, "Organizational Structure, Design, and Technology," focuses on the impact of organizational structure on behavior in organizations; how organizational design is connected to organizational behavior; and how technology is integrated into organizational structure and design.

ANCILLARIES

Personalized Learning Tools and Easy-to-Use Teaching Resources

Designed to enhance each student's learning experience, **SAGE edge** is a robust online environment featuring carefully crafted tools and resources that encourage review, practice, and critical thinking to give students the edge they need to master course content.

SAGE edge for Instructors supports teaching with quality content, featuring:

- **Course management system integration** that makes it easy for student test results to seamlessly flow into your gradebooks so you can track your students' progress
- **Test banks built on Bloom's Taxonomy** to provide a diverse range of test items, which allow you to save time and offer a pedagogically robust way to measure your students' understanding of the material
- **Sample course syllabi** with suggested models for structuring your course
- Editable, chapter-specific **PowerPoint slides** that offer flexibility when creating multimedia lectures
- EXCLUSIVE access to full-text **SAGE journal articles** to expose students to important research and scholarship tied to chapter concepts
- **Video and multimedia content** that enhances student engagement and appeal to different learning styles
- **Lecture notes** that summarize key concepts on a chapter-by-chapter basis to help you with preparation for lectures and class discussions
- Sample **answers to in-text questions** that provide an essential reference
- Additional **critical-thinking challenges,** including suggested writing prompts and assignments
- Lively and stimulating **experiential exercises** that can be used in class to reinforce active learning
- **Teaching notes for the cases** to guide analysis
- **Ethical dilemmas** for each chapter require students to respond to real-world scenarios and decide what they would do in those situations
- Suggested film clips showing **OB in the movies** that include analysis and critical-thinking questions
- **Web resources** that provide further research and insights.

SAGE edge for Students helps students accomplish their coursework goals in an easy-to-use, rich learning environment that offers:

- Mobile-friendly **flashcards** to strengthen understanding of key concepts
- Mobile-friendly practice **quizzes** to encourage self-guided assessment and practice
- Carefully selected **video** and **multimedia content** that enhance exploration of key topics
- EXCLUSIVE access to full-text **SAGE journal articles** and other readings, which support and expand on chapter concepts
- **Web resources** that provide further research and insights
- **Learning objectives** with summaries that reinforce the most important material
- Online **action plans** that allow you to track your progress and enhance your learning experience

ENDNOTE

1. Kuncel, Nathan R., and Sarah A. Hezlett. "Fact and Fiction in Cognitive Ability Testing for Admissions and Hiring Decisions." *Current Directions in Psychological Science* 19, no. 6 (December 2010): 339–345.

ACKNOWLEDGMENTS

The authors thank all those people who have supported our efforts in writing this book. There are a plethora of people who contributed to making this text a reality. First, we thank all of the students who over the years have encouraged us to leave our teaching comfort zone to explore new and innovative ways of teaching. It was through these experiences that we obtained the courage to attempt to write such a book as *Organizational Behavior: A Critical-Thinking Approach*. We also thank our respective deans Amy Hillman at Arizona State (W. P. Carey School of Business) and Nancy McIntyre at West Virginia University's College of Business & Economics for their support for this project. We thank our department heads (Trevis Certo, Arizona State, and Abhishek Srivastava, West Virginia University) for their encouragement as well. Chris Neck thanks Duane Roen (Dean of the College of Letters and Sciences at Arizona State University) for his steadfast support and encouragement to excel in the classroom.

For their thoughtful and helpful comments and ideas on our manuscript, we sincerely thank the following reviewers. Our book is a better product because of their insightful suggestions.

Tracy H. Porter, Cleveland State University

Samira B. Hussein, Johnson County Community College

Lisa M. Nieman, Indiana Wesleyan University

Tommy Nichols, Texas Wesleyan University

Steven D. Charlier, Georgia Southern University

Daniel S. Marrone, Farmingdale State College

Linda Hefferin, Columbia College of Missouri

Robert D. Gulbro, Florida Institute of Technology

Deborah S. Butler, Georgia State University

Christine R. Day, Eastern Michigan University

Janice S. Gates, Western Illinois University

Nathan Himelstein, Essex County College

Harriet L. Rojas, Indiana Wesleyan University

Andrea E. Smith-Hunter, Siena College

Maria D. Vitale, Brandman University, Chaffey College, and UCLA Extension

Audrey M. Parajon, Wilmington University

Frederick R. Brodzinski, The City College of New York

Michael J. Alleruzzo, Saint Joseph's University

Jacqueline Mayfield, Texas A&M International University

Milton Mayfield, Texas A&M International University

Bob Waris, University of Missouri-Kansas City

Ann Snell, Tulane University

Mike Shaner, Saint Louis University

Susan Knapp, Kaplan University

Jason Jackson, Kaplan University

Palaniappan Thiagarajan, Jackson State University

Maria Minor, Kaplan University

David J. Biemer, Texas State University

Marla Lowenthal, University of San Francisco

Avan Jassawalla, SUNY Geneseo

Warren Matthews, LeTourneau University

Eric B. Dent, Fayetteville State University

It takes a team to write a textbook, and we thank those behind-the-scenes individuals who assisted in the research, development, and/or editing of various parts of this book. Specifically, we thank Elizabeth Parsons, Marisa Keegan, Amanda Rogers, Rachel Wilkerson, Nishant Mahajan, Varun Parmar, Kyle Helmle, Erich Weber, and Prakrut Desai.

In addition, we thank the fine folks at SAGE for bringing this book to fruition. Our dream of creating an innovative OB textbook and ancillary package has become a reality because of our amazing, energetic, and encouraging acquisitions editor, Maggie Stanley. She has been a champion for this book and our ideas (and there were many!) every step of the way. We can't thank her enough for her dedication and support. Elisa Adams, our talented developmental editor, pushed us to explore new ideas and our associate editor, Abbie Rickard, kept us on track to write the best book possible. David Felts, our production editor, made sure that everything that needed to happen did indeed happen and kept all of us on track. We appreciate all of his hard work, creativity, and attention to detail. We are also grateful to Ashlee Blunk and Mark Achenbach from SAGE, who planted the seeds for this book many years ago.

We are grateful to Harriet Rojas (Indiana Wesleyan University), Milton R. Mayfield (Texas A&M International University), and Jacqueline R. Mayfield (Texas A&M International University) for contributing valuable, hands-on experiential exercises.

Designer Gail Buschman came up with an elegant and contemporary look for this book that visually brings to life our ideas more than we could have ever imagined. Nicole Mangona took care of a myriad of tasks during the development of the manuscript with an energy and enthusiasm that was inspiring. Liz Thornton, our marketing manager, did a great job coordinating the promotion of our book, from organizing focus groups to overseeing all of the professor outreach efforts. And we thank our families for "living without us" as we worked diligently on completing this textbook.

Christopher P. Neck
Jeffery D. Houghton
Emma L. Murray

ABOUT THE AUTHORS

Christopher P. Neck, PhD

Dr. Christopher P. Neck is currently an associate professor of management at Arizona State University, where he held the title "University Master Teacher." From 1994 to 2009, he was part of the Pamplin College of Business faculty at Virginia Tech. He received his PhD in management from Arizona State University and his MBA from Louisiana State University. Dr. Neck is author of the books *Beyond Self-Leadership: Empowering Yourself and Others to Personal Excellence* (forthcoming, SAGE); *Fit To Lead: The Proven Eight-Week Solution for Shaping Up Your Body, Your Mind, and Your Career* (St. Martin's 2004; Carpenter's Sons Publishing 2012); *Mastering Self-Leadership: Empowering Yourself for Personal Excellence,* sixth edition (Pearson 2013); *The Wisdom of Solomon at Work* (Berrett-Koehler 2001); *For Team Members Only: Making Your Workplace Team Productive and Hassle-Free* (Amacom Books 1997); and *Medicine for the Mind: Healing Words to Help You Soar,* fourth edition (Wiley 2012). Dr. Neck is also the coauthor of the principles of management textbook, *Management: A Balanced Approach to the 21st Century* (Wiley 2013); and the upcoming introduction to entrepreneurship textbook, *Entrepreneurship* (SAGE forthcoming).

Dr. Neck's research specialties include employee/executive fitness, self-leadership, leadership, group decision-making processes, and self-managing teams. He has more than 100 publications in the form of books, chapters, and articles in various journals. Some of the outlets in which his work has appeared include *Organizational Behavior and Human Decision Processes, Journal of Organizational Behavior, Academy of Management Executive, Journal of Applied Behavioral Science, Journal of Managerial Psychology, Executive Excellence, Human Relations, Human Resource Development Quarterly, Journal of Leadership Studies, Educational Leadership,* and *Commercial Law Journal.*

Because of Dr. Neck's expertise in management, he has been cited in numerous national publications, including the *Washington Post,* the *Wall Street Journal,* the *Los Angeles Times,* the *Houston Chronicle,* and the *Chicago Tribune.* Additionally, each semester Dr. Neck teaches an introductory management course to a single class of anywhere from 500 to 1,000 students.

Dr. Neck was the recipient of the 2007 *Business Week* Favorite Professor Award. He is featured on www.businessweek.com as one of the approximately 20 professors from across the world receiving this award.

Dr. Neck currently teaches a mega-section of management principles to approximately 500 students at Arizona State University. He recently received the Order of Omega Outstanding Teaching Award for 2012. This award is awarded to one professor at Arizona State by the Alpha Lambda chapter of this leadership fraternity. His class sizes at Virginia Tech filled rooms with up to 1,000 students. He received numerous teaching awards during his tenure at Virginia Tech, including the 2002 Wine Award for Teaching Excellence. Also, Dr. Neck was the 10-time winner (1996, 1998, 2000, 2002, 2004, 2005, 2006, 2007, 2008, and 2009) of the Students' Choice Teacher of The Year Award (voted by the students for the best teacher of the year within the entire university).

Some of the organizations that have participated in Dr. Neck's management development training include GE/Toshiba, Busch Gardens, Clark Construction, the US Army, Crestar, American Family Insurance, Sales and Marketing Executives International, American Airlines, American Electric Power, W. L. Gore & Associates, Dillard's Department Stores, and Prudential Life Insurance. Dr. Neck is also an avid runner. He has completed 12 marathons, including the Boston Marathon, New York City Marathon, and the San Diego Marathon. In fact, his personal record for a single long distance run is a 40-mile run.

Jeffery D. Houghton, PhD

Dr. Jeffery D. Houghton completed his PhD in management at Virginia Polytechnic Institute and State University (Virginia Tech) and is currently an associate professor of management at West Virginia University (WVU). Dr. Houghton has taught college-level business courses at Virginia Tech, Abilene Christian University (Texas), Lipscomb University (Tennessee), The International University (Vienna, Austria), and for the US Justice Department-Federal Bureau of Prisons. Prior to pursuing a full-time career in academics, he worked in the banking industry as a loan officer and branch manager.

A member of the Honor Society of Phi Kappa Phi, Dr. Houghton's research specialties include human behavior, motivation, personality, leadership, and self-leadership. He has published more than 40 peer-reviewed journal articles and book chapters, and his work has been cited more than 1,600 times in academic journals. He currently teaches undergraduate-, master's-, and doctoral-level courses in management, organizational behavior, and leadership. Dr. Houghton was named the 2013 Beta Gamma Sigma Professor of the Year for the WVU College of Business and Economics, awarded annually to one faculty member within the college as selected by a vote of the student members of Beta Gamma Sigma; and he received the 2008 Outstanding Teaching Award for the WVU College of Business and Economics, awarded annually to one faculty member for outstanding teaching.

In addition to his research and teaching activities, Dr. Houghton has consulted and conducted training seminars for companies including the Federal Bureau of Investigations, Pfizer Pharmaceuticals, and the Bruce Hardwood Floors Company. In his spare time, Dr. Houghton enjoys traveling, classic mystery novels, racquetball, and snow skiing. Finally, Dr. Houghton has trained for and completed two marathons, the Marine Corps Marathon in Washington, DC, and the Dallas White Rock Marathon in Dallas, Texas.

Emma L. Murray, BA, Hdip, DBS IT

Emma Murray completed a bachelor of arts degree in English and Spanish at University College Dublin (UCD) in County Dublin, Ireland. This was followed by a Higher Diploma (Hdip) in business studies and information technology at the Michael Smurfit Graduate School of Business in County Dublin, Ireland. Following her studies, Emma spent nearly a decade in investment banking before becoming a full-time writer and author.

As a writer, she has worked on numerous texts, including business and economics, self-help, and psychology. Within the field of higher education, she has assisted in creating and writing business course modules for students in the United States and the United Kingdom. She worked with Dr. Christopher P. Neck and Dr. Jeffery D. Houghton on *Management: A Balanced Approach to the 21st Century* (Wiley 2013); and is the coauthor of *Management: A Balanced Approach to the 21st Century,* second edition (Wiley 2016).

She is the author of *The Unauthorized Guide to Doing Business the Alan Sugar Way* (Wiley-Capstone, 2010) and coauthor of *How to Succeed as a Freelancer in Publishing* (How To Books, 2010). She lives in London.

Chapter 1 Why Organizational Behavior Matters

PART 1

INTRODUCTION

1 Why Organizational Behavior Matters

The success of your organization doesn't depend on your understanding of economics, or organizational development, or marketing. It depends, quite simply, on your understanding of human psychology: how each individual employee connects with your company and how each individual employee connects with your customers.

——Curt Coffman and Gabriela Gonzalez-Molina, authors of *Follow This Path: How the World's Greatest Organizations Drive Growth by Unleashing Human Potential*

WHAT IS ORGANIZATIONAL BEHAVIOR AND WHY IS IT IMPORTANT?

1.1 Explain the basic concept of organizational behavior (OB) and its value in organizations

Today's continually changing economic world needs managers who can understand, anticipate, and direct people in a fast-paced competitive market. In the past, organizations focused on numbers and how to achieve those numbers without paying too much attention to motivating and understanding their staff. However, fast-paced organizations need the right people with the right skills to achieve success. This is why organizational behavior has taken on a new level of importance; people with organizational behavior skills are now regarded as a valuable and essential commodity. In an environment in which competition is fiercer than ever, people will differentiate your business from anyone else's. No matter what area of business you work in, people are the cornerstone of success.

We define **organizational behavior** (OB) as a field of study focused on understanding, explaining, and improving attitudes of individuals and groups in organizations.[1] An **organization** is a structured arrangement of people working together to accomplish specific goals. In short, OB focuses on figuring out how and why individual employees and groups of employees behave the way they do within an organizational setting. Researchers carry out studies in OB, and managers or consultants establish whether this research can be applied in a real-world organization.

How will studying organizational behavior benefit you in the workplace? Understanding the ways people act and interact within organizations provides three key advantages:

1. You can *explain* behavior. You can explain why your boss, coworkers, or subordinates are doing what they are doing.
2. You can *predict* behavior. You can anticipate what your boss, coworkers, or subordinates will do in certain circumstances and situations.

LEARNING OBJECTIVES

By the end of this chapter, you will be able to:

1.1 Explain the basic concept of organizational behavior (OB) and its value in organizations

1.2 Describe the key role of managing human capital in creating a sustainable competitive advantage for organizations

1.3 Identify the major behavioral science disciplines that contribute to OB

1.4 Demonstrate the value of critical thinking in the context of OB

1.5 Identify the major challenges and opportunities in the field of OB

1.6 Describe the importance of ethical behavior in global organizations

1.7 Differentiate the three basic levels of analysis at which OB may be examined

1.8 Outline the benefits of positive OB and high-involvement management

Master the content.
edge.sagepub.com/neckob

SAGE edge™

3. You can *influence* behavior. You can shape the actions of your subordinates, as well as your boss and coworkers in order to help them accomplish their goals and achieve organizational objectives.

Although explaining and predicting behavior are undoubtedly useful skills, *influencing* behavior is probably of the greatest interest to a practicing manager. Once you are equipped with knowledge about your employees' work behaviors, you can use it to optimize performance by providing effective direction and guidance. This explains why managing organizational behavior (i.e. focusing on the behavior and actions of employees and how they apply their knowledge and skills to achieve organizational objectives) is so important in today's organizations.

Let's remind ourselves what a manager actually does in the workplace. Typically, managers carry out four main functions: planning, organizing, leading, and controlling.[2] (See Figure 1.1.)

In *planning*, a manager evaluates an organization's current position and where it wants to be in the future, and sets goals, designs strategies, and identifies actions and resources needed to achieve success. *Organizing* means arranging resources such as people and functions to implement the strategy made during the planning stage. Managers ensure goals are achieved by *leading* teams and individuals effectively, which means motivating and communicating with people to achieve goals. The *controlling* function allows managers to monitor employee performance, ensure milestones are being reached, and take corrective or preventative action where necessary.

Managers need to be equipped with specific skills to carry out their roles effectively.[3] First, they must have technical skills. A **technical skill** is an aptitude for performing and applying specialized tasks.[4] Today's managers need to be proficient in using the latest technologies, including databases, spreadsheets, email, and social networking tools.

Ciaran Griffin/Photodisc/Thinkstock

Studying organizational behavior can help you to understand how and why individuals and groups interact.

Technical skill: The aptitude to perform and apply specialized tasks

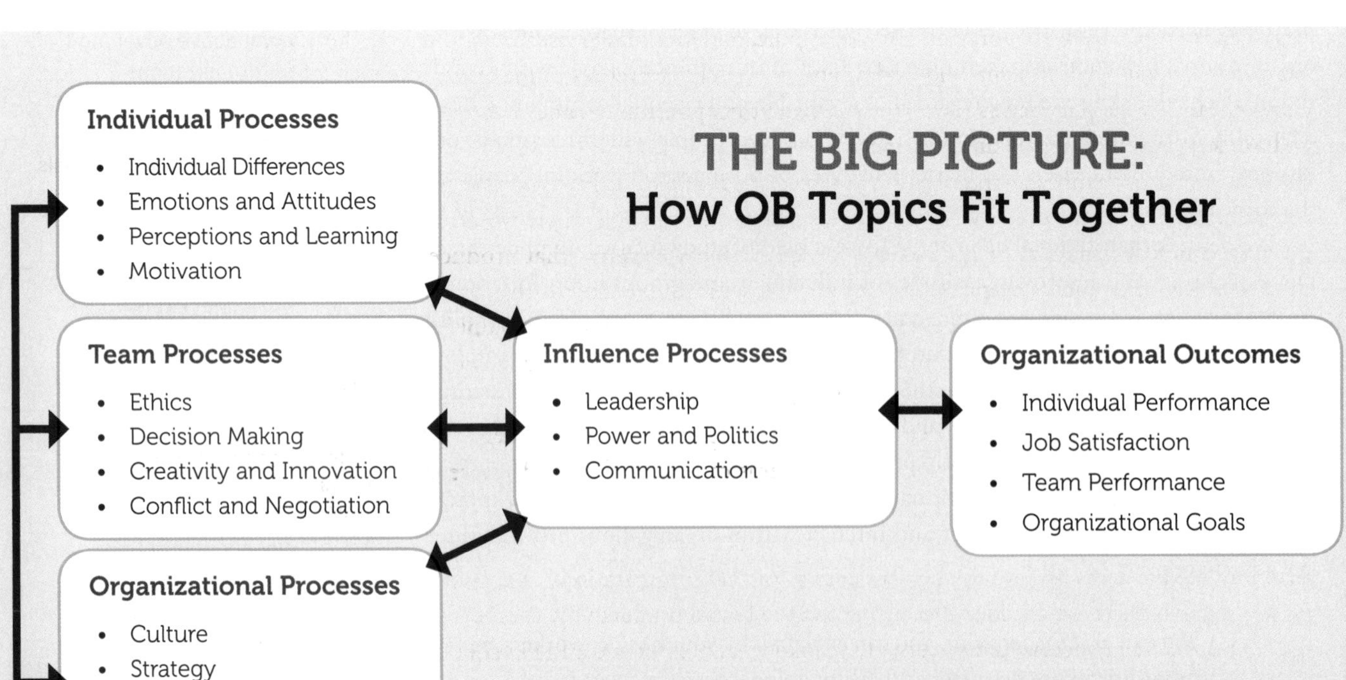

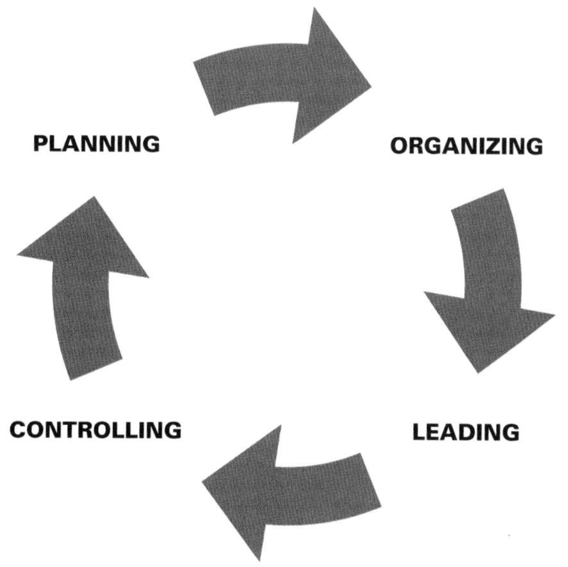

■ FIGURE 1.1 The Four Functions of Managers

SOURCE: http://2012books.lardbucket.org/books/management-principles-v1.1/s19-the-essentials-of-control.html.

Although technical skills are important, they can be learned on the job; to be really effective, managers need to possess **human skills** or the ability to relate to other people.[5] People with effective human skills take the feelings of others into account and are adept at dealing with conflict. A key facet of human skills is **emotional intelligence** (EI), which is an awareness of how your actions and emotions affect those around you and the ability to understand and empathize with the feelings of others.[6]

Managers need to be technically proficient and know how to get along with people, but what about dealing with the complexities of the organization itself? Managers also need **conceptual skills** in order to see the organization as a whole, visualize how it fits into its overall environment, and understand how each part relates to the others.[7] Conceptual skills help managers solve problems, identify opportunities and challenges, and think creatively when making decisions.

Managers who embrace organizational behavior principles understand that the success of an organization lies with its people, and without people, there would be no companies, businesses, or industries. You may have a business that produces the highest-quality, most competitively priced product in the market or that prides itself on excellent customer service. However, if you don't have the right people in place to manufacture, market, and sell your product and take care of your customers, the business will suffer. Similarly, if some of your coworkers lose motivation and provide lower levels of customer service, the company will lose business, and perhaps even its reputation. Either of these problems can bring about a decrease in profits, reduced employee wages and bonuses, staff layoffs, and in extreme cases, bankruptcy.

How do managers achieve the best outcomes for their organizations? A **strategic OB approach** is based on the idea that people are the key to productivity, competitive edge, and financial success. This means that managers must place a high value on **human capital**, which is the sum of people's skills, knowledge, experience, and general attributes.[8] Let's take a closer look at where human capital fits into organizations, and how it is managed.

Organizational behavior: A field of study focused on understanding, explaining, and improving attitudes of individuals and groups in organizations

Organization: A structured arrangement of people working together to accomplish specific goals

Human skills: The ability to relate to other people

Emotional intelligence: The ability to understand emotions in oneself and others in order to effectively manage one's own behaviors and relationships with others

Conceptual skill: The capacity to see the organization as a whole and understand how each part relates to each other and how it fits into its overall environment

Strategic OB approach: The idea that people are the key to productivity, competitive edge, and financial success

Human capital: People's skills, knowledge, experience, and general attributes

THINKING CRITICALLY

1. OB helps managers explain, predict, and influence behavior in the workplace. Identify the types of behavior you are most interested in explaining, understanding, and predicting in the workplace.
2. Of the four main functions managers fulfill (planning, organizing, leading, and controlling), which do you think is most likely to be enhanced by an understanding of organizational behavior? Why?
3. Managers need technical, human, and conceptual skills in order to succeed. Which of these skills are least likely to be learned on the job? Explain your position.
4. Compare the book's argument that the success of an organization lies with its people with the argument that every employee is replaceable and expendable. Which argument do you consider more compelling? Why?

MANAGING HUMAN CAPITAL

1.2 Describe the key role of managing human capital in creating a sustainable competitive advantage for organizations

Organizations have two kinds of resources: tangible and intangible. Physical assets such as equipment, property, and inventory are examples of *tangible* resources. *Intangible* resources include an organization's reputation and culture, its relationships with customers, and the trust between managers and coworkers. Although it is difficult to measure intangible resources because of their subtle nature, they remain crucial for organizations competing in a global economy.

Human capital falls into the category of critical intangible resources. Today's managers focus on enriching their human capital by nurturing and enhancing their employees' knowledge and skills. The possibilities of building on human capital are endless—empowered, satisfied, knowledgeable employees can achieve so much for the organization and its customers. Human capital is essential for gaining **competitive advantage**, the edge that gives organizations a more beneficial position than their competitors and allows them to generate more profits and retain more customers.[9] (See Figure 1.2.) Three main aspects of human capital enhance true competitive advantage: value, rareness, and inimitability.[10]

Value

Employees can add value in many different ways, but there is a difference between merely fulfilling the requirements of your job and working with an eye on company

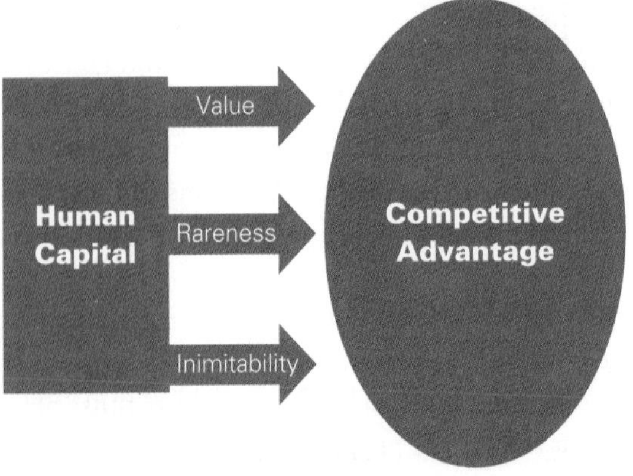

■ FIGURE 1.2 How Human Capital Enhances Competitive Advantage

Competitive advantage: The edge that gives organizations a more beneficial position than their competitors and allows them to generate more profits and retain more customers

strategy. **Human capital value** accumulates when employees work toward the strategic goals of an organization to achieve competitive advantage. Although it is essential that employees have the skills and the abilities to execute a company strategy, they must also have a genuine willingness to contribute to the performance and success of an organization. Therefore, it is critical that managers make every effort to continuously nurture their high-performing employees, because regardless of labor market conditions, outstanding employees are always in short supply.

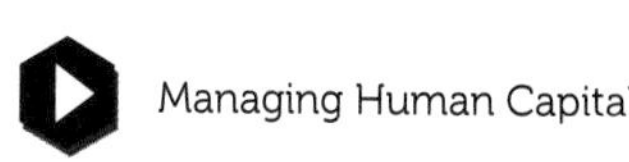

Rareness

Not everyone has the right skillset to further the progress of an organization. **Human capital rareness** is the level of exceptional skills and talents employees possess in an industry. For example, you may be an excellent computer programmer with an outstanding eye for detail, or you could have a gift for dealing with customer complaints and creating resolutions to resolve dilemmas. These are rare skills that employees may bring with them into an organization, but they can also be learned given the right training and encouragement.

Inimitability

Employees may be able to add real value and possess rare and important skills, but these attributes must be inimitable (i.e., unique and difficult to copy or replicate) for an organization to achieve success. **Human capital inimitability** is the degree to which the skills and talents of employees can be emulated by other organizations. The higher the level of inimitability, the more competitive an organization will be. For example, what's to prevent an excellent computer programmer from going to a competitor that offers the same services and opportunities? Successful organizations ensure that their talented employees possess skills and talents that are difficult to imitate. This means employees have a degree of *tacit knowledge:* they have a feel or an instinct for a method or a process but can't easily articulate it; they just know it is right. An organization's culture or values are also difficult to imitate and often determine why employees choose to work for one company over another that offers similar produces and services. Usually, this comes down to the organization's shared values, attitudes, and type of culture.

Take a look at how former Human Resources (HR) Director Meredith Soleau managed human capital at Ed Schmidt Auto, a car dealership in Ohio, to address high turnover within the company, in the OB in the Real World feature.

THINKING CRITICALLY

1. Compare the relative importance of tangible and intangible resources. Can an organization succeed without adequate resourcing in both areas? Why or why not? **[Apply]**
2. Explain in your own words how value, rareness, and inimitability in human capital contribute to an organization's competitive advantage. **[Understand]**

BEHAVIORAL SCIENCE DISCIPLINES THAT CONTRIBUTE TO OB

1.3 Identify the major behavioral science disciplines that contribute to OB

In the early days of management theory, studies focused on how workers could perform manual labor more efficiently (on a factory assembly line, for example), and how physical working conditions could be improved for better employee performance. There

Human capital value: The way employees work toward the strategic goals of an organization to achieve competitive advantage

Human capital rareness: The skills and talents of an organization's people that are unique in the industry

Human capital inimitability: The degree to which the skills and talents of employees can be emulated by other organizations

MEREDITH SOLEAU,

Former human resources director, Ed Schmidt Auto

OB in the Real World

© Meredith Soleau/Eric Schmidt

In volume and growth, Ed Schmidt Auto is one of the leading car dealerships in northwest Ohio. It has been in business since 1937 and currently has nearly 200 employees. When Meredith started working in the human resources (HR) department in 2006, her biggest concern was the high employee turnover, which had reached a rate of 66 percent annually.

Not only was high turnover costing the company a lot of money in recruiting and training, but it was affecting the experience their customers were having. "In order to keep customers happy we needed to have the best employees working for us and we needed to treat them well. We weren't hiring the best people. That was our first mistake."

Meredith quickly changed the company's recruiting practices. Many car dealerships hire a high percentage of employees who don't have a college education, but CEO Ed Schmidt started recruiting from community colleges and local universities. This change increased the caliber of employees coming in the door and resulted in a high number of employees who viewed their time at the company as a career rather than just another job. This change in employee attitude allowed managers to focus more of their time on helping outstanding employees move up the ladder and contributed to the development of a strong company culture. Leadership has taken full advantage of this opportunity by continuously soliciting feedback from employees, managers, and customers about ways they can make their organization even stronger.

"It's important for leaders to know when someone is struggling and, more importantly, why they are struggling. It's equally important to know when someone is happy and why they are happy. This information helps drive positive changes within an organization."

At Ed Schmidt Auto, management works hard to engage employees from all over the company in projects that employees are passionate about. "We realized that we have a lot of employees who love to write, so we started a blog and let any interested employee contribute to it. There is an employee who loves Pinterest so we've made her our Pinterest employee."

A few years ago the company discovered that one of its service technicians "souped-up" Volkswagens in his spare time. Leadership, including HR, called him into the office for a meeting.

> He thought he was going to get in trouble for doing side-work and was shocked when we asked him if he wanted to help us create a completely new performance division within Ed Schmidt Auto. We knew that if we offered our customers the ability to have their cars "souped up" we'd be able to increase sales of our specialty car parts. Since Joe loved doing this kind of work, the new division just made sense. Today, sales of our specialty car parts and accessories are booming, Joe is happy, and our customers can't stop talking about their fast and furious cars.
>
> When you know what makes your employees tick, you can find all kinds of projects for them to work on within your business. People love working here because they know that when they have an idea they can tell their manager, and their manager will say, "Cool, we can do this together."

Today, the turnover rate at Ed Schmidt Auto has dropped from 66 percent to 8 percent. Meredith has attributed the decline to the company's strong new focus on the type of people hired, the way managers interact with their employees, and the CEO's dedication to understanding the needs of everyone on the team.

Critical-Thinking Questions

1. What aspect(s) of human capital did Ed Schmidt Auto capitalize on to reduce turnover?
2. What else could Ed Schmidt have done to influence employee turnover behavior?

SOURCE: Interview with Meredith Soleau, May 15, 2013.
Meredith is currently founder and CEO of online digital marketing and recruitment agency, 424 Degrees.

was little focus on the human element (i.e. how individual characteristics, communication, and interpersonal relationships effect organizations.). Over the past one hundred years, however, researchers have carried out a host of studies on the practice and application of OB, taking full advantage of its strong links to five main behavioral science disciplines: psychology, sociology, social psychology, political science, and anthropology (see Figure 1.3).

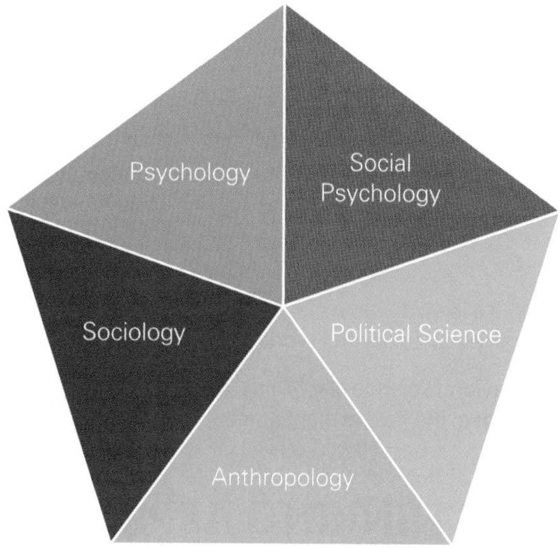

■ FIGURE 1.3 Disciplines Contributing to the Field of Organizational Behavior

Psychology

Psychology is the scientific study of the human mind that seeks to measure and explain behavioral characteristics. Early organizational psychological research and theory focused on the factors affecting work performance and efficiency, such as lethargy and boredom. More recently, psychologists have focused on the mental health and well-being of employees in relationship to their work performance and created methods to help employees deal with challenges such as job stress. Psychologists have also helped design performance appraisals, decision-making processes, recruitment techniques, and training programs.

Sociology

While psychology focuses on the individual, **sociology** looks at the way groups behave and they communicate and exchange information in a social setting. Sociologists have made valuable contributions to OB within areas such as group dynamics, communication, power, organizational culture, and conflict.

Social Psychology

Social psychology mixes concepts from sociology and psychology and focuses on the way people influence each other in a social setting. Social psychologists look at behaviors, feelings, actions, beliefs, and intentions and how they are constructed and influenced by others. They have made significant contributions to reducing the level of prejudice, discrimination, and stereotyping by designing processes to change attitudes, build communication, and improve the way groups work together.

Political Science

Political science studies the behavior of individuals and groups within a political environment. Political scientists focus particularly on how conflict is managed and

Psychology: The scientific study of the human mind that seeks to measure and explain behavioral characteristics

Sociology: The study of the behavior of groups and how they relate to each other in a social setting

Social psychology: The social science that blends concepts from sociology and psychology and focuses on how people influence each other in a social setting

Political science: The study of the behavior of individuals and groups within a political environment

structured, how power is distributed, and how power is abused or manipulated for the purposes of self-interest. Their studies have helped improve our understanding of how different interests, motivations, and preferences can lead to conflict and power struggles between individuals and groups.

Anthropology

Anthropology is the study of people and their activities in relation to societal, environmental, and cultural influences. In a global organizational environment, anthropological research has become even more significant because it increases our understanding of other cultures and the types of values and attitudes held by others from other countries and organizations.

THINKING CRITICALLY

1. What factors are likely to have played a role in early management theory's emphasis on physical tasks and working conditions? **[Understand]**
2. Of the five behavioral science disciplines listed, which one do you consider to be the most relevant to the field of management today? Explain your answer. **[Analyze]**

A CRITICAL-THINKING APPROACH TO OB

1.4 Demonstrate the value of critical thinking in the context of OB

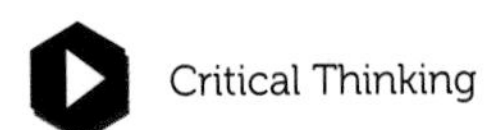

Critical Thinking

In the section "What Is Organizational Behavior and Why Is It Important?" we outlined the four main functions of management (planning, organizing, leading, and controlling) and the skills (technical, human, and conceptual) managers need to be effective in an organization. However, another skill is becoming increasingly important for managers in the workplace: critical thinking. **Critical thinking** is the use of your intelligence, knowledge, and skills to question and carefully explore situations and arrive at thoughtful conclusions based on evidence and reason.[11] Increasingly used in business as a problem-solving tool, the critical-thinking approach is a powerful analytical method that helps managers consider intended and unintended consequences of individual behaviors on their teams and within their organizations and communities. Organizations need managers who think independently without judgment and bias, predict patterns of behaviors and processes, and ask the right questions—"How?" and "Why?" and not just "What?"—in order to make effective and thoughtful decisions.

At the moment, there is a skilled labor shortage in the United States, yet unemployment is still on the rise.[12] How can this be? Surely, if there are enough people available for work, then companies should be able to fill their vacancies. However, as the business environment changes, so do the types of skills expected from employees. New and recent graduates may find that their educational backgrounds do not fulfill the requirements of organizations and may be forced to change, adapt, or learn new skillsets to secure a job. Furthermore, many organizations are becoming more selective; for some positions a degree is not enough.

Your ability to think critically will differentiate you from other job applicants. In an interview situation, critical thinkers take the time to think carefully about the questions they are asked, base their responses on facts or experience rather than emotion or bias, consider different viewpoints or perspectives equally, and compare their responses with similar examples that have occurred in the past. Once hired, critical thinkers are more likely to succeed. After all, most companies do not employ graduates to simply go through the motions or to be a mere cog in the wheel. They expect their employees to play a pivotal role in helping the company achieve its organizational goals. And when a company does well,

Anthropology: The study of people and their activities in relation to societal, environmental, and cultural influences

Critical thinking: The ability to use intelligence, knowledge, and skills to question and carefully explore situations and arrive at thoughtful conclusions based on evidence and reason

Rank	Basic Knowledge and Applied Skills	Percentage	Rank	Basic Knowledge and Applied Skills	Percentage
1	Critical Thinking/Problem Solving*	77.8%	11	Lifelong Learning/Self-Direction*	64.0%
2	Information Technology Application*	77.4	12	Foreign Language	63.3
3	Teamwork/Collaboration*	74.2	13	Mathematics	48.8
4	Creativity/Innovation*	73.6	14	Writing in English	45.4
5	Diversity*	67.1	15	Reading Comprehension	41.0
6	Leadership*	66.9	16	Science	38.7
7	Oral Communications*	65.9	17	English Language	32.8
8	Professionalism/Work Ethic*	64.4	18	Government/Economics	24.8
9	Ethics/Social Responsibility*	64.3	19	History/Geography	17.9
10	Written Communications*	64.0	20	Humanities/Arts	9.5

* INDICATES AN APPLIED SKILL.

■ TABLE 1.1 Ranking of the Most Important Skill for Employees by HR Professionals

SOURCE: *Are They Really Ready to Work? Employers' Perspectives on the Basic Knowledge and Applied Skills of New Entrants to the 21st-Century U.S. Workforce.* Study conducted by the Conference Board, Partnership for 21st-Century Skills, Corporate Voices for Working Families, and the Society for Human Resource Management, 2006.

NOTE: Number of respondents varied for each question, ranging from 398 to 424. Percentages calculated out of total number of respondents electing "increase" in importance over the next five years.

everyone benefits. You don't need to be an expert in critical thinking to get a job. Many of these skills can be learned in the workplace. However, employers look for candidates who have a questioning mind, a willingness to embrace change, and a keen desire to learn.

Indeed, as research shows, businesses are desperate to attract employees with critical-thinking skills.[13] Why? Because organizations are undergoing such rapid change that they need their employees to consistently introduce new, fresh ideas to stay ahead of the competition. Consider the following:

1. When more than 400 senior HR professionals were asked in a survey to name the most important skill their employees will need in the next five years, critical thinking ranked the highest—beating out innovation and information technology (see Table 1.1).[14]
2. Senior executive development professionals report that future leaders are lacking chiefly in strategic thinking skills—which are closely related to critical-thinking skills.[15]
3. A 2009 study by Ones and Dilchert found that the most successful senior executives scored higher on critical-thinking skills than did the less successful ones.[16]
4. *Forbes* recently analyzed data from online databases of occupations and necessary skills in order to identify the skills most in-demand in 2013. Then the magazine went further and analyzed the key skills necessary for success in those roles. The number one skill should be no surprise at all: it was critical thinking.[17]

Business leaders use critical thinking when making decisions, solving problems, gathering information, and asking questions. Time and again, research has shown the effectiveness of critical thinking in the workplace. A recent article published in the journal *Current Directions in Psychological Science* reports that "cognitive ability tests, including critical-thinking tests . . . are among the strongest and most consistent predictors of performance across academic and work settings."[18]

Daniel Ek, founder of Spotify, shows critical thinking by asking "How?" and "Why?" and seeking out the answers.

Andrew Burton/Getty Images

Entrepreneur Daniel Ek, founder of Spotify, is a good example of a critical thinker.[19] Launched in 2008, Spotify is a digital music service that allows people legal paid access to millions of songs streamed directly from major and independent record labels. As a child, Daniel was fascinated by computers and computer games: "When he asked his mother what to do when one of his computer games broke, she told him, 'I don't know, why don't you figure it out?' So he did. 'And that was basically my life story,' says Mr. Ek." By using critical thinking and asking "How?" and "Why?" Ek has managed to build a cutting-edge company worth $3 billion with more than 24 million active users.

The process of critical thinking provides you with the tools to make better decisions as a manager and help you to predict the effects and consequences of those decisions. Most important, you will be better able to manage the complexities of human behavior and initiate behavioral changes by following the critical-thinking process. There are five steps to applying critical thinking in order to manage and change behavior (Figure 1.4): *observe* (recognize the behavior), *interpret* (understand the cause and effects of behavior), *analyze* (investigate the causes and effects of behavior), *evaluate* (assess the consequences of changing behavior), and *explain* (justify a change to behavior).

Let's use an example to illustrate the five steps of critical-thinking methodology. Suppose you are the manager of a restaurant owned by a local businesswoman. Samir, one of your wait staff, has failed to show up for several shifts without giving any meaningful reason. Since Samir is usually reliable, you are puzzled by his absenteeism. Because you don't have all the facts, you decide to use critical-thinking skills to investigate the real source of the problem.

The next time Samir comes to work, you *observe* the situation objectively, suspending all bias and judgment. You notice that he is abrupt with customers, doesn't attempt to communicate with his fellow colleagues, and walks across the restaurant with a heavy gait. This helps you to *interpret* the situation better, giving you enough evidence to deduce that your employee is not happy. You might *analyze* these effects and think of a way to deal with the behavior. What should you do? You decide to *evaluate* the situation and assess the consequences of trying to change his behavior. Based on his performance, your boss, Jessica, the restaurant owner, tells you to fire Samir but you *explain* to your boss why you believe an attempt to change his behavior might be justified and she agrees to give Samir another chance.

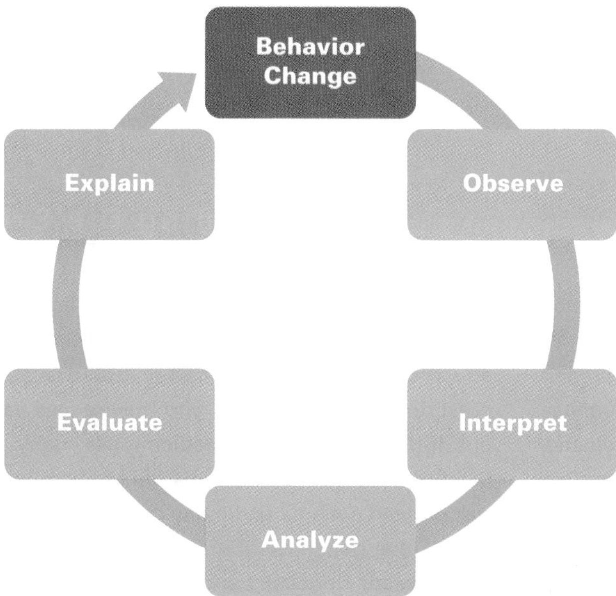

■ FIGURE 1.4 Five-Step Critical-Thinking Framework for Managing and Changing Behavior

SOURCE: Neck, C., et al., *Management* (Hoboken, NJ: Wiley, 2014): 5.

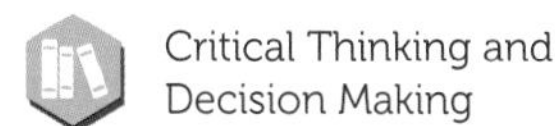

You set up a meeting with Samir to discover the reasons behind his unexplained absences and unmotivated behavior at work. Samir apologizes and tells you he has become dissatisfied with his job and would much rather work on the front desk of the restaurant, greeting customers and taking reservations. He says he has been afraid to tell you because he has been worried he would be letting you down by switching roles. You explain that his absences have already disappointed you but that you are willing to give him a second chance. Following a trial period at the front desk, Samir immediately becomes more motivated, and his attendance is impeccable.

Of course, there could be many ways to handle this dilemma, but it is clear that critical thinking can help to find the best solution for each situation when dealing with the complexities of real-life challenges.

In the next section, we explore how managers use OB research findings to enhance their critical-thinking skills.

The Scientific Method

Researchers use the scientific method to conduct research that managers can use to understand their employees and enhance critical thinking in OB. Researchers often begin with a **theory**, a set of principles intended to explain behavioral phenomena in organizations.[20] OB researchers may also use **models**, simplified snapshots of reality, to summarize and illustrate the reasons behind certain behaviors such as absenteeism or employee turnover. Connecting the elements of these models are **independent variables**, which are factors that remain unchanged, and **dependent variables**, factors affected by independent variables. Researchers then write a prediction called a **hypothesis**, a statement that specifies the relationships between the two variables. For example, much OB research has been carried out on the **correlation**, or the reciprocal relationship between two or more factors, between job satisfaction (independent variable) and absenteeism (dependent variable).

Theory: A set of principles intended to explain behavioral phenomena in organizations

Model: A simplified snapshot of reality

Independent variables: Factors that remain unchanged

Dependent variable: Factor affected by independent variables

Hypothesis: A statement that specifies the relationships between the two variables

Correlation: A reciprocal relationship between two or more factors

Researchers discovered that employees who were more satisfied in their jobs had higher attendance at work than those who had lower levels of job satisfaction. At first

EVIDENCE-BASED MANAGEMENT

Examining the Evidence

One of the strongest proponents of applying research evidence to management practice, Denise M. Rousseau, H. J. Heinz II University Professor of Organizational Behavior at Carnegie Mellon University, defines evidence-based management (EBMgt) as "the systematic, evidence-informed practice of management, incorporating scientific knowledge in the content and processes of making decisions."* EBMgt employs valid scientific findings in the context of critical thinking, decision making, and judgment to help managers obtain and use the best and most reliable information available to increase managerial and organizational effectiveness.*

But why is it important for managers to think critically about and incorporate current research findings into their management practices and decision making? A good parallel comes from the field of medicine. You may naturally assume that medical doctors and health care practitioners use the latest and best research evidence available in the field of medicine to make their decisions. Yet despite the thousands of studies conducted and published in the field of medicine each year, studies suggest that only about 15 percent of doctors make evidence-based decisions.^ Instead, they rely on obsolete information they learned in school, unproven traditions, personal experiences, and information provided by vendors selling medical products and services.^ During the past two decades, however, evidence-based medicine has begun to revolutionize the way medical practitioners make decisions and prescribe treatments.

Stanford Professors Jeffrey Pfeffer and Robert I. Sutton argue that managers should take a similar evidence-based approach in making decisions, taking actions, and prescribing cures for organizational ills: "Managers are actually much more ignorant than doctors about which prescriptions are reliable—and they're less eager to find out. If doctors practiced medicine like many companies practice management, there would be more unnecessarily sick or dead patients and many more doctors in jail or suffering other penalties for malpractice."^

Professor Rousseau suggests that EBMgt consists of four basic activities:* (1) obtaining the best scientific information available, (2) systematically assessing organizational facts, (3) using critical thinking and reflective judgment to apply the research evidence, and (4) considering key ethical issues. Throughout the remainder of the text, you will be presented with current research evidence from the field of OB and asked to think critically about how you might apply these findings in your current or future career as a management practitioner.

Critical-Thinking Questions

1. **What are some of the primary advantages of evidence-based management practices?**
2. **What makes it difficult for managers to be evidence-based in their actions and decision making?**

* Rousseau, Denise M. "Envisioning Evidence-Based Management." In *The Oxford Handbook Of Evidence-Based Management*, 3–24 (New York: Oxford University Press, 2012).

^ Pfeffer, Jeffrey, and Robert I. Sutton "Evidence-Based Management." *Harvard Business Review* 84, no. 1 (January 2006): 62–74.

glance, this seems pretty reasonable—you may feel more inclined to call in sick when you dislike your job. But it doesn't end there. OB researchers used critical thinking to examine the theory further in order to provide a solution to this work dilemma. What are the factors affecting job satisfaction? What makes employees happy or miserable in their jobs? How can organizations improve conditions to increase job satisfaction and decrease levels of absenteeism? By drilling down deeply into proposed theories, researchers have created practical resolutions to address these problems. OB researchers apply critical thinking to facets of an organization by questioning and exploring the reasons behind issues such as work stress, unethical behavior, lack of team cohesion, poor relationships between individuals and groups, and many more.

Similarly, we could apply the same critical-thinking method to the issue of work/life balance (independent variable) and its relationship to stress (dependent variable), which is one of the main issues facing today's organizations. Employees who sacrifice their personal lives for too many hours in the office may be subject to higher levels of stress. Conversely, workers who achieve a balance between their personal and working lives may have lower levels of stress. We may conclude from this that an acceptable work/life balance leads to higher levels of job satisfaction. Using critical thinking, managers explore how they can help their employees achieve a balance between work and play.

Yet, for all the research that exists on OB and the debates it continues to inspire, it is still universally agreed that there is no one best way of managing people. In fact, there is a theory for that too. It's called **contingency thinking**, and it states that our actions must be dependent on the nature of the situation. In other words, one size does not fit all. Every single circumstance brings about a whole new set of questions and solutions—this is where critical thinking comes into play. By asking the right questions to fit each scenario, managers have a better chance of resolving problems. Related to contingency thinking is **evidence-based management**, which relies on research-based facts to make decisions.[21] Successful OB managers use this wealth of research findings as a basis for understanding different situations.

Open Systems Theory

A key OB research finding that has had a significant impact on the use of critical thinking by managers is called **open systems theory**. According to this theory, organizations are systems that interact with (are *open* to) their environments and use their environments to obtain resources, or inputs, and transform those inputs into outputs that are returned to the environment for consumption.[22] Open systems theory maintains that all organizations are unique and subject to internal and external environmental influences that can affect their efficiency. To ensure the smooth running of an organization, a defined structure should be in place that can accommodate problems and opportunities as they arise. Let's take a look at how a car manufacturing company might operate, according to this theory (see Figure 1.5).

In this example, a car manufacturing company takes inputs from suppliers of certain goods or materials and then uses these resources to manufacture cars within the organization itself ("throughput" in the figure), before exporting them back into the environment as outputs. Put into a general context, this means organizations use input from their resources, such as technology, people, money, raw materials, information, and processes, and transform them into the finished product or output, which they sell.

When open systems work well, they create a **value chain**, the sequence of activities carried out by organizations to create valued goods and services to consumers.[23] In the car example, if every link in the chain is working efficiently, suppliers are satisfied with the way they have been treated by the car company and continue to meet its specifications, employees are productive and manufacture the car in good time and within budget, and consumers are gratified with their new purchase. However, a poorly managed value chain can have disastrous consequences. Suppliers that go out of business, high employee turnover, and a dissatisfied consumer base can all lead to the decline of an organization.

Open systems strive to find a balance between themselves and their environment and to remain harmonious, especially in the face of environmental changes. A strong open system can be crucial to organizational survival, especially in today's organizations that are continually adjusting to meet the demands of global challenges and opportunities.

Contingency thinking: The approach that describes actions as dependent on the nature of the situation; one size does not fit all

Evidence-based management: The practice of using research-based facts to make decisions

Open systems theory: The assumption that organizations are systems that interact with their environments to obtain resources or inputs and transform them into outputs returned to the environment for consumption

Value chain: The sequence of activities carried out by organizations to create valued goods and services to consumers

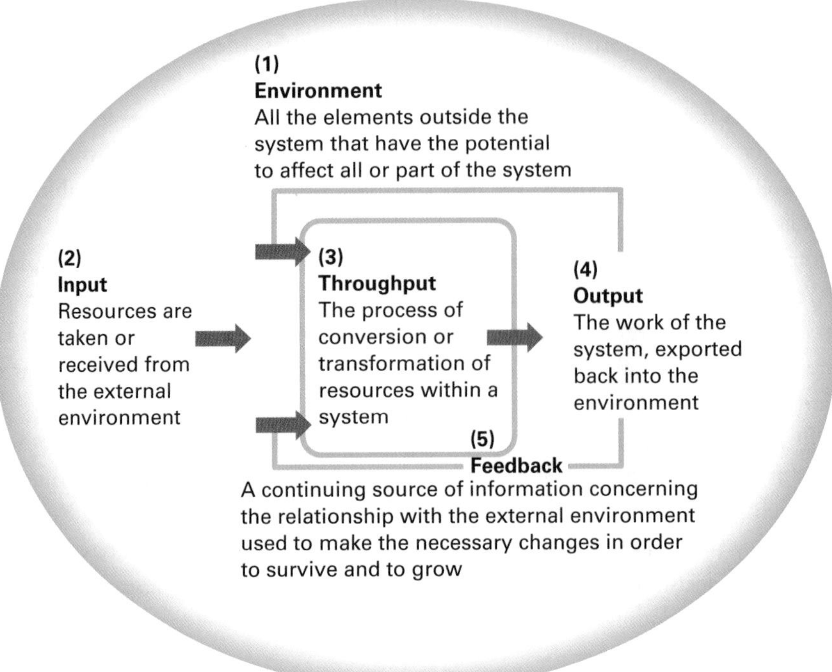

■ FIGURE 1.5 Open Systems Theory: Inputs and Outputs

SOURCE: Basic Open System Model. CSAP Institute for Partnership Development. US Department of Health and Human Services. n.d. Public domain. https://commons.wikimedia.org/wiki/File:Basic_Open_System_Model.gif.

THINKING CRITICALLY

1. Explain in your own words how critical thinking can be used as a problem-solving tool in the workplace. **[Understand]**
2. Create a list of behaviors and skills that contribute to a manager's ability to think critically. **[Apply/Create]**
3. Imagine that you manage two employees who dislike each other and have engaged in heated arguments in front of customers. What specific steps could you take, following the 5-step critical-thinking model (observe, interpret, analyze, evaluate, and explain), to resolve the situation? **[Apply/Analyze]**
4. Identify the inputs, throughput, and outputs of a fast food chain according to Open Systems Theory. **[Apply]**
5. Explain the meaning of "value chain" and provide an example of one way that a value chain may be enhanced and one way a value chain may be harmed. **[Apply]**

OB CHALLENGES AND OPPORTUNITIES

1.5 Identify the major challenges and opportunities in the field of OB

Organizations are in a continual state of flux and transformation. In addition, within the past decade, the financial world has been in turmoil because of a lingering recession and high unemployment. The resulting uncertainty has immeasurably influenced the behavior of people and organizations. So what can you expect when you enter

In an increasingly global economy with more companies expanding internationally, having a strong grasp of organizational behavior can help individuals to relate to and respect their colleagues.

■ FIGURE 1.6 Challenges and Opportunities Facing Today's Organizations

the workforce? Next we discuss some of the main challenges and opportunities facing organizations today (see Figure 1.6).

Globalization

Globalization is a process by which the world has become increasingly interconnected through trade, culture, technology, and politics. It has had a huge influence on OB. Many organizations now have offices all over the world, and it's not uncommon for employees to move between them. For example, you may be placed on a foreign assignment where you are expected to learn a different language and work with people from different cultures and backgrounds. Even at home, you are very likely to be working with people from abroad or from backgrounds different from yours. It is essential to be able to work well with others regardless of their location or cultural background. Communicating effectively across time zones and via the latest technological methods is equally important.

Economic Factors

Economic events have had a significant effect on the workplace. Recessions and financial crises have led to layoffs, reduced wages, unemployment, bankruptcy, and labor shortages. Organizations are continuously strategizing to overcome economic stumbling blocks by seeking out talent and focusing on the skill set of their workforce to find innovative ways to differentiate themselves from the competition. To flourish in a work environment that is continually in flux, you will need to be agile, adaptable, and open to learning new skills when required.

Workforce Diversity

The demographic profile of the United States is changing, and the resulting diversity in the workforce is encouraging organizations to foster inclusive working environments that do not discriminate against employees regardless of gender, race, ethnicity, age, sexual orientation, or disability.[24] In most large organizations, employees are educated about diversity and taught the importance of respecting individual differences. Forming and building good working relationships is central to achieving professional success. You will need to respect others and accept people without prejudice if you want to get ahead in the workplace.

Customer Service

Organizations are creating customer-responsive cultures to meet the increasing needs and changing demands of their customer bases. Companies are striving to understand the customers' needs first and then tailor the product to customer requirements. In most businesses, you will carry out some level of customer service, whether you are dealing with external clients (customers) or internal ones (coworkers). In doing so, you will need to develop a customer-focused attitude and think creatively about how to satisfy customers' needs.

People Skills

Managers and employees must have excellent people skills, such as the ability to communicate and interact with others, in order to work harmoniously with their colleagues. Being able to relate to other people has just as much impact on success as your technical skills, especially when you are leading and managing teams.

Innovation and Change

Organizations need to simulate innovation and change by becoming faster and more agile than the competition. Tangible resources such as physical equipment are no longer the mainstay of an organization. The organization's most important assets are its people and their ability to continuously create, strategize, innovate, and convert their ideas into quality products and processes. Critical thinking is imperative in innovation; you will need to question, analyze, and create to come up with new, original ideas that will appeal to your customers to secure a competitive advantage.

Sustainability

Sustainability

Many organizations are striving to build a more sustainable and responsible global marketplace by taking environmental factors into consideration during decision making and goal setting. Whatever role you play, you will need to take into account the effects your decisions and the decisions of others may have on the environment, your community, and the organization itself.

Throughout this book, we explore these and other factors that influence OB, including leadership, and the effects of a new generation of workers on the workplace. In the next section, we analyze one of the most important elements of global OB: ethical behavior in organizations.

THINKING CRITICALLY

1. Of the seven challenges discussed in this section, which do you consider the most difficult to address? Which do you consider the easiest to address? Why? **[Understand]**
2. Based on your own work or volunteer experience, have you ever experienced any of these seven challenges? Describe your experience and brainstorm ways for overcoming these challenges. **[Apply]**
3. Select a company and research online to learn more about their sustainable business practices. Do they have a sustainability plan? What are some recommendations you might make that would benefit the organization as well as the environment and society? **[Apply/Analyze]**

GLOBAL ETHICS

1.6 Describe the importance of ethical behavior in global organizations

Ethics are moral principles that guide our behavior. Although ethics are useful in helping us make decisions and come to certain conclusions, they don't always give a clear answer to every moral question. For example, complex issues such as abortion and euthanasia have been the subject of strong debate over many years, yet people do not agree on a "right" or "wrong" moral answer to these issues. By following a code of ethics, however, we can make many decisions based on sound guiding principles.

More than a decade ago, the unethical behavior of some major US-based organizations hit the headlines worldwide. One of the most infamous cases brought about the fall of energy giant Enron. In 2001, it was discovered that Enron's CEO Kenneth Lay had used unethical accounting practices and led his team to commit one of the largest corporate frauds in US history. One of the biggest corporate casualties of the Enron scandal was the company's auditors, the accounting and consultancy firm Arthur Anderson, which until then had enjoyed a sterling reputation. Because of the unethical choices made by a few members of the Enron team, such as the decision to destroy evidence of wrongdoing, the company was eventually dissolved.

More recently in 2015 Volkswagen came under fire for developing software designed to ensure some cars meet emissions standards during emissions testing but not during normal operation. Consumers were led to believe they were making an environmentally responsible choice by choosing Volkswagen vehicles. As a result of this scandal, stock prices have fallen and consumer trust in the Volkswagen brand has weakened. This scandal illustrates the economic, reputational, and financial damages that unethical behavior can cause.

Ethics: Moral principles that guide our behavior

Former Enron CEO Kenneth Lay was convicted of conspiracy and fraud after the company went bankrupt in 2001.

Global Ethics

Company scandals have also made many people more aware and less tolerant of perceived unethical behavior. For example, Naked Juice, owned by PepsiCo, was sued in 2011 for deceptively labelling its products "all natural" despite their including some synthetic ingredients.[25] PepsiCo refuted the claim but dropped the word *natural*; the firm has pledged to pay a total of $9 million in compensation to consumers who purchased the juice in the past.

As the Enron, Volkswagen, and other scandals prove, making unethical decisions can have huge consequences. Yet it is not only enormous organizations that deal with ethical problems. Breaches of ethics happen all over the world; in many countries corruption is prevalent, and instances of bribery to win business are commonplace. Similarly, some organizations exploit labor by hiring children, paying very low wages, and forcing employees to work in poor conditions. An organization is unethical if it violates the basic rights of its employees and ignores health, safety, and environmental standards.

One of the more recent ethical debates springs from the rapid development of artificial intelligence (AI) technology. With enhanced speech recognition available, robot dogs in development, and solar-powered drones and self-driving cars on the horizon, the risks associated with AI have quickly come to the fore. Tesla Motors founder Elon Musk and the noted physicist Stephen Hawking are among those who have expressed concern about the ethical consequences of advanced technology. Still to be answered are questions about the danger of building robots for military use, the safety of self-driving cars, the possibility that jobs will be lost to drones and robots, and the general risk of creating software designed to help computers think like humans. Google, owner of several robotics companies, has set up an ethics board to ensure that AI technology is not exploited.

However, Google is not the only company conscious of ethical risks. In many organizations, employees attend training programs, workshops, and seminars that present ethical dilemmas and how to overcome them. In most workplaces there is a growing intolerance for unethical behavior, and there is an expectation that employees will align their work practices with the organization's code of ethics. Indeed, such is the demand for a better understanding of ethical organizational behavior that many business schools, including the Catholic University of America, have integrated ethics into their business and economics courses on a daily basis to teach students the importance of behaving ethically in the workplace.[26]

One of the ways to ensure the practice of good ethical behavior in organizations is to understand the actions and behavior of people and how they work together. In the next section of the chapter, we explore the three underlying levels of analysis in the organizational behavior model.

THINKING CRITICALLY

1. Analyze the relationship between ethics and technology. How might technology lead to unethical behavior? How might technology help businesses develop more ethical and transparent business practices? **[Apply/Analyze]**

2. Recall a recent news story related to unethical behavior by a company. What were the effects of the ethical breach in terms of their reputation and profitability? **[Analyze]**

3. Research a company that is making a positive ethical impact in the business world. How is that company making a difference? How do you think this affects their reputation and profitability? **[Analyze]**

THREE LEVELS OF ANALYSIS IN OB

1.7 Differentiate the three basic levels of analysis at which OB may be examined

There are three main levels of analysis within the OB model: individuals, teams, and organizations.[27] (See Figure 1.7.) Each level builds on the previous one. For example, individuals working well together lay the foundation for effective teams, which in turn work together to achieve organizational goals.

Individuals

Individuals are the foundation of organizations, and the way they work and behave makes or breaks a business. The role of managers is to integrate individuals into the organization, nurture their skills and attributes, and balance their needs and expectations accordingly. When managers do this successfully, individuals will achieve high levels of job satisfaction, motivating them to work toward attaining organizational goals. For

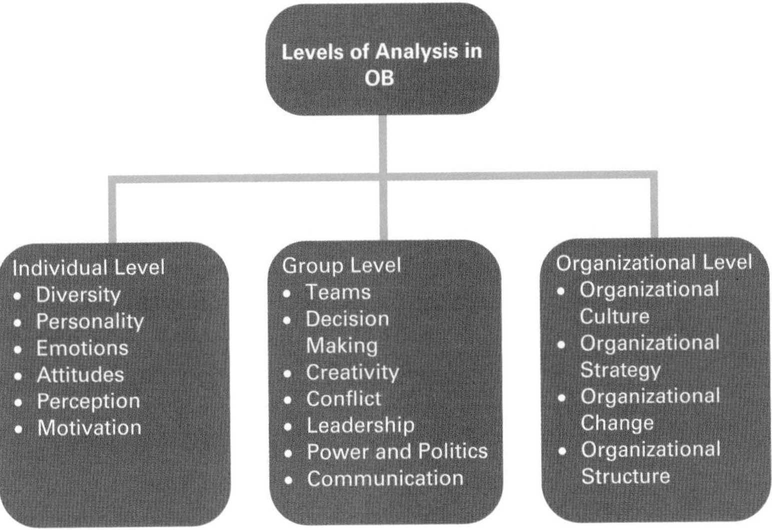

■ FIGURE 1.7 The Three Main Levels of Analysis

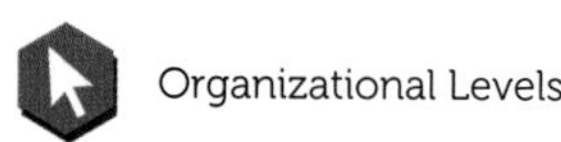

instance, the management at Ed Schmidt Auto, featured in OB in the Real World, strives to engage employees from all over the company in projects they are passionate about.

Teams

Teams or groups exist in all organizations, large or small, and their effective functioning is essential to the success of any organization. Teams are complex because they consist of many different personalities and attitudes. Managers who understand the dynamics of a team and the way it is structured also better understand the underlying behaviors of individuals within the group. A good example is the British football team Manchester United, whose players continually cooperate with each other in pursuit of a common goal, in spite of well-documented personality differences and the occasional feud.[28]

Organizations

Organizations provide individuals and groups with the tools and systems to achieve objectives and goals. The attitudes and behavior of employees are influenced by the way organizations are structured. For instance, Google's organizational structure is centered around employees from all disciplines working together to meet goals and generate innovative ideas. Google employees derive job satisfaction from a flexible working structure that provides them the freedom to set their own goals and standards.[29]

With organizations continually juggling market changes and customer demands, the success of a business depends on its workforce as never before. But how do managers get the best from individuals, teams, and the organization itself?

THINKING CRITICALLY

1. Discuss the relationship among the three levels of analysis in OB. How might individuals influence organizations? How might organizations influence individuals? **[Understand/Apply]**

2. Teams play a critical role in OB. What are some of the benefits of working in teams? What are some of the challenges? **[Understand/Apply]**

POSITIVE OB AND HIGH-INVOLVEMENT MANAGEMENT

1.8 Outline the benefits of positive OB and high-involvement management

Drawing from a range of organizational research and theories, scholarship on **positive organizational behavior** focuses on the strengths, virtues, vitality, and resilience of individuals and organizations.[30] The idea is that nurturing the strengths of individuals rather than attempting to "fix" their weaknesses is far more beneficial to achieving organizational goals. Employees will gain more self-confidence and feel more positive about their skills and abilities, leading to better performance. Managers who practice positive OB value human capital as their most important resource.

Positive organizational behavior: The strengths, virtues, vitality, and resilience of individuals and organizations

Say you are the manager of a sales and marketing department. You need your sales team to reach a specific sales target by the end of each month. However, one of your new hires, a recent business graduate, is regularly failing to meet objectives, bringing down the department's sales total. When you arrange a one-to-one meeting with him, he admits he is finding the role tougher than he thought it would be. He

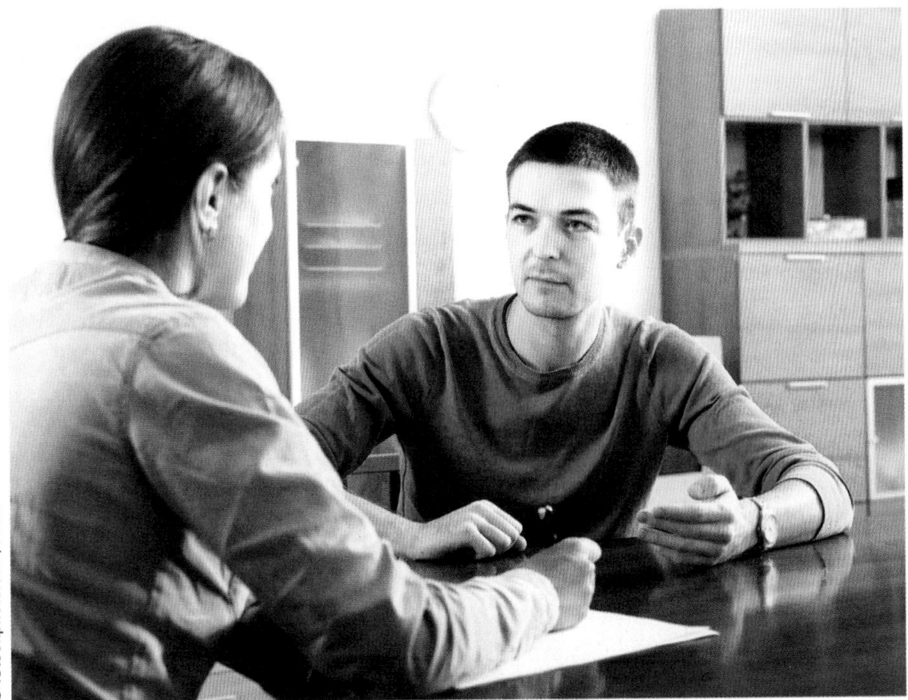

© iStockphoto.com/JackF

Managers who practice positive OB will communicate with their employees and learn their strengths to discover the position that is best suited to their skills.

knows the products and services inside out but finds it difficult to persuade people to meet with him to discuss a potential sale. As his manager, you arrange additional training to improve his sales technique and build his confidence in selling. Following extensive training, he succeeds in securing a couple of meetings with prospects but fails to sell anything. When you hired him, you felt he had potential. Do you fire him for not bringing in the business, or do you consider another position for him in the organization?

Managers who practice positive OB will choose the second option. This employee may not be a good fit for sales, but what else can he do that would benefit the organization? Perhaps he loves to write and feels more comfortable communicating through media rather than over the phone. As a Web content assistant, writing articles for the company website and working with project teams, designers, and developers to ensure information is presented in the best way, he can thrive.

This is just one example of how managers get the best from (and for) their employees using positive behavior. Most people are hired for a reason, but it is entirely possible that some may not be the best fit in the role for which they were hired. In such a case, managers who value their human capital should make every effort to match employees' skill sets with a more appropriate position. Otherwise, organizations could face the dilemmas of low job satisfaction and reduced productivity, leading to an increase in absenteeism and high turnover.

High-Involvement Management

Positive OB places the highest priority on the well-being of employees. This style of management is closely linked with **high-involvement management**, a strategy in which managers empower employees to make decisions, provide them with extensive training and opportunities to increase their knowledge base, share important information, and provide incentive compensation.[31] Increasing employee involvement in this way is a very democratic approach to management, giving all employees, including those who carry out basic duties, a say in how the work is conducted. They are then more likely to work hard, and more willing to adapt to new processes and learn new tasks. Empowered, satisfied employees strive to achieve organizational goals.

High-involvement management: The way managers empower employees to make decisions, provide them with extensive training and the opportunities to increase their knowledge base, share important information, and provide incentive compensation

Again, this type of approach works only when the right employees are selected to work in an organization. They must be the right cultural fit and believe in the values

Brandon Steiner of Steiner Sports is a high-involvement manager.

AP Photo/Kathy Willens

and mission of the company. Equally, managers must treat employees with respect, listen carefully to their ideas, and be willing to admit to themselves and their employees that they don't have all the answers. When high-involvement management is effective, it helps to build strong relationships between employees and managers, fosters trust, and increases job satisfaction and productivity.

High-involvement managers have different ways of empowering their employees. Take Brandon Steiner, for instance. Steiner is the founder and CEO of Steiner Sports and a professional sports marketer, speaker, and author. He believes the well-being of his employees begins with the food they eat, and that there is a strong correlation between a healthy diet and work performance.[32] When new hires join Steiner Sports, he tells them, "I don't care about a lot of the things other managers do, but one thing you cannot do here is eat unhealthily."[33] How does Steiner encourage his employees to be healthy? The company pays for gym membership, ensures a continuous supply of fresh fruit is available in the break room, and makes personal side bets with heavily overweight employees to see who can lose the most weight in the healthiest way within a specified period of time. One of Steiner's mottos is, "If you don't feel your best, you can't do your best work."[34] Would you like to work for a company like Steiner Sports that strongly promotes employee health and well-being? Do you think you would fit in and buy into the ethos of this type of organization? If you are not the type of person who places as high a value on healthy living as Steiner, then perhaps this might not be the right work culture for you. Remember, high-involvement management works best when employees are a good fit for the organization.

Throughout this text, we present a number of case studies and scenarios to demonstrate a critical-thinking perspective in relation to OB. Some of the characters you will meet in our OB stories include Laura Pierce, who is beginning her new role as marketing and development manager for the West Texas Regional Theatre (WTRT); Katie O'Donnell, a college MBA student working as a server at the Waterfront Grill restaurant in upstate New York; Brian Stevens, plant manager of a tractor assembly plant in the Midwest; and Langston Burrows, a recent college graduate working in the leadership development program (LDP) in a mid-sized regional bank. Based on real-life scenarios, the stories illustrate the types of situations and people you may come across within organizations and to provide you with clear insights and strategies to deal with complexities as and when they arise.

We have structured this book to explore the challenges and opportunities facing OB on an individual, group, and organizational level. Throughout the text, we explore the complexities of human behavior, including individual behaviors, emotions, and attitudes. We also examine OB in the context of leadership, motivation, teamwork, and culture.

At the heart of every job, regardless of the industry, lies the need to get along with people and to fit in with the values and culture of the organization. However, in today's organizations, fitting in does not mean agreeing with everything to maintain the status quo, nor does it mean laughing at your boss's jokes (especially when you don't think they are very funny!). Instead, applying critical thinking by asking questions, suspending bias, and providing creative solutions, all of which you'll experience in this book, form the new norm. Understanding and gaining knowledge about OB is a lifelong learning process. Your career success depends on your ability to learn from your everyday experiences and on the way you conduct your relationships with others, behave, and communicate.

In a world where the only constant is change, it is more important than ever to manage our own behavior and understand the feelings, attitudes, and behaviors of others around us in order to work harmoniously and productively and succeed in a complex working environment.

THINKING CRITICALLY

1. Identify your top five strengths. Describe how each of these strengths might benefit an organization. **[Understand/Apply]**

2. Could there be a downside or unintended consequences for managers who focus primarily on the findings of positive organizational behavior research? Explain your answer. **[Analyze]**

3. List three concrete ways a high-involvement manager could empower employees. **[Apply]**

IN REVIEW

Learning Objectives

1.1 Explain the basic concept of organizational behavior and its value in organizations

Organizational behavior studies how and why individual employees and groups of employees behave the way they do within an organizational setting. The three main reasons for studying organizational behavior in your organization are to be able to *explain* it, *predict* it, and *influence* it.

1.2 Describe the key role of managing human capital in creating a sustainable competitive advantage for organizations

Human capital is essential for gaining **competitive advantage**, the edge that gives organizations a more beneficial position than their competitors and allows them to generate more profits and retain more customers. Three main aspects of human capital enhance true competitive advantage: **value, rareness,** and **inimitability.**

1.3 Identify the major behavioral science disciplines that contribute to OB

Psychology is the scientific study of the human mind that seeks to measure and explain behavioral characteristics. **Sociology** is the study of the behavior of groups and how they relate to each other in a social setting. **Social psychology** blends concepts from sociology and psychology and focuses on how people influence each other in a social setting. **Political science** studies the behavior of individuals and groups within a political environment. **Anthropology** is the study of people and their activities in relation to societal, environmental, and cultural influences.

1.4 Demonstrate the value of critical thinking in the context of OB

Critical thinking is the ability to use intelligence, knowledge, and skills to question and carefully explore situations and arrive at thoughtful conclusions based on evidence and reason. The critical-thinking approach is a powerful analytical method that helps managers consider intended and unintended consequences of behaviors on their teams, organizations, and communities.

1.5 Identify the major challenges and opportunities in the field of OB

The process of *globalization* has had a huge influence on OB. The *economy* has had a significant effect on OB. Organizations are continually strategizing to overcome economic stumbling blocks by hiring talent and focusing on the skill sets of their workforce to find new, innovative ways to differentiate themselves from the competition. Workforce diversity develops when organizations foster working environments that do not discriminate against others regardless of gender, race, ethnicity, age, sexual orientation, and disability. Organizations are creating *customer-responsive cultures* to meet the increasing needs and changing demands of their customer base. Managers and employees must have excellent people skills to use on the job to work harmoniously with their fellow colleagues. Organizations need to simulate *innovation* and *change* by becoming faster and more agile than the competition. There is a growing commitment to fostering an *ethical culture* and improving ethical behavior in the *workplace*. Many organizations are striving to build a more *sustainable* and responsible global marketplace by taking environmental factors into consideration during decision-making and goal-setting practices.

1.6 Describe the importance of ethical behavior in global organizations

Ethics are moral principles that guide our behavior. Ethical scandals in recent years have made many people more aware and less tolerant of perceived unethical behavior. An organization is unethical if it violates the basic rights of its employees and ignores health, safety, and environmental standards. In many organizations, employees attend training programs, workshops, and seminars that present ethical dilemmas and how to overcome them. In most workplaces there is a growing intolerance for unethical behavior and an expectation that employees will align their work practices with the organization's code of ethics.

1.7 Differentiate the three basic levels of analysis at which OB may be examined

There are three main levels of analysis within the OB model: individuals, teams, and organizations. Individuals are the foundation of organizations: the way they work and behave either makes or breaks a business. The role of managers is to integrate individuals into the organization, nurture their skills and attributes, and balance their needs and expectations accordingly. Teams or groups exist in all organizations, large or small, and have a significant influence on the behavior of individual team members. Managers who understand the dynamics of a team and how it is structured gain more knowledge about the underlying behaviors of individuals within the group. Individuals and groups work within the formal structure of organizations. Organizations provide employees with the tools and systems to achieve objectives and goals. The attitudes and behavior of employees are influenced by the way organizations are structured.

1.8 Outline the benefits of positive OB and high-involvement management

Positive organizational behavior focuses on the strengths, virtues, vitality, and resilience of individuals and organizations. **High-involvement management** occurs when managers empower employees to make decisions, provide them with extensive training and the opportunities to increase their knowledge base, share important information, and provide incentive compensation. This type of approach works only when the right employees are selected to work in an organization. When high-involvement management is effective it helps to build strong relationships between individuals and teams, fosters trust, and increases job satisfaction and productivity.

KEY TERMS

EXERCISE 1.1: OB ON SCREEN

Think of at least two movies or television shows about the president or CEO of a large business. How does the leader treat his or her employees? What changes could be made to foster better employee relations?

EXERCISE 1.2: WHAT YOU WERE THEN

Morris Massey, a marketing professor at the University of Colorado, developed a video series expounding the concept "You Are What You Were When." The idea behind this was that the culture, the significant world events, and your own personal life experiences during your youth contribute significantly to your identity. To better understand the differences in individuals with whom you work, it may be helpful to understand what was happening in the world when they were young.

Objective:

To better understand OB and practice understanding the individual differences that exist in people.

Instructions:

Interview two people who are from different generations than yourself. You can interview family, friends, or acquaintances. Ask them the following questions about life when they were 8–14 years old:

1. Where did you grow up? (State or country)
2. How did your closest friendships develop?
3. What was happening in the world? How did these world events affect you?
4. What was the economic situation of your family?
5. What was the most important thing to you during that time of your life?

Now, ask yourself those same questions and write down your responses.

As a class or in groups, aggregate the responses and address the following questions.

Reflection Questions:

1. What patterns do you see in the aggregated responses?
2. What differences do you see based on where individuals grew up?
3. What types of world events had the most impact?
4. How might someone's economic situation growing up influence the way she or he thinks about work and approach her or his job?
5. How can you use the knowledge of what people were experiencing in their youth to better work with them now?

Exercise contributed by Harriet Rojas, Professor of Business, Indiana Wesleyan University.

EXERCISE 1.3: YOUR EXPERIENCE WITH OB

Objective:

This exercise will help you to better *understand* organizational behavior, its concepts, and its uses by helping you to *explain* and *discuss* your organizational experiences in terms of Chapter 1 concepts.

Instructions:

Step 1 (10 minutes): Think about an organization that you are or have been a member of. This organization can be any type of organization as discussed in the first chapter of this text (i.e. a social, religious, charitable, or other type of organization). After selecting your organization, think about some problem that the organization has had. Write down a brief (no more than one half of a page) narrative describing this problem. Be sure to explain the problem using the concept terms from Chapter 1. Also, try to identify the level at which this problem existed: individual, group, organizational, or across multiple levels.

Step 2 (10 minutes): Find a partner and read each other the problem you each wrote about. Select the most interesting of the two write-ups. Together re-write the description so that it clarifies any points that are unclear and is more concrete in its use and application of chapter concepts.

Step 3 (10 minutes): Each pair should find another pair to form a quad. Each pair should read the situation write-up selected in step 2 to the other pair. Again, select the situation that is the most interesting, and work together as a group to improve the situation description. Clarify any misuse of terms, and be sure that as much of the situation as possible is described using chapter concepts.

Step 4 (10 to 30 minutes): Select one person from the quad to read the write-up chosen by the entire quad as the most interesting to the entire class. The person who reads the situation should be someone other than the person who initially wrote about the situation, but everyone should be prepared to help clarify any points about the write-up using chapter concepts.

Reflection Questions:

Think about the process of identifying organizational problems in terms of the organizational behavior concepts you are learning.

1. How did identifying the problem in this way change the way you thought about the problem?
2. How did linking the problem to the concepts help you think about methods for dealing with the problem?
3. How did thinking about the level of the problem shape the way you thought about the problem?
4. When listening to other groups, note how their descriptions used chapter concepts. Were there any usages that surprised you or you were uncertain about?

Exercise contributed by Milton R. Mayfield, Professor of Business, Texas A&M International University and Jaqueline R. Mayfield, Professor of Business, Texas A&M International University.

CASE STUDY 1.1: PFIZER PHARMACEUTICALS

Researchers at the Gallup-Healthways Well-Being Index estimate that employee unhappiness costs US businesses a mind-boggling $300 billion per year in lost productivity. And although worker productivity—what drives it, what quashes it—is a topic of some debate, certain correlations show up again and again: unhappy workers have high levels of absenteeism and produce less in both quality and quantity. According to a 2011 *Harvard Business Review* article, workers' creativity, productivity, commitment, and collegiality are all affected by their level of happiness, and the corporate bottom line either suffers or flourishes as a result.

Discussions about the world's "happiest places to work" might bring to mind some now-famous companies like Zappos, with its focus on hiring only the right employees, or any number of technology-based start-ups creating unusual workspaces to foster creativity. The seemingly cold and faceless world of pharmaceuticals is perhaps an unlikely candidate for a happy place to work. Yet for the second year in a row, 165-year-old New York City-based Pfizer Pharmaceuticals grabbed the number one spot on the 50 Happiest Companies in America list published on career website CareerBliss. With annual revenue exceeding $67 billion, driven by more than 110,000 employees, Pfizer—the maker of Advil, ChapStick, Zoloft, Viagra, Dimetapp, and hundreds of other drugstore products found both behind and over the counter—not only ranks as the world's largest pharmaceutical company, it also employs the happiest workers.

Job satisfaction at Pfizer is the result of forward-thinking, innovative policies that seek to create a meaningful, engaging environment for colleagues (as Pfizer employees are called)—and one in which those colleagues enjoy working with each other. The most prominent strategy used in creating such an environment is ownership. Pfizer CEO Ian Read promoted the ownership culture in 2012 with the goal of engaging each employee in improving the company for all its stakeholders, from consumers to shareholders. The ultimate goal was the creation of a work environment that was a birthplace not only of new products, but of new pathways leading to those products. In turn, this environment would support the employees within it and foster in them a deep sense of responsibility to fellow colleagues and every company stakeholder.

The idea of the ownership model was born of candid research within the company among employees at every level. That led to the creation of a corporate culture that fosters independent and innovative thinking, provides opportunity for growth and movement within the company, gives meaningful feedback to employees, and encourages responsible risk taking while placing a high emphasis on personal responsibility. Failure is treated as an inevitability that provides an opportunity for learning or problem solving—and pharmaceutical research is no stranger to failure. By accepting failure and providing meaningful, constructive feedback, the company encourages employees to innovate, and innovation is something Pfizer considers an imperative for continued success in a crowded industry.

The ownership model isn't the only aspect of Pfizer employment that leads to contented workers; the company has also taken great strides to ensure that its colleagues spend most of their time at work able to focus on what they were hired to do. Although at first glance this seems an obvious step, Pfizer's own reviews of employee activity found that a significant chunk of valuable time was spent on "support tasks," like creating Microsoft PowerPoint presentations or handling correspondence, instead of on the appropriate use of the employee's talents and primary job roles. To address this issue, Pfizer turned to outsourcing, which is the practice of transferring work to other companies to save on costs. Pfizer employees can outsource presentations, data mining and analysis, document creation, scheduling, and other tasks so they can spend more time developing and implementing new research strategies, conducting research, and all the other tasks that allow Pfizer to remain a leading innovator in the industry. The result of this strategy is a tangible increase in productivity over shorter periods of time. This means a shorter path from idea to research to execution, not only for new products but for new business strategies as well.

Pfizer has worked hard to be an innovator, not only in the pharmaceutical development that sustains the bottom line but also in the creation of a corporate environment filled with happy, productive employees. The company's own stated outlook is that even in an industry driven by patents and products, "Pfizer's most important assets leave our building at the end of each workday." This company is a primary example of the value gained by having employees who believe in what they do and feel encouraged to produce high-quality, innovative work, not because they fear the consequences of underperforming but because they feel like a part of the company in a meaningful way. Pfizer's corporate policy treats employees as people rather than numbers, and the success of this strategy is evident in its continued reign as the largest pharmaceutical company in the world—and now the happiest, too.

Case Questions

1. Describe how Pfizer enriches its human capital in value, rareness, and inimitability.
2. Show how Pfizer is utilizing three levels of analysis to its practice of strategic organizational behavior.
3. In what ways does Pfizer utilize positive organizational behavior?

Sources

Breen, Bill. "The Thrill of Defeat." *Fast Company*, June 1, 2004. www.fastcompany.com/49239/thrill-defeat.

The Career Bliss Team. "CareerBliss 50 Happiest Companies in America for 2014." *Careerbliss*, December 9, 2013. www.careerbliss.com/facts-and-figures/careerbliss-50-happiest-companies-in-america-for-2014/.

Cohen, Adrienne. "Scuttling Scut Work." *Fast Company*, February 1, 2008. www.fastcompany.com/641153/scuttling-scut-work-1/10/2013.

Dishman, Lydia. "Secrets of America's Happiest Companies." *Fast Company*, January 10, 2013. www.fastcompany.com/3004595/secrets-americas-happiest-companies.

"Pfizer." *Forbes*, April 2012. www.forbes.com/companies/pfizer/.

Pfizer Annual Report 2011. www.pfizer.com/investors/financial_reports/annual_reports/2011/colleagues.jsp.

Tam, Marilyn. "A Happy Worker Is a Productive Worker." *Huffington Post*, July 31, 2013. www.huffingtonpost.com/marilyn-tam/how-to-be-happy-at-work_b_3648000.html.

SELF-ASSESSMENT 1.1

Follow the flow chart below to see what kind of a leader you are!

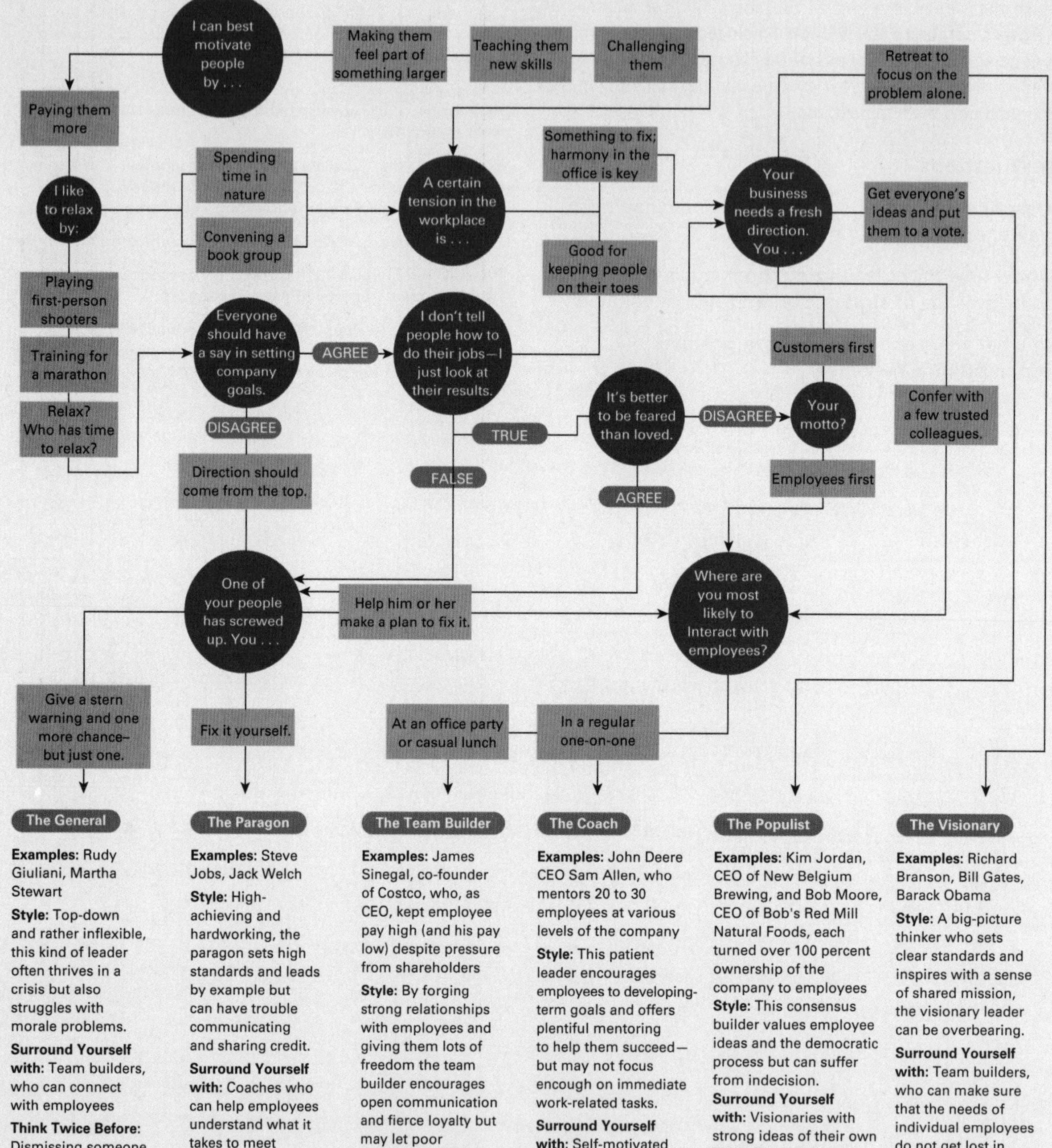

The General

Examples: Rudy Giuliani, Martha Stewart

Style: Top-down and rather inflexible, this kind of leader often thrives in a crisis but also struggles with morale problems.

Surround Yourself with: Team builders, who can connect with employees

Think Twice Before: Dismissing someone else's idea

The Paragon

Examples: Steve Jobs, Jack Welch

Style: High-achieving and hardworking, the paragon sets high standards and leads by example but can have trouble communicating and sharing credit.

Surround Yourself with: Coaches who can help employees understand what it takes to meet standards and team builders who help boost morale

Think Twice Before: Taking control of other people's projects

The Team Builder

Examples: James Sinegal, co-founder of Costco, who, as CEO, kept employee pay high (and his pay low) despite pressure from shareholders

Style: By forging strong relationships with employees and giving them lots of freedom the team builder encourages open communication and fierce loyalty but may let poor performance go uncorrected.

Surround Yourself with: Paragons, and who will enforce high standards, and generals, who can focus on details

Think Twice Before: Giving unqualified praise

The Coach

Examples: John Deere CEO Sam Allen, who mentors 20 to 30 employees at various levels of the company

Style: This patient leader encourages employees to developing-term goals and offers plentiful mentoring to help them succeed—but may not focus encough on immediate work-related tasks.

Surround Yourself with: Self-motivated paragons and generals, who can deal efficiently with crises

Think Twice Before: Devoting too much time to employees who resist mentoring

The Populist

Examples: Kim Jordan, CEO of New Belgium Brewing, and Bob Moore, CEO of Bob's Red Mill Natural Foods, each turned over 100 percent ownership of the company to employees

Style: This consensus builder values employee ideas and the democratic process but can suffer from indecision.

Surround Yourself with: Visionaries with strong ideas of their own

Think Twice Before: Calling another meeting

The Visionary

Examples: Richard Branson, Bill Gates, Barack Obama

Style: A big-picture thinker who sets clear standards and inspires with a sense of shared mission, the visionary leader can be overbearing.

Surround Yourself with: Team builders, who can make sure that the needs of individual employees do not get lost in pursuit of a grand vision

Think Twice Before: Showing the smart people who work for you how much smarter you are

SOURCE: www.inc.com/magazine/201310/adam-bluestein/what-kind-of-leader-are-you.html.

PART 2

INDIVIDUAL PROCESSES

2 Diversity and Individual Differences

We all should know that diversity makes for a rich tapestry, and we must understand that all the threads are equal in value no matter what their color.

—Maya Angelou, American author

DIVERSITY IN OB

2.1 Explain the importance of diversity in OB

In Chapter 1, we took a brief look at workforce diversity and the importance of respecting individual differences in order to form and build successful professional relationships. In broader terms, **workplace diversity** refers to the degree to which an organization includes people from different cultures and backgrounds; it involves recognizing, respecting, and valuing both individual and group differences by treating people as individuals in an effort to promote an inclusive culture.[1]

One of the most effective ways organizations can encourage acceptance of differences and create a harmonious workforce is through the management of diversity. Today's workplace welcomes more people from different backgrounds and different experiences than ever before. Combined, these individuals create a powerful force—studies have shown diverse groups working well together perform better and are more innovative, creative, and productive; factors essential for organizations when gaining competitive advantage in the workplace.[2] Similarly, a diverse workforce can increase market share by helping the organization more effectively communicate with customers from different backgrounds and cultures. Looking into the future, recent reports on demographics project that groups currently classified as minorities will become the majority in the United States by 2050. In a recent survey of the Top 50 Companies for Diversity run by DiversityInc, pharmaceuticals giant Novartis took the number one spot; Verizon Communications came last on the list.[3] Organizations that do not currently foster a diverse workforce need to harness all the talent available and commit to these changing demographics or risk being left behind.[4]

LEARNING OBJECTIVES

By the end of this chapter, you will be able to:

- 2.1 Explain the importance of diversity in OB
- 2.2 Discuss why individual differences are important
- 2.3 Contrast the nature and nurture explanations of personality development
- 2.4 Describe the Myers-Briggs Type Indicator Types and the Four Temperaments
- 2.5 Identify the five personality factors of the Big Five Model
- 2.6 Differentiate among the most common personality attributes

Surface-Level and Deep-Level Diversity

There are two main types of diversity: surface-level diversity and deep-level diversity.[5] (See Figure 2.1.) **Surface-level diversity** describes the easily perceived differences between us, such as age and generation, race and ethnicity, gender and sexual orientation, and physical and/or mental ability. This type of diversity can lead to discrimination when managers or recruiters judge or stereotype others on the basis of superficial differences. For example, if they believe performance declines with age, they will choose a younger candidate over an older candidate.

In contrast, **deep-level diversity** describes verbal and nonverbal behaviors that are not as easily perceived because they lie below the surface. Deep-level diversity

Workplace diversity: The degree to which an organization represents different cultures

Surface-level diversity: Easily perceived differences between people, such as age/generation, race/ethnicity, gender, and ability

Deep-level diversity: Differences in verbal and nonverbal behaviors that are not as easily perceived because they lie below the surface, such as differences in attitudes, values, beliefs, and personality

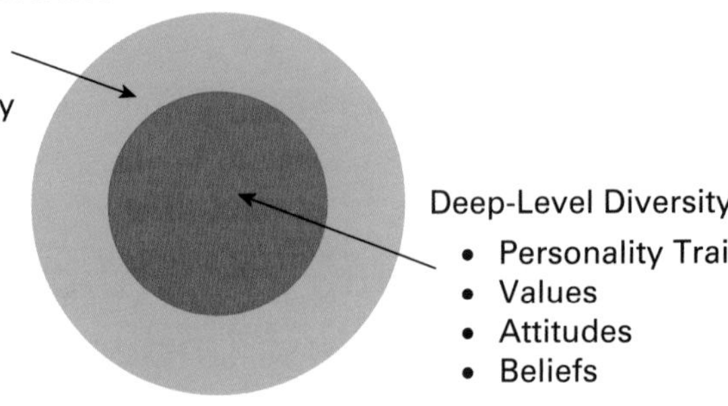

■ FIGURE 2.1 Surface-Level and Deep-Level Diversity

SOURCES: Huszczo, G., and Megan Endres. "Joint Effects of Gender and Personality on Choice of Happiness Strategies." *Europe's Journal of Psychology* 9, no 1 (February 2013).

may include attitudes, values, beliefs, and personality traits. People first identify surface-level differences in others, and then become aware of deep-level differences as they get to know someone. For example, initially Myra and Jorge might treat one another with caution because of dissimilarities between their cultural background or native languages. As their relationship deepens and they learn about each other's underlying attitudes, values, and beliefs, however, their surface-level perceptions of difference may subside. Myra and Jorge may begin to find common ground and recognize the similarities they share with one other.

Age/Generation Diversity

Age diversity: People of all different ages included within the workplace

With workforce demographics shifting and the number of mature people in the workplace rising, many organizations are finding ways to leverage **age diversity**, which is

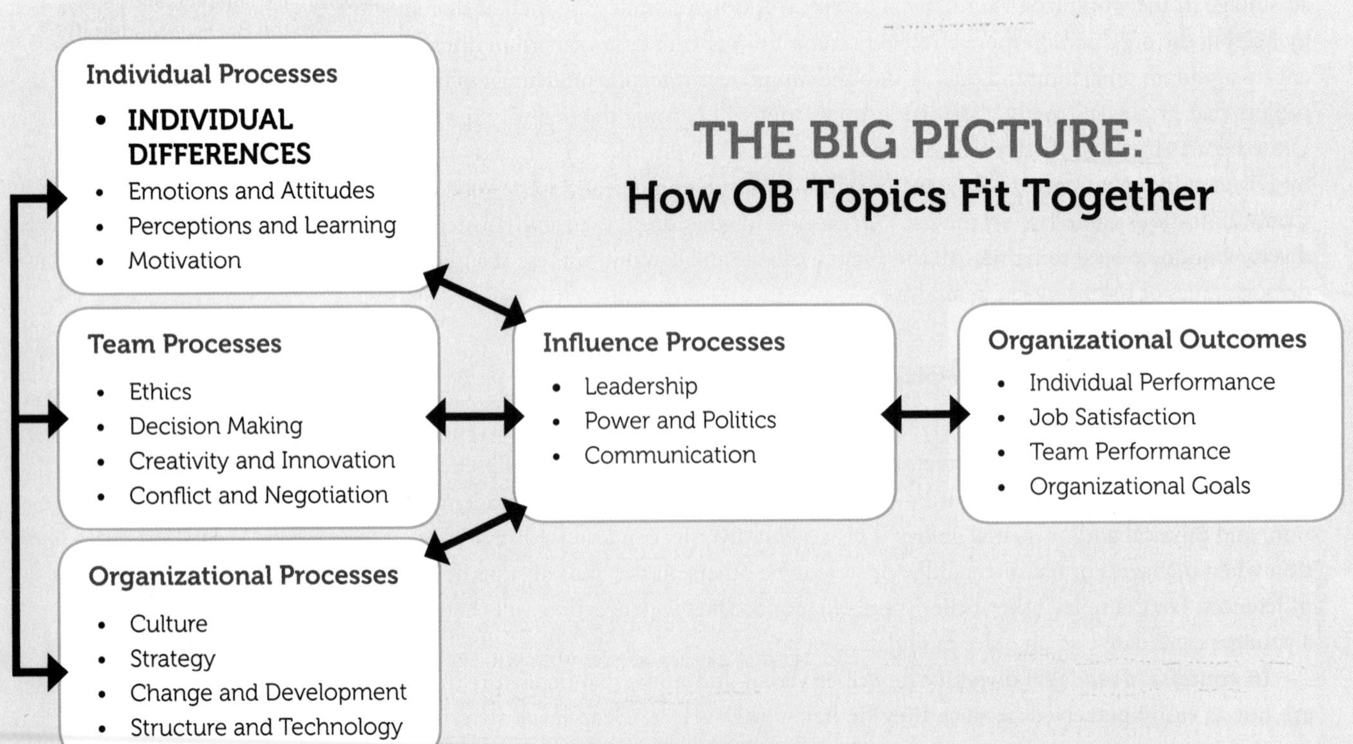

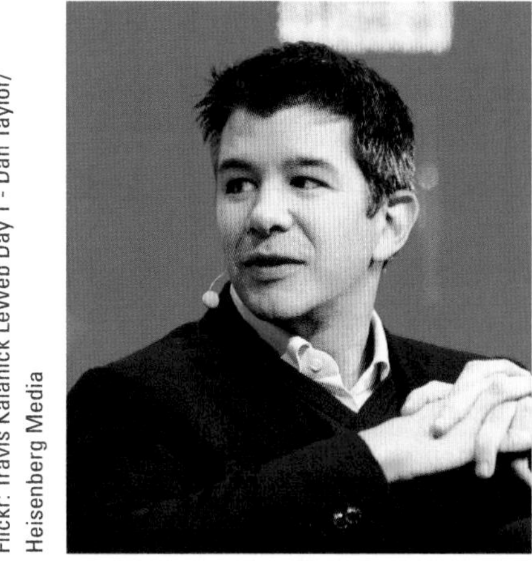

Hillary Rodham Clinton is a notable member of the baby boomer generation; Uber founder Travis Kalanick belongs to generation X; Facebook founder Mark Zuckerberg is quite possibly the posterboy for the generation deemed millenials.

including people of all different ages within the workplace.[6] This is no easy task given that today's workforce spans four generations: traditionalists (born before 1946); baby boomers (born 1946–1964); generation Xers (born 1965–1981); and millennials (born 1982–2000). Managers need to treat age-diverse workforces thoughtfully, without falling prey to stereotypes often portrayed by the popular media. For example, traditionalists and baby boomers are often described as "old school," conservative, and not up to date with the latest technology, while younger employees such as gen Xers and millennials are thought to be technology savvy yet lazy and with a tendency to flit from one job to the next. Applying these stereotypes to individuals could lead to bias and conflict among differently aged workers in an organization. Organizations dealing with a multigenerational workforce need to focus on the strengths and weaknesses of their individual employees and should be able foster the transfer of knowledge across age groups while bridging differences and building on commonalities in order to create a cohesive, dynamic workforce.

Race and Ethnicity

Diversity in the Gaming Industry

Today's workplace is made up of people from different racial groups and ethnicities, yet racial and ethnic prejudice still persist. Sometimes the terms *race* and *ethnicity* are used interchangeably, but **race** is related to factors of physical appearance such as skin, hair, or eye color, whereas **ethnicity** is associated with sociological factors such as nationality, culture, language, and ancestry.[7]

No one should ever feel uncomfortable because of their race or ethnicity. Racial and ethnic prejudice often stems from ignorance and stereotypes that individuals may not even be aware influence them. Racial and ethnic discrimination has played a prominent role in U.S. history and it is only in the last few decades that significant strides have been made to overcome such discrimination. Making an effort to develop a deeper sense of racial and cultural awareness by becoming familiar with the history of racial and ethnic discrimination in the U.S. and learning about different languages and cultural traditions goes a long way toward building group harmony in the workplace. And, as with all workplace relationships, treating every person with whom you work as an individual rather than a collection of predetermined labels goes a long way toward establishing trust and understanding.

Race: Identifying biological factors such as skin, hair, or eye color

Ethnicity: Sociological factors such as nationality, culture, language, and ancestry

Gender Diversity and Sexual Orientation

Gender diversity is the equal representation of both men and women in the workplace.[8] As with racial and ethnic minorities in the U.S., the treatment of women in the workplace has come a long way during the past fifty years. In the past, wealthier women were often expected to take care of their children and their home rather than having a career, while poorer women often did double-duty caring for their own households as well as working to supplement their family's income. The jobs available to women were limited, paid less than similar jobs available to men, and most employers considered women to be physically, emotionally, and mentally inferior to men in their ability to contribute to the workplace.

Today, women occupy positions and roles in every industry, and laws and regulations have been put in place to counteract discrimination against them. However, though women have made great strides in achieving equality, differences in salary and hiring practices remain. For example, many women are still hampered by a **glass ceiling**, an invisible barrier that limits their ability to progress to more senior positions.[9] In addition, in 2015 women are still paid less than men for comparable jobs and remain under-represented in more senior roles.[10]

Like race, ethnicity, and gender, the organizational approach to **sexual orientation**, which refers to a person's sexual identity and the gender(s) to which she or he is attracted, in the United States has come a long way during the past few decades, yet achieving equal rights and protections in the workplace regardless of sexual orientation have only partially occurred. According to the 2014 Out and Equal Workplace Survey conducted by the Harris Poll, though there is increasing support from organizations for workplace equality in the United States and around the world, in 32 states employees can legally be fired by their employers for being lesbian, gay, bisexual, or transgender (LGBT).[11] (See Figure 2.2.)

Diversity of Abilities

Ability diversity is the representation of people with different levels of mental and physical abilities within an organization. More than 50 million people in the United States have a disability and more than 50 percent of those people are unemployed.[12]

Although people with physical and mental impairments may not be able to carry out certain tasks, there is still a huge range of tasks at which they can excel. Skills can be taught, and people can be trained to improve their skills; jobs may or may not require particular physical abilities, like the ability to walk unaided. Managing ability diversity begins with selecting employees with abilities that best fit the role. This, in turn, leads to increased productivity and job satisfaction.

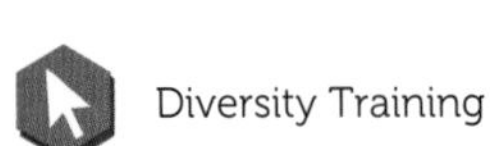

Diversity Training

Diversity Training

Diversity training can help reduce bias and break down prejudices or psychological barriers among those who struggle to accept coworkers they perceive as different. Many organizations institute mandatory diversity training programs with an emphasis on inclusion, in which each employee is asked whether he or she feels valued, respected, and welcomed in the organization. This provides a safe forum for employees to openly discuss diversity issues and consider the actions they would take when presented with different scenarios.

Although most organizations would agree that all employees should be treated fairly and equally, the rising number of lawsuits citing discrimination and bias has led some experts to question whether diversity training programs are as effective as organizations would like to believe. For example, a 2007 study of more than 800 companies over the course of 31 years showed that despite millions spent on diversity training, no positive impact was made on the workplace. In fact, in organizations with lawsuits made against them, diversity training had a negative influence.[13]

Gender diversity: The way different genders are treated in the workplace

Glass ceiling: An invisible barrier that limits one's ability to progress to more senior positions

Sexual orientation: A person's sexual identity and the gender(s) to which she or he is attracted

Ability diversity: The representation of people with different levels of mental and physical abilities within an organization

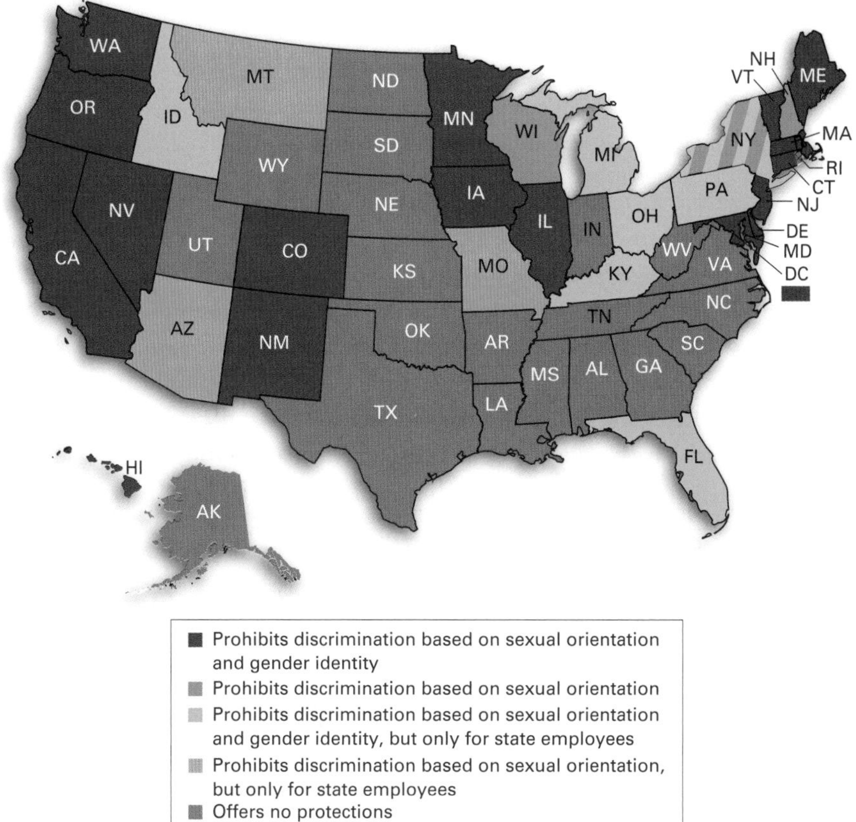

■ FIGURE 2.2 Where Are LGBT Employees Most Vulnerable?

SOURCE: www.vocativ.com/culture/lgbt/lgbt-rights-kansas/.

Despite the debate surrounding the effectiveness of diversity training programs, it is still vital that organizations create environments that embrace every employee, regardless of background, age, culture, ethnicity, or other difference.

Introducing the Case of Laura Pierce: Differences at the West Texas Regional Theatre

In the following sections of this chapter, we introduce a fictionalized scenario that further illustrates and provides an opportunity to apply and evaluate topics related to diversity and individual differences in the workplace. This fictionalized case is written from the perspective of Laura Pierce, who is beginning her new role as development and marketing director at the West Texas Regional Theatre (WTRT) in Texas.

The WTRT team is a diverse group representing different ages, ethnicities, and genders, factors that sometimes contribute to tension within the group. Let's meet some of these employees.

The West Texas Regional Theatre is a well-respected, nonprofit professional theatre company that presents eight to ten shows each year in the historic Paramount Theatre in downtown Abilene, Texas. With a full-time office staff of four, WTRT employs more than 100 part-time artists and technical workers per year and has a contract with the Actors Equity Association.

Laura Pierce, development and marketing director. An arts major in college, Laura left her job as the former development director of a National Public Radio (NPR) station in her home state of Tennessee because she was overlooked by a promotion in favor of a male coworker who was less qualified than her. Frustrated by the glass ceiling barrier at NPR, 28-year-old Laura has accepted the newly created role of development and marketing director at WTRT to address a decline in ticket sales and donations. She is spontaneous, smart, and enthusiastic. Laura is black and comes from a middle-class background.

Abigail Swenson, founder and chair of the board of directors. Baby boomer Abigail Swenson is white and in her sixties. She won the title of "Miss Oklahoma" as a teenager and later married into an old and wealthy Texas family. She firmly controls the theatre's hand-picked board of directors, composed mainly of her friends, and allows others little initiative or creative freedom. Gregarious and flamboyant, she insists on having a small speaking part in every WTRT production. She tends to spend money freely and has landed the theatre in a substantial degree of debt. Many in the community have begun to question her judgment and business decision making.

Tony Arroyo, producing artistic director. Tony Arroyo is Hispanic, age 47 and, like Abigail, a native of Oklahoma. He has a tendency to break into Spanish when he is enthusiastic about something, which frustrates Abigail because she speaks only English. Generally level-headed and highly creative, he dresses in jeans and T-shirts and has an easy confidence about him.

Cheryl Kooser, accountant and office manager. Originally from Louisiana, baby boomer Cheryl Kooser is a white, 45-year-old no-nonsense working mother. Conscientious, intelligent, and responsible, she prefers harmonious environments and has trouble handling difficult situations. With a track record of seven years, she is the longest-standing employee of WTRT and earlier held a number of mid-level corporate jobs in accountancy firms.

Joey Hernandez, box office manager and administrative assistant. Joey Hernandez is a 23-year-old millennial, a native Texan who still lives at home. He likes to wear jeans to work (even though the dress code forbids denim) and takes a lot of "me time" on the job. Upset with the way Cheryl and Abigail regard him as a kid, he is often late to work and has an absentee problem. Frustrated by his poor work ethic, Abigail overloads him with work, which upsets him. Joey gives some of the work to Cheryl, who reluctantly helps him out.

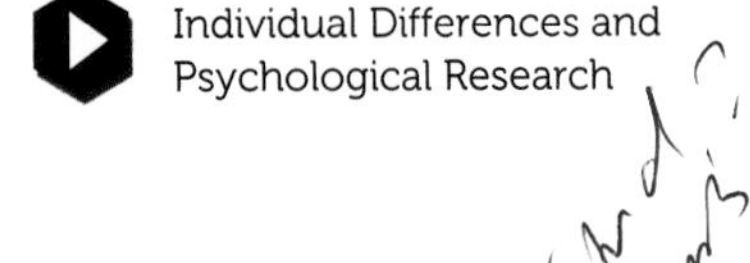

Individual Differences and Psychological Research

Today's organizations must cultivate a diverse workforce. Employees from different cultures with different languages provide companies with a greater reach into global markets because of their ability to communicate with people from similar backgrounds. A wide range of diverse employees with different perspectives and knowledge also offer a variety of solutions that help boost creativity and productivity, and increasingly, organizations with diverse workforces have become desirable places to work because they are perceived as being fair and nondiscriminatory. More important, it is essential to our own personal and professional relationships to be tolerant of our individual differences. Let's see why.

THINKING CRITICALLY

1. Explain why a diverse work group might score higher on innovation, creativity, and productivity than a group made up of similar individuals. **[Understand]**
2. Identify and list at least 3 surface-level and 3 deep-level aspects of diversity that describe you. Then list 3 surface-level and 3 deep-level aspects of diversity that describe one of your good friends. How do the similarities and differences between you and your friend affect your friendship? **[Understand/Apply]**
3. Imagine that you work in an organization with a variety of people who differ from you in terms of age, race, ethnicity, gender, sexual orientation, and physical or mental ability. Which diversity category would you find it most

difficult to understand and bridge? Which diversity category would you find it easiest to understand and bridge? Explain your answer. **[Analyze/Evaluate]**

4. What criteria would you use to determine the effectiveness of a workplace diversity training program? List at least three separate measurable variables that you could evaluate if you were conducting research in this area. **[Evaluate/Create]**

THE IMPORTANCE OF INDIVIDUAL DIFFERENCES

2.2 Discuss why individual differences are important

Individual Differences

Diversity is not the only thing that makes us feel different from each other. Have you ever been teamed up with someone for a school or work project who just seemed so different from you? What made that person unique? Maybe he or she had opinions or beliefs different from your own, liked music you hated, or had hobbies you considered strange. How did you handle working together? Did you just focus on getting the job done, or did you make an effort to find some common ground?

In class and at work you are surrounded by a multitude of individual personalities and behaviors and are expected to work well with others regardless of how different they seem to you. As we mentioned in Chapter 1, people are the key to ensuring competitive advantage and organizational success, and today's managers keep a close eye on team dynamics and the relationships among team members. Hostility or tension between workers is simply not tolerated. Working in a harmonious organizational environment is the ultimate goal, but to realize this goal we need to understand more about the differences and similarities between us and the way they guide our behavior.

Being different from each other makes us each unique. We define **individual differences** as the behavioral and cognitive similarities and differences among people.[14] In short, we need to understand not only people who are like us (which is relatively easy), but also people who are not like us and who think, behave, and make decisions differently than we do. When you can analyze the differences and similarities among your coworkers, you will have a better idea why people act the way they do. Take a look at how Rackspace manager Ben Hubbard champions individual differences to inspire and motivate his employees in athe OB in the Real World feature.

To understand individual differences, we must also have a high degree of **self-awareness**, or awareness of our own feelings, behaviors, personalities, likes, and dislikes.[15] We must also possess an **awareness of others**, a consciousness of other people's feelings, behaviors, personalities, likes, and dislikes.[16] But how easy is it to define ourselves?

We generally have a perception of ourselves as distinct human beings. This is called our **self-concept**, the belief we have about who we are and how we feel about ourselves.[17] Social and academic influences and the culture in which we are raised play a significant role in our belief system. For example, we might be influenced by the beliefs held by our parents, friends, teachers, or coworkers.

Our self-concept can be divided into two key components: self-esteem and self-efficacy. **Self-esteem** is the belief we have about our own worth.[18] People with high self-esteem perceive themselves to be confident, have a high sense of self-worth, and be capable of taking on challenges. In contrast, people with low self-esteem are full of self-doubt, have a rather low opinion of themselves, and tend to shy away from challenges.

The other part of self-concept is **self-efficacy**, our belief in our ability to succeed in a specific task or situation.[19] However, just because you have high self-esteem doesn't mean you have a strong sense of self-efficacy. For example, you may be confident about completing coursework but have a low sense of self-efficacy when taking the exams.

Individual differences: The degree to which people exhibit behavioral similarities and differences

Self-awareness: Being aware of our own feelings, behaviors, personalities, likes, and dislikes

Awareness of others: The way we are aware (or unaware) of the feelings, behaviors, personalities, likes, and dislikes in other people

Self-concept: The beliefs we have about who we are and how we feel about ourselves

Self-esteem: The beliefs we have about our own worth following the self-evaluation process

Self-efficacy: The belief we have in our ability to succeed in a specific task or situation

BEN HUBBARD, *Manager, Rackspace Hosting*

OB in the Real World

© Ben Hubbard

Rackspace is an IT provider focusing on open-cloud hosting. To achieve the fanatical level of customer support for which it is known, its managers have to lead, coach, motivate, and inspire their employees to "volunteer to do their best" every day.

Ben Hubbard has been with Rackspace for more than ten years. He started as one of the founders in the Email Hosting Division and has since become chief of staff for the entire product team for the Cloud. He has managed hundreds of employees and is well respected for his straightforward management, coaching, and leadership style.

Ben is known for his philosophy that you should "treat every employee equally differently," which comes from his days as a soccer coach. He says, "Players are motivated by different coaching styles. One player might struggle with confidence. If he messes up on the field and you immediately start yelling at him, he'll crumble. Instead, you have to pull him aside, talk him through the mistake, and tell him that you know he can do it better next time. Another player might respond better to a challenge. When that player messes up, you tell him that if he does it again, he's off the field. That player is energized by proving you wrong."

Hubbard has learned that though some employees like public recognition, others despise it. For example, a "Straitjacket Award" is given to Rackers who are so over-the-top fanatical that they can't be contained. It's presented at a ceremony at which the recipient is put in the straitjacket and runs around the office while all the employees cheer, clap, and carry on. It's a highly sought-after award that gives a glimpse into the company's nationally recognized culture. But Ben says, "I would never give that award to someone who hates being in the spotlight. Instead, I'd slip them a note and a gift certificate or reward them in a more private way. That's what it means to treat every employee equally differently."

Critical-Thinking Questions

1. **What are some management behaviors that might result in treating everyone equally differently but that will still drive performance?**
2. **What action did Ben Hubbard take to get the best out of his employees?**

SOURCES: B. Hubbard, personal interview, April 11, 2013, and the author's knowledge of the organization.

THINKING CRITICALLY

1. Identify at least 3 types of individual differences related to each of the following categories: behavior, thought, and decision making. **[Apply]**
2. To illustrate your level of self-awareness and your awareness of others, imagine a scenario in which you are working under a tight deadline and a new coworker stops by your office and asks for help understanding a key report she needs to submit to her manager. How are you likely to respond given your stress level and overall personality? How would your response affect a new employee who didn't know you well? **[Understand/Apply]**
3. Briefly discuss your levels of self-esteem and self-efficacy. What sort of an impact do these factors have on your ability to meet school and job expectations? **[Analyze/Evaluate]**

NATURE VERSUS NURTURE

2.3 Contrast the nature and nurture explanations of personality development

We often regard people as having "good personalities" or "bad personalities," but what does that really mean? Is someone's personality "good" because we have something in common with that person and get along with him or her? Or is someone's personality "bad" because he or she ignores or offends us? What is personality after all?

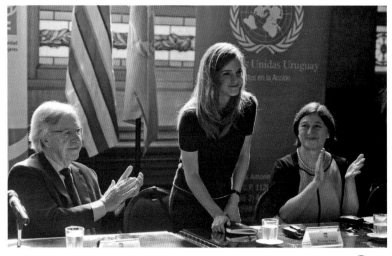

AP Photo/Matilde Campodonico

Actress and model Emma Watson demonstrates self-esteem and self-efficacy through serving as the UN Women Goodwill Ambassador.

The Blank Slate

We define **personality** as a stable and unique pattern of traits, characteristics, and resulting behaviors that gives an individual his or her identity.[20] When we understand different personalities, we can better understand the behaviors and motivations of others rather than making snap judgments that are often inaccurate. Researchers have spent decades carrying out different studies of **personality traits**, the characteristics that describe our thoughts, feelings, and behaviors.[21] But we are such complex creatures that no one theory has yet established a clear definition of personality.

Where does personality come from? Research has proven that we inherit some physical characteristics from our parents; you may have your father's blue eyes or your mother's curly hair, for example. However, the origins of our personality traits have yet to be fully determined, and the nature versus nurture debate still rages. Is personality inherited (nature) or is it influenced by our environment and upbringing (nurture)? In an effort to differentiate the impacts of nature and nurture on personality, researchers have studied identical twins adopted by different sets of parents at birth. They discovered that though 40 percent of personality traits can be attributed to inheritance, the 60 percent that remain suggest that personality is more likely to be shaped by environmental and situational factors such as culture, religion, and family life. In the next section, we explore how many organizations use assessment tools to get a better understanding of their employees' personality traits.

THINKING CRITICALLY

1. Describe your personality by listing 7–10 adjectives that illustrate your behavior and approach to life. Now imagine your opposite personality type by listing 7–10 adjectives that are diametrically opposed to those you listed for yourself. **[Understand]**

2. If you were a researcher who believed that individual differences were primarily determined by nature (i.e. inherited and hard-wired) what common-sense arguments could you use to support your belief? **[Apply/Analyze]**

3. If you were a researcher who believed that individual differences were primarily determined by nurture (i.e. shaped by one's upbringing and environment) what common-sense arguments could you use to support your belief? **[Apply/Analyze]**

4. Argue for a middle ground to the nature vs. nurture debate. How would you support the belief that BOTH genetic and environmental influence personality and differences? **[Apply/Analyze]**

Personality: A stable and unique pattern of traits, characteristics, and resulting behaviors that gives an individual his or her identity

Personality traits: Characteristics that describe our thoughts, feelings, and behaviors

MYERS-BRIGGS TYPE INDICATOR AND THE FOUR TEMPERAMENTS

2.4 Describe the Myers-Briggs Type Indicator Types and the Four Temperaments

The Myers-Briggs Type Indicator (MBTI) is a psychometric questionnaire used to evaluate four psychological preferences that combine to describe 16 personality types.[22] It was originally created by Katharine Cook Briggs and her daughter Isabel Briggs Myers during World War II to test a theory of psychological types advanced by the noted psychologist Carl Jung.[23] Initially drafted as a questionnaire, the test was developed into the official MBTI in 1962. It is the most widely used personality assessment instrument in the world.[24]

Although countless organizations all over the world still use the MBTI, it has been criticized by academics for providing a simplified, limited view of personality. It can be a valuable tool for increasing self-awareness and understanding others, but it is limiting in that it tends to box individual personalities into two main categories: introverts or extraverts. Whatever results you get after completing the questionnaire, remember they are not a definitive description of your personality type—they are merely suggestions based on psychological preferences, and are open to interpretation.

Myers-Briggs Preferences

Each MBTI profile is made up of four psychological preferences, each of which is one of a pair (see Figure 2.3). According to the theory, we have a tendency to lean toward one of the characteristics within each pair, which determines our preference in each case.

The four pairs of preferences are as follows:

- Extraversion (E) versus Introversion (I)
- Sensing (S) versus Intuitive (N)
- Thinking (T) versus Feeling (F)
- Judging (J) versus Perceiving (P)

Extraversion (E) Versus Introversion (I)

This pair of traits looks at how energy is directed by extraverts and introverts.

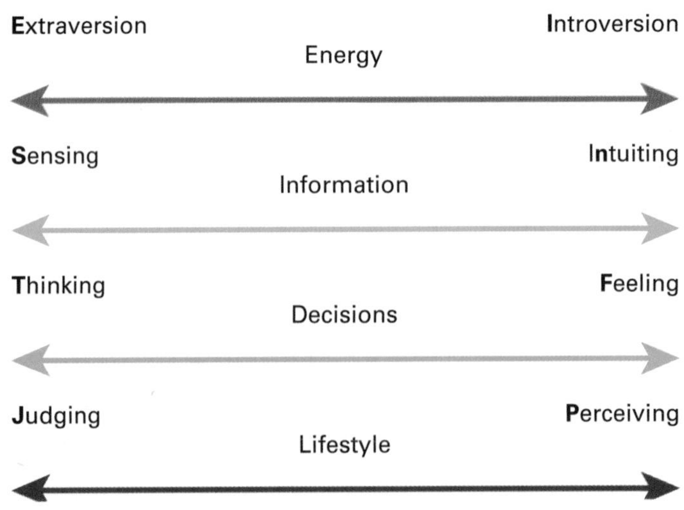

■ FIGURE 2.3 Myers-Briggs Preferences

- Extraverts are energized and stimulated by external events and other people. They tend to be talkative and expressive, and they work well in teams.
- Introverts draw their energy from being alone. Usually quite reserved, they keep their feelings hidden and tend to engage in self-examination and self-discovery. They like to work by themselves and learn through observing others.

Sensing (S) Versus Intuitive (N)

The sensing–intuitive continuum explores the way we understand and interpret information.

- Sensing people interpret information by using their five physical senses (sight, hearing, touch, taste, and smell). They prefer tangible, concrete, real-life information based on known facts.
- Intuitive people tend to use their instincts and prefer to look for alternatives rather than work with facts. They are imaginative, creative, and insightful. However, by interpreting information purely through hunches and feelings, they may miss some of the facts.

Thinking (T) Versus Feeling (F)

The comparison of thinking and feeling studies the way we make decisions.

- Thinking people use reason and logic to make decisions. They tend to ask lots of questions and like to debate ideas with others.
- Feeling people draw from their own values when making decisions. They tend to conform to others and prefer union and harmony.

Judging (J) Versus Perceiving (P)

Our tendency to judge or perceive describes the way we cope with the world around us.

- Judging people are focused, determined, and decisive. They prefer order, structure, plans, and rules.
- Perceiving people take a relaxed approach. They're flexible and adaptable and like to keep their options open.

The Sixteen Myers-Briggs Types

To identify personality type, the four psychological preferences have been developed into a Preference Clarity Index (PCI) made up of 16 different typologies (Table 2.1).[25]

For example, if you think you are an introvert rather than an extravert, a sensing person rather than an intuitive one, a thinking person rather than a feeling person, and a judging person rather than a perceiving person, then you would be known as an ISTJ. Each type is associated with a list of personal characteristics. For instance, ISTJ people

ISTJ 11–14%	ISFJ 9–14%	INFJ 1–3%	INTJ 2–4%
ISTP 4–6%	ISFP 5–9%	INFP 4–5%	INTP 3–5%
ESTP 4–5%	ESFP 4–9%	ENFP 6–8%	ENTP 2–5%
ESTJ 8–12%	ESFJ 9–13%	ENFJ 2–5%	ENTJ 2–5%
Estimated percentages of the 16 types in the US population, 2010			

■ TABLE 2.1 Sixteen Myers-Briggs Types

SOURCE: www.capt.org/mbti-assessment/estimated-frequencies.htm.

tend to be thorough, practical, determined, and calm in a crisis. However, they can be impatient and sometimes make impulsive decisions.

The MBTI can be beneficial in understanding yourself and increasing your self-awareness. It is also useful for identifying individual differences between us that can be a source of conflict and misunderstanding. The MBTI theory holds that by broadening our perspectives of others, knowing what motivates them, and why they behave and communicate in the way they do, we will build better relationships.

In the next section, we explore another popular personality test and observe our characters in action as they meet Laura for the first time.

THINKING CRITICALLY

1. How might knowing a coworker's Myers-Briggs type help you to more effectively work with her or him? How might knowing a coworker's Myers-Briggs type might hinder your ability to work together? **[Analyze/Evaluate]**

2. What other preference categories in addition to energy, information, decisions, and lifestyle that you think could be helpful in typing personality? List at least two. **[Evaluate/Create]**

THE BIG FIVE MODEL

2.5 Identify the five personality factors of the Big Five Model

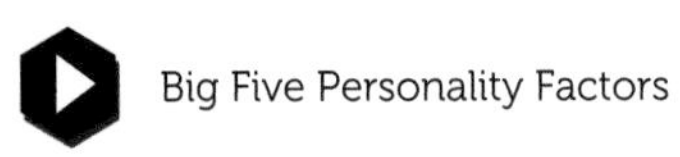

Big Five Personality Factors

One important area of personality is **emotional stability**, the extent to which we can remain calm and composed. At the opposite end of the spectrum for this trait is **neuroticism**, a tendency to be tense, moody, irritable, and temperamental. The more emotionally stable you are, the lower your level of neuroticism. The MBTI tells us very little about these traits. However, researchers have created another, broader personality test by condensing personality traits into one list. This model is widely accepted in academia and used more frequently in academic research. The **Big Five Model**, outlined in Table 2.2, describes five basic dimensions of personality, including neuroticism, and is frequently used to evaluate and assess people in the workplace.[26]

The Big Five personality test scores these personality dimensions from low to high, and a combination of these traits gives us an idea of what type of personality the individual possesses. For example, a person may score high in extraversion (very sociable), but low on conscientiousness (not very responsible). This analysis gives employers a better idea of the worker's profile and how he or she might fit into a certain role, and it is a useful way of assessing and predicting job performance. It also provides a more complete view of personality traits than earlier theories that saw traits as contradictory rather than as different in degree, because it allows for the many complexities of the human temperament.

Yet the search for the most accurate personality test continues. The consultancy firm Deloitte teamed up with scientists from the fields of neuro-anthropology and genetics to create a 70-question personality test called "Business Chemistry." Devised with CFOs in mind, Business Chemistry helps people identify their own personality traits and recognize qualities in their colleagues. Deloitte believe this new personality test helps CFOs engage with stakeholders, manage the strengths and weaknesses of their teams, and use their capabilities to handle multiple tasks.[27]

Emotional stability: The extent to which we can remain calm and composed

Neuroticism: A personality trait that involves being tense, moody, irritable, and temperamental

Big Five Model: Five basic dimensions of personality to include neuroticism and frequently used to evaluate and assess people in the workplace

In the section "Diversity in OB," we presented the diverse characters who will feature in the West Texas Regional Theatre (WTRT) case. As we have since learned, the diversity of a group is not the only thing that can cause challenges to working relationships—personality also plays a huge part. Let's observe the WTRT characters

Openness to Experience	The dimension of being curious, creative, and receptive to new ideas
Conscientiousness	The dimension of being thoughtful, organized, responsible, and achievement oriented
Neuroticism	The dimension of being tense, moody, irritable, and temperamental
Extraversion	The dimension of being outgoing, sociable, assertive, and talkative
Agreeableness	The dimension of being trusting, good natured, tolerant, forgiving, and cooperative

■ TABLE 2.2 The Big Five Model

SOURCE: Based on Barrick, Murray R., and Michael K. Mount. "The Big Five Personality Dimensions and Job Performance: A Meta-Analysis." *Personnel Psychology* 44, no. 1 (Spring 1991): 1–26; John, Oliver P., and Sanjay Srivastava. "The Big Five Trait Taxonomy: History, Measurement, and Theoretical Perspectives." In *Handbook of Personality: Theory and Research* (2nd ed.), 102–138 (New York: Guilford, 1999).

in action as they exemplify some of the MBTI traits, as well as the Big Five dimensions of personality.

The Big Five and Job Stress

On her first day of work at WTRT in Abilene, Texas, Laura Pierce arrives with a smile on her face. Although she had left her previous role as development director for her local National Public Radio station back in Tennessee because she had been unfairly passed over for a promotion, she is still thrilled to finally be working in the theatre industry. Because she is the first marketing and development director the theatre has hired, Laura believes she has an opportunity to make a difference. She can't wait to share her ideas with her new boss, Abigail Swenson.

So far, all Laura's communication with Abigail has taken place over the phone because Laura was living in Tennessee when she applied for the position. During the phone interviews, Laura had been blown away by Abigail's passion and love for the theatre, a passion rivaled only by her own. She believes Abigail has been vague about the responsibilities of the position. But she was so overwhelmed by Abigail's enthusiasm and faith in her abilities that she deduced it would be up to her to create the position based on her previous experience. Laura hopes that when she finally meets Abigail she will be given the creative freedom to showcase her talents and introduce new initiatives. She is looking forward to meeting her new boss in person.

Laura walks up the steps of the WTRT and into the lobby and sees a young man slumped behind the ticket office desk. "I'm Laura Pierce, the new marketing and development director. Today is my first day of work here."

"Welcome to WTRT. I'm Joey Hernandez, the box office manager and administrative assistant. I'd show you around but I have a pile of work to get through," Joey says, gesturing to the paperwork scattered all over his desk.

"Oh, that's okay," Laura says with a smile. "Just point me in the direction of Abigail's office, and I'll introduce myself."

"I can show you where her office is," Joey sighs, getting up slowly, "but she isn't here yet." Laura's smile falters. She is sure Abigail arranged to meet her at 9:00 a.m. "Don't worry," Joey says, noticing her trepidation. "She always shows up late for work the day after a performance."

"Why is that?" asks Laura.

"Because she has a small part in every play we put on, and she tends to mingle with the rest of the cast and members of the board until late into the night," Joey mutters.

Laura thinks Joey seems miserable, but she shakes off her first impression and follows him upstairs. When Joey opens the door of the office, there is a woman standing by a desk. Laura presumes it is Abigail Swenson and walks forward confidently and introduces herself.

"I'm not Abigail. I'm Cheryl Kooser, the accountant and office manager," the woman says curtly. "I was just leaving some documents on Abigail's desk for signing."

"I'm glad to meet you," says Laura. "Abigail mentioned that we'll be working closely together on the marketing budget."

Before Cheryl can respond, Joey says, "Cheryl, Abigail overloaded me with work again. Can you help me out?"

Cheryl glares at him. "Fine. Come to my office later and we'll discuss it," she snaps. Joey mutters his thanks and leaves the room without saying anything more to Laura. Laura watches him as he leaves. He looks like a little boy who has just been scolded.

"That kid is always offloading his work on me," Cheryl grumbles. "Anyway, I'll bring you through the accounts later today. I have everything filed, organized, and prepared for your arrival. I'm sure Abigail has filled you in on the difficult financial situation we're going through at the moment."

"What do you mean?" Laura says. Abigail hasn't mentioned anything about the theatre's financial state during their phone conversations. Laura is taken aback when Cheryl sighs and rolls her eyes. But just then a voice booms from the direction of the lobby.

"I'm here! I have arrived! Never fear!"

"That's Abigail," Cheryl says resignedly. "She announces her arrival the same way every morning. Take a seat, Laura. Abigail will be here in little while. She likes to have her coffee in the staff kitchen before she starts work."

Laura sits down on the chair closest to her. Cheryl excuses herself and leaves, ending Laura's hopes of finding out more about the financial state of the theatre. At 9:30 a.m, Abigail Swenson breezes into her office in a whirl of white—white hair, a white flowing dress, and impossibly high-heeled white shoes.

"Laura!" She booms enthusiastically, embracing her heartily, and planting an effusive kiss on both cheeks. Then Abigail takes a step back, assumes a grave expression, and raises her arms slowly, thundering, "Welcome to WTRT—the theatre that will never be upstaged!"

Laura smiles and nods in recognition. She had noted the theatre's tagline on the WTRT website.

Although Laura is slightly overwhelmed by this dramatic figure, she can't help but be impressed with Abigail's energy and enthusiasm.

"She is clearly as passionate about the theatre as I am," Laura thinks.

"Now, let's sit down like civilized creatures, and I'll tell you all about the greatest theatre in town!" Abigail says. Laura is relieved that Abigail is finally going to fill her in on the duties of her new role. She can't wait to get started! Abigail begins.

"As you know from our phone conversations, we need more people to come to the theatre to see our fabulous shows!"

Laura nods enthusiastically. "Yes, I have some ideas about how we can attract more theatre-goers to WTRT. When I was development director of NPR radio in Tennessee, I used a number of marketing strategies that really helped to increase our listener base. For example, I . . ."

Abigail interrupts. "I hired you because you seem to love theatre as much as I do. I'm sure you have some wonderful ideas, but this the *theatre* not *radio*. They are poles apart in terms of well . . . everything . . . as I'm sure you will soon learn."

Laura is stumped. She hadn't intended to compare radio to theatre; she merely wanted to share her marketing strategies that have proved successful in the past and that she feels could easily translate to the theatre. Not wanting to get off on the wrong foot on her first day, she doesn't push the issue. There will be other opportunities to share her ideas. Laura reminds herself that this is only an introductory meeting, after all.

Before the meeting can continue, a tall man, casually dressed, knocks on the door. "Tony!" Abigail roars. "Come over here and meet our new marketing and development manager, Laura Pierce!"

Tony crosses the room in two quick strides and firmly shakes Laura's hand. "I'm Tony Arroyo, producing artistic director. Good to meet you." Laura is fascinated by how quickly Tony walks and speaks. He is clearly a man in a hurry!

"Fabulous show last night!," Abigail booms. "I loved playing my little part. It was so much fun!"

Tony looks at her and says flatly, "Yes, you were great, Abigail, as usual." Abigail beams, but Laura detects a lack of sincerity in Tony's compliment—it seems rehearsed, and she is guessing that Tony has made this statement many times before. Tony continues, "Excuse me, Laura, for interrupting your meeting, but I had to share with Abigail that I have the best idea for the opening show of the next season. I wanted to run it by you, and I think you're going to love it!"

To Laura's surprise, Tony breaks into an excited flurry of Spanish—a language she studied extensively in high school and college, and she nods and smiles at his enthusiasm.

Abigail looks down and ruffles some papers on her desk. "Tony, that sounds great, but I have a ton of work to get through, and I am in the middle of a meeting, so maybe we could talk about this later?"

Tony looks crestfallen. "No problem," he says, brusquely. "Nice to meet you, Laura. I'm sure we will catch up properly a bit later."

"Yes, I look forward to it!" Laura says, noticing how disheartened he seems. As Tony reaches the door of the office, Abigail calls to him.

"You know everyone on the board of directors that came to the show last night said it was the best performance they had ever seen. They think you're a wonderful producer!"

Tony smiles broadly. "Well, let's see if we can make the next one even better!," he says, and instantly the spring is back in his step.

No sooner has Tony left the office than Abigail gestures to Laura, beckoning her to come closer. When Laura leans forward, Abigail says in a loud whisper, "Tony always has these big ideas about what shows to choose for every season. He's a talented producer, don't get me wrong, but he still doesn't get that *I* am the one who chooses the shows—not him!"

Laura has no idea how to respond to this. She doesn't even know Tony, so she thinks she is in no position to comment. "Besides," Abigail continues, "I can never understand a word Tony is saying when he speaks Spanish. Why does he do that when he knows I can't understand him?"

Again, Laura is shocked at Abigail's attitude toward Tony's Hispanic culture. If Abigail is so bothered by this, why doesn't she discuss it with Tony directly? Laura makes a mental note to raise this issue when she is more settled into her new job. For now, she has more pressing issues to address.

Abigail leans back in her chair and Laura decides to take advantage of the pause to ask more questions about her new role.

"Abigail, I am really excited about my position here at WTRT, and once I see the marketing budget, I'll be in a better position to create some new initiatives to make WTRT the most successful theatre in Texas!" Abigail's expression clouds over, and she drums her fingers on the desk, almost impatiently. Slightly unnerved by Abigail's change in demeanor, Laura continues nonetheless. "I met Cheryl Kooser earlier, and she mentioned she could bring me through the theatre's finances to help work out a marketing budget. Do you think that would be the best place for me to start?"

Laura instinctively feels it is best not to repeat Cheryl's low opinion of the financial state of the theatre. Even with this omission, the expression on Abigail's face is grim. Laura is dismayed.

"Laura, you'll be given the marketing budget in due course," Abigail says, stiffly. Then she returns to the loud whisper she used earlier. "But don't listen too much to what Cheryl has to say. She's a great accountant manager, but she likes to think things are worse than they really are."

"How are things, then?," Laura asks.

Abigail stares at her for a minute and then a smile spreads across her face. "Why things are fabulous! We just need a few more people to come to our magical theatre, and a few more patrons to keep us in this business we call 'show,' and we'll be back on track again! It's just fate that things aren't going our way at the moment, but we can turn it around. And that's where you come in! In fact you're the best thing that's happened to this place, I just know it!" Then Abigail takes an exaggerated look at her watch. "Is that the time? I scheduled a breakfast meeting with the board of directors 30 minutes ago!"

Laura deduces that Abigail doesn't make it a habit to arrive at her meetings on time.

"Have to run!" Abigail sweeps out the door as majestically as she entered.

Although she is a little stunned, Laura can't help feeling flattered and energized by Abigail's confidence in her. "She may be a little eccentric, but I think I can make a real difference here," she thinks. Laura strides out of the office, determined to figure out a way she and her new team can improve ticket sales at the theatre.

Applying the Big Five

Drawing from the previous scenario and going on first impressions, we may deduce that Laura rates highly on openness, extraversion, and agreeableness, and low on neuroticism. For example, she is looking forward to her new experience at the theatre, introduces herself confidently to her coworkers, is tolerant of Abigail's temperamental behavior, and remains composed throughout the first few couple of hours on her new job.

In contrast, we might say that Abigail and Cheryl score highly on neuroticism. Abigail seems to be prone to mood swings, and Cheryl comes across as being tense and irritable. Joey would score low in conscientiousness; it seems that he is not the most organized worker. Finally, like Laura, Tony would score highly on extraversion and openness. He is friendly, outgoing, and willing to create and implement new ideas. Of course, these conclusions are based on initial impressions, which are not always accurate. In the next section, we explore additional personality attributes exemplified by the characters in the story.

THINKING CRITICALLY

1. Rank each of the Big Five dimensions of personality (Openness to Experience, Conscientiousness, Neuroticism, Extraversion, and Agreeableness) in order of importance to workplace performance. Then rank them in order of importance to getting along well with others. Provide an explanation and defense for the two sets of rankings and discuss the similarities and differences between the two. **[Apply/Analyze/Evaluate]**

2. Pick one of the Big Five dimensions of personality and describe a possible work scenario where an employee who rates high on the dimension you have chosen would be more effective at solving a conflict or problem than an employee who rates low on the dimension. Next, describe a different scenario where an employee rating low on the dimension would be more effective in solving a problem or conflict than an employee rating high on the dimension. **[Analyze/Evaluate/Create]**

THE HEXACO MODEL OF PERSONALITY

Examining the Evidence

Although the Big Five Model of personality has become a standard framework for personality in the field of OB, in recent years a competing model of personality has emerged that adds a sixth personality dimension to the basic five factors. The HEXACO model of personality consists of the six dimensions of Honesty-Humility (H), Emotionality (E), Extraversion (X), Agreeableness (A), Conscientiousness (C), and Openness to Experience (O).* Although aspects of all five factors are interpreted somewhat differently in the HEXACO model, the addition of the Honesty-Humility dimension represents the biggest departure from the classic framework.

The Honesty-Humility factor includes trait descriptors such as honesty, sincerity, fairness, and modesty, as opposed to greediness, conceitedness, deceitfulness, and pretentiousness—concepts that were traditionally elements of Agreeableness in the Big Five Model.* Focusing on honesty-humility as a separate personality dimension may have important implications for managerial practice. For example, the results of a recent study by Professors Jocelyn Wiltshire and Kibeom Lee of the University of Calgary and Joshua S. Bourdage of Western University suggests that employees rating low on the honesty–humility dimension may be more likely to engage in counterproductive work behaviors and impression management behaviors and to experience greater job stress and decreased job satisfaction when working in a highly political work environment,^ while another recent study found that low levels of honesty–humility were related to the intention to commit premeditated and calculated vengeful acts.#

Critical-Thinking Questions

1. **Why might it be important to consider the honesty-humility personality dimension in addition to the traditional Big Five dimensions?**
2. **What are some possible implications of the research findings outlined above for managerial practice?**

*Ashton, Michael C., Kibeom Lee, and Reinout E. de Vries. "The HEXACO Honesty-Humility, Agreeableness, and Emotionality Factors: A Review of Research and Theory." *Personality and Social Psychology Review* 18, no. 2 (May 2014): 139–152.

^Wiltshire, Jocelyn, Joshua S. Bourdage, and Kibeom Lee. "Honesty-Humility and Perceptions of Organizational Politics in Predicting Workplace Outcomes." *Journal of Business and Psychology* 29, no. 2 (June 2014): 235–251.

#Lee, Kibeom, and Michael C. Ashton. "Getting Mad and Getting Even: Agreeableness and Honesty–Humility as Predictors of Revenge Intentions." *Personality and Individual Differences* 52, no. 5 (April 2012): 596–600.

OTHER PERSONALITY ATTRIBUTES

2.6 Differentiate among the most common personality attributes

Personal conception is the degree to which individuals relate to and think about their social and physical environments and their personal beliefs regarding a range of issues. A person's conception of himself or herself is dependent on the following personality dimensions shown in Figure 2.4.

- Locus of Control

Locus of control is the extent to which people believe they have influence over events.[28] There are two types: **internal locus of control**, which allows people to believe they are responsible for influencing events; and **external locus of control**, which allows people to believe outside influences are responsible for their fate. Abigail's blaming fate for the theatre's current situation is an example of external locus of control.

Personal conception traits: The degree to which individuals relate to and think about their social and physical environment and their personal beliefs regarding a range of issues

Locus of control: The extent to which people feel they have influence over events

Internal locus of control: The degree to which people believe they control the events and consequences which affect their lives

External locus of control: The extent to which people believe their performance is the product of circumstances which are beyond their immediate control

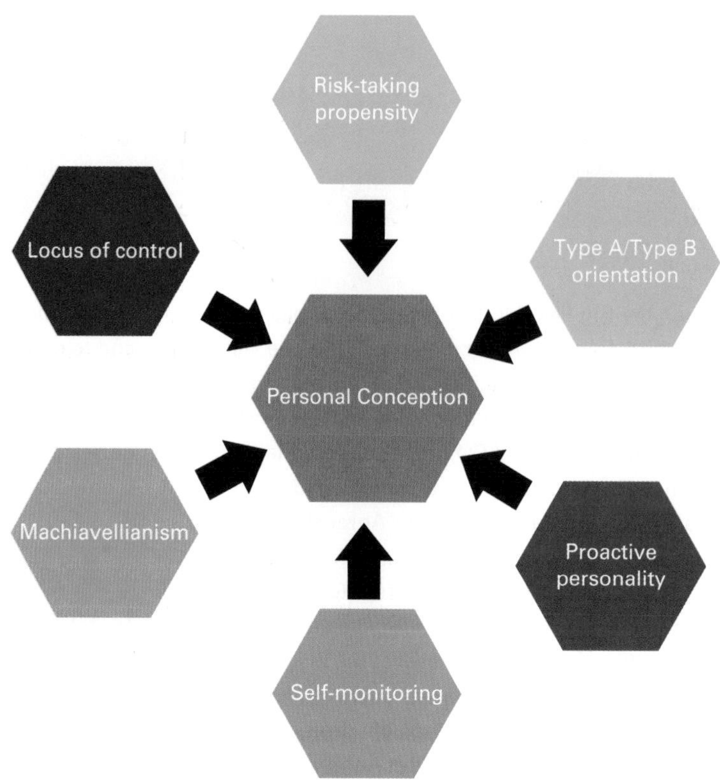

■ FIGURE 2.4 Dimensions of Personality

Machiavellianism and Career Success

- Machiavellianism

Some psychologists and sociologists use the term **Machiavellianism** to describe the behavior of people who manipulate others and use unethical practices for personal gain.[29] The term owes its origins to the 16th century author Nicolo Machiavelli, whose book *The Prince* describes the true nature of power and its acquisition through cunning and ruthless means. People with high levels of Machiavellianism tend be pragmatic, may be prone to lying to achieve goals, are good at influencing others, and have the ability to distance themselves from conventional morality. Conversely, people with low levels of Machiavellianism are more likely to maintain moral standards and use ethical practices to achieve objectives.

Abigail displays medium levels of Machiavellianism—she demonstrates that she is capable of manipulating people to get what she wants. For example, by flattering Laura and telling her she is the "best thing" to happen to WTRT, she distracts Laura from asking any further questions about the true financial state of the theatre, a topic she seems determined not to discuss.

Self-Monitoring

- Self-Monitoring

Self-monitoring is the degree to which people adjust their behavior to accommodate different situations.[30] High self-monitors might hold back on expressing their true feelings and behaviors if they think the situation does not call for it, or that others might not approve. In short, they match their behavior to the requirements of the situation. In contrast, low self-monitors do not disguise their behaviors, have little regard for how others perceive them, and refuse to change any aspect of themselves to accommodate any given situation. Their attitude is "What you see is what you get." Laura is a high self-monitor. She remains composed when Abigail makes negative remarks about other members of the staff.

Machiavellianism: A philosophy that describes people who manipulate others and use unethical practices for personal gain

Self-monitoring: Adjusting our behavior to accommodate different situations

- Proactive Personality

Proactive personality is the extent to which individuals take the initiative to change their circumstances.[31] Those who are high in proactive personality look for opportunities to change events and take action to ensure the desired change takes place. People who are low in proactive personality are generally more accepting of the status quo and take very little action to change the circumstances surrounding them. Today's organizations actively seek out proactive people because they are more likely to react positively to and adapt to an ever-changing work environment. Joey is an example of someone who is low in proactive personality. He is passive and seems defeated when Cheryl snaps at him.

- Type A/Type B Orientation

The way employees react to stressful situations is of particular interest to OB managers. For example, some people thrive under pressure and perceive tight deadlines as a challenge, whereas others may struggle and react negatively. Researchers have defined two main personality types to gauge how workers cope under pressure: Type A and Type B orientation.[32] People with a **Type A orientation** are characterized as competitive, impatient, aggressive, and achievement oriented. Conversely, those with a **Type B orientation** are characterized as relaxed, easygoing, more patient, and less competitive. Most of the characters in our story display a Type A orientation. Only Joey falls into the Type B category; he appears to be more relaxed and patient.

- Risk-Taking Propensity

Risk-taking propensity is the tendency to engage in behaviors that might have positive or negative outcomes.[33] High risk-takers make faster decisions based on less information, but they risk making mistakes if they don't adequately assess the consequences of their decisions. For example, excessive risk-taking was one of the main causes of the housing market crisis between 2007 and 2008, because lenders granted high-risk mortgages loans to subprime (poorly qualified) borrowers who could not afford to pay back the loans. When the housing market bubble burst, prices dropped, resulting in high volumes of defaults, leaving the banks with foreclosed houses that were worth less than the amount of the original loan. This had a devastating effect on the lenders, banks, and investment institutions that were involved in selling or trading mortgage loans, many of which collapsed.[34]

Low risk-takers tend to take more time with their decision making and require more information to assess the potential level of risk, yet they may become paralyzed by indecision if they spend too much time gathering information. Similarly, people can become paralyzed by having too much choice. For example, in an experiment known as the "jam studies," researchers set up some samples of jams in a gourmet food market. Every few hours, they switched from 6 to 24 jams on display. The results showed that 60 percent of customers were attracted to the larger display, but only 40 percent were drawn to the smaller one. Yet out of the 60 percent, only 3 percent bought the jam, while out of the 40 percent of customers who sampled the smaller selection of jams, 30 percent bought the jam. This research shows that consumers are more likely to buy products when they have less choice, leading to the theory that too much choice can be demotivating because it puts consumers at a higher risk of making the wrong choice.[35]

In our story Laura has taken a risk by accepting a new job and moving from Tennessee to Texas, and Abigail may have taken on a certain amount of financial risk with the theatre's funds.

Proactive personality: The tendency for individuals to take the initiative to change their circumstances

Type A orientation: The way people are characterized as competitive, impatient, aggressive, and achievement oriented

Type B orientation: The way people are characterized as relaxed, easygoing, patient, and noncompetitive

Risk-taking propensity: The tendency to engage in behaviors that might have positive or negative outcomes

Richard Branson, owner of Virgin Group, is a notorious risk taker.

D@LY3D via Flickr.com

As we have seen, despite the amount of research and theories carried out, the human personality still remains something of a mystery. However, by applying some of the research toward understanding our own differences and the differences of others, we have a better chance of building productive relationships inside and outside the workplace.

In the next chapter, we follow Laura on her quest to unify a team of very different personalities to restore WTRT to its former glory.

THINKING CRITICALLY

1. Imagine your ideal coworker based on where you fall on each of the dimensions of personality. Identify the dimensions where similarity would be most beneficial to an effective working relationship. Identify the dimensions where difference would likely benefit the relationship. Defend your answers. **[Analyze/Evaluate]**

2. What sorts of industries or types of businesses would most value workers rating high on each of the six dimensions of personality. What sorts of industries or types of businesses would most value employees rating low on the six dimensions of personality. Are there any dimensions where a particularly low or particularly high rating would be an obstacle to satisfactory work performance regardless of the type of industry or business? **[Apply/Analyze/Evaluate]**

IN REVIEW

Learning Objectives

2.1 Explain the importance of diversity in OB

Workplace diversity can be defined as the degree to which an organization includes people from different cultures and backgrounds, and recognizes, respects, and values both individual and group differences by treating people as individuals in an effort to promote an inclusive culture. One of the most effective ways organizations can encourage acceptance of differences and create a harmonious workforce is through the management of diversity. **Surface-level diversity** describes the easily perceived differences between us, such as **age/generation, race/ethnicity, gender, sexual orientation,** and **ability**. **Deep-level diversity** describes verbal and nonverbal behaviors that are not as easily perceived as they lie below the surface, such as differences in attitudes, values, beliefs, and personality.

Discuss why individual differences are important

Individual differences are defined as the effort to find behavioral similarities and differences. We don't need to just understand people who are different from us, but also those who are similar to us in the way they think, make decisions, and behave. When you figure out the differences and similarities of your coworkers, it will give you a better idea of why people act the way they do.

Contrast the nature and nurture explanations of personality development

Personality is defined as a stable and unique pattern of traits, characteristics, and resulting behaviors that gives an individual his or her identity. The origins of our personality traits have yet to be fully determined, and the nature versus nurture debate still abounds. The nature side of the debate argues that personality is inherited while the nurture side argues that personality is influenced by the environment.

Describe the Myers-Briggs Type Indicator Types and the Four Temperaments

The **Myers-Briggs Type Indicator (MBTI)** is a psychometric questionnaire used to evaluate four psychological preferences, and developed into 16 personality types. The four psychological preferences are as follows:

- Extraversion (E) versus Introversion (I): How the flow of energy is directed
- Sensing (S) versus Intuitive (N): How information is understood and interpreted
- Thinking (T) versus Feeling (F): How decisions are made
- Judging (J) versus Perceiving (P): How we cope with our surroundings

2.5 Identify the five personality factors of the Big Five Model

The Big Five Model describes five basic dimensions of personality to include neuroticism and is frequently used to evaluate and assess people in the workplace. The five traits are as follows:

1. *Openness to experience*: The dimension of being curious, creative, and receptive to new ideas
2. *Conscientiousness*: The dimension of being thoughtful, organized, responsible, and achievement oriented
3. *Neuroticism*: The dimension of being tense, moody, irritable, and temperamental
4. *Extraversion*: The dimension of being outgoing, sociable, assertive, and talkative
5. *Agreeableness*: The dimension of being trusting, good-natured, tolerant, forgiving, and cooperative

The Big Five personality test scores these personality dimensions from low to high; a combination of these traits gives us an idea of what type of personality the individual possesses.

2.6 Differentiate among the most common personality attributes

Personal conception is the degree to which individuals relate to and think about their social and physical environment, and their personal beliefs regarding a range of issues. A person's conception of himself or herself is dependent on the following personality dimensions:

- **Locus of control:** The extent to which people feel they have influence over events
- **Machiavellianism:** A philosophy that describes people who manipulate others and use unethical practices for personal gain
- **Self-monitoring**: Adjusting our behavior to accommodate different situations
- **Proactive personality:** The tendency for individuals to take the initiative to change their circumstances
- **Type A/Type B orientation:** The way people are characterized as possessing certain personality attributes
- **Risk-taking propensity:** The tendency to engage in behaviors that may have positive or negative outcomes

KEY TERMS

THINKING CRITICALLY ABOUT THE CASE OF LAURA PIERCE

Put yourself in Laura Pierce's position as a new employee at WTRT and apply the Five-Step Critical-Thinking Framework introduced in Chapter 1 in relation to diversity and individual differences within the theatre company.

Behavior Change

5. Explain

1. Observe

4. Evaluate

2. Interpret

3. Analyze

OBSERVE

What cultural and background differences do you observe among the existing staff (Abigail, Tony, Cheryl, and Joey) based on the chapter's descriptions of these characters and Laura's first-day interactions with them? How does Laura's culture and background compare to the others?

What individual differences do you observe among the existing staff and Laura? List at least 3 individual differences for each character.

INTERPRET

Based on the diversity and range of individual differences among the characters as well as the description of Laura's first day, what types of conflicts is Laura likely to encounter at WTRT? What conflicts is Laura likely to cause as she tries to do her job?

ANALYZE

Laura seems to have managed to keep an optimistic perspective on the challenges her new job will bring, but provide your own analysis of ways she may be able to forge positive relationships with her new boss and coworkers despite her differences with them.

EVALUATE

Evaluate which colleagues Laura should approach first as she begins her work at WTRT. What are three things she could do to learn more about her job and have a chance to interact with her colleagues? What potential problems could arise as Laura begins to reach out to her coworkers in order to learn more about the organization in which she is working?

EXPLAIN

Choose the first action you listed above and explain how you, as Laura, would approach accomplishing this task. If a problem arose, explain how you would attempt to handle it.

EXERCISE 2.1: PERSONALITY: THINKING VERSUS FEELING

1. Write five sentences about your college or university.
2. Describe a good movie you have seen recently. What did you like about it?
3. If you were on a TV dating show, how would you decide who to keep and who to eliminate?

Complete Self-Assessment 2.1 and then read the below interpretation of your results: Feeling types generally describe how they feel about the college and describe movies that involve feelings such as romances. They usually eliminate the date based on feelings.

The thinking types often describe a map of the campus. They generally like action movies with complex plots. They analyze dates on criteria such as physical appearance, compatibility, and matching personal characteristics.

EXERCISE 2.2: DIMENSIONS OF DIVERSITY

Objective:

Differentiate between surface-level diversity and deep-level diversity

Instructions:

You have one minute to write down on a 3x5 card as many words as possible that come to mind when you hear the term "diversity."

As a class or in small groups, compared your responses and note the number of times each word is used. Categorize the words into two categories: surface-level diversity and deep-level diversity.

Reflection Questions:

1. How many of the words were the surface-level? What aspects of surface-level diversity were mentioned the most?
2. How many of the words were deep-level? What aspects of deep-level diversity were mentioned the most?
3. Did your group list more surface-level or deep-level dimensions of diversity? Why do you think that was the case?

Exercise contributed by Harriet Rojas, Professor of Business, Indiana Wesleyan University.

EXERCISE 2.3: MY EXPERIENCE WITH INDIVIDUAL DIFFERENCES

Objectives:

In this exercise you will explore and *describe* the concept of diversity and its importance-including its benefits. In addition you will *develop* an understanding of the significance of individual differences.

Instructions:

This exercise consists of four steps.

Step 1. Individually think about then write about an experience where you were unfairly treated for being different in an organizational group. The group can have been in any type of organization (i.e. work, school, social, religious, volunteer, etc.). Be as specific as possible about the following aspects of this experience and answer the following questions (10 minutes):

- In what way were you different from the group?
- How were you treated unfairly?
- What were the consequences of the unfair treatment? Describe the effectives in terms of how you were effected as an individual as well as how the group and organization were effected.
- What could the group have gained if that person had been treated fairly?

Step 2. Choose a partner, preferably someone who you do not know very well, and compare your situation and responses. Identify what your experiences share in common and how they differ. (10 minutes)

Step 3. Partners should now join groups of five to seven people. Repeat the comparison process among all team members. Be sure to focus on each of the four preceding specific questions. As a group, identify commonalities and divergence in member experiences. Finally, select one member's experience to be presented to the entire class. Choose a team spokesperson (the spokesperson should not be the author of the selected experience) to describe the situation and the answers to the four specific questions. (10 to 20 minutes)

Step 4. Each team spokesperson should be prepared to present the team's findings to the entire class. Again, the class should identify through discussion common points and differences in the various group's interpretations of unfair treatment based on differences from a group. (10 to 20 minutes)

Reflection Questions:

1. How does your new understanding of chapter concepts better help you to grasp the negative consequences of excluding people based on non-performance related differences?
2. Did you identify any structural or cultural issues in the exclusion process?
3. What similarities did you notice between different team presentations?
4. What concrete, specific behaviors and mindsets could help ensure that such unfair treatment does not happen?
5. How can individuals, groups, and organizations themselves benefit from helping all members maximize their potential contributions?

Exercise contributed by Milton R. Mayfield, Professor of Business, Texas A&M International University and Jaqueline R. Mayfield, Professor of Business, Texas A&M International University.

CASE STUDY 2.1: W. L. GORE AND ASSOCIATES

He was ready for anything—or so he thought. Dressed in his finest and armed with an MBA degree fresh off the press, Jack Dougherty walked in for his first day of work at Newark, Delaware–based W. L. Gore and Associates, the global fluoropolymer technology and manufacturing giant that is best known as the maker of Gore-Tex.

But it turned out he wasn't ready for this: "Why don't you look around and find something you'd like to do," founder and CEO Bill Gore said to him after a quick introduction. Although many things have changed over the course of W. L. Gore and Associates' 50+ years in business, the late Gore stuck to his principles regarding organizational structure (or lack thereof), a legacy he passed down to subsequent generations of management. Gore wasn't fond of thick layers of formal management, which he believed smothered individual creativity. According to Gore, "A lattice (flat) organization is one that involves direct transactions, self-commitment, natural leadership, and lacks assigned or assumed authority."

In the 1930s, Gore received a bachelor's degree in chemical engineering and a master's degree in physical chemistry. During his career, he worked on a team to develop applications for polytetraflurothylene (PTFE), commonly known as Teflon. Through this experience, Gore discovered a sense of excited commitment, personal fulfillment, and self-direction, which he yearned to share with others. Spending nights tinkering in his own workshop, he did what he had previously thought to be impossible: he created a PTFE-coated ribbon cable. It occurred to Gore that he might be able to start his own business producing his invention, so he left his stable career of 17 years, borrowed money, and drained his savings. Though his friends advised him against taking such a risk, W. L. Gore and Associates was born in January 1958. The basement of the Gore home was the company's first facility.

Although no longer operating from a family basement (Gore boasts more than $3 billion in annual sales and 9,000 employees in more than 45 facilities worldwide), the sense of informality has stuck. "It absolutely is less efficient upfront," said Terri Kelly, chief executive of W. L. Gore. (Her title is one of the few at the company.) "[But] once you have the organization behind it . . . the buy-in and the execution happens quickly," she added.

Structure and Management of Unstructure and Unmanagement

Even as Gore started to grow, the company continued to resist titles and hierarchy. It had no mission statement, no ethics statement, and no conventional structures typical of companies of the same size. The only formal titles were "chief executive" and "secretary-treasurer"—those required by law for corporations. There were also no rules that business units within the company couldn't create such structures, and so some of them did create their own mission statements and such. Many called Gore's management style "unmanagement." What had started as 12 employees working in the Gore basement eventually evolved into a thriving company by the 1960s, with multiple plants.

There were 200 employees working at a plant in Newark, Delaware. One day, Gore was walking around the plant, and it occurred to him that he didn't know all the employees there. Based on this realization, Gore established a policy that said no plant was to be larger than 150 to 200 workers per plant, to keep things more intimate and interpersonal. He wanted to "get big while staying small."

Understanding and Leveraging Differences

With a global recession on the horizon in 2007, the company prepared for tough times by hunkering down, self-assessing, and embarking on a journey of self-improvement. A diversity leadership program was developed that focused on Gore's most important asset: people. The Gore team sought to understand "when, why, if, and how differences affect relationships, because the quality of relationships [among employees] has a lot to do with how well our business performs," adding that improving relationships [could] "decrease reactivity; increase professional capacity; and [help associates] learn about self while helping to make a more cohesive, diverse, and cross-discipline system." Intense analysis and discussion led to bold change:

> Workshops, lunch and learn sessions and other programs help promote a more inclusive environment and encourage associates to listen to and learn from each other on a regular basis.... [We created] space for self-exploration, learning from differences dialogues; meeting with enterprise diversity affinity groups; monthly 15 engagement survey; building space in global business meetings to talk about individual belief systems and the connection to enterprise belief systems; proactively ensuring that learning from difference dialogues are built into global and local business meetings; and once a year, teams form to create and raffle off diversity baskets, filled with items that celebrate their culture, ethnicity, religion, etc. In addition, these teams speak at plant meetings about the items and traditions represented in their baskets.

As the objectives were set into motion, monthly and annual employee survey results began to reflect increased satisfaction.

People Helping People

As the company grew, Gore also realized that there had to be some kind of system in place to assist new people on the job and to track progress. Instead of a formal management program, Gore implemented a "sponsor" program. When people applied for jobs with the company, they were screened and then interviewed by associates. An associate who took a personal interest in the new associate's contributions, problems, and goals would agree to act as a mentor, or sponsor. The new hire's sponsor would coach and advocate for him, tracking progress, encouraging the person, and dealing with weaknesses while focusing on strengths. Sponsors were also responsible for ensuring that their associates were fairly paid. The result of all this focus on mentoring and the right-sized teams has cultivated a feeling of intimacy and appreciation that attracts and retains a strong workforce.

"You feel like you're part of a family," said Steve Shuster, part of Gore's enterprise communication team. "I have been working at Gore for 27 years, and I still get excited coming to work each day."

Case Questions

1. How did Bill Gore structure management within his company and why is this relevant to personality and individual differences?
2. Explain why the diversity leadership program developed by W. L. Gore and Associates is a positive way to better understand and foster individual differences.
3. Describe how the sponsor program developed higher levels of employee satisfaction as well as maintained the "unmanagement" culture.

Sources

"About Us," www.gore.com/en_xx/aboutus/culture/index.html.

Mayhew, Ruth, "Cons of a Lattice Organizational Structure," *Houston Chronicle*, http://smallbusiness.chron.com/cons-lattice-organizational- structure-3836.html.

Sacconey Townsend, Gail, and William Aubrey Saunders, "Cross-Functional Teaming through the Lenses of Differences: W. L. Gore & Associates, Inc., Case Study," October 8, 2013; http://c.ymcdn.com/sites/www.odnetwork.org/resource/resmgr/2013_education/gailt_aubreys_handout_whitep.pdf.

Shipper, Frank, and Charles C. Manz, "Classic 6: W. L. Gore & Associates," www.academia.edu/964711/Classic_Case_6_WL_Gore_and_ Associates_Inc; n.d.

"Workplace Democracy at W.L. Gore & Associates," *workplacedemocracy.com*, July 14, 2009; http://workplacedemocracy.com/2009/07/14/work- place-democracy-at-w-l-gore-associates.

SELF-ASSESSMENT 2.1

How Accurately Can You Describe Yourself?*

Describe yourself as you generally are now, not as you wish to be in the future. Describe yourself as you honestly see yourself in relation to other people you know of the same sex as you are, and roughly your same age.

For each statement, check the circle that best describes you based on the following scale:

	Not at all Accurate	Somewhat Accurate	A Little Accurate	Mostly Accurate	Completely Accurate
1. Am the life of the party	O	O	O	O	O
2. Am interested in people	O	O	O	O	O
3. Am always prepared	O	O	O	O	O
4. Am relaxed most of the time	O	O	O	O	O
5. Have a rich vocabulary	O	O	O	O	O
6. Feel comfortable around people	O	O	O	O	O
7. Sympathize with others' feelings	O	O	O	O	O
8. Pay attention to details	O	O	O	O	O
9. Don't get stressed out easily	O	O	O	O	O
10. Have excellent ideas	O	O	O	O	O
11. Feel comfortable around people	O	O	O	O	O
12. Have a soft heart	O	O	O	O	O
13. Get chores done right away	O	O	O	O	O
14. Seldom feel blue	O	O	O	O	O
15. Have a vivid imagination	O	O	O	O	O
16. Start conversations	O	O	O	O	O
17. Take time out for others	O	O	O	O	O
18. Like order	O	O	O	O	O
19. Seldom feel blue	O	O	O	O	O
20. Am full of ideas	O	O	O	O	O

Scoring

Extraversion (add items 1, 6, 11, 16 and write your score in the blank) ____________

The extent to which you are outgoing, sociable, talkative, and able to get on well with others

Agreeableness (add items 2, 7, 12, 17 and write your score in the blank) ____________

The extent to which you are able to relate to others by being trusting, forgiving, kind, affectionate, and cooperative

Conscientiousness (add items 3, 8, 13, 18 and write your score in the blank) ____________

The extent to which you exhibit thoughtfulness, organization, and responsibility

Emotional Stability (Neuroticism reverse scaled) (add items 4, 9, 14, 19 and write your score in the blank) ____________

The extent to which you are calm, relaxed, and not tense, moody, irritable, or anxious

Openness to Experience/Imagination (add items 5, 10, 15, 20 and write score in the blank)

____

The extent to which you are able to have fun, experience elation and delight, foster a diverse sharing of ideas, and learn from contradictory points of view.

What was your strongest decision-making style? What are the advantages and disadvantages of this style?

What was your weakest decision-making style? What are the advantages and disadvantages of this style?

*These five scales were developed to measure the Big-Five factor markers reported in Goldberg, L. R. "The Development of Markers for the Big-Five Factor Structure." *Psychological Assessment* 4 (1992): 26–42.

3 Emotions, Attitudes, and Stress

If your emotional abilities aren't in hand, if you don't have self-awareness, if you are not able to manage your distressing emotions, if you can't have empathy and have effective relationships, then no matter how smart you are, you are not going to get very far.

—Dr. Daniel Goleman, psychologist, scientist, and author

LEARNING OBJECTIVES

By the end of this chapter, you will be able to:

3.1 Describe the basic concept of emotions in the context of organizational behavior

3.2 Discuss the various roles of emotions in the workplace

3.3 Explain the ways in which attitudes influence behavior in organizations

3.4 Identify some common workplace attitudes and related outcomes

3.5 Illustrate the ways in which stress can affect behavior in the workplace

3.6 Discuss different outcomes of stress and the benefits of wellness programs

EMOTIONS IN ORGANIZATIONAL BEHAVIOR

3.1 Describe the basic concept of emotions in the context of organizational behavior

One morning your professor hands you an important, complex assignment and tells you it has to be completed by the end of the day. How do you feel? Are you excited at the thought of a new challenge? Or fearful because the task is so complex? Do you feel angry with your professor because you have been given such a tight deadline?

People or events elicit a variety of feelings that cause us to respond in different ways. These feelings are called **affects**, a broad term covering a wide range of feelings, including emotions and moods.[1] We may react to certain situations with sadness, anger, or elation. These responses are **emotions**, intense feelings directed at a specific object or person.[2] Emotions are numerous and intense, but they are usually also short-lived. For example, in the scenario described, it's likely that your intense feeling of anger toward your professor will dissipate as soon as you begin to focus on the task.

But what if your professor has caught you on a day when you feel like you can't be bothered with working at all? In fact, now that you think about it, you've felt a bit down for the past few days and feel like a short deadline is the last thing you need since you're feeling so unmotivated. In this case, you are probably experiencing a negative **mood**, which consists of less intense and more generalized feelings not directed at a specific object or person.[3] Moods last longer than emotions. Of course, moods can also be positive, and we often categorize ourselves and others as being in a "good mood" or a "bad mood."

OB researchers have identified two basic types of mood dimensions: positive affect and negative affect. **Positive affect** includes emotions such as excitement, cheerfulness, and self-assurance, while **negative affect** includes emotions such as boredom, lethargy, and depression.[4] The sources of moods and emotions are complex. Factors such as lack of sleep and exercise, the weather, and the amount of stress we are under might play a part, but there are no concrete answers to explain the underlying reasons for our feelings and moods.

Although there are clear differences between emotions and moods, they do influence each other. Emotions can turn into moods when you lose focus on what caused

Affects: The range of feelings in form of emotions and moods that people experience

Emotions: Intense feelings directed at a specific object or person

Moods: Generalized positive or negative feelings of mind

Master the content.
edge.sagepub.com/neckob

the feeling in the first place, and good or bad moods can trigger a stronger, more intense emotional response. For example, your feelings of anger toward your professor for giving you a complex assignment on short notice may put you in a bad mood, which distracts you from focusing on the task. Conversely, if you were already in a bad mood before you were handed the project, your angry feelings may intensify even more after you receive the last-minute assignment. While your negative feelings are justified from your perspective, what about your classmates, friends, and others around you? How does your mood affect them?

Measuring Happiness

THINKING CRITICALLY

1. Identify and list five separate emotions and five separate moods. **[Understand]**
2. Imagine and describe a work situation where positive affect would be more effective in accomplishing key tasks. Imagine and describe a work situation where negative affect would be more effective in accomplishing key tasks. **[Apply]**
3. In general, which type of affect (positive or negative) do you think would be more effective overall in a situation where you need to collaborate with a large team? Defend your response. **[Evaluate]**

Positive affect: A mood dimension that consists of emotions such as excitement, self-assurance, and cheerfulness at the high end and boredom, sluggishness, and tiredness at the low end

Negative affect: A mood dimension that consists of emotions such as nervousness, stress, and anxiety at the high end and relaxation, tranquility, and poises the low end.

EMOTIONS IN THE WORKPLACE

3.2 Discuss the various roles of emotions in the workplace

Awareness of our emotional state is paramount when making important career decisions. For example, people who are in heightened emotional states and are unhappy

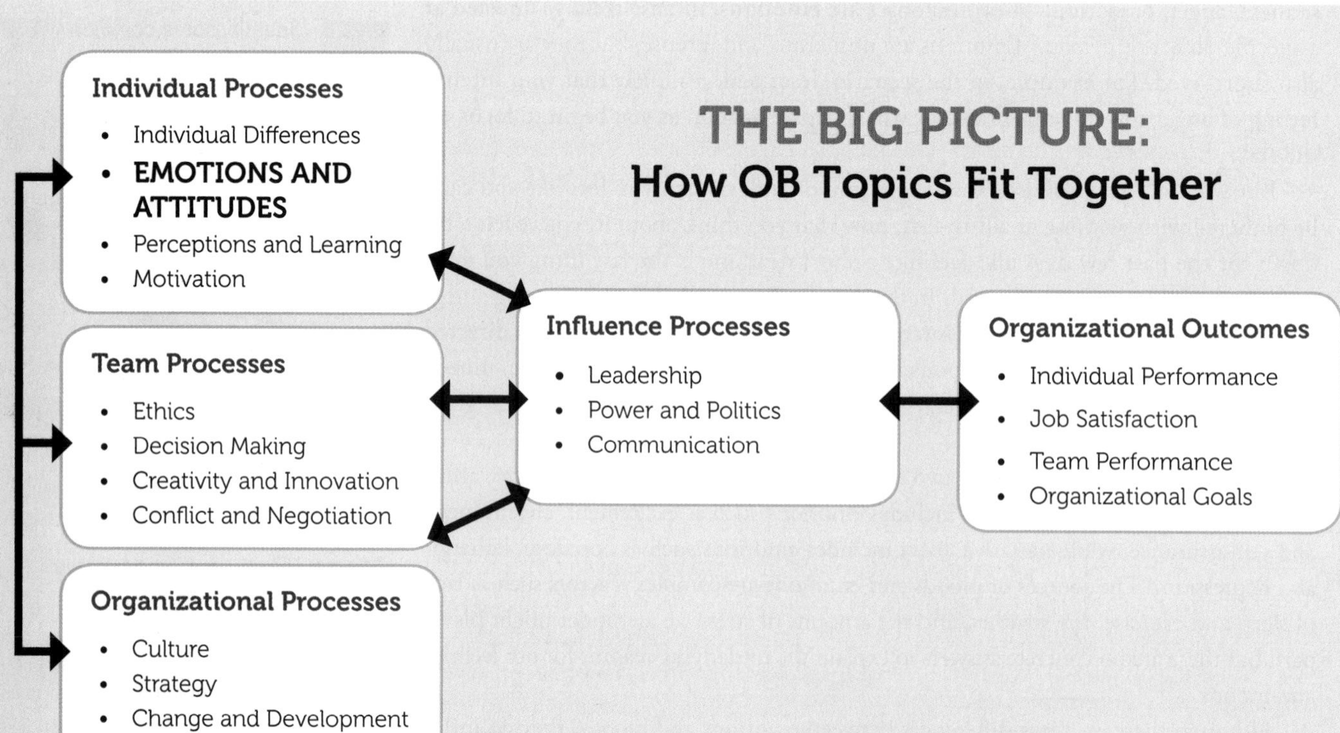

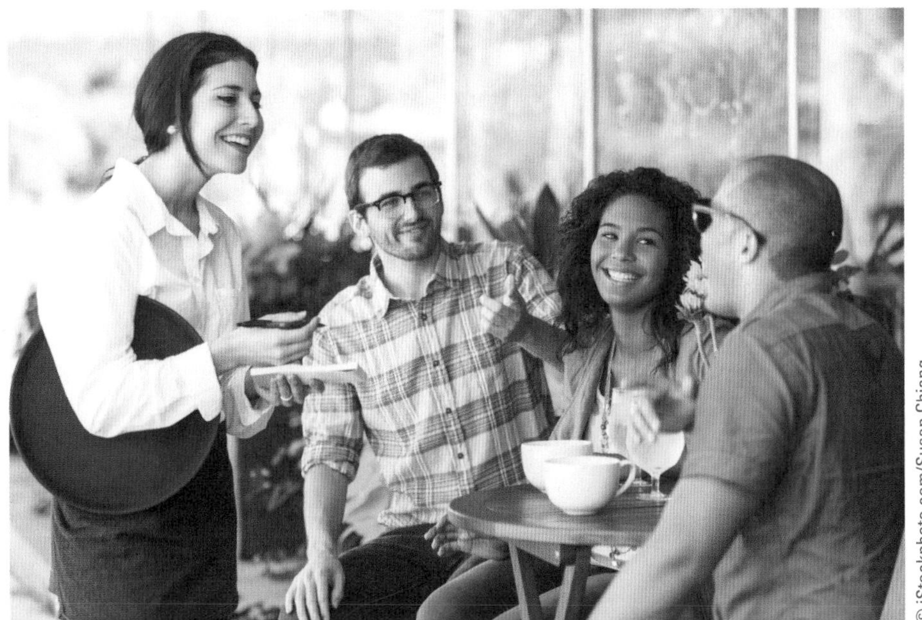

Waiters are expected to be friendly and approachable even when they are tired or dealing with difficult situations. This can create a burden of emotional labor for the employee.

with their current roles sometimes jump into new positions without fully assessing the realities of what the new job has to offer. In this situation, job seekers need to think about how they would feel about taking the job now and into the future.[5]

Most of us experience heightened emotional states at least once in a while. When we are feeling frustrated, angry, or disappointed, we may choose to shout, storm out of a room, or curl up in a quiet place to calm down for a while. However, in the workplace, emotional outbursts could seriously damage your professional reputation and affect your work performance. A lack of self-control over your emotions not only affects you, but your negative responses can spread to others around you and disrupt the function of work groups.[6]

Emotional Contagion

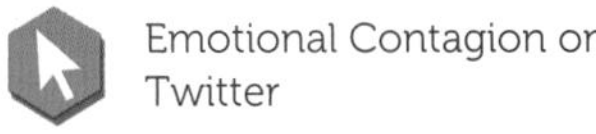

Emotional Contagion on Twitter

Moods and emotions are contagious and have a strong influence on group behavior. **Emotional contagion** is a phenomenon in which emotions experienced by one or more individuals in a work group spread to the others.[7] Researchers have found that negative emotions tend to spread more quickly than positive emotions, which can affect morale, productivity, and motivation. Positive emotional contagion creates an environment in which people work better together, experience less conflict, and experience higher levels of work performance. Managers and leaders who have positive attitudes generally have the ability to inspire their employees to work well together.

Emotional Labor

The concept of **emotional labor** refers to the process of managing our feelings so that we present positive emotions even when they are contrary to our actual feelings.[8] Hotel employees, salespeople, flight attendants, wait staff, and tour operators are all examples of the types of service workers who are expected to smile and be pleasant even in the most demanding circumstances. Today's organizations are increasingly customer oriented, and many managers expect their employees to present a positive face when interacting with their external customers as well as with their internal clients and coworkers.

Emotional contagion: A phenomenon in which emotions which are experienced by few people of a work group are spread to the others

Emotional labor: The process of managing one's feelings to present positive emotions even when they are contrary to one's actual feelings

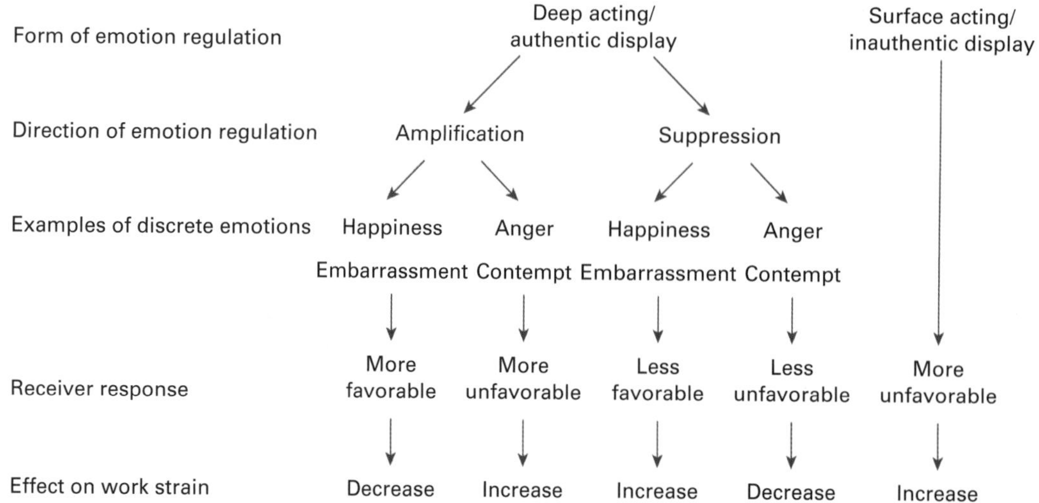

■ FIGURE 3.1 Social Interaction Model

SOURCE: Côté, Stéphane. "A Social Interaction Model of the Effects of Emotion Regulation on Work Strain." *Academy of Management Review* 30, no. 3 (July 2005): 509–530.

Display Rules

Many organizations teach their employees **display rules**, the basic norms that govern which emotions should be displayed and which should be suppressed.[9] Different organizations have different rules that accord with their company culture. For example, call center workers may be given a script to read to customers and be instructed to be enthusiastic and conceal their frustration. Rules for retail or wait staff may require them to greet customers with a smile and treat them as if they are always right.

Emotional Dissonance

It is challenging to put on a happy face all the time, especially if you are experiencing emotional upheaval at home or dealing with work stress. When you feel this way, sometimes the last thing you want to do is to be cheerful and helpful to difficult customers. Under these circumstances, you might experience **emotional dissonance**, a discrepancy between the emotions a person displays and the emotions he or she actually feels.[10] For example, you may feel angry with a particularly demanding and rude customer, but you are compelled to be polite regardless of your true feelings.

Surface Acting Versus Deep Acting

Display rules: Basic norms that govern which emotions should be displayed and which should be suppressed

Emotional dissonance: A discrepancy between the emotions a person displays and the emotions he or she actually feels

Surface acting: A person suppresses their true feelings while displaying the organizationally desirable ones

Deep acting: Efforts to change your actual emotions to better match the required emotions of the situation

When you engage in emotional labor, you are expected to regulate your true feelings in order to achieve organizational goals. People tend to use two emotional labor techniques to control their real emotions: surface acting, and deep acting.[11] **Surface acting** occurs when a person suppresses his or her true feelings while displaying the organizationally desirable ones. For example, you may fake a smile or use a soft tone of voice when dealing with a difficult customer even when, underneath, you are offended. In **deep acting** you try to change your emotions to better match the emotions your employer requires in the situation. For example, rather than feeling irritated by the demanding customer, you attempt to empathize by putting yourself in the customer's position and trying to feel his or her frustration.

Both surface acting and deep acting through social interaction can affect the level of work strain felt by individual employees (see Figure 3.1). As shown in the figure, people who amplify positive emotions like happiness or even embarrassment through deep acting will generate a favorable response from others which decreases work strain. Those who display high levels of anger or contempt will receive a negative response, thus increasing work strain. Similarly, those who put on a fake display of surface acting will also receive an unfavorable response from others, which again increases work strain.

Emotional Regulation

Every day we are exposed to situations that can trigger a range of strong emotions. Most of us try and control our feelings through **emotional regulation**, a set of processes through which people influence their own emotions and the ways in which they experience and express them.[12] The two main kinds of regulation strategies are antecedent focused and response focused.

Antecedent-Focused Strategies

Antecedent-focused strategies[13] come into play before the emotional response has been fully triggered. They include the following.

- *Situation selection* lets you choose or avoid situations that have the potential to generate certain emotional responses. For example, if you dislike a coworker, you might avoid going by his desk so you don't have to engage with him.
- *Situation modification* involves altering a situation to change its emotional impact. For example, you might move physically closer to a person if you want to positively engage him or her in a serious discussion.
- *Attention deployment* consists of refocusing your attention to an area of a situation that results in a more positive emotional outcome. For example, if you are anxious about a looming deadline, you might distract yourself by taking a short break to recharge your energy levels and refresh your focus.
- *Cognitive change* lets you reassess an event or situation to see the bigger picture and bring about a more positive emotional reaction. For example, instead of being frustrated with your boss for being late for your meeting, you could use the extra time to do additional preparation or even take a moment to relax.

Antecedent-focused strategies help us to prevent strong emotional responses when we are confronted with certain situations. In the next section, we take a look at the second type of regulation strategies: response-focused strategies.

Response-Focused Strategies

We use response-focused strategies[14] after an emotional response has been fully triggered. There are two types.

- *Reappraisal* involves reevaluating a potentially emotional situation in a more objective way. For example, you are about to give a speech and you feel very nervous. Rather than allowing nerves to overcome you, you might take a few deep breaths or think about how interested your audience will be in what you have to say.
- *Suppression* occurs when we consciously mask inward emotional reactions with more positive or neutral behavioral responses. For example, you may feel inclined to laugh when a colleague mispronounces someone else's name, but you keep your emotions in check so as not to appear insensitive.

Emotional regulation: A set of processes through which people influence their own emotions and the ways in which they experience and express them

Photo by Joe Raedle/Getty Images

The Aflac booth at a job fair in Southern Florida. When recruiting new employees, Aflac looks for people who display high levels of emotional intelligence in addition to technical skills.

Response-focused strategies help us to prevent any outwardly perceivable expression of emotion in order to support us in coping with certain situations.

Emotional Intelligence

Imagine you are working on a complex project and one of your teammates is having such difficulty carrying out his role that he slows down the rest of the team and jeopardizes the deadline. Do you complain to your boss that this employee is letting the team down? Or do you try and manage the situation by supporting your teammate and helping him learn the right skills? If you chose the latter option, you probably have high levels of emotional intelligence (EI), the ability to understand emotions in ourselves and others in order to effectively manage our own behaviors and our interpersonal relationships.[15] Organizations are beginning to base hiring and promoting decisions on EI, and it is considered as important to professional success as other abilities such as technical skills.[16] For example, American Insurance Company Aflac recruits people who can provide specific examples to illustrate their ability to stay calm in stressful situations.[17]

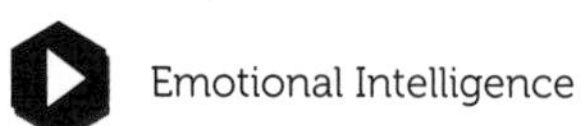

Emotional Intelligence

It is equally important to consider cultural variations in emotional expression. For example, in the United States it is acceptable to show enthusiasm in work when the situation is appropriate, and to debate points with passion in a meeting. However, in Japan and China, this sort of emotional expression is not tolerated and may be perceived as showing off. Similarly, people in the United Kingdom can be quite reserved and understated and tend to play down their emotions in a business setting. When dealing with different cultures, it is extremely important to learn the language of emotion in order to gain a greater understanding of emotional expression. Just because a person from a different culture may not seem enthusiastic doesn't mean they are not excited; they might just be showing their emotions in a different way.[18]

Related to EI is the use of "soft skills," or competencies that rely on personality traits such as empathy, listening abilities, and good communication to build work relationships. Job candidates with soft skills are in demand because they are generally better at conducting self-assessment, managing their emotions, and accepting feedback.[19]

There are four dimensions[20] of EI (see Figure 3.2):

1. *Self-Awareness*: A good understanding of your own emotions
2. *Self-Management*: The ability to control and regulate emotions and impulses
3. *Social Awareness*: Skills in perceiving, empathizing with, and reacting appropriately to the emotions of others
4. *Relationship Management*: The ability to manage the emotions of others to build strong and healthy relationships with them

Despite its popularity during the past decade, some theorists question the validity of the EI concept, citing lack of evidence and criticizing the ways in which EI is tested

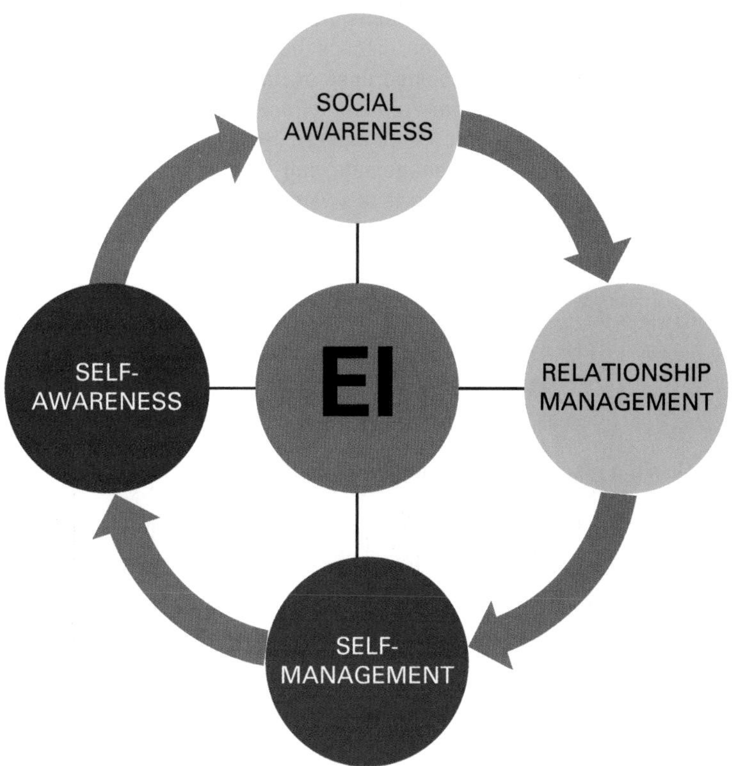

■ FIGURE 3.2 The Four Dimensions of EI

and measured and the resulting conclusions.[21] Despite these criticisms, EI is becoming more popular in the workplace. For example, the US Air Force uses EI to select recruiters, and cosmetics giant L'Oréal chooses its salespeople on the basis of their emotional competencies.[22]

THINKING CRITICALLY

1. Crowds at large sporting events, concerts, or in a movie theatre typically experience emotional contagion in one form or another. Assume that your favorite professional sports team is in a close game and unexpectedly wins. What positive aspects of emotional contagion would you be likely to experience? If your team unexpectedly lost, perhaps to a bad call, what negative aspects of social contagion might you experience? **[Understand]**

2. Take a close look at Figure 3.1. Describe an experience you have had with a friend, classmate, or coworker who displayed surface acting. What was your response to his or her display? How did your response affect her or his likelihood of displaying surface acting in the future? **[Apply/Analyze]**

3. You are the manager of a publishing group of 20 employees. Your parent company is closing your organization and you must inform your employees that they are being laid off. While you will receive a bonus for staying on an additional two weeks, you will also be losing your job. Discuss the antecedent-focused strategies (situation selection, situation modification, attention deployment, cognitive change) and/or response-focused strategies (reappraisal, suppression) you would use to regulate your emotions and behavior in this situation. Which strategy or strategies do you believe would be most effective? Least effective? **[Apply/Analyze/Evaluate]**

4. While emotional intelligence is considered an important and desirable quality in employees, discuss the ways in which emotional intelligence may be used in unscrupulous or unethical ways. For example, imagine you are running a Ponzi scheme similar to the one Bernie Madoff created and ran. How would social awareness, relationship management, self-awareness, and self-management benefit your efforts to swindle people and foundations? Rank the usefulness of each of the four dimensions of IE in this context and explain your rationale. **[Analyze/Evaluate]**

ATTITUDES AND BEHAVIOR

3.3 Explain the ways in which attitudes influence behavior in organizations

In the OB in the Real World feature, hrQ Manager Kathy Rapp stresses the importance of possessing a good attitude. But what is attitude and why is it so important in the workplace? We define **attitude** as a learned tendency to consistently respond positively or negatively to people or events.[23] Attitudes determine our likes and dislikes and help us to make judgments about other people or events. Our beliefs provide us with the necessary information to shape our attitudes, which in turn shape our behaviors.

How Attitudes Are Created

To truly understand attitudes, we need to understand how they are created (Figure 3.3). Three main elements form our attitudes.[24]

1. *Cognitive appraisal* reflects the sum total of a person's underlying beliefs, opinions, information, and knowledge about a specific object, person, or event. For example, my professor is overbearing; my girlfriend is smart and beautiful; the Steelers are the best team in the NFL.
2. *Affective evaluation* reflects a person's positive and negative feelings toward a specific object, person, or event. For example, I don't like my professor; I love my girlfriend; I like the Steelers.
3. *Behavioral intention* is the perceived likelihood that someone will behave in a particular way toward a specific object, person, or event. For example, I will not take another course with my professor; I will kiss my girlfriend; I will root for the Steelers.

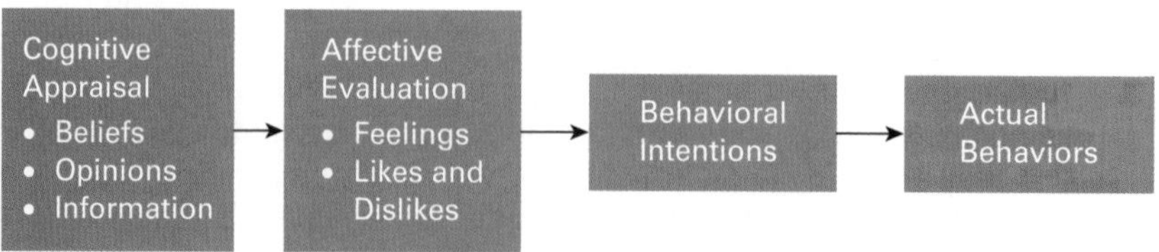

FIGURE 3.3 The Relationship between Attitudes and Behaviors

SOURCE: Adapted from Fishbein, M., & I. Ajzen. *Belief, Attitude, Intention, and Behavior: An Introduction to Theory and Research* (Reading, MA: Addison-Wesley, 1975).

Attitude: A learned tendency to consistently respond positively or negatively to people or events

KATHY RAPP, *president, hrQ*

OB in the Real World

© Kathy Rapp

hrQ is a professional services firm focused exclusively on human resources (HR) search, interim HR staffing, and HR consulting.* It has more than twenty employees in its corporate office and managed 103 HR searches and 161 interim assignments and consulting projects in 2012. The company strives to "elevate HR" by assisting organizations in finding the best HR professionals and solutions to help them achieve their desired results. The goal is to match the most capable, talented, diverse, and qualified HR professional to clients' needs.

Kathy has an interesting vantage point from which to understand how attitude and emotions can influence a person's success in the workplace. She sees firsthand how they affect employees within her company as well as candidates looking for jobs with her clients' organizations.

"For us, employees have to be very self-motivated and they have to be able to keep their emotions in check," she says. For instance, when hrQ was working with a client that wanted to hire two senior HR professionals, the prep work was extensive and time consuming. It included getting to know the client's company, culture, and hiring needs. As soon as the contract was signed, the employees at hrQ got to work diligently reaching out to candidates. Less than forty-eight hours later, however, the client asked to put the searches on hold because of internal restructuring. Because hrQ's employees were emotionally invested in their searches, it might have been easy for them to get emotional about losing credibility with the candidates and losing out on a financial reward that would have come at the end of a successful search. However, "instead of getting emotionally worked up," says Kathy, "my employees try to focus on the bigger picture and understand that waiting until the client is ready to make those hires is the best move for everyone."

Kathy stresses that it's acceptable for hrQ staff to show enthusiasm and passion for their positions. "I would much rather work with an employee who has less experience but shows energy, enthusiasm, and a passionate attitude than someone who has more experience but an ego to go with it." About 90 percent of the employees are seasoned HR professionals who have spent many years in corporate HR. This is a key competitive advantage, because hrQ's employees truly understand what their clients are going through. One of Kathy's employees broke the mold, however. She was hired despite her lack of extensive HR experience, and she knew she had a lot to learn. Rather than getting overwhelmed, she jumped in enthusiastically, reading everything she could find about hrQ's clients, asking a lot of questions, doing her homework, and going the extra mile to learn industry jargon. Her positive attitude allows her to meet any challenge she's given. "A client called us with a completely unreasonable request. They needed us to find 25 to 30 HR interim professionals and they needed the people in two weeks. I was about to turn the project down when this employee told me she wanted to take on the challenge. Not only did she find 30 people for our client but she exceeded their expectations. Her attitude is her differentiator."

Critical-Thinking Questions:

1. **How would you describe Kathy's approach to encouraging a group to adopt a positive attitude in the face of a challenging situation?**
2. **Which do you think is more important in a new hire, experience or a positive attitude? Why?**

SOURCE: Interview with Kathy Rapp conducted on May 14, 2013.

While behavioral intention is the strongest predictor of actual behavior, it does not *necessarily* predict our behavior. Social norms and other behavioral controls may intervene, stopping us from carrying out our intended or most desired action. For example, perhaps Neda's boss has belittled her in front of her coworkers. While her behavioral intention may be to defend herself by telling her boss that his behavior is unprofessional and destructive, social norms suggest that telling off your boss will be considered professionally inappropriate. Meanwhile, in this example an especially relevant behavioral control is the knowledge that Neda might be fired if she responds to her boss in the way that her behavioral intention demands!

Cognitive Dissonance

Originally coined by psychologist Leon Festinger, **cognitive dissonance** is the stress and discomfort individuals experience when they face an inconsistency among her or his beliefs, attitudes, values, and behaviors.[25] Festinger observed that people prefer consistency and thus tend to alter their attitudes, beliefs, or behaviors in order to restore harmony.

For example, despite the evidence that smoking is detrimental to health, Matt likes to smoke and has a positive attitude toward smoking. However, it also makes Matt uneasy that he may be carrying out a behavior that has a negative effect on his health. To alleviate the psychological discomfort associated with his cognitive dissonance in relation to smoking, Matt has a number of choices:

- Change the behavior (Matt will stop smoking)
- Change the belief or attitude (Matt says he doesn't believe the evidence that suggests smoking is dangerous to his health)
- Rationalize the inconsistency in his knowledge that smoking is unhealthy and his behavioral choice to keep smoking (Matt believes smoking is dangerous for most people, but not for him)

As this example illustrates, although we strive to quell the discomfort we feel when attitudes and behaviors contradict each other, the manner in which we try to reconcile dissonant beliefs, values, or attitudes may not be very rational.

THINKING CRITICALLY

1. Discuss the cognitive appraisal, affective evaluation, and behavioral intention that might contribute to your decision not to dress down on casual Friday in your workplace. **[Apply/Analyze]**

2. You work long hours at a startup, routinely working weekends and while on vacation. Although you miss spending time with your family and friends, you believe that by working hard and exhibiting company loyalty you will be promoted as the company grows. When you are passed over for the promotion, you experience cognitive dissonance. List 2-3 options per category (changing your behavior, changing your belief or attitudes, or rationalizing away inconsistencies) that you could pursue in order to reduce the cognitive dissonance you feel. **[Apply/Analyze]**

Cognitive dissonance: The inconsistency between a person's beliefs, attitudes or behaviors

COMMON WORKPLACE ATTITUDES

3.4 Identify some common workplace attitudes and related outcomes

Returning to the Case of Laura Pierce

In Chapter 2, we followed New Development and Marketing Director Laura Pierce during her first day of work at the West Texas Regional Theatre (WTRT). Laura has been assigned the task of increasing ticket sales and creating new marketing initiatives to drive more business to the theatre. However, she suspects her boss Abigail Swenson is not telling her the whole truth about the theatre's financial state, and she is determined to get to the bottom of it. The attitudes we bring to the workplace are critical for three main areas: job satisfaction, organizational commitment, and employee engagement.

Let's follow Laura as she tries to understand the attitudes and behaviors of the different staff members.

On her second day at WTRT, Laura meets with Accountant and Office Manager Cheryl Kooser to work out a marketing budget. Laura is looking forward to completing this step so she can start implementing some new marketing initiatives. She can't help but notice how neat everything in Cheryl's office is. Files are stacked meticulously and there are just a few documents on Cheryl's desk.

"So, you're here about the marketing budget," Cheryl says with an impatient sigh.

Laura is surprised at her negative attitude but chooses to ignore it. "Yes, I'd like to start implementing some ideas that I think will increase ticket sales and publicity."

Cheryl pushes a pile of files toward Laura. "These documents will tell you everything you need to know about our current financial situation," she says. "I'll cut to the chase. The theatre is in a huge amount of debt, close to a million dollars."

Laura gasps. She had suspected from her previous exchange with Cheryl that things are not great, but a million dollars in debt? Laura tries to compose herself. She needs to see what the options are for getting the theatre's finances back on track.

"This is a shock," she begins. "Abigail didn't mention the extent of the theatre's financial difficulties when I was interviewing for the position or when we met yesterday."

Cheryl gives a rueful smile and says, "I thought as much. Fond as I am of Abigail, she tends to bury her head in the sand when it comes to the finances. I have asked her repeatedly to tell the board members about the situation, but she keeps telling me she can handle everything herself."

"But how has the theatre managed to accrue so much debt?" Laura asks.

"It's Abigail. She overspends on everything and doesn't think about the consequences. The donor events we put on are held in lavish hotels and she hires pricey caterers. Every time she meets with the board, she insists on reserving conference rooms in top hotels and paying for lunch. And then there are the extravagant after-show parties. It all adds up," Cheryl says.

"I can see why Abigail is so focused on attracting more patrons to the theatre," Laura says, digesting what she has heard.

Cheryl says, "We definitely need initiatives to get out of this debt, but we can't afford a marketing budget, let alone a salary for a new employee."

Laura is taken aback. So far this morning she has been told that the theatre has a huge amount of debt, there is no marketing budget, and the theatre may not be able to afford her salary.

Before she can respond, Cheryl continues.

"I told Abigail many times that I could help implement some new initiatives that would not only save the theatre money and increase ticket sales, but would also save us having to pay another employee. Abigail told me she would think about it, but the next thing I know, you turn up!"

Laura sees how bitter and agitated Cheryl appears after this revelation. Did Cheryl want the job of development and marketing director and Abigail wouldn't give it to her? If that is the case, how will this affect her working relationship with Cheryl? Laura is thinking about how excited she was just a few days ago to start the dream job that would combine her marketing skills with her love of theatre. It is only two days in, and already her future at WTRT looks bleak. She is finding it difficult to hide her disappointment.

Cheryl looks at her and sighs. "Laura, I'm not sure what else there is left to say. I've been with WTRT for over five years but we're sinking under the weight of the debt. We have a whole season of plays ahead of us and I'm not sure we can even afford to stage them. If things continue to plummet, we'll all be out of a job in six months."

"What about the rest of the staff?" Laura says. "Do they know how close WTRT is to bankruptcy?"

"No," Cheryl replies. "Abigail doesn't want them to know. She's afraid they'll leave when they find out."

Laura needs some time to think through everything Cheryl has told her, so she asks Cheryl whether they can arrange another meeting after she has had a chance to review the financials.

From this narrative, let's assume Cheryl is experiencing low levels of **job satisfaction**, the degree to which an individual feels positive or negative about a job.[26] Table 3.1 lists common characteristics of job satisfaction in the United States. As Table 3.1 illustrates, factors such as relations with coworkers, job security, and the amount of on-the-job stress are correlated with job satisfaction. Cheryl appears to be frustrated not only because of the theatre's financial situation but also because Abigail appears unwilling to take her advice or allow her to help. Laura is also experiencing low levels of job satisfaction, because she has quickly learned that this is not the job she signed up for!

Employee Engagement

Cheryl seems to have high levels of organizational commitment, the loyalty an individual feels to the organization.[27] After all, she has stayed with the theatre through a period of mounting debt and has tried to persuade Abigail to implement some of her ideas about attracting more business and improving the financial situation. We could also say Cheryl has a strong sense of **employee engagement**, which is a connection with the organization and passion for the job.[28] Cheryl refuses to abandon the theatre even though the level of debt means she could be out of a job soon.

Job satisfaction and job performance are strongly related. As the WTRT story unfolds, we can see how job satisfaction influences the work behavior of the staff.

When Laura arrives at work the following day, she is disheartened. She feels misled by Abigail and wonders why Abigail hired her if there is no marketing budget to pay her salary let alone implement her initiatives. Cheryl hadn't exaggerated the financial state of WTRT— the theatre is only a few months away from bankruptcy. Laura knows she needs to talk to Abigail and get answers.

But when she knocks on Abigail's office door, there is no response. Laura gets a cup of coffee and sits in the staff kitchen to gather her thoughts. Before she started

Job satisfaction: The degree to which an individual feels positive or negative about a job

Employee engagement: A connection with the organization and passion for one's job

US Workers' Satisfaction with All Job Aspects (2014)	% Completely Satisfied
The physical safety conditions of your workplace	74
Your relations with coworkers	71
The flexibility of your hours	63
Your boss or immediate supervisor	60
The amount of vacation time you receive	59
Your job security	58
The amount of work that is required of you	56
The recognition you receive at work for your work accomplishments	53
Your chances for promotion	38
The health insurance benefits your employer offers	39
The retirement plan your employer offers	36
The amount of money you earn	31
The amount of on-the-job stress in your job	27

■ TABLE 3.1 Characteristics of Job Satisfaction

SOURCE: Adapted from Riffkin, R. "Americans' Satisfaction with Job Security at New High." *Gallup*. August 20, 2014. www.gallup.com/poll/175190/americans-satisfaction-job-security-new-high.aspx.

NOTE: Sorted by % completely satisfied in 2014

working at WTRT she had done a great deal of research and come up with a list of marketing initiatives to increase ticket sales at the theatre. As Laura is thinking that it will be impossible to implement her ideas without a budget, she has a breakthrough and springs out of her chair.

"Some of these initiatives can be done on a shoestring budget. All I need is the right support!"

Laura realizes it's time to talk to the rest of the staff. She finds Tony stage-side.

"Laura! How's your first week at WTRT going?" he asks, smiling. "I'm just trying to arrange the first show of the next season."

"Did you choose the show?" Laura asks, remembering Tony's exchange with Abigail.

Tony's face clouds over. "No. I went with Abigail's idea," he says. "My choice would have been one that was more appropriate for a younger audience, while Abigail prefers the classic stage shows."

Laura feels appealing to younger people is exactly what WTRT needs to attract a wider audience, especially with the large university close by in Abilene. She makes a mental note to talk to Abigail about it.

Tony seems deflated and unhappy. Laura wonders whether any of the staff are satisfied with their jobs at the moment.

"Anyway, what can I do for you?" Tony says, making an effort to sound cheerful.

Laura asks whether he has a few minutes to listen to some of her marketing ideas for the theatre. Tony says he is happy to help and they head to his office to talk. Laura starts by outlining her marketing ideas that won't be costly to implement. Tony listens intently as she describes:

- Asking the local radio station for free on-air time to advertise WTRT in exchange for a free ad in the WTRT playbills
- Partnering with local restaurants to offer patrons "dinner and a show" discounts

- Asking a local graphic design firm to revamp the WTRT website so they can post video clips of their shows in exchange for free advertising on the playbills and the WTRT website
- Creating new sponsorship categories to encourage more people to make donations to the theatre
- Using Twitter to generate more publicity and provide updates about the latest shows and news at WTRT
- Creating a WTRT Facebook page to promote the upcoming shows and provide information about ticket deals
- Setting up a booth at the local craft fair on Saturday mornings to sell theatre tickets and attract new patrons and sponsors

"Laura, those are excellent ideas! I would be happy to help you implement them, especially setting up a booth at the craft fair every weekend. We have lots of props we could use to make it eye-catching, and we could even wear costumes to promote the essence of the theatre!"

Laura is delighted with Tony's enthusiastic attitude and willingness to get involved. She is particularly impressed by his high levels of **organizational citizenship behavior** (OCB), which is discretionary and voluntary behavior that is not a part of the employee's specific role requirements and is not formally rewarded.[29] Tony's offer to make time to help out at the craft fair booth every Saturday is really "going the extra mile," she thinks.

Buoyed by Tony's energy, Laura outlines her plans for implementing the rest of her ideas. "I can get in touch with the radio station. Maybe my past experience working for NPR in Tennessee will help me get my foot in the door. I can also have a chat with some of the local restaurant owners to see whether we can work out a deal, and I'll put a call in to a few local graphic design firms to see whether anyone is interested in working with us. I just need someone on the staff who can do regular Twitter and Facebook updates. I'd like us to have a presence on Instagram and Pinterest too."

"Joey would be perfect!" Tony replies instantly. "He's a whiz at social media."

Laura is surprised. If Joey is so great at social networking, why hasn't he mentioned it before?

Tony continues, "Joey has approached Abigail with innovative ideas several times, but she prefers that he focus on the administrative side of things. Maybe you can persuade her otherwise."

Laura is struck by the increasing examples of poor management practices going on at the theatre. There seems to be very little communication between Abigail and her staff, as well as low morale thanks to Abigail's "My way is the only way" type of leadership style. The staff seems to be continuously confined to their roles and their ideas continually rejected. Tony gets knocked back for suggesting more modern theatre productions, Joey is steered away from using his social media skills, and Cheryl is dissuaded from suggesting cost-saving initiatives. On top of all that, Abigail's refusal to admit the level of debt and its implications to her staff strikes Laura as downright unethical. Laura can't help but think that such poor management practices are setting a very bad example for the rest of the staff.

Laura realizes she needs to get Abigail on board with her ideas as soon as possible if there is any chance of turning around WTRT.

After her productive discussion with Tony, she heads off to find Joey and see whether she can gain his support, too. She sees him sitting glumly at his desk, surrounded by a stack of papers.

Organizational citizenship behavior: Discretionary and voluntary behavior that is not a part of the employee's specific role requirements and is not formally rewarded

"That looks like quite a large pile of work you have there!" Laura says with a smile.

Joey looks at the stack of papers and sighs heavily. "Some days I don't make it to work, and then it's all piled up when I get back," he says.

Laura doesn't want to pry but wonders why Joey isn't showing up to work on a regular basis. The theatre can't afford to be without every one of the staff, and the ticket desk needs to be covered at all times. She looks at his expression of hopelessness and wonders whether there is anything Joey likes about his job at WTRT. She knows from experience that low levels of job satisfaction tend to lead to withdrawal behaviors such as *absenteeism* and *turnover*.[30] She worries that if Joey is absent from work so often he might eventually quit, which means recruiting and training a replacement—an expense WTRT could do without. It's all the more reason for her to try and boost Joey's spirits a little.

She asks him whether he has a few minutes to talk about marketing. He's happy to take a break from all the paperwork and motions for her to sit down next to him in the ticket office. As she outlines some of her marketing initiatives, Joey begins to sit up and look her straight in the eye for the first time since she arrived at WTRT. "I'd love to be in charge of social networking for the theatre!" he says enthusiastically. Laura smiles at his sudden energy; he seems much more motivated than he was a few minutes ago.

A few minutes later, Cheryl arrives with a pile of files and glares at Joey, who is showing Laura some of his favorite Instagram feeds and discussing the best time of day to post updates. "I wouldn't be smiling if I were you, Joey. You have a lot of work to make up after being out so often. I have too much of my own work to do and am not going to help you out anymore. You're on your own." Cheryl drops the files on the pile of papers on Joey's desk, causing it to topple over onto the floor, and walks away.

Laura is shocked at Cheryl's **counterproductive work behaviors (CWBs)**, voluntary behaviors that purposefully disrupt or harm the organization.[31] CWBs include avoiding work or taking shortcuts, creating conflict, harassing coworkers, being physically or verbally aggressive, and stealing or sabotaging work efforts. Embarrassed, Joey bends down to pick up the papers, and Laura immediately starts to help him.

"I don't want to lose my job or be a burden to Cheryl," Joey mutters, straightening the papers on his desk. "It's just that I have commitments at home, which means there are times I can't be here— then when I get back, all this is waiting for me." He gestures, hopelessly, at the stack of paperwork. Before Laura can offer any words of comfort, the phone rings, and Joey turns to pick it up.

Laura signals good-bye and walks back to her office to go through her notes. Now that she has Tony's and Joey's support, she feels more confident about presenting her marketing initiatives to Abigail. However, Abigail doesn't show up to work at all that day and is not answering her cell. Laura's positivity fades—she is beginning to feel even more overwhelmed and stressed.

THINKING CRITICALLY

1. Discuss the level of organizational commitment and employee engagement exhibited by each character in the narrative case (Laura, Cheryl, Tony, Joey, and Abigail). To what extent can organizational commitment and employee engagement contribute to a successful organization? Do situations exist where organizational commitment and employee engagement are counterproductive to organizational success? Explain. **[Understand/Apply/Analyze]**

2. List at least five specific behaviors that illustrate organizational citizenship behavior (OCB). How are coworkers likely to view and collaborate with those who display high levels of OCB? Defend your answer. **[Apply/Analyze/Evaluate]**

3. List at least five specific behaviors that illustrate counterproductive work behaviors (CWBs). How are coworkers likely to view and collaborate with those who display high levels of CWBs? Defend your answer. **[Apply/Analyze/Evaluate]**

Counterproductive work behaviors: Voluntary behaviors that purposefully disrupt or harm the organization

High levels of workplace stress can lead to loss of productivity and even illness.

© iStockphoto.com/Martinan

STRESS IN THE WORKPLACE

3.5 Illustrate the ways in which stress can affect behavior in the workplace

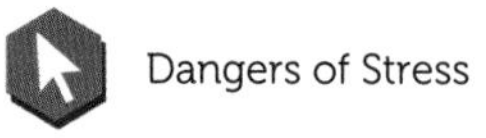

Dangers of Stress

Most of us know what it feels like to be stressed. We may feel under pressure about making a deadline, taking an exam, or giving a presentation in front of a large audience. We define stress as a response that occurs when a person perceives a situation as threatening to his or her well-being when his or her resources have been taxed or exceeded.[32] Stress in the workplace can affect the behavior of people working in an organization, leading to poor health and absenteeism. Statistics show that 60 percent of illnesses are caused by stress, which costs the United States $300 billion every year on medical bills and loss of productivity.[33] Let's explore how Laura and the other members of the WTRT staff manage different types of stress.

When Laura arrives at work the next day, she is determined to sit down with Abigail and discuss the financial dilemma at WTRT, as well as request her support for the marketing initiatives she would like to implement. But by 10:00 a.m., Abigail still hasn't arrived at work.

Laura feels frustrated but is determined not to let stress get the better of her. She decides to take matters into her own hands and picks up the phone. The first call she makes is to the station manager at the local radio station to see whether she can trade on-air time for free advertising in the theatre playbill. She carefully outlines her idea, but without giving any reason the station manager politely tells her he is unable to grant her request. Before she can attempt to change his mind, he wishes her luck and hangs up. Laura is puzzled, but she's not going to give up.

She picks up the phone again and calls a local restaurant to see whether they would be interested in collaborating on a "dinner-plus-theatre" deal. The restaurant manager seems friendly enough at first, but when Laura mentions Abigail's name, his tone changes. "You tell Abigail she still has an outstanding bill to pay from the last party she had here," he says angrily and hangs up.

Taken aback but undeterred, Laura makes some more calls to local businesses around town, and every time she gets the same response. Apparently, Abigail owes money to everyone in Abilene. Laura is deeply upset. If there is no goodwill in the community, how is she supposed to make her ideas work? Just then, she hears Abigail announce her arrival. Laura takes a moment to calm down. She needs to ensure her emotions are under control in order to handle the coming confrontation with her boss. After a few minutes, she makes her way to Abigail's office and knocks on the door. "It's show time," she thinks, frustrated and nervous at the same time.

"Oh Laura, my angel! How are you settling in?" Abigail rushes over to her and gives her an enthusiastic hug.

Despite her frustration, Laura smiles. Abigail's energy is contagious. At Abigail's invitation she sits down and gives her an account of everything she has discovered over the last few days, starting with the huge amount of debt owed by WTRT.

"I told you not to listen to Cheryl," says Abigail, her smile fading quickly. "She likes to exaggerate."

Laura is prepared for this response and replies, "I've seen the documents myself, Abigail. Cheryl gave me all the files. The theatre is in real trouble."

Suddenly the words rush out of Abigail in a torrent. "You have no idea how much stress I am under! Do you know how we stayed afloat for the last six months? I have been personally bankrolling WTRT by mortgaging my home. I spent all day yesterday trying to persuade the bank not to take away my house. I haven't slept in months and I'm exhausted from worrying about it. The theatre means everything to me, but I don't know how much longer I can carry on. Maybe I should just let someone else deal with it, because I'm pretty much out of steam."

Laura gives the tearful Abigail some time to compose herself. She can't believe what she has heard— Abigail has been pouring her own money into keeping WTRT afloat? What about the theatre's patrons, sponsors, and donors?

Abigail snickers when Laura asks her about them. "Money from them? They owe *me* money. They send checks whenever they feel like it, but never the full amount they originally promised. Sometimes months pass before the donations come in, if at all. Our corporate sponsor went bankrupt, so that line of financing has been cut off too."

Laura sits back, thinking about her new coworkers. Cheryl is stressed because Abigail refuses to listen to her repeated warnings about the mounting debt, and she appears to be taking her frustrations out on Joey. Tony is stressed because Abigail won't let him choose the shows for the next season, and Joey is stressed because Abigail dismisses his social networking ideas and he has more work than he can keep up with. Abigail is stressed because her beloved theatre is in trouble and she has run out of resources to save it. Laura realizes she has been stressed since she started the job, but she thinks she has figured out a way to manage it.

"The key to fixing the problem is Abigail," Laura says to herself. "Although she has great charisma and the staff seems to be loyal to her, she needs to champion other people's ideas if she wants the theatre to succeed. I need to take the stress out of the situation, beginning with her." If she can get persuade Abigail to get on board with some of her ideas, she knows she can make a difference.

Stressors

There are many sources of stress in the workplace. **Stressors** are environmental stimuli that place demands on individuals. There are two main types:[34]

Stressors

- *Challenge stressors* are associated with workload, job demands, job complexity, and deadlines and are positively related to motivation and performance. For example, although Laura faces a number of challenges to implementing her marketing initiatives, she still feels motivated to accomplish tasks.

Stressors: Environmental stimuli that place demands on individuals

- *Hindrance stressors* inhibit progress toward objectives; examples are role ambiguity or conflict, hassles, red tape, and highly political environments. These stressors are negatively related to motivation and performance. For example, Joey in particular seems to lack motivation; he is often absent from work, and when he does show up, he does not perform well because of the constraints placed on him by Cheryl and Abigail.

However, stress doesn't have to always be negative, nor is it a permanent condition. In the next section we explore different aspects of stress and ways of managing it.

THINKING CRITICALLY

1. Briefly discuss the level of stress each of the narrative case's characters is working under. Do you agree with Laura's assessment that changing Abigail's management style is the best solution to the problems facing WTRT? Why or why not? **[Apply/ Evaluate]**
2. List the challenge stressors and the hindrance stressors affecting each of the narrative case characters. Is it possible for the same stressor to be a challenge stressor to one person and a hindrance stressor to another? Explain your answer. **[Analyze/ Evaluate]**

STRESS-RELATED OUTCOMES AND WELLNESS

3.6 Discuss different outcomes of stress and the benefits of wellness programs

Although high degrees of stress can be destructive to our behaviors and harmful to our health, stress isn't always negative. For example, when Laura objectively evaluates the stressful situation she is in and realizes there can be positive outcomes if she can get Abigail's support, she experiences **eustress**, a moderate level of stressors that have constructive and positive effects on effort and performance.[35] Conversely, Abigail is experiencing **distress**, high levels of stressors that have destructive and negative effects on effort and performance.[36]

There are three elements to distress:[37]

- The *physiological element* is manifested as negative physical health effects. For example, Abigail tells Laura she suffers from insomnia and exhaustion.
- The *psychological element* appears as negative attitudes and emotions that can lower job satisfaction, among other results. For example, Abigail is overwhelmed by the theatre's financial burden and seems anxious and irritable.
- *Job burnout* consists of emotional exhaustion, cynicism, and loss of interest in the job that can result from ongoing exposure to high levels of stressors. For example, Abigail appears to be on the point of giving up because of the stress she is under.

Eustress: Moderate levels of stressors that have constructive and positive effects on effort and performance

Distress: High levels of stressors that have destructive and negative effects on effort and performance

Managing Stress

Yet the good thing about stress is that it can be managed. Let's explore how Laura helps Abigail manage her stress levels.

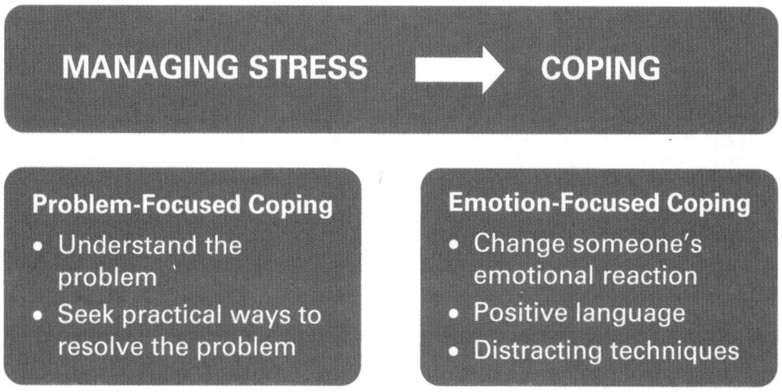

MANAGING STRESS → COPING

Problem-Focused Coping
- Understand the problem
- Seek practical ways to resolve the problem

Emotion-Focused Coping
- Change someone's emotional reaction
- Positive language
- Distracting techniques

FIGURE 3.4 Managing Stress

Now that Abigail has revealed the truth about her personal and financial stress, Laura is determined to help her eliminate some of the stressors and cope with the distress in her life. **Coping** is the effort to manage, reduce, or minimize stressors.[38] There are two types of coping:[39] **problem-focused coping**, which aims at reducing or eliminating stressors by attempting to understand the problem, and seeking practical ways in which to resolve it; and **emotion-focused coping**, which is an effort to try to change a person's emotional reaction to a stressor by using positive language and distracting techniques (see Figure 3.4).

Laura takes control of the meeting and uses some *problem-focused coping* strategies to try to remove the cause of Abigail's distress. A subdued Abigail listens while Laura talks her through the marketing initiatives she has in mind, all the time reassuring her they will require very little financing to implement. When she has finished, Abigail stands up and starts pacing around the room.

Then she turns to face Laura and says, "I like your ideas about creating new sponsorship programs and setting up a booth at the local crafts fair, but you won't get any help from the local businesses around here. They never support WTRT!"

Laura replies, "I contacted a couple of restaurants earlier today and each of them mentioned outstanding bills that need to be paid by the theatre."

Abigail is upset that Laura now has this information, but she catches Laura's steady gaze and sighs. "Yes, it's true I owe them money, too."

Laura changes tack and tries to distract Abigail from her money problems for a minute by telling her about the staff's willingness to help implement the initiatives. Abigail protests when Laura tells her Joey is going to handle the online publicity. "He can barely do his own job as it is, and he never shows up for work!" But Laura is insistent. After a short debate, Abigail grudgingly agrees to give Joey a month's trial to prove he can be a reliable employee as well as adept at handling social media for the theatre.

Laura also broaches the subject of Tony choosing at least one of the shows for the next season in order to attract a wider market of theatregoers, citing the university students as a prime example. Abigail initially refuses to entertain the idea, insisting that she is the only one who can choose the shows. To resolve this conflict, Laura uses *emotion-focused strategies* by telling Abigail how supportive the team has been and how passionate they are about WTRT. Abigail softens, "I guess I have nothing to lose," she says quietly. Laura also persuades her to tell the staff the truth about WTRT's financial state and agrees to organize a staff meeting for the following day.

"Let's start by building goodwill in the community. We need to improve our reputation and our profile if we're going to attract new theatregoers," Laura says. "The more customers we can attract, the higher the ticket sales, and the sooner the theatre will be able to pay off its debts."

Coping: The effort to manage, reduce, or minimize stressors

Problem-focused coping: A type of coping that aims at reducing or eliminating stressors by attempting to understand the problem and seeking practical ways in which to resolve it

Emotion-focused coping: An effort to try to change a person's emotional reaction to a stressor by using positive language and distracting techniques

EMOTION-FOCUSED COPING STRATEGIES AND EMOTIONAL INTELLIGENCE

Examining the Evidence

When faced with stressors in the workplace, employees often choose problem-focused coping, tackling the problems head-on in an effort to eliminate or reduce stressors. However, recent research suggests that emotion-focused coping strategies may be very useful in helping employees to maintain their immediate task-performance levels. Researchers Janaki Gooty and Jane S. Thomas of the University of North Carolina at Charlotte, Mark B. Gavin of West Virginia University, and Neal M. Ashkanasy of the University of Queensland suggest that emotion-focused coping strategies such as denial, mental and behavioral disengagement, and venting could be effective short-term responses for dealing with discrete emotions such as anger, guilt, or joy. Their findings not only showed a significant positive relationship between emotion-focused coping strategies and task performance; they also indicated that people with high levels of emotional intelligence were more likely to choose emotion-focused strategies in response to their anger, guilt, and joy than were people with low levels of emotional intelligence.

Critical-Thinking Questions

1. **What are the primary implications of this research regarding employee coping strategies?**
2. **What specifically can managers do to ensure that employees are using the most appropriate coping strategies to deal with their emotions in the workplace?**

SOURCE: Gooty, Janaki, Mark B. Gavin, Neal M. Ashkanasy, and Jane S. Thomas. "The Wisdom of Letting Go and Performance: The Moderating Role of Emotional Intelligence and Discrete Emotions." *Journal of Occupational and Organizational Psychology* 87, no. 2 (June 2014): 392–413.

"But how are we supposed to generate that many audience members in such a short period of time? The actors will be arriving next month to begin rehearsals for the next season. Honestly, I'm not sure we can even pay them," Abigail says, anxiously.

"To start, I think we should start chasing the outstanding monies the patrons owe the theatre," Laura says.

"I can't do that," Abigail gasps. "The patrons who owe the most money . . . some of them are board members— they're my friends! What will they think?"

"Abigail, you need to be honest with the board members about the state of the finances. They need to know you've been personally keeping the theatre afloat and that you need their help. If they truly are your friends and supporters of WTRT, they'll help us get the theatre back on track again. Cheryl will support you in the meeting— you won't be alone."

Abigail puts her head in her hands and sighs before regaining her composure. "Okay, Laura— we will do it your way for now. Let's hope it pays off!"

"So do I!" Laura thinks to herself.

When she goes home that evening, she thinks about everything that has happened and all that is to come. Although she is pleased that Abigail is supporting her ideas, she can't help but feel a bit apprehensive about the difficult conversations with the board members that lie ahead.

Wellness

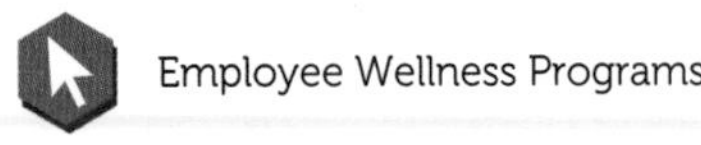

We've seen that there are different degrees and types of stress and various ways of managing it. In recognition of the implications of stress, some organizations offer wellness programs as a way of helping their employees manage stress and otherwise protect and improve their health. A **wellness program** is a personal or organizational effort to promote health and well-being[40] through providing access to services like medical screenings, weight management, health advice, and exercise programs. The main aim of the wellness program is to cultivate a healthier and more productive workforce that are more satisfied with their jobs.

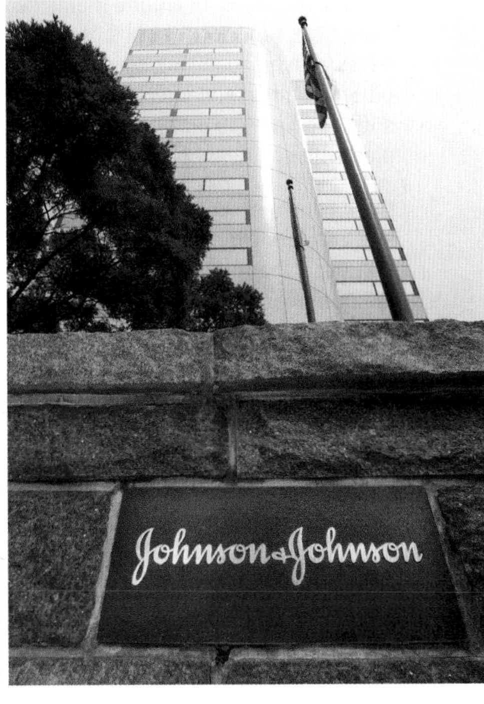

AP Photo/Daniel Hulshizer

By providing their employees with health benefits and wellness programs, Johnson & Johnson not only improved the lives of their employees but also saved $250 million in healthcare costs over 10 years.

Another major benefit of wellness programs is that they save organizations money by reducing absenteeism and lower the cost of providing medical insurance, both of which are major motivators for companies. For example, pharmaceutical company Johnson & Johnson claim that its wellness programs have saved the company $250 million on health care costs over a ten-year period.[41] Studies have also shown that effective wellness programs increase morale and reduce employee turnover. Nelnet, an education finance firm, asked employees in exit interviews what they would miss most about working at Nelnet. Most of the departing employees responded that they would miss the wellness program the most.[42]

However, to be effective, wellness programs should be carefully planned. The most successful programs engage employees by inviting feedback and getting their buy-in through meetings, suggestion boxes, or staff surveys, and by tracking the level of employee participation and its impact on absenteeism, turnover, insurance costs, morale, and overall employee well-being. Managers are essential to a program's success, because they can communicate the many benefits to employees and lead by example by showing real commitment to the wellness program. The program's activities should also be attractive to employees and be designed to promote healthy eating and raise awareness of and knowledge about health. For example, the Capital Metropolitan Transit Authority promoted overall health and wellness by providing a corporate wellness program that offered access to two 24-hour fitness centers, personal trainers, smoking cessation workshops, and tailored nutrition assessments and advice. As a result of the program, absenteeism fell by 25 percent and morale increased.[43]

More important, wellness programs should be fun! Walking and cycling clubs, golf, onsite fitness classes such as yoga, Pilates, Zumba, and corporate challenge events such as half-marathons are popular activities run by organizations.

In this chapter we have explored the impact of emotions, attitudes, and stress on individuals and organizations. As you have seen, reducing stress and resolving conflicts requires the ability to communicate with people with different attitudes, behaviors, and personalities.

THINKING CRITICALLY

1. Consider what factors contribute to your own level of stress. Under what circumstances are you most likely to experience eustress? Under what circumstances are you most likely to experience distress? Do individual personalities play a role in how people experience stress? Support your answer. **[Apply/Analyze]**

Wellness program: A personal or organizational effort to promote health and wellbeing through providing access to services like medical screenings, weight management, health advice, and exercise programs

2. Vikram, the father of a good friend, has been coaching Little League for over a decade. You attend a game and notice that Vikram is unusually harsh with his team, is making cynical remarks about their performance to other coaches, and seems lacking in energy or enthusiasm. Clearly he is suffering from job burnout. Discuss what physiological and psychological elements could be contributing to Vikram's burnout. **[Analyze/Evaluate]**

3. Based on your answer to Question 2 above, devise a list of at least 5 steps you and your friend could take to help Vikram manage his stress and job burnout. What problem-focused and emotion-focused coping strategies would you use? Do you believe that one type of strategy would be better than another in this situation? Why or why not? **[Evaluate/Create]**

4. Imagine that you are the human resources manager for a large non-profit food bank that distributes groceries to hungry families and also offers cooking lessons, nutritional advice, and strategies for making scarce financial resources stretch further at the grocery store. Demand for your services is high and employees and volunteers are showing increased signs of stress as they struggle to meet the needs of hungry children and families. A wealthy patron offers to provide funding for wellness program that benefits food bank employees and volunteers and becomes self-sustaining after one year. What will the wellness program you create look like? **[Create]**

IN REVIEW

Learning Objectives

3.1 Describe the basic concept of emotions in the context of organizational behavior

Emotions are intense feelings directed at a specific object or person. They are numerous and intense but they are usually fleeting and short-lived. **Moods** are less intense and more generalized feelings not directed at a specific object or person; they last longer than emotions.

Emotions can turn into moods when we lose focus of what caused the feeling in the first place; both good and bad moods can trigger stronger, more intense emotional responses.

3.2 Discuss the various aspects of emotions in the workplace

In the workplace, emotional outbursts could seriously damage your professional reputation as well as your work performance. **Emotional contagion** is a phenomenon in which emotions experienced by a few people of a work group are spread to the others. **Emotional labor** takes place when in the course of the job service industry employees must display emotions different from those they are actually feeling. **Emotional regulation** is a set of processes through which people influence their own emotions and the ways in which they experience and express them. **Emotional intelligence (EI)** is the ability to understand emotions in ourselves and others in order to effectively manage our own behaviors and relationships with others.

3.3 Explain the ways in which attitudes influence behavior in organizations

An **attitude** is a learned tendency to consistently respond positively or negatively to people or events. *Cognitive appraisal* reflects the sum total of a person's underlying beliefs, opinions, information, and knowledge about a specific object, person, or event. These appraisals lead to *affective evaluation*, which reflects a person's attitudes and his or her positive and negative feelings toward a specific object, person, or event. This then leads to the individual's *behavioral intention,* the intention to behave in a particular way toward a specific object, person, or event. Attitudes do not necessarily predict behavior; social norms and other behavioral controls may intervene.

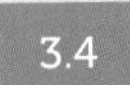

3.4 Identify some common workplace attitudes and related outcomes

Our workplace attitudes are critical in three main areas: job satisfaction, organizational commitment, and employee engagement. **Job satisfaction** is the degree to which an individual feels positive or negative about a job. **Organizational commitment** is the loyalty of an individual to the organization. **Employee engagement** is a connection with the organization and passion for one's job. There is a strong relationship between job satisfaction and job performance. **Organizational citizenship behaviors (OCBs)** are discretionary and voluntary behaviors that are not a part of the employee's specific role requirements and are not formally rewarded.

3.5 Illustrate the ways in which stress can affect behavior in the workplace

Stress is a response that occurs when a situation is perceived as threatening to a person's well-being when the person's resources are taxed or exceeded. **Stressors** are environmental stimuli that place demands on individuals. The outcomes of stress can be either positive or negative.

3.6 Discuss different outcomes of stress and the benefits of wellness programs.

Eustress is a moderate level of stressors that have constructive and positive effects on effort and performance. In contrast, **distress** is characterized by high levels of stressors that have destructive and negative effects on effort and performance. **Coping** is the effort to manage, reduce, or minimize stressors. **Problem-focused coping** aims at reducing or eliminating stressors by attempting to understand the problem, and seeking practical ways in which to resolve it; **emotion-focused coping** is an effort to try to change our emotional reaction to a stressor by using positive language and distracting techniques. Many organizations offer wellness programs as a way of helping their employees manage stress. A **wellness program** is a personal or organizational effort to promote health and wellbeing.

KEY TERMS

THINKING CRITICALLY ABOUT THE CASE OF LAURA PIERCE

Coping with Stress at WTRT

Put yourself in Laura Pierce's position as a new employee at WTRT and consider the five critical-thinking steps in relation to stress within the theatre company.

OBSERVE

What differences do you observe among Cheryl, Tony, Joey, and Abigail's response to workplace stress? How does Laura's response to her stress in her new position compare to their responses as long-term workers at WTRT? List the challenge stressors and hindrance stressors experienced by each character, including Laura.

INTERPRET

Based on the actions of the characters discussed in this chapter, what factors of Abigail's management style are contributing to workplace stress for Cheryl, Tony, and Joey? How does Abigail's personality and management style contribute to Abigail's workplace stress?

ANALYZE

The steps Laura takes to help Abigail cope with her stress are discussed in the chapter. List a series of problem-focused coping strategies and emotion-focused strategies that Laura could employ with each of the remaining characters: Cheryl, Tony, and Joey.

EVALUATE

Based on the strategies you devise for helping Cheryl, Tony, and Joey cope with workplace stress, do you consider problem-focused coping strategies or emotion-focused coping strategies more likely to be helpful to Laura in reducing her coworkers' stress and enlisting their support? Why?

EXPLAIN

Explain the best course of action you believe Laura can take to manage her own level of stress as she continues to work with Abigail and the staff at WTRT to get the company out of debt. What coping strategies should she continue to use? What strategies might she need to begin using as the amount of time she is undergoing stress increases?

EXERCISE 3.1: ANTECEDENT-FOCUSED STRATEGIES

Antecedent-focused strategies take place before the emotional response has been fully triggered. Apply an example from your past work experiences to each of the four types. (Do not use the examples from the text.)

1. Situation Selection ______________________________
____
____
____
____

2. Situation Modification ______________________________
____
____
____
____

3. Attention Deployment ______________________________
____
____
____
____

4. Cognitive Change ______________________________
____
____
____
____

EXERCISE 3.2: AIRPORT ROLE PLAY: EMOTIONAL LABOR AT WORK

Objective:

Discuss the various roles of emotions in the workplace.

Instructions:

Break into groups of three. One person will play the role of an airline passenger, one person will be in the role of the gate agent for an airline, and the final person will be an observer.

The scenario is one in which the airline passenger absolutely MUST get to the destination tonight and the flight has been cancelled. The passenger needs to be as frustrated as possible and the gate agent needs to be as pleasant and provide as much customer service as possible. This role play scenario should be played out for 3-5 minutes.

Reflection Questions:

1. If you were the airline passenger, how did you feel when you were trying to express your frustration?
2. If you were the airline gate agent, how did you feel as you were trying to resolve the issue for the passenger?
3. If you were the observer, what emotions were evident in the passenger and the gate agent?
4. If you were the passenger, what more could the gate agent have done to resolve the issue?
5. If you were the gate agent, what were the emotions you felt during the exchange and which of those had to be suppressed in order to provide good customer service?

Exercise contributed by Harriet Rojas, Professor of Business, Indiana Wesleyan University

EXERCISE 3.3: MOURNING AT THE DECO CHOCOLATE COMPANY

Objective:

In this exercise, you will develop your ability to *describe* emotions in an organizational context, *discuss* the roles these emotions play in the workplace, and *develop examples* of the effects of workplace stress.

Background:

You are a manager at the Deco Chocolate Company. Deco Chocolate is a small, boutique chocolate company that specializes in high-end, custom designed, hand crafted chocolates for special events such as large weddings and corporate banquets. The company has been highly profitable, but due to the nature of its service, it has remained relatively small with only 118 employees.

The company is very close knit, with all current employees having been personally selected by one of the founders, the former President (Mary Washington) or Vice President of HR (her husband Hank Washington). The founders would regularly invite workers at all levels to their home for dinners or parties. Reciprocally, there was rarely a wedding, birth, bar mitzvah, or other major life event that the founders were not invited to as well. In brief, Mary and Hank had developed the company into a true family.

This made the car crash and subsequent death of Mary and Hank last week a truly devastating loss to everyone in the company. A strong succession plan created by Mary Washington has ensured a smooth operational transition for the company, but the emotional fallout is quite different. There have been noticeable signs of grief, depression, and a general drop in worker morale and performance. In addition, more withdrawal behaviors such as absenteeism, lateness, and even looking for external employment have occurred.

While the company has provided grief counseling for the workers, the acting president realizes that the managers need to take an active role in helping the workers process their feelings and continue to sustain the company. To facilitate this process, the acting president has called a meeting of all company managers to discuss the situation, and how to best proceed.

Instructions: For the exercise, form into small groups (5 to 7 people). One person should take the role of the acting company president. This person's task will mainly be to make sure that everyone in the group has a chance to contribute to the discussion and to encourage exploration of ideas. Everyone else will assume the role of a company manager. In the group, discuss the expected emotional issues that company workers – and yourselves – are experiencing. Discuss the role of how the company's family atmosphere both aids and hinders workers in processing the situation. You may want to have a special discussion about the extra emotional labor that workers (especially those who have to interact with the public as part of their jobs and the managers who have to maintain smooth business processes) are encountering. Also, discuss the role of stress in the situation. Finally, be sure to ground your discussion in concrete steps that can be taken to improve affected workplace outcomes such as performance, turnover, absenteeism, loyalty, and job satisfaction.

At the end of the discussion, have one person prepared to present an overview of the group's discussion and recommended steps to the class.

Reflection Questions:

1. How did using chapter terms and concepts help shape how you understood and what you thought about the situation?
2. Did use of these concepts provide you with better insights into dealing with the situation? Also, look for differences between your group's presentation and other groups' presentations.
3. Were there any insights brought up that your group did not see?
4. Finally, while this exercise dealt with a negative situation, there are also many positive situations and attendant emotions at work. How could you use chapter concepts to recognize and promote such positive emotions?

Exercise contributed by Milton R. Mayfield, Professor of Business, Texas A&M International University and Jaqueline R. Mayfield, Professor of Business, Texas A&M International University.

CASE STUDY 3.1: THE STARBUCKS EXPERIENCE

According to *CNN Money*, *barista* carries the dubious dual distinction of being one of the nation's most stressful jobs and among those with the lowest pay. Baristas face many challenges: not only do they have to deal with the physical demands of making and serving coffee, they also have the emotional stress of coping with early morning lines of impatient customers in a hurry. In a recent poll surveying coffee workers, 55 percent of respondents reported upper-body repetitive stress injuries, 37 percent complained of persistent sore muscles, 29 percent said they suffered from anxiety attacks, and 44 percent lamented high stress levels. Considering that the median pay of baristas is $20,300, is the stress really worth it? How might their employers help baristas cope?

Howard Shultz is CEO of Starbucks Coffee, which is worth about $72.4 billion at the time of this writing and is projected to grow. There are more than 21,000 stores in 65 countries with 191,000+ employees, the bulk of whom are serving up your morning joe. After slashing jobs and closing stores in 2009, Shultz and Starbucks are brewing up new business again. The company's China/Asia Pacific business grew revenue at 85 percent year over year as reported at close of 2014.

When Starbucks was conceived by three friends on the Seattle waterfront in 1971, the number one principle of its mission statement was bold: "To provide a great work environment and treat each other with respect and dignity." Forty-plus years later, Starbucks continues to provide an exception to *CNN Money*'s suggestion that the barista job is generally awful. The company frequently tops *Fortune*'s "100 Best Companies to Work For" list and has legions of fierce brand loyalists, many of them employees past and present. You can read employee testimonials on Glassdoor.com ("When I first started [with Starbucks] I had no intention of making a career out of Starbucks. Now, I have no intention of having a career without Starbucks"), plus numerous glowing blogs and the 2007 bestseller, *How Starbucks Saved My Life: A Son of Privilege Learns to Live Like Everyone Else*, by Michael Gates Gill.

Managers know that happy, healthy employees make for a better workforce, and a better workforce means a better experience for customers. To keep the money rolling in—while remaining true to its founding principles—Starbucks has had to be proactive about battling the barista blues. In the late 1990s, after conducting its own internal studies, Starbucks enlisted the help of La Marzocco, the Italian maker of espresso machines. La Marzocco in turn reached out to an osteopath and a physical therapist for insight into the company's concerns about the repetitive actions performed by the baristas. They found that lifting milk jugs and steaming milk, tamping, inserting and removing portafilters, and simply standing for long periods had serious health implications. The demands also placed a dampener on staff "happiness and effectiveness." To combat the effects, Starbucks worked with La Marzocco to develop a number of new employee-friendly technologies, including the auto-dosing and tamping Swift grinder. Throughout the decades, Starbucks has continued to innovate and automate processes with its employees' health and safety in mind.

In Peter Ubel's article in *Forbes*, "Do Starbucks' Employees Have More Emotional Intelligence Than Your Physician?" the author suggests that doctors have a lot to learn from Starbucks' baristas in terms of managing stress and communicating with constituents. He points out that, unlike physicians, Starbucks' employees are trained to be emotionally sensitive and intuitive and to act accordingly. In the "Latte Method," they undergo rigorous training on how to recognize and respond to customer needs. When a customer is unhappy, the Latte Method suggests, "We *Listen* to the customer, *Acknowledge* their complaint, *Take* action by solving the problem, *Thank* them, and then *Explain* why the problem occurred."

With a framework in place to manage customer anxiety, Starbucks also succeeds in soothing employees' nerves by providing the employee a basis for managing customers that reduces the fear of the unknown. The framework also empowers the employee (gives them tools) to handle stressful customer situations.

There are other ways in which Starbucks helps ameliorate employee stress—physical, emotional, and financial, too. Part-time employees who work at least 20 hours a week receive health care benefits. Salaries are higher than average for store managers and plans are in the works to raise wages for employees across the board; Starbucks' CEO, in fact, has been a vocal proponent of raising the minimum wage for workers in the service industry. The company recently revised its practices to give employees more consistent hours, which helps with financial planning, not to mention the demands of family life. What's more, Starbucks employees are eligible for bonuses, 401(k) matching, and tuition reimbursement, and most recently, a free college education through online portals. Employees (called "partners") are also encouraged to move up the ladder. All these benefits help relieve the typical stress associated with service jobs. An employee who feels valued and who is encouraged to grow will be more invested in his or her job.

Schultz and Starbucks are clearly doing something right. Restaurant industry insider Eric Levine writes, "I'm fascinated how each and every Starbucks, while all corporately owned and part of a billion-dollar company, makes you feel that the owner and his wife are there, and that's why they care." Curious about what made Starbucks employees so happy, he decided to launch an informal poll. "I would have thought that the No. 1 reasons would have been benefits and stock options or growth and opportunity. To my surprise, the No. 1 answer—from eight out of 10 employees—was that they love the product, people and culture."

The service industry is a notoriously stressful one, which Levine knows well. "I have seen servers yell at customers, 'I have five tables just seated. I'm doing the best I can.' This energy becomes anxiety and frustration, stressing customers, and costing both the company and the server money. . . . Starbucks employees deal with lines and stress like all the employees in our industry, but their stress is channeled into motion and productivity, not resentment and aggression."

Case Questions

1. Starbucks' core agenda is to provide an excellent work environment and for employees to treat each other with respect and dignity. How were they able to make this happen?
2. Describe the "Latte Method." How did it help grow Starbucks?
3. Employees say that they love Starbucks' company culture, and Starbucks regularly tops *Fortune*'s "100 Best Companies to Work For." How does Starbucks promote organizational commitment and job satisfaction?

SELF-ASSESSMENT 3.1

Emotional Intelligence Self-Assessment

Emotional intelligence is the ability to understand emotions in oneself and others in order to effectively manage one's own behaviors and relationships with others. More and more organizations are basing their hiring and promoting decisions on EI, and it is as important to professional success as other abilities such as technical skills. This assessment will help identify your EI strengths and areas for development.

Rank each statement as follows:

	Never 0	Rarely 1	Sometimes 2	Often 3	Always 4
Self-Awareness					
I have a good understanding of my feelings.	0	1	2	3	4
I am aware of my individual strengths and weaknesses.	0	1	2	3	4
I usually know how I feel and understand why I feel that way.	0	1	2	3	4
I think about my own emotional reactions to the things that happen to me.	0	1	2	3	4
I analyze how my emotions may influence my behaviors.	0	1	2	3	4
Total: ______					

	Never 0	Rarely 1	Sometimes 2	Often 3	Always 4
Self-Management					
I am able to effectively control negative feelings and impulses.	0	1	2	3	4
I am a person that other people can depend upon and trust.	0	1	2	3	4
I tend to be flexible when I encounter changing situations or difficult obstacles.	0	1	2	3	4
I always try to see the positive or the good in the things that happen to me.	0	1	2	3	4
I try to take advantage of opportunities when they are presented to me.	0	1	2	3	4
Total: ______					
Social Awareness					
I try to understand other people's emotions.	0	1	2	3	4
I am effective in reading and understanding the actions and decisions of others	0	1	2	3	4
I recognize and respond to the needs of other people.	0	1	2	3	4
I try to see things from other people's perspectives.	0	1	2	3	4
I show an interest in the concerns of other people.	0	1	2	3	4
Total: ______					
Relationship Management					
I can effectively guide and motivate other people.	0	1	2	3	4
I provide feedback and guidance to help others develop their abilities.	0	1	2	3	4
I am good at leading people in new directions.	0	1	2	3	4
I can effectively develop and maintain relationships with other people.	0	1	2	3	4
I enjoy cooperating with others in a team setting.	0	1	2	3	4
Total: ______					

You can assess your effectiveness on each EI dimension using the following scale:

0–12 *Needs Improvement*: These dimensions should be targeted for additional consideration and refinement.

13–17 *Adequate Functioning*: These dimensions are acceptable but could use additional strengthening.

18–20 *Advanced Strengths*: These dimensions are key areas of strength that may be used to help develop lacking skills in other areas.

4 Perception and Learning

©iStockphoto.com/TommL

> Studies have shown that 90% of error in thinking is due to error in perception. If you can change your perception, you can change your emotion and this can lead to new ideas.
>
> —Edward de Bono, author and psychologist

PERCEPTION: INTERPRETING OUR ENVIRONMENT

4.1 Describe the basic concept of perception

In early 2007, the *Washington Post* carried out an experiment in perception by placing world-famous violinist Joshua Bell, disguised as a street musician, in a Washington Metro station.[1] Wearing a baseball cap, T-shirt, and jeans, Bell performed a 43-minute set of six classical pieces for unsuspecting commuters. Of the 1,097 who passed by, only seven stopped for just over a minute to listen to his virtuoso performance before continuing their journey. By the end of his performance, the virtuoso Bell had made a grand total of $30 and a few cents—hardly enough to buy a ticket to one of his own sell-out concerts.

So what does this experiment tell us about perception? Was it because Bell was dressed as a street musician that the commuters didn't stop to listen? Or was it because of the setting—after all, how likely is it that a world-famous musician would perform for free in a Metro station? Whatever the reason, we can conclude that most people perceived Bell to be someone other than who he was, which affected their ability to recognize and appreciate his talent as a musician.

We define **perception** as the process by which we receive and interpret information from our environment.[2] Take a look at the Figure 4.1. What do you see?

You might say you see three bars while someone else sees four. In this trick drawing neither answer is the "right" one. The cartoon illustrates the fact that we often perceive things differently from one another.

LEARNING OBJECTIVES

By the end of this chapter, you will be able to:

4.1 Describe the basic concept of perception

4.2 Explain the different types of perceptual distortions

4.3 Apply attribution theory to more effectively interpret behavior

4.4 Use reinforcement theory to understand learning and modify behavior

4.5 Apply social cognitive theory to social learning and cognitive processes

COMPONENTS OF THE SELECTION PROCESS

A number of factors may influence and distort perception, including the perceiver, the environment, and the focal object.

Perception: The process by which we receive and interpret information from our environment

Master the content.
edge.sagepub.com/neckob

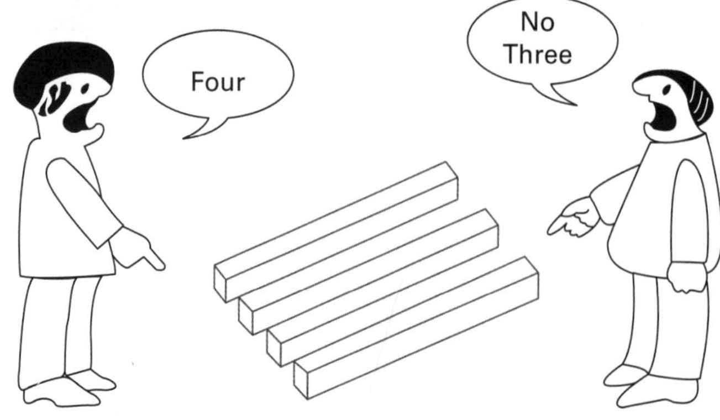

■ FIGURE 4.1 Optical Illusion

SOURCE: http://www.goillusions.com/2015/05/three-or-four-perspective-matters.html.

The Perceiver

Perceptions are shaped by past experiences, culture, attitude, values, upbringing, and more. This means the nature of the perceiver has a strong influence on the perceptual process. For example, say you were raised in an environment where working hard and being on time were considered very important. You might have a negative attitude toward a coworker who comes to work late or takes long work breaks. Once you have formed this perception, it might be difficult for you to change your mind about your coworker even if he performs well.

The Environment

The context or the setting also affects the perception process. For example, you may not notice a person dressed in athletic attire running on the street, but if she turned up at a

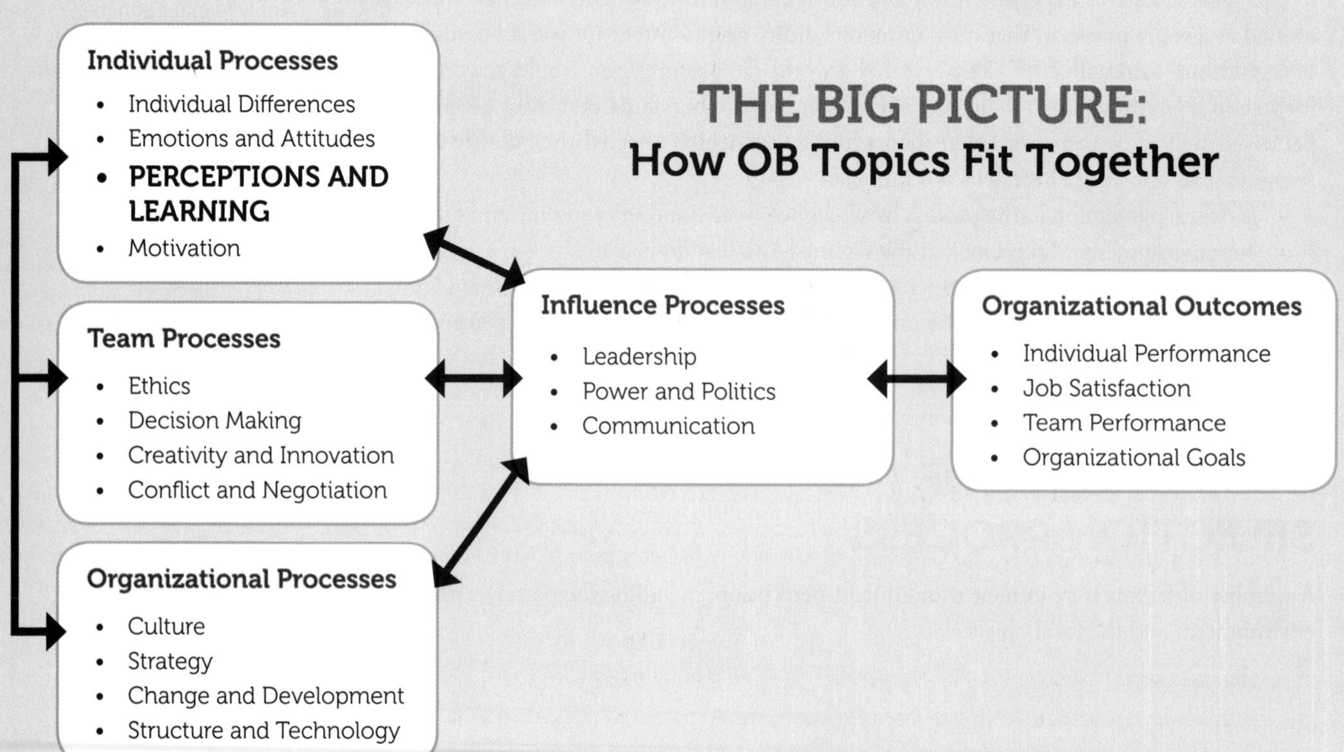

high-level work meeting in the same clothes, she would definitely look out of place. People flocked to see Joshua Bell perform in a concert hall but failed to recognize him in the Metro station. The person remained the same, but the situation or context had changed, which in turn influenced the perception of him.

Michael Williamson/The Washington Post via Getty Images

Violinist Joshua Bell posed as a street performer in a Washington Metro station as part of an experiment by *The Washington Post.* At the end of the day, he had made just over $30 for performing six classical pieces.

The Focal Object

The person, thing, or event being interpreted also affects our perception. Many business people choose to drive expensive cars because they feel it makes a good impression on others, who they hope will perceive them as wealthy, successful, and professional. However, in today's social context, do people really perceive owners of expensive cars in this way, or do they resent them for flaunting their success?[3] We tend to perceive objects in terms of contrast. For example, we might interpret the driver of the expensive car in a different way to someone else depending on their situation. Similarly, we perceive people who stand out differently from others—a work colleague who is vocal in meetings might be perceived differently from one who says very little.

WHY IS PERCEPTION IMPORTANT?

In 1936, psychologist Kurt Lewin observed that people act not upon the basis of reality, but upon their *perceptions* of reality.[4] In other words, we tend to interpret events differently from what actually happens in our environment. Therefore, understanding perception is a critical part of understanding behavior. In the workplace, the way we are perceived and the way in which we perceive others are crucial for career progress and for building our relationships. For example, a salesperson's success or failure depends on how he is perceived by prospective customers. He could have all the knowledge in the world about a product, but if he is perceived as overeager or too talkative, he is unlikely to make the sale. This is why many people in sales roles use self-critiquing techniques such as videoing themselves or seeking feedback from others in order to perceive themselves as others do. Salespeople who actively listen, communicate sincerely, and show a genuine interest in the person to whom they are selling tend to excel and to have more successful customer relationships.[5]

Returning to the Case of Laura Pierce

Let's return to our West Texas Regional Theatre (WTRT) story from Chapters 2 and 3. In Chapter 3, Development and Marketing Director Laura Pierce, discovers that WTRT is almost a million dollars in debt. She confronts her boss, Abigail Swenson, about the financial state of the theatre, and Abigail confesses that she has been personally bankrolling the business to keep it afloat. In a bid to save the theatre from bankruptcy, Laura convinces Abigail to allow her and the rest of the team to implement some of Laura's marketing initiatives. Laura also persuades Abigail to tell the board and the rest of the staff the truth about the theatre's finances. In the next section, we explore the ways in which differing perceptions affect the relationships among the different characters at WTRT.

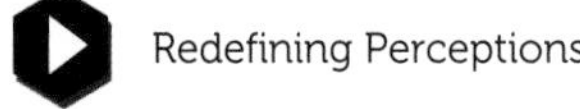

Uncritically allowing our perceptions to take control can create distorted versions of reality that can be very harmful to working relationships. Let's see how differing perceptions affect Laura, Abigail, and Cheryl as they meet with the board members to tell them the truth about the financial decline of WTRT.

Determined to make a good first impression on the board, Laura walks into Abigail's office the following morning dressed in a simple gray suit. She is pleased to see that everything is arranged for the breakfast meeting with the three WTRT board members. Abigail makes an unusually quiet entrance at exactly 9:00 a.m. Laura greets her and immediately notices how tired she looks. Moments later, Cheryl enters, holding some files.

Not long after, the three board members, Hilary, Gary, and Fiona, file in and sit down. Hilary is married to one of Abilene's wealthiest businessmen and is a well-known contributor to many arts-related organizations in the city. Gary is a retired entrepreneur who successfully ran his own property development business for 30 years, and Fiona owns a chain of flower shops in several cities in Texas. Each has known Abigail for more than 20 years and they are united in their love of the theatre. Laura introduces herself to the board and the group engages in a few minutes of polite discussion.

Then Abigail rises to her feet, takes a deep breath, and tells them everything: the long-term decline of ticket sales; the loss of the WTRT corporate sponsor because of bankruptcy; the cost of putting on the shows and the after-parties; and finally, the amount of debt WTRT is in. When she is finished, she collapses back into her chair and dramatically puts her head in her hands.

Gary is the first to react. "I can't believe what I'm hearing! Almost a million dollars in debt!" he says angrily. "How long has this been going on?"

"It's been going on for almost a year," she says, clearly embarrassed.

"But why didn't you tell us?" Fiona asks, softly.

"I thought I could handle it," Abigail replies, wiping a tear from her eye. "But I'm almost bankrupt myself."

The board members exchange incredulous looks.

Cheryl joins the discussion. "Abigail has been supporting WTRT with her own personal finances for almost a year," she says. "She's been struggling financially without any support." Cheryl casts an accusing glare at the board members.

Hilary turns to Cheryl. "But we didn't know anything about it! You're the office manager and accountant—if you were so concerned about Abigail, why didn't you tell us?"

"It wasn't my place. I wanted to wait until she was ready to tell you herself," Cheryl says.

Hilary says, "All this time I thought that accountants were supposed to be on top of the finances of the organization. Talk about poor management practice. I guess I was wrong!"

Cheryl flushes and frowns at Hilary.

Fearing the situation is getting out of hand, Laura speaks up.

"I understand this all comes as a bit of a shock, but I have some ideas that I think can improve the situation if you would hear me out."

The board members look skeptical, but Gary signals her to go ahead. Laura outlines the initiatives she has discussed with Abigail and the team to increase ticket sales and raise WTRT's profile in the community, from setting up a booth at the local crafts fair to partnering with local businesses, advertising on the radio, and creating an online presence to attract another segment of the market.

"These are all really good ideas," Fiona says, enthusiastically. "I think they'll really attract attention to WTRT and bring in more theatregoers."

Laura is encouraged but feels she needs to be honest. She tells the board members how she has been rebuffed by the local radio station and confesses that because of unpaid debts she has been unable to persuade some of the local restaurants to partner with WTRT in a "dinner-and-a-show" deal.

"Which restaurants are we talking about?" Hilary asks.

Laura gives her the names of the local restaurants and is surprised when Hilary smiles and says, "I know the owners of both those restaurants very well—I'll talk them around."

Gary joins in. "That website company built my property development company site a few years ago; I'm sure I can convince them to support WTRT."

"That's great!" Laura says. "We appreciate all your support. Do you have any ideas for how we can persuade the station manager to help us advertize WTRT?"

All three board members look at Abigail.

Abigail sighs. "Fine! I'll apologize to him!"

Laura has no idea why Abigail needs to apologize to the station manager and has no intention of finding out—building a relationship with the radio station is all that counts.

Cheryl, who has remained silent during the conversation, speaks up.

"Laura's ideas are good, but we have less than six months to save WTRT from bankruptcy. Quite frankly, we need money as soon as possible. Going by the figures I have here, we don't even have enough funds to put on the shows for next season. What do you suggest?"

"I think we can start by collecting outstanding patron payments," Laura suggests. "We can also create new patron arrangements with attractive incentives that I hope will encourage more sponsors to sign up with WTRT."

Fiona smiles at Laura. "You're right, Laura. I'm a patron and I'm ashamed to say I owe money to WTRT too."

Gary and Hilary nod their heads in agreement.

"Cheryl—if you could provide each of us with an invoice detailing the outstanding monies, we'll make sure WTRT receives the funds right away. In my case, I know it's a substantial amount," Hilary admits.

Cheryl nods. Laura can't help noticing how angry she looks, but she needs to focus on the positive. Frankly, Laura can't believe how well the meeting is going. She expected more of a battle, especially when discussing the sensitive topic of the debts owed by the board members themselves, but they seem to be willing to offer WTRT their support.

"As Abigail mentioned, we've also lost our corporate sponsorship," Laura adds. "We need to find a new corporate sponsor as soon as possible—that will make a big difference to raising the funds we need to cover the next season."

All three of the board members agree to call their respective contacts to see what they can do to acquire new sponsorship.

"Finally, I would like to discuss with you the shows that have been chosen for the next season," Laura says.

When she shares Tony's choice with the group, Gary claps his hands. "I've wanted WTRT to do that show for years! The younger generation will love it!"

"Well, it's not my first choice by a long shot," Abigail says. "I was railroaded into agreeing to let Tony choose the first show of the season, and I'm not happy about it!"

Abigail voices her disapproval for the theatre company's new plan, even though Laura thinks the staff should appear to be united to give the board members confidence in them.

©iStockphoto.com/mediaphotos

Laura is concerned about Abigail's reaction—she wants the theatre staff to appear united as a team; otherwise the board may have second thoughts about giving their support. But the members don't seem to have noticed anything Abigail has said; instead they are chatting among themselves, talking about other shows they have seen and how students are sure to flock to the show.

As the conversations wind down, Hilary speaks up. "I think Tony's choice of show is inspired. I was just telling Fiona and Gary that I saw an outstanding show a couple of months ago in Dallas. WTRT put on the same show last week, and I thought it was mediocre to say the least. We could do with a fresh line-up for next season."

Laura doesn't think Hilary is being fair. She saw the WTRT production the previous week and thought it was excellent—far from mediocre. However, now is not the time to object; there's too much work to do!

Noticing Abigail's outraged expression, Laura decides to employ a distraction technique and offers the members more refreshments. Gary and Hilary request coffee.

"No problem!" Laura says. "I'll just see whether Joey can make us a fresh pot."

"That's if he is still in the building! I'm surprised he even showed up to work today," says Cheryl.

The board members exchange looks.

"It doesn't sound like Joey is the most committed employee," Hilary says.

Laura ignores Hilary and refuses to allow any negativity to spoil what is turning out to be a productive meeting.

"That's okay," she says. "I'll just head to the kitchen and make it myself." When Laura returns, she senses a different atmosphere in the room. Abigail is looking sullenly at the ground, and nobody is speaking. Puzzled but determined to end the meeting on a high note, Laura encourages more discussion on how the initiatives should be implemented and sets some timelines for the goals to be achieved.

Laura ends the meeting by thanking the board members for their support and committing to make WTRT a success once more. As they are filing out of Abigail's office, each member thanks Laura profusely. She is so delighted with the outcome of the meeting that she gives each of them a hug.

When the door closes, Laura is left with Cheryl and Abigail. "Well, I think that went well!" she says.

Abigail spins around in her chair. "Do you?" she shouts. "That was the most humiliating experience of my life! They barely even listened to me—my own friends. They don't care what I think. You wanted all the attention for yourself!"

"I agree with Abigail," Cheryl says, darkly. "You completely hijacked the meeting and did everything you could to get the board on your side, including sucking up to them. Hugging—really? In their eyes you can do no wrong. Are you trying to usurp Abigail?"

"I don't understand," Laura says.

"While you were getting the coffee, Hilary suggested that running WTRT has become too much for Abigail and that perhaps she should consider taking a break," Cheryl says.

"I had to convince Hilary and the others that I'm still competent enough to be chairperson. Do you know how embarrassing that is?" Abigail says.

Laura is shocked. Clearly, Abigail and Cheryl think she has a hidden agenda. She has suspected that Cheryl resents her for being hired to do marketing for WTRT, and now both Cheryl and Abigail think she is trying to oust Abigail as chairperson. Laura struggles to keep calm.

"It has been a very emotional morning," she says, trying to stop her voice from shaking. "Personally, I'm very pleased with how the meeting went. We have full support from all three board members, and we have a plan in place to address some of the debt problems and generate more income and publicity for WTRT. I suggest we reconvene later this afternoon and discuss the next steps."

On that note, Laura turns and walks out of the office.

THINKING CRITICALLY

1. Consider the text's point that we often perceive things differently from others and that no one perception is necessarily right. What, from an OB perspective, are the benefits of differences of perception when a team of people is working on a project? What are the potential drawbacks of perceptual differences when a team is working together on a project? **[Understand/ Apply]**

2. Daya and Robert are interviewing candidates for an administrative assistant position at their consulting firm. They narrow their preferred candidates to two people: Anthony and Elaine. Both agree that Elaine has superior experience and seems more knowledgeable and enthusiastic about the company, but Daya believes that Elaine's "dressed down" appearance for the interview (she wore a dressy top, pants, and casual flats) in comparison to Anthony's more formal attire (he wore a suit and dress shoes) is problematic. She wants to offer the position to Anthony. Robert considers Elaine's attire a small matter and would prefer to make an initial offer to Elaine. Discuss Daya's perception of Elaine versus Robert's perception by focusing on the components of perception: the perceiver, the environment, and the focal object. **[Apply/Analyze]**

3. Describe Laura, Abigail, and Cheryl's meeting with the three board members from Cheryl's perspective. While Laura believes that Cheryl's accusations stem from Cheryl's interest in Laura's marketing job, what other events during the meeting likely had an impact on Cheryl's negative reaction? **[Analyze/Evaluate]**

4. Consider the Board members' favorable perception of Laura at the meeting. What aspects of the environment and Laura as focal object likely have led to their positive assessment? Try to list at least five items for each perceptual component. **[Analyze/Evaluate]**

5. Imagine that Laura, Cheryl, and Abigail have worked with one another for years and trust and respect one another. How might their positive perceptions of one another have made the meeting go more smoothly? **[Analyze/Evaluate]**

COMMON PERCEPTUAL DISTORTIONS

4.2 Explain the different types of perceptual distortions

Each and every day we take in and process a huge amount of complex information. Our attempts to organize and sift this information can lead to inaccuracies and clouds our perceptions of different people, situations, and events. Using the WTRT scenario as an example, let's explore some common perceptual distortions:

Optimism Bias

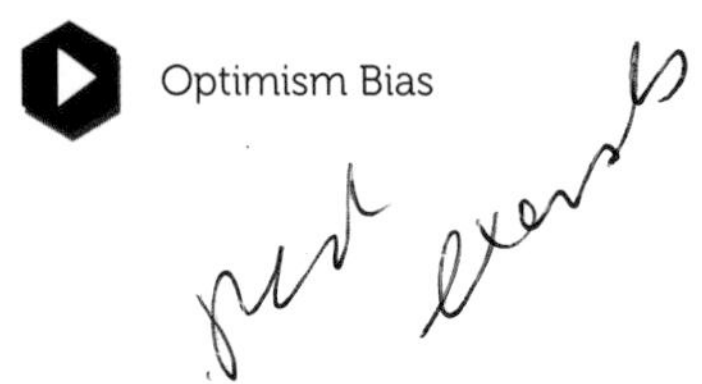

- **Stereotypes** are an individual's fixed beliefs about the characteristics of a particular group.[6] When we have a particular feeling or attitude (often negative) toward members of a specific group, we call this *prejudice*. For example, Hilary stereotypes accountants when she berates Cheryl for not telling the board about the financial situation.
- **Selective attention** is the tendency to selectively focus on aspects of situations that are most aligned with our own interests, values, and attitudes.[7] For example, the board doesn't pay any attention to Abigail when she protests Tony's choice of show for the next season; instead they focus on their shared interest in staging a show they each feel strongly about.
- **Halo effect** is a perception problem in which we form a positive or negative view of one aspect of an individual based on our overall impressions of that person.[8] By claiming Laura can "do no wrong" in the eyes of the board, Cheryl is suggesting that the board has fallen prey to the "halo effect."
- **Primacy effect** is a perception problem in which an individual assesses a person quickly on the basis of the first information encountered.[9] Cheryl seems to fall out of favor with the board as soon as she tells them Abigail has been bankrolling the theatre herself and glares at them in an accusing manner. After that, they don't warm to her at all.
- **Recency effect** is a perception problem in which we use the most recent information available to assess a person.[10] For example, when Hilary hears that Joey is frequently absent from work, she jumps to the conclusion that he is not committed to WTRT.
- **Contrast effect** takes place when people rank something higher or lower than they should as a result of exposure to recent events or situations.[11] Hilary rates WTRT's show as "mediocre" because she has seen a better performance of the same show in Dallas.
- **Projecting** is a process in which people transfer their own thoughts, motivations, feelings, and desires to others.[12] When Abigail accuses Laura of "wanting all the attention" in the meeting, she is projecting onto Laura her own personal need for attention.
- **Self-fulfilling prophecy** occurs when a person bases behavior on preexisting expectations about another person or situation in order to create an outcome aligned with those expectations.[13] Laura predicts a positive outcome from the meeting and exhibits behavior that makes the board members warm to her; in the end her prophecy comes true.
- **Impression management** is the process by which we attempt to influence the perceptions others may have of us. Laura wants to create a good impression with the board by dressing professionally and remaining calm, positive, and knowledgeable throughout the meeting.[14] A facet of impression management is **ingratiation**, in which an individual attempts to influence others by becoming more attractive or likeable. Cheryl accuses Laura of "sucking up" to the board members when she gives each of them a hug.

Stereotypes: An individual's fixed beliefs about the characteristics of a particular group

Selective attention: The tendency to selectively focus on aspects of situations that are most aligned with our own interests, values, and attitudes

Halo effect: A perception problem through which we form a positive or negative bias of an individual based on our overall impressions of that person

Primacy effect: A perception problem through which an individual assesses a person quickly on the basis of the first information encountered.

Recency effect: A perception problem through which we use the most recent information available to assess a person

Contrast effect: An effect that takes place when people rank something higher or lower than they should as a result of exposure to recent events or situations

Projecting: A process through which people ascribe their own personal attributes onto others

Self-fulfilling prophecy: The way a person behaves based on preexisting expectations about another person or situation so as to create an outcome that is aligned with those expectations

Impression management: The process by which we attempt to influence the perceptions others may have of us

Ingratiation: A strategy of winning favor and putting oneself in the good graces of others before making a request

Forming accurate perceptions of others is a complex process. Awareness of these common perceptual distortions may help you to avoid making them about others and may also allow you to combat inaccurate perceptions others may form about you. In addition to perceptual distortion, it's also important to understand attribution theory.

THINKING CRITICALLY

1. Choose one of the perceptual distortions discussed (stereotypes, selective attention, halo effect, primary effect, recency effect, contrast effect, project, self-fulfilling prophecy, and impression management) and briefly describe a situation where your perception of another person was impacted by that distortion. **[Understand/ Apply]**

2. What do you think are the top three perceptual distortions that managers are most likely to be affected by when forming perceptions of their direct reports? Explain your answer. **[Apply/Analyze]**

3. What do you think are the top three perceptual distortions that employees are most likely to be affected by when forming perceptions of a new manager? Defend your answer. **[Apply/ Analyze]**

COMMON ATTRIBUTION ERRORS

4.3 Apply attribution theory to more effectively interpret behavior

When we see someone behave in a certain way, we tend to try and make sense of it or at least attach some meaning to it. **Attribution theory** holds that people look for two causes to explain the behavior of others: *internal attributions,* which are personal characteristics of others, and *external attributions*, which are situational factors.[15]

Let's use Joey from the WTRT management as an example to illustrate the use of attribution theory. Joey has a problem with absenteeism. How would you make sense of his behavior? Do you think he is lazy and indifferent? Or do you think he is so overloaded with responsibilities that he finds the prospect of coming to work overwhelming? If you choose the first option, you would ascribe Joey's behavior to internal causes: you believe Joey's absenteeism is a result of laziness and apathy. However, if you choose the latter option, you are attributing Joey's behavior to external causes: you blame overwhelming amounts of work for his poor attendance record.

Three factors influence our internal and external attributions: consistency, distinctiveness, and consensus, as outlined in Figure 4.2.[16]

Consistency is the extent to which a person responds in the same way over a period of time. For example, if Cheryl is late arriving at work every morning (high consistency in the same situation), we tend to ascribe her tardiness to internal causes and assume she is just not a punctual person. If, however, she is only late to work on Fridays (low consistency in the same situation), then we might assume an external cause, such as her husband must be at work early on Fridays and she must drop her children off at school.

Distinctiveness is the extent to which a person behaves consistently in similar situations. For example, if Joey tends to be frequently late to work, late returning from lunch, and late to mid-morning staff meetings (low distinctiveness across situations), we might ascribe his behavior to internal factors such as being lazy and indifferent. Conversely, if Joey is punctual in most situations but is sometimes late returning from lunch (high distinctiveness across situations), we might ascribe his tardiness in that particular situation to the fact that he sometimes visits his aging grandmother during lunch to see if she needs any heavy chores done around her house.

Attribution theory: A theory that holds that people look for two causes to explain the behavior of others: internal attributions, which are personal characteristics of others, and external attributions, which are situational factors

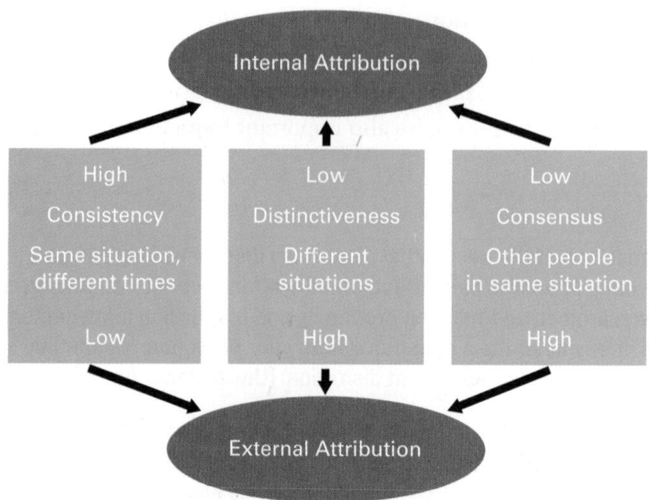

■ FIGURE 4.2 Determinants of Attribution

SOURCE: Based on Mehlman, Rick C., and C. R. Snyder. "Excuse Theory: A Test of the Self-Protective Role of Attributions." *Journal of Personality and Social Psychology* 49, no. 4 (October 1985): 994–1001.

Consensus looks at how everyone else responds in the same situation. For example, if several people in the office are absent or late on the same day (high consensus with other people in the same situation), we might ascribe this behavior to an external attribution such as a dust storm that has slowed the morning commute for everyone or a virus or flu that has spread through the office. Conversely, if everyone else but Tony has arrived on time and is not absent on a given day (low consensus with other people in the same situation), we are more likely to attribute Tony's tardiness or absence to internal factors.

It is important to try and make sense of the behaviors of others in order to form the most meaningful conclusion. However, as the following section shows, it is also easy for us to make wrong judgments.

When Laura leaves Abigail's office after the meeting with the board, she thinks, "How dare they accuse me of trying to undermine Abigail? I'm the one who successfully persuaded the board to support WTRT in spite of the huge amount of debt. If it weren't for Abigail's lavish overspending, lack of discipline, and sheer carelessness with the financials, WTRT wouldn't be in this mess in the first place."

Laura goes into the office kitchen to calm down and think about her next move. Should she resign? After all, there is no point in working with a boss who doesn't support her. Yet she loves the theatre and has high hopes for her new job. Joey and Tony are enthusiastic about her initiatives and the board seems to back her. "I'm not a quitter!" she thinks. "It's time to sort this business out with Cheryl and Abigail once and for all."

When Laura reaches the door of Abigail's office, she sees Abigail addressing the rest of the WTRT staff, including Joey. Not wanting to interrupt, Laura stays in the background and listens. Abigail tells the staff about the debt and explains how it has accumulated to such a degree.

"I do believe factors outside my control have contributed to the debt," Abigail says. "We still haven't recovered from the global economic recession. Many people are on a tight budget and perhaps they perceive the arts as a luxury they simply can't afford. Our patronage base is not only shrinking but it's also aging, which means many of our most loyal patrons either don't go to the theatre any more or have passed away. Finally, our corporate sponsor has gone bankrupt, which has had an enormous impact on our funding. Yet I've made WTRT a success in the past, and I will do so once again!"

As Laura listens, she realizes she has made an incorrect judgment about Abigail. Yes, Abigail has been careless and lavish, but factors outside her control have also contributed to WTRT's difficult financial circumstances. After all, Abigail has been running the theatre for decades, and it was a thriving business until a couple of years ago. Yet Abigail couldn't have done it without Cheryl, her financial expert and most loyal supporter. Abigail's biggest mistake was refusing to heed Cheryl's persistent warnings about overspending. Laura begins to change her perspective of Abigail and Cheryl; each of them in her own way has tried her very best to keep WTRT afloat.

When perceiving others, we sometimes make erroneous judgments when assessing their behaviors. There are two common attribution errors: fundamental attribution error, and self-serving bias. **Fundamental attribution error** is the inclination to attribute internal factors to the behavior of others more than external factors.[17] For example, Laura initially thinks Abigail's carelessness is mostly to blame for WTRT's debt. It is only when she calms down and listens to Abigail addressing the rest of the staff that she realizes other factors that are out of Abigail's control are also at play.

Fundamental Attribution Error

Self-serving bias is the tendency for individuals to attribute external factors more than internal factors for one's own failures.[18] For example, Abigail blames external factors such as the economic recession and the aging patron base for her woes and never accepts responsibility for her carelessness and overspending, instead perceiving herself as the true savior of WTRT.

Abigail tells the staff about the meeting with the board (leaving out that Hilary suggested Abigail "take a break"), the responsibilities each board member has agreed to take on to generate more income and win public favor for WTRT, and their support for Tony's choice of show and Laura's marketing initiatives. When she is finished, Joey raises his hand. "Abigail, Laura mentioned that I might be responsible for the social networking initiative. Is this still the case?"

Abigail looks at him and sighs. "Joey, until a few months ago, I would have wondered what I would do without you. However, now you hardly ever bother coming into work and you're unloading all your work onto Cheryl."

Laura doesn't like the way this discussion is going. Joey may have a problem with absenteeism but she feels he has the potential to be the social networking guru for WTRT.

Red-faced, Joey responds, "Abigail, I used to love working here, but now I feel completely overwhelmed. You've been giving me more and more work that technically doesn't even fall under my job description. Sometimes I get so stressed about it that I can't face coming in."

Abigail says quietly, "Joey, the reason I've been giving you more responsibility is that I thought you could handle it, but if you feel overwhelmed, then let's sit down later today to discuss how we can improve the situation."

Joey nods in agreement, and Laura exhales in relief. The last thing they need is to lose a valuable member of staff.

After the meeting, the staff files out of the room, chatting about the plans to revive WTRT. Tony is excited to be putting on his favorite show, Joey hangs back briefly to arrange a time with Abigail so they can discuss managing his workload and new social networking duties, and Cheryl gathers her files, smiles only at Abigail, and leaves the room. Only Abigail remains.

Laura looks at Abigail and says, "I think we need to talk."

She sits down across from Abigail and begins by explaining her position, stating that her only intention is to save WTRT from going under.

To her surprise, Abigail agrees with her. "That meeting was very difficult for me, but I know you're not trying to take my place, Laura. I took my embarrassment and

Fundamental attribution error: The tendency to underestimate the influence of external factors and overestimate the impact of internal factors when making judgments about the behavior of others

Self-serving bias: The tendency for individuals to attribute their own successes to internal factors and put the blame for failures on external factors

anger out on you and that was unfair. Cheryl and I jumped to the wrong conclusion; Cheryl is very protective of me."

"I am concerned that Cheryl believes she could be handling the marketing initiatives and resents my having been hired," Laura says.

"Yes, she wanted your position before I hired you," Abigail replies, "but I didn't give it to her because I wanted someone to come in with a fresh perspective and a proven history in marketing. I respect Cheryl and appreciate her talents and dedication but she wasn't the right fit for the job. She wasn't happy when I told her, and I think she may be taking her frustrations out on you, although by nature she is pretty prickly."

Laura tells Abigail about Cheryl's refusal to help Joey with his work and the way she threw files onto his desk. "I'll speak to her about that later today," Abigail says.

By the end of the meeting, Abigail and Laura have reached a resolution. They agree to work together to make sure the initiatives are implemented as quickly and efficiently as possible. Laura knows it isn't going to be easy working with Cheryl, but she feels more confident knowing she has Abigail's support and understanding.

Six months later, WTRT is showing hopeful signs of recovery. The first show of the season is a huge hit with younger and older audiences, and Joey has started an online campaign that has attracted new customers to the theatre. The theatre booth at the local arts fair, meal deals with the local restaurants, and local radio advertizing have also helped to boost the theatre's profile and ticket sales. New sponsorship programs have drawn patrons to the theatre. However, Cheryl is still chasing some of the theatre's patrons to pay their outstanding debts, and the board members have yet to find a new corporate sponsor.

Attribution Errors

Abigail and Laura have built a relationship of mutual respect, but Laura still finds Cheryl abrupt and difficult to deal with. However, she is gratified to see Cheryl making an effort to mentor Joey and helping him to prioritize his work. The theatre has a long way to go before the debt is cleared, but Abigail and the team are determined to work together until WTRT is the best, most financially sound, theatre in Texas once again.

THINKING CRITICALLY

1. Imagine that you are waiting in line to purchase groceries. You notice that your line is moving very slowly because the high school aged student who is bagging groceries is flirting with the cashier rather than working quickly and paying attention to customers. What internal and external attributions might you apply to this behavior? Try to generate at least 3 options for each type of attribution. **[Understand/ Apply]**

2. Briefly discuss distinctiveness, consistency, and consensus as they apply to Laura's professional demeanor during the board meeting and in this section of the chapter. Do you agree or disagree with the statement that Laura's behavior appears to be primarily determined by internal factors? Support your answer. **[Apply/Analyze]**

3. Based on Laura's experience recognizing that she has unfairly pinned all the blame for WTRT's debt on Abigail's poor management skills, describe what you could do in a similarly difficult work situation to protect yourself from falling prey to fundamental attribution error. **[Analyze/Evaluate]**

4. Based on the chapter's discussion of self-serving bias, devise a list of questions you could ask yourself in order to determine whether you are attributing all positive outcomes to your own internal attributes and all negative outcomes to external attributes. **[Evaluate/Create]**

LEARNING PROCESSES: BEHAVIORAL THEORY

4.4 Use reinforcement theory to understand learning and modify behavior

Perception is shaped by **learning**, an ongoing process through which individuals adjust their behavior based on experience.[19] Understanding the way we learn is essential to OB because it has a direct influence on our work performance, our ability to relate to others, and our career progression. We all learn in different ways, and it is never too late to learn new skills. In fact, recent studies have shown that contrary to common thought, it is not just children who can easily absorb new languages; adults are just as capable of learning new linguistic skills with the same ease. Indeed, studies demonstrate that we are capable of learning any new skill, or even a few at a time, as long as we change our mind-set and focus on the task at hand.[20]

Learning opens up so many opportunities for us in every aspect of our daily existence. In the OB in the Real World feature, we see how learning can also save lives.

To better understand learning behaviors, it is useful to evaluate the behavioral interpretations provided by different theorists over the past century. The behavioral view holds that behavior is shaped and learned as a result of external environmental stimuli. There are three important contributions within the behavioral perspective: classical conditioning, operant conditioning, and reinforcement theory.

Classical Conditioning

The concept of **classical conditioning** was developed by Russian physiologist Ivan Pavlov. Classical conditioning suggests that learning can be accomplished through the use of stimuli.[21] Pavlov's most famous experiment used different stimuli to elicit a behavioral response in dogs. Pavlov found that dogs began to salivate in response to the ringing of a bell—a *neutral stimulus*—before they were given food—an *unconditioned stimulus*. Eventually, the bell became a *conditioned stimulus* that caused the dogs to salivate (*conditioned response)* without the food being present. The steps are outlined in Figure 4.3.

We find evidence of classical conditioning in the workplace during fire drills. Most companies carry out fire drills to instill safety procedures in their employees in the event of a fire. When we hear the fire alarm (conditioned stimulus) we respond by leaving the building (conditioned response). However, if we saw a fire (unconditioned response) in

Learning: An ongoing process through which individuals adjust their behavior based on experience

Classical conditioning: A conditioning concept developed by Russian physiologist Ivan Pavlov that suggests that learning can be accomplished through the use of stimuli

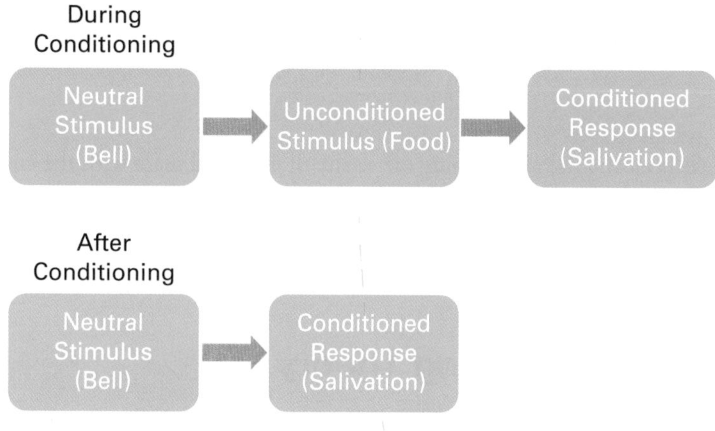

FIGURE 4.3 Classical Conditioning

CHARLIE RAPPAZZO, *manager, Town of Colonie Emergency Medical Services*

OB in the Real World

Colonie is a suburb of Albany, New York, and has a population of about 80,000 residents. Its Emergency Medical Services (EMS) team is more than 100 people strong and is made up of both paid and volunteer staff members who work 12-hour shifts. Each year they respond to more than 9,000 emergency calls using a fleet of 20 emergency vehicles.

With more than 35 years of experience as a paramedic, manager Charlie Rappazzo isn't new to the world of EMS. He has held roles as crew leader, supervisor, and even acting captain when circumstances required it. He knows how to take charge of an ambulance, help employees work through conflict, ensure that calls are responded to quickly and smoothly, and, of course, save lives.

When Charlie first became a paramedic, protocol dictated that paramedics weren't allowed to do any work on a patient unless instructed by a doctor over the phone. Today paramedics are much more knowledgeable and better trained. They are exam-certified in trauma treatment, emergency medical services operations, cardiac management, and pediatrics. They continue to attend certification and medical training sessions to learn the newest practices for handling emergency situations, and doctors see them as being in partnership. "Now," says Charlie, "the only time I'm on the phone with a doctor is when I'm letting them know who is coming in and what we've done."

Charlie knows firsthand that perceiving a tough call as stressful can make people panic. "When an emergency responder perceives a situation to be overwhelming it can make them panic and forget what they're supposed to do. When you panic you don't pay attention to your skills. It is my job to step in and remind them that they are capable of handling the situation."

Charlie's team was once called to the scene of an accident in which a jogger was hit by a truck and her legs were pinned between the truck and a guard rail. Both legs were severed and she was bleeding badly. He knew he had to calm his crew down before they started working on the woman. He pulled them aside and said, "You are going to do this. Before you panic think of what you've learned in the classroom and in the field. You have the skills you need so be calm, think carefully, and do what your instinct is telling you to do." Thanks to the crew's ability to do those things, they saved her legs and her life.

Good paramedics truly want to help people, are confident that they can handle tough situations, and are continuously learning. Furthermore, as Rappazzo states, "paramedics like the adrenalin rush they get from taking a traumatic experience and creating a positive outcome for someone."

Critical-Thinking Questions

1. **What does this story about the paramedics have to do with perception?**
2. **How does ongoing medical training for paramedics affect their job performance and the lives of their patients?**

SOURCE: Charlie Rappazzo, personal interview, June 30, 2013.

the office without the fire alarm going off, many of us would react with the conditioned response of running away from the perceived danger. Although classical conditioning explains a great deal about why we react to certain stimuli, researchers have developed more sophisticated theories to explain why we behave the way we do.

Operant Conditioning Theory

Operant conditioning: The process of forming associations between learning and behavior by controlling its consequences

Operant conditioning is the process of forming associations between learning and behavior that occurs when the consequences of behavior are being controlled.[22] At the root of operant conditioning is the law of effect theory devised by US psychologist

©iStockphoto.com/skynesher

Operant conditioning follows the idea that a behavior followed by positive results is likely to be repeated. Rewarding employees for a job well done can encourage further positive performance.

E. L. Thorndike, which states that behavior followed by pleasant results is more likely to be repeated, whereas behavior followed by unpleasant results is not.[23] For example, if your boss reprimands you for being late to work, you are less likely to repeat the behavior. Theorists have since refined operant conditioning into the more comprehensive reinforcement theory.

Reinforcement Theory

Pioneered by psychologist B. F. Skinner and his colleagues, reinforcement theory is the most fully developed theory of operant conditioning to date.[24] We define **reinforcement** as the application of consequences for the purpose of establishing patterns of behavior. Within **reinforcement theory**, behavior is a function of its consequences and is determined exclusively by environmental factors such as external stimuli and other reinforcers. The steps in the reinforcement process, sometimes referred to as the ABCs of behavior, are outlined in Figure 4.4.

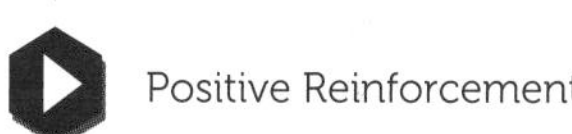

Positive Reinforcement

For example, a curious child sees a hot stove (stimulus); the child touches the stove (response); the child gets burned and cries out in pain (consequence); the child avoids touching hot stoves in the future (future responses).

The practical application of reinforcement in the workplace is called **organizational behavior modification**, which is the use of behavioral techniques to reinforce positive work behavior and discourage unhelpful work behavior.[25] Research has shown that when employees are permitted to design their own roles in accordance with their skills, passion, and values—in organizations like Google, for example—it leads to a more positive work performance.[26] There are four main types of behavioral reinforcement techniques: positive reinforcement, negative reinforcement, punishment, and extinction.

Reinforcement: The application of consequences to establish patterns of behavior

Reinforcement theory: A theory that states that behavior is a function of its consequences and is determined exclusively by environmental factors such as external stimuli and other reinforcers

Organizational behavior modification: The use of behavioral techniques to reinforce positive work behavior and discourage unhelpful work behavior.

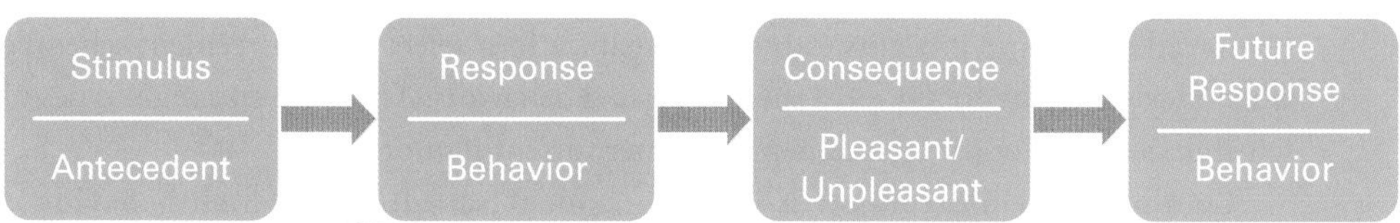

FIGURE 4.4 Reinforcement Theory

Positive and Negative Reinforcement

Many managers use **positive reinforcement**, in which positive consequences are used to reinforce positive behaviors to make the employee more likely to behave in similar ways in the same or similar situations.[27] Conversely, **negative reinforcement** is the removal of previously experienced negative consequences, resulting in the likelihood that positive behaviors will occur again in the same or similar situations.[28]

In a recent example of positive and negative reinforcement, a group of university psychology students carried out a behavioral experiment on their professor. The professor had a habit of pacing back and forth and up and down the classroom during lectures, which the students found distracting and frustrating. To encourage him to remain in the center of the room where all the students could see and hear him, whenever he wandered there, the students applied the positive reinforcement of behaving as if they were fully engaged and focused on what he was saying. However, when the professor wandered to another point in the room, the students behaved as if they weren't listening until he returned to the center of the room, at which time they refocused their attention, thereby providing negative reinforcement. A quarter of the way through the semester, the students noticed a change in the professor's lecturing habit: he remained in the center of the classroom from then on.[29]

Punishment

Punishment is the administration of unpleasant consequences or removal of positive ones for the purpose of discouraging undesirable behavior.[30] There are two types of punishment: positive punishment—the administering of unpleasant consequences—and negative punishment—the removal of pleasant consequences.[31] For example, say your manager reprimands you for interrupting him during a meeting—this is positive punishment because your manager has administered unpleasant consequences that decrease the likelihood of your interrupting him again. Conversely, suppose that after the interruption your manager stops addressing comments to you and asking for your input; this is negative punishment because your manager has removed positively reinforcing consequences in an effort to eliminate your unappreciated behavior.

Extinction

Using punishment techniques in the workplace can be risky and demotivating, which is why many managers often choose **extinction**, the absence of any consequences, which reduces the likelihood that the behavior will be repeated in the same or similar situations.[32] In one example, an employee continually makes jokes during important meetings, resulting in disapproving frowns from some of his teammates and laughter from others. In this situation, the employee may be seeking attention, which both the positive and negative reactions are rewarding. The manager instructs the rest of the team to pay no attention to this person during meetings. As a result, he no longer makes jokes because the reinforcing consequences of that behavior have been removed.

Schedules of Reinforcement

Schedules of reinforcement determine how often specific instances of behaviors will be reinforced. In the real world, it is unrealistic to think that every single behavior will be reinforced every time it occurs, but some organizations select a reinforcement schedule when they are trying to reinforce specific desired behaviors. There are two main types of schedules: continuous reinforcement and intermittent reinforcement.

Continuous reinforcement is a reinforcement schedule in which behavior is rewarded every time it takes place.[33] For example, some companies reward their sales teams with commissions every time they make a sale.

Positive reinforcement: A reinforcement contingency through which behaviors followed by positive consequences, are more likely to occur again in the same or similar situations

Negative reinforcement: A reinforcement contingency through which behaviors are followed by the removal of previously experienced negative consequences, resulting in the likelihood that the behavior will occur again in the same or similar situations

Punishment: A reinforcement contingency that discourages undesirable behavior by administering unpleasant consequences

Extinction: A reinforcement contingency in which a behavior is followed by the absence of any consequence, thereby reducing the likelihood that the behavior will be repeated in the same or similar situations

Continuous reinforcement: A reinforcement schedule in which a reward occurs after each instance of a behavior or set of behaviors

In **intermittent reinforcement**, behavior is not rewarded every time it occurs.[34] There are four types of intermittent schedules:

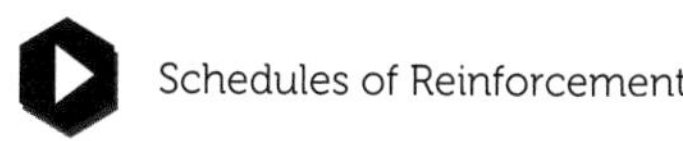

- Many companies use a *fixed interval schedule*, a reward provided only after a certain period of time has elapsed, as the most common form of reinforcement schedule.[35] For example, employees receive a monthly or annual paycheck for working during a fixed period of time or interval.
- A *fixed ratio schedule* is followed when desired behaviors are rewarded after they have been exhibited a fixed number of times.[36] For example, production line workers may be rewarded with a cash incentive every time they produce a certain number of items.
- A *variable interval schedule* is designed to reinforce behavior at varying times.[37] For example, an employee may be rewarded with high praise following desirable behavior during periods of different length. However, employers need to ensure that too much time does not pass between reinforcements, because this might reduce the schedule's effectiveness.
- Finally, a *variable ratio schedule* rewards people after the desired behavior has occurred after a varying number of times.[38] For example, in a call center, the more calls workers make, the higher the chance of closing a sale, leading to greater financial compensation.

Behavioral theory provides a greater understanding of workplace behavior that occurs in response to external environmental stimuli. However, cognitive theorists believe the behavioral view is too limited, arguing that behavioral theorists do not take into account the mental processes behind the behavior. In the next section, we explore the cognitive view and the role it plays in shaping human behavior.

THINKING CRITICALLY

1. Re-read the fire alarm example in the classical conditioning section. Develop a different example of a type of classical conditioning response. **[Understand/Apply]**

2. Praise can be a type of positive reinforcement used by managers. List at least 3 additional positive reinforcements that are used in the workplace. Of the reinforcements you list, which do you find most personally motivating and why? **[Understand/Apply]**

3. You are the CTO of an educational startup focused on building a learning management system that out-performs Blackboard. You're concerned that your programmers are sticking to the same tried and true methods to improve your platform. What negative reinforcements might you apply in order to foster more creative and novel solutions? What positive reinforcements might you apply? Which of the two types of reinforcement do you believe would be most successful in fostering a spirit of innovation among your programmers? **[Apply/ Analyze/ Evaluate]**

4. You are an African American woman who has been hired to lead an all-white, all-male team of programmers. They don't have difficulty accepting your authority, but they do seem to have a hard time getting over the novelty of reporting to a woman and minority in an industry in which most workers are white and male. You're getting tired of their jokes and quips. How could you use the concept of extinction to reduce and eventually put a stop to this behavior? How could you use negative punishment to reduce the behavior? Do you believe one approach or the other would be more effective in diminishing the behavior? Why or why not? **[Apply/Analyze]**

Intermittent reinforcement: Reinforcement schedule in which a reward does not occur after each instance of a behavior or set of behaviors

5. Compare continuous reinforcement strategies to intermittent reinforcement strategies. What benefits would a company receive from implementing intermittent reinforcement strategies rather than continuous reinforcement strategies to achieve sales goals? What potential problems might arise as a result of this decision? **[Analyze/Evaluate]**

LEARNING PROCESSES: THE COGNITIVE VIEW

4.5 Apply social cognitive theory to social learning and cognitive processes

In **social cognitive theory,** psychologist Albert Bandura proposed that we learn by observing, imitating, and modeling the behavior of others within our social context.[39] The theory holds that our cognitive processes, which include awareness, perception, reasoning, and judgment, play important roles in how we learn new knowledge and skills.

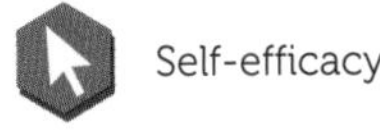
Self-efficacy

This type of learning is particularly significant in the workplace, where employees tend to model the behavior of their managers. For example, a manager who demonstrates commitment, works late when needed, and completes projects on time is likely to lead a team with a similar work ethic. Conversely, if a manager arrives to work late, leaves early, and takes long lunch breaks, then employees are likely to imitate this behavior, leading to a decrease in work productivity and performance. CEO of PepsiCo Indra Nooyi has managed to cultivate a very friendly, loyal, and collaborative work environment by wholly committing to the organization and leading by example, stating, "I wouldn't ask anyone to do anything I wouldn't do myself."[40]

Social cognitive theory: A theory that proposes that learning takes place through the observation, imitation, and the modeling of others within a social context

Self-efficacy: The belief we have in our ability to succeed in a specific task or situation

Vicarious learning: A process of learning by watching the actions or behaviors of another person

There are several important aspects of social cognitive theory. The first is **self-efficacy,** which describes our personal belief in our ability to perform certain tasks or behaviors.[41] For example, if you feel very confident speaking in public, then you have high self-efficacy with regard to public speaking; however, if you feel very nervous about giving a speech in front of an audience, you have low efficacy in this area.

The second component of social cognitive theory is **vicarious learning,** a process of learning by watching the actions or behaviors of another person. Vicarious learning influences our degree of self-efficacy.[43] For example, if you see a colleague on a similar career path successfully giving the weekly presentation during a meeting, you might be

Indra Nooyi, CEO of PepsiCo, demonstrates social cognitive theory by operating the way she expects her employees to act on the job.

SNAKES, SELF-EFFICACY, AND TASK PERFORMANCE

Too Much of a Good Thing?

Examining the Evidence

Some very interesting early classic studies examining the concept of self-efficacy focused on people with a fear of snakes.* Albert Bandura and his colleagues set up an experiment using both an experimental group and a control group, with a pre-test indicating that both groups had strong fear of snakes and low self-efficacy for approaching and handling them. The researchers then carried out an intervention with the experimental group. They explained that the snakes were not poisonous and would not bite, and they described how the snakes would react when the subjects handled them. They also informed the group that the snakes were not cold and slimy, but actually dry and scaly. The researchers then measured the fear and self-efficacy levels in both groups again. Both groups still had a high fear of snakes, but the experimental group had a much higher level of self-efficacy for approaching and handing the snakes. Consequently, when members of both groups were asked to approach and handle the snakes, those from the experimental group whose level of self-efficacy had increased were able to do so at a much higher rate than those with low self-efficacy.

Although hundreds of studies have shown similar positive effects for self-efficacy on task performance, some recent studies have called this relationship into question.# These studies suggest that high levels of self-efficacy within an individual could cause that person to become overconfident and to allocate fewer resources and less effort to the task at hand, thereby resulting in lower levels of task performance. For example, one study of students playing an analytical game showed a negative relationship between self-efficacy and performance.[42] Self-efficacy resulted in overconfidence and the increased likelihood of making a logical error in the game.

Critical-Thinking Questions

1. **Given the conflicting research evidence, how can self-efficacy affect individual task performance in the workplace?**
2. **What can managers do to try to enhance the positive effects of self-efficacy in their employees?**

SOURCES

*Bandura, Albert, and Nancy E. Adams. "Analysis of Self-Efficacy Theory of Behavioral Change." *Cognitive Therapy and Research* 1, no. 4 (December 1977): 287–310; Bandura, Albert, Linda Reese, and Nancy E. Adams. "Microanalysis of Action and Fear Arousal as a Function of Differential Levels of Perceived Self-Efficacy." *Journal of Personality and Social Psychology* 43, no. 1 (July 1982): 5–21.

#Vancouver, Jeffrey B., Charles M. Thompson, E. Casey Tischner, and Dan J. Putka. "Two Studies Examining the Negative Effect of Self-Efficacy on Performance." *Journal of Applied Psychology* 87, no. 3 (June 2002): 506–516.

more inclined to volunteer to do the next one, because you have observed this event as a positive experience, thereby increasing your self-efficacy for doing presentations. However, if you observe the same colleague stumble nervously through the presentation, it might give you second thoughts about doing one yourself, resulting in low self-efficacy for giving presentations.

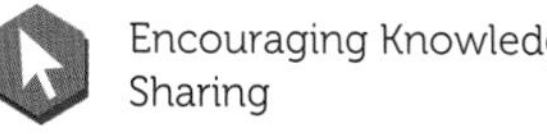
Encouraging Knowledge-Sharing

Without being aware of it, UPS worker Jacob Mitchoff, of Concord, California, employed vicarious learning. In 2013, Mitchoff made a resolution to keep fit in an effort to avoid injuries at work. Observing a friend keeping a strict fitness regime gave him the confidence to know that he could do the same. As a result of this vicarious learning, Mitchoff was able to commit to a workout schedule that required four to seven days a week at the gym in order to achieve the desired level of fitness.[44]

The third factor of social cognitive theory is **self-regulation**, the process in which we set goals that create a discrepancy between a desired state and a current state.[45] This discrepancy creates tension, which drives us to increase effort to reduce tension and reach the goal. For example, your manager sets a goal for you to complete a complex project within two weeks; you might feel uncomfortable or nervous about your ability

Self-regulation: A process whereby people set goals, creating a discrepancy between the desired state and the current state

to achieve the goal within the allotted time frame, so you work harder in order to reduce your feelings of discomfort and to successfully complete the assignment on time.

THINKING CRITICALLY

1. You join a company where managers regularly reprimand their direct reports in front of others, play favorites, and encourage co-workers to report one another for making small mistakes. Based on Bandura's social cognitive theory, what sort of company culture is likely to spring from these practices? How would a new employee seek to "get ahead" at such a company and to what extent would efforts to succeed in this culture directly benefit the company's shareholders? **[Apply/Analyze]**
2. Of the three key aspects of social cognitive theory (self-efficacy, vicarious learning, and self-regulation) which do you think is most import in adjusting to a new and particularly challenging job? Defend your response. **[Analyze/Evaluate]**
3. Apply the Triadic Reciprocal Model of Behavior to Joey's difficulties in adjusting to a heavier workload at WTRT. How does the model explain Joey's increased absenteeism from work? **[Understand/Apply]**

Triadic Reciprocal Model of Behavior

Bandura also believed human functioning is shaped by three factors that are reciprocally related: reinforcement, cognitive processes, and behavior.[46] The relationship is shown graphically in the **triadic reciprocal model of behavior** (Figure 4.5).

Figure 4.5 shows how cognitive processes mediate the effects of reinforcers on behavior and how behavior influences both reinforcers and cognitive processes. Consider two quarterbacks in a football game. The first throws an interception. This causes him to think that he is not an effective passer and lowers his self-efficacy for completing passes. Lower self-efficacy causes him to become tentative, make more mistakes, and throw more incompletions and interceptions. His poor play encourages the defensive players to try even harder, which creates more negative reinforcers in the form of pressure.

In contrast, the second quarterback also throws an interception. However, unlike the first, he acknowledges his mistake and is determined to try harder; his self-efficacy remains constant. He increases his efforts, which leads to a touchdown pass. This success increases his self-efficacy even further. The defensive players become tentative because of his good play, which leads to even more success for the quarterback.

In this chapter, we have focused on the nature of perception and the differing ways in which we perceive each other and ourselves. We have also explored learning and its importance to our working, personal, and professional lives. In the next chapter, we look at the topic of motivation as we seek to understand what drives us towards desired goals.

Triadic reciprocal model of behavior: A model that shows human functioning shaped by three factors that are reciprocally related: reinforcement, cognitive processes, and behavior

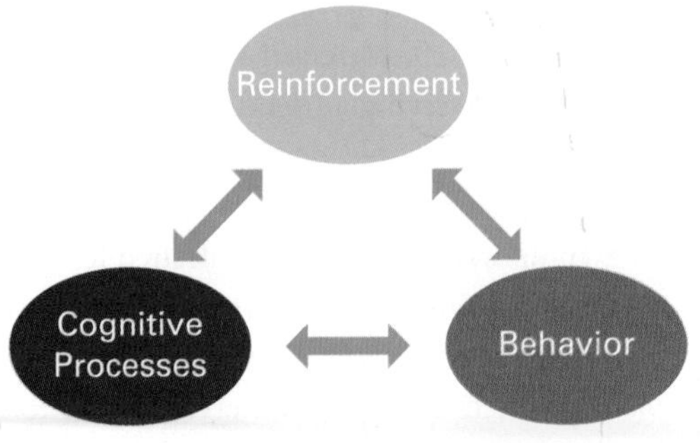

■ FIGURE 4.5 Triadic Reciprocal Model of Behavior

IN REVIEW

Learning Objectives

4.1 Describe the basic concept of perception

Perception is the process by which we receive and interpret information from our environment. A number of factors influence and perhaps distort perception, including the perceiver, the environment, and the focal object. Perceptions are shaped by past experiences, culture, attitude, values, upbringing, and so on. This means that the nature of the *perceiver* has a strong influence on the perceptual process. The context or the setting also affects the perception process. The person, thing, or event being interpreted also affects our perception.

4.2 Explain the different types of perceptual distortions

People process a huge amount of complex information, and their attempts to organize and sift this information can lead to inaccuracies. There are a number of common perceptual distortions. **Stereotypes** are an individual's fixed beliefs about the characteristics of a particular group. **Selective attention** is the tendency to selectively focus on aspects of situations that are most aligned with our own interests, values, and attitudes. **Halo effect** is a perception problem through which we form a positive or negative view of one aspect of an individual based on our overall impressions of that person. **Primacy effect** is a perception problem through which an individual assesses a person quickly on the basis of the first information encountered. **Recency effect** is a perception problem through which we use the most recent information available to assess a person. **Contrast effect** takes place when people rank something higher or lower than they should as a result of exposure to recent events or situations. **Projecting** is a process through which people transfer their own thoughts, motivations, feelings, and desires to others. **Self-fulfilling prophecy** occurs when a person bases behavior on preexisting expectations about another person or situation in order to create an outcome aligned with those expectations. **Impression management** is the process by which we attempt to influence the perceptions others may have of us. A facet of impression management is **ingratiation,** by which an individual attempts to influence others by becoming more attractive or likeable.

4.3 Apply attribution theory to more effectively interpret behavior

Attribution theory holds that people look for two causes to explain the behavior of others: *internal attributions,* which are personal characteristics of others, and *external attributions,* which are situational factors. The theory holds that people tend to use two types of causal attributions to look for ways to explain the behavior of others: internal attributions, which are personal characteristics; and external attributions, which are situational factors.

There are three types of determinants of attribution that influence our internal and external attributions: distinctiveness, consensus, and consistency. *Distinctiveness* is the extent to which a person behaves consistently in similar situations. *Consensus* involves looking at how everyone else responds in the same situation. *Consistency* is the extent to which a person responds in the same way over a period of time.

4.4 Use reinforcement theory to understand learning and modify behavior

Learning is an ongoing process through which individuals adjust their behavior based on experience. **Reinforcement** is defined as the application of consequences to establish patterns of behavior. Within reinforcement theory, behavior is determined exclusively by environmental factors such as external stimuli and other reinforcers.

The practical application of reinforcement process in the workplace is called **organizational behavior modification,** which is the use of behavioral techniques to reinforce positive work behavior and discourage unhelpful work behavior.

4.5 Apply social cognitive theory to social learning and cognitive processes

The **social learning theory** proposes that learning takes place through the observation, imitation, and the modeling of others within a social context. There are several important components to social learning theory. The first is **self-efficacy,** which describes our personal conviction in our ability to perform certain tasks or behaviors. The second component to social learning is **vicarious**

learning, a process of learning that involves watching the actions or behaviors of another person. Vicarious learning influences our degree of self-efficacy. The third factor of social learning is **self-regulation,** in which people set goals that create a discrepancy between the desired state and the current state.

KEY TERMS

THINKING CRITICALLY ABOUT THE CASE OF LAURA PIERCE

Perception and Learning at WTRT

Keeping in mind that how we perceive and learn from co-workers has a significant impact on our success in the workplace, consider the five critical-thinking steps in relation to how the WTRT staff perceive and learn from one another.

OBSERVE

What aspects of WTRT's work culture might a new employee like Laura have vicariously learned from Cheryl, Joey, and Abigail if she were a less experienced employee with a lower sense of self-efficacy? What perceptual mistakes is Laura able to avoid as a result of her self-efficacy and self-regulation?

INTERPRET

Review the narrative case discussions in the chapter and then list the perceptual distortions Laura, Cheryl, and Abigail fall prey to during the course of the described events. What perceptual distortions do the three board members exhibit during the meeting?

ANALYZE

How might Abigail employ reinforcements in order to reduce Cheryl's abruptness and reward her loyalty and dedication? How might Abigail employ reinforcements in order to foster a more cooperative relationship between Cheryl and Joey and Cheryl and Laura?

EVALUATE

Discuss Abigail's suitability as the continuing head of WTRT. To what extent is the board correct in suggesting Abigail should take a break from running the company? To what extent are perceptual distortions impacting the board's reactions to Abigail in an unfair way?

EXPLAIN

To what extent should Laura be responsible for trying to change Abigail's negative perception of Laura's motives? To what extent is Abigail, as Laura's manager, responsible for thinking critically about her reaction to and perception of Laura? Put another way: to what degree should we as individuals proactively defend ourselves from the inaccurate perceptions of colleagues and to what extent should all members of a work group seek to guard against perceptual distortions?

EXERCISE 4.1: THE POWER OF PERCEPTION

This exercise shows the phenomenal perceptive power of the human mind! The following text circulated widely on the Internet in September 2003:

Aoccdrnig to a rscheearch at Cmabrigde Uinervtisy, it deosn't mttaer in waht oredr the ltteers in a wrod are, the olny iprmoatnt tihng is taht the frist and lsat ltteer be in the rghit pclae. The rset can be a taotl mses and you can sitll raed it wouthit a porbelm.

Tihs is bcuseae the huamn mnid deos not raed ervey lteter by istlef, but the wrod as a wlohe. Amzanig huh? And I awlyas tghuhot slpeling was ipmorantt!

Were you able to read the text despite the jumbled letters? The perceptive power of the human mind is impressive! But if you were able to read the statement, you are probably now holding a couple of misperceptions about reading words with jumbled letters:

1. No research on reading words with jumbled letters has ever been conducted at Cambridge University.[1] However, research on this topic has been conducted by researchers at other universities.[2]
2. It does matter what order the letters are in, and some jumbled letter words are much easier to read than others. Consider the following sentences:

---

[1]http://www.mrc-cbu.cam.ac.uk/people/matt.davis/cmabridge/

[2]Rawlinson, G. E. (1976) The significance of letter position in word recognition. Unpublished PhD Thesis, Psychology Department, University of Nottingham, Nottingham UK.

A vheclie epxledod at a plocie cehckipont near the UN haduqertares in Bagahdd on Mnoday kilinlg the bmober and an Irqai polcie offceir

A dootcr has aimttded the magltheuansr of a tageene ceacnr pintaet who deid aetfr a hatospil durg blendur

You will probably agree that the first sentence is much easier to read than the second, although both follow the same "rules" for jumbling the letters described above. The first and last letter are not all you use when reading text. If this were true, how would you tell the difference between the words *salt* and *slat*?

> Write a brief essay explaining how your power of perception has been applied in other school, work, or personal situations that you have experienced. For example, you might focus on a time when your perception allowed you to find a creative solution to a difficult problem that other people could not solve. Or you might focus on a time when you perceived a situation differently than your professor, boss, or coworkers, leading to positive (or negative) outcomes for you and/or your organization. As you will see from the examples in your essay, the power of perception has many practical applications beyond jumbled letter reading!

This exercise helps to illustrate that perception is a complicated and nuanced process of making sense of the world around us!

EXERCISE 4.2: PERCEPTUAL ERRORS

Objective:

This exercise will help you to be better able to *describe* the basic concepts of perception, *explain* different types of perceptual distortions, and *apply* attribution theory in interpreting behavior.

Instructions:

Step1: Write down a description of a time when your perceptions of someone were completely wrong. Write about a situation that you are willing to share with everyone in the class. Describe this situation in as much detail as possible and make sure you also describe the reasons (internal and external) that you misperceived the person. (5 minutes)

Step 2: Find a partner (ideally someone who you do not regularly interact with), and read them your situation. After you have both read your situations, select one and analyze the reasons for the misperception using chapter terms and concepts. Specifically, you should use concepts related to the perceptual *selection process, common perceptual distortions,* and *common attribution errors.* Be sure to write down your analysis of the situation. (10 minutes)

Step 3: Be prepared to discuss your analysis if your instructor calls on you. (2 to 5 minutes)

Reflection Questions:

1. How did using chapter terms and concepts better help you to understand the perceptual error you had made?
2. Thinking about other misperceptions you have made about people, are there any perceptual errors that you tend to fall into?
3. How could you use your understanding of common perceptual errors and the perceptual selection process to avoid future errors?
4. How can thinking about perceptual errors help you to avoid perceptual errors?
5. What roles do perceptual errors play in the workplace?

Exercise contributed by Milton R. Mayfield, Professor of Business, Texas A&M International University and Jaqueline R. Mayfield, Professor of Business, Texas A&M International University.

EXERCISE 4.3: USING OB TO IMPROVE YOUR LIFE

Objectives:

After completing this exercise you will be able to better *understand* reinforcement theory concepts, and be able to *apply* reinforcement theory and social cognitive theory concepts to your personal and professional life.

Instructions:

Step 1: Think about some behavior in your life you would like to improve and that you feel comfortable discussing with members of your class. Write down this behavior, and classify (i.e., does it relate to your school, personal, or work life?). Then decide if it is a behavior that you would like to increase the frequency of (such as exercising), or reduce the frequency of or eliminate (such as smoking). Note the key reasons you would like to change this behavior. Be sure to include what benefits the change would bring to you, friends, family, and colleagues. Then, using the reinforcement concepts you have learned in the chapter, set up a self-reinforcement plan for changing your behavior. Clearly define the behavior you want to change, set intermediate goals for your behavioral change (e.g. initially work out once a week, then advance to three times a week, and then reach five times a week). Next, set self-rewards for achieving and sustaining these behavioral changes. Be sure to specify the reward schedule and specific rewards that you will apply, and give the rationale behind your chosen schedule. Are there any natural rewards (related to changing the behavior) that might help? For example, would working out to your favorite music be more motivational? If possible, include ways that you can recruit friends, family, and other people to help you in your change plan. (10 minutes)

Step 2: Form into six groups based on behavioral change goal similarity. The groups are as follows:

- Behavior Frequency Increase – Work
- Behavior Frequency Increase – Social
- Behavior Frequency Increase – School
- Behavior Frequency Decrease – Work
- Behavior Frequency Decrease – Social
- Behavior Frequency Decrease – School

Once everyone has joined the appropriate group, each person should read their goal(s) and plan. In turn, the others should provide feedback on ways to improve the plan. (20 to 30 minutes)

Step 3: Be prepared to present your plan to the class, including any improvement suggestions from your group members. In your presentation, use chapter terms to describe your plan, and explain why you expect the plan to be effective using chapter concepts. (10 to 15 minutes)

Reflection Questions:

This exercise is a good opportunity for you to think about and apply chapter concepts to personal, work, and educational goals and behaviors.

1. For your selected behavior, have you tried to change these behaviors before? How effective were you in making these changes?
2. Based on chapter concepts, if you implement your behavioral change plan, do you expect to see a different outcome?
3. Did the social cognitive aspect (discussing your plan with other people with similar behavioral plans) help you in the process?
4. As a manager, how might you apply similar methods to help workers reach their full potential at work?

Exercise contributed by Milton R. Mayfield, Professor of Business, Texas A&M International University and Jaqueline R. Mayfield, Professor of Business, Texas A&M International University.

CASE STUDY 4.1: KEMPINSKI HOTELS

Kempinski Hotels, headquartered in Switzerland, is Europe's oldest luxury hotel group, specializing in five-star properties that include the Emirates Palace in Abu Dhabi, the Hotel Taschenbergpalais Kempinski in Dresden, and the Çiragan Palace Kempinski in Istanbul. Founded in 1897, the Kempinski brand has an intriguing story to tell. "Our employees have been a part of creating history around the world," the website reads. "From historic buildings to the most avant-garde of modern architecture, our properties are the setting for some of life's greatest moments. We've witnessed historic meetings between world leaders, celebrities taking sanctuary in the world of calm we create for them, and created incredible memories for guests on a 'once-in-a-lifetime' journey."

In 2008, Kempinski was ready for a journey of its own: its portfolio of hotels was set to double by 2015, and its workforce was expected to grow from 7,500 to 37,500. How could Kempinski expand so dramatically without losing the soul that made it so unique?

Mia Norcao, vice president of corporate communication, realized that it was time to do some serious company soul-searching. Did employees understand the Kempinski brand? Were they armed with the knowledge and loyalty they needed to be true ambassadors to guests and to the world?

Norcao was part of a team that devised and implemented an elaborate plan to give every Kempinski employee a solid, intuitive understanding of what Kempinski was all about. The challenges were monumental. First and foremost, what *was* Kempinski all about? Despite its long, rich history, corporate values had never been consistently articulated—not in the Geneva -based boardroom, and certainly not at the front desk of any of its hundreds of hotels. Once those values had been identified, how could Norcao and her team communicate them to employees throughout the organization, given their widely varying levels of responsibility and education and the dozens of different languages they spoke?

Norcao knew she needed resources and buy-in from every level of the organization, starting with the top. "This last task was especially crucial—top management [the management board and regional presidents] had to commit their time and assign company resources to this program if we were to be successful with senior management on a group wide basis. They had to understand the link between delivering a consistent brand promise and guest experience, and actively managing our corporate culture," Norcao said. Explaining the benefits in dollars and sense was important. "We were able to demonstrate in business terms that when employee engagement is higher than 60 percent, total shareholder return can almost double, and conversely that if engagement drops below 25 percent, total shareholder return can be negatively impacted." Norcao's team showed that the organization already had 29 percent engagement—compared to the industry standard of 21— a solid start but with much room for improvement.

Once the top brass was on board, Norcao and her team conducted intensive interviews across the organization. Listening to the staff who lived the Kempinski experience every day helped shape what would eventually become five core values: "Being people oriented, being straightforward, encouraging entrepreneurial performance amongst staff, having the freedom to create traditions and being passionate about European luxury." The DNA of Kempinski's corporate culture had been identified. Now came the hard part: implementation.

How to reach every member of the organization in a meaningful way? How to make an impression on the concierge in Cairo and the maid in Munich? Clearly, an all-saturating, trickle-down approach was needed. But what was the model? "Our aim throughout was to create a corporate culture, which would empower staff to know instinctively what would be an appropriate way at Kempinski to solve a challenge, work with colleagues or serve our guests—not to limit them with strict rules," said Norcao.

Her team eventually opted for storytelling. "All cultures in the world have some form of story-telling tradition," Norcao said. Stories were collected from employees about emotional or memorable happenings at the hotel that represented one or more of the five core values. Campaigns were designed around the best of them, with "artwork and colors [that] were associated with each value, so that all collateral could have a consistent visual language—important again in helping illiterate staff identify values or stories."

Norcao started a storybook as her team built a wealth of tools to support managers: presentations, games, activities, session plans, Q&As, plus posters and brochures. A storytelling mini-site, "myStory", was constructed to collect touching, personal stories from employees all over the world. "The myStory space is among the most visited areas online and we've collected nearly 300 stories," Norcao commented. "This is very positive in an industry where most staff don't have time to regularly access a computer. Anecdotal evidence from sessions shows that staff often believe some or all of the original stories are about their hotel, which exhibits their pride, and belief in and ownership of these stories."

Today, Kempinski's growth plan is well underway, with more than 70 hotels worldwide and counting. "When I look back at the road we've traveled," Norcao continued, "I'm amazed to see how much we've accomplished with a relatively small budget but using a powerful storytelling approach to propagate our core values. . . . As part of my role, I spend time with senior managers when they first arrive at the company and often ask for their initial impressions of Kempinski (before mentioning our values) and am reassured that we haven't lost our soul—they always remark on how friendly, welcoming and practical everyone is. Some have even already heard of our values and can tell me their own stories."

Case Questions

1. Why did Norcao think that employee engagement was important? Can you explain the importance of perception in this case?
2. Describe how Kempinski used social cognitive theory to establish their corporate culture and core values.
3. What reinforcement activities were chosen to support the growth plan at Kempinski Hotels?

Sources

"About Us." *Kempinski.com.* www.kempinski.com/en/hotels/information/about-us/.

MacDiarmid, Ann. "Encouraging Employee Engagement." *CMA Management* (June/July 2004).

Mitchell, Colin. "Selling the Brand Inside." *Harvard Business Review.* http://hbr.org/2002/01/selling-the-brand-inside/ar/1.

Norcao, Mia. "Using Storytelling to Engage a Diverse Workforce at Kempinski Hotels," Melcrum, n.d.; www.melcrum.com/research/employee-engagement/using-storytelling-engage-diverse-workforce-kempinski-hotels#sthash.k23PPOU8.dpuf.

Rydberg, Isabella, and Lyttinen, J. P. "Internal Marketing in Hotel Chains" (Luleå University of Technology, 2005); http://epubl.ltu.se/1404-5508/2005/183/LTU-SHU-EX-05183-SE.pdf.

SELF-ASSESSMENT 4.1

General Self-Efficacy

Although Bandura originally conceptualized self-efficacy as a person's belief that he or she is capable of performing a *specific* task, many researchers have subsequently found it useful to expand it to describe general self-efficacy, our perceived ability to cope with daily hassles and adapt after experiencing stressful events.

For each statement, circle the number that best describes you based on the following scale:

	Not at all True	Hardly True	Moderately True	Exactly True
1. I can always manage to solve difficult problems if I try hard enough.	1	2	3	4
2. If someone opposes me, I can find the means and ways to get what I want.	1	2	3	4
3. It is easy for me to stick to my aims and accomplish my goals.	1	2	3	4
4. I am confident that I could deal efficiently with unexpected events.	1	2	3	4
5. Thanks to my resourcefulness, I know how to handle unforeseen situations.	1	2	3	4
6. I can solve most problems if I invest the necessary effort.	1	2	3	4
7. I can remain calm when facing difficulties because I can rely on my coping abilities.	1	2	3	4
8. When I am confronted with a problem, I can usually find several solutions.	1	2	3	4
9 If I am in trouble, I can usually think of a solution.	1	2	3	4
10. I can usually handle whatever comes my way.	1	2	3	4

Scoring: Add the numbers you circled and write your score in the blank: ______________

Interpretation

30 and above = You have very strong general self-efficacy. You are likely to be quite effective in coping with daily challenges and adapting to stressful events.

20 – 29 = You have a moderate level of general self-efficacy. Your confidence in your ability to perform difficult tasks and cope with adversity, though generally steady, may falter in certain situations.

19 and below = You have a low level of general self-efficacy. As a result, you may be more susceptible to the effects of stress, anxiety, burnout, and depression. You could benefit from the self-leadership strategies discussed in Chapter 13. Research has linked self-leadership with higher self-efficacy perceptions.

SOURCE: Adapted from Schwarzer, R., & Jerusalem, M. (1995). "Generalized Self-Efficacy Scale." In J. Weinman, S. Wright, & M. Johnston (Eds.), *Measures in Health Psychology: A User's Portfolio. Causal and Control Beliefs* (pp. 35–37). Windsor, UK: NFER-NELSON.

5 Motivation: Concepts and Theoretical Perspectives

> Motivation is the art of getting people to do what you want them to do because they want to do it.
>
> —Dwight D. Eisenhower, 34th president of the United States

THE MOTIVATION PROCESS

5.1 Explain the basic motivation process

Have you ever successfully completed a goal such as passing an exam or getting a job and wondered how you did it? Think about the behaviors you exhibited to achieve your objectives. To pass the exam, you probably studied hard for long periods of time, and to get the job you likely prepared for the interview by researching the company and practicing responses to potential interview questions. Whatever your intended goal, you would not have achieved it without motivation. We define **motivation** as forces from within individuals that stimulate and drive them to achieve goals.[1]

But how does motivation affect the way we behave? Motivation is a process by which behavior is *energized*, meaning we are willing to work hard; *directed*, meaning we've chosen what to work at; and *maintained*, meaning we intend to work for some period of time to achieve objectives.[2] Take a look at how the cofounders of Evolve Architecture, Randy Blankenship and RoseMarie Bundy, motivate their employees in the OB in the Real World feature.

The motivation process is shaped by unsatisfied needs and the resulting tension, as shown in detail in Figure 5.1. For example, you may have an unsatisfied goal to achieve a high grade in an exam, which creates tension. The demand to satisfy this

LEARNING OBJECTIVES

By the end of this chapter, you will be able to:

- 5.1 Explain the basic motivation process
- 5.2 Compare the various needs theories of motivation
- 5.3 Examine equity theory in the context of organizational justice and distinguish among the predictable outcomes of perceived inequity
- 5.4 Apply goal-setting theory in organizational contexts
- 5.5 Describe the expectancy theory of motivation and its practical implications

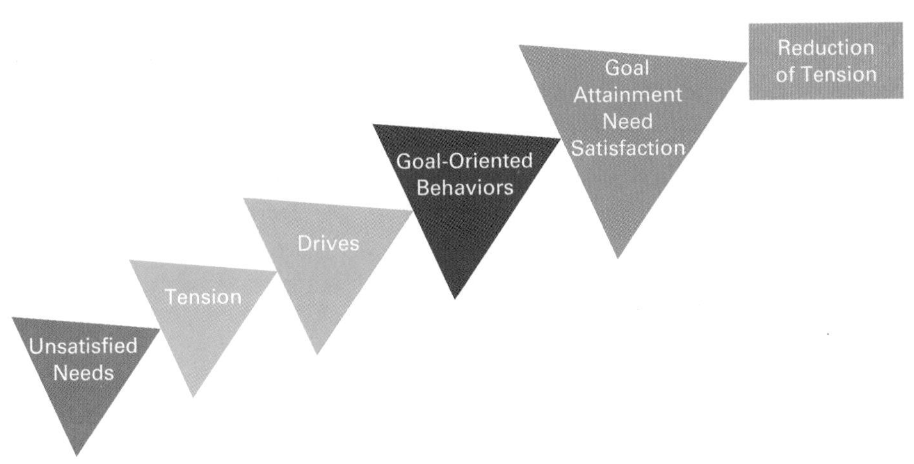

■ FIGURE 5.1 The Motivation Process

Motivation: Forces from within individuals that stimulate and drive them to achieve goals

Master the content.
edge.sagepub.com/neckob

SAGE edge™

need and relieve the discomfort drives you to study hard, which helps you to attain your goal, thus reducing tension.

There are many theories about motivation, but most focus on the idea that motivation is based on different needs and the behavioral outcomes of those needs.

Researchers have spent decades attempting to identify the underlying factors that motivate people. Needs motivation theories are generally divided into two categories: content theories and process theories.[3] **Content theories** explain why people have different needs at different times and how these needs motivate behavior. There are four main content theories: Maslow's hierarchy of needs, Alderfer's ERG theory, McClelland's need theory, and Herzberg's two-factor theory. **Process theories** describe the cognitive processes through which needs are translated into behavior. The process theories we investigate in this chapter are equity theory, goal-setting theory, and expectancy theory.

Content theories: Theories that explain why people have different needs at different times and how these needs motivate behavior, such as Maslow's hierarchy of needs, Alderfer's ERG theory, McClelland's need theory, and Herzberg's two-factor theory

Process theories: Theories that describe the cognitive processes through which needs are translated into behavior, such as equity theory, expectancy theory, and goal-setting theory

THINKING CRITICALLY

1. List at least ten forces that have motivated you to attain simple and complex goals in your life. These forces may include those that affect your daily behavior such as preparing a meal or walking your dog or forces that affect work behavior such as meeting deadlines or arriving on time. **[Understand]**

2. Apply the six-step motivation process shown in Figure 5-1 to a need in your own life (e.g. need to secure a job, need to improve your grades). **[Apply]**

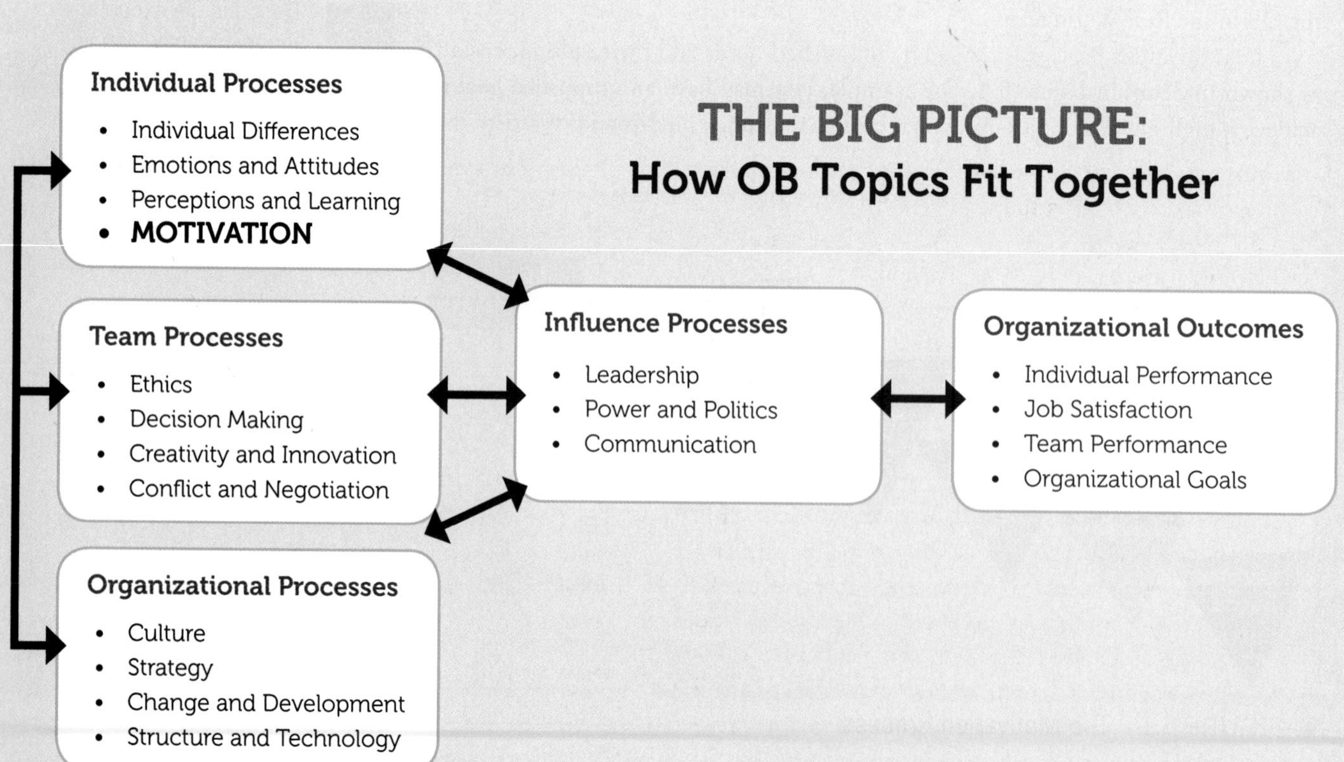

ROSEMARIE BUNDY AND RANDY BLANKENSHIP, *joint founders and partners*

OB in the Real World

© Randy Blankenship and Rose Marie Bundy

Evolve Architecture is an architecture and interior design firm founded in 1990 with the mission of bringing unsurpassed service and creativity to clients. The company prides itself on its ability to transform a client's vision into a unique workspace that fosters innovation and excellence and has succeeded with such clients as American Family Fitness, Pfizer, and Snagajob (a Top 10 Best Small Company to Work for in America).

Evolve was founded by Randy Blankenship and RoseMarie Bundy. RoseMarie had spent 12 years in the design industry and knew she wanted to start a company that diverged from the prevalent "live to work" corporate mentality. "I've worked at companies where there was a lot of pressure to spend long hours at the office which took away from time with my family. I wanted to start a company where employees were truly encouraged to have a life outside work."

Randy was also interested in starting a business and running his own company. The two sat down early to talk about the type of environment they wanted to create and the type of employees they wanted to hire. "We want employees who have good manners, understand the Golden Rule, treat people kindly, value their family, and are happy." Evolve's founders have found that by hiring people who fit this criteria they have not only produced good work for their clients but have also created a culture in which employees enjoy being at work.

RoseMarie and Randy understand that every employee is motivated by something different. An employee who has young children at home might be motivated by a flexible work schedule. Someone looking to gain new skills and experiences may be excited to tackle something new, like attending client meetings or using a new technology. And an employee eager for leadership experience may be motivated by the opportunity to manage a new project or a new team. "When it comes to motivation we don't just pigeonhole employees or assume the same thing motivates everyone. Instead, we work hard to get to know our employees as individuals." In addition to a traditional performance review, Evolve leaders and managers often take employees to lunch and ask questions such as:

- How are things going?
- What are you working on that is making you happy?
- What do you think our company needs to change in order to be more successful?
- What types of projects do you wish you were working on?

Randy and RoseMarie talk openly about their lives, careers, career and personal aspirations, and mistakes they've made along the way. RoseMarie says, "We strive to break down the perception that we're the boss and they are our employees. We don't feel that way at all, and as leaders we're willing to do the same jobs our people are doing and are willing to work just as hard as our employees are working. . . . That being said, we also make sure that our employees see us creating a work/life balance for ourselves."

Monthly team-building events for the entire company include river boat trips, Segway tours, and meals at local restaurants. Leaders take time off work to relax and make sure everyone in the company does the same. "The measure of success for our employees is the work they produce, not the number of hours they are at their desks. We want our employees to see that our actions support that philosophy."

By viewing their employees as individuals, demonstrating and encouraging the achievement of work/life balance and supporting personal and professional development, Evolve Architecture's founders have built an organization of loyal and motivated employees who offer high-quality solutions to their clients.

Critical-Thinking Questions:

1. **The founders of Evolve Architecture believe treating their employees as individuals is a key motivator. What do you think would be helpful in motivating a group of people?**
2. **How important do you think a work/life balance is for motivating employees?**

SOURCE: Personal interview with RoseMarie Bundy, May 2013.

NEEDS THEORIES

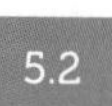

Compare the various needs theories of motivation

In this section we'll explore several needs theories of motivation: Maslow's hierarchy of needs, Herzberg's two-factor theory, McClelland's acquired needs theory, and money as a motivator

Maslow's Hierarchy of Needs

Psychologist Abraham Maslow developed one of the most popular needs theories, referred to as the **hierarchy of needs theory**,[4] which is visually depicted as a pyramid of five levels of individual needs with physiological needs at the bottom and self-actualization needs at the top (Figure 5.2). Maslow's theory teaches that each need must be satisfied before we can move up the pyramid to satisfy the the need above it. For example, at the base of the pyramid, we need to satisfy the physiological need to eat food and drink water in order to survive before we can satisfy our safety needs such as looking after our families or getting a job. Maslow's hierarchy is based on the belief that successfully accomplishing the lower-level needs leads to the achievement of higher-level needs such as gaining confidence, self-esteem, and finally self-actualization.

Though Maslow's theory is useful for identifying categories of needs, there has been much debate about its implication that each need loses its importance as soon as it has been satisfied.[5] For example, according to the hierarchy, people who reach self-actualization won't be as concerned with gaining the respect of others. Researchers have also argued against the step-by-step sequence of Maslow's hierarchy, proposing that people may be motivated to satisfy these needs in a number of different ways or even simultaneously.[6]

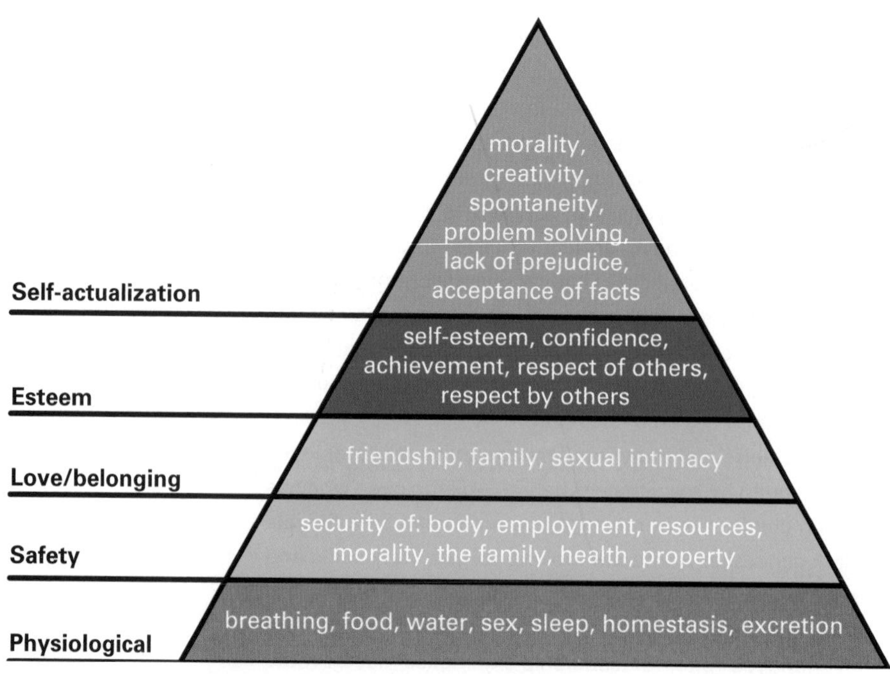

■ FIGURE 5.2 Maslow's Hierarchy of Needs

SOURCE: Factoryjoe (Mazlow's Hierarchy of Needs.svg) [CC BY-SA 3.0 (http://creativecommons.org/licenses/by-sa/3.0)], via Wikimedia Commons.

Hierarchy of needs theory: Maslow's theory that suggests people are motivated by their desire to satisfy specific needs, and that needs are arranged in a hierarchy with physiological needs at the bottom and self-actualization needs at the top

ERG Theory

Developed by psychologist Clayton Alderfer, **ERG theory** also suggests that people are motivated by categories of needs arranged in the form of a hierarchy.[7] Instead of Maslow's five need categories, however, Alderfer includes only three: existence needs (E), relatedness needs (R), and growth needs (G). *Existence needs* are similar to Maslow's physiological and safety needs, *relatedness needs* are comparable to Maslow's love/belonging needs, and *growth needs* bear similarities to Maslow's esteem needs and self-actualization needs. Alderfer proposed that instead of satisfying needs one step at a time, we can satisfy different levels in any order or even at the same time depending on the circumstances. ERG theory has received more support from researchers than Maslow's hierarchy of needs, but further research needs to be carried out to fully test the validity of Alderfer's model.

Herzberg's Two-Factor Theory

A third theory of motivation, developed by psychologist Frederick Herzberg, is called **two-factor theory** (or *motivation-hygiene theory* or *dual theory*). It explores the impact of motivational influences on job satisfaction.[8] Herzberg conducted interviews with hundreds of workers before identifying two main factors influencing employee behavior: hygiene factors and motivators (Figure 5.3). **Hygiene factors** are sources of job satisfaction such as salary, status, and security. Herzberg found that the first step to employee satisfaction was to eliminate poor hygiene factors. For example, if employees don't feel they are being paid enough in comparison to industry standards, employers can remedy the situation by introducing fair and competitive wages. While eliminating poor hygiene factors will reduce job dissatisfaction, two-factor theory states that taking such steps will not increase increase job satisfaction.[9] To correct this, managers need to use **motivators** such as achievement, recognition, and responsibility to build job satisfaction.

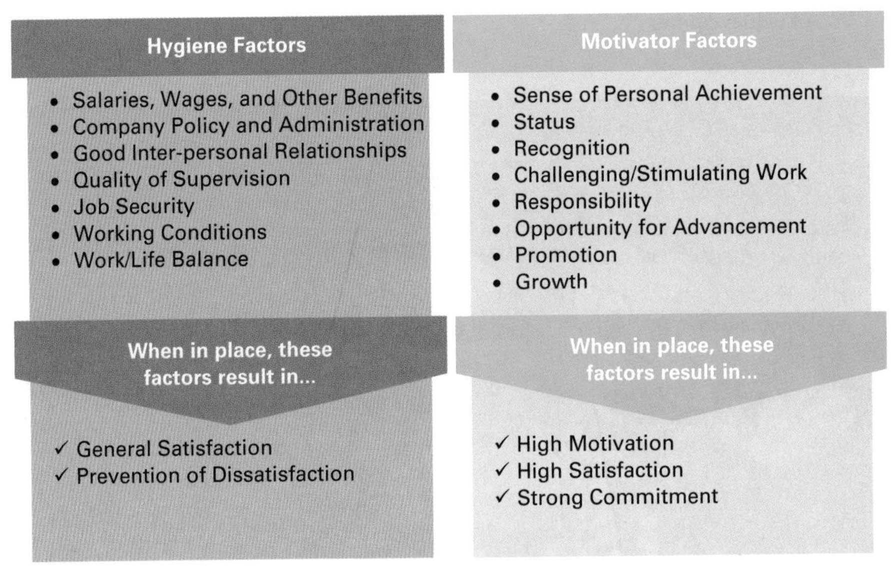

■ FIGURE 5. 3 Herzberg's Two-Factor Theory

SOURCE: Figure created based on Herzberg, F., B. Mausner, and B. Snyderman. *The Motivation to Work* (2nd ed.) (Oxford: Wiley, 1959); Herzberg, Frederick, "One More Time: How Do You Motivate Employees?" *Harvard Business Review* 81, no. 1 (January 2003): 87–96.

ERG theory: Theory that suggests that people are motivated by three categories of needs arranged in the form of a hierarchy

Two-factor theory (*motivation-hygiene theory* or *dual theory*): The impact of motivational influences on job satisfaction

Hygiene factors: Sources of job satisfaction such as salary, status, and security

Motivators: Sources of job satisfaction such as achievement, recognition, and responsibility

According to Herzberg, effective motivators lead to a highly stimulated, motivated workforce, whereas in the absence of motivators, employees can become ambivalent or apathetic toward their roles. Over the years, Herzberg's two-factor theory has received a number of criticisms for being too narrow in scope. Some theorists have questioned Herzberg's assumption that satisfied employees are more productive. Others have argued that what motivates one person might not necessarily motivate another. The theory has also been criticized for not accounting for individual differences, meaning that some individuals may respond differently to hygiene or motivator factors.[10]

Despite these criticisms, Herzberg's two-factor theory has been an important influence on the motivational techniques employed by managers with their workforce in the areas of job security, job enrichment, and job satisfaction.[11]

McClelland's Acquired Needs Theory

Developed by psychological theorist David McClelland, **acquired needs theory** holds that our needs are shaped over time and formed by our experiences and cultural background. McClelland classified needs into three main categories: need for achievement, need for affiliation, and need for power.[12] Although McClelland believed that in each of us one of these needs is the dominant motivator, he also believed that all three, in particular the need for achievement, can be learned through training.

- **Need for achievement** is the desire to excel. People who are achievement oriented are generally positive in nature, tend to set their own goals, thrive on feedback, and take ownership of their work. High achievers do well in challenging environments but may lose motivation in routine roles. Walt Disney is a good example of a person with a desire to excel. While he lost his first character Oswald the Lucky Rabbit to distributors who stole the rights, his high need for achievement, in part, led him to follow his own path inventing subsequent characters such as Mickey Mouse, creating the first full-length animated motion picture, *Snow White and the Seven Dwarfs,* and creating Disneyland, the first theme park—a remarkable series of achievements.[13]

Acquired needs theory: Theory that suggests three main categories of needs: need for achievement, need for affiliation, and need for power

Need for achievement: Need to perform well against a standard of excellence

© iStockphoto.com/Bastiaan Slabbers

Before creating his empire, Walt Disney lost his first character, Oswald the Lucky Rabbit, to distributors. His high need for achievement drove him to go on to create some of the most recognized characters in the world.

- **Need for affiliation** is the desire to belong to a group and to be liked. Generally, people who possess this need as a dominant motivator like to maintain the status quo; they tend not to make good managers because they don't like to make unpopular decisions or give orders for fear of falling out of favor with their colleagues. Without daily contact with others, people with strong affiliation needs might lose motivation, which may lead to job dissatisfaction.
- **Need for power** is the desire to control and influence the behavior of others. There are two types of power. *Institutional power* is the power an individual exerts for the good of the organization and its employees, and *personal power* is power focused on controlling and manipulating others for personal gain. Dictators Kim Jong-un, Fidel Castro, and Adolf Hitler are examples of leaders who used their power to coerce and control their followers.

Vandrad at the German language Wikipedia

Fidel Castro's need for personal power drove him to control his followers and become one of the most notorious dictators in the world.

Each of the content theorists—Maslow, Alderfer, Herzberg, and McClelland—focused on our human needs and what motivates us to satisfy those needs (Figure 5.4). Yet, in many organizations, money is used as a prime motivator for employees.

Money as a Motivator

Money is one of the primary mechanisms managers use for motivating people in the workplace. But how does money fit in with the content theories? Generally, money sits with lower-level needs: safety and physiological for Maslow's hierarchy of needs, existence for Alderfer's ERG theory, and hygiene factors for Hertzberg's two-factor theory. Money provides us with food, housing, clothing, and all the necessities of life. If money is so important, why did the theorists not consider it a high-level need?

Need for affiliation: Need to be liked and to stay on good terms with most other people

Need for power: Desire to influence people and events

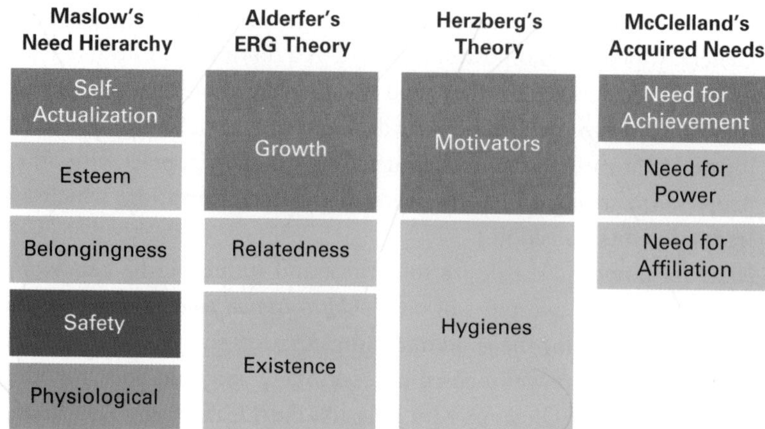

■ FIGURE 5.4 Comparison of the Four Content Theories of Motivation

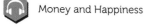

Money and Happiness

Most people who live in modern societies and work in contemporary organizations receive a pay check that affords them a certain standard of living. This means their lower-level needs are already being satisfied. Instead, people focus on higher-level needs such as belongingness, esteem, self-actualization according to Maslow, relatedness and growth for Alderfer, and Hertzberg's motivator factors. Money is not as important here according to these theorists. As the Beatles said, "I don't care too much for money, 'cause money can't buy me love."

Money can sometimes become a status symbol or an indication of success, and some people are paid far more than others. For example, CEO of Discovery Communications

MONEY AS A MOTIVATOR

Examining the Evidence

Few behavioral researchers would argue that money has no motivational effect on employees. Indeed, a number of studies suggest that financial incentives can increase certain types of work performance.* However, a group of researchers conducted a series of experiments in which subjects completed basic tasks under different financial reward conditions ranging from relatively small to moderate to very large and across different types of tasks involving motor skills, creativity, and memory respectively. The researchers concluded that "one cannot assume that introducing or raising incentives will always improve performance."^ In short, these findings suggest that financial incentives—especially very large ones—could increase task motivation to a higher than optimal level, leading to "choking" under pressure and reduced performance. In contrast, small-to-moderate financial inducements may work best, especially when used to motivate the performance of noncognitive tasks that don't require employees to learn or develop specialized skills or work collaboratively with others. These researchers conclude that "perhaps there is good reason why so many workers continue to be paid on a straight salary basis."

Critical-Thinking Questions

1. **Many companies offer large financial incentives for tasks that require creativity, problem solving, and memory. Based on the research findings described here, what is a possible limitation to this approach?**
2. **How can managers most effectively use nonfinancial incentives to increase employee performance?**

*Rynes, Sara I., Barry Gerhart, and Laura Parks. "Personnel Psychology: Performance Evaluation and Pay for Performance." *Annual Review of Psychology* 56, no. 1 (February 2005): 571–600.

^Ariely, Dan, Uri Gneezy, George Loewenstein, and Nina Mazar. "Large Stakes and Big Mistakes." *REVIEW OF ECONOMIC STUDIES* 76, NO. 2 (APRIL 2009): 451–469.

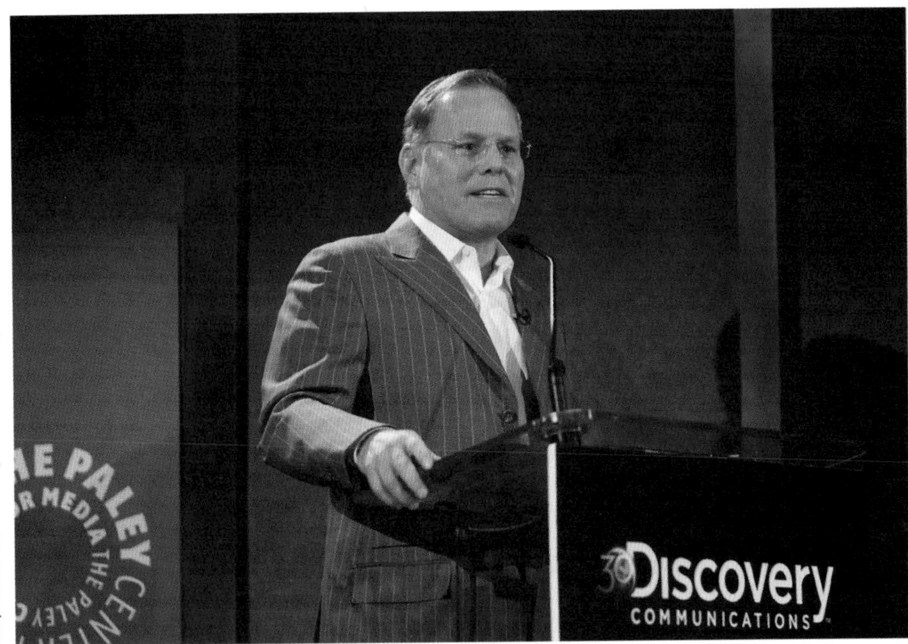

Amy Sussman/AP Images for Discovery Communications

David Zaslav of Discovery Communications was the highest paid CEO in the US in 2014, but this does not mean that he was the most effective or successful.

David Zaslav earned $150 million in 2014, making him the highest-paid CEO in the United States.[14] However, appealing as it might be to earn millions, money generally does not relate directly to the needs that people are trying to satisfy in the workplace. This is not to say that money is unimportant, but rather that it may not be the most important or most effective motivator. For example, promising an employee a 10 cent per hour raise or a $300 year-end bonus may not necessarily increase motivation. Instead, these theories suggest, people are motivated by their affiliation with others and the opportunity to achieve, grow, and be recognized for their accomplishments.

Drew Greenblatt, president of Marlin Steel, a US-based builder of steel wire baskets and sheet metal material-handling containers, uses a combination of lower-level and higher-level needs to motivate his workforce. An advocate of cross-training, Greenblatt ensures his employees undergo rigorous training courses in order to learn the skills necessary to carry out a variety of tasks and operate multiple machines. Each employee is rewarded with a bonus for every additional skill he or she acquires. Greenblatt believes his employees are motivated not only by the cash incentive but also by the opportunity to acquire new skills that increase their productivity and commitment.[15]

Marlin Steel is a large company, but what about smaller companies that cannot afford to pay cash bonuses or give monetary rewards, especially in difficult economic times? How do they motivate their employees? Universal Information Services, a news-media analysis company in Nebraska, offers “Free Beer Fridays” as a way of rewarding their employees for their hard work during the week; they also offer free sodas. The San Francisco software maker 15Five offers telecommuting as a motivator. 15Five employees can work remotely anywhere in the world. VoIP Supply, which sells voice-over Internet protocol equipment, allows pets in the office from time to time.[16] These small companies have managed to create a committed and loyal workforce through their application of innovative motivators in lieu of high salaries and cash bonuses.

THINKING CRITICALLY

1. Write a brief biography that assumes your development over time is following Maslow’s hierarchy of needs precisely. To what extent does this version of your life story seem accurate? What problems and distortions do you perceive from this biography? **[Analyze/Evaluate]**

2. Revise your biography according to Alderfer's ERG theory so that it reflects the assumptions and categories (existence needs, relatedness needs, growth needs) of that theory instead. To what extent is this version of your life story more or less accurate than the version based on Maslow's hierarchy of needs? What aspects of your life are difficult to address when the main means of shaping/describing your life is based on your motivation to have particular needs met? **[Analyze/Evaluate]**
3. Based on your understanding of Herzberg's two-factor theory of job satisfaction, what types of incentives or employee programs are most likely to reduce job dissatisfaction? What types of incentives or employee programs are most likely to increase job satisfaction? **[Understand/Apply]**
4. Compare McClelland's acquired needs theory and its emphasis on needs being shaped by experience and cultural background over time to Maslow's hierarchy of needs and ERG theory. Of these three theories, which do you think provides the most useful and realistic explanation for human development and motivation? Why? **[Analyze/Evaluate]**
5. Assume that you are the CEO of a midsize company that needs to increase employee retention and productivity. Based on the theories in this section and the text's discussion of money as a motivator, what sorts of payment/bonus strategies and benefits would you focus on providing or improving? Why? **[Apply/Analyze]**

EQUITY THEORY

5.3 Examine equity theory in the context of organizational justice and distinguish among the predictable outcomes of perceived inequity

But what happens when managers have done very little to motivate employees? In the following narrative we meet a group of dissatisfied restaurant employees whose motivation has been affected by their perception of their roles and rewards within the organization.

Introducing the Case of Katie O'Donnell: Motivating Staff at the Waterfront Grill

The Waterfront Grill is a restaurant owned by manager Kamal Williams and located in Ithaca, in upstate New York. The restaurant is among the first in the state to cater to the craze for bubble tea (a Taiwanese milk- or fruit-based tea with tapioca) that has swept the country. Boasting a dedicated bubble tea bar staffed with bubble tea experts, the Waterfront Grill is a unique restaurant in town.

Katie O'Donnell has been a server at the restaurant for the past two years, working three evening shifts during the week and full days on weekends. Server turnover has been high at the Waterfront Grill. Katie, one of the most experienced servers, has just accepted the job of assistant manager. She sees her promotion as an opportunity to identify and solve a number of problems she has experienced at the restaurant during the past two years.

Katie is frustrated by the lack of motivation and the conflicts among the staff in the restaurant, many of whom are students like herself. There are major divisions among the hostesses, servers, food runners, bar staff, and cooks regarding monetary rewards. She hopes her new position as assistant manager will give her the authority to address some of the issues.

Katie is only two weeks in to her role as assistant manager when she faces her first major challenge. One of the servers, Diego, takes her aside after a late shift and tells her he is thinking about quitting. Katie is frustrated. Turnover is a huge problem at the Waterfront Grill, and she knows that staff is expensive to replace because of advertising and training costs. Diego is a hard-working server and has been at the restaurant full time for almost a year. Katie hopes she can find some way to persuade him to stay. Because it's near closing time and the restaurant is almost empty, Katie sits down with Diego in a corner booth to discuss the situation.

"Diego, you're one of the best servers on staff; we don't want to lose you," Katie begins.

"Look Katie, I'm just not getting enough tips anymore," Diego says. "It's not worth working this hard for so little compensation."

Katie is puzzled. The servers' base pay is the lowest in the restaurant, but the tips servers earn usually ensure them high overall compensation. She asks Diego why he is unhappy with his tips.

"A couple of the servers, Kim and Lucia, have agreed to share their tips with the hostesses if they give them the best tables and keep their sections filled before anyone else's. They boast about how much they make and it's just not fair. My section isn't being seated as quickly and my tables aren't turning over as quickly as Kim and Lucia's, so I'm collecting fewer tips."

"Is that the reason you want to quit?"

"Partly, but that's not all of it. The Waterfront Grill is not a fun place to work—most of the staff has a bad attitude. One of the runners, Evan, approached me the other day and asked me if I'd share my tips with him. I asked him, 'Why would I do that? It's not my fault runners don't get tips.' Since then he's been bussing my tables in my section slowly and not very well, because he knows if my tables aren't ready, the hostesses will seat customers in another section instead."

Katie can relate to everything Diego is saying, and she agrees that many of the employees have an indifferent attitude that could certainly have a negative impact on the customers. In addition, she is aware of the rift among the servers, the runners, and the hostesses. It's clear that the hostesses and food runners are envious of the servers' tips.

Although she wasn't aware of it when she was a server, she isn't surprised that some of the other servers have struck an arrangement with the hostesses. Katie believes the compensation structure in the restaurant is partly to blame for the conflict and jealousy between the staff. After listening to Diego's complaints, Katie is ready to empathize with him, but quickly realizes Diego isn't finished yet.

"And don't get me started on the kitchen staff. They get upset when the restaurant is full because they have to work harder for no extra pay, and then they take it out on us because we make more tips on a busy night. When they screw up a food order, which happens a lot, or they take too long getting the food ready, the customers complain, and guess whose tip is affected yet again? That's right—mine!" Diego crosses his arms angrily.

"You've told me about what's going on with the other servers, the hostesses, the kitchen staff. . . . What about the bubble tea bar staff?" Katie asks.

Diego leans forward. "The bubble tea bar staff has always been a pretty decent group, but they're miserable these days because the bar has become quieter over the last few months—they aren't getting good tips either. In fact, the other day one of the bar staff, Yuan, was telling me he's looking for a new job."

Katie knew many of the staff were dissatisfied but had hoped her new position would give her a chance to change things before people started quitting. Yuan is the most efficient in the group, yet she can't blame him for looking for a new job. Despite the initial craze for bubble tea, bar bills have fallen by 20 percent over the past six months. Because bubble tea sells for $7 a serving, this decline has affected not just the bar staff's tips but the overall profitability of the business.

Diego interrupts her train of thought and says, "Look, Katie, the bottom line is I don't like the way things are being run around here. Management should be paying us fairly and making sure there are no unfair practices going on between the staff members."

Katie nods and replies, "Diego, have you spoken to Kamal about these issues? I think that as manager and owner of the Waterfront Grill, he would really like to know what's going on."

Diego shakes his head, "I liked Kamal when he hired me, but he has barely looked my way since I started. I decided to talk to you since I know you and Kamal has promoted you. You're getting a business degree so you must have some thoughts about how to fix this mess."

Katie promises to make an appointment with Kamal to discuss the challenges facing the restaurant. But first she needs to persuade Diego not to leave the restaurant. After more discussion he agrees to stay on for another six weeks on the provision that Katie will initiate changes that improve the working conditions in the restaurant.

As soon as Diego leaves, Katie writes down notes about their conversation in preparation for her meeting with Kamal. She needs to work out some solutions to the problems Diego outlined before the rest of the workforce threatens to quit.

In this narrative, one of the main reasons Diego wants to quit his job is that he doesn't feel he is being treated fairly. The concept of **equity theory**, introduced by psychologist J. Stacey Adams, holds that motivation is based on our perception of how fairly we are being treated in comparison with others.[17] According to this theory, our perception of what is fair depends on the ratio O/I where O equals outcomes like the recognition, pay, and status we enjoy and I equals inputs like our effort, experience, and ability (Figure 5.5).

People tend to compare their own perceived O/I ratio to their perceptions of the O/1 ratio of *referent others,* or people whose situation is comparable to their own. As long as the ratios are similar there is no problem, but someone who perceives the other person's ratio as greater than his or her own will feel an inequity. For example, Diego believes he is under-rewarded because the restaurant hostesses are giving two other servers preferential treatment and he is making less tips as a result. People adopt several behaviors in the face of such **perceived inequity**. Let's explore how Diego and the restaurant staff have responded to the perceived inequity at the Waterfront Grill:

- Change inputs

People may increase or decrease their inputs depending on the situation. For example, because Diego perceives that others are getting more tips than he is through unfair means, he has decided it isn't worth continuing to work hard and he feels unmotivated and is considering quitting to find a different job.

Equity theory: Theory that holds that motivation is based on our perception of fairness in comparison with others

Perceived inequity: The sense of feeling under-rewarded or over-rewarded in comparison with others

Equity theory says we perceive the fairness of rewards as a ratio of input to outcome and compare our ratio to other people's.

Person		**Referent Other**
$\frac{\text{Outcomes}}{\text{Inputs}}$	=	$\frac{\text{Outcomes}}{\text{Inputs}}$

■ FIGURE 5.5 Equity Theory

- Attempt to change outcomes

Employees might try to change the outcomes to restore O/I balance. For example, Katie decides to approach her manager to work out a solution to the problems highlighted by Diego.

- Carry out cognitive reevaluation

Workers may change their perspective on the other person. If Diego spoke with the servers who were sharing tips with hostesses and discovered that their tips had not increased despite their arrangement, he would likely be less dissatisfied (at least initially) with his own tips.

- Attempt to get to change inputs or outcomes

Employees might try and convince others to reduce or give up other outcomes. For example, one of the runners asks Diego for a cut of Diego's tips, which will reduce Diego's outcomes but increase his own. Alternatively, the kitchen staff might try to similarly force servers to provide them with a cut of their tips in order to provide timely, accurate food orders.

- Pick another "Other"

Employees might compare themselves to different coworkers to perceive a more equitable situation. For example, if Diego stopped comparing himself to the other servers in the restaurant and instead compared his tips to the bubble tea bar staff, he might become more satisfied with the tips he was earning as a result.

- Leave the field

When employees feel strongly enough about the inequity, they will quit their jobs. As Katie recognizes, organizational turnover can cost a company significant amounts of money. Diego is on the verge of quitting because he feels a high level of inequity at the Waterfront Grill.

Organizational Justice

Organizational Justice

Equity theory includes the concept of **organizational justice**, which focuses on what people perceive as fairness in workplace practices.[18] There are two main kinds of organizational justice: distributive and procedural.

Distributive justice is the degree to which people perceive outcomes to be fairly allocated. For example, employees doing the same job as others expect to be compensated equally. When equal work does not produce equal outcomes, or when one employee is paid more or less than another for doing the same job, then there is a lack of distributive justice.

In the Waterfront Grill scenario, Diego is unhappy that two servers have worked out an unofficial arrangement with the hostesses that reduces his income and is upset that his refusal to share tips with Evan, a runner, is further reducing his income since Evan is purposefully working less hard to bus Diego's tables. Diego perceives a lack of distributive justice and believes the restaurant's management should provide a solution to these issues.

Procedural justice is the degree to which people perceive the implementation of company policies and procedures to be fair. For example, most restaurants have a strict policy regarding tardiness and absenteeism. Those who are repeatedly late for work or who miss work without covering their shift will eventually lose their jobs. If such a policy applies to all staff at every level, then employees will be more likely to accept it as fair. If some workers are exempt, then employees are unlikely to believe they are being treated equally.[19]

Organizational justice: The perception of fairness in workplace practices

Distributive justice: The degree to which people think outcomes are fair

Procedural justice: The degree to which people perceive the implementation of company policies and procedures to be fair

In our narrative, Diego is upset by the ways that employees are undermining the compensation plan distributed by the Waterfront Grill, as well as the lack of managerial oversight by the owner and manager, Kamal.

THINKING CRITICALLY

1. Compare the input to outcome ratios of Katie, Diego, and Evan (the runner who approached Diego about a portion of his tips) and discuss how each character's perception of the fairness of his or her job rewards is affecting their job performance. **[Understand/Apply]**
2. Based on the compensation situation at Waterfront Grill and the employee problems and perceived inequities Diego describes to Katie, discuss the reasons why Kamal may want to listen carefully to Katie's proposals to make changes at the restaurant. What are the likely long-term outcomes of the allocation of tips to just the servers and of the drop in bubble tea orders? What impact are the inequities employees perceive already having on customers? **[Analyze/Evaluate]**
3. To what extent are perceptions of procedural justice versus distributive justice a matter of perception? Do you think the allocation of tips at Waterfront Grill be considered BOTH a matter of distributive and procedural justice? Why or why not? **[Analyze]**

GOAL-SETTING THEORY

5.4 Apply goal-setting theory in organizational contexts

Setting Goals

In the following section of the narrative, we continue to follow Katie's experiences as assistant manager as she attempts to develop solutions to the problems at the Waterfront Grill.

The more Katie thinks about the difficulties at the Waterfront Grill, the more she believes the staff should be given goals to achieve. She thinks this will increase motivation and encourage employees to work as a team. That evening, she spends a couple of hours thinking about what realistic goals for the staff would look like.

Goal-setting theory, developed by Edwin Locke and Gary Latham, suggests that human performance is directed by conscious goals and intentions.[20] Studies of the effects of goal setting in the workplace showed that employees are motivated by clear goals accompanied by appropriate feedback.[21]

Goals can have both direct and indirect effects. *Direct effects* motivate and energize us, helping to achieve objectives, and *indirect* effects encourage us to use cognitive skills such as planning and strategizing to attain goals. For example, the direct effect of buying a house involves the ownership of the house, but it also has the indirect effect of working out how to pay the mortgage.

Katie believes the employees at the Waterfront Grill might be more satisfied and encouraged to work as a team if they were given a pay increase, but revenue is down because of declining bubble tea sales and the restaurant can't afford to pay higher wages right now. Katie concludes she needs to find a way for the staff to earn more tips and to generate additional income for the restaurant at the same time. If the servers and bubble tea staff are all trained to promote and sell additional items at the Waterfront Grill, she reasons, everyone will benefit, and if servers receive a percentage of all restaurant checks that include bubble tea, they'll be motivated to sell more. She also believes that if she sets goals for the servers and bar staff to sell a certain amount of drinks per shift, they will become more motivated and energized. To effectively set goals for the restaurant staff, Katie considers several characteristics of goals.

Goal-setting theory: Theory that suggests that human performance is directed by conscious goals and intentions

Specific Goals

Research has shown that people respond more to clear, well-defined goals and produce better results than vague, or "Do Your Best," goals.[22] Managers can set specific goals by making them clear and easy to understand, ensure they are challenging but attainable, make them measurable, and set them within a distinct time frame. Katie devises specific goals for the servers to sell 50 cups of bubble tea per shift.

Difficult Goals

Similarly, researchers found that goals set at a high but not unreasonable level of difficulty produce better results than less challenging or easier goals.[23] Katie realizes the servers may feel apprehensive about trying to sell such a large number of bubble tea in the space of a shift, but she believes the challenge will motivate them into achieving the goal.

Goal Acceptance and Commitment

In general, employees who accept and commit to goals set by or developed in participation with their managers have higher levels of performance and are more motivated to achieve the objectives.[24] As soon as Katie gets the go-ahead from Kamal, she is going to have a chat with the servers to ensure their acceptance and commitment to the goal.

Feedback

Goals that are accompanied by regular feedback are more likely to motivate employees.[25] Katie plans to develop a spreadsheet to record the amount of bubble tea sales per individual server per shift so she can monitor the progress of each member of staff and provide feedback after every shift.

Finally, Katie reviews the concept that goals are often arranged in hierarchies in order to assess which ones take priority.[26] For example, **behavioral goals**, which are short-term goals that provide employees with frequent feedback about their performance, are positioned further up the hierarchy than **performance goals**, which are long-term goals set into the future. From her experience as a server, Katie knows that setting goals too far into the future can be demotivating for employees. Katie is satisfied that the behavioral goals she has set will motivate the servers to increase their income and help reach the long-term goals of achieving overall profit for the restaurant.

Katie spends the rest of the evening drafting an email about her proposal to change the tipping structure at the restaurant.

THINKING CRITICALLY

1. Assess Katie's focus on setting goals related to sales of bubble tea. What problems among the staff is this focus likely to address? What business problems for the restaurant is this approach likely to address? **[Analyze/Evaluate]**

2. The kitchen staff's dissatisfaction is not being addressed by this approach. Do you think this will create an obstacle in Katie's efforts to improve staff morale and productivity at Waterfront Grill? Why or why not? **[Analyze/Evaluate]**

3. Pretend that you are Katie and devise a set of goals to improve customer satisfaction at Waterfront Grill. What goals would you introduce? How would your goals differ from group to group? What would be the direct effects on the staff of seeking to improve customer satisfaction? What would be the indirect effects on the staff? **[Evaluate/Create]**

Behavioral goals (proximal goals): Short-term goals

Performance goals (distal): Long-term goals set into the future

EXPECTANCY THEORY

5.5 Describe the expectancy theory of motivation and its practical implications

When Katie knocks on Kamal's office door the following morning, she is nervous but enthusiastic. This is her first initiative as assistant manager and she hopes Kamal agrees to give her ideas a try.

Kamal greets Katie and invites her to sit down. She shares her discussion with Diego and what she has learned about the different problems among staff that exist in the restaurant. She finishes by proposing that the servers be trained to increase bubble tea sales and receive a percentage of the additional sales. Kamal listens carefully and then sits back in his chair.

"Katie, part of the reason I appointed you as assistant manager is that I need someone on the floor the staff can relate to. They don't always come to me with their problems and I'm not always available to hear them, so I'm glad Diego feels he can confide in you."

Katie smiles. "This is a good start," she thinks.

Kamal continues, "I think your goal-setting strategy to increase bubble tea revenue sales makes sense. I'm going to give it a trial run. Let's set a goal to increase bubble tea sales by 15 percent using the methods you have proposed to me. I'm giving you six weeks to achieve that goal."

Katie is delighted. Kamal has given her an opportunity to try out her goal-setting technique with the servers and she can't wait to get started. But then she realizes she has been focusing only on the servers.

"What about the rest of the staff?" she asks. "From what I have been told, it's not just the servers who are unhappy with their pay. The kitchen staff, the runners, the hostesses, the bubble tea bar staff . . . everyone is disappointed with their pay."

"If revenue increases, then I'm happy to address the pay issues experienced by the rest of the staff. But at the moment profits are down, and I can't afford to increase everyone's base pay right now," Kamal replies.

Katie understands—she needs to make her plan work if things are going to change.

That afternoon she gathers the four servers—Kim, Theo, Diego, and Lucia—in the staff room to present the new goals. Kim and Lucia, college students who have been working at the Waterfront Grill part time for the past six months, are efficient workers but aren't connecting with their customers. They are the servers who struck a deal with the hostesses to share their tips provided the hostesses gave them preferential treatment. Katie believes that setting a team goal the servers must achieve will discourage this practice since having the hostesses treat any one server preferentially is likely to cut down on number of tables seated during a shift. Theo, also a college student, is Katie's replacement; he has been at the restaurant for only two weeks and is still learning the ropes.

In preparation for the meeting, Katie spent some time researching Vroom's **Expectancy theory**, which holds that people will choose certain behaviors over others with the expectation of a certain outcome.[27] The theory describes motivation as a function of an individual's beliefs concerning effort-to-performance relationships (expectancy), work–outcome relationships (instrumentality), and the desirability of various work outcomes (valence).

Expectancy theory: Theory that holds that people will choose certain behaviors over others with the expectation of a certain outcome

Expectancy: The probability that the amount of work effort invested by an individual will result in a high level of performance

Expectancy is the probability that the amount of work effort invested by an individual will result in a high level of performance. In other words, it could be phrased as "What's the probability that, if I work very hard, I'll be able to do a good job?" It is measured in a range from zero to +1. If someone believes strong effort will not result in a higher performance level, his or her expectancy is zero; however, if the person believes a good effort *will* lead to high performance, expectancy is +1. For example, for Katie's plan to succeed, the servers need to expect that their hard work will result in an increase in bubble tea sales.

Instrumentality is the probability that good performance will lead to various work outcomes. Another way of saying this is "What's the probability that, if I do a good job, that there will be some kind of outcome in it for me?" It can range from −1 to +1. An instrumentality of +1 would apply to people who believe that their performance would make an outcome likely, whereas people who think their performance will not result in outcomes would have an instrumentality of −1. For example, Katie needs to reassure the servers that meeting their bubble tea sales targets will result in their receiving a percentage of sales for each ticket.

Expectancy Theory and Analytics

Valence is the value individuals place on work outcomes. Phrased a different way, "Is the outcome I get of any value to me?" Valences range from −1 to +1 and are positive or negative depending on the nature of the outcome. For example, Katie hopes the servers will value the opportunity to make more money and see the advantages of working closely as a team. The theory is summarized in Figure 5.6.[28]

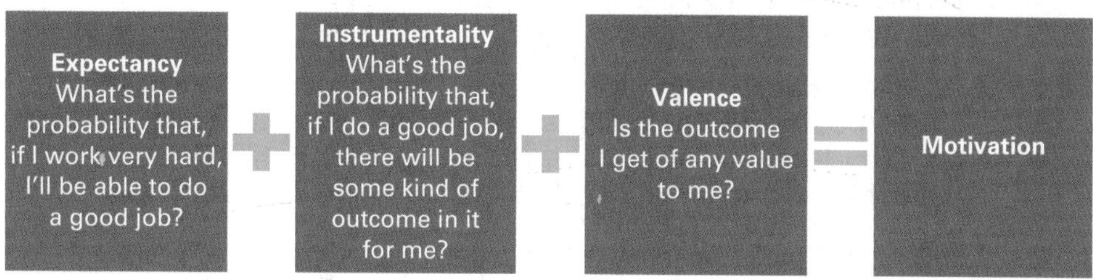

■ FIGURE 5.6 Expectancy Theory

During the meeting, Katie does her best to convince the servers that their increased efforts will lead to higher performance and outcomes that will eventually result in rewards. She also makes the point that this initiative is not just about making more money, but also about everyone pulling together to make the restaurant a success. When she is finished, Diego is the first to speak.

"I think trying to sell 50 bubble tea per shift is going to be difficult, but I think it can be done," he says. The other servers murmur in agreement.

"What if we don't meet the target?" Theo asks. "I'm new here and I'm not too sure if I'll be able to increase my sales when I'm just learning the menu and how to do the job."

"Theo, you've picked up things really quickly," Katie says, "and I have no doubt you'll meet the goals. If you feel you're struggling in any way, you can talk to me any time. In fact, I'll be providing each of you with feedback after every shift for the next six weeks, so you'll have an opportunity to discuss any concerns you have. I'll be there for you every step of the way."

Theo thanks her and tells her he will do his best. Then Kim speaks up.

"Say we reach our sales targets and meet our quotas, which I do think is achievable. We make more money for the restaurant, and we each receive an additional percentage of those sales on top of the tips we already earn." Katie nods and gestures for her to continue. "The bubble tea bar staff take 30 percent of our tips for tables that purchase bubble tea. So where is the incentive for us to sell more bubble tea when most of the tip goes to the bubble tea bar?"

Lucia joins in. "Kim's right. There's no point in us working like crazy when we won't see much of a reward!"

Katie feels the color drain from her face. She is at a loss for words. In her zeal to apply goal setting for the servers she has completely forgotten about the 30 percent tip-out to the bubble tea bar staff. Of course the servers have no incentive to strive for this goal because they don't think they will get the rewards. In expectancy theory terms, the link between effort and performance is strong—the servers believe if they put the effort in they can reach the bubble tea goal—but the link between performance and reward is

Instrumentality: The probability that good performance will lead to various work outcomes.

Valence: The value individuals place on work outcomes

weak. The servers don't believe they will get the rewards; in fact, adding two bubble tea drinks to a ticket will actually *reduce* the servers' total tip because of the 30 percent tip-out to the bartenders. Katie is mortified at her oversight—it's even more embarrassing because she has spent two years as a server herself—she should know how the tips are distributed!

She gathers herself and addresses the group. "Team, I've made a mistake. Kim and Lucia, you're both absolutely right. I'm going to have to revise my plan. Before I do this, would any of you like to contribute your own ideas regarding a new, more achievable goal?"

The servers are silent, and Katie promises them a solution by the end of the week.

In this chapter, we have explored the different concepts and theories associated with motivation. Motivating employees can be complex and depends on a number of factors such as knowing what drives employees to achieve goals. In the next chapter, we further analyze the application of these motivational theories and how they affect employees.

THINKING CRITICALLY

1. Assess Katie's meeting with Kamal. Should she have worked harder to come up with additional ideas to address all staff needs? How realistic is it to expect the servers to increase revenue by themselves for the good of the overall restaurant and restaurant staff? Defend your answers. **[Analyze/Evaluate]**

2. Describe Katie's proposal to the servers and their response to it in terms of expectancy theory. How does her proposal stack up in terms of expectancy, instrumentality, and valence? What changes to her approach would you suggest given the valence issue Kim points out? **[Analyze/Evaluate/Create]**

3. Revisit the set of customer satisfaction goals you created in the last "Thinking Critically" section. Evaluate the utility of your goals in relation to expectancy theory? **[Apply/Analyze/Evaluate]**

IN REVIEW

Learning Objectives

5.1 Explain the basic motivation process

Motivation is a process by which behavior is *energized*, meaning how hard we work; *directed*, meaning what we choose to work at; and *maintained* meaning how long we intend to work for to achieve objectives. **Content theories** of motivation explain why people have different needs at different times and how these needs motivate behavior. Maslow's hierarchy of needs, Alderfer's ERG theory, McClelland's need theory, and Herzberg's two-factor theory are all examples of content theories. **Process theories** describe the cognitive processes through which needs are translated into behavior. Examples of process theories include equity theory, expectancy theory, and goal-setting theory.

5.2 Compare the various needs theories of motivation

Maslow's hierarchy of needs identifies five levels of individual needs, with physiological needs at the bottom of the hierarchy and self-actualization needs at the top. **ERG theory** suggests that people are motivated by three categories of needs—existence, relatedness, and growth needs— that can be satisfied in any order or at the same time depending on the circumstances. **Herzberg's two-factor theory** proposes that the first step to employee satisfaction is to eliminate poor *hygiene factors*. Managers then need to use *motivators* such as achievement, recognition, and responsibility to build job satisfaction. **McClelland's acquired needs theory** suggests three main categories of needs: need for achievement, need for affiliation, and need for power. We all have a dominant motivator, and each of the motivators, in particular achievement, can be learned.

5.3 Examine equity theory in the context of organizational justice and distinguish among the predictable outcomes of perceived inequity

The concept of **equity theory,** introduced by psychologist J. Stacey Adams, holds that motivation is based on our perception of how fairly we are being treated in comparison with others. According to this theory, our perception of what is fair depends on the ratio O/I where O = their outcomes like the recognition, pay, and status we enjoy and I = inputs like our effort, experience, and ability.

Organizational justice describes how people perceive fairness in workplace practices. **Distributive justice** is the degree to which people perceive outcomes to be fairly allocated. **Procedural justice** is the degree to which people perceive the implementation of company policies and procedures to be fair.

5.4 Apply goal-setting theory in organizational contexts

Goal-setting theory suggests that human performance is directed by conscious goals and intentions. Effective goals are specific, difficult, accepted by employees, and accompanied by regular feedback.

5.5 Describe the expectancy theory of motivation and its practical implications

Vroom's **Expectancy Theory** holds that people will choose certain behaviors over others with the expectation of a certain outcome. The theory describes motivation as a function of an individual's beliefs concerning effort-to-performance relationships (expectancy), work–outcome relationships (instrumentality), and the desirability of various work outcomes (valence).

KEY TERMS

THINKING CRITICALLY ABOUT THE CASE OF KATIE O'DONNELL

Equity and Employee Motivation at Waterfront Grill

Put yourself in Katie O'Donnell's position as the new assistant manager at Waterfront Grill and consider the five critical-thinking steps in relation to workplace equity and motivation.

OBSERVE

What inequities does each group of workers (servers, hostesses, runners, kitchen staff, bubble tea bar staff) perceive at Waterfront Grill? To what extent are the perceptions of each group accurate or inaccurate in your opinion? Does the accuracy of each group's perception matter from a managerial standpoint? Why or why not?

INTERPRET

Based on the inequities perceived by each group, what sorts of conflicts do you expect to see at the restaurant? Are these conflicts likely to increase or decrease over time? What are the likely long-term costs to the restaurant's profitability if management does not address the perceived inequities?

ANALYZE

Katie decides to set a quota on bubble tea sales to address staff problems. Assuming her initial proposal was workable, what problems among what group or groups of staff would her proposal solve? What problems among what group or groups of staff would her proposal fail to solve?

EVALUATE

Evaluate the effectiveness of Katie's decision to solve the problems at her restaurant by setting staff goals. Assuming that Katie can change her goal-setting proposal to account for the tip percentage that goes to the bubble tea bar staff, how successful do you believe her effort will be in reducing perceived inequities among all groups of staff?

EXPLAIN

If you were Katie, what steps would you take to solve the perceptions of inequity and dissatisfaction at Waterfront Grill?

EXERCISE 5.1: HOW SHOULD MERIT RAISES BE ALLOCATED?

Small State University is located in the eastern part of the United States and has an enrollment of about 8,000 students. The College of Business has 40 full-time faculty members and over 30 part-time faculty.

The College is divided into five departments: Management, Marketing, Finance and Accounting, Decision Sciences, and Information Technology. Profiles of the Management Department faculty members are presented in Table 1. Management faculty is evaluated each year based on three primary criteria: Teaching, Research, and Service. Teaching performance is based on student course evaluations over a two-year period. Service to the university, college, profession, and community is also based on accomplishments over a two-year period. Research is based on the number of journal articles published over a three-year period. Teaching and research are considered more important than service to the university. In judging faculty performance, the department chair evaluates each professor in terms of four standards: far exceeds standards, exceeds standards, meets standards, and fails to meet standards. The results of this year's evaluations are shown in Table 2.

This year the state has agreed to give raises to state employees totaling 3%, or $17,400 to the management department. Your task as department chair is to divide the $17,400 among the faculty members. Keep in mind that these raises will likely set a precedent for future years and that the professors will view the raises as a signal for what behavior is valued and what is not.

Prof. Housman:
55 years old; 25 years with the university; teaches Principles of Management mass sections; teaches over 400 students per year; has written over 40 articles and given over 30 presentations since joining the College; wants a good raise to catch up with others.
Prof. Jones:
49 years old; 10 years with the university; teaches Human Resource Management and Organizational Behavior; stepped down as Department Chair three years ago; teaches about 200 students a year; has written over 30 articles and 2 books since joining the College; recently received an $80,000 grant for the College from a local foundation. Wants a good raise as a reward for obtaining the grant.
Prof. Ricks:
61 years old; 6 years with University; teaches Labor Relations and Organizational Development; stepped down as Dean of the College of Business two years ago and took a $20,000 pay cut; teaches about 180 students per year; has written only 2 articles in the last 6 years due to administrative duties; very active in the community and serves on several charity boards. Wants a good raise to make up for loss of $20,000 stipend.
Prof. Matthews:
28 years old; new hire—only four months with University; teaches Employee Relations and Compensation Management; just graduated with a Ph.D.; will teach about 110 students this year. To be competitive in the job market, the College needed to pay Prof. Matthews $87,000 plus provide a reduced teaching load for two years and a $6,000 per year summer stipend; none of the other faculty received this when they were first hired or subsequently; had 2 minor publications while a doctoral student but none since joining the College. Wants a good raise to pay student loans and establish a new residence.
Prof. Karas:
32 years old; 4 years with University; teaches International Business and Honors sections of Management Principles; teaches about 150 students per year; won Teacher of the Year Award this year; published 12 articles in last 4 years; has been interviewing for a new job at other universities and may leave if good raise is not forthcoming.
Prof Franks:
64 years old; 18 years with University; teaches Principles of Management and Human Resource Management; teaches about 150 students per year; principle advisor for Management major students; has not written any articles during the last 4 years; plans on retiring within 2-3 years. Wants a good raise to enhance pension plan.

■ TABLE 5.1 Professor Profiles

Professor	Current Salary	Teaching	Research	Service
Housman	$82,000	Exceeds	Exceeds	Meets
Jones	$106,000	Exceeds	Far Exceeds	Exceeds
Ricks	$135,000	Meets	Meets	Far Exceeds
Matthews	$87,000	New Hire	New Hire	New Hire
Karas	$90,000	Far Exceeds	Exceeds	Meets
Franks	$80,000	Meets	Fails to Meet	Exceeds

■ TABLE 5.2 Department Chairs Rating of Job Performance

SOURCE: This exercise was developed by R. Bruce McAfee and Marian W. Boscia and was published in *Developments in Business Simulation and Experiential Learning*. 31 (2004): 116–119.

EXERCISE 5.2: TAKE A CARD

Objective:

Completing this exercise will help you to better *compare* the different needs theories of motivation, *examine* equity theory, *apply* goal setting theory, and *describe* the expectancy theory of motivation.

Instructions:

Your instructor will hand you a random card with the name of one of the major motivation concepts from this chapter. Take approximately 10 minutes to write a brief summary and overview of the theory, along with at least one example of how the theory can be used to improve or better understand workplace situations.

Be prepared for your instructor to call on you to present your overview and example(s) in the class.

Reflection Questions:

1. What new insights into the motivation theories did you gain from listening to your classmates´ explanations?
2. What insights did you gain from having to write an overview of the theory?
3. In what areas did you discover you did not understand a concept as well as you thought you did?

Exercise contributed by Milton R. Mayfield, Professor of Business, Texas A&M International University and Jaqueline R. Mayfield, Professor of Business, Texas A&M International University.

EXERCISE 5.3: YOUR MOTIVATION FOR SELECTING YOUR MAJOR

Objective:

This exercise will help you develop your ability to *explain* the basic motivation process, *compare* the different needs motivation theories, and *select* a needs motivation theory that is most useful in understanding situations.

Instructions:

This exercise will help you to apply chapter concepts for analyzing your decisions, and give you a foundation to make choices that are more likely to fulfill your expectations. In this exercise, you will be applying decision-making models and concepts that you have learned in this chapter to better analyze the process of selecting a major.

Step 1. Select a partner for the exercise. Ideally this person should be someone who you do not know well or work with on a regular basis. The person who has had a birthday most recently will take the role of the *teller* and the other person will be the *analyzer*. Both partners will have a chance to play each role. Introduce yourselves to each other, and tell each other your majors. (5 minutes)

Step 2. The *teller* should tell the process by which he or she chose a major. The *teller* should be as explicit as possible about this decision making process. It may be that the decision about a major was not a direct decision about a major—the person may have been following the advice of a parent or older sibling. If this is the case, then the decision to be analyzed is why the person chose to follow someone else´s advice on major selection. (10 to 15 minutes)

The *analyzer* should restate the major selection in terms of chapter concepts. Specifically, select one of the chapter needs theories, and describe the *teller's* needs in terms of the theory. Once you and the *teller* agree on the needs, describe the selection process based on *the motivation process* model.

Step 3. Switch roles and repeat step 2. (10 to 15 minutes)

Step 4. Be prepared to report your analyses to the class. (10 to 20 minutes)

Reflection Questions:

1. How conscious and rational was your major selection?
2. Does your major selection meet the needs identified in this exercise?
3. After examining your major selection choice using chapter concepts, do you see any way to improve future decision processes to better meet your needs?
4. How could you apply this process to selecting a career or new job?

Exercise contributed by Milton R. Mayfield, Professor of Business, Texas A&M International University and Jaqueline R. Mayfield, Professor of Business, Texas A&M International University.

CASE STUDY 5.1: THE WHOLE CULTURE OF WHOLE FOODS

There's a palpable delight in the atmosphere of a business whose employees are actually *happy*. Smiles come naturally. Help is offered without reservation. Prices may be a little steeper, but customers are less likely to balk. They know they are getting more for their money—an experience with their product.

Whole Foods Market is a prime example of what can happen when you create a culture that keeps employees happy, empowered, and engaged. The organic grocery super-chain booked $14 billion in fiscal year 2014 and currently has 414 stores in the United States, Canada, and the United Kingdom with another 100 stores under development. By 2017, the company wants to reach 500 locations; the ultimate goal is said to be 1,000. Yet despite its mammoth size and the notoriously staffing-challenged industry it occupies, Whole Foods has a remarkably low turnover rate—about 26 percent annually compared to the 90 percent standard. It's been named one of *Fortune* magazine's "100 Best Companies to Work For" every year since the list began in 1998; the distinction is earned, in large part, by independent surveys of its employees.

How does Whole Foods keep its 87,000+ team members motivated? Founder and co-CEO John Mackey says it doesn't. You can't really motivate someone, he told a student audience in 2011; it's better to focus on selecting the right people from the start, and create a "conscious culture" in which motivation perpetuates itself. If that sounds a bit philosophical, it is. Mackey studied philosophy during the 1970s is the author of *Conscious Capitalism*, a book whose title has since become a buzzword in business. "Conscious capitalism" refers to an "evolved" capitalism, shaped by humanistic and environmental principals. This approach is not just a reflection of Mackey's social leanings; he argues that it is smart business. Increasingly, consumers want to purchase from businesses they can feel good about. And Whole Foods' principles are aligned with the desire of the millennial workforce to make a difference in the world; they help Whole Foods attract motivated, high-quality employees.

Mission (Not Profit) Driven

Whole Foods makes money, to be sure, but Mackey makes it clear that profit is not his company's primary motivation. It's telling that among Whole Foods' eight core values (Table 5.1), only one of them is tied to the quality and performance of the physical goods in consumers' grocery carts, and there is not a single mention of price or convenience (compare that to the focus of a traditional grocery chain, like Safeway). Although "We create wealth through profits and growth" gets the number four spot, the other core values focus on ethical pursuits: sustainable and ecological farming practices, fair trade, and helping the community. In this way, Whole Foods positions itself more as the leader of a food/product *movement* rather than simply a food/product provider.

Employees as Stakeholders

Investors are important, but Whole Foods stresses they are not the most important of stakeholders. For Whole Foods, *stakeholder* is defined broadly: it means anyone who has "an investment in what we do or sell," which includes customers, employees, suppliers, and the communities within which they operate. Decisions are made, ideally, with the interests of all these stakeholders in mind—not just those of the investors, as is the case in traditional capitalism.

1.	We sell the highest quality natural and organic products available.
2.	We satisfy, delight, and nourish our customers.
3.	We support team member excellence and happiness.
4.	We create wealth through profits and growth.
5.	We serve and support our local and global communities.
6.	We practice and advance environmental stewardship.
7.	We create ongoing, win-win relationships with our suppliers.
8.	We promote the health of our stakeholders through healthy eating education.

■ TABLE 5.3 Whole Foods' Core Values

SOURCE: www.wholefoodsmarket.com/mission-values/core-values.

And to keep its employee stakeholders happy, Whole Foods aims to empower them: employees at every level have input on decisions about policy, including benefit options, plus product offerings and more. Robust compensation doesn't hurt, and a stock option plan is available to workers at all levels, even the front-line staff manning cash registers or stocking shelves. A whopping 94 percent of the company's stock options are distributed to nonexecutives. At the same time, Whole Foods' open-book policy gives team members access to the firm's financial records, including compensation information for all associates, including the top management team and the CEO. Since 2007, Mackey himself earns a symbolic $1 per year, and executives may make no more than 19 times that of the lowest-paid associate (the US average for top executive-to-worker pay ratio is 30:1). Together, these policies help to enforce a shared identity under which everyone feels equal and valued.

Other stakeholder-benefiting programs includes the distribution of $10 million in grants to small food producers each year. Whole Foods holds seminars that teach small farmers and producers how to get their products onto its shelves. The company also donates 5 percent of its annual profits to a variety of nonprofit and community organizations. In the stores, employees are encouraged to recycle and reuse (a nod to the community in which a store operates, another stakeholder). Whole Foods was also the first to build its stores to meet Leadership in Energy and Environmental Design (LEED) Green Building Rating System.

Cultivating Conscious Leadership

From empowering employees with fair pay, ample benefits, and decision-making powers, to grants that benefit small farmers, Whole Foods aims to be a corporation with a conscience. To that end, Mackey created the Academy for Conscious Leadership, located in Austin, Texas. With conscious capitalism as the guiding principle, the academy is another opportunity for Whole Foods to reinforce the culture it's worked so hard to build, through courses on sustainable agriculture, whole and organic foods, and fair trade. During four-day retreats and other special events, the academy "prepares leaders to lead from a place of service by guiding them through experiences that identify their higher purpose and create cultures of meaning."

Whole Foods Brand of conscious capitalism is no longer the relative novelty it was in 1997—it's hard to find a large company these days without some sort corporate social responsibility program or a philanthropic arm. Though skeptics may argue the shift is all about marketing or positioning, paying attention to a broad swatch of "stakeholders"—with a special focus on employees—can be a win-win. As Mackey's co-CEO Walter Robb told Snagajob in 2015: "[Whole Foods'] strong culture of empowerment is really the secret to the company's success. . . . Culture is the living, breathing heart of the company."

Case Questions

1. What role does personal motivation play in Whole Foods' success?
2. How does Whole Foods help employees fulfill the needs in Maslow's Hierarchy?

Sources

"Academy for Conscious Leadership Mission Statement." http://academyforconsciousleadership.com/our-mission.

Egan, John. "Despite Falling Share Prices, Whole Foods Envisions Massive Expansion in U.S." *Austin Culture Map*. February 13, 2014. http://austin.culturemap.com/news/innovation/02-12-14-whole-foods-envisions-1200-stores-in-us-expansion-grocer/.

Farfan, Barbara. "Kroger Supermarkets Mission Statement—Being the Leader with Values." *Retail Industry*. n.d., http://retailindustry.about.com/od/retailbestpractices/ig/Company-Mission-Statements/Kroger-Mission-Statement.htm.

Katchen, Joe. "Whole Foods CEO: I Don't Think Obamacare Comment Will Hurt Sales." *NBCNews.com*, January 18, 2013, http://www.nbcnews.com/id/50508631/t/whole-foods-ceo-i-dont-think-obamacare-comment-will-hurt-sales/.

Layton, Joe. "Whole Foods CEO Lectures about Business Philosophy." *Daily Texan Online*. March 28, 2011. www.dailytexanonline.com/news/2011/03/28/whole-foods-ceo-lectures-about-business-philosophy.

"100 Best Companies to Work For." *CNNMoney.com*. http://money.cnn.com/magazines/fortune/best-companies/2013/snapshots/71.html.

"Opening Case Study: Whole Foods, Whole People." *Mysafaribooksonline.com*. http://my.safaribooksonline.com/book/hr-organizational-management/9780470528532/opening-case-study-whole-foods-whole-people/opening_case_study_colon_whole_foods_com.

"Our Core Values." *Wholefoods.com*. http://www.wholefoodsmarket.com/mission-values/core-values.

"Our Visions, Our Mission." *Safeway.com*. www.careersatsafeway.com/why-work-for-us/missionvision-statement.

Sriram, S. "Whole Foods' John Mackey among CEOs Drawing $1 Salary." *Citybizlist*. March 26, 2013. http://dallas.citybizlist.com/article/whole-foods%E2%80%99-john-mackey-among-ceos-drawing-1-salary.

"Whole Foods Market® Celebrates 17 Years on *Fortune*'s '100 Best Companies to Work For' List." *Businesswire.com*. January 14, 2014. www.bloomberg.com/article/2014-01-16/aufPXNX7AyfU.html.

"Whole Foods Market Q1 2014 Earnings Conference Call Summary," Thompson Reuters, February 12, 2014, www.alacrastore.com/thomson-streetevents-transcripts/Q1-2014-Whole-Foods-Market-Earnings-Conference-Call-B5273163.

SELF-ASSESSMENT 5.1

Leadership Motivation Assessment

For each statement, circle the number that best describes you based on the following scale:

	Strongly Disagree	Somewhat Disagree	Neutral	Somewhat Agree	Strongly Agree
1. I take pride in my ability to influence others.	1	2	3	4	5
2. I am often the "creator" or "idea generator" in group or team projects.	1	2	3	4	5
3. I enjoy providing feedback and/or praise to my coworkers as we work toward achieving a goal or objective.	1	2	3	4	5
4. People look to me for ideas and direction.	1	2	3	4	5
5. When working in a team context, I tend to share my ideas and thoughts about how best to proceed.	1	2	3	4	5
6. I often challenge my team or coworkers when we are working on projects or tasks.	1	2	3	4	5
7. Seeing my team or those around me succeed is more important to me than my own personal gain.	1	2	3	4	5
8. I enjoy providing recognition and rewards for other people's achievements.	1	2	3	4	5
9. I enjoy serving as a mediator in resolving conflict among my coworkers.	1	2	3	4	5
10. When working in a team context, I often work to build team cohesion and shared norms.	1	2	3	4	5
11. When working in a team context, people often advance and refine ideas that I originated.	1	2	3	4	5
12. When working in a team context, I enjoy coaching and mentoring other members of the team.	1	2	3	4	5
Total Score: ______					

Score Interpretation

12–23	This implies a low motivation to lead.
24–47	This implies some uncertainty over your motivation to lead.
48–60	This implies a strong motivation to lead.

6 Motivation: Practices and Applications

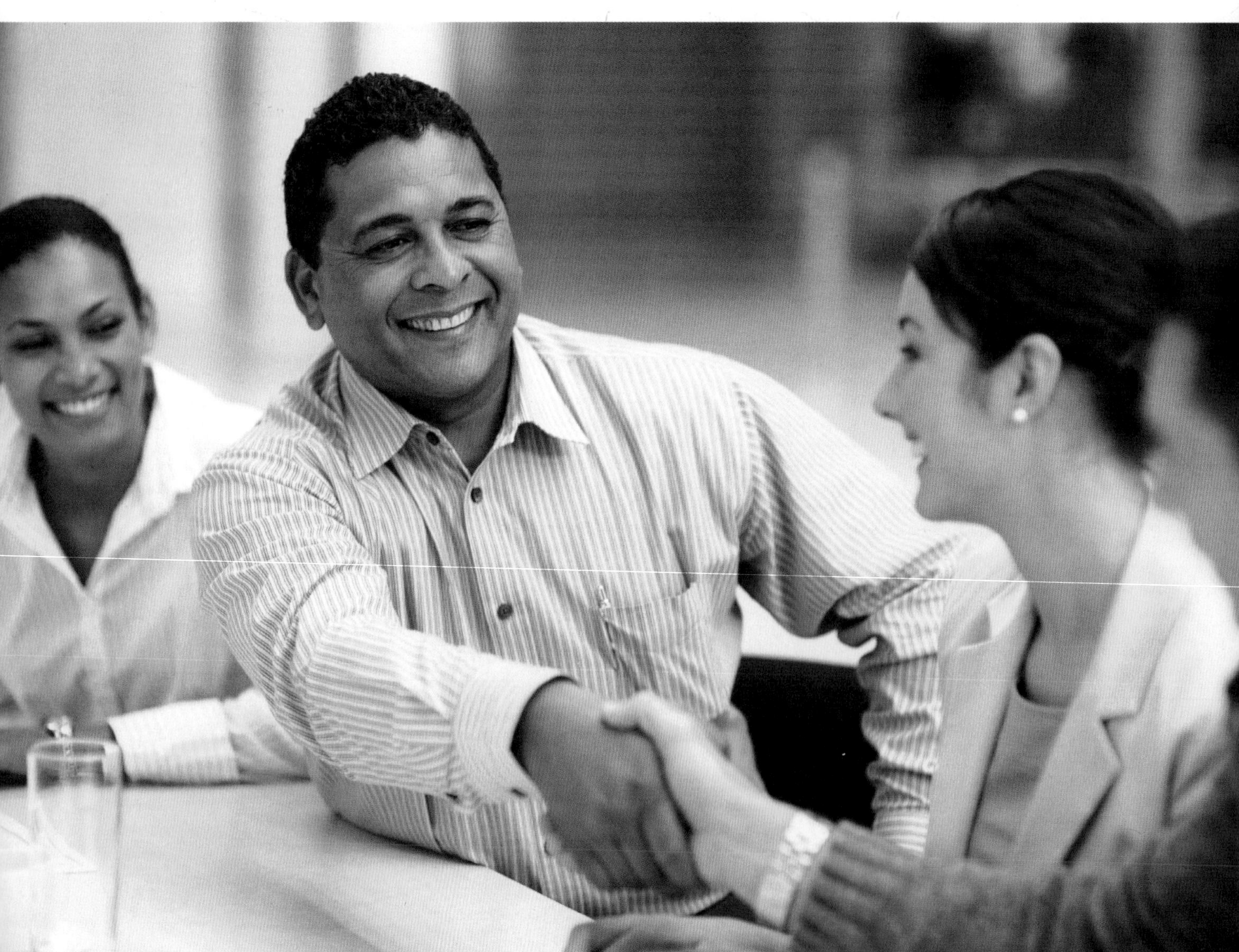

*Ability is what you're capable of doing.
Motivation determines what you do.
Attitude determines how well you do it.*

*—Raymond Chandler,
American novelist and screenwriter*

LEARNING OBJECTIVES

By the end of this chapter, you will be able to:

6.1 Explain the concept of intrinsic motivation and its primary determinants

6.2 Differentiate among the various types of extrinsic rewards

6.3 Discuss the various facets of job design

6.4 Discuss psychological empowerment and its components

6.5 Evaluate various approaches to nontraditional work schedules

INTRINSIC MOTIVATION

6.1 Explain the concept of intrinsic motivation and its primary determinants

In Chapter 5, we explored the motivation process, the theories behind it, and the way it affects our behavior.

Back to the Case of Katie O'Donnell

We were also introduced to newly appointed assistant manager Katie O'Donnell, who wants to motivate the staff at the Waterfront Grill, a struggling restaurant in Ithaca, New York. Katie created a goal-setting plan for the servers to increase bubble tea sales, hoping it would generate more income for the restaurant and increase financial rewards for the staff. However, she overlooked the fact that the bar staff takes 30 percent of server tips for bubble tea sales, so there is very little financial incentive for the servers to strive for these goals. In this chapter, we continue to chart Katie's progress as she puts different types of motivational concepts into practice in collaboration with Kamal, the manager and owner of the Waterfront Grill.

Despite her oversight regarding the tipping structure, Katie is determined to come up with an alternate solution to low employee motivation at the Waterfront Grill. But why is Katie so concerned about the restaurant? After all, she is only working there part-time while she studies for an MBA. She could just go through the motions of her role as assistant manager and then walk away as soon as she completes her degree. Why does Katie care so much about what happens at a college town restaurant where she is only working temporarily? From an OB perspective, Katie is inspired by **intrinsic motivation**. She performs tasks for her own innate satisfaction. Katie finds the business interesting and wants both the restaurant and herself to succeed. Her reward comes from finding solutions to different problems she encounters at the restaurant. Intrinsic motivation consists of two main mechanisms: need for competence, and need for self-determination.[1] In carrying out her duties as assistant manager, Katie is satisfying both her **need for competence**, which is the motivation we derive from stretching and exercising our capabilities, and her **need for self-determination**, or the feeling of

Intrinsic Motivation

Intrinsic motivation: The performance of tasks for our own innate satisfaction

Need for competence: The motivation derived from stretching and exercising our capabilities

Need for self-determination: The state of motivation and control gained through making efforts that are not reliant on any external influences

Master the content.
edge.sagepub.com/neckob

SAGE edge™

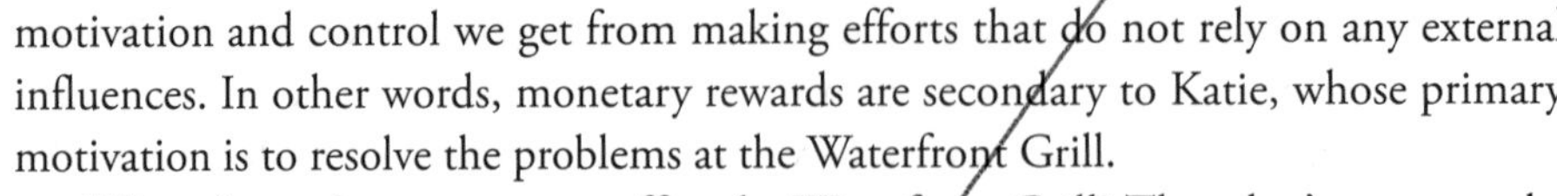

motivation and control we get from making efforts that do not rely on any external influences. In other words, monetary rewards are secondary to Katie, whose primary motivation is to resolve the problems at the Waterfront Grill.

What about the restaurant staff at the Waterfront Grill? They don't appear to be intrinsically motivated. In fact, the problem seems to be that they are unhappy with the current pay structure. Katie realizes that unless she devises a fair payment structure, there will be very little opportunity for the staff to feel intrinsically motivated.

Darrin Klimek/Photodisc/Thinkstock

Poor extrinsic rewards can demotivate employees by failing to show them their value to the organization.

Extrinsic rewards: External awards to employees such as salary, bonuses, and paid vacations

By addressing the problem of pay, Katie is focusing first on **extrinsic rewards**, which are external awards to employees such as salary, bonuses, and paid vacations. Extrinsic rewards can either increase intrinsic motivation, if the rewards are high, or decrease it if they are low. On the one hand, extrinsic rewards act as a source of competency information. That is, financial rewards directly and concretely show the employee he or she is valued and thus increase employee feelings of competence and self-determination and increase intrinsic motivation. On the other hand, when people feel they are being under-rewarded, their feelings of self-determination decrease, as does their intrinsic motivation.[24] The current pay structure at the Waterfront Grill is a prime example of how poor extrinsic rewards can serve as a demotivator. Katie's theory is that better extrinsic rewards will increase performance and job satisfaction, leading to increased intrinsic motivation.

THE BIG PICTURE:
How OB Topics Fit Together

Individual Processes
- Individual Differences
- Emotions and Attitudes
- Perceptions and Learning
- **MOTIVATION**

Team Processes
- Ethics
- Decision Making
- Creativity and Innovation
- Conflict and Negotiation

Organizational Processes
- Culture
- Strategy
- Change and Development
- Structure and Technology

Influence Processes
- Leadership
- Power and Politics
- Communication

Organizational Outcomes
- Individual Performance
- Job Satisfaction
- Team Performance
- Organizational Goals

Katie is also aware, however, that improved compensation will not address the divisions and poor relationships between the staff members. She needs to resolve the other concerns raised by the staff in order to increase levels of performance and satisfaction. However, because the pay issue seems to be the most pressing, Katie decides to focus first on extrinsic rewards and how to apply them to create a better payment structure.

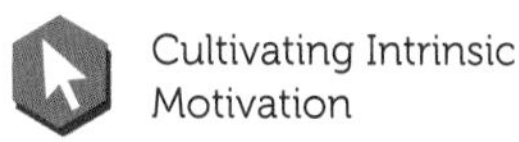

How do real-world managers inspire intrinsic motivation in their employees? Take a look at how Ben Hannam at the marketing and design agency Futprint motivates his employees by appealing to their desire for self-determination and competence in the OB in the Real World feature.

BEN HANNAM, *former creative director, Futprint*

OB in the Real World

© Ben Hannam

Before Ben Hannam became the creative director at Futprint, he spent three years teaching art and design classes to young women at the Virginia Commonwealth University in Qatar Doha in the Middle East. During this time, Hannam witnessed the positive impact the art and design program had on his students' lives. "When I got back from the Middle East it took me a while to figure out how I could help change more lives. I would ask myself, 'What are you working on? Does it really matter? Is it going to change someone's life for the better?' Ben decided that work was not his goal in life. His goal was to be fulfilled. "I wanted to continue changing lives, and I knew I could do that by being a good leader, mentor and manager to the people around me. What I want to do is support my students and coworkers by giving them challenges and projects they're interested in and then giving them the space to come up with a creative solution. I might tell someone they're in charge of making sure a product works in every browser and operating system. Then I back off and let them come up with their strategy for testing."

Ben knows how important it is to manage people in a way that allows them to feel intrinsically motivated and inspired to deliver good work. "Being the kind of manager who micromanages and cracks the whip to get people to jump isn't conducive to creativity," he says. "In a creative environment like Futprint where you're supposed to come up with new ideas and angles to create improvement for customers we have to inspire people, get them working with their strengths, challenge them in a healthy way, and create positive team dynamics."

He wants the quality of the environment and the type of work to be what keeps people around and changes their lives. "When you give people challenges and put them in an environment that is conducive to creativity, they feel like they are contributing as individuals to something greater, and that creates motivation."

Critical-Thinking Questions

1. **How do you describe Ben Hannam's approach to motivating his employees?**
2. **How would you help to inspire intrinsic motivation in a group of people?**

SOURCE: Ben Hannam, personal interview, September 26, 2013.

1. The text describes Katie O'Donnell as intrinsically motivated, but does not mention the extrinsic reward of her recent promotion to a newly created position as a possible factor in her level of motivation. In your opinion, how closely is intrinsic motivation tied to extrinsic reward in most job situations? What other factors might have an impact on intrinsic motivation? **[Understand/Apply]**
2. Imagine that you are a senior manager who has recently promoted one of your best, most intrinsically motivated employees to manage a group of five people. Like Ben Hannam in the OB in the Real World feature, you employ a fairly hands-off approach in order to allow each individual to exercise competence and self-determination (the key components of intrinsic motivation) in performing their roles. Your newly promoted manager is employing a different approach and appears to believe that dictating not only the goal of a given task but also all the steps needed to accomplish it is the best way to manage people. Write a memo to this new manager explaining why your preferred managerial style is a better approach to motivating employees than a micro-managing approach where employees have little say in how tasks are accomplished. **[Analyze/Evaluate/Create]**

TYPES OF EXTRINSIC REWARDS

6.2 Differentiate among the various types of extrinsic rewards

Katie turns to her MBA studies as a foundation for her research into extrinsic rewards. First, she explores several types of extrinsic rewards.

Seniority-Based Pay

Guaranteed wages and salary increases based on the amount of time the employee has spent with the organization are called **seniority-based pay**.[3] These wages, which are paid at fixed intervals such as monthly or weekly, tend to encourage longevity and commitment, which reduces turnover. However, seniority-based pay can also be demotivating because employees know they will get paid regardless of how they perform, which also encourages poor performers to stay in an organization much longer.

After some thought, Katie dismisses seniority-based pay increases. Even though they might encourage longevity and help reduce turnover, the fact is that turnover will always be reality at the Waterfront Grill because it is based in a college town and most of the employees are students.

Job Content–Based Pay

Job content–based pay is based on an evaluation of a job's worth to the organization and its relationship to other jobs within the organization.[4] Many organizations use this compensation structure because it is thought to be one of the best ways to maintain pay equity. Employees also tend to be more motivated to compete for promotions and a higher rate of pay. At the same time, employees who are competing against each other may exaggerate their duties to their managers to try and impress, or they may hoard resources to get ahead. These activities can also create a psychological distance across teams and hierarchies.

The pay system at the Waterfront Grill is job content–based, but since the staff is having so many problems with the compensation structure, Katie feels that this type of extrinsic reward is not working effectively.

Seniority-based pay: Guaranteed wages and salary increases based on the amount of time the employee has spent with the organization

Job content–based pay: A salary paid based on the evaluation of a job's worth

Bloomberg/Getty Images

Employees of Marlin Steel are rewarded with bonus pay each time they learn a new skill.

Skill-Based Pay

Skill-based pay rewards employees for the acquisition of new skills that lead to enhanced work performance.[5] As we learned in Chapter 5, Marlin Steel uses this type of extrinsic reward by paying its employees bonuses every time they acquire a new skill. Skill-based pay can be a useful way to motivate employees while providing them with an opportunity to showcase their new skills and competencies. As a result, workers are more flexible and productive. However, there can be some disadvantages. There is the high cost of additional bonuses and training to consider, as well as the possibility that employees may max out their skill levels, which means they cannot receive any additional pay increases unless they change jobs.

Katie knows some of the larger restaurants in the area give servers skills tests and award them for each new skill they acquire. However, because the Waterfront Grill is an independently owned enterprise, with a small staff and a lower overall skill level than larger restaurants, Katie doesn't feel that this approach is realistic. Next, she considers the fourth type of extrinsic reward, performance-based pay.

Performance-Based Pay

Performance-based pay is a financial incentive awarded to employees for meeting specific goals or objectives.[6] Two levels of performance-based pay exist: individual level and team and organization level.

Individual-Level Performance-Based Pay

Individual-level pay includes:

- **Piece rate** is a pay plan in which workers are paid a fixed sum for each unit of production completed. In other words, people are rewarded for the quantity of goods they produce regardless of how long it has taken them.

Skill-based pay: A system of pay that rewards employees for the acquisition and the development of new skills that lead to enhanced work performance

Performance-based pay: A financial incentive awarded to employees for meeting certain goals or objectives

Piece rate: A pay plan in which workers are paid a fixed sum for each unit of production completed

- **Merit pay** links pay increases directly to performance. In other words, it rewards performance by increasing the employee's salary on a long-term basis.
- **Bonus pay** rewards employees for good performance in addition to their base salary.

Katie spends a long time trying to figure out how to apply one of the individual-level performance-based pay plans to the restaurant staff without any success. The next morning she sits down with Kamal, the restaurant's owner and manager, and describes the past 24 hours, starting with her conversation with the servers and the flaw they pointed out in the tipping structure.

"Don't the servers realize they're still keeping 70 percent of the tips they collect on bubble tea sales? Don't they think 70 percent of something is better than 100 percent of nothing?" Kamal says, throwing his hands in the air in frustration.

"Actually, I did the figures and the servers are correct. Under the current tip-out policy, increasing bubble tea sales could actually reduce server tips," Katie replies. (See Figure 6.1.)

Katie spends the next few minutes bringing Kamal through her calculations and in the end he agrees that the current tip-out structure needs to be reviewed. He brings up an Excel spread sheet and starts typing. After a short while, he stops and turns back to Katie.

"I think I've worked out a new tipping policy that could work," Kamal says thoughtfully. "How about if we reduce the bubble tea bar staff's tip from 30 percent of all checks with bubble tea to 9 percent of all checks?"

"So that means the bubble tea bar staff will get 9 percent of *all* checks, rather than just 30 percent of the ones with bubble tea?" Katie says, slowly, trying to absorb Kamal's new plan.

Kamal shows Katie the calculations he has made on the spread sheet and she agrees they make sense. They are shown in Figure 6.2.

With a tip-out on *all* checks, both bartenders and servers make the same average tips, but now there is incentive for the servers to sell more bubble tea and, in turn, make more money.

Katie is excited about the new policy, but she has a few questions.

"I think the new policy needs to be explained carefully to the bar staff, otherwise they might feel they're losing tips. They need to see the value of receiving a percentage of all checks, not just those that include bubble tea," Katie says.

"I agree we need to communicate the message properly, so I'll have a talk with them later on today and answer any concerns they may have," Kamal replies.

"What about the rest of the staff?" Katie asks. "The runners, hosts, and kitchen staff don't get any tips."

She walks Kamal through the different types of individual performance-based pay structures. Kamal dismisses merit pay because he feels that reaching the sales targets instead is not only indicative of the servers' performance but also allows them to earn

Scenario A: $30 check (no bubble tea) × .15 tip = $4.50
A check with no bubble tea and the standard server 15 percent tip generates a tip of $4.50 for the server.
Scenario B: $42 check (with bubble tea) × .15 × .70 = $4.41
NOTE: A larger check with a bubble tea bar tab gets the standard 15 percent but 30 percent of the tip goes to the bubble tea bar staff generating a tip of $4.41 for the server (which is less tip for the server than Scenario A).

■ FIGURE 6.1 Current Tip-Out Structure

Merit pay: A pay plan consisting of a pay rise which is linked directly to performance

Bonus pay: A pay plan that rewards employees for recent performance rather than historical performance

Current policy (example: 30 percent tip-out to bubble tea bartenders on checks with bubble tea)

Tip-out to bubble tea bartender

$100 × .30 (average percentage of checks with bubble tea) =

$30 × 0.15 (tip to server) × 0.30 (tip-out to bubble tea bartender) =

$1.35 to bubble tea bar tender

Tip-out to server

($100 × .70 × .15) + ($100 × .30 × .15 × .70) = $13.65 to server

NOTE: After the 15 percent tip goes to the servers on checks with bubble tea, bubble tea bar staff take 30 percent of the tip, equaling $1.35 for bubble tea bartender tips.

New policy (example: 9 percent tip-out on ALL checks)

Tip-out to bubble tea bartender

$100 × .15 (tip) × .09 (tip-out to bubble tea bartender) = $1.35 to bubble tea bartender

Tip-out to server

$100 × .15 × .91 = $13.65 to server

NOTE: After the 15 percent tip goes to the servers, bubble tea bar staff take 9 percent of the tip, equaling $1.35. At this tip-out rate on all checks, the average tip remains the same for both servers and bubble tea bartenders as under the existing policy.

■ FIGURE 6.2 New Versus Current Tip-Out Policy

generous tips at the same time. He also discards the idea of piece-rate pay as more appropriate to manufacturing and farming industries than to the restaurant business. But he does consider the idea of bonuses.

"Maybe if the restaurant's performance improves," he says, "I can afford to give each member of the staff a small bonus at the end of the year to reward good performance."

Katie thinks bonuses based on performance are a great idea and believes they will help increase loyalty. She suggests introducing a "Waterfront Grill Employee of the Year Award," which Kamal promises to consider. But Katie still has a question.

"While I think bonuses are a good idea," Katie says, "I'm not sure a small annual bonus is enough of an incentive for those who don't receive tips on a regular basis."

"Let me talk to the kitchen staff," Kamal replies. "They don't usually earn tips, but if the restaurant starts to turn over more profit, then I would consider giving them a wage increase. As for the runners, perhaps we could give them 2 percent of the servers' tips."

"I'm not sure the servers will be happy giving away an additional 2 percent of their tips," Katie says, thinking about her conversation with Diego about the runner who wanted to share his tips.

"It's in their best interests," Kamal points out. "If the runners share in the tips they'll be more motivated to bus tables quickly and efficiently. The tables will be turned around faster and that will benefit the servers."

Katie isn't convinced. "I'm not sure 2 percent of tips will motivate the runners to that degree," she says.

"I think it's better than nothing!" Kamal says, frustrated.

Katie doesn't want to appear negative, so she decides to change the subject.

"That just leaves the hosts. . ." Katie says. She fills Kamal in about the side deals Kim and Lucia have with the hosts, and how they boast about their tips in front of the rest of the staff.

Kamal agrees the arrangement needs to come to an end because he believes the hosts already receive a fair base rate. "The hosts won't be pleased that I'm putting an end to their arrangement, but they shouldn't be cutting deals in the first place. Their behavior is unethical and demotivating for the other staff."

Katie agrees to relay this message to the hosts and servers involved and asks Kamal's opinion about the second level of performance-based pay for teams and organizations, which includes gain sharing, profit sharing, and employee stock ownership plans.

Team- and Organization-Level Performance-Based Pay

There are three types of team and organization performance-based plans:

- **Gain sharing** is a system whereby managers agree to share the benefits of cost savings with staff in return for their contribution to the company's performance.[7] When Katie discusses this pay plan with Kamal, he says he has noticed the servers often provide customers with far more packets of ketchup, mustard, and mayonnaise and servings of complimentary bread than they really need. Kamal agrees to look into the possibility of sharing 50 percent of any food cost savings with servers on a quarterly basis if they play their part in helping to reduce costs.
- **Profit sharing** is a pay system in which the organization shares its profits with employees.[8] Kamal agrees to consider introducing a profit-sharing plan for all staff when the restaurant becomes profitable once more so employees can receive a portion of the profit they helped create. The hope is that such a plan will encourage employees to stay longer.
- **Employee stock ownership plans (ESOPs)** allow employees to purchase company stock, often at below-market price, as one of their benefits.[9] Many small businesses use ESOPs because of their big tax benefits and because they allow the owner to keep control of the business until the time comes to hand over the reins to eligible employees. Since Kamal is a small-business owner, he finds the idea of ESOPs interesting. He thinks they are a good way to motivate employees and give them a sense of ownership and says he will give the idea further thought.

Profit Sharing

Although she is pleased that the staff can look forward to promising financial incentives, Katie knows this will not be enough to motivate them to work together as a team. She suggests some job design strategies to increase motivation.

Gain sharing: A system whereby managers agree to share the benefits of cost savings with staff in return for their contribution to the company's performance

Profit sharing: Sharing profits with employees of an organization by the owners

Employee stock ownership plans (ESOPs): Plans in which employees purchase stock, often at below market price as a part of their benefits

THINKING CRITICALLY

1. Create a chart that lists the types of extrinsic rewards discussed in the section. Provide an example of a useful application and a detrimental application for each type of reward. For example, Kamal notes in the narrative case that piece-rate pay is applicable to manufacturing jobs but not to restaurant jobs. **[Analyze/Create]**

2. Imagine that you are the manager of a small clothing manufacturer. You wish to retain your more senior employees, who typically work faster in completing each item of clothing than newer employees. Nevertheless, because 80% of your current workforce is over 50 you need to incentivize new hires in order to be sure you have an adequate supply of skilled workers in 10 years time. Devise an extrinsic reward plan that rewards skilled workers as well as new workers who need to acquire skills. **[Analyze/Create]**

MOTIVATION THROUGH JOB DESIGN

6.3 Discuss the various facets of job design

Job design is a method of setting forth the duties and responsibilities of a job with the intention of improving productivity and performance.[10] The concept of job design can be traced back to the theory of **scientific management**, introduced in the early 20th century by Frederick Taylor and his colleagues, who analyzed workflow through systematic observation of the tasks to be performed. Taylor designed experiments to calculate the motions and time required to complete workplace tasks in order to improve efficiencies. For example, he tested the various motions required for laying bricks to understand how workers could complete the task more quickly.

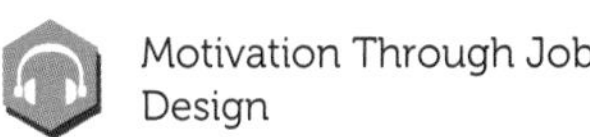
Motivation Through Job Design

Through these "time and motion" studies Taylor not only discovered better and faster ways to complete tasks; he also found that certain people could work more efficiently than others. Therefore, he advocated selecting the right people for the job as another important part of workplace efficiency.

Also known as "Taylorism," scientific management focused on how to make people, assembly line workers in particular, more efficient at their jobs through training, monitoring, and detailed planning.

Though Katie is all for improving efficiency, she also wants the Waterfront Grill to be a fun place to work, not just an assembly line of repetitive boring tasks. Kamal agrees, and with this in mind, they take a look at **job enlargement**, a method of job design that increases the range of tasks and duties associated with a job in order to make it more challenging and varied.[11] Katie hopes the servers will feel more challenged and motivated by the extra tasks they are taking on to increase sales. But what about the rest of the staff?

Kamal suggests the runners could help out in the kitchen during quiet periods, washing dishes or chopping vegetables. Similarly, the hosts could leave their stations when it's not busy to collect glasses from tables for the bar staff, and perhaps the kitchen staff could swap duties now and then, or, following some training, take turns working as sous chef for the night. Katie agrees, believing the expanding roles will lead to more positive interaction among the staff and contribute to effective relationship building, strengthening the team.

Next, Katie and Kamal focus on **job rotation**, which is a process of periodically moving employees from one job to another.[12] Because the server and bubble bar tender positions are the most lucrative, Katie reasons, what about giving hosts and runners the opportunity to work shifts as servers and bartenders to cover absent staff or to fill in on a busy night? If they prove successful, they'll have the first option of moving into these roles as they become available. She also suggests that new hires should come in at the base level and work as runners and hosts until a server or bartender vacancy arises. They will also be given the opportunity to rotate roles. This means everyone will have a chance to work their way into more lucrative positions if they are interested.

Kamal is excited about this plan. He and Katie discuss rotation in more depth before moving on to the concept of **job enrichment**, or increasing the scope of a job to make it more complex, stimulating, and satisfying for employees.[13] Kamal believes he can implement job enrichment by creating a "lead server" position. On any given night, the most experienced server would be the lead server, a sort of quasi-manager who has additional responsibilities and authority. He or she would be empowered to make decisions and resolve problems for customers and fellow employees, especially if Kamal or Katie were not available.

Job design: A method of setting duties and responsibilities of a job with the intention of improving productivity and performance

Scientific management: Early 20th century theory introduced by Frederick Taylor and his colleagues that analyzes workflow through systematic observation or reasoning

Job enlargement: An increase in the range of tasks and duties associated with a job

Job rotation: A process of periodically moving staff employees from one job to another

Job enrichment: An increase in the scope of a job to make it more complex, interesting, stimulating, and satisfying for employees

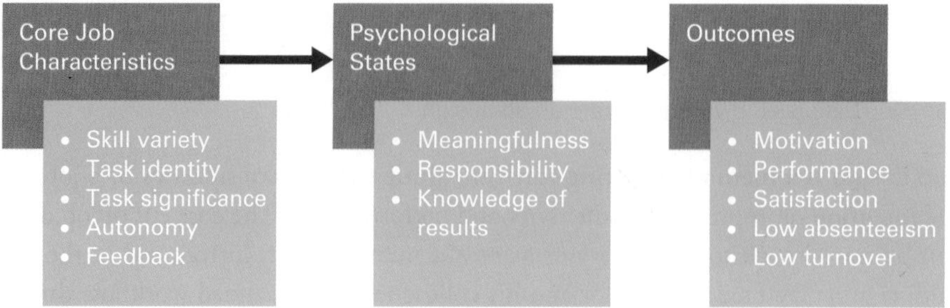

FIGURE 6.3 Job Characteristics Model

SOURCE: Hackman, J. R., and G. R. Oldham. *Work Redesign* (Reading, MA: Addison-Wesley, 1980).

Finally, in order to ensure that their plan will have a positive outcome, Katie and Kamal apply what they have discussed to the Hackman and Oldham **job characteristics model**, (see Figure 6.3) which identifies five core dimensions of jobs: skill variety, task identity, task significance, autonomy, and feedback.[14] Hackman and Oldham created a scoring system based on these five characteristics. The higher the score for each of the characteristics, the more positive are employees' psychological states and outcomes.

Skill variety is the extent to which workers utilize a variety of skills. For example, everyone on the restaurant staff will now have the opportunity to learn and use a variety of skills.

Task identity is the extent to which an employee completes an entire piece of work from start to finish. For example, employees will be able to carry out their different roles from beginning to end without any outside interference.

Task significance is the extent to which employees see meaning in the impact of their roles on the organization. As business at the Waterfront Grill improves, the staff will be able to see the impact their extra effort has made.

Autonomy is the extent to which employees are given the freedom and independence to schedule and perform tasks. Katie works with Kamal to create a more flexible scheduling process whereby employees can, within limits, set their own hours, including longer work days on non-class days for employees who are students.

Feedback is the extent to which employees are provided with timely information regarding their job performance. Katie has already agreed to provide feedback to the servers after every shift to discuss bubble tea sales targets. Kamal commits to providing monthly constructive feedback in the form of a personal meeting with each member of staff in an effort to motivate and build relationships between management and staff.

Katie and Kamal are satisfied that once the plan they have agreed upon is enacted jobs will score more highly on the job characteristics model, resulting in a happier staff. Katie is delighted that in one meeting, albeit a very long one, she and Kamal have managed to create a new payment structure, worked through some job design concepts, and applied the five job characteristics to the major issues and challenges at the restaurant. Katie believes that the new ideas have the power to intrinsically motivate and empower the staff at the Waterfront Grill. Now all she has to do is put the new plan into action.

THINKING CRITICALLY

1. Consider the details of the plan Katie and Kamal intend to put in place at the Waterfront Grill. What positive outcomes do you predict will occur once the aspects of the plan related to job enlargement, job rotation, and job enrichment are implemented? What objections or obstacles could Katie and Kamal encounter in seeking to implement their plans with the staff? **[Understand /Analyze]**

Job characteristics model: Five core dimensions of jobs: skill variety, task identity, task significance, autonomy, and feedback

2. Use Hackman and Oldham's job characteristics model to assess the ways in which each group of staff (kitchen employees, runners, hosts, and servers) will be affected by Katie and Kamal's plan. Discuss the impact of the plan on each of the five core dimensions (skill variety, task identity, task significance, autonomy, and feedback) for each job. Based on your assessment, what pitfalls and obstacles to developing teamwork and intrinsic motivation among individual staff do you predict? **[Apply/Analyze/Evaluate]**

PSYCHOLOGICAL EMPOWERMENT

6.4 Discuss psychological empowerment and its components

Another facet of the job characteristics model is the concept of **psychological empowerment**, the extent to which employees feel a sense of personal fulfillment and intent when carrying out tasks, along with a belief that their work contributes to some larger purpose.[15] There are four main factors associated with psychological empowerment: *competence, self-determination, impact,* and *meaningfulness.*

Katie hopes that the new plan will provide increased psychological empowerment for the staff. She schedules a meeting to talk to the servers, hosts, and runners in individual groups to advise them of the changes she and Kamal are making.

At the meeting the servers seem pleased with the new tipping policy. Kim and Lucia shift uncomfortably when she tells them to cut out the side deals with the hosts, but both eventually agree it's best for the team and the restaurant. Katie also reminds the servers not to boast about their tips in front of the hosts and kitchen staff.

Theo is pleased with the new compensation structure but tells Katie he is nervous about meeting his sales targets. Katie observes that Theo is lacking in **competence**, which is a ability to perform work tasks successfully.[16] She reassures him by telling him she believes in him and will provide frequent feedback on his performance, give him more sales training if necessary, and discuss any other concerns on an ongoing basis. Theo thanks her and tells her he will make as much effort as he can to meet his targets. Katie hopes she has said enough to help Theo feel more empowered about reaching his goals.

Next Katie tells the servers the runners will receive 2 percent of the servers' tips. There is a short silence, then Diego says the runners "deserve something because they work so hard." The other servers agree. "Now that we have the opportunity to make more money, it's only fair that we give the runners a portion of it," Lucia says. "Besides, it's not going to make a huge difference to our earnings."

Katie thanks the servers for their level-headedness and moves on to the newly created lead server position, telling Diego he is management's choice to take on the role that very night. Diego enthusiastically agrees, and Katie asks him to stay behind after the meeting so she can talk him through his new responsibilities. She also reassures Kim, Lucia, and Theo that they will each be given a chance to be lead servers in the future. After a few minutes of discussion, the servers agree to the changes and Katie brings the meeting to a close. As she watches Theo, Kim, and Lucia file out, Katie hopes that all the changes related to extrinsic rewards and job design will motivate the staff to be more productive and satisfied with their roles at the Waterfront Grill.

After the meeting, Diego thanks Katie for putting a stop to the unfair side deals and for working out a new tipping structure that he thinks is fair and will help to increase tips. Diego tells Katie he understands what is involved in the lead server role, but he would like to clarify one point: "Do I have the ability to train the other servers in the art of customer service?"

Psychological empowerment: The extent to which employees feel a sense of personal fulfillment and intent when carrying out tasks, together with a belief that their work contributes to some larger purpose

Competence: The ability to perform work tasks successfully

When a problematic issue in the workplace is resolved, employees are motivated to work harder.

© iStockphoto.com/Steve Debenport

Katie hasn't thought about this angle, but she thinks Diego has a good point.

Diego says, "Although Theo is new and lacks confidence, he is polite to customers and probably doesn't need too much training. But as I mentioned before, I don't think Kim and Lucia treat customers the way they should be treated. They barely give them a smile or even look them in the eye. I know this new tipping structure should motivate them to be more enthusiastic and ambitious about increasing their tips, but my concern is that they will simply put on a fake smile which customers can spot a mile away! I think I have the skills to teach the staff how the customers should be treated."

Katie is delighted by Diego's **self-determination**, which is the understanding of skills, knowledge, and strengths that enable a person to make choices and initiate work tasks.[17] She is also impressed that Diego is aware of his own abilities and their application in improving the customer service skills of the two servers. Clearly Diego feels empowered enough to see that his actions can make a real **impact**.[18]

Meaningfulness at Work

Katie is relieved that Diego has reacted positively to the new plan and she hopes he will stay on at the restaurant long term.

When Katie has finished talking to the runners and the hosts, she heads off to find Kamal to tell him the outcome. When she walks into his office, instead of his usual welcome, he greets her with a terse nod.

"Yuan quit," Kamal reports, sighing heavily.

Yuan is the best bubble tea bartender they have at the Waterfront Grill, and he will be costly to replace.

"I tried to persuade him to stay," Kamal continues. "I told him how the bubble tea bar staff would be receiving a 9 percent tip from all the servers' tickets including bubble tea and food sales, but he didn't seem to understand what that meant for him or the restaurant. Yuan just said he was bored working here and had received a better opportunity at a larger restaurant."

Katie perceives that Yuan lacked a sense of **meaningfulness**, which is the value of work tasks in line with a person's own self-concepts and ideals.[19] Though Katie is disappointed that Kamal has not been successful in convincing Yuan to stay on at the restaurant, she also knows that as a long-term employee Yuan may have "mentally checked out" from his job a while ago. Once an employee is ready to move to a new job, it can be difficult, if not impossible, to persuade them to change their minds.

Over the next six months, profits at the Waterfront Grill begin to improve, but it is not all smooth sailing at the restaurant. Katie is dismayed when both hosts quit their jobs

Self-determination: The understanding of skills, knowledge, and strengths that enable a person to make choices and initiate work tasks

Impact: The feeling of making a difference

Meaningfulness: The value of work tasks in line with a person's own self-concepts and ideals

at the restaurant at the same time and with very little notice. The rest of the staff have been pulling together and covering their shifts and responsibilities temporarily until the positions are filled. Though Katie is impressed by the way the staff has come together, it has been difficult to find new hosts and she has received little support from Kamal during the process.

Because of the success of the servers promoting items and increasing sales, and the restaurant becoming more profitable, Kamal is busier than ever. High volumes of paperwork and calls means he has neglected his promise to connect with the staff on a regular basis. His office door is kept firmly shut to avoid any disturbance, which has frustrated some of the employees who believe they have some good ideas to share with him. Even Katie is finding it impossible to get some time with him, which she finds irritating. After repeated requests to meet in the wake of the hosts' departures, Kamal tells Katie that he does not have the time for personal meetings and that she and the other employees should email him with any concerns instead of trying to speak with him in person. Katie follows orders, thinking there are no other options for communicating with Kamal, but her emails remain unanswered.

Katie begins to feel disheartened and starts questioning her loyalty to the Waterfront Grill. Her level of intrinsic motivation decreases markedly.

Though she is pleased with the positive impact her ideas have had at the restaurant, Katie realizes this is only the beginning of the changes that are needed and that there is much more work to be done. She has many other ideas to improve things, but she cannot act on them without Kamal's support. Katie begins to seriously consider quitting her job as assistant manager at the Waterfront Grill. Kamal's lack of support and her inability to move forward with new initiatives reduces her sense of psychological empowerment to the point where she believes she would be better off focusing on her studies and finding a less demanding part-time job.

THINKING CRITICALLY

1. Analyze the level of psychological empowerment Katie appeared to feel when she was developing the extrinsic reward and job design plan with Kamal. Give examples of the ways in which her behavior illustrated each of the four main beliefs (competence, self-determination, impact, and meaningfulness). **[Understand/Analyze/Apply]**

2. To what extent do you believe Katie's lack of motivation at the end of this section is Kamal's fault? In other words, is the nature of Katie's job inevitably going to lead to demotivation over time or could better management have ensured a longer-term commitment from Katie? What about Yuan's job as a bubble tea bartender? Do certain types of job automatically lead to lower motivation over time? Why or why not? **[Analyze/Evaluate]**

NONTRADITIONAL WORK SCHEDULES

6.5 Evaluate various approaches to nontraditional work schedules

Flexible work schedules are becoming more popular with today's workers and their employers. Rather than putting in the traditional 40-hour week, many employees are permitted to work from home, choose their own working hours, and even work remotely from different countries. Free agents and part-time workers are two types of workers who adhere to nontraditional work schedules. **Free agents** are independent workers who supply organizations with short-term talent for projects that need to be completed within a certain amount of time.[20] A freelancer is a type of free agent who can work for multiple employers, giving a limited amount of time to each. Similarly, **part-time workers** are independent workers who supply organizations with part-time

Free agents: Independent workers that supply organizations with short-term talent for projects or time-bound objectives

Part-time workers (similar to *free agents*): Independent workers who supply organizations with part-time talent for projects or time-bound objectives

PSYCHOLOGICAL EMPOWERMENT

Examining the Evidence

We've seen that psychological empowerment is a motivational state in which a person senses control of and active orientation to his or her work as manifested in meaningfulness, self-determination, competence, and impact. But how can managers help employees feel psychologically empowered in the workplace? Researchers Scott E. Seibert, Gang Wang, and Stephen H. Courtright of the University of Iowa conducted a meta-analysis of more than 140 research studies in an effort to identify key originators and consequences of psychological empowerment.* Their results suggest that high-performance managerial practices, sociopolitical support, effective leadership practices, and the five core job characteristics of the job characteristics model were all relatively strongly related to employee psychological empowerment. Furthermore, these factors were more related to employee psychological empowerment than were individual traits and characteristics. Their analysis also demonstrated a positive relationship between psychological empowerment and employee attitudes such as job satisfaction and organizational commitment, and employee behaviors including task performance and organizational citizenship behavior (OCB). Taken together, this research evidence suggests that managers and organizations should consider taking proactive steps to facilitate perceptions of psychological empowerment among their employees.

Critical-Thinking Questions

1. **What specific actions can managers take to help employees feel psychologically empowered? Why would these actions be effective?**
2. **What factors could limit the effectiveness of interventions designed to increase psychological empowerment? How could these limitations be overcome?**

*Seibert, Scott E., Gang Wang, and Stephen H. Courtright. "Antecedents and Consequences of Psychological and Team Empowerment in Organizations: A Meta-analytic Review." *Journal of Applied Psychology* 96, no. 5 (September 2011): 981–1003.

talent for projects that need to be completed within a certain amount of time. Part-time workers work fewer hours than full-time workers but may supplement these hours by working for other employers.

Why are more companies implementing flexible working arrangements for their employees? According to recent studies, members of generation Y, or the millennials, are driving the change. One report shows that 45 percent of Millennials choose work flexibility over pay, prefer jobs where they can make a real impact, and value roles that provide them with personal fulfillment.[21] Because 60 percent of these young employees switch employers every three years, companies seeking to avoid the high cost of turnover are looking for ways to keep their employees satisfied so they'll stay longer. Yet, despite the recent surge of flexible work arrangements, not every organization is keen to implement them. Yahoo is one company that has bucked the trend by announcing an end to working from home, with CEO Marissa Mayer stating that Yahoo employees need to be "physically together" in order for the organization to be at its most productive.[22] These are the four main nontraditional work schedules commonly adopted by employers in today's workplace (see Figure 6.4.).

Flextime: Flexible working hours in which employees customize their own work hours within limits established by management

Compressed workweeks: A work arrangement that gives employees the benefit of an extra day off by allowing them to work their usual number of hours in fewer days per pay period

Flextime means flexible working hours whereby an employee can customize his or her own work hours within limits established by management.[23] For example, an employee might work a 7:00 a.m. to 3:00 p.m. shift rather than the more traditional 9:00 a.m. to 5:00 p.m. workday.

Compressed workweeks give employees the benefit of an extra day off by allowing them to work their usual number of hours in fewer days per pay period.[24] For example,

Work Schedule	Monday	Tuesday	Wednesday	Thursday	Friday
Flextime	7 a.m.–3 p.m.	8 a.m.–4 p.m.	10 a.m.–6 p.m.	8 a.m.–4 p.m.	9 a.m.–5 p.m.
Compressed Workweek	9 a.m.–7p.m.	9 a.m.–7 p.m.	9 a.m.–7 p.m.	9 a.m.–7 p.m.	off
Job Sharing	Lucy 9 a.m.–2 p.m., Nathan 2 p.m.–6 p.m.	Lucy 9 a.m.–2 p.m., Nathan 2 p.m.–6 p.m.	Lucy 9 a.m.–2 p.m., Nathan 2 p.m.–6 p.m.	Lucy 9 a.m.–2 p.m., Nathan 2 p.m.–6 p.m.	Lucy 9 a.m.–2 p.m., Nathan 2 p.m.–6 p.m.
Telecommuting	9 a.m.–5 p.m.	9 a.m.–5 p.m.	9 a.m.–5 p.m.	Work from home	Work from home

■ FIGURE 6.4 Examples of Nontraditional Work Schedules

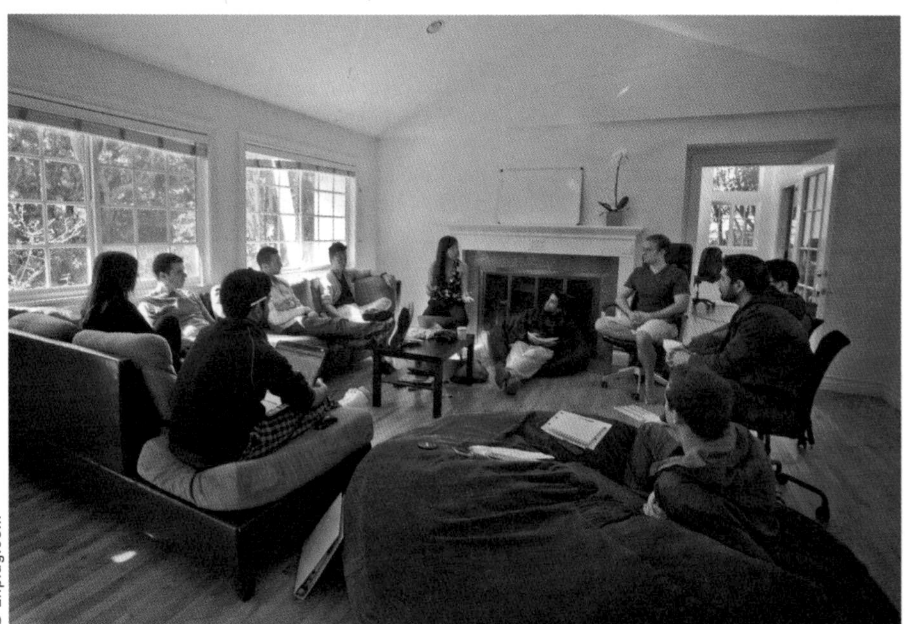

Employees of Los Angeles-based startup Enplug live and work in a large company-owned house where the lines of work life and home life are blurred to create a more efficient and connected environment.

the employee might work four 10-hour days each week and then enjoy a three-day weekend, or work 80 hours in nine days with an extra day off every other week.

Job sharing divides one full-time job among two or more people who work pre-determined hours.[25] Job sharers can hand over their work to the next person when their part of the shift ends and the next begins.

Telecommuting means working from home or from a remote location on a computer or other advanced telecommunications system linked to the main office.[26] This gives workers greater flexibility of working hours and location. Though more companies are using at least one of these alternative work schedules, other businesses are coming up with even more creative ways to meet the needs of their employees.

Telecommuting

Take the start-up advertising-technology company Enplug, based in Los Angeles, California. Twelve of Enplug's 37 employees, including the CEO, live and work together in a large ranch-style house owned by the company. There are no formal working hours; some software developers code until the early hours and wake up late the following day, while account managers rise early to attend business meetings at their clients' premises. Along with free lodging and food, employees (typically recent college graduates) receive a modest salary. They also save money by not having a daily commute. CEO Nanxi Liu believes that while the lifestyle is a "little cultish," Enplug's working model makes for a very efficient workforce because it helps employees bond

Job sharing: An employment option in which one full-time job is divided among two or more people according to predetermined hours

Telecommuting: Working from home or from a remote location on a computer or other advanced telecommunications that are linked to the office and provides them with an environment that combines work and home life with very few outside distractions.[27]

Telecommuting Effectiveness

Yet even the most flexible working arrangements have their drawbacks. Some people who work remotely or telecommute may feel isolated or cut off from coworkers, while others may not be suited to working from home and the potential distractions of family life. Job sharing can be frustrating if the sharers don't work well together; and holding down a multitude of part-time or free agent jobs can lead to overwork and stress. This is why companies need to tailor their alternate work schedules to their employees with a view to retaining a productive, efficient, and committed workforce.

In this chapter, we have explored the application of motivation and its impact on employees. As we have seen, motivation is unsustainable without the support of teams and managers. In Chapter 7, we explore the nature of teams and the way people actively work together to achieve organizational goals.

THINKING CRITICALLY

1. List each of the work schedules discussed in the section and provide a list of the strengths and weaknesses of each approach. **[Understand/Apply]**
2. Imagine you are considering funding Enplug. What likely outcomes of its integration of work and life would you consider a positive factor in your funding decision? What likely outcomes of this arrangement would you consider a negative factor in your funding decision? **[Analyze/Evaluate]**
3. Imagine that you have replaced Marissa Mayer as CEO of Yahoo. Based on what you have learned in this chapter about intrinsic motivation, extrinsic rewards, and the job characteristics model would you continue or rescind the no telecommuting policy she implemented? Why or why not? **[Analyze/Evaluate]**

IN REVIEW

Learning Objectives

6.1 Explain the concept of intrinsic motivation and its primary determinants

Intrinsic motivation moves us to perform tasks for our own innate satisfaction. The two main mechanisms of intrinsic motivation are *need for competence* and *need for self-determination.* The **need for competence** motivates us to gain satisfaction by stretching and exercising our capabilities. The **need for self-determination** motivates us to achieve the feeling of satisfaction and control gained through making efforts that are not reliant on any external influences.

6.2 Differentiate among the various types of extrinsic rewards

Extrinsic rewards are external contributions awarded to employees such as salary, bonuses, paid vacations, and so on. **Seniority-based pay** is guaranteed wages and salary increases based on the amount of time the employee spends with the organization. **Job content-based pay** is a salary paid based on the evaluation of a job's worth. **Skill-based pay** rewards employees for the acquisition and the development of new skills that lead to enhanced work performance. **Performance-based pay** is a financial incentive awarded to employees for meeting certain goals or objectives.

6.3 Discuss the various facets of job design

Job design is a method of setting duties and responsibilities of a job with the intention of improving productivity and performance. **Job enlargement** increases the range of tasks and duties associated with a job. **Job rotation** is a process of periodically moving staff employees from one job to another. **Job enrichment** entails increasing the scope of a job to make it more complex, interesting, stimulating and satisfying for employees.

6.4 Discuss psychological empowerment and its components

Psychological empowerment is the extent to which employees feel a sense of personal fulfillment and intent when carrying out tasks, together with a belief that their work contributes to some larger purpose. There are four main beliefs associated with psychological empowerment. **Competence** is a belief in a person's ability to perform work tasks successfully. **Self-determination** is the understanding of skills, knowledge, and strengths that enable a person to make choices and initiate work tasks. **Impact** is the feeling of making a difference. **Meaningfulness** is the value of work tasks in line with a person's own self-concepts and ideals.

6.5 Evaluate various approaches to nontraditional work schedules

Free agents are independent workers that supply organizations with short-term talent for projects or time-bound objectives. **Part-time workers** (similar to free agents) are independent workers that supply organizations with part-time talent for projects or time-bound objectives.

There are four main nontraditional work schedules commonly adopted by employers. **Flextime** means flexible working hours where you customize your own work hours within limits established by management. **Compressed workweeks** give you the benefit of an extra day off by allowing you to work your usual number of hours in fewer days per pay period. **Job sharing** is when one full-time job is divided among two or more people according to predetermined hours. **Telecommuting** means working from home or from a remote location on a computer or other advanced telecommunications that are linked to the office.

KEY TERMS

THINKING CRITICALLY ABOUT THE CASE OF KATIE O'DONNELL

Staff Management and Motivation at the Waterfront Grill

Using the five critical-thinking steps, evaluate Kamal and Katie's performance as managers of the Waterfront Grill.

OBSERVE

What qualities does Kamal exhibit as a manager when he first meets with Katie about changes to pay and tipping at his restaurant? How does Katie respond to Kamal as a result of his approach? How does Kamal's response to Yuan's decision to leave the restaurant suggest he handles stress and disappointment?

INTERPRET

How do you explain Kamal's initial willingness to meet with Katie and agree to regular one-on-one feedback meetings with individual staff in comparison to his subsequent decision to only communicate with staff via email? Are you sympathetic to Kamal's decision? Why or why not?

ANALYZE

Assume that Katie O'Donnell decides to quit her job as assistant manager and gives Kamal two weeks' notice. What steps could Kamal take to convince Katie to remain at Waterfront Grill? If you were Kamal, would you try to keep her on staff? Explain your reasoning.

EVALUATE

List what you perceive to be Kamal's strengths and weaknesses as a manager. List what you perceive to be Katie's strengths and weaknesses as a manager. How might Kamal and Katie work together to offset each other's weaknesses as managers and more effectively run the restaurant?

EXPLAIN

What steps would you as Katie have taken to secure a face-to-face meeting with Kamal after the hosts resigned? What steps as Kamal would you have taken to ensure that employees stayed positive, collaborative, and on track?

EXERCISE 6.1: INTRINSIC REWARDS VERSUS EXTRINSIC REWARDS

What are your intrinsic motivators? List five or more and rank them in order with 1 being the most influential.

1. ______________________________
2. ______________________________
3. ______________________________
4. ______________________________
5. ______________________________

What are your extrinsic motivators? List five or more and rank them in order with 1 being the most influential.

1. ______________________________
2. ______________________________
3. ______________________________
4. ______________________________
5. ______________________________

Describe an instance in which your extrinsic motivators conflicted with your intrinsic motivators.

What steps can you take in the future to ensure balance between your extrinsic and intrinsic motivators?

EXERCISE 6.2: ROUND ROBIN

Objectives:

After completing this exercise, you will better able to and more confident about *discussing* the facets of job design, and the component of psychological empowerment.

Instructions:

Form into quads (groups of four people), and complete the following steps:

Step1. Choose a person to go first, and have that person say and write down *one* specific job design aspect, and how that aspect can either increase or decrease motivation (depending on the job design aspect). Then move to the person to the right of the initial speaker and repeat the process. Continue the process until time runs out or no one has more ideas. (5 minutes)

Step 2. Repeat this process, but for this round everyone should say and write down a way to better psychologically empower workers. (5 minutes)

Step 3. Be prepared to discuss the ideas generated in the quads during the class lecture. (Remainder of the class)

Reflection Questions:

1. In which round did you have the most trouble coming up with ideas?
2. Which ideas presented by your colleagues were most surprising or intriguing?
3. Which ideas helped you to better understand the chapter concepts?

Exercise contributed by Milton R. Mayfield, Professor of Business, Texas A&M International University and Jaqueline R. Mayfield, Professor of Business, Texas A&M International University.

EXERCISE 6.3: CHARITY BEGINS WITH MOTIVATION

Objectives:

In completing this exercise, you will have practiced your ability to *explain* intrinsic motivation and its determinants, *differentiate* between various types of extrinsic rewards, and *discuss* work duties in terms of a job design.

Background:

You are part of a group that is in charge of recruiting and staffing a charity car wash to raise money for a university scholarship fund. The car wash is expected to last from 8:00 a.m. to 5:00 or 6:00 p.m., with lunch provided on a rotating basis for each volunteer. In addition to the free lunch, the university can provide a small fund for compensation (approximately five to ten dollars per volunteer) to be used in any reasonable way the committee decides is appropriate. In addition to this fund, the university is planning on posting the volunteers' names and pictures on the university website along with a brief story about the event.

From your OB class, you realize the importance of a good job design in motivating people: both in terms of quality work outcomes and in being able to better recruit people for tasks. Using this knowledge, you were able to convince everyone to hold a meeting just to develop a clear plan for maximizing the volunteers' motivation for this event. You are about to go into that meeting.

Instructions:

Step 1. Form into groups (maximum of seven members), and create a motivation plan for the volunteers. This plan should include intrinsic and extrinsic motivations, as well as any job design aspects that are appropriate. Be creative in developing this plan, but also be sure to link your ideas back to chapter concepts, and use chapter terms in your descriptions. Then use this plan to make suggestions of how the job aspects can be used to promote the recruitment process. Also, provide information on how the job design and motivational aspects of the task are likely to affect volunteer outcomes. (20 minutes)

Step 2. Select a spokesperson to present your plan. (If possible, the spokesperson should be someone who has not had an opportunity to speak in front of the class before. If everyone has presented in front of class, select the person who has presented the least.) Before the person presents, give your group a unique name. (20 to 30 minutes)

Step 3. Vote on the plan that should be the most motivational. (You cannot vote for the team you were a member of.) In addition to writing the group's name on a sheet of paper, write down why you believe the plan will be the most motivational using chapter terms. (10 to 15 minutes)

Reflection Questions:

1. What difficulties did you encounter in developing motivational methods with such constrained resources? How are these difficulties similar to what supervisors for entry level personnel face?
2. Which type of motivations do you expect to be stronger in this situation—intrinsic or extrinsic?
3. How might that motivational balance differ for supervisors of entry-level personnel?
4. How did using chapter terms and concepts better help you frame and understand this situation?
5. What other teams came up with creative ways to motivate the volunteers? Were there motivators that you found difficult to classify as intrinsic or extrinsic?

Exercise contributed by Milton R. Mayfield, Professor of Business, Texas A&M International University and Jaqueline R. Mayfield, Professor of Business, Texas A&M International University.

CASE STUDY 6.1: NETFLIX

Netflix's new employee practices have grabbed attention, to put it mildly. In 2012, a simple internal PowerPoint explaining them went viral and was viewed more than 5 million times on the Web. Sheryl Sandberg, chief operating officer of Facebook, said it "may well be the most important document ever to come out of [Silicon] Valley." Dozens of bloggers and journalists scrambled to analyze its contents. And Netflix is surely doing something right: In 2013, the company's stock value tripled. It reached a record 29 million subscribers and won three Emmy Awards for its original show *House of Cards*.

What was revealed in that game-changing PowerPoint? It was simply a "commonsense" approach, according to Patty McCord, then Netflix's chief talent officer and one of the presentation's authors. Netflix treats the people it hires as grownups. It grants them a great deal of freedom, and it expects them to use it wisely.

Game Changers

Conventional human resources (HR) is full of structure and documentation. Directors spend hours drafting standard operating procedures about time off, performance appraisals, training, and more. Netflix has simplified the process by doing away with many of these policies and focusing on results rather than processes.

McCord realized that motivating employees to produce outstanding results had a lot to do with trusting them with greater independence. That didn't mean installing an arcade or skateboard park, as other tech companies have done. Instead, Netflix started doing away with formal procedures. Among the first to go was the leave procedure. Gone were the standard 10 days of vacation, 10 holidays, and handful of sick days. The new policy? Take what you need when you need it.

Giving employees the leeway to take as much vacation time as they'd like might strike many HR professionals as reckless. Wouldn't people abuse such a liberal leave plan? McCord, however, had shifted to a different philosophy. Written policies, she reasoned, were mainly designed to eliminate problems created by a very small percentage of employees. The vast majority of people, and particularly the type of person Netflix tries to recruit, could be counted on to use common sense in their decision making.

This approach was extended to other areas. Travel and expense accounts are generally kept under a watchful eye, policed by HR or accounting to ensure that money is being spent in an acceptable manner, with plenty of documentation and accountability. Netflix turned tradition on its head, creating what may be the shortest expense policy any company has ever set: "Act in Netflix's best interests." Employees are also allowed to book their own travel online rather than going through a designated travel agent, allowing them to choose the best price.

Netflix compensates its employees very well, but there's freedom there, too. People can choose what portion of their pay they would like to receive in direct compensation and what portion in stock options. This allows them to consider what sort of risk level they're comfortable with (the value of any company's stock will fluctuate over time) and what is best for them and their families. Netflix also eliminated performance-based bonuses, preferring to pay people fairly and trust them to do good work. There are no "golden handcuffs"—a form of retention plan that does not allow employees to receive stock options or other incentives until they've reached a certain number of years of service. Employees are also encouraged to research and interview with competitor companies and then have frank discussions with HR. This helps both the department *and* the employee know what is are good salaries for various positions.

The company also decided to forego conventional performance reviews. It eliminated the performance metrics typical of many companies' evaluations, like grading an employee on a five-point scale in a variety of different tasks and expectations. Instead, a "360-degree review" is performed, which is an open conversation between employees and their managers about feedback from people inside (and occasionally outside) the company who have any contact with the employee. The evaluation is largely centered on one question for the manager, known as the "keeper test": "Which of my people, if they told me they were leaving in two months for a similar job at a peer company, would I fight hard to keep at Netflix?" If someone's skills and abilities are no longer a match for the company, the person is given a generous severance package upon exit. As CEO Reed Hastings told the *Harvard Business Review*, paraphrasing a section of the now-famous PowerPoint: "'Adequate performance gets a generous severance package.' It's a pretty blunt statement of our hunger for excellence."

The document is "our version of *Letters to a Young Poet* for budding entrepreneurs," Reed continued. "It's what we wish we had understood when we started." He goes on to argue that a relatively new industry—online, on-demand entertainment—demands new paradigms. "As a society, we've had hundreds of years to work on managing industrial firms, so a lot of accepted HR practices are centered in that experience. We're just beginning to learn how to run creative firms, which is quite different. Industrial firms thrive on reducing variation (manufacturing errors); creative firms thrive on increasing variation (innovation)."

The Payoffs

Netflix's overhaul of its HR policies has yielded positive results. Despite the lack of carefully outlined procedures, the expectations are still clear: you have the freedom to make decisions, but keep in mind what is best for the company. The HR department at Netflix has realized that it isn't necessary to beat its people over the head with exactly *how* to make good decisions.

Freedom equals reduced stress, arguably. The level of flexibility and self-management that Netflix also offers creates more efficiency. Employees don't have to worry about whether they've racked up enough days off to take a trip or whether they've worked long enough hours to impress the boss. They aren't fretting over how the big annual review will go, or whether they'll get the score that will earn the bonus they've been counting on. Eliminating these typical workplace stressors motivates employees to stay focused on creating ideas and solutions for the business.

At Netflix, clear and honest communication thrives. Employees don't fear retribution for looking into openings with other companies; they can go to HR and openly discuss other possibilities. Managers no longer have to spend time "in the weeds" developing improvement plans and riding mediocre workers for results. Likewise, employees are less likely to have to pick up slack for colleagues who are not performing. While Netflix lets people go whose knowledge and skills are no longer relevant, it's candid about why. As McCord puts it, "People can handle anything as long as they're told the truth."

Being straightforward has costs, but having direct conversations with and offering a generous severance package to employees who are no longer a good fit has resulted in *zero* lawsuits over termination to date. HR is also empowered to find someone who fits the bill rather than continuing to invest in someone who cannot do what's needed while risking the morale and motivation of fellow coworkers.

By allowing its employees plenty of liberty to make decisions for themselves, Netflix has reaped great rewards in employee motivation, efficiency, and productivity. While the premise may have seemed risky, it proved to be a commonsense solution for issues most HR departments face. Considering the way it revolutionized and streamlined the movie rental process for changing times, it is hardly surprising that Netflix seems to have done the same for employee motivation.

Case Questions

1. How does Netflix use intrinsic motivation to support its HR practices?
2. Why would a creative firm choose to use intrinsic motivation where an industrial firm would probably choose to use extrinsic rewards?
3. Explain the appeal of nontraditional work schedules and how Netflix has chosen to implement them.

Sources

Baer, Drake. "Netflix's Major HR Innovation: Treating Humans Like People." *Fast Company.* March 13, 2014. www.fastcompany.com/3027124/lessons-learned/netflixs-major-hr-innovation-treating-humans-like-people.

Fenzi, Francesca. "3 Big Ideas to Steal from Netflix." *Inc.* February 5, 2013. www.inc.com/francesca-fenzi/management-ideas-to-steal-from-netflix.html.

Grossman, Robert J. "Tough Love at Netflix." *HR.*. April 1, 2010. www.shrm.org/Publications/hrmagazine/EditorialContent/2010/0410/Pages/0410grossman3.aspx.

Kamensky, John. "Netflix's 5 Tenets of HR." *Government Executive.* February 14, 2014. www.govexec.com/excellence/promising-practices/2014/02/netflixs-5-tenets-hr/78827/.

McCord, Patty. "How Netflix Reinvented HR." *Harvard Business Review* (January–February 2014). http://hbr.org/2014/01/how-netflix-reinvented-hr.

Nisen, Max. "Legendary Ex-HR Director from Netflix Shares 6 Important Lessons." *Business Insider.* December 30, 2013. www.businessinsider.com/netflix-corporate-culture-hr-policy-2013-12.

No Author. "Netflix Wins Three Emmys." *Huffington Post.* September 23, 2013. www.huffingtonpost.com/2013/09/22/netflix-emmys-house-of-cards-wins_n_3973794.html.

SELF-ASSESSMENT 6.1

Is Job Enrichment Motivational to Me?

For each statement, circle the number that best describes you based on the following scale:

	Strongly Disagree	Somewhat Disagree	Neutral	Somewhat Agree	Strongly Agree
1. I prefer a job that requires me to use a number of complex and high-level skills.	1	2	3	4	5
2. I prefer a job in which the work is arranged so that I have the chance to complete an entire work process from beginning to end.	1	2	3	4	5
3. I prefer a job that provides many chances for me to figure out how well I am doing.	1	2	3	4	5
4. I do not prefer work that is quite simple and repetitive.	1	2	3	4	5
5. I prefer a job in which a lot of other people can be affected by how well the work gets done.	1	2	3	4	5
6. I prefer a job that provides me the opportunity to use my own personal initiative and judgment in carrying out the work.	1	2	3	4	5
7. I prefer to completely finish the work processes that I begin.	1	2	3	4	5
8. I enjoy work that provides information about how well I am performing.	1	2	3	4	5
9. I prefer considerable independence and freedom in how I do my work.	1	2	3	4	5
10. I am interested in work that is very significant or important in the broader scheme of things.	1	2	3	4	5
11. I prefer a job that allows me to decide on my own how to go about doing the work.	1	2	3	4	5
12. I prefer a job that provides me with information about my performance.	1	2	3	4	5

Scoring

Add the numbers circled above: ____________

Interpretation

48 and above = You have a strong desire for complex, challenging work. You would find an enriched job to be very motivational.

25–47 = You have moderate desire for complex, challenging work. You would find an enriched job to be moderately motivational.

24 and below = You have a low desire for complex, challenging work. You would not find an enriched job to be motivational. You would prefer a job that is more simple, straightforward, and uncomplicated.

SOURCE: Adapted from Hackman, J. R., and G. R. Oldham. *The Job Diagnostic Survey: An Instrument for the Diagnosis of Jobs and the Evaluation of Job Redesign Projects.* Technical Report No. 4 (New Haven, CT: Yale University, Department of Administrative Sciences, 1974).

B

PART 3
TEAMS AND TEAMWORK

7 Teams

I am a member of a team, and I rely on the team, I defer to it and sacrifice for it, because the team, not the individual, is the ultimate champion.

—Mia Hamm, American professional soccer player

TEAMS AND TEAMWORK IN CONTEMPORARY ORGANIZATIONS

LEARNING OBJECTIVES

By the end of this chapter, you will be able to:

- 7.1 Distinguish between a team and a group
- 7.2 Compare the various types of teams in organizations today
- 7.3 Apply the model of team effectiveness to evaluate team performance
- 7.4 Explain how team processes affect team outcomes
- 7.5 Identify the advantages and disadvantages of different team decision-making approaches

7.1 Distinguish between a team and a group

There is no doubt that teams and teamwork play a critical role in the success of 21st century organizations. The most successful organizations value and understand the nature of teams and create a productive environment in which teams flourish. A **team** is a collection of people brought together to apply their individual skills to a common project or goal.[1]

Regardless of the type of organization, most employees work in some form of a team in today's workplace. Compared to a few decades ago, teamwork has become commonplace in contemporary organizations. But what has caused this dramatic shift to team structures? Global competition means that organizations need to respond quickly to competitive pressures. Efficient, collaborative teams are one way for organizations to meet the growing demands of their customers and stay ahead of the competition. Some organizations take collaboration so seriously that they are changing the traditional office layout and replacing cubicles with low walls or no walls between desks. Many are creating small, informal areas designed to encourage spontaneous discussion and problem solving.[2]

Organizational restructuring and downsizing have brought leaner, more efficient and more productive structures to many companies. Rather than viewing layoffs as a negative, some companies perceive a trimmer organization as an optimal way for employees to collaborate more intensely, to become more engaged in the decision-making processes, and to contribute their own ideas and initiatives. In addition, employees have become more empowered through **decentralization**, the distribution of power across all levels of the organization.[3] Employees are encouraged to be creative and innovative and given more freedom to make decisions.

Decentralization

Finally, many employees, especially in the United States and Europe, are working in high technology or knowledge information industries where close collaboration is viewed as a positive forum for innovation and creativity. Take Taco Bell, for instance. Its efforts to reinvent the taco as the DLT (Doritos Locos Taco) called on the knowledge, creative input, and close collaboration of members of the development team to come up with the flavor and seasoning, the engineering team to find a way to make the shells bend without cracking, and manufacturing teams to make the shells as quickly as possible. The result of this teamwork was such a success that 450 million DLTs have been sold since launching, in 2012.[4]

Team: A group of people brought together to use their individual skills on a common project or goal

Decentralization: The distribution of power across all levels of the organization

Master the content.
edge.sagepub.com/neckob

Teams and Groups

Group: Three or more people who work independently to attain organizational goals

Teams Versus Groups

The terms *teams* and *groups* are often used interchangeably, but there are subtle differences between them.[5]

A **group** usually consists of three or more people who work independently to attain organizational goals.[6] For example, in a small business, there might be three people in the marketing department; one might be focused on sales, another on branding, and a third on the administration associated with those tasks. In contrast, teams consist of a number of people, usually between three and seven, who use their complementary skills to collaborate in a joint effort. Teams with fewer than three people tend not to derive the benefits of a collaborative team, and teams with more than seven tend to have communication and control issues. In this chapter we focus on teams.

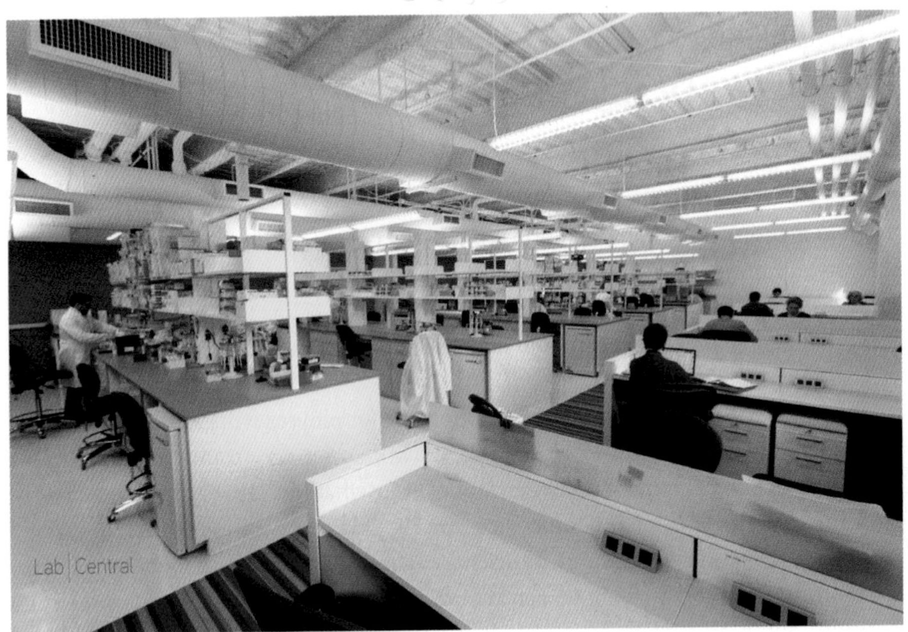

PRNewsFoto/LabCentral

LabCentral in Cambridge, MA is a unique shared lab space for up-and-coming life science startups, specifically designed to spark innovation and foster collaboration.

THE BIG PICTURE: How OB Topics Fit Together

Individual Processes
- Individual Differences
- Emotions and Attitudes
- Perceptions and Learning
- Motivation

Team Processes
- Ethics
- Decision Making
- Creativity and Innovation
- Conflict and Negotiation

Organizational Processes
- Culture
- Strategy
- Change and Development
- Structure and Technology

Influence Processes
- Leadership
- Power and Politics
- Communication

Organizational Outcomes
- Individual Performance
- Job Satisfaction
- **TEAM PERFORMANCE**
- Organizational Goals

Jim R. Bounds/AP Images for Taco Bell

Taco Bell COO Rob Savage poses for a photo with the winner of a social media contest promoting Doritos Locos Tacos.

Are Teams Effective?

The effectiveness of work teams depends on how well they are managed and treated within the organization. A well-run team is usually productive, innovative, loyal, and adaptable. Organizations that consistently nurture teams tend to experience reduced turnover and absenteeism. However, teams can fail if they are mismanaged; if they are not implemented properly, they can cause more harm than good. Explore the concept of teams further from the point of view of Tanya Faidley, former curriculum coordinator at the Virginia School for the Deaf and the Blind (VSDB) in the OB in the Real World feature.

THINKING CRITICALLY

1. What types of tasks are best suited to a group? What types of tasks are best suited to a team? **[Understand/Apply]**
2. Which of the four aspects of a well-run team (productive, innovative, loyal, adaptable) do you think is the most important? Which do you think is least important? Explain your response. **[Analyze/ Evaluate]**

TYPES OF TEAMS

7.2 Compare the various types of teams in organizations today

Virtual Teams

The technological revolution has turned the original concept of what a team means on its head. Many global companies now operate in **virtual teams**, whose members are in different locations and work together through email, video conferencing, instant messaging, and other electronic media.[7] Virtual team members have great flexibility because they are able to work anywhere, including their own homes. Organizations value the virtual team model because it saves on travel costs by eliminating in-person meetings and allows for greater sharing of information between employees from different countries. However, there are a few disadvantages to working in a virtual team. Time differences between countries can cause confusion, lack of face-to-face contact

Virtual teams: Groups of individuals from different locations work together through e-mail, video conferencing, instant messaging, and other electronic media

TANYA FAIDLEY, *curriculum coordinator, the Virginia School for the Deaf and the Blind (VSDB)*

OB in the Real World

© Tanya Faidley

The Virginia School for the Deaf and the Blind is one of the oldest schools in Virginia and the second if its kind in the world. It was established in 1839 and serves students from pre-kindergarten through 12th grade. Residential and day students are deaf/hard of hearing, blind/vision impaired, or deaf and blind, and some have secondary disabilities as well. VSDB strives to create an environment that fosters self-confidence and helps to develop contributing citizens and lifelong learners. The staff consists of 45 teachers and 15 support staff including occupational therapists, speech therapists, audiologists, counselors, and behavioral specialists.

Tanya was the curriculum coordinator at the VSDB for 38 years before retiring in the summer of 2013. During her time at the school, she supervised the teaching assistants, made sure teachers had necessary resources, established budgets, set up new projects, and ensured that blind students had access to Braille textbooks.

At VSDB, the team meets every week to discuss students' progress with standardized tests, schoolwork, language, and writing development. They work hard to ensure that students are integrating into the school, making friends, and if they are residential students, managing being away from their families. "We're all here for the same reason—to provide the best education possible and to raise the bar as high as we can for students with disabilities," Tanya comments. "These children achieve their best when we are supporting them as a team. Communication is paramount in everything we do, and in-person communication trumps e-mail."

Recently, one student was thriving in some of her classes but struggling in others. A meeting was called with all her teachers (science, social studies, English, math, music, daily living skills, orientation and mobility, Braille, and physical education) along with the school psychologist, school counselor, and vice principal.

"By open communication and teamwork, we discovered that specific teaching strategies used in one particular classroom were really effective," Tanya says. They figured out how to implement the successful strategies into all this student's classes and she flourished.

Another student, William, had been attending his public high school and was really struggling. One day he came home and told his mom he just couldn't do it anymore. His parents sent him to VSDB, and the team put together a plan that would allow William to catch up and graduate from high school. Staff members quickly realized that William loved police work. His job coordinator made an arrangement with the local police department and an officer would pick him up from the school, take him on their beats, bring him to the station, and teach him more about the criminal justice system.

Thanks to the team approach and individual attention he received at VSDB, William graduated from high school and is currently studying criminal justice at a local community college. "That's what we're here for. When you see this type of success story you can't help but feel proud of how much work our team did to offer the resources to these kids so they could be successful," Tanya comments.

"It's amazing when you walk into the school and you see the expertise level of the people working there. Everyone is working as a team to meet the goals for the students and it goes beyond just the teachers and support staff. From the employees in the front office to the maintenance crew, everyone cares. We have a security guard named Charlie, who has really taken to the kids, learning sign language so he can communicate with them. When he's not around the kids will always ask, 'Where's Charlie. Where's Charlie!?' That teamwork and connection that we all feel is what makes this place so special."

Critical-Thinking Questions

1. **In your view, how do members of the VDSB team work together to meet their goals for the students?**
2. **How would you cultivate a team where "everyone cares"?**

SOURCE: Tanya Faidley, personal interview.

© iStockphoto.com/LDProd

Virtual teams can communicate with each other more easily with video conferencing software like Skype.

can result in miscommunication, and cultural differences can also compound misunderstandings related to distance.

However, in many instances, virtual teams work successfully. Take the author team of this book, for example. Chris Neck lives in Arizona; Jeff Houghton is in West Virginia; and Emma Murray lives in London, United Kingdom. Despite their locations, the team has managed to successfully work together over a number of years thanks to e-mail and Skype.

Self-Managing Teams

Other types of teams include self-managing teams, problem-solving teams, and cross-functional teams. A **self-managing team** is a group of workers who manage their own daily duties under little to no supervision.[8] Systems engineering and management company Semco is composed of highly effective self-managing teams, in which team members are expected make decisions without consulting higher management.[9]

A **problem-solving team** consists of a small group of workers who come together for a set amount of time to discuss and resolve specific issues.[10] Small teams at global design firm IDEO use design thinking to solve complex problems.[11] Finally, a **cross-functional team** is comprised of a group of workers from different units with various areas of expertise to work on certain projects.[12] The cross-functional model can be effective in both large and small companies. For example, small business Reprint Management Services of Lancaster, Pennsylvania, successfully uses cross-functional teams to manage special projects.[13]

In the following continuing narrative, we explore these three types of teams in more detail and examine how they commonly operate in the workplace.

Introducing the Case of Brian Stevens: Trouble at the Tractor Assembly Plant

Human resources (HR) manager Brian Stevens has been working in a tractor engine manufacturing plant in the Midwest. He recently received a promotion to plant manager at the company's tractor assembly plant, located a few miles from his current location, and reports directly to the president of the company, Hans Wagner. Brian is both excited and apprehensive about his new role, which brings added responsibilities. Still, he is looking forward to the challenge and hopes his new colleagues will be supportive.

Self-managing team: A group of workers who manage their daily duties under little to no supervision

Problem-solving team: A group of workers coming together for a set amount of time to discuss specific issues

Cross-functional team: A group of workers from different units with various areas of expertise, assembled to address certain issues

On his first day on the new job, Brian meets with the plant's HR manager, Maria Gonzalez, to discuss the current situation at the assembly plant.

"We have a problem," Maria begins. "The purchasing department is underperforming and it's costing us a lot of money."

Brian knows how crucial the purchasing department is to the daily operation of the plant. The staff in this department is responsible for buying the parts, materials, and components for the machine assembly. They are also in charge of evaluating the price of the materials to maximize profitability, negotiating with vendors, and shopping around for better rates when necessary. The purchasing department also deals with the necessary paperwork and works closely with the accounts department to ensure orders have been received and paid for on time.

"What's the problem in purchasing?" Brian asks.

"Purchase orders are missing or being sent to the vendors late. The inventory that does show up is either too much or too little for the production line's needs. Sometimes the quality of the components is below our standards, which means we have to return them, yet the team keeps making repeat orders to the same vendors instead of shopping around," Maria says.

"The employees in the warehouses are going crazy because they don't have the space for over-ordered inventory; the assembly line is affected when material is under-ordered or flawed; and the production and planning department is frustrated because of the poor quality of some of the components."

"How long has this been going on?" Brian asks.

"About four months," Maria responds. "Clearly there's a problem within the team but so far we haven't been able to identify it."

When Maria explains that the purchasing department is a *self-managing team,* Brian is skeptical. In his career to date, he has never witnessed a successful self-managing team. He's seen conflict among team members, lack of accountability, and poor commitment, leading to low morale, high absenteeism, and increased turnover.

Maria agrees to some extent but explains that the situation with the purchasing department isn't as clear-cut as Brian suggests. "The team used to work really well together and has been our highest performing team. In fact, their self-managing model has been so successful that we've been thinking of applying it to the rest of the team structures in the plant," she explains.

"But now there are problems with this team . . . ," Brian says, thoughtfully. "What did the previous plant manager do to address it?"

"He didn't feel it was appropriate to challenge a self-managing team," Maria replies. Though Brian understands that managers must adopt a "hands-off" policy toward self-managing teams, he is curious to know why his predecessor didn't step in, especially when the team's errors are costing the organization so much money.

"Did Hans Wagner agree with this decision?" Brian says.

"Hans is busy and just wants the problem fixed," Maria says. "He told me and the previous plant manager to do whatever we could to sort out the problem, but it's been difficult."

"What have you done so far?" Brian says.

"Since the team is self-managing, they expect very little interference," Maria explains. "But we did implement one initiative to try and find the source of the problem."

Maria explains that she set up a *problem-solving team.* The group included employees from different areas of the production department.

"The meetings didn't go as planned, however," Maria says. "There was very little talk about the work issues and lots of joking around. Nobody took responsibility for the problems and the meetings went nowhere."

Brian is puzzled. "Have there been any changes to the purchasing team over the last few months?" Brian says.

Maria hesitates. "Six months ago Nathan Jackson joined the team, replacing a long-standing team member who left for health reasons."

"Is Nathan a poor fit for the team? Do you think that's why there have been so many problems recently?" Brian asks.

"That's what I thought initially, but Nathan is one of our most popular employees. Although high performing, the team was a little isolated before, and social communication was lacking between team members and the rest of the department. Since Nathan's arrival, the team members have become much more social. Morale has really improved!" Maria replies.

Brian frowns. "So morale is up and productivity is down. What is going on?" he wonders.

In his earlier role with the company, Brian had set up a *cross-functional team.* Because the team members had different skills and came from different areas, they were able to contribute a variety of solutions and objectively address the problems with the project. Brian wonders whether Maria's problem-solving team had too many members from the same area with similar skills who were too friendly with the purchasing team to be objective. He thought a cross-functional team might be able to provide a fresh perspective on the situation.

When he suggests the idea to Maria, she says, "I'm not sure whether the self-managing team will welcome any more outside involvement, but it's your call."

Brian agrees she has a point. He needs to learn a lot more about the purchasing team before he forges ahead with any ideas.

THINKING CRITICALLY

1. Imagine that you are assigned to work with a virtual team. What challenges and drawbacks might you encounter? What technological methods of communication would you use most often to communicate? Why? **[Understand/Apply]**
2. What industries and types of businesses would be most likely to be open to the use of self-managing teams? What industries and types of businesses would be least open to the use of self-managing teams? Explain your answers. **[Analyze/Evaluate]**
3. What criteria would you as a manager use in determining whether a problem-solving team should also be a cross-functional team? In other words, what types of issues would a problem-solving team from the same functional area solve most efficiently and what types of issues would a problem-solving team that is also cross-functional solve most efficiently? **[Analyze/Evaluate]**
4. Review the case about Brian Stevens' management challenge at the tractor assembly plant. Generate a list of at least five possible explanations for the problems affecting the self-managing team responsible for purchasing. Pick the two explanations and explain what you believe Brian's next steps should be in each case. **[Evaluate/Create]**

A MODEL OF TEAM EFFECTIVENESS: CONTEXT AND COMPOSITION

7.3 Apply the model of team effectiveness to evaluate team performance

As the tractor plant case demonstrates, not all teams are effective. Effective teams in an organization are characterized by their ability to improve quality, reach goals, and change processes. One classic way of understanding teams and their effectiveness is to

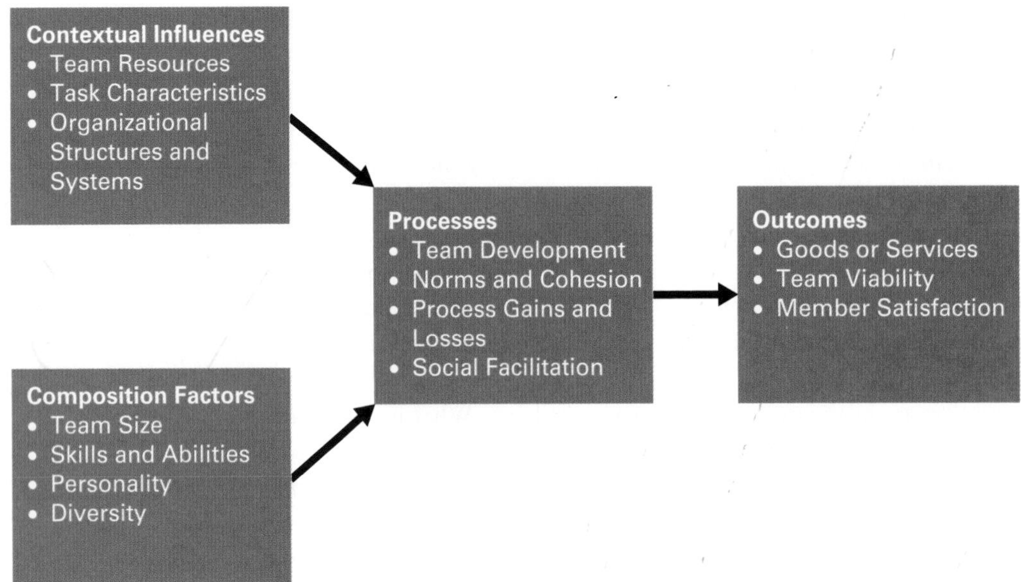

■ FIGURE 7.1 A Model of Team Effectiveness

SOURCE: Figure adapted from Hackman, J. R. "The Design of Work Teams." In *Handbook of Organizational Behavior*, edited by J. W. Lorsch, 315–342 (Englewood Cliffs, NJ: Prentice-Hall, 1987); McGrath, J. E. *Social Psychology: A Brief Introduction* (New York: Rinehart and Winston, 1964); Resick, C. J., M. W. Dickson, J. K. Mitchelson, L. K. Allison, and M. A. Clark. "Team Composition, Cognition, and Effectiveness: Examining Mental Model Similarity and Accuracy." *Group Dynamics: Theory, Research, and Practice* 14, no. 2 (June 2010): 174–191; Doolen, Toni L., Marla E. Hacker, and Eileen M. Van Aken. "The Impact of Organizational Context on Work Team Effectiveness: A Study of Production Team." *IEEE Transactions on Engineering Management* 50, no. 3 (August 2003): 285–296.

consider teams in terms of the contextual influences that affect their functioning, their composition, the processes they use, and the outcomes they achieve.[14] Figure 7.1 shows how these factors influence team effectiveness.

In the next section, we explore contextual influences and composition factors through Brian's and Maria's continued discussion about the problems with the purchasing team.

Team Contextual Influences

Later in the day, Brian and Maria sit down to discuss the extent of team contextual influences on the purchasing group. There are three main contextual influences: team resources, task characteristics, and organizational systems and structures.

Team resources are important for effective teams because they equip the team members with the tools to successfully perform their roles. Resources consist of the equipment, materials, training, information, staffing, and budgets the organization supplies to support the team's goals. The purchasing team has the appropriate amount of materials and training and is fully staffed, thanks to the addition of the new team member, Nathan Jackson.

Tasks are the specific steps the team must perform to achieve its goals. They can be structured or unstructured, complex or simple, and characterized by more or less interdependence among team members. **Interdependence** is the extent to which team members rely on each other to complete their work tasks.[15] There are three levels of interdependence:

Interdependence: The extent to which team members rely on each other to complete their work tasks

Pooled interdependence: An organizational model in which each team member produces a piece of work independently of the other members

- **Pooled interdependence** occurs when each team member produces a piece of work independently of the others. Sandwich fast-food restaurant Subway is an example of pooled interdependence. Though each restaurant unit is a part of the overall Subway organization, the units work independently of each other.[16]

- **Sequential interdependence** takes place when one team member completes a piece of work and passes it on to the next member for his or her input, as on an assembly line. Car manufacturer Toyota's production system is partly based on sequential interdependence.[17]
- **Reciprocal interdependence** happens when team members work closely together on a piece of work, consulting with each other, providing each other with advice, and exchanging information. For example, the teams at Parkland Memorial Hospital rely on reciprocal interdependence to manage the intense coordination of the different services provided to patients and the movement between those services.[18]

AP Photo/Ted S. Warren

Subway restaurants are an example of pooled interdependence. While all Subway restaurants are part of the larger organization, they operate independently of one another.

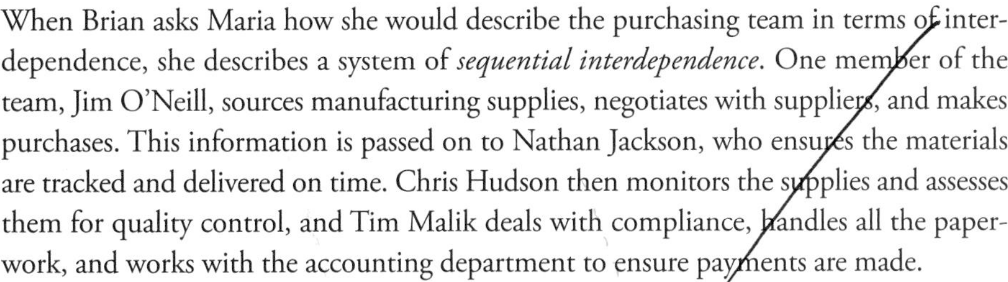

When Brian asks Maria how she would describe the purchasing team in terms of interdependence, she describes a system of *sequential interdependence*. One member of the team, Jim O'Neill, sources manufacturing supplies, negotiates with suppliers, and makes purchases. This information is passed on to Nathan Jackson, who ensures the materials are tracked and delivered on time. Chris Hudson then monitors the supplies and assesses them for quality control, and Tim Malik deals with compliance, handles all the paperwork, and works with the accounting department to ensure payments are made.

"Ideally, that's the way it should work," Maria says. "But clearly something isn't right, because there are flaws in each of the areas and yet nobody is willing to take responsibility for the problems."

Brian is determined to find the flaw in the purchasing team's workflow, but he knows there is more analysis to do first. He and Maria move on to the next team contextual influence: organizational systems and structures. Brian knows from his experience as an HR manager that performance management systems, compensation and reward systems, and

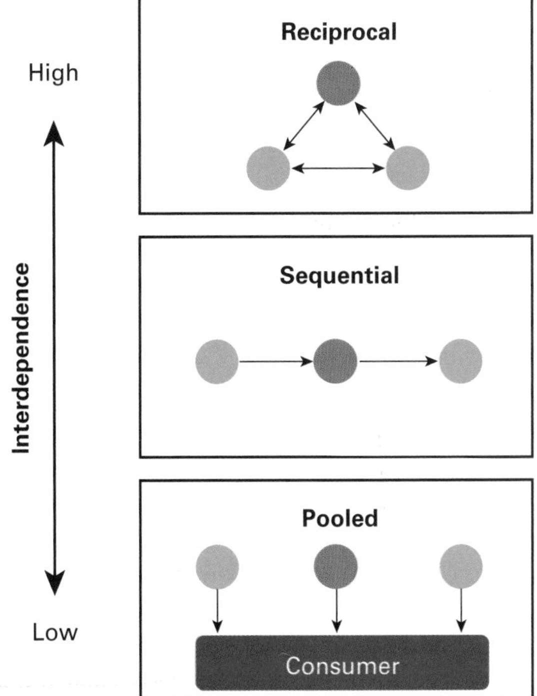

■ FIGURE 7.2 Levels of Task Interdependence

Sequential interdependence: An organizational model in which one team member completes a piece of work and passes it on to the next member for their input, similar to an assembly line

Reciprocal interdependence: An organizational model in which team members work closely together on a piece of work, consulting with each other, providing each other with advice, and exchanging information

While it may be tempting to congratulate or reward individual employees, this could create conflict or resentment among team members.

organizational and leadership structures must be aligned with team structures to maintain smooth running of operations. If these systems and structures are out of place it could cause problems. For example, rewarding or evaluating one team member for performance rather than the whole team may cause conflict and resentment, and strict hierarchical structures or authoritative leaders can sometimes disempower teams if often decisions are made without consulting them.

Maria tells Brian the purchasing team evaluates performance and rewards on a team basis, recruits and selects new hires, and monitors individual performance of team members. Because they are self-managing, there is no authoritarian leader watching over them or making demands. Satisfied that he has a better understanding of the team's structure and its organization, Brian moves on to team composition.

Team Composition

Typically, a team is characterized by four qualities: its size as well as the skills and abilities, personalities, and diversity of its members.

The appropriate *size* of a team depends on the task the team needs to perform. In general, teams tend to consist of four to seven members. Maria tells Brian the purchasing team needs only four members to function efficiently.

If all that being a team player meant was having *skills* and *abilities*, professional baseball teams with the highest payrolls (like the New York Yankees) would win the World Series every year. Instead, however, it's the way talent interacts in the context of team processes that brings results. Maria tells Brian she feels all the members of the purchasing team have the right skills for the roles they are performing.

In terms of *personality,* teams typically need a balance between extraverts and introverts.[19] Having too many extraverts can mean too much talking and not enough listening, and having too many introverts can mean very little communication among the team members. Generally, people who are agreeable and conscientious are effective team members.[20]

Brian asks Maria to describe the individual personalities of each team member.

"Nathan is a real extravert, no doubt about that!" she says. "He's always making everyone laugh. He has a real bond with the team. I would say Chris, Jim, and Tim fall into the introvert category. In fact, the employee Nathan replaced was also an introvert. They were a quiet bunch but they got along well and got the job done." Brian nods, wondering whether the imbalanced personality types have something to do with the problems within the team. Still, he knows he needs to gather all the facts before he starts making assumptions.

Ensuring *diversity* on a team can be a challenge. Recall from Chapter 2 that diversity include surface-level factors such as race and ethnicity, gender, sexuality, and age as well as deep-level factors such as personality and beliefs. From a team composition perspective managers are most concerned with the ways that deep-level diversity factors, like introversion and extraversion, affect team functioning. Typically, team members who share similarities in values, personalities, and interests tend to have positive social relationships with each other, which helps the team to be more effective.

Psychologist Benjamin Schneider's attraction-selection-attrition (ASA) model (see Figure 7.3) states that people are functions of three interrelated dynamic processes: attraction, selection, and attrition, all of which influence organizational culture.[21] For example, new employees are *attracted* to a team because of a perceived similarity in values, interests, and goals. New hires are *selected* based on how well they fit in to an organization. Over time, *attrition* occurs when employees feel they do not fit in, causing them to leave the organization.

This theory explains why team members who are perceived as sharing similarities are selected as a good "fit," while those who do not fit in tend to leave the team.[22] However, there must be a balance between diversity and similarity, because too many people behaving in a similar way can stunt growth and have a negative effect on insight and creativity due to the lack of unique viewpoints.

Brian asks Maria why she believes Nathan Jackson is a good fit for the team, since she describes him as an outgoing, outspoken individual who does not seem to share the same quiet focus and concentration as the other members.

Maria smiles. "Nathan is the kind of person who fits in anywhere. He has a big personality and he's really likable. In fact, he seems to find common ground with anyone he meets. The others on the team are definitely a happier bunch when he's around. I guess you just have to meet the team and decide for yourself."

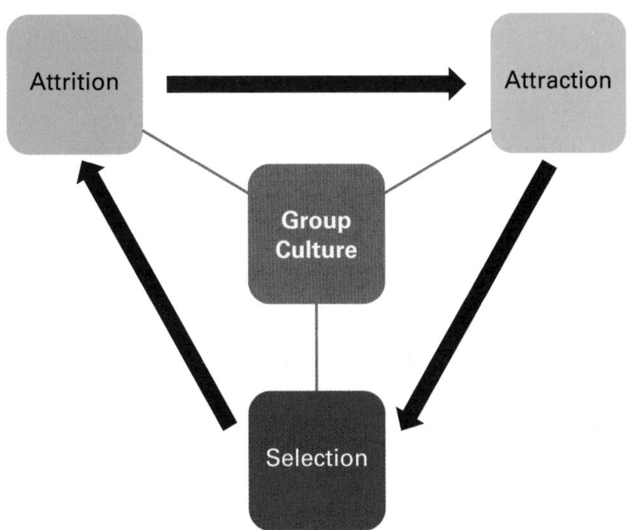

■ FIGURE 7.3 Attraction-Selection-Attrition Model

SOURCE: Based on Schneider, Benjamin. "The People Make the Place." *Personnel Psychology* 40, no. 3 (September 1987): 437–453; Schneider, Benjamin, Harold W. Goldstein, and D. Brent Smith. "The ASA Framework: An Update." *Personnel Psychology* 48, no. 4 (Winter 1995): 747–773.

THINKING CRITICALLY

1. Based on this section and Figure 7.1, the model of team effectiveness, explain how problems in each one of the three contextual influences (team resources, task characteristics, and organizational structure and systems) could affect team success. Provide an example for each of the three influences. **[Apply/Analyze]**

2. Explain how problems in each one of the composition factors (team size, skills and abilities, personality, and diversity) could affect team success. Provide an example for each of the four composition factors. **[Apply/Analyze]**

3. Do you think there are any types of situations where either contextual influences or composition factors would have a bigger influence on successful team functioning? Explain. **[Analyze/Evaluate]**

4. Assume you work in a restaurant that specializes in a broad variety of Chinese-style dumplings and potstickers. Identify the likely level of task interdependence (pooled, sequential, or reciprocal) for each of the groups involved with the operation of the restaurant (dumpling makers, hosts, servers, runners, bartenders). **[Understand/Apply]**

5. Consider diversity as it was discussed in Chapter 2 and its impact on and interplay with the ASA Model. How might a lack of surface-level diversity in a team affect the attraction and selection process discussed in the ASA Model? What are the potential weaknesses of teams that lack diversity in these areas? **[Apply/Analyze]**

A MODEL OF TEAM EFFECTIVENESS: PROCESSES AND OUTCOMES

7.4 Explain how team processes affect team outcomes

When teams first come together they go through a number of stages in the process of becoming a team. In his original model of group development in 1965, psychologist Bruce Tuckman named the stages "forming, norming, storming, and performing" (Figure 7.4).[23] Twelve years later, Tuckman created a fifth stage called "adjourning."

Forming: A process whereby team members meet for the first time, get to know each other, and try to understand where they fit in to the team structure

Storming: A phase during which, after a period of time, tension may arise between members and different personalities might clash, leading to tension and conflict in the team

Norming: The process by which team members resolve the conflict and begin to work well together and become more cohesive

Performing: The way in which a team is invested towards achieving its goals and operates as a unit

Adjourning: The stage when individuals either leave the team or have no reason to be in further contact with their teammates

Forming. In the first stage of group development the members meet for the first time, get to know each other, and try to understand where they fit within the team structure. During this period, team members are polite to each other and tend to avoid conflict.

Storming. After a period of time, tensions may arise between members and different personalities might clash, leading to conflict within the team.

Norming. The team members resolve the conflict and begin to work well together and become more cohesive.

Performing. The team becomes invested in achieving its goals and operates as a unit. At this stage, there is high loyalty and trust between members.

Adjourning. The final stage takes place when individuals either leave the team or have no reason to be in further contact with their teammates—successfully completing a group project, for example.

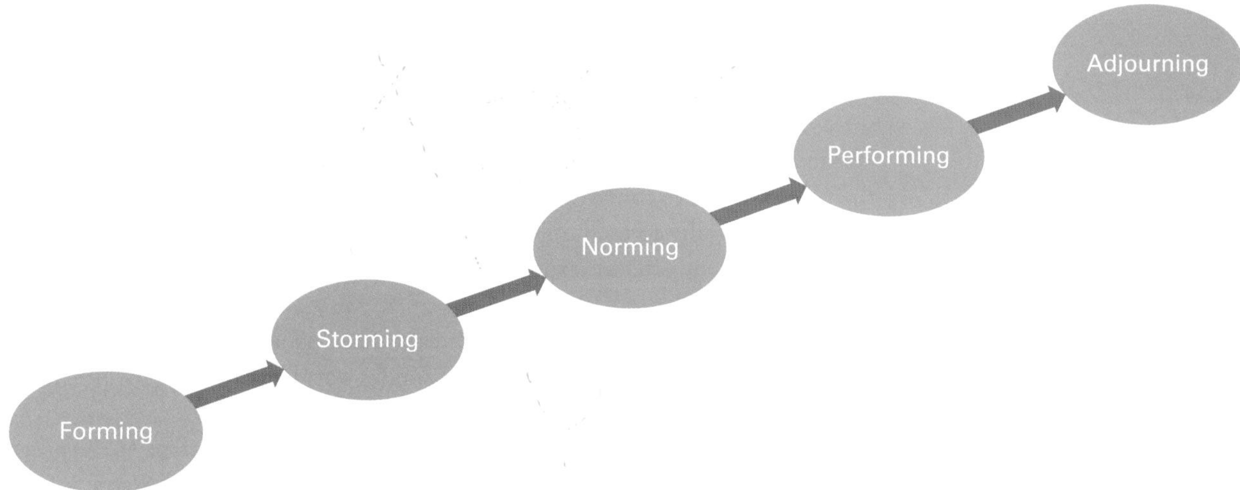

■ FIGURE 7.4 The Tuckman Model of Team Development

SOURCE: Tuckman, Bruce. "Developmental Sequence in Small Groups." *Psychological Bulletin* 63 (1965): 384–399.

Maria has told Brian that in the five years she has been HR manager, there has been very little conflict within the team. Although he wasn't there to see it, Brian imagines the team went through a new *forming* stage when Nathan arrived six months ago, treating him politely and taking time to get to know him. But what about the *storming* stage? According to Maria, the other team members clicked instantly with Nathan, and there has never been any tension that she knows of between them.

When he walks over to the purchasing team's bank of desks, Brian notes that three team members are hunched over one computer screen, laughing at a YouTube video, while another sits apart, tapping away at his computer. Brian greets the team and one of the members looks up from the video, holds out his hand and says, "Hi, Brian. I'm Nathan Jackson. Great to meet you!"

Brian firmly shakes Nathan's hand. The team members watching the video with Nathan follow suit, greeting Brian warmly and introducing themselves as Chris Hudson and Tim Malik. The team member working at his computer introduces himself as Jim O'Neill.

Brian asks the group to gather in a meeting room. When everyone is seated, Brian tells the team a little bit about his background and that he is excited to have been named plant manager. He says he would like to get to know them and explore any challenges they have been experiencing in their current roles.

Nathan Jackson is the first to answer. "Hey, my job isn't rocket science but I like it!" he says with a grin. The other three members laugh in response. "I track orders and deliveries, and that's pretty much it," he adds.

When Brian asks him about the missing or late arrival of deliveries, Nathan answers in the same easy manner. "We've had the odd blip as you probably know, but we're sorting it out now."

Brian turns to Chris Hudson, who is responsible for making purchases and negotiating with suppliers. "What about you, Chris? How are things going with you?" Brian asks.

Chris glances at Nathan, then shrugs and says, "What can I say, Brian? As Nathan mentioned, a number of mistakes have been made, but we're taking steps to address them."

It strikes Brian that Chris has given the same response as Nathan. He moves on to Jim O'Neill, who is in charge of paperwork and compliance and was working separately from the rest of the group when Brian first met the team. Jim doesn't seem happy to be put on the spot, and before he can reply, Nathan jumps in. "Hey Brian, we're all human; we all make mistakes. Give the team a chance to address them," he says, reasonably.

Brian looks at Jim, hoping he will speak up, but after glancing gratefully at Nathan, Jim avoids eye contact. Brian is getting frustrated. While he appreciates the team members' loyalty to each other, he is disappointed that nobody seems to want to be accountable or offer an explanation for the recent problems with inventory and billing.

Brian turns to the final member of the team, Tim Malik, who monitors supplies and oversees quality control. Tim replies in a similar way; he is aware of the problems but the team is addressing them.

Brian doesn't feel like he is getting anywhere so he ends the meeting. As the other team members file out, Nathan hangs back and says in a friendly manner, "Brian, we're a self-managing team; we don't really need a boss or someone looking over our shoulders. We work well together and I'm sure any problems are a thing of the past. Each of us knows how to do his job and works very independently; we all do our own thing, and we're happy that way—no worries." Brian smiles noncommittally and thanks Nathan for his and the rest of the team's time.

Nathan is right: the team doesn't have a boss, they seem to be happy working together, and they are not used to outside interference. Yet their lack of accountability with regard to the errors they have made is a major concern. Brian knows that he will have to pursue a solution to the team's underperformance.

Team Norms and Cohesion

For the rest of the day, Brian mulls over his meeting with the purchasing team and thinks about its **norms**, or the informal rules of behavior that govern the team.[24] He realizes that Nathan Jackson is the team's unofficial spokesperson, and the other members seem to take their cues from him. Nathan is certainly a charismatic character. Maria is right; he's just one of those people you can't help liking, and the other three members clearly feel a strong affiliation to him.

Brian is struck by the high level of **cohesion**, the degree to which team members connect with each other, within the purchasing team.[25] In most cases, cohesiveness is essential for team effectiveness because it encourages members to work together to reach the same goal. However, too much cohesion can lead to lack of accountability and decision making. In Brian's view the purchasing team members are so loyal to each other they are reluctant to monitor each other or point out mistakes, for fear they will be perceived as being critical, controlling, or not a team player.

Brian needs to figure out how the purchasing team can work effectively so that they can perform at optimal levels once again.

Synergy: Process Gains and Losses

The following day, Brian sits down and looks at the model of process gains and losses, shown in Figure 7.5, to analyze the purchasing team's **synergy**, or the interaction that makes the total amount of work produced by a team greater than the amount of work produced by individual members working independently.[26] From what Maria has told him, the team should be working at a level of sequential interdependence in an assembly line format, but Nathan suggested that each member works independently. This leads Brian to believe the members are working at a lower level of pooled interdependence, and possibly communicating only on a social level.

Norms: The informal rules of a team's behavior that govern the team

Cohesion: The degree to which team members connect with each other

Synergy: The concept that the total amount of work produced by a team is greater than the amount of work produced by individual members working independently

TEAM COHESION: Is Too Much More Than Enough?

Examining the Evidence

Team cohesion is a necessary prerequisite for effective team performance, as indicated by the model of team development. But is it possible to have too much team cohesion? The answer is yes!

In 1951, Solomon Asch of Swarthmore College published the results of his now-famous conformity study. In the study, college students were asked to participate in a perceptual activity. Eight participants were shown a card with a single line, followed by another card with three lines (labeled A, B, and C as shown).

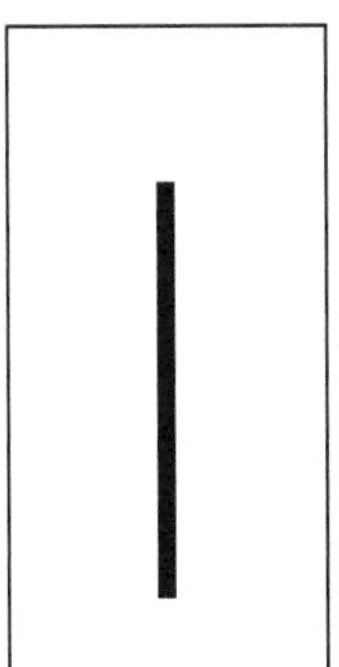

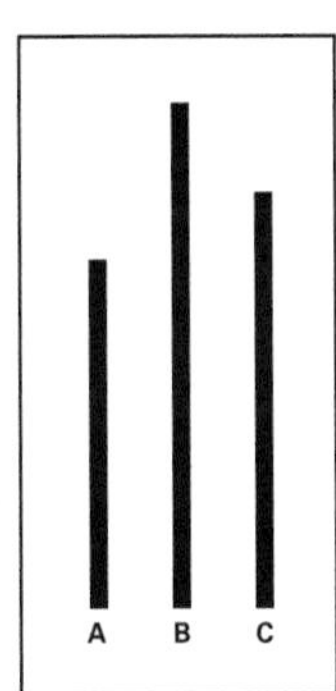

Participants were then asked to state which of the three lines matched the line on the first card in length. In the first couple of trials, all eight participants agreed it was C. However, in the third trial, the first seven participants all gave the same obviously incorrect answer, because they were actually confederates working in collusion with the researchers. The only true participant was the eighth student, and the real focus of the study was on how this student would react to the confederates' behavior. Remarkably, one of every three true participants responded with an obviously incorrect answer in order to conform to the answers given by the seven confederates! If there is that much pressure to conform in an ad hoc group brought together temporarily for a research study, imagine how much pressure there might be to conform in a permanent and highly cohesive work group. It's certainly possible that too much cohesion could be a bad thing.

Critical-Thinking Questions

1. **How can managers recognize when there is too much cohesion on their teams?**
2. **What specific actions can managers take to reduce ineffective levels of team cohesiveness?**

SOURCE: Asch, Solomon E. "Effects of Group Pressure upon the Modification and Distortion of Judgments." In *Groups, Leadership and Men: Research in Human Relations,* 177–190 (Oxford: Carnegie Press, 1951).

In his analysis of the purchasing team, Brian looks at **process gains**, which are the degree to which certain factors contribute to team effectiveness.[27] Process gains include a sense of shared purpose, plans, and goals; the confidence team members have in their own abilities to achieve objectives; a shared vision of the way the work should be carried out; and constructive task-focused conflict, which can help teams with their problem solving and decision making. Brian concludes that the purchasing team members have the skills to complete their tasks but do not share a vision of how these tasks should be performed.

Next, Brian looks at **process losses**, the factors that detract from team effectiveness.[28] Process losses include **social loafing**, which is the reduced effort people exert in a group compared to the amount they supply when working independently; personality clashes or unproductive conflict; and the inability to focus on certain tasks. Brian thinks about the social loafing side of the purchasing team. Maria has told him the team likes to joke around, and he saw three members laughing at a YouTube video during working hours. Although there has been no apparent conflict on the team, he wonders whether the explanation is that three members are introverts who avoid confrontation. Brian remembers how uncomfortable Jim appeared in the meeting and how he sat apart from the others when

 Social Loafing

Process gains: Factors that contribute to team effectiveness

Process losses: Factors that detract from team effectiveness

Social loafing: A phenomenon wherein people put forth less effort when they work in teams than when they work alone

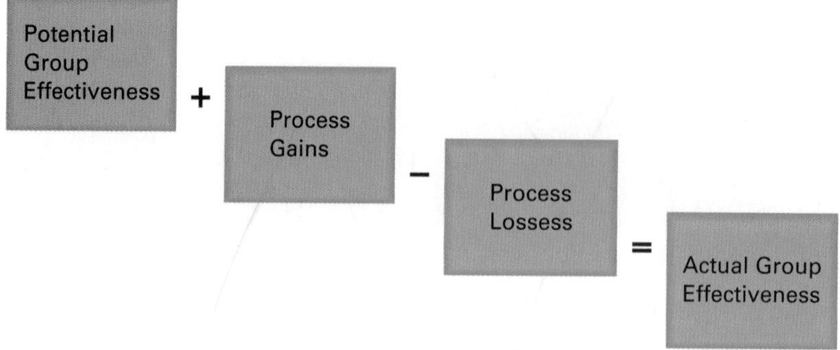

■ FIGURE 7.5 A Model of Process Gains and Losses

SOURCES: Based on Miner, Frederick C. "Group versus Individual Decision Making: An Investigation of Performance Measures, Decision Strategies, and Process Losses/Gains." *Organizational Behavior and Human Performance* 33, no. 1 (February 1984): 112–124; Steiner, Ivan D, "Models for Inferring Relationships Between Group Size and Potential Group Productivity," *Behavioral Science* 11, no. 4 (1966): 273–283.

they were watching the video. He wonders whether Jim has a problem with the team but is too loyal to voice his concerns.

Finally, Brian turns to the factors that contribute to group effectiveness. The first factor is **social facilitation,** which occurs when individuals perform tasks better in the presence of others.[29] However, social facilitation applies to simple rather than complex or novel tasks. For example, you may play soccer better when people are watching, but you might not be able to cook a meal as easily in front of an audience!

Another factor that contributes to group effectiveness is the number of favorable outcomes a team engineers. Effective teams usually produce high-quality goods and services, a satisfied customer base, a capacity to consistently work well together, and a high degree of team member satisfaction.

Because the purchasing team members seem to function independently of each other, Brian doesn't think they have experienced the benefits of social facilitation. Furthermore, their inability to perform well has had a negative impact on the quality of materials, as well as the other plant staff. Brian looks at the wealth of information before him. "Whatever happens, I'm not going to ignore this situation like the previous plant manager did," he thinks. "It's time to start making some decisions."

THINKING CRITICALLY

1. Brian appears to believe that the purchasing team has skipped over the storming stage of Tuckman's Model of Team Development. Do you agree with Brian's assessment? Why or why not? **[Apply/Analyze]**

2. Discuss the ways in which team cohesion can contribute to overall team effectiveness. Discuss the ways in which team cohesion can undermine overall team effectiveness. What questions would you ask to determine whether a team was suffering from too much team cohesiveness? **[Analyze/Evaluate]**

3. Apply the Model of Process Gains and Losses to the purchasing team. What gains and losses has Brian potentially identified? Based on Brian's assessment of the purchasing team, how do you think Brian should proceed in improving the team's performance? **[Analyze/Evaluate]**

Social facilitation: The tendency for individuals to perform tasks better when they are in the presence of others

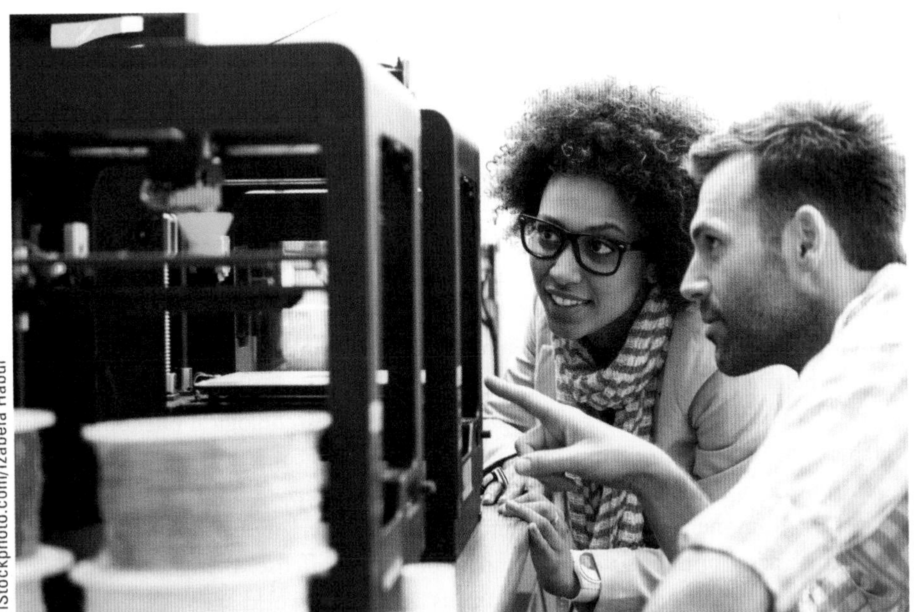
© iStockphoto.com/Izabela Habur

A group's effectiveness can be attributed to social facilitation, when individuals perform better in the presence of others.

TEAM DECISION MAKING

7.5 Identify the advantages and disadvantages of different team decision-making approaches

Brian concludes that the purchasing team is too close-knit to make an objective decision about how to resolve their problems. Ideally, they need an opportunity to confront the individual or individuals they feel is responsible for the disruption to the team. He thinks about his idea to gather a cross-functional team together that would include people from across different departments of the plant with a variety of skills to objectively explore issues with the purchasing team and make decisions about what to do next.

Advantages and Disadvantages of Team Decision Making

Based on his previous experience as HR manager, Brian is a big believer in team decision making and its advantages. He believes that it gives everyone a broader perspective, provides more alternatives, clarifies ambiguities, and brings about team satisfaction and support. However, Brian is also aware of the disadvantages of team decision making. In the past, he has been in meetings in which the process has been time consuming; too much attention has been paid to simple matters; nobody takes responsibility for the decision; and worst of all, team members end up agreeing on a compromise that satisfies nobody.

Brian spends the next week meeting the rest of the plant's employees, getting to know them better, and attempting to get a basic understanding of each of their roles. The following week, he chooses Head of Engineering Joan de Salis, Head of Sales Paul Rahman, and Head of Systems Aidan Murphy for his cross-functional team.

When Brian tells the purchasing team about the meeting, to his surprise, they all express their support. Brian opens the meeting the following morning, explains the reason for the cross-functional group, and discusses the goal of generating decisions to help resolve the challenges the purchasing team has been facing.

Nathan cuts in, "Just to clarify for the folks that don't know us too well, the purchasing team has a great track record for performance and delivery, but we have made a few missteps that we are trying to rectify."

Brian has expected this from Nathan and he is prepared for it. "Nathan, the facts show that over the last four months the team has been underperforming, leading to lost orders, poor-quality materials, and inconsistent stock levels. We are all here today to discuss how to resolve those issues."

"I appreciate that, Brian, but the team knows the right way to handle these issues ourselves," Nathan replies. Chris and Tim nod in agreement, but Jim simply shrugs. Brian wants to hear from Jim, but when he gestures for him to speak, Jim clams up and looks at the ground.

Groupthink

Brian suspects the team is a victim of **groupthink**, a psychological phenomenon in which people in a cohesive group go along with the group consensus rather than offering their own opinions.[30] Groupthink is a major disadvantage to team decision making, because the team members are more concerned with preserving harmony in the group than with risking opinions that may cause conflict or offense. Being in this kind of group confers an illusion of immunity, an "us against the world" view that the group members know better than outsiders even given evidence to the contrary.

Brian suspects Jim doesn't want to rock the boat by expressing a conflicting opinion, and he is exasperated. Without any dissenting voices within the purchasing team, nothing will ever change because they will think that every decision they make is the right one. But what can he do? He can't force Jim to speak up.

Team Decision Approaches

Before Brian can attempt a different tack, Joan de Salis interjects.

"Over the course of my 20 years at the plant, I have seen a number of issues occur in the engineering department. One team decision-making approach I've found useful is the brainstorming technique," she says.

Brian is grateful for Joan's suggestion. He likes the idea of **brainstorming**, which is generating creative, spontaneous ideas from all members of a group without making any initial criticism or judgment of them.[31] "I think that's a great idea!," he says. "What do you think?," he asks the rest of the group, who nod in response. "We'd like to hear all your ideas. The more imaginative and creative, the better. We're looking for original solutions here."

The brainstorming gets off to a slow start. The members of the purchasing team are silent, but the departmental heads start to throw out ideas. Joan suggests that the team make a shared checklist of their duties and tick each item off as they accomplish it. Paul suggests implementing a weekly purchasing team discussion group to talk about any challenges they might come across and how to solve them. But it is Aidan's idea to appoint a team leader or supervisor to the purchasing team that finally gets a reaction.

Jim raises his hand. "I think having an official leader or supervisor is a good idea."

Nathan, Chris, and Tim turn to look at him with wide eyes.

Jim takes a deep breath and continues, "The team is struggling at the moment. Important stuff is slipping through the net. Personally, I feel I've been shouldering a lot of the responsibility." Brian looks at the three members for their response, but for the first time they are speechless.

"You know what? Jim is right," Nathan finally says. "There's too much goofing around. I take responsibility for that. I find my job pretty boring and I guess I'm looking for distractions to make the day go faster. These guys were a pretty serious bunch when I arrived and I suppose I wanted to liven up the team and have a bit of fun. I may have gone a bit overboard in that regard," Nathan finishes.

Groupthink: A psychological phenomenon in which people in a cohesive group go along with the group consensus rather than offering their own opinions

Brainstorming: The process of generating creative, spontaneous ideas from all members of a group without any criticism or judgment

"Nobody forced us to joke around or goof off. It's great having you as part of the team," Chris says, looking up.

"I agree with Chris," Tim adds. "It's been a lot more fun since you arrived, but I do think Jim has taken on more than he should, although he's never complained about it before."

"That's because I didn't want to be the one to ruin all the fun," Jim replies.

"Honestly, Jim, if you have a problem, I'd rather you told us. We're a team—we're there to support each other," Nathan says.

Brian is pleased with the honest exchange between the team members. This is what he has hoped the meeting would achieve—a safe, nonjudgmental environment in which team members could confront each other in a nonthreatening way. He is also impressed that Nathan, Chris, and Tim are willing to take responsibility for slacking off on the job.

The group spends more time discussing the problems within the team and how to address them. Eventually, they agree to adopt an assembly line structure with more communication among team members rather than working independently of each other. They also agree that a checklist is a good idea and commit to enforcing it beginning the following day. Brian is pleased, but he hasn't heard yet whether the team likes the idea of a supervisor.

"But if we have a supervisor, it means that we won't be a self-managing team anymore," Nathan says.

Joan replies, "Not exactly. It means you would be semi-autonomous. Basically, a team leader would be appointed to oversee the functioning of the team."

"Exactly," says Paul. "This not a typical 'boss' role; the team retains a significant amount of autonomy, but the team leader will be in place to supervise and help resolve any conflicts or issues in the team."

"In a nutshell, you want someone to keep an eye on us!," Nathan says, half-jokingly.

Joan smiles. "That's one way of looking at it, but I would think of it as extra support," she replies.

"I think there's some merit in knowing that the burden of responsibility doesn't necessarily fall on anyone's shoulders," Aidan adds. "A supervisor can guide you when needed and even offer you advice about your career and the direction it's taking."

"I agree with Aidan," Paul says. "Jim, you've told us you're carrying the team to a certain degree, and Nathan, you said you find your role boring. A team leader or supervisor could help you both address some of these issues and offer guidance."

After some further discussion, everyone agrees that some level of monitoring is an idea worth exploring further. Brian promises to broach the idea of a team supervisor with Hans Wagner when he returns to the plant. Although there is more work to be done, Brian is glad that, for now, things seem to be heading in the right direction.

The cross-functional team at the tractor assembly plant found brainstorming to be a useful way to make decisions. Many organizations use other team decision-making techniques. The **nominal group technique** is a structured way for team members to generate ideas and identify solutions.[32] Each member is asked the same question in relation to a work issue and requested to write down as many solutions as possible. Answers are read aloud and recorded for discussion. Then the ideas are put to the vote. No criticism or judgment of any ideas is allowed.

Nominal group technique: A structured way for team members to generate ideas and identify solutions in which each member is asked the same question in relation to a work issue and requested to write as many answers as possible. Answers are read aloud and voted upon

The **Delphi technique** is a method of decision making in which information is gathered from a group of respondents within their area of expertise.[33] Questionnaires are sent to a select group of experts, whose responses are collated and reviewed, and then a summary is returned to the group with a follow-up questionnaire. Again, the experts provide their answers. The process continues until the group agrees on a common answer and a

Delphi technique: A method of decision making in which information is gathered from a group of respondents within their area of expertise

decision is reached. Through team models and analysis, Brian has succeeded in getting the team to cooperate and communicate with him and the cross-functional team to come up with some decisions and solutions to make the team work better together. In the next chapter, Brian is forced to make an ethical decision that could put his career at risk.

THINKING CRITICALLY

1. What aspects of brainstorming as a team decision-making approach helped Jim to voice his concerns about the purchasing group's functioning? Would the Nominal Group Technique have had a similar outcome? Why or why not? **[Analyze/ Evaluate]**

2. Do you think a more authoritarian manager than Brian have had a similar, more effective, or less effective impact on the purchasing group's performance? Explain your response. **[Analyze/ Evaluate]**

3. Discuss the pros and cons of having a team leader for the purchasing group in light of their willingness to institute a checklist and regular meetings to ensure performance levels. What issues could a team leader solve for the group? What problems might the addition of a team leader create for the group? **[Analyze/ Evaluate]**

IN REVIEW

Learning Objectives

7.1 Distinguish between a team and a group

A **team** is a group of people brought together to use their individual skills on a common project or goal. Regardless of the type of organization, most employees work in some form of team in today's workplace. A **group** usually consists of three or more people who work independently to attain organizational goals.

7.2 Compare the various types of teams in organizations today

Many global companies now operate in **virtual teams,** whose members are from different locations and work together through e-mail, video conferencing, instant messaging, and other electronic media. A **self-managing team** is a group of workers who manage their own daily duties under little to no supervision. A **problem-solving team** is a group of workers coming together for a set amount of time to discuss and resolve specific issues. A **cross-functional team** is a group of workers from different units with various areas of expertise.

7.3 Apply the model of team effectiveness to evaluate team performance

Team contextual influences include team resources, task characteristics, and organizational structures and systems. Team resources are the level of support provided by the organization, such as equipment, materials, training, information, staffing, budgets, and such. Task characteristics can be structured or

unstructured; complex or simple; and measured by a degree of interdependence. Performance management systems, compensation and reward systems, and organizational and leadership structures must be aligned with team structures to maintain smooth running of operations.

Typically, a team has four main elements: team size, skills and abilities, personality of team members, and team diversity. Teams tend to consist of four to seven members. The skills and abilities of the team members are very important, but the way this talent interacts in the context of team processes is also important. Typically, teams need a balance between extraverts and introverts. Team members who share common interests or certain similarities tend to have positive social relationships with each other that help the team to be more effective.

7.4 Explain how team processes affect team outcomes

Process gains are factors that contribute to team effectiveness. They include a sense of shared purpose, plans, and goals; the confidence team members have in their own abilities to achieve objectives; a shared vision of how the work should be carried out; and constructive task-focused conflict that can help teams with their problem solving and decision making.

Process losses are factors that detract from team effectiveness. They include social loafing, wherein people in a group put in less effort than when working independently; personality clashes or conflict; and the inability to focus on certain tasks.

7.5 Identify the advantages and disadvantages of different team decision-making approaches

Groupthink is a psychological phenomenon in which people in a cohesive group go along with the group consensus to preserve harmony rather than offering their own opinions.

Brainstorming generates creative, spontaneous ideas from all members of a group without any criticism or judgment.

The **nominal group technique** is a structured way for team members to generate ideas and identify solutions. Each member is asked the same question in relation to a work issue and requested to write as many answers as possible. Answers are read aloud and recorded for discussion. Then the ideas are put to the vote. No criticism or judgment of any ideas is allowed. **The Delphi technique** is a method of decision-making in which information is gathered from a group of respondents within their area of expertise.

KEY TERMS

THINKING CRITICALLY ABOUT THE CASE OF BRIAN STEVENS

Put yourself in Brian Stevens' position as the new manager of the tractor assembly plant and consider the five critical-thinking steps in relation to the purchasing team's underperformance.

OBSERVE

While Brian speaks directly with Maria Gonzalez, the plant's HR Manager, the purchasing team, and other heads of department, what additional steps might he have taken to better observe and understand the impact of the purchasing team's underperformance at the plant?

INTERPRET

Consider the purchasing team's interactions and their reaction to Brian's statements about the team's underperformance. What features of Jim's personality and responsibilities likely contribute to his support of the idea of a team leader for the group? What features of Nathan's personality and responsibilities likely contribute to his emphasis on the team's ability to police itself without outside interference.

ANALYZE

Consider the two solutions to the team's performance that they agree to implement near the end of the chapter: a shared checklist of team duties and a weekly team discussion group. What aspects of the team's process will each solution improve?

EVALUATE

Are there any other potential solutions (in addition to the team leader suggestion) that might help this team function more efficiently? Please list them. With regard to the team leader position, what attributes would you look for in selecting the person to fulfill this role?

EXPLAIN

How would you, as Brian Stevens, go about broaching the subject of the purchasing team's underperformance, the solutions it is going to implement, and the possibility of a team leader to Hans Wagner, the company's president? Would you advocate for the team leader position or simply present the option as a possibility?

EXERCISE 7.1: THE SHOE BOX EXERCISE

This exercise will help you to understand the differences between individual, group, and team performance.

Instructions:

Step 1: Individual Performance. Your instructor will show each individual in the class the inside of a shoe box filled with 30–40 miscellaneous items. You will have three seconds to observe the items and remember as many of them as you can. The instructor will then ask everyone in the class to say how many of the items they can remember (without actually naming the items). Use the honor system. Your instructor will record the maximum, minimum, and average number of items on the board or screen.

Step 2: Ad Hoc Group Performance. Now form a group of three to five people with other members of your class. Talk together and come up with a list of items from the box that you can collectively recall (no duplications). The instructor will then poll the groups and record their maximum, minimum, and average number of items on the board or screen.

Step 3: Organized Team Performance. Groups must put away their list of items. You will be allowed to look in the box for another three seconds, but this time as an organized team. Your team will have a few minutes to create a strategy and organize your efforts. The instructor will once again record the maximum, minimum, and average number of items on the board or screen.

Relection Questions

1. Did performance increase from individual to group to team? If so, why? If not, why not?
2. What strategy did your team implement to take advantage of individual members' skills and increase performance?
3. In what ways can an organized team effort lead to better results than individual effort or simply pooling information and knowledge in a group?

EXERCISE 7.2: A NOMINAL BRAINSTORM ABOUT THE DELPHI TECHNIQUE

Objectives:

This exercise will help you to *identify* the advantages and disadvantages of different team decision-making approaches.

Instructions:

Form into a group of six to eight members. Your task is to develop a set of recommendations on using the Delphi Technique and explain its appropriateness for generating management ideas. You will be developing these recommendations using the brainstorming and nominal group methods. To complete this task, complete the following steps:

Step1. Select a person to write down the ideas generated in this exercise and to tally votes in the later steps. (1 to 2 minutes)

Step 2. Use the brainstorming method to generate ideas about when using the Delphi technique would not be successful. These ideas can either be statements about the general characteristics of a situation or about a specific job situation. (5 minutes)

Step 3. Combine ideas where appropriate. Soliciting feedback from everyone in your group, determine whether an idea is relevant or not for your guidelines. In order to be considered relevant, an idea must be true (based on chapter concepts) and useful in a business setting. Write down the list of ideas that are voted as being relevant. (1 to 2 minutes)

Step 4. Use the nominal group technique to generate ideas about when the Delphi technique would be successful. These ideas can either be statements about the general characteristics of a situation or a specific job situation. (5 to 10 minutes).

Step 5. Repeat step 3. (1 to 2 minutes).

Reflection Questions:

1. Which idea generation method did your prefer? Why?
2. Which idea method generation method generated the most ideas?
3. Which idea generated the most relevant ideas?
4. What new ways of employing the Delphi technique did you discover?

Exercise contributed by Milton R. Mayfield, Professor of Business, Texas A&M International University and Jaqueline R. Mayfield, Professor of Business, Texas A&M International University.

EXERCISE 7.3: CONSULTING AT BELLA NOTA

Objective:

This exercise will help you to *distinguish* between teams and groups, *compare* different types of teams, and *apply* the team effectiveness model.

Background:

You are in a consulting group who is working with Bella Nota—a company in Austin, Texas, that provides background and incidental music for commercials and industrial videos. The company has enough steady business to sustain ten musicians, two composers, two sound engineers, and one conductor as full-time employees. The musicians and conductor usually work together on a regular basis, rotating between the composers and engineers. When business picks up or there is a call for a larger set of musicians, the local talent pool provides an easy source for short-term hires. While many of the same people are hired frequently, none of these people work for Bella Nota on an ongoing basis.

The company president, Natalie Bell, realizes how critically important high-quality team processes is to her business. She has brought in your consulting group to help develop guidelines for developing effective teams. To develop these guidelines, you will need to provide information the following:

- Create a guideline that distinguishes between groups and teams. Include the differences between a team and a group, and when the use of teams would be more appropriate at Bella Nota.
- Develop a guideline for classifying different types of teams. While not all team types will be represented in the musical side of the company, there are other business activities and teams that will find these guidelines useful.
- Develop a guideline for evaluating the musical teams/groups on process. This guideline will be used for developing suggestions for future team/group improvements.

Instructions:

Step 1. Form into teams to complete the three tasks outlined in the background section. (20 to 30 minutes)

Step 2. Present your guidelines to the class and be prepared to answer questions from the class and the instructor. (20 to 30 minutes)

Reflection Questions:

1. How did using chapter terms and concepts help you to better structure your thinking about teams and team processes?
2. If you have been working in a team in this or another class, how can you use the guidelines in improving team outcomes?
3. How do processes differ in team work situations compared with individual work situations? How do team processes differ between different types of teams?

Exercise contributed by Milton R. Mayfield, Professor of Business, Texas A&M International University and Jaqueline R. Mayfield, Professor of Business, Texas A&M International University.

CASE STUDY 7.1: INTERNATIONAL GAME TECHNOLOGY (IGT)

You may not know the company by name, but if you've ever been to a casino, chances are you've had an IGT experience. The global powerhouse Nevada-based International Game Technology (IGT) specializes in computerized gaming machines and is the designer and manufacturer of well-known slot machines such as Red White & Blue, Double Diamond, and the ever-popular Wheel of Fortune games. Although IGT was acquired in 2015 by Italy-based GTECH—uniting the world's largest provider of lottery systems (GTECH) with the world's largest slot-machine maker—IGT's manufacturing hub remains stationed in its hometown of more than 40 years, Reno, Nevada. A formidable player in the $430 billion global gambling business, the combined company retains the iconic IGT name and boasts 13,000+ employees and thousands of gaming machines in casinos all over the world. As longtime GTECH executive and IGT CEO Marco Sala told *Bloomberg Business* at the time of the acquisition, "This is a transaction that we firmly believe will transform the gaming industry. We will have a library of games that will surpass that of any other company in the industry."

But during the Great Recession, IGT had experienced significant cuts in revenue and profit and worrying drops in share price. Competitors like Bally Technologies were eager to step in and grab market share, and grab they did. Like many companies, IGT was struggling to regain its footing in 2009—and its approach to team management on several different fronts is among one of its key strategies for recovery.

Streamlining Teamwork in "The Shop"

IGT had been focusing on teams since the early 2000s to keep its market position and to stay on top. In 2004, the company invested in iMaint, which helps IGT's maintenance crew team manage work orders, scheduling, parts and inventory, and purchasing, as well as track costs and budget and project progress with easy-to-use graphs and charts—no small feat in a global company whose maintenance department alone is spread over a 1.2 million-square-foot facility. Although the system cuts out paperwork and streamlines streamlined processes, there is a very human element involved: its users. John Butterfield, facilities maintenance supervisor based in Reno, praised the system but insisted that training is the key. "Investing in training is money well spent for two reasons. First, it helps employees understand how important their data is and thus provides better data and better history. Second, it enhances the mechanics' overall knowledge in the maintenance field. Now they not only know how to turn wrenches, but also have an understanding of how all the maintenance processes are put together (scheduling, parts ordering, contractor work) which in turn increases the entire team's effectiveness." Butterfield dedicated every second Friday of the month to continued training. "At our once a month training the employees learn more and I learn more. It's a win-win."

iMaint gave IGT an additional advantage: what would otherwise be costly and potentially disruptive—the testing of new processes—can could occur in the virtual environment first. When Butterfield's crew wants to implement something new—be it changes to parts ordering, inventory management, scheduling, or codes—they could test it in iMaint's training database first. Initiatives are either quashed or implemented, with the added benefit that those rolling it out have already developed a comfort level with the new process, and could anticipate possible challenges.

Virtual Teams

Enter virtual teams. In 2009, Chris Satchell was hired by as chief technology officer (CTO) to help battle IGT's financial woes. Satchell's job was to keep an eagle eye trained on the competitive marketplace, to make sure IGT-wannabes weren't out-innovating the gaming giant. One of Satchell's strategies was deploying virtual teams throughout the organization. He started small-scale efforts within his information technology (IT) department, perhaps the ideal testing ground, because its members were already accustomed to working on problems remotely and through machines.

Satchell found that the IT experiment proved his case: the benefits of virtual teams were tangible. Beyond the obvious benefits, like the ability to rely on top talent the world over without travel costs (because meetings could take place online), working remotely helped the company realize faster time to market. Satchell also noticed greater innovation, because the online environment, by its very nature, skirts bureaucratic interference, allowing employees a level of semi-autonomy.

Yet Satchell found that, as in the face-to-face workplace—and perhaps more so—building relationships among team members was vital. "We're always pushing employees to understand that people in other groups have different perspectives. They have something you need, and you have something they can use." And even as virtual teams move beyond the IT department, traveling for occasional "face time" is still necessary, although not as frequently, and not for the whole team. "It's a misconception to think that you can do away with your travel budget," Satchell noted.

Teamwork and Emergenetics

IGT has implemented technology to help with its human resources strategy as well. Emergenetics Solutions utilizes research in brain science, psychometric evaluation, and organizational development to help analyze the way people think and behave, providing actionable solutions and suggestions for better teamwork. Specifically, Emergenetics' ESP System helps companies match candidate profiles against the job description, while the Emergenetics Profile offers companies (and individuals) a portrait of individual strengths and weaknesses, predicting how these might play out in different team arrangements.

Emergenetics helped IGT generate a "picture" of who they were as an organization—and, with deeper analysis, "extract performance themes, identify strengths and opportunities across the organization and formulate groups to better meet specific business needs." Although not a requirement, many IGT employees displayed their Emergenetics profiles in their workspaces, which IGT says helps create a feeling of openness, stimulate dialogue, and encourage collaboration.

IGT also used Emergenetics tools during the hiring on-boarding process, helping potential team members and leaders recognize strengths and potential pitfalls in the team the former may be joining. "Specific practices are then developed based on the team's overall Emergenetics make-up and the team's objectives," Emergenetics authors noted in a case study on their work with IGT. Goals and benchmarks can could be developed, and tracked, accordingly.

The IGT of today is far removed from its struggles of the mid- and late 2000s. IGT's official headquarters have shifted to London. Asked how the new IGT will compare to the "IGT as Reno knew it," CEO Marco Sala responded, "[It] will be a combination of the two companies. We're putting in teams of different experiences, and some guys will join Nevada. I think these combinations will bring new ideas for future innovation. That is what we intend to pursue."

Case Questions

1. What role did competition play in IGT's decision to implement stronger team management for recovery?
2. Describe the benefits as well as shortcomings that IGT saw after implementing virtual teams.
3. Explain how IGT used systems like iMaint and Emergenetics to increase team effectiveness.

Sources

"Case Study: IGT." *Emergentics.com*. www.emergenetics.com/wp-content/uploads/2010/12/Emergenetics-International-Case-Study-IGT.pdf.

"How to Deploy Collaborative Virtual Teams." Economist. www.economistinsights.com/technology-innovation/analysis/next-generation-cios/casestudies.

"Success Stories: International Game Technology," *DSPI.com*. www.dpsi.com/success-stories/international-game-technology/.

"What Is Emergentics?" *Emergentics.com*. www.emergenetics.com/whatis.

SELF-ASSESSMENT 7.1

Communicating with a Problem Team Member

What do you do when a team member arrives late for or misses meetings, does not contribute a fair share toward the team's effort, is offensive or disruptive, or has some other problem? The following self-assessment will provide you with some feedback that may help you improve your ability to communicate with a difficult team member.

For each statement, circle the number that best describes how you would talk to a problem team member based on the following scale:

	Not at all Accurate	Somewhat Accurate	A Little Accurate	Mostly Accurate	Completely Accurate
1. I am specific rather than general, giving good, clear, and recent examples of the problem behavior.	1	2	3	4	5
2. I present the situation as a problem that disrupts the whole team not just one individual.	1	2	3	4	5
3. My comments focus on things that the team member has control over and can actually do something about.	1	2	3	4	5
4. I try to provide constructive criticism at a time when the team member is prepared to receive it, rather when they are busy doing something else.	1	2	3	4	5
5. I don't try to embarrass or put my team member on the spot, but remember that the purpose of my comments is to improve the team member's behavior.	1	2	3	4	5
6. I try to keep feedback professional, avoiding labels such as *stupid* or *incompetent*.	1	2	3	4	5
7. I make sure that my criticisms are concise and complete enough that the team member understands the problem.	1	2	3	4	5
8. I talk to the team member as an equal, not as a controlling parent, supervisor, or boss.	1	2	3	4	5

Scoring

Add the numbers circled above and write your score in the blank ____________

Interpretation

32 and above = You have very strong skills for communicating with a problem team member. You are likely to be naturally effective at constructively influencing the behaviors of your problem team member.

24–31 = You have a moderate level of skills for communicating with a problem team member. You may want to consider reshaping your approach to communicating with a difficult team member based on the previous statements.

23 and below = You have room to improve your team communication skills. You and your team will be more effective if you can successfully reshape your communication approaches based on the previous statements.

SOURCE: Adapted from Manz, C. C., C. P. Neck, J. Mancuso, and K. P. Manz. *For Team Members Only: Making Your Workplace Team Productive and Hassle-Free* (New York: AMACOM, 1997).

8 Decision Making and Ethics

It's not hard to make decisions when you know what your values are.

—Roy E. Disney, former Disney executive and nephew to Walt Disney

DECISION MAKING AND PROBLEM SOLVING

LEARNING OBJECTIVES

By the end of this chapter, you will be able to:

8.1 Identify the primary types of decisions managers make to solve problems

8.2 Apply a rational model of decision making to solve problems and make decisions

8.3 Identify factors that influence the way we make decisions in the real world

8.4 Explain a basis for resolving ethical dilemmas in organizations

8.5 Contrast various approaches to ethical decision making

Management Decision Making

8.1 Identify the primary types of decisions managers make to solve problems

The ability to make decisions and solve problems is a key aspect of organizational behavior. We make decisions, big and small, every single day in our professional and personal lives. Living in the technology era means we are subject to a continuous flow of information that needs to be processed and absorbed. When we are deciding what to do with this abundance of information, our understanding of a rational decision-making process can guide us toward the right course of action. **Decision making** is the action or process of identifying a strategy to resolve problems.[1]

There are two main types of decisions: programmed decisions and non-programmed decisions.[2]

Programmed decisions are automatic responses to routine and recurring situations. Usually these situations have occurred in the past and are familiar to the people dealing with them. Decisions are generally made by following company policies and guidelines that have been put in place to deal with specific issues. For example, Amazon is a market leader in customer service because of its excellent policy for responding to customer queries and resolving customer complaints.[3]

Non-programmed decisions respond to new or nonroutine problems for which there are no proven solutions. In these situations employees will not find the answer they are looking for in the company handbook or policy guidelines. Very often, the problems are complex in nature with few past occurrences for employees to draw on. For example, Apple's decision to invest in new manufacturing technology for its products would have required a great deal of research, information, and judgment.[4]

Decision making: The action or process of identifying a strategy to resolve problems

Programmed decisions: Automatic responses to routine and recurring situations

Non-programmed decisions: New or nonroutine problems for which there are no proven answers

THINKING CRITICALLY

1. Briefly discuss the ways in which a more experienced employee could excel in comparison to a new employee with regard to programmed decisions. **[Understand/Apply]**

2. What qualities and habits would you expect an employee who excels at making non-programmed decisions to exhibit? **[Apply/Analyze]**

3. Do you believe an employee's ability to make programmed decisions would decrease in importance as they advanced in level of responsibility? Why or why not? **[Analyze/ Evaluate]**

Master the content.
edge.sagepub.com/neckob

SAGE edge™

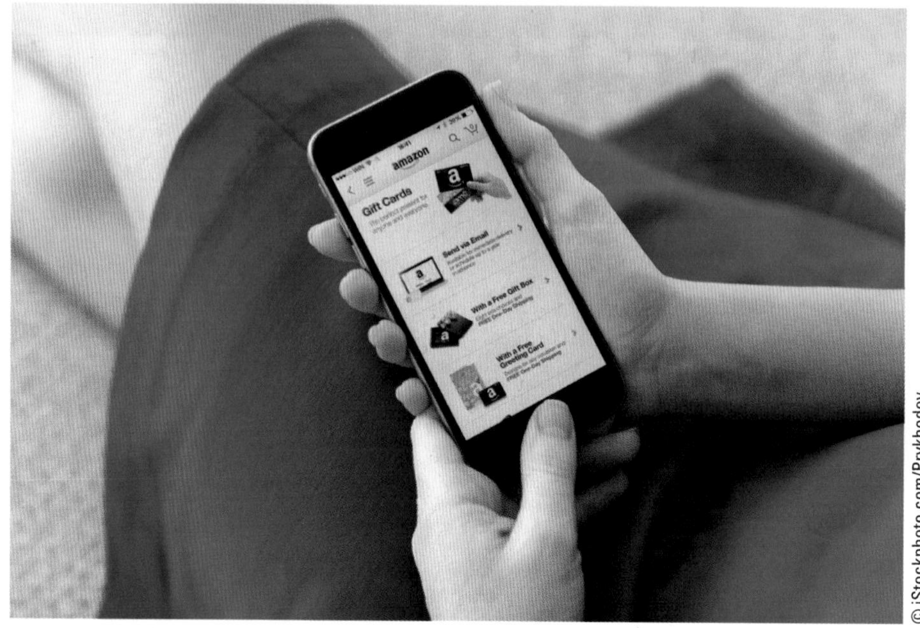

Amazon has a reputation for having high-quality customer service.

© iStockphoto.com/Prykhodov

A RATIONAL MODEL OF DECISION MAKING

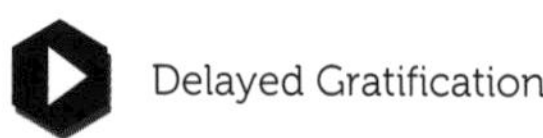

Delayed Gratification

8.2 Apply a rational model of decision making to solve problems and make decisions

Back to the Case of Brian Stevens

In Chapter 7, we met Brian Stevens, a newly appointed manager at a tractor assembly plant. We explored his efforts to improve the performance of the self-managing purchasing team consisting of team

THE BIG PICTURE: How OB Topics Fit Together

Individual Processes
- Individual Differences
- Emotions and Attitudes
- Perceptions and Learning
- Motivation

Team Processes
- **ETHICS**
- **DECISION MAKING**
- Creativity and Innovation
- Conflict and Negotiation

Organizational Processes
- Culture
- Strategy
- Change and Development
- Structure and Technology

Influence Processes
- Leadership
- Power and Politics
- Communication

Organizational Outcomes
- Individual Performance
- Job Satisfaction
- Team Performance
- Organizational Goals

members Jim O'Neill, Chris Hudson, Tim Malik, and Nathan Jackson. Thanks to a brainstorming session with the team members and three other departmental heads, the team has decided a supervisor might prove to be a welcome support. Brian has promised to run the idea past the company president, Hans Wagner, when he returns to the plant.

A week after the brainstorming session, Brian is pleased to see Hans Wagner back in his office. He gets straight to the point. "The purchasing team and key departmental heads have decided a supervisor would be useful to oversee the daily operations of the group." He explains that the team could benefit from some additional support and guidance.

"I don't have the budget to put a full-time supervisor in place. I'll get the head of production, Doris Nakamura, to keep an eye on them," Hans responds. "Now I need to talk you about the number of work-related injuries we have at the plant," he continues. "I've just come back from a Health and Safety manufacturing management conference, and we need to do something. There were ten injuries here this year. That's unacceptable."

Brian agrees this is a big problem. If the plant doesn't address it, the company could be in danger of violating rules set by the Occupational Health and Safety Administration (OSHA), the federal agency that regulates workplace safety and health. OSHA defines recordable incidents as those that result in death, absences from work, medical treatment beyond first aid, and loss of consciousness.

"People are getting careless on the assembly line. It makes us look bad in front of the board and shareholders, and having all these injured people miss work is costing us a lot of money. Since you're the new plant manager, I want you to sort this out. We need to decrease the numbers of injuries as soon as possible," Hans says.

Brian is surprised that Hans puts cost reduction and impression management ahead of employee welfare in his approach to at-work injuries, but he heads to the tractor engine assembly line to find out what has been causing the increase. First, he

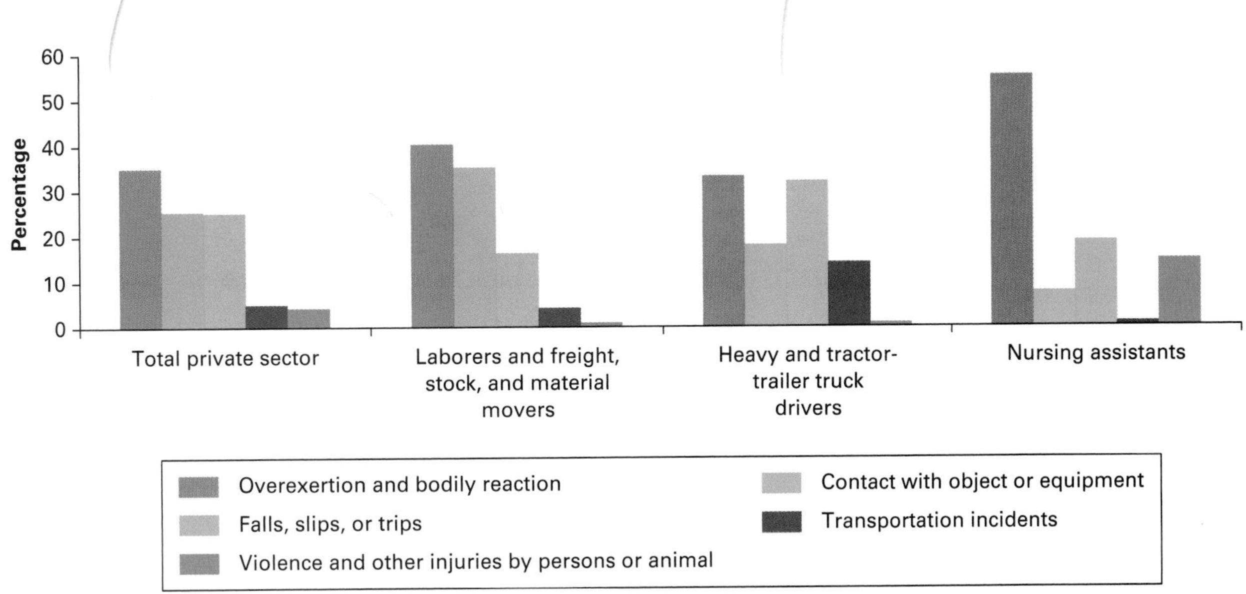

■ FIGURE 8.1 Distribution of Selected Occupational Injuries for Selected Private Sector Occupations, 2013

SOURCE: Bureau of Labor Statistics. *Nonfatal Occupational Injuries and Illnesses Requiring Days Away From Work, 2013,* p. 2 (Washington, DC: US Department of Labor, 2014). www.bls.gov/news.release/pdf/osh2.pdf.

seeks out the assembly line team leader, Jacob Siegel, to see what light he can shed on the situation.

"It's a real problem," Jacob says. "I can't get my people to take safety seriously around here. Some of them think they know it all just because they've been doing the same tasks for years, but even with repetitive work there are still steps that can be missed."

"What kinds of injuries have we seen in the past year?" Brian asks.

"A few of the workers have had to take time off for muscle stress and back injuries from standing in one spot and repeating the same actions day after day, one employee had a bad fall, and we've had some employees burnt or shocked during their shift," Jacob replies.

"What happens when they return to work?" Brian says.

"They go back in the assembly line," Jacob responds as if this is a very obvious answer to Brian's question.

Brian asks some more questions about the causes of the injuries. Jacob tells him that out of the ten employees injured the previous year, four of them missed work because of various muscle problems; one of them had a serious fall while painting a tractor; and five employees suffered burns and electric shocks from malfunctioning machinery they tried to "patch up" rather than reporting the problems.

Brian is upset at the seriousness of the injuries and asks Jacob's permission to observe the assembly line workers in action for an hour or so.

"Sure thing!" Jacob says. "Just be sure you don't distract them."

Brian starts by spending time watching the engine production line. Everything appears to move smoothly enough, but he notices that there isn't much space between the workers. Some workers unconsciously pause to stretch or massage their shoulders in between tasks, while others simply look uncomfortable as they hunch over their work. Brian also finds that there is no communication between the workers; in fact most of them look bored and disconnected from one another.

When Brian gets back to his desk, he spends some time mulling over what to do next. To support him in his quest for a solution, he uses the five-step model of decision making (Figure 8.2).[5]

Define the Problem

First, Brian needs to state the problem in clear and concise terms. Despite their different perspectives, he and Hans have the same goal: to reduce the number of work-related injuries in the plant as soon as possible.

Identify and Weigh Decision Criteria

Now that Brian has defined the problem, he needs to identify and weigh the criteria in the decision. He defines his criteria as follows: his solution must increase employee focus on safety and encourage employees to care about safety procedures in a way that will not be viewed as a threat or a negative.

Generate Multiple Alternatives

Next, Brian thinks of alternate solutions to his defined problem. Perhaps stricter sanctions and punishments should be imposed for violations of safety standards. Alternatively, he could implement a reward system such as bonuses or vacation time for low injury rates.

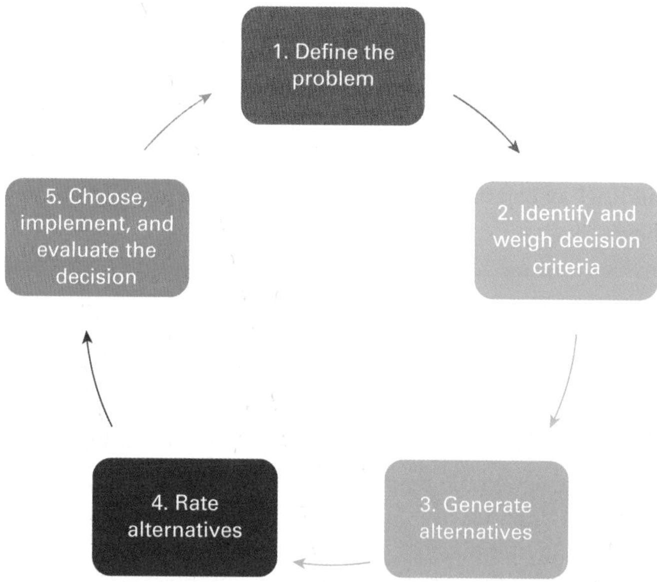

■ FIGURE 8.2 The Five-Step Model of Decision Making

Rate Alternatives on the Basis of Decision Criteria

Brian spends time weighing these two possible solutions against each other and finds they both rate poorly on the basis of the criteria. For example, sanctions and punishments could be viewed negatively and as a threat, and employees might fail to report injuries for fear of punishment. Similarly, though the reward system might be viewed more positively, Brian is also concerned that because rewards would be contingent on achieving a lower number of reported injuries, there is less incentive to report incidents that should be legally reported.

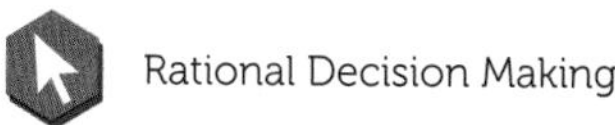

Choose, Implement, and Evaluate the Best Alternative

As far as Brian can tell from his continuing research into the problem, the majority of injuries seem to arise from employees trying to repair malfunctioning machinery themselves, so he comes up with one possible solution that focuses on a critical-thinking strategy. He spends a couple of hours outlining a program he decides to call Safety Critical Thinking (SCT) based on the plant's health and safety manual. Many injuries are caused by exposure to energy sources and failure to take proper precautions to mitigate the risks they represent. SCT asks each employee to think critically about the work environment in terms of potential energy sources including the plant's machines, which produce pressure, mechanical, chemical, electrical, gravity, and heat/cold energy. Brian hopes SCT will encourage all employees to do three things relative to these energy sources: identify-act-review. First *identify* the energy source, and then take mitigation *actions* to eliminate it, control it, or if necessary protect yourself from it. If that is not possible, for example, if the machine is malfunctioning, then the employee should stop, call, and wait for a supervisor to *review* the situation. Brian thinks this is the best choice relative to his criteria and an effective and nonthreatening way of encouraging employees to care about safety processes at the plant.

Brian is also concerned about the employees who have been forced to take time off to recover from repetitive strain injuries. He knows these injuries can be avoided with the use of adjustable work benches, foot rails, and elbow supports and the provision of plenty of room to move around and change position. From what he has seen, nothing like this has been put in place for the assembly line workers. Finally, he needs to address the low morale and lack of communication down the line. How can he make a tedious job more rewarding?

Brian carries out some research into other manufacturing plants, noting a number of ways that organizations strive to improve morale. Some pipe music in; others encourage workers to socialize by holding game nights or bowling after work; and some give their assembly line workers more responsibility and opportunities to provide feedback. Over the course of a week, Brian organizes his new initiative for Hans's approval.

After Hans has reviewed the proposal, he asks Brian, "How much is all this going to cost the company?"

Brian has done his homework, and thanks to the head of finance, he has all the figures ready for Hans's review. He has calculated the cost of redesigning the workspace to give the workers more room, as well as the expense of providing more supportive equipment, creating brochures for the SCT program together with additional employee training opportunities, playing music in the plant, and scheduling a game night once a month as well as a company bowling team to help employees bond.

"I'll agree to most of it. Not the music though—it might distract the employees," Hans says. "Let's see how all this affects the injury rates and morale."

Brian's safety measures are implemented and he is extremely pleased a year later when the number of work-related injuries has dropped to two. Workers who neglected to wear their protective gear properly caused both of the recently reported injuries. Brian has arranged for a special training session to ensure these incidents will not be repeated. All in all, he is happy with the progress made on the assembly line; the team seems more communicative and invested in their tasks. Jacob has told Brian he sees a marked improvement in their attitudes and performance. Hans Wagner congratulates him for "saving the company significant costs" by successfully decreasing the number of injuries. Depite Brian's happiness with the success of the SCT initiative, he remains concerned about Hans Wagner's prioritizing profit over the welfare of the plant's employees.

THINKING CRITICALLY

1. Review Brian's reasoning as he develops a plan to reduce workplace injuries at the plant. If you were Brian, what steps in the 5-Step Model of Decision Making would you have spent the most time exploring? What plant personnel would you have consulted with in formulating and finalizing a plan? **[Analyze/ Evaluate]**

2. Defend the perspective that the first step in the 5-Step Decision Making Model is the most important. **[Evaluate]**

3. Defend the perspective that generating and evaluating alternatives (steps 3 and 4) are the most important steps in the model. **[Evaluate]**

4. Do you believe that any one step is more or less important than any other step in the model? Why or why not? **[Evaluate]**

DECISION MAKING IN THE REAL WORLD

8.3 Identify factors that influence the way we make decisions in the real world

We've seen that decision making requires taking multiple steps to arrive at a clear solution. But what other factors affect an individual's ability to make rational decisions?

Bounded Rationality

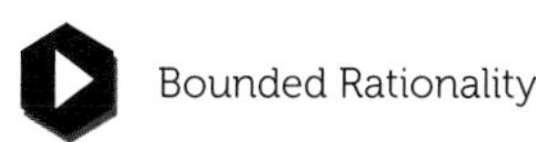

Bounded rationality is the idea that we are restricted by a variety of constraints when making decisions.[6] This concept is in contrast with **complete rationality**, which assumes we take in to account every single criterion or possible alternative to make a decision.[7] (See Figure 8.3.) In reality, most of us don't have the time or mental processing capacity to deal with so much information; instead, we tend to narrow the options to a few key criteria. For example, when buying a new car, we are more likely to use bounded rationality. First, we identify a few main benchmarks, like mileage, options, and price, and then we choose the models that meet our benchmarks to test drive. However, if we were to adopt a completely rational approach, we would need to consider every single car in production as a viable option, which is not realistic.

Satisficing Decisions

Satisficing decisions aim for acceptable results rather than for the best or optimal solutions.[8] Satisficing is useful for less important decisions. For example, when purchasing a pack of chewing gum, we tend to choose something that looks good. We don't spend time researching the merits of all the different chewing gum brands and flavors on the market. If it turns out that we made a bad decision in choosing that particular brand, it's not a big deal because gum isn't expensive. We simply make a different decision the next time. However, satisficing is not appropriate for important decisions. For example, when diagnosing illness, doctors cannot afford to make an incorrect decision that causes harm; they need to consider a great deal of information to establish the right course of treatment for the patient.

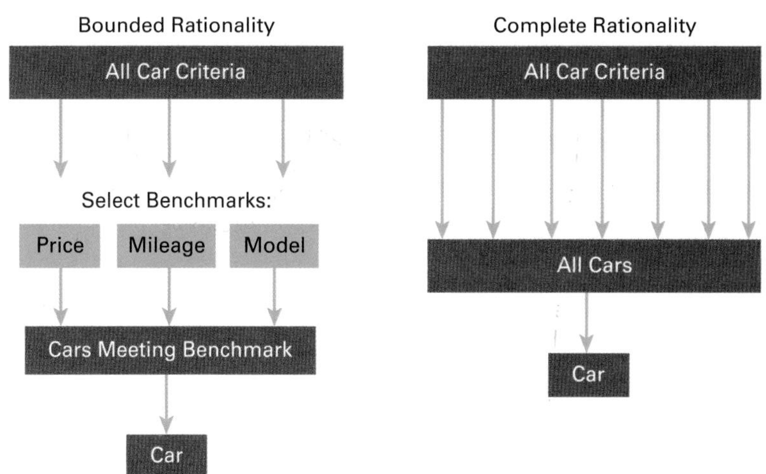

■ FIGURE 8.3 Bounded Versus Complete Rationality

Bounded rationality: The idea that we are restricted by a variety of constraints when making decisions

Complete rationality: The assumption that we take in to account every single criterion or possible alternative to make a decision

Satisficing decisions: Solutions that aim for acceptable results rather than for the best or optimal ones

Rob Janoff via Wikimedia Commons

Apple's classic slogan, "Think Different," alludes to founder Steve Jobs' tendency to rely on his intuition to make creative decisions and innovations.

Intuition

Intuition is the unconscious process of making decisions based on imagination and possibilities.[9] Relying on "a feeling" may not seem a totally reliable decision process. Some research suggests, however, that intuitive decisions often represent information we are already holding at an unconscious level, and thus it may lead to effective decisions.[10] The late Steve Jobs, cofounder of Apple, famously relied on his intuition to "think different" when designing Apple products and help him anticipate what users might want next.[11]

Heuristics

Another aspect of decision making is **heuristics**, shortcuts or "rules of thumb" that allow us to make judgments and decisions quickly and efficiently.[12] There are three types of heuristics: availability heuristic, anchoring and adjustment heuristic, and representativeness heuristic.

© iStockphoto.com/alvarez

We use representative heuristics to make decisions, using our existing expectations or experiences to predict an outcome. For example, you may expect someone dressed in a suit when interviewing for an office job to be a better fit for the company than someone who shows up in a sleeveless shirt and jeans.

Availability heuristics allow us to make judgments based on examples and events that are available and immediately spring to mind.[13] Sometimes we can make incorrect judgments about certain issues because of our reliance on information that is more readily available to us. This is called *availability bias.* Extensive media coverage can also bias our opinion; for example, a plane crash that is widely reported could lead many people to believe flying is unsafe, whereas it's more likely that one would be killed in a car accident than in the air.[14]

Anchoring and adjustment heuristics lead us to base decisions on the first piece of information and then adjust it, leading to *anchoring bias*, which is the tendency to over-rely on initial information while overlooking other important criteria.[15]

For example, a shopper might "anchor" on the discount of 25 percent on a pair of jeans worth $150, rather than considering that even with the discount the jeans are still more money than the shopper intended to spend.

With **representativeness heuristic** we base a decision on our existing mental prototype and similar representative stereotypes.[16] For example, two candidates turn up for an interview; one is well groomed, neatly dressed in a shirt and trousers, and the other has untidy hair and dresses in jeans and an old T-shirt. Based on past experience, you might assume the better-groomed candidate to be the more serious and committed person.

Intuition: An unconscious process of making decisions based on imagination and possibilities

Heuristics: Shortcuts or "rules of thumb" that allow us to make judgments and decisions quickly and efficiently

Availability heuristic: A rule of thumb for making judgments on examples and events that immediately spring to mind

Biases and Errors

Our decision making is often influenced by different types of bias. Recognizing and minimizing these biases is crucial for making accurate decisions.

Common-information bias is the inclination to overemphasize information held by the majority of group members while failing to consider other perspectives held

THE PARADOX OF CHOICE

Examining the Evidence

Bounded rationality suggests that humans are limited in their decision-making capabilities by the amount of information they can consider at a given time and by their mental capacity to process this information. Researcher Barry Schwartz of Swarthmore College conducted a study that showed that shoppers at a grocery store who were given a choice of six types of jam to purchase were more likely to make a purchase decision and actually buy some jam than shoppers who were given a choice of 24 different types. Schwartz labeled this phenomenon "The Paradox of Choice" and noted that our cherished freedom of choice may actually lead to decision-making uncertainty and dissatisfaction with decision outcomes. In other words, having too many choices may cause people to be unhappy with their decisions or to have difficulties in making any decision at all. Decision making can be especially difficult for "maximizers"—those individuals determined to make only the best choices.

Critical-Thinking Questions

1. **What are the implications of the Paradox of Choice for managerial decision making?**
2. **How can managers simplify their decision making so that they will not be paralyzed by choices?**

SOURCE: Schwartz, Barry. *The Paradox of Choice: Why More is Less* (New York: HarperCollins, 2004).

by the minority.[17] For example, in a voting situation, people often go along with the common or majority view rather than take the time to learn about and discuss other views.

Confirmation bias is the tendency to seek out information that fuels or confirms our preexisting views and to discount information that conflicts with them.[18] For example, say you want to move to a country in Europe for a couple of years. During your research, you only look at the aspects that support your own beliefs about that country (historic, scenic, cultural) and overlook information that presents alternate viewpoints (unpredictable weather conditions, cultural differences, cost of living).

Ease-of-recall bias is the propensity to over-rely on information recollected from memory when making a decision.[19] For example, an investor might provide inaccurate information about a stock by plucking figures from his memory instead of taking the time to locate the exact information.

Hindsight bias is the tendency to overestimate our ability to predict an outcome of an event.[20] For example, before a baseball game you "predict" that your favorite team is going to win. When your team does win, you might say, "I knew that was going to happen!," even though it is clearly impossible to predict these things.

Projection bias is the inclination to believe that other people think, feel, and act the same way we do (we project our thoughts and attitudes onto them).[21] For example, you might assume that all of your coworkers agree with your opinion of the company CEO, even though you've never asked them their opinion.

Escalation of commitment is the increased commitment we may make to a decision despite receiving negative information about the consequences.[22] For example, a manager may choose to invest in more and more training for an underperforming

Anchoring and adjustment heuristic: A process whereby people base their decisions on the first piece of information they are given without taking other probabilities into account

Representativeness heuristic: A shortcut that bases a decision on our existing mental prototype and similar stereotypes

Common-information bias: The inclination to overemphasize information held by the majority of group members while failing to consider other perspectives held by the minority

Confirmation bias: The tendency to seek out information that fuels our preexisting views and to discount information that conflicts with our worldview

Ease-of-recall bias: The propensity to over-rely on information recollected from memory when making a decision

Hindsight bias: The tendency to overestimate the ability to predict an outcome of an event

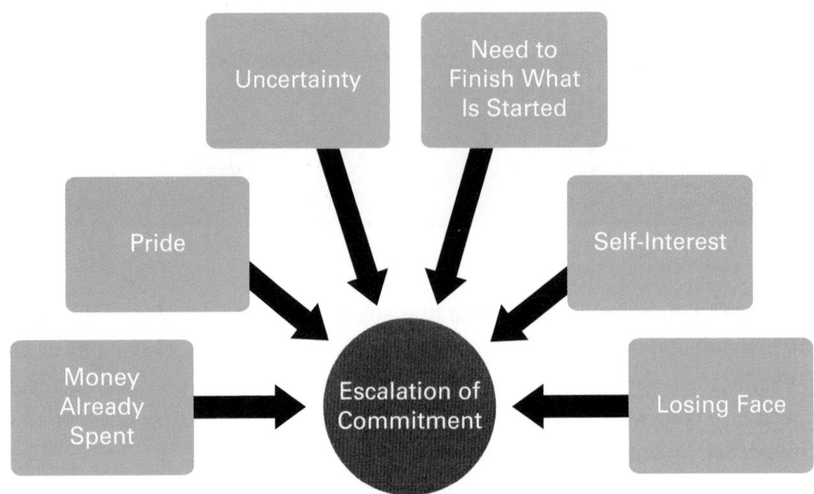

■ FIGURE 8.4 Escalation of Commitment Effect

SOURCE: Adapted from Staw, B. M. "The Escalation of Commitment to a Course of Action." *Academy of Management Review* 6 (1981): 577–587.

employee even though the evidence suggests that the employee's work is unlikely to improve. Figure 8.4 suggests a number of factors that can contribute to the escalation of commitment effect.

Sunk cost bias is the decision to continue an unwise investment based on past investments of time, effort, and/or money.[23] For example, you might be reluctant to sell your car for a reasonable price because you spent so much to fix it (your sunk cost) and you think it's worth more than it is.

Framing error is the tendency to highlight certain aspects of a situation, either positive or negative, to solve a problem while ignoring other aspects.[24] For example, suppose the company president tells her executive team that the company, which employs 2,000 workers, has an annual turnover of 2 percent. A positive frame views this percentage as low, requiring very little action, whereas a negative frame perceives the loss of 40 employees a year as unacceptable and is likely to spark discussions about how to resolve this perceived problem.

Lack of participation error is the inclination to exclude certain people from the decision-making process. For example, in hierarchical companies, most of the lower-level employees are not invited to partake in decision making even though their feedback may prove very useful.

Randomness error is the tendency for people to believe they can predict the outcome of chance events based on false information or superstition. For example, people believe it is possible to have a run of luck at the poker table, when in fact the probability of winning is the same every game.

Projection bias: The inclination to believe other people think, feel, and act the same way we do

Escalation of commitment: The increased commitment to a decision despite negative information

Sunk cost bias: The decision to continue an investment based on past investments of time, effort, and/or money

Framing error: The tendency to highlight certain aspects of a situation depending on whether they are positive or negative to solve a problem while ignoring other aspects

Lack of participation error: The inclination to exclude certain people from the decision-making process

Randomness error: The tendency for people to believe they can predict the outcome of chance events based on false information or superstition

THINKING CRITICALLY

1. Discuss the ways in which Brian Stevens' decision making process with regard to reducing injuries at the plant illustrates bounded rationality. **[Understand/Apply]**

2. In what types of work situations would satisficing be appropriate? List at least three occupations or industries where satisficing would not be an appropriate strategy for decision making? **[Apply/Analyze]**

3. Provide two examples of each of the three heuristics (availability, anchoring and adjustment, and representative) that are not discussed in the text. **[Understand/Apply]**

4. Which of the biases and errors discussed do you think are most likely to lead to miscommunication issues with colleagues and friends? Devise a series of questions you could ask yourself in order to avoid falling prey to the biases and errors you identify. **[Analyze/Evaluate/Create]**

5. Which of the biases and errors discussed are most likely to lead to budget and time-line problems in an organization? Defend your answer. **[Analyze/Evaluate]**

ETHICAL DECISION MAKING IN ORGANIZATIONS

8.4 Explain a basis for resolving ethical dilemmas in organizations

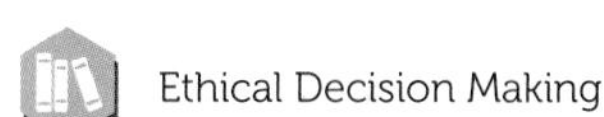
Ethical Decision Making

In Chapter 1, we introduced ethics and showed how it can be useful in helping us make decisions in cases where there may not be easy answers. We described bad ethical decisions in organizational settings may result in harm to employees as well as lost profits, bankruptcy, and litigation. Because of these instances, many of today's organizations have committed to fostering an ethical culture and improving ethical behavior in the workplace by providing employee training programs, workshops, and seminars on dealing with ethical dilemmas.

Many decisions include some sort of ethical choice. For instance, what would you do if you saw a good friend in your class cheating on an exam? It's tough to know the right decisions to make in certain circumstances. This is where ethical decision making can be useful in guiding us to do the right thing. Take a look at how Stuart Mease, director of Undergraduate Career Services at Virginia Tech, deals with ethical decisions in the OB in the Real World feature.

Individuals and companies frequently face large and small **ethical dilemmas**, or conflicts between two or more morally unpleasant alternatives.[25] The cheating example mentioned earlier represents an ethical dilemma. You could tell the professor you witnessed the student cheating, but then you might feel guilty for betraying a friend. However, you could keep quiet, but you might feel bad allowing the cheater to gain an unfair advantage over you and the rest of the students in the class. So how do you make the right choice?

The key to being an ethical person or organization is to *consistently* choose to do the right thing. Most people have strong values and the character to make morally correct decisions, and even people who are immoral can be sensible enough to know that cheating, lying, and breaking trust will not help them get very far in the workplace in the long term.[26]

In the next installment of our narrative, Brian is faced with a situation that challenges his personal ethics.

A few months after Brian's one-year anniversary at the plant, Hans Wagner calls him into his office.

"Brian, our third-quarter reports show that profits are down by two percent," Hans begins. "We need to make sure we end this fiscal year in the black."

Brian nods in agreement. "What do you have in mind?" he asks.

"I am thinking about cost-saving initiatives that have to do with our chemical waste," Hans replies. "We pay Johnsons Waste to collect and dispose of the plant's chemical wast on a monthly basis," Hans says.

Ethical dilemma: A conflict between two or more morally unpleasant alternatives

STUART MEASE, *Director of Undergraduate Career Services, Virginia Tech.*

OB in the Real World

© Stuart Mease

As director of Undergraduate Career Services for the Pamplin College of Business at Virginia Tech for several years, Stuart Mease has been connecting employers with college students who are looking for jobs after graduation. He is proactive in his approach and welcomes metrics and accountability. He actively seeks to engage employers in new and innovative ways so they feel invested in the students at Virginia Tech. One of his most recent projects is to increase the diversity of the student base, at prospective employers' request. Stuart's team approached employers with a two-page strategy document and asked them to donate to a scholarship fund that would specifically go toward helping diverse students attend Virginia Tech. Within the first two months of the campaign, ten companies had committed $22,000 to the program.

Stuart works closely with students on a daily basis to prepare them to be successful both in their future jobs and in their lives. When giving advice to students about making sound ethical decisions, Stuart says,

> I've made my fair share of bad decisions, but the worst decision you can make is not acting at all and thinking time will make something go away. I'm more comfortable dealing with the consequences than letting something sit there. If you make a bad decision, how do you make up for it? 'Fess up to it. Hey it's my fault I made a bad decision. If you make a good decision you want to be applauded for what you did. If you make a bad decision you have to be willing to step up and admit to doing a wrong.

Stuart also tells students that it's up to them to decide the nature of their ethics and values and to check them against the decisions they make. "For example," Stuart says,

> if the university system says that when you go out of town for two days you are allowed a $75 per diem, how you spend that money is up to you. However, let's say I go on business and every single one of my meals is paid for by an employer. To me, I don't feel comfortable taking the $75 because it was really meant to cover my expenses and I didn't have any. Sure, if I took that per diem someone can say "That's the right thing to do," but the system contradicts my values and I choose to live up to my values because I believe they are more important than laying down to a system that might be flawed.

Critical-Thinking Questions

1. **How do you explain Stuart's attitude toward expenses?**
2. **What would you do in his situation?**

SOURCE: Stuart Mease, personal interview

"I think we could cut the significant costs of hiring a waste disposal company by storing our chemical waste in steel drums on-site," Hans says. "The chemicals are corrosive, but we will be fine storing the waste for six to nine months and then we could arrange for Johnsons to take the waste away next fiscal year. Moving the waste disposal expenditure into next year will make it appear to the board and the shareholders that our profits are up and and everyone's a winner!" Hans finishes.

"Your job is to make all this happen."

Brian struggles to remain calm. Storing harmful chemicals on site is not only a direct violation of Environmental Protection Agency (EPA) guidelines, but because

© iStockphoto.com/hansenn

Brian is worried about Hans' short-term solution to store waste on-site because it is dangerous and ethically irresponsible.

the waste is corrosive, the barrels could leak, with severe consequences to employee health and the environment. Brian wants to make sure Hans realizes the implications of his actions.

Ethics at Work

"Hans, while I understand you need to cut costs, I don't believe that chemical waste is the area where we want to take short cuts. Storing hazardous chemicals on-site is against the company's corporate social responsibility reporting guidelines and standards. What if those barrels leak? And what if there's a surprise EPA inspection?"

"You're such a worrier, Brian! The waste will be on-site for only nine months at the most, and the steel drums won't corrode in that time. And what are the chances of the EPA dropping by in the next nine months? We haven't had an inspection in years!"

Brian is incredulous. "That's not the point!" he says, but Hans continues as if he hasn't heard.

"Besides, even if the EPA were to drop in, what's to say they are going to find the steel drums anyway? We'll make sure they're properly concealed," he says reassuringly.

"I'm sorry, Hans, but I can't play any part in this," Brian says. "Storing waste on-site is not only dangerous but in direct violation of EPA guidelines. You're putting the health and livelihood of your employees at risk."

Now it's Hans's turn to look taken aback. "Relax, Brian," he says in a surprised tone. "Let's not be too dramatic here. This is just a short-term solution to lower our costs. Both of us will receive better bonuses if we follow my plan."

"It's a short-term plan that has far-reaching and and potentially serious consequences," Brian says. "Let me be very clear: I'm not against your idea just because I'm afraid of getting caught. I'm against it because it's the wrong thing to do. It's ethically and morally wrong."

"Well, hey, I'm sorry if I've trampled all over your personal values," Hans says, sarcastically.

Brian can barely control his temper. Clearly Hans hasn't recognized the seriousness of the matter at all. He thinks back to his first conversation with Hans regarding the high numbers of employee injuries, and how Hans wanted to reduce the number only because injuries were costing the company money and making it look bad. And Hans is again willing to put his employees at risk. How can Brian justify working for someone who values profit over human safety? He knows what he has to do.

"My resignation letter will be on your desk within the hour," Brian says calmly and gets up to leave.

To his surprise, Hans jumps up from his chair. "Come on, Brian! Let's not be too hasty here. Let's talk about this some more." Brian hesitates. "Please," Hans says, gesturing for Brian to sit back down. Brian is reluctant but sits down waits to hear what Hans has to say.

"Look, Brian, you've achieved a lot over the last 15 months. The employees respect you and I don't want to lose you. But I'm under a huge amount of pressure from the board to deliver profits. You're right—cutting costs on chemical waste isn't an ideal option, but what else can I do?" Hans says.

Brian thinks for a moment and gives Hans the benefit of the doubt. Maybe this is his opportunity to help his boss see the situation from a different point of view. He considers less drastic options for reducing expenditures at the plant. Suddenly, Brian has a thought.

"When was the last time we did a competitive analysis to compare Johnson's rates with those of other waste disposal companies in the area?" Brian asks.

"I have no idea," Hans says. "Certainly not in my time, and I've been here 11 years."

Brian thinks he might be on to something. "Do you think it's worth reviewing other competitors to evaluate their fees?"

"I guess we could," Hans says, slowly. "Do you think we could get a better deal elsewhere?"

"It's worth a try," Brian replies.

"Can you please look into it?" Hans asks.

Brian pauses. He is surprised how quickly things have turned around. A minute ago he was ready to resign, but now Hans is depending on him to find a way to cut costs.

"Yes, I'll look into it and get back to you later today," Brian replies.

Hans leans forward and shakes his hand. "Thanks for sticking it out with me, Brian," he says.

After Brian leaves Hans's office, he heads to meet with the purchasing team. Jim O'Neill is responsible for purchasing and negotiations, and Brian hopes Jim will be able to advise him. As he approaches the team's bank of desks, Jim is on the phone and everyone is focused on their tasks. Brian can't help but think back to the first time he met the purchasing team and it seemed to him that they were spending more time joking around than working.

When Jim gets off the phone, Brian explains that he needs him to compare the plant's current waste disposal company's charges with those of others in the area to see whether they can get a more competitive rate. Jim is reluctant at first. "I've known the waste disposal people for years. They do a great job and it seems disloyal to start digging around for better rates," Jim says.

Brian understands Jim's position. It is always difficult to mix friendship with business, but he believes there are times when things need to change for the greater good.

"It's great to have good relationships with long-standing contractors, Jim, but we need to make sure we're getting the best deal possible," Brian replies.

"Ok, I'm on it," Jim sighs.

Two hours later, Jim knocks on Brian's office door with a sheaf of papers in his hand.

"Here's the information about the waste disposal companies around the area and a listing of their costs," Jim says as he hands the papers to Brian. "It turns out that we can get a better deal elsewhere. But Johnsons does a great job for us and understands the drill. I'm not sure replacing them and having to try out and train someone new is the best solution," Jim blurts out.

Brian considers Jim's point. "Jim, I know you have a great relationship with Johnsons. Why don't you negotiate with them? Ask them to match the most competitive rate you found, and if they agree then we'll keep them on as the plant's waste disposal company. How does that sound?" Brian says.

"They're not going to like it," Jim replies.

"They'll take it better from someone they know and trust—like you," Brian says, encouragingly. "They're a business too and they have to be realistic about market rates to stay competitive."

Jim nods. "Let me talk to them now and I'll see what I can do."

An hour later, Jim is back in Brian's office, looking pleased and relieved.

"Johnsons agreed to match the lowest competitor's rate!" he exclaims. "That means we can keep them on as our contractors, right?"

"Absolutely," Brian replies. As soon as he finishes working out the details with Jim, Brian goes to Hans's office to share the good news. Brian is relieved that he managed to resolve a major work dilemma with both his personal ethics and his job intact.

THINKING CRITICALLY

1. Describe the process you would use to resolve the ethical dilemma related to seeing a friend cheat on an exam. How would you define the problem? What ethical decision criteria would you apply? What alternative actions could you take? How would you evaluate each alternative action and what would you ultimately do? **[Apply/Analyze/Evaluate]**

2. Write a mission statement or list of rules that sums up what "consistently doing what's right" means to you. **[Create]**

3. In the case, Brian comes up with an alternate, ethical way to save costs related chemical waste disposal when confronted by Hans' unethical cost-saving strategy. Assume that Johnsons Waste is actually cheaper than its competitors. What other strategies (think back to what you learned in the previous chapter) could Brian employ to come up with an alternate cost saving solution? **[Apply/Analyze/Evaluate]**

ETHICAL DECISION-MAKING APPROACHES

8.5 Contrast various approaches to ethical decision making

Organizations often face ethical dilemmas in which they have to choose a certain course of action. There are three main ethical decision making approaches: utilitarian approach, rights approach, and justice approach.

The **utilitarian approach** focuses on taking action that results in the greater good for the majority of people.[27] For example, an organization that is struggling financially may choose to outsource some of its operations more cheaply overseas in order stay in business and retain its US workforce.

Utilitarianism

The **rights approach** fosters decisions made on moral principles that infringe as little as possible on the entitlements of others.[28] For example, a business owner might believe it is morally wrong to pay overseas workers low wages and decide to close down his US-based company rather than betray his principles.

The **justice approach** advocates basing decisions on fairness.[29] For example, a struggling organization might choose to turn down the best candidate for CEO if that person expected compensation that wasn't in line with the company's fairness-based compensation structure.

There are no easy answers to most ethical decisions. The organization that saves its domestic workforce by outsourcing some functions to inexpensive labor overseas may

Utilitarian approach: Action that results in the greater good for the majority of people

Rights approach: A decision-making method based on using moral principles that least infringe on the entitlements of others

Justice approach: A way to base decisions on the basis of the fairness

discover that the overseas workers don't receive a fair wage or work in unsafe conditions. Similarly, the business owner who refuses to hire inexpensive labor because of ethical concerns will nevertheless lose his company and leave his current employees jobless. A struggling organization may choose a less-qualified candidate who is willing to accept their compensation structure, but to what extent is justice served if they are failing to hire the best-qualified candidate who is more likely to save the business?

Despite the challenges of ethical decision making, having a clear ethical code that guides your actions will make it easier to choose the most appropriate path.

The Josephson Institute was founded in 1987 with a mission to change personal and organizational decision making and improve ethics and character development in society.[30] CHARACTER COUNTS! is a program established by the institute to promote and teach the Six Pillars of Character it believes define ethical behavior.[31] Today, this program is the most widely used approach to character education in the United States, reaching millions of young people through thousands of affiliated schools, agencies, and organizations.[32] Both Democratic and Republican presidential administrations have proclaimed the third week of October as CHARACTER COUNTS! Week, while a bipartisan group of US senators form the congressional CHARACTER COUNTS! Working Group.[33] In addition, dozens of mayors and governors have endorsed the CHARACTER COUNTS! framework and programming in their communities.[34]

The Six Pillars of Character are not based on political, religious, or cultural leanings in making ethical decisions. The six pillars are:

> ***Trustworthiness.*** Be trustworthy and willing to build trust with others. Honesty, sincerity, and loyalty are core qualities necessary for ethical behavior.
>
> ***Respect.*** Treat others with courtesy, appreciation, and tolerance. Avoid judging others and using aggressive language.
>
> ***Responsibility.*** Work hard, and be conscious of the way you behave and communicate toward others. Practice self-awareness and always strive toward self-improvement.
>
> ***Fairness.*** Be impartial and make decisions based on sound knowledge. Follow the rules but question injustices when they arise.
>
> ***Caring.*** Exercise forgiveness, compassion, gratitude, and kindness in relationships with others.

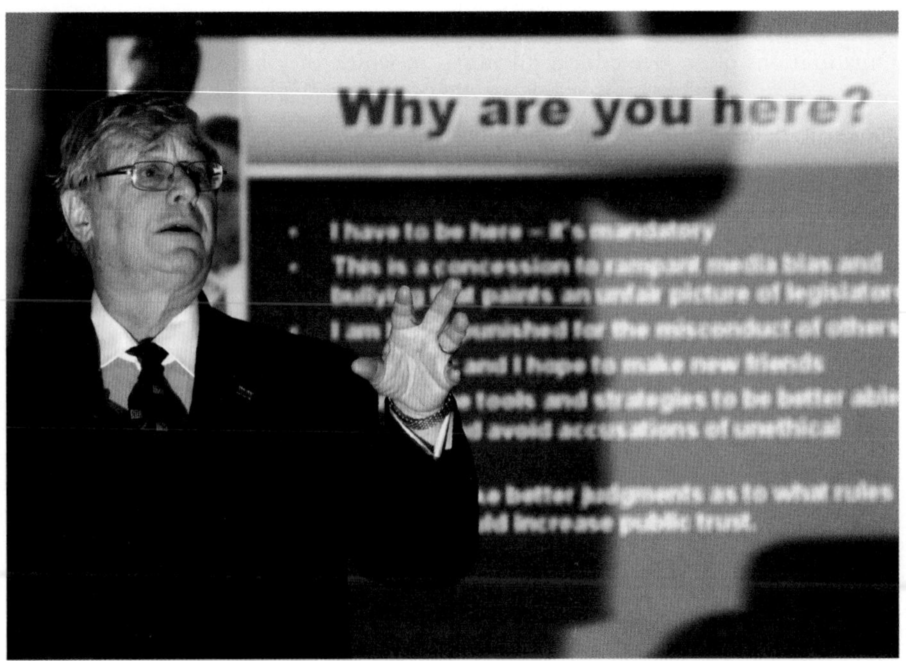

Michael Josephson of the Josephson Institute presents the Six Pillars of Character that are the foundation of his CHARACTER COUNTS! training program.

AP Photo/Chris Miller

Citizenship. Be sure to vote and play your part in improving the lives of the people in your community. Be kind to the environment and make time to volunteer in social enterprises.

The Six Pillars of Character offer a framework of commonly held ethical values that may be useful in discussing ethical issues and making ethical decisions in the workplace. Josephson suggests the following process for making ethical decisions:[35] First, take into account the interest and well-being of all stakeholders. Next, put the core ethical values (the Six Pillars) above all other values. For example, a person may value money, success, or winning, but these values should not be put above core values such as integrity, courtesy, or kindness. Finally, this approach suggests that if you must violate one core value in order to honor another, do what you believe will provide the greatest amount of good in the long run (apply the utilitarian approach). It is rare that the core values in the Six Pillars will conflict with one another, but it is possible, for example, that honesty might conflict with kindness and compassion; for example, if any employee asks for feedback from their boss on a new idea, the boss does not want to stifle the employee's creativity in the long run and may suggest to the employee that the idea is okay when in fact it is not.

In this chapter we have explored the importance of decision making, the different types of decision making, and described difficult situations that challenge personal ethics. In the next chapter, Brian and his employees' innovation and creativity is tested as they work to develop an innovative product.

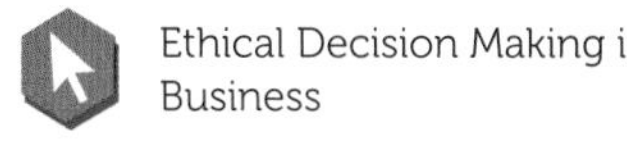

THINKING CRITICALLY

1. Consider the strengths and weaknesses of each of the three ethical decision making approaches (utilitarian, rights, and justice). Is one of the three more appealing to you than the other two? Why or why not? **[Understand/Apply]**

2. Think back to the case of Brian Stevens. Under what circumstances, given Hans's emphasis on profitability, could enacting an ethical decision making process at the plant change Hans's outlook? **[Evaluate]**

3. Imagine that the only way to reduce costs at your manufacturing plant is to lay people off. Fewer people will lose their jobs if you choose to lay off more senior staff, but more senior staff will be less likely to find employment elsewhere and all have a track record of extreme loyalty to the company. A number of senior staff members, meanwhile, are supporting aged parents, while the less senior staff are mostly single. Apply the model of ethical decision making advocated by the Josephson Institute to this ethical dilemma. Which of the Six Pillars of Character (trustworthiness, respect, responsibility, fairness, caring, citizenship) would you take most into account in making your decision? **[Understand/Apply/Analyze]**

IN REVIEW

Learning Objectives

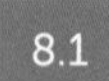

Identify the primary types of decisions managers make to solve problems

The ability to make decisions and solve problems is a key aspect of organizational behavior. **Programmed decisions** are automatic responses to routine and recurring situations. **Non-programmed decisions** address new or nonroutine problems for which there are no proven answers.

Apply a rational model of decision making to solve problems and make decisions

The first step in the five-step decision-making model is to define the problem in clear and concise terms. Second, we identify and weigh decision criteria. Next, we generate multiple alternatives to solve the defined problem. The fourth step is to rate the alternatives on the basis of defined decision criteria. Finally, we choose, implement, and evaluate the decision.

Identify factors that influence the way we make decisions in the real world

Bounded rationality is the idea that we are restricted by a variety of constraints when making decisions. This is in contrast with **complete rationality,** which assumes that we take into account every single criterion or possible alternative to make a decision. **Satisficing decisions** aim for acceptable results rather than for the best or optimal solutions. **Intuition** is an unconscious process of making decisions based on imagination and possibilities.

Heuristics are shortcuts or "rules of thumb" that allow us to make judgments and decisions quickly and efficiently. **Availability heuristics** allow us to base judgments on examples and events that immediately spring to mind. The **anchoring and adjustment heuristic** is a process of basing decisions on the first piece of information we are given without taking other probabilities into account. **Representativeness heuristic** bases a decision on our existing mental prototype and similar stereotypes.

Confirmation bias is the tendency to seek out information that fuels our preexisting views and to discount information that conflicts with our worldview. **Ease-of-recall bias** is the propensity to over-rely on information recollected from memory when making a decision. **Hindsight bias** is the tendency to overestimate the ability to predict an outcome of an event. **Projection bias** is the inclination to believe that other people think, feel, and act the same way we do. **Escalation of commitment** is the increased commitment to a decision despite negative information. **Sunk cost bias** is the decision to continue an investment is based on past investments of time, effort, and/or money. **Framing error** is the tendency to highlight certain aspects of a situation depending on whether they are positive or negative to solve a problem while ignoring other aspects. **Lack of participation error** is the inclination to exclude certain people from the decision making process. **Randomness error** is the tendency for people to believe they can predict the outcome of chance events based on false information or superstition.

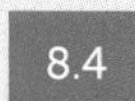

Explain a basis for resolving ethical dilemmas in organizations

We define **ethics** as moral principles that manage our behavior. Most individuals and companies frequently face large and small **ethical dilemmas,** which are conflicts between two or more morally unpleasant alternatives. The key to being an ethical person or organization is to *consistently* choose to do the right thing.

Contrast various approaches to ethical decision making

The **utilitarian approach** focuses on taking action that results in the greater good for the majority of people. The **rights approach** bases decisions on moral principles that least infringe on the entitlements of others. The **justice approach** encourages making decisions on the basis of the fairness.

KEY TERMS

Anchoring and adjustment heuristic 198
Availability heuristic 198
Bounded rationality 197
Common-information bias 198
Complete rationality 197
Confirmation bias 199
Decision making 191
Ease-of-recall bias 199
Escalation of commitment 199
Ethical dilemma 201
Framing error 200
Heuristics 198
Hindsight bias 199
Intuition 198
Justice approach 205
Lack of participation error 200
Non-programmed decisions 191
Programmed decisions 191
Projection bias 199
Randomness error 200
Representativeness heuristic 198
Rights approach 205
Satisficing decisions 197
Sunk cost bias 200
Utilitarian approach 205

THINKING CRITICALLY ABOUT THE CASE OF BRIAN STEVENS

Ethical Decision Making

Put yourself in Brian Stevens' position as the manager of the tractor assembly plant and consider the five critical-thinking steps in relation to ethical decision making and the need to cut costs at the plant.

OBSERVE

What differences do you perceive between Brian and Hans's attitude towards the plant's workers? As company president, is it fair to assume that Hans is operating within a different set of ethical considerations than Brian? Does he owe more loyalty to his shareholders and board than to his employees? Why or why not?

INTERPRET

How do you interpret Brian's initial decision to resign from his position rather than follow Hans's proposal to store corrosive waste on-site? What greater good would be served if Hans had allowed Brian to resign and gone ahead with his scheme to store the chemical waste on site? Assuming this outcome, could Brian's decision to resign be interpreted as a self-serving gesture? Why or why not?

ANALYZE

To what extent is Brian's critical-thinking ability as important as his ethical decision making in this scenario? Put another way: Hans appears less wedded to his unethical proposal than he is to cutting costs. He backs down quickly when Brian refuses to go along with his idea. Could Brian have avoided a showdown on ethics altogether by proposing alternatives from the get-go? Would this have been a better or more efficient approach?

EVALUATE

Based on Hans's reaction to Brian's refusal to behave unethically, what steps could Brian take going forward to ensure that Hans doesn't propose similarly unethical strategies in the future?

EXPLAIN

How would you respond if you were faced with a challenge similar to Brian's? In what ways would you handle things differently and in what ways would you handle things the same?

EXERCISE 8.1: ETHICAL DILEMMA IN THE JUNGLE

This exercise presents you with an ethical dilemma, a conflict between two or more morally unpleasant alternatives. Read the following scenario and carefully consider the two available options.

The Scenario

You are a botanist doing research in Central America. You find yourself in a small rural village where members of a drug cartel have captured and lined up 20 villagers who are accused of helping government officials in their efforts to crack down on illegal drug trafficking. The cartel *sicarios* (hit men) plan to shoot all 20 villagers as an example of what could happen to others who aid the government in their fight against the cartel. Because you are an outsider and not from the village, you will not be killed. You plead with the leader of the *sicarios* not to kill the villagers. Finally, the leader takes a gun, removes all the bullets except one, and puts the gun in your hand. "We will only kill only one villager as an example to the rest," he says. "As our honored guest, you will decide who will be killed and you will execute that person." He concludes with this warning: "If you refuse to kill a villager, we will go back to our original plan of killing all 20. And if you try any tricks, we will kill the 20 villagers and then kill you."

What should you do?

Your Options

1. Take the gun, choose a villager, and kill him or her.
2. Refuse and walk away.

Step 1: Carefully consider the scenario and decide which option you would choose. Be prepared to justify your choice.

Step 2: Divide into small groups of three to five members. Each member should present his or her choice and justification to the group. Next, attempt to reach a group consensus on the choice and justification. Be prepared to either present your decision or discuss the disagreements that prevented you from reaching consensus.

SOURCE: Based on a scenario described by English philosopher Sir Bernard Williams.

EXERCISE 8.2: SO, WHAT IS FAIR?

Objectives:

After successfully completing this exercise, you will be able to better *explain* different methods for resolving ethical dilemmas, and *contrast* different approaches to ethical decision making.

Instructions:

Background – You are the member of the board of directors for a medium-sized light aircraft parts manufacturing plant. The company has been in operations for over 50 years, and has been moderately successful throughout its history. However, due to changes in manufacturing processes, your current manufacturing methods are becoming obsolete and relatively costly compared to your competitors. You can upgrade your current manufacturing methods, but that will mean that 20 percent of your workforce will no longer be needed.

Your company has always prided itself on supporting the community through providing well-paying jobs, and strong employment guarantees to all of your workers. If you put the automation processes in place, you will not need to hire new workers for the foreseeable future. Additionally, all workers were promised (though not contractually guaranteed) lifetime employment as long as they did a good job.

If you do not implement the technological changes, your projections show a 20 percent chance of going bankrupt (and ceasing all operations) in the next five years due to increased competition.

Due to the nature of this decision, the company president has asked the company's board for advice on the ethical dimensions of this decision. You and the other board members have decided to meet to examine the situation using the utilitarian, rights, and justice approaches to the situation.

Step 1. Form into groups of five to seven members. Examine the decision from all three ethical approaches and make a recommendation on what steps to take from one selected approach. You can bring up alternative solutions to those currently being considered, but those alternatives must fall within the presented business constraints, and also be evaluated for ethical considerations. You will need to report your recommendation, and you will also need to report which approach you finally decided to use, why you chose it, the elements you used in making your decision, and if you would have made a different choice if you used another approach. (30 to 40 minutes)

Step 2. Choose a spokesperson to make your report to the entire class. However, all group members should be prepared to answer questions from the instructor and classmates. (5 minutes)

Reflection Questions:

1. What difficulties did you have in making your recommendation?
2. Did using the different ethical approaches help you in making your decision?
3. What were the major ways in which your discussions differed using the different approaches?

Exercise contributed by Milton R. Mayfield, Professor of Business, Texas A&M International University and Jaqueline R. Mayfield, Professor of Business, Texas A&M International University.

EXERCISE 8.3: I'VE DECIDED TO LET YOU MAKE THAT DECISION

Objective:

This exercise will help you to understand how to *apply* the rational decision making model, and *identify* ways in which we make more rational decisions in everyday situations.

Instructions:

Find a partner to work with on this exercise. Ideally, this person should be someone you do not work with on a regular basis. Work together to list and briefly describe the steps in the rational decision making model. As you are creating this description, note how each of the *Decision making in reality* concepts can influence the steps. You do not have to apply each *reality* concept to each rational decision making step (and you are unlikely to have time to do so in any case), but you should apply at least one *reality* concept to each step. Ideally, you will be able to link each *reality* concept to at least one step in the decision making process.

You can use your text when developing your write-up, and you should complete the task in about five to ten minutes. Be prepared to present your write-up or portions of your write-up during the class.

Reflection Questions:

1. How does linking the *reality* concepts to the decision making process help you better understand the problems that people have in making decisions?
2. What new insights into decision-making did you have from examining both idea sets together?
3. What poor decision-making processes can you better identify after reading the chapter and completing this exercise?
4. When and why might it be necessary to depart from the rational decision-making process?

Exercise contributed by Milton R. Mayfield, Professor of Business, Texas A&M International University and Jaqueline R. Mayfield, Professor of Business, Texas A&M International University.

CASE STUDY 8.1: CHIPOTLE

Fast food in the United States serves up $200 billion in sales annually, and its rapidly growing sibling is the "fast casual" industry, which strives to offer all the quality and freshness of traditional restaurants but with quicker turn-around times and lower costs. Fast casual, in fact, is expected to gobble up $62 billion in sales by 2019, skyrocketing up from 2014's still-formidable $39 billion—and Denver-based Chipotle Mexican Grille is one of the movement's most successful pioneers. Founded in 1993, today Chipotle opens a new store every other day and was recently valued at a staggering $21 billion. As Andrés Cardenal wrote in the *Motley Fool*, Chipotle is "perhaps the most successful growth story in the restaurant industry in recent years." When pundits talk fast casual, Chipotle is inevitably mentioned in the same breath.

And yet, despite being a capitalist's dream, Chipotle sees itself as more. Its commitment to "food with integrity" sets it apart from its competitors. According to Chipotle's website, "food with integrity" is a commitment to "the very best ingredients" that are ethically sourced; "to vegetables grown in healthy soil, and pork from pigs allowed to freely root and roam outdoors or in deeply bedded barns." Chipotle says food with integrity is based on an understanding of "the connection between how food is raised and prepared, and how it tastes," and it's been integral to the company's story since the late 1990s. It was then that Steve Ells, Chipotle's founder, co-CEO, and a classically trained chef, read about the Niman Ranch pork farmers. As Ells told the *Wall Street Journal*, the farmers "had a very special protocol about raising animals humanely, feeding them a vegetarian diet and not giving them growth hormones." Ells ordered a sample of the meat and made *carnitas* with it—he found the dish to be tastier than his previous efforts with factory-farmed meat. The chef-turned-entrepreneur had also toured factory farms and confinement hog operations, and he knew he "didn't want my success or Chipotle's to be based on the exploitation I saw. Not only the brutal treatment of the animals but the disregard to the environment, to the displacement of the family farmer and to the working conditions."

Ethical food became Ells's passion, and though he had opened his first Chipotle as a means to an end—to fund his then-dream of starting a fine dining restaurant—eventually it "clicked" that he could satisfy that passion with casual fare. Chipotle took off over the years (charged in part by an investment from McDonald's); Ells has yet to open his fine dining restaurant, and perhaps never will. Ingredients like hormone- and antibiotic-free meats "were only available in high-end restaurants [at the time], not mainstream places," he said in the same interview. "Today, we buy more naturally raised meat than any other restaurant company in the world. I don't know if I would ever have that kind of impact with one full-scale restaurant."

Though publicly Ells insists that what keeps customers coming back is Chipotle's great-tasting food, he and his team must have realized along the way that the "integrity" message had marketing power. The company takes every opportunity to reinforce it, after all; "it is what animates every decision the company makes, every strategic move," as Robert Safian wrote in a piece on Chipotle in *Fast Company*. For example, in 2012, Chipotle rolled out a massive, multitiered marketing campaign emphasizing both the healthful and ethical considerations inherent to food choices. The message was introduced across an array of media: a smartphone game called Pasture Pandemonium; large-scale sustainable food festivals in cities like Chicago; and a two-minute animated film, *Back to the Start*, that portrayed a family farmer deliberating between factory farming and a more sustainable approach. The narrative "humanized the devastating statistic that hundreds of families quit working their farms in the United States every week due to competition from big agriculture," wrote Danielle Sacks, also in *Fast Company*.

In addition to educating consumers—while keeping Chipotle top-of-mind when hunger strikes—the efforts helped to fund the chain's Cultivate Foundation. Ells started the charitable nonprofit in 2011 to promote and encourage sustainable and family farming "realized through the support of family farmers and their communities, educators and programs that teach younger generations about food matters, along with support for ranchers and farmers who are working to develop more sustainable practices," according to its website. The Cultivate Foundation's first major award of $250,000 went to Farm Aid, founded in the 1980s to promote family farms. Other beneficiaries have included the California State Parks Foundation, Jamie Oliver's Food Revolution, and the Nature Conservancy. The foundation has doled out more than $2 million in grants to date.

Chipotle's latest expression of its commitment to food with integrity came in 2015, when the restaurant announced it will stop serving foods made with genetically modified ingredients, which have come under scrutiny in recent years because of health and ethical concerns. "This is another step toward the visions we have of changing the way people think about and eat fast food," said Ells at the time. Though the restaurant chain has backed off its promise somewhat, acknowledging that some of Chipotle's meat and dairy "are likely to come from animals given at least some GMO feed" given GMO pervasiveness in the United States, the move was largely praised by industry watchers and business press. "The decision can be viewed as a bet on the younger generations in America," wrote Steve Kell in *Forbes*. In an additional show of their commitment to ethically sourced products, the company also decided to temporarily remove pork from the menu at one-third of their restaurants in early 2015 after discovering one of their suppliers had been violating pig-housing policies.

Chipotle has been forced to raise its prices more than once this decade—a dicey decision in 2012 especially, with the country still smarting from the economic downturn—but its gangbuster sales remain largely unaffected. Will it last? Chipotle and fast casual peers like Panera are no longer the only game in town. Traditional fast food chains are eager to get in on the trend—Wendy's now offers "natural cut" fries dusted in sea salt; McDonald's serves "bistro gourmet" burgers; and in 2013, Taco Bell introduced its "Cantina Bell" line, a not-so-subtle bid to lure customers away from Chipotle. Yet Chipotle offers something that Taco Bell (for now) cannot, which may help it keep its corner on the market: a conscience. Its "food with integrity" positioning is attractive to consumers who want their dollars to go toward a mission, not just a meal.

Ells certainly doesn't seem worried about his restaurant chain losing ground. An interviewer for *Fast Company* asked him, "If traditional fast-food chains begin changing their practices, in reaction to Chipotle's success, would [Ells] see that as a good thing overall, because it broadens the food-with-integrity culture? Or would he view it as a threat?" "It's a joke," Ells replied. "You know those guys, right? They can't change. The culture is just too ingrained. Which bodes very well for Chipotle."

Case Questions

1. Explain the type of decision making Chipotle used to develop its marketing campaign.
2. Describe how Chipotle became an example for ethical decision making in the fast casual restaurant industry.
3. Explain why Chipotle may experience more ethical dilemmas than Taco Bell or McDonald's in trying to maintain success.

Sources

Cardenal, Andres. "Chipotle Mexican Grill Inc. Stock Falls After Earnings: Time to Buy?" *Motley Fool*. May 13, 2015. www.fool.com/investing/general/2015/05/13/chipotle-mexican-grill-inc-stock-falls-after-earni.aspx.

Safian, Robert. "'I Didn't Know What the Fast-Food Rules Were': Steve Ells." *Fast Company*. October 14, 2014. www.fastcompany.com/3036584/generation-flux/i-didnt-know-what-the-fast-food-rules-were-steve-ells.

Kell, John. "Chipotle Just Went GMO-free—A Savvy Move to Impress Millennials." *Fortune*. April 27, 2015. http://fortune.com/2015/04/27/gmo-free-chipotle-millennials/.

"Chipotle Start-up Story." *Fundable.com*. n.d. www.fundable.com/learn/startup-stories/chipotle.

Debaise, Nicole. "Starting Chipotle from Scratch." *Wall Street Journal*, September 22, 2009. www.wsj.com/news/articles/SB125319598236119629.

Gasparro, Annie. "Chipotle Shares Sink on Outlook." *Wall Street Journal*. January 4, 2013. http://online.wsj.com/article/SB1000087239639044368410457806648403730132 0.html?KEYWORDS=chipotle.

Olson, Elizabeth. "An Animated Ad with a Plot Line and a Moral." *New York Times*. January 4, 2013. www.nytimes.com/2012/02/10/business/media/chipotle-ad-promotes-sustainable-farming.html?_r=0.

Serrao, John. "Does McDonalds Own Chipotle?" Mailbag, *Nutrition Wonderland* June 29, 2009. http://nutritionwonderland.com/2009/06/does-mcdonalds-own-chipotle-mailbag/.

Sacks, Danielle. "The World's 50 Most Innovative Companies: Chipotle, For Exploding All the Rules of Fast Food." *Fast Company*. January 4, 2013. www.fastcompany.com/most-innovative-companies/2012/chipotle.

"Fast Casual Restaurant Franchise Industry Report." *Franchise Direct*. January 22, 2010. www.franchisedirect.com/foodfranchises/2010foodfranchiseindustryreport/14/267.

Jargon, Julie. "Fast Food Aspires to 'Fast Casual.'" *Wall Street Journal*. October 10, 2012. http://online.wsj.com/article/SB1000087239639044465780457804865177366916 8.html?KEYWORDS=chipotle.

"Chipotle Donates $100K to California State Parks." May 30, 2012. *QSR*. www.qsrmagazine.com/news/chipotle-donates-100k-california-state-parks.

Giammona, Craig. "Chipotle Halts Pork Sales at a Third of U.S. Locations." *Bloomberg Business*. January 14, 2015. www.bloomberg.com/news/articles/2015-01-14/chipotle-halts-pork-sales-at-a-third-of-u-s-locations.

SELF-ASSESSMENT 8.1

What Is My Decision-Making Preference?

This assessment will help you to determine the extent to which you tend to be rational, satisficing, or intuitive in your decision making processes.

For each statement, circle the number that best describes how you would approach a decision of average importance based on the following scale:

	Not at All Accurate	Somewhat Accurate	A Little Accurate	Mostly Accurate	Completely Accurate
1. I tend to establish specific criteria before I make a decision.	1	2	3	4	5
2. I tend to select the first option I find that meets my needs.	1	2	3	4	5
3. I tend to trust my instincts when making decisions.	1	2	3	4	5
4. I generally consider a significant number of possible alternatives before I decide on the best course of action.	1	2	3	4	5
5. I generally select a course of action that meets most of my needs, rather than searching for an "optimum" solution.	1	2	3	4	5
6. I am more likely to follow a given course of action if it "feels right" to me.	1	2	3	4	5
7. I always take the time to clearly identify the situation and/or problem I am facing before I decide how to handle it.	1	2	3	4	5
8. When working in a group, I tend to look toward a solution everyone can agree on even if it may not be the best.	1	2	3	4	5
9. If I were faced with a life and death situation, I would trust my immediate reactions on how to respond.	1	2	3	4	5

Preference for Rational Decision Making

Total for items 1, 4, and 7 ___________

Preference for Satisficing Decision Making

Total for items 2, 5, and 8 ___________

Preference for Intuitive Decision Making

Total for items 3, 6, and 9 ___________

What was your strongest decision-making preference?

What are some of the strengths and weaknesses to this approach?

Under what circumstances might if be beneficial for you to attempt to incorporate more of your weakest decision-making preference?

9 Creativity and Innovation

Creativity comes from trust. Trust your instincts. And never hope more than you work.

—Rita Mae Brown, author

CREATIVITY AND INNOVATION IN INDIVIDUALS, TEAMS, AND ORGANIZATIONS

LEARNING OBJECTIVES

By the end of this chapter, you will be able to:

9.1 Discuss the critical nature of creativity and innovation in today's organizations

9.2 Describe the three-component model of creativity

9.3 Identify the three types of support for creativity

9.4 Outline the steps in the innovation process

9.5 Distinguish among the various types of innovation in organizations

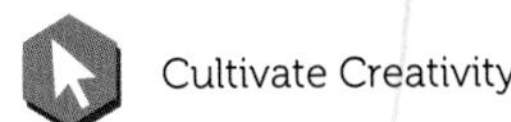

9.1 Discuss the critical nature of creativity and innovation in today's organizations

Imagine a world without the innovation brought to us via laptops, tablets, smartphones, social technologies, and digital media—a world in which we are no longer connected. Is it difficult to visualize?

Organizations like Apple, Facebook, and Google have transformed the way we live and interact with others and encouraged us to want more. What do these organizations have in common, and why are they so wildly successful? The reason is that their business models are largely based on promoting **creativity**, which is the generation of meaningful ideas by individuals or teams,[1] and **innovation**, which is the creation and development of a new product or service.[2] Creativity and innovation affect organizational behavior in those organizations in which employees are expected to generate creative products, processes, and strategies. The contribution from a group of individuals with varying knowledge, skills, backgrounds, and experiences can be a powerful force in creating innovative ideas and solutions. It is not just technology companies that have embraced this business model. Most successful organizations, whether in media, fashion, architecture, medicine, or engineering, are emphasizing creativity and innovation in order to stay competitive. They recognize the need to redefine, reinvent, and repurpose brands and products to keep up with market demand. One example is Cirque du Soleil, which describes itself as a dramatic mix of circus arts and street entertainment. Thanks to the creativity and innovative work of its members, it has reinvented the traditional circus by drawing on the worlds of theatre and opera to attract a larger, higher-spending customer base. Other organizations have mirrored or adopted its innovation strategy to help them think differently about their products and services.[3]

Every business, large or small, needs to innovate in order to compete. Fortunately, with the right training and a willingness to learn, every one of us has the ability to be creative on an individual level. "Business as usual" is no longer an option. Creativity and innovation are the lifeblood of successful organizations.[4]

THINKING CRITICALLY

1. Discuss the relationship between creativity and innovation. Is it possible to innovate without creativity? Is it possible to be creative without innovating? Defend your position. **[Analyze/Evaluate]**

Creativity: The generation of meaningful ideas by individuals or teams

Innovation: The creation and development of a new product or service

Master the content.

edge.sagepub.com/neckob

2. List at least three key technological advances and how they have affected consumer behavior within the last decade. Then discuss the ways in which consumer behavior changes have put more pressure on businesses to be more innovative and creative. **[Analyze/Evaluate]**

3. Read the OB in the Real World feature on the opposite page. When Attack! CEO Andrew Loos comments that "you don't just innovate with technology and create with people," what does he mean? **[Evaluate]**

Cirque du Soleil constantly reinvents and innovates what we traditionally think about the circus, drawing on more high-end concepts like opera and theatre, to attract a higher-paying customer base.

© iStockphoto.com/Arpad Benedek

THE BIG PICTURE: How OB Topics Fit Together

Individual Processes
- Individual Differences
- Emotions and Attitudes
- Perceptions and Learning
- Motivation

Team Processes
- Ethics
- Decision Making
- **CREATIVITY AND INNOVATION**
- Conflict and Negotiation

Organizational Processes
- Culture
- Strategy
- Change and Development
- Structure and Technology

Influence Processes
- Leadership
- Power and Politics
- Communication

Organizational Outcomes
- Individual Performance
- Job Satisfaction
- Team Performance
- Organizational Goals

ANDREW LOOS, CEO, Attack!

OB in the Real World

© Andrew Loos

Attack! is an experiential marketing agency founded in 2001. It brings traditional advertising campaigns to life by creating experiences for the target consumers to interact in real time and face to face with brands at beaches, concerts, malls, or office buildings where they can touch, try, or sample the product. One of Attack!'s recent successes was undertaken for Matrix, creator of high-end hair care and styling products marketed to salons. Attack! designed custom kiosks, developed and launched an iPad app, and sent "brand ambassadors" into salons to educate stylists and distribute coupons. During the campaign, data was collected, free samples were distributed, and the Attack! staff made sure the stylists were engaged with the Matrix brand. The campaign resulted in a substantial increase in sales of Matrix products and an extension into five additional markets.

Andrew Loos, Attack!'s CEO, says, "First and foremost, we have to constantly reinvent ourselves in our space to stay relevant. Our clients trust that we're going to spend their money wisely and in order to do that we have to be thought leaders in the industry. We have to have our finger on the pulse of trend and we can *never* be told about a new trend by our clients. It's our job to be the innovators."

Creativity and Innovation go hand in hand. "Creativity is what you use to drive innovation," says Andrew. "Creativity comes from being in the right mind-set and trusting your team. If you ask anyone out there where they are when they feel the most creative, they'll tell you it's when they are working with people they trust in an environment they mesh with."

Innovation means adapting and evolving. Sometimes it has to do with the technology you're using but "you don't just innovate with technology and create with people. We've become more innovative by changing up our think tank." Attack! encourages employees from all over the company to participate in brainstorming sessions.

Andrew believes that one of the best ways to increase creativity and innovation is to build a company with a strong corporate culture. In order to do this Attack! has developed a strong vision, story, and core values that remind employees to "deliver excellence in every aspect of your work," "build a positive team and family spirit," and "remember to laugh a lot." Employees also have a lot of fun at the office, with their life-size Jenga tournaments, team outings in Attack!'s custom-stretch limo, and Ping-Pong tournaments.

"The one phrase I utter more than anything else these days is 'spread the floor' and it means that I want our employees to be mixing together so our VP and directors are working closely with people from across the company." Not only does "spreading the floor" help innovation and creativity but it eliminates silo building between teams and helps Andrew achieve his goal of creating a great company culture.

Critical-Thinking Questions

1. **How does Andrew Loos use creativity to drive innovation?**
2. **How would you explain Attack!'s approach to reinventing itself as an organization?**
3. **What sort of creative outlets does Loos use to bring his team closer together?**

SOURCES: Andrew Loos, personal Interview, July 17, 2013; Attack! website, www.attackmarketing.com.

A THREE-COMPONENT MODEL OF CREATIVITY

9.2 Describe the three-component model of creativity

When Nick Woodman discovered surfing, he also discovered that catching waves wasn't enough for him. He wanted to capture on camera the daring surfing stunts he

Nick Woodman invented the GoPro camera as a creative solution to the lack of sports-oriented camera equipment on the market.

cellanr via Flickr.com and Wikimedia Commons

and his peers performed. First he tried tying a waterproof camera to his wrists, but this experiment and many others failed. Finally Nick realized he would need to build a custom camera himself. He called his tiny invention GoPro, and today it generates more than $500 million per year in all types of sports including snowboarding, cycling, and sky diving.[5] Many of us would describe Nick Woodman as a creative person. He created an innovation that filled a gap in the market and succeeded admirably. But what makes someone creative?

Researchers have spent years trying to figure out what makes a person creative. Some theorists have focused on the personalities of history's most creative geniuses, such as Einstein, Plath, Edison, Plato, and Mozart, to try and find the common thread associated with creativity. Other theorists argue that the study of personality traits is not sufficient to explain the foundations of creativity. Creativity researcher Teresa Amabile believes that creativity is a process rather than a list of traits, and she proposes a **three-component model of creativity** to describe the factors necessary for an individual to be creative. The three components of Amabile's model are domain-relevant skills and expertise, creativity-relevant processes, and task motivation (Figure 9.1).[6]

Inspiring Creativity

Domain-Relevant Skills and Expertise

Amabile argues that we must have what she calls *domain-relevant skills and expertise,* that is, knowledge about the subject and the skills and talent to provide the most creative and productive responses. An increase in knowledge leads to higher levels of creativity. For example, say you work in the graphics section of your firm and your boss asks you to come up with a new product logo. If you are a brand expert, you will draw on your knowledge and experience of certain brands to come up with creative responses that accurately represent the product. Even without any brand knowledge, you can still produce creative responses because such knowledge can be learned, but it usually takes longer to generate creative suggestions because it takes more time to acquire the relevant knowledge.[7]

Creativity-Relevant Processes

According to Amabile, *creativity-relevant processes*, work methods dependent on particular personality characteristics, methods of thinking, and knowledge of heuristics, are a second component needed for creativity. Personality traits such as self-discipline, perseverance, delayed gratification, and independence, for instance, appear to be associated with creative minds.[8] In addition, creative people tend to adopt a work style consisting of long periods of concentration and focus. They also have the ability to use **productive forgetting**, which allows them to abandon a solution that isn't working in favor of a new one.[9] People with creativity-relevant skills can also suspend judgment, adopt viewpoints different from their own persist in overcoming

Three-component model of creativity: A model proposing that individual creativity relies on domain-relevant skills and expertise, creativity-relevant processes, and intrinsic task motivation

Productive forgetting: The ability to abandon a solution that isn't working in favor of a new one

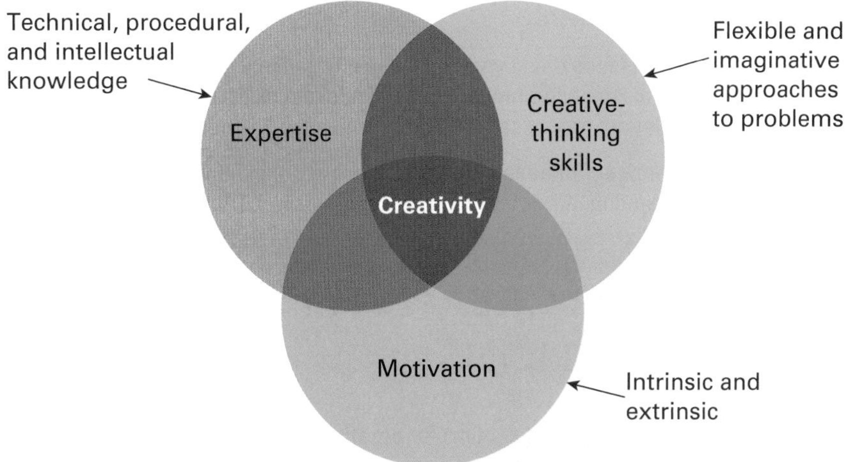

■ FIGURE 9.1 Three Components of Creativity

SOURCE: Adapted from Amabile, Teresa M. "How to Kill Creativity." *Harvard Business Review* 76, no. 5 (September 1998): 76–87.

obstacles, and ignore social approval. Finally, they use mental shortcuts or heuristics rather than strict rules to find creative ways to resolve a problem. For example, if you spend most of your day manually inputting data into a computer system, you might try and find practical ways to make the process more efficient. Like domain knowledge, creativity-relevant skills and processes can be learned through training and on-the-job experience.

Intrinsic and Extrinsic Motivation

People who have an innate interest in a chosen task tend to be more motivated to produce creative ideas. It stands to reason that if we find a task interesting and stimulating, then we will be more inclined to engage with it. In contrast, a task that we perceive to be tedious and boring will not provoke the same degree of attention or inspiration.

In the past, it was believed that extrinsic or external factors that control the way a person deals with the task tend to inhibit creativity. For example, you might feel intimidated or overly cautious if your manager is looking over your shoulder while you answer e-mails. This level of control may indeed stifle your creativity and your willingness to take risks, while people who are given the freedom to explore creative options may feel less inhibited and more inclined to share their ideas. Similarly, extrinsic rewards such as bonuses or other monetary rewards may stunt employee creativity, because many people have a tendency to focus solely on the steps it takes to obtain the reward rather than thinking of creative ways to reach their work goal.

More recent research suggests that extrinsic motivation, when used in the right way, could support intrinsic or inner motivation, especially when the levels of intrinsic motivation are already high.[10] For example, you might be told that your team is going to participate in a brainstorming session during which each of you is expected to come up with at least five ideas to redefine a product. You are likely to find this task creatively stimulating, particularly if you have a real interest in the product already. In other words, people who are explicitly told exactly what they need to do to be creative tend to produce creative responses.

THINKING CRITICALLY

1. What types of issues could you tackle most creatively given the three components of Amabile's model (domain-relevant skills and expertise, creativity-relevant processes, and task motivation)? **[Understand/Apply]**
2. To what extent can Amabile's model of creativity explain varying levels of creativity among individuals? Explain your answer. **[Apply/Analyze]**

SUPPORT FOR CREATIVITY IN ORGANIZATIONS

9.3 Identify the three types of support for creativity

Back to the Case of Brian Stevens

In Chapter 8, we followed tractor assembly plant manager Brian Stevens as he addressed an ethical issue with his boss, Hans Wagner. Hans had proposed storing hazardous chemical materials on site to cut the cost of using the plant's long-term waste contractor to increase profits, but Brian saw the proposal as unethical and dangerous.

Following a tense exchange, Brian suggested an alternate solution: check to see if other waste contractors charged less than the plant's existing contractor. With comparative price information, the purchasing department was able to renegotiate its contract for waste disposal, saving the plant money in an ethical way and alleviating Hans's concerns about profitability.

In this section, we explore a problem Brian encounters that requires creativity and innovation to solve.

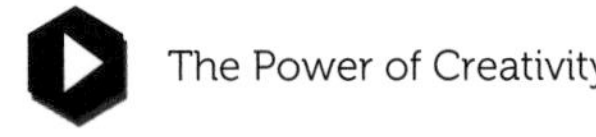
The Power of Creativity

Shortly after Brian's ethical disagreement with Hans, he is approached by assembly line team leader, Jacob Siegel. Jacob informs Brian that he has a serious problem requiring an immediate solution.

"Brian, our team just received a big order for a line of huge agricultural tractors. The assembly tools are big and heavy, and our workers really struggled to handle them last time we had an order for these. There's no way we'll be able to assemble this even larger number on time. If we hire more workers, we still have to train them, and that takes time we don't have. The deadline for delivery is tight under any circumstances, and I don't know how we're going to manage."

"The last time your team made these tractors, did they have any ideas about how to make the process more efficient?" Brian asks.

"Actually, a couple of the assembly team members came up with a few creative ideas. One particular innovation stood out, but it needed sign-off from the top," Jacob explains. "I tried to talk to the plant manager at the time, but he said he didn't have time to discuss it and told me to just get the job done. It's a shame because I work with a great team and we thought the innovation could work in the long term."

"Have you tried sharing these ideas with Hans Wagner?" Brian asks.

"The top guy? Are you kidding me?" Jacob laughs. "All Hans Wagner wants from us is to keep quiet, work hard, and save money where we can."

Brian starts to protest but stops when he realizes that Jacob is right. The chain of command dictates that all ideas have to go through the plant manager first, and if he or she vetoes them they don't go any further.

ZUMA Press,Inc./Alamy

Pixar Studios has an environment that fosters open communication, creativity, and playfulness.

"I want to hear about this idea," Brian says.

"The idea came from the team and they should be the ones to tell you," Jacob says.

Brian admires Jacob's loyalty to his team. He and Jacob work out a time to meet with the assembly team.

Creative Potential Versus Practiced Creativity

Creative Potential

People with **creative potential** tend to possess the skills and capacity to generate ideas. In contrast, **practiced creativity** is the ability to spot opportunities to apply these skills in the workplace.[11] In the tractor plant case, Jacob and some of the assembly team members have creative potential, because they have exchanged a number of ideas regarding the challenge of assembling huge tractors. However, because the earlier plant manager disregarded their ideas, practiced creativity is lacking; Jacob does not perceive that there is an opportunity to put the team's innovations into practice. He has not made the effort to pursue the ideas.

Research shows that creative people are more likely to flourish in a work environment that supports creativity.[12] For example, animation studio Pixar fosters a culture of open communication and constructive feedback and creates a work environment where everyone's opinions and ideas matter, all of which encourage its employees to be creative.[13] Those who perceive their work environment to lack support for creative expression may feel reluctant to express their ideas. This may create a gap between the person's creative potential and the application of their creative skills.[14]

Organizations that do not cultivate an environment open to creativity are at a disadvantage because they are neglecting resources that could help the company operate and compete more effectively. Organizations can narrow the creativity gap by fostering an environment that employees perceive as supportive to creative expression.[15]

Three Types of Support for Creativity

There are three main types of support for creativity in organizations: organizational support, supervisory support, and workgroup support, all of which have an influence on whether and how creativity flourishes in an organization.

Creative potential: The skills and capacity to generate ideas

Practiced creativity: The ability to seize opportunities to apply creative skills in the workplace

ORGANIZATIONAL SUPPORT AND CREATIVITY

Examining the Evidence

Research findings support the idea that employee perceptions of a supportive organization help to facilitate creativity.* But exactly how does organizational support translate into employee creativity? Researchers Chongxin Yu and Stephen J. Frenkel of the University of New South Wales examined this question in a study of 206 bank employees in China.^ Their findings demonstrate that perceived organizational support, which is the extent to which employees perceive that they are valued and cared for by the organization, as delivered by middle managers, affected employee creativity by strengthening two factors: employees' identification with their work unit and their expectations of career success. These results suggest that factors that engage intrinsic motivation—as heightened work group identification and career success expectations do—will be more likely to result in creative behaviors than extrinsic motivational factors such as felt obligation to care about and to assist the organization in the process of achieving its goals. To facilitate more creativity in the workplace, then, managers should engage in supportive behaviors that encourage employees to feel connected to their peers and to anticipate the possibility of a successful career path in the organization.

Critical-Thinking Questions

1. **In what ways can managers help employees feel more connected to their work group and to have expectations a successful career path?**
2. **What can managers do to try to avoid feelings of obligation among employees that could undermine creativity?**

*Amabile, Teresa M., Regina Conti, Heather Coon, Jeffrey Lazenby, and Michael Herron. "Assessing the Work Environment for Creativity." *Academy of Management Journal* 39, no. 5 (October 1996): 1154–1184.

^Yu, Chongxin, and Stephen J. Frenkel. "Explaining Task Performance and Creativity from Perceived Organizational Support Theory: Which Mechanisms Are More Important?" *Journal of Organizational Behavior* 34, no. 8 (November 2013): 1165–1181.

Organizational Support for Creativity

Researchers have identified a range of environmental factors controlled by the organization that can either stimulate or stifle creativity.[16] Creativity flourishes when employees are provided with the autonomy and resources they need to implement their concepts and when they are given license to take risks. In addition, organizations that provide appropriate rewards and feedback and that encourage a collaborative environment tend to possess a more creative culture.[17]

In contrast, organizations that impose too many constraints or controls over their employees, and that do not provide feedback, resources, or sufficient rewards, tend to create an environment that fails to encourage teamwork and collaboration. This type of organization stifles creativity. Though Brian believes the tractor assembly plant has improved in terms of teamwork and collaboration, he realizes the company has a long way to go before it can be considered an environment that fosters creativity. Although teams and employees tend to swap ideas, there is no real means of implementing them because feedback is not encouraged by senior management.

Supervisory Support for Creativity

A good role model, Brian realizes, is essential to fostering a creative working culture. Employees who perceive their supervisor as supportive will feel more comfortable about speaking up and making suggestions. Supervisors who communicate, set clear goals, and are confident and protective of their teams tend to nurture a creative environment.[18] Brian considers Jacob to be a good role model for his team. He knows Jacob encourages ideas and feedback, appears to have real respect for his group, and experienced disappointment when the team's ideas to improve the huge tractor's assembly process were not supported by the previous plant manager.

Work Group Support for Creativity

Finally, Brian considers the assembly team itself. Do they communicate well and help each other out? Do they like and respect each other? Are they committed to their work? Are their backgrounds diverse enough to provide a range of different perspectives? From what Brian has seen of the team, they are, as Jacob says, a group of "really good people." Brian has come to know a few members of the team through the monthly game nights that were implemented shortly after he took over managing the plant. He is impressed by how well they work together on the assembly line and how committed they are to each other and to the tasks they perform.

All in all, Brian concludes that both the supervisor and the work group are supportive of creativity and that the problem is the organization's hierarchical culture. As supervisor, Jacob has a certain amount of power to execute and sign off on ideas, especially those that save the company money. However, for the huge tractor assembly problem, Hans is the only one who can provide Jacob and his team with the approval and the financial support they need to implement a solution. In order to champion their cause, Brian needs to know more about the idea and the supporting evidence that proves it will work.

THINKING CRITICALLY

1. Under what organizational circumstances would you choose a job candidate who exhibited creative potential but lacked practiced creativity experience, over a candidate who had worked in an environment where opportunities to developed practiced creativity were extensive, but who exhibited less creative potential? Under what organizational circumstances would you choose a candidate with obvious practiced creativity skills over someone with creative potential? **[Evaluate]**

2. Reviewing Brian's interaction with Jacob as well as his interactions with other employees in the case installments in previous chapters, to what extent is he a supervisor who encourages creativity? Provide support for your answer. **[Analyze/ Evaluate]**

3. Can work group support for creativity make up for lack of organizational or supervisory support? Why or why not? **[Apply/Analyze]**

THE INNOVATION PROCESS

9.4 Outline the steps in the innovation process

Every innovation starts with an idea. Take the innovative website Free Rice, founded by computer programmer John Breen and launched in 2007. Breen's idea was to help end world hunger by finding a way to give people in disadvantaged countries free rice. The site presents visitors with simple multiple-choice questions. For every correct answer they give, 10 grains of rice are automatically donated to impoverished countries via the UN World Food Program and paid for by the banner ads that appear below the questions. To date, the site has donated more than 93 billion grains of rice, which has helped feed about five million people.[19]

The Innovation Process

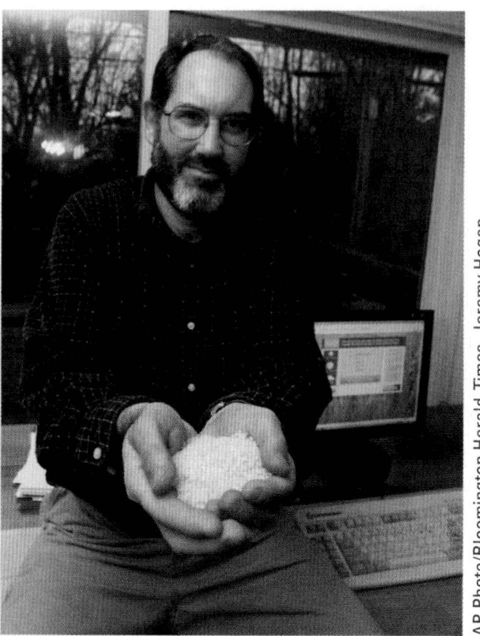
AP Photo/Bloomington Herald-Times, Jeremy Hogan

John Breen created Free Rice in 2007 as a new way to send food to people in disadvantaged countries.

Let's explore how Brian and the tractor assembly team follow the innovation process to devise a unique solution to ensure the large tractor order is filled on time.

The day after Brian's discussion with Jacob, 14 assembly line workers gather in the meeting room to discuss the large tractor assembly issue. Brian hopes to find out more about their thoughts and then follow the three steps in the innovation process: idea generation, problem solving, and implementation and diffusion[20] as shown in Figure 9.2. He hopes that this approach will help the team to produce a practical innovation to resolve the assembly problem.

Idea Generation

The first step in the innovation process is the creation of the idea itself. Usually an idea is born out of the recognition of a need for a solution and generated from existing information, experience, and knowledge. It is clear from Brian's discussion with Jacob that the assembly line team already has an idea to make the large tractor assembly process more efficient.

"As I said to you yesterday, Brian, our main problem is the size and weight of the assembly tools needed to build these tractors," Jacob begins. "Also, because the tractors are so large, it takes a considerable amount of strength, time, and effort to tighten the screws, which slows down the whole process. The first time we worked on these tractors, we started to think about what would speed things up and make the whole process more efficient, and that's where Jared comes in," Jacob finishes, gesturing for Jared to take the floor.

"Well," says Jared, "I got to thinking about how great it would be if we could create handling arms that could be suspended above the assembly line.[21] The arms would bear the weight of the heavy tools and give us freedom to move around," Jared says.

Zara joins in. "I'm in the break room having a cup of coffee with Jared one day, and he starts drawing a sketch of the handling arms. I thought it was a great innovation, so we swapped ideas and then went to the rest of the team to see what they thought," Zara finishes.

"That's when they came to me," Jacob explains. "And the idea got the whole team talking. The handling arms could be rotatable, which would help us maneuver the heavy tools more easily. We figured they'll help us to work faster and increase our capacity to fulfill any orders for the large tractors."

The rest of the workers join the discussion, offering their own opinions and ideas on the innovation. Brian, impressed by the team's ingenuity and enthusiasm, listens carefully, giving everyone a chance to share his or her thoughts. "I think your idea has a lot of potential, but we need to work together and look at every possible angle before I present it to Hans."

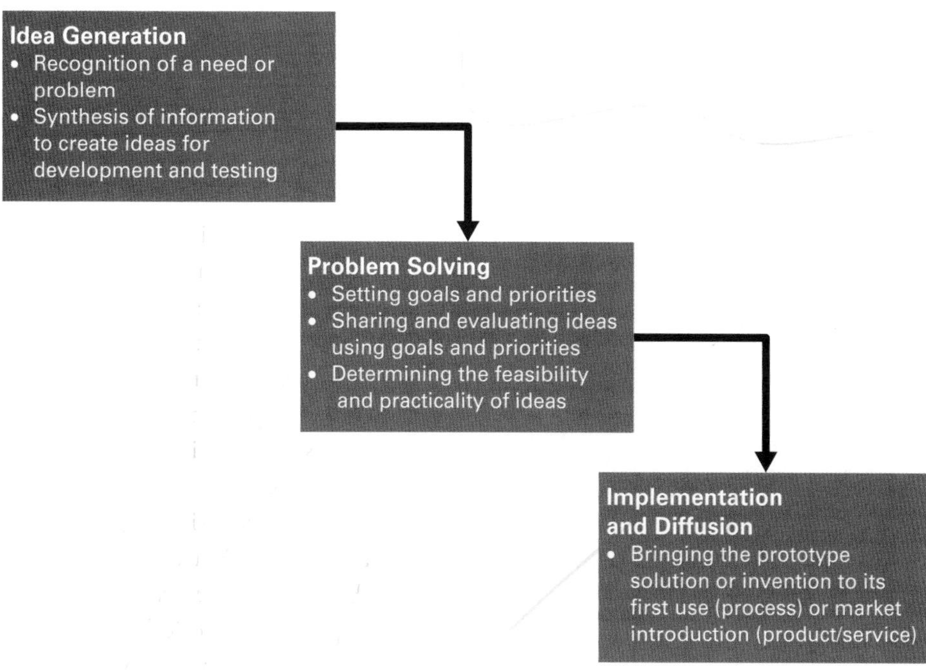
Idea Generation
• Recognition of a need or problem
• Synthesis of information to create ideas for development and testing
Problem Solving
• Setting goals and priorities
• Sharing and evaluating ideas using goals and priorities
• Determining the feasibility and practicality of ideas
Implementation and Diffusion
• Bringing the prototype solution or invention to its first use (process) or market introduction (product/service)

■ FIGURE 9.2 A Model of the Innovation Process

SOURCE: Based on Utterback, James M. "The Process of Technological Innovation within the Firm." *Academy of Management Journal* 14, no. 1 (March 1971): 75–88.

The assembly team agrees to help Brian as much as they can. Confident that he has the team's support, Brian moves on to the next stage of the innovation process.

Problem Solving

The second step of the innovation process is to identify any advantages and disadvantages associated with the innovation, explore costs and value, and set goals and priorities. Since the team has already explained the benefits of the new system, Brian decides to focus on potential problems and the feasibility of the innovation.

"How do you propose we bring this innovation to life?" Brian asks.

"We were thinking of asking the plant engineers to build us a prototype," Jacob replies. "Then we can test it and see whether it works the way we want it to."

"But that's a problem because a prototype is going to take time, and if we want to fulfill the order for the large tractors, we don't have a lot of time," Pedro replies.

Charlie speaks up from the back of the room. "It's also going to take up the engineers' time, and I know they're snowed under at the moment," he says.

Brian senses the shift in mood and decides to set some clear goals that he hopes will help motivate the team. "Okay, here's what we need to do. Jared, I want you to sketch an outline of the handling system. Put in as much detail as you can, making sure to incorporate feedback from the team. Then get someone on the design team to help you refine it. Jacob, once the sketch is finished, I want you to sit down with the head of engineering and discuss the time and budget they need to make a prototype. I know the engineering department is busy, but it's worth a shot," Brian says. Then he addresses the rest of the assembly line workers.

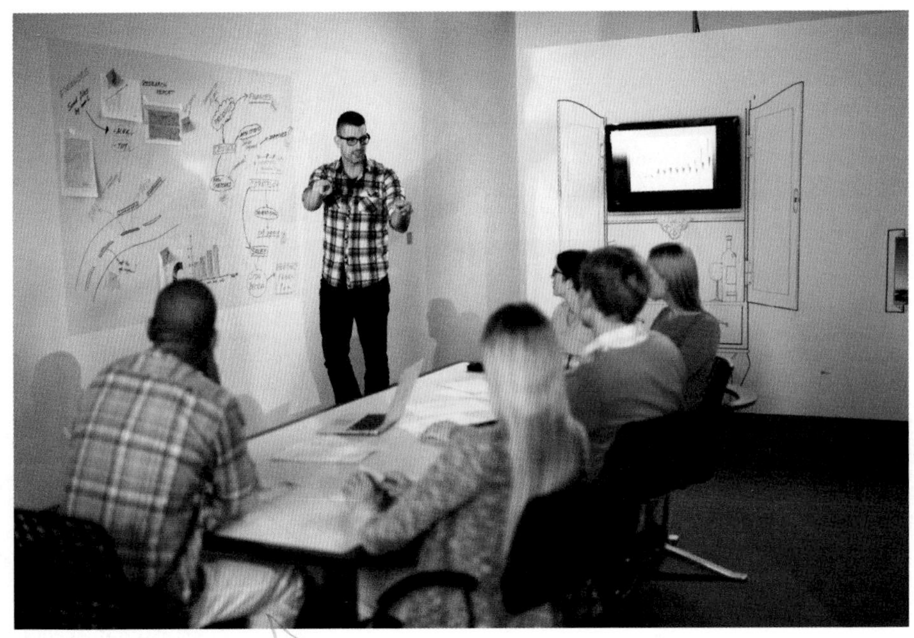

Brainstorming and sketching out ideas as a group is one way to involve everyone on your team in the creative process.

"While Jared is working on the design, I want you all to do some research to see whether this invention already exists," Brian says. "Talk to anyone you know working in assembly in other plants. Go online and see whether other companies like ours use them."

"But if the handling arms already exist, what's the point of doing all this work? It just means someone else has thought of our idea and we should drop it," Jared says despondently.

Brian is quick to respond; he doesn't want the team to lose sight of their purpose. "The main goal is to find a solution to the assembly task of creating the large tractors. If other plants use handling arms, then it might be quicker and make more sense financially to buy them rather than investing the time and money to create the prototype here on site. Also, if they do exist, I want to see whether our model is better in any way," Brian finishes.

Jacob agrees, "We know we have a good idea; we just need to do our homework. So let's get started!"

The assembly team follows Brian's instructions to the letter. Handling arms do exist, but those on the market are rigid and difficult to maneuver. Brian feels the team has a good chance of building on an existing product to produce a unique and more efficient innovation.

He asks the purchasing department to get prices for purchasing the existing handling arms from an external supplier and to work with engineering to estimate the time and cost of manufacturing a custom model of the arms themselves. The difference in cost is staggering; manufacturing the team's custom rotatable model will be significantly less expensive.

When Brian is confident that he has a strong case for developing the innovation, he arranges a meeting with Hans Wagner. He goes in with the idea that he won't take no for an answer.

Implementation and Diffusion

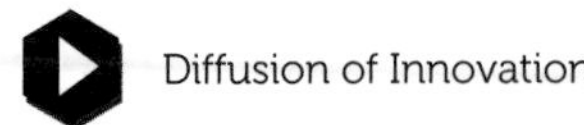

Diffusion of Innovation

The final stage of the innovation process is producing and distributing the new product or idea.

© iStockphoto.com/PeopleImages

After coming up with solutions to a problem, you must research how to implement it to ensure that it is the best option.

Early the next morning, Brian walks into Hans Wagner's office with his tablet containing spreadsheets of all the team's facts and figures. He explains the difficulties the assembly line experienced when it assembled the huge machines the previous year, and how they had come up with a solution to make the process more speedy and efficient.

Hans folds his arms and says, "I suppose they want me to hire more people to help them out? "Well, you can tell them I don't have the budget to put anyone else on the assembly line. They're just going to have to manage."

"No, Hans, that's not what they're suggesting at all," Brian says. He brings up the design of the handling arms on his tablet and turns the screen to face Hans. "This is what they're proposing," he says proudly.

Hans looks at the screen and nods, "Oh—handling arms. I've seen them in operation in other plants and industries, aerospace and automotive in particular. They're pretty common in Europe."

Brian is pleased that Hans is familiar with the concept, but his happiness is short-lived.

"I looked into this before and found they were inflexible and expensive," Hans says, turning the tablet back to Brian. "I'm afraid the team will have to come up with another solution."

But Brian describes in great detail how the team's innovative handling arms are different from the others on the market in that they are rotatable and easy to maneuver. He explains how cost-effective it will be to build the handling arms on site by sourcing their own parts. Then he takes Hans through all the facts and figures provided by the engineering and purchasing departments for the arms and the prototype.

When Brian is finished, Hans looks at him thoughtfully. "I'm impressed," he says. "Everyone has done their research, and I can see this innovation might really help improve the large tractor assembly process without our investing too much money."

"If the handling arms work the way the team has envisioned, we can take on even bigger orders for the largest machines, which could be very profitable," Brian adds, appealing to Hans's quest for profit.

Hans nods his head. "I have another idea," he says slowly. "If we can get this innovation right, it might have the potential to be a product we can sell to other industries. We could branch out into an entirely new market."

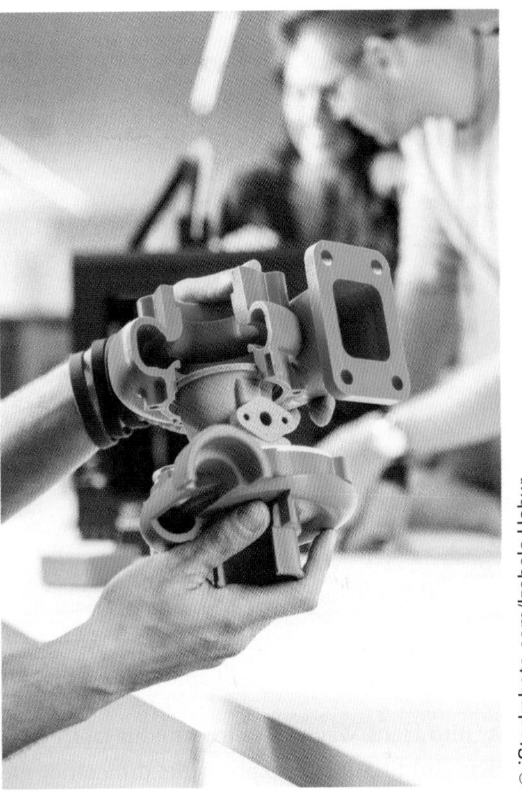
© iStockphoto.com/Izabela Habur

Constructing prototypes of an idea will give you and your managers a better sense of how the final product will work.

"Any industry that uses heavy tools would probably appreciate our flexible design," Brian agrees.

"We could tap into the aerospace and automotive market, Brian. The sky's the limit!" Hans says, slapping his desk. "But to make this happen, we need a prototype right away."

"I'll get on it," Brian replies. "The assembly team will be thrilled to have your support," he adds. He decides to focus his energy on getting the prototype built and tested as soon as possible. There isn't a moment to lose.

The assembly team puts in overtime during the course of a month, working alongside the engineering team to ensure their vision is realized. The teams test the prototype repeatedly, fixing problems and adding extra flexibility to the arms where necessary. The prototype is then attached to a tracking system above the assembly line so each assembly worker can test the model on the tractors and provide feedback. At the end of the testing period, the team believes they have the product they need to help them assemble the large tractors. A month later, the model is presented to and approved by the board, and the manufacturing plant is given the order to put the handling arms into production.

Once equipped with a number of handling arms suspended above the assembly line, the workers find it much easier and more convenient to build the huge agricultural tractors, and they complete the large order in advance of the deadline. In the meantime, the marketing department is working overtime to build a brand for the revolutionary handling arms with the goal of selling them to other heavy machinery assembly and manufacturing plants. The handling arms create a buzz when they are demonstrated at the annual agricultural trade show a couple of months later, and orders begin to trickle in.

The marketing team creates a video of the handling arms in action and posts it online, where it generates tens of thousands of views. Demand for the rotatable handling arms is so high that the manufacturing plant needs to hire more workers to fulfil orders. Thanks to increased profits, the company has the funds to do so. Hans is so pleased he gives the assembly workers a year-end bonus as a reward for their creativity and hard work.

On Brian's recommendation, Hans begins to hold monthly meetings with the assembly line workers to listen to their feedback and encourages them to contribute their ideas for innovation at the plant. Brian is pleased that the workers have been given more license to be creative, resulting in an organizational culture that is more supportive of creative effort and innovation. The entire development process of the control arms has reinforced his belief in the power of creativity and in establishing an environment that nurtures ingenuity.

THINKING CRITICALLY

1. Does one of the three steps (idea generation, problem solving, or implementation and diffusion) in the Innovation Process Model strike you as being more difficult to accomplish successfully than the other steps or is each step equally difficult? Explain your answer. **[Analyze/Evaluate]**

2. Developing, implementing, and selling the rotatable handling arms described in the case was a collaborative effort, but was one of the case characters more responsible for this innovative product's successful launch than other team members? Why or why not? **[Analyze/Evaluate]**

TYPES OF INNOVATION IN ORGANIZATIONS

9.5 Distinguish among the various types of innovation in organizations

We often think of innovation as a process that produces a tangible product, but in fact there are six main types of innovations in organizations: product innovation, process innovation, organizational structure innovation, people innovation, exploitative innovation, and exploratory innovation (see Figure 9.3). Let's apply the six types of innovation to the tractor assembly plant case.

Product and Process Innovation

Product innovation is the development of new or improved goods or services that are sold to meet customer needs.[22] One of the main difficulties of product innovation is getting the right teams in place to turn an idea into reality. In the tractor plant case, three teams are involved in developing the product—the assembly team, the marketing team, and the engineering team. If any of those teams had lacked commitment, it is likely that the product would not have been successful. Moreover, if Brian had failed to secure Hans's support, the innovation would not have occurred. In short, product innovation takes considerable time, effort, hard work, and dedication by everyone involved in order to succeed.

Process innovation is the introduction of new or improved operational and work methods.[23] Originally the assembly workers set out to devise a method to improve the way they worked on assembling large agricultural tractors. They found that manually putting these machines together was time consuming and physically draining. The handling arms address these challenges and improve the tractor assembly process making it faster and more efficient.

Organizational structure innovation is the introduction or modification of work assignments, authority relationships, and communication and reward systems.[24] As we have learned in the tractor assembly plant case, the plant is operated as a hierarchical organizational structure. Hans Wagner runs the company and calls the shots. Thanks to Brian's thorough presentation of the team's findings, Hans agrees to support the handling arms idea, which results in better communication between Hans and the rest of the workers, a new product, and an unexpected year-end bonus for the tractor plant's assembly team.

People innovation includes the changes in beliefs and behaviors of individuals working in an organization.[25] Organizations use a variety of training methods to foster positive behavioral change in their employees. In the tractor plant case, it is Hans Wagner whose behavior changes to the greatest degree. He becomes more accessible to his lower-level employees. This change, in turn, encouraged the employees to share their creative ideas.

Product innovation: The development of new or improved goods or services that are sold to meet customer needs

Process innovation: The introduction of new or improved operational and work methods

Organization structural innovation: The introduction or modification of work assignments, authority relationships, and communication and reward systems within an organization

People innovation: Changes in the beliefs and behaviors of individuals working in an organization

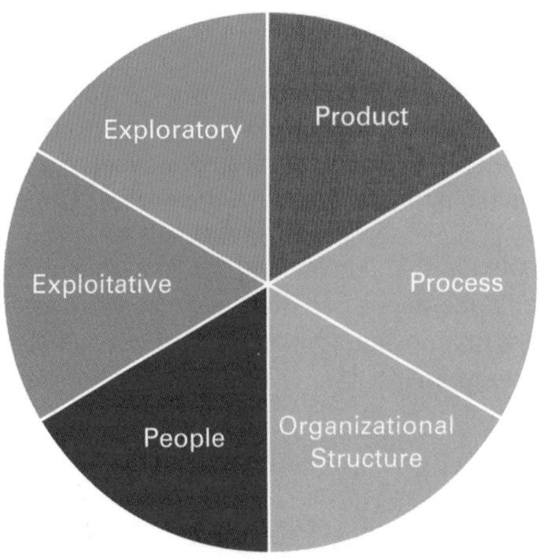

■ FIGURE 9.3 Types of Innovations in Organizations

Exploitative innovation focuses on the enhancement and reuse (exploitation) of existing products and processes.[26] The tractor assembly team has managed to refine an existing process and devise a product that not only supports and enhances its own work performance but can also be packaged to sell into a new market.

Exploratory innovation focuses on risk taking, radical thinking, and experimentation.[27] To work, exploratory innovation has to be supported by a management team that advocates the freedom of radical thinking. Thanks to Hans's eventual support, the assembly team is provided with the opportunity to explore their vision for an enhanced set of handling arms. Hans also takes the risk of packaging it into a new product to market and sell to a different target market. This level of exploratory innovation can bring about big changes within an organization, altering its culture, structure, and the way decisions are made.

Researchers believe organizations need to strike a balance between the contradictory natures of exploitative and exploratory innovation. Many organizations play it safe by focusing on the refinement of existing products rather than taking risks to explore new avenues. This approach can lead to **organizational cultural lag**, an effect that occurs when organizations fail to keep up with emerging innovations and so risk missing lucrative opportunities to capitalize upon.[28] To avoid cultural lag, organizations need to continuously focus on their existing products and processes at the same time they are investigating new innovations. For example, when enhancements to the Web made it possible to deliver news online, some newspapers capitalized on this opportunity and sought to attract readers through creatively presenting the electronic news while maintaining their traditional paper editions.[29]As a result, those newspapers remained successful. In contrast, newspapers with managers who perceived the delivery of news online as a threat rather than an opportunity lost readers.

To achieve the desired combination of exploitation and exploration, senior managers need to achieve a balance; encourage their employees to think in terms of sustaining an existing product while developing innovation; provide a forum for creative discussion; assign roles and set goals to get the process in motion; and introduce a reward system to help motivate teams and reinforce the importance of the organization's strategy.

In this chapter we have explored the differences between creativity and innovation, the different types of innovation and creativity and their importance to organizational success, and the process of innovation. In the next chapter, we reach the final installment of our tractor assembly plant case and observe how Brian Stevens manages major conflict at the plant.

Exploitative innovation: The enhancement and reuse of existing products and processes

Exploratory innovation: Risk taking, radical thinking, and experimentation

Organizational cultural lag: The deficit in organizations that fail to keep up with new emerging innovations

THINKING CRITICALLY

1. Provide at least two real-world examples of each of the six types of innovation (product, process, organizational structure, people, exploitive, and exploratory). To what extent do you believe that innovation in organizational structure and people enhances the likelihood of other types of innovation in an organization? **[Understand/Apply/Analyze]**

2. Consider the newspaper illustration used to explain cultural lag in the section. Newspapers are heavily dependent on advertising revenue for their profitability. A complicating factor for the newspaper industry has been the move of advertising dollars from traditional print products to the Internet. Using this additional information about the newspaper industry, revise the text's illustration to provide a more complex explanation of the factors spurring newspaper innovation over the past decade. **[Apply/Analyze/Evaluate]**

3. While the section discusses the need to balance exploitive and exploratory innovation in a successful organization, do you believe it is possible for an organization to remain profitable by focusing solely on one of these two types of innovation? Why or why not? **[Apply/Analyze]**

IN REVIEW

Learning Objectives

9.1 Discuss the critical nature of creativity and innovation in today's organizations

Creativity is the generation of meaningful ideas by individuals or teams. Innovation is the creation and development of a new product or service. Organizations need to redefine, reinvent, and repurpose brands and products to keep up with market demand. Creativity and innovation are the lifeblood of successful organizations.

9.2 Describe the three-component model of creativity

The three-component model of creativity proposes that creativity depends on the presence of domain-relevant skills and expertise, creativity-relevant processes, and intrinsic task motivation. *Domain-relevant skills and expertise* provide knowledge about the relevant subject and the skills and talent to provide the most creative and productive responses. *Creativity-relevant processes* are work methods dependent on certain personality characteristics, methods of thinking, and knowledge of heuristics. Personality traits such as self-discipline, perseverance, delayed gratification, and independence appear to be associated with creative minds. *Intrinsic task motivation* ensures that people who have an innate interest in a chosen task will be more motivated in producing creative ideas.

9.3 Identify the three types of support for creativity

People with creative potential tend to possess the skills and capacity to generate ideas. In contrast, practiced creativity allows people who perceive the appropriate opportunities to apply these skills in the workplace. Organizations that do not cultivate an environment for creativity are at a disadvantage because they are neglecting potential resources that could help them operate and compete more effectively.

The three types of support for creativity are organizational, supervisory, and work group. Organizations that provide support for creativity, appropriate rewards and feedback, and encourage a collaborative environment tend to possess a more creative culture. Supervisory support for creativity takes place when supervisors have the ability to communicate, set clear goals, and are confident and protective of their teams. Work group support for creativity takes place when the work group members communicate well, respect each other, are committed to their work, have diverse backgrounds and perspectives, and are willing to help each other out.

9.4 Outline the steps in the innovation process

In the first step an idea is born out of recognition of a need for a solution and generated from existing information, experience, and knowledge. The second step is to identify any advantages and disadvantages associated with the innovation, explore costs and value, and set goals and priorities. The final stage is the production and distribution of the innovation. It is in this stage that the idea is brought to life.

9.5 Distinguish among the various types of innovation in organizations

Product innovation is the development of new or improved goods or services sold to meet customer needs. **Process innovation** is the introduction of new or improved operational and work methods. **Organizational structure innovation** is the introduction or modification of work assignments, authority relationships, and communication and reward systems.

People innovation includes changes in the beliefs and behaviors of individuals working in an organization. **Exploitative innovation** focuses on the enhancement and reuse of existing products and processes. **Exploratory innovation** focuses on risk taking, radical thinking, and experimentation.

KEY TERMS

Creative potential 221
Creativity 215
Exploitative innovation 230
Exploratory innovation 230
Innovation 215
Organizational cultural lag 230
Organization structural innovation 229
People innovation 229
Practiced creativity 221
Process innovation 229
Product innovation 229
Productive forgetting 218
Three-component model of creativity 218

THINKING CRITICALLY ABOUT THE CASE OF BRIAN STEVENS

Consider the five critical-thinking steps in relation to the rotatable handling arms innovation process at the tractor assembly plant.

OBSERVE

The creativity of each of the key characters in this chapter's case (Brian, Jacob, Jared, and Hans) can be broken down differently based on the three-component model discussed in the chapter. List the domain-relevant skills and areas of expertise, the creativity-relevant processes, and the extrinsic and intrinsic motivating factors affecting the creativity of each character.

INTERPRET

How do the creativity differences among the characters, especially the factors motivating them to innovate, help or hurt the product's development? Focus specifically on Jared, Brian, and Hans.

ANALYZE

The description of the actual innovation process and the ways in which the assembly team, engineering team, and marketing teams collaborate to bring the rotatable handling arms to market is described briefly in the chapter. Develop an illustrative sketch of the idea generation, problem solving, and innovation and diffusion process that takes into account how each phase of the process is led and the ways in which the teams must collaborate with one another.

EVALUATE

Based on the different goals and areas of responsibility of each group, identify the types of obstacles they might encounter in working effectively with one another. How might inter-group conflicts result in better solutions?

EXPLAIN

What overall lessons related to creativity and innovation can you draw from this case? Keeping in mind that the handling arms innovation is based on a real-world example, what are the organizational practices you would implement if you were managing a company that needed to raise profits through the expansion of market share?

EXERCISE 9.1: THE CANDLE PROBLEM

You must affix a lit candle on a wall so the candle wax will not drip onto the table underneath it. As shown in the following picture, on the table you have a candle, a box of matches, and a box of thumb tacks. No other items are available to you. What do you do?

Solution

Empty the box of thumbtacks, put the candle into the box, use the thumbtacks to attach the box (with the candle in it) to the wall, and light the candle with a match. Most people will create a self-imposed constraint and see the box only as a device for holding the thumbtacks instead of seeing it as a separate component that could be used in solving the task.

SOURCE: Based on a scenario described by Karl Dunker.

EXERCISE 9.2: WATCH ME GET CREATIVE HERE

Objective(s):

This exercise will help you to better *understand* the various creativity and innovation concepts presented in this chapter.

Instructions:

Step 1. Find a partner and select a concept you want to present to the class. (1 to 2 minutes)

Step 2. Develop a creative way to present this concept to the class. You will need to present the following elements of the concept:

- An overview of the concept.
- The importance of the concept to organizations.

The presentation needs to be brief (1 to 3 minutes), but it can take any creative form you want. Some examples include writing a short story about the concept, singing a song about the concept, writing a poem about the concept, or performing a short skit demonstrating the concept.

When selecting a concept, you may want to use the major chapter headings as a guideline. (15 minutes)

Step 3. Present your concept in the selected creative way. (1 to 3 minutes)

Reflection Questions:

1. How did the process of having to present a concept in a creative way aid your understanding of the creative process?
2. Which creative presentations of others were most memorable and why?
3. What barriers did you face in developing a creative presentation?
4. How did completing a creative activity increase your confidence about future creative activities?
5. How could organizations use similar exercises to increase overall creativity in the organization?

Exercise contributed by Milton R. Mayfield, Professor of Business, Texas A&M International University and Jaqueline R. Mayfield, Professor of Business, Texas A&M International University.

EXERCISE 9.3: WATCHING YOUR GARDEN GROW

Objectives:

This exercise will give you practice *discussing* the role of creativity and innovation in organizations, *describing* the three-component model of creativity, and *identifying* the three types of creativity support.

Background:

Creativity and innovation can occur in many different forms, and be used for multiple purposes. While creativity and innovation are often discussed in terms of high-level activities such as designing new products, they can also be used in more day-to-day ways. For example, when someone comes up with a new way to display products in a store, or finds a new way to recruit college graduates, such activities are also creative. The term for such activities is garden variety creativity (Stafford, 1998).

Instructions:

Step 1. Find a partner, and help each other think about and write down a garden variety creativity activity that each of you have done. Your tasks will be to help each other in recognizing garden variety activities since it is easy to overlook your own creative accomplishments.

Describe your creative accomplishment using the three component model of creativity. Also, describe which of the three types of support for creativity were available in your creative task. (10 minutes)

Step 2. Form into groups of six (composed of three of the original pairs). Discuss what types of support for creativity were most common and useful for the various garden variety creativity accomplishments. Also, make note of any barrier to creativity that arose. (20 minutes)

Step 3. Present your discussion on what creativity support was most common and useful, as well as the barriers to creativity that group members faced. (20 to 30 minutes)

Reflection Questions:

1. In what ways did using chapter terms and concepts help you to better understand your own creative process?
2. What insights did you gain into how support for or barriers hindering creativity can impact workplace outcomes?
3. Can you think of different ways that managers could structure a work environment to encourage workplace creativity and innovation?

Stafford, S. (1998). "Capitalizing on careabouts to facilitate creativity." *Creativity and Innovation Management*, 7(3), 159–167.

Exercise contributed by Milton R. Mayfield, Professor of Business, Texas A&M International University and Jaqueline R. Mayfield, Professor of Business, Texas A&M International University.

CASE STUDY 9.1: INNOVATION AT APPLE

There's the typical job. Punch in, push paper, punch out, repeat. Then there's a career at Apple. Where you're encouraged to defy routine. To explore the far reaches of the possible. To travel uncharted paths. And to be a part of something far bigger than yourself. Because around here, changing the world just comes with the job description.

—The Apple Career Website

"Think Different" is more than a slogan to push Apple products. It's at the company's core, so to speak—the expression of a drive that has attracted 80,000 of the world's brightest and most driven minds, disrupted then dominated industry after industry, and made Apple stock the most valuable on the planet. Apple began in 1976 as a computer company (it was once "Apple Computer"), but has since blazed paths in music (iPod and iTunes), smartphones, and tablet devices (the iPhone and iPad), and has entered the "wearable" technology market with the Apple Watch. How does Apple continue to innovate? Its hyper-focus on intentionally unorthodox product and team management strategies is one of the factors that gives Apple the edge.

Product Obsessed

Apple's unprecedented success in the world of technology has long made it the subject of breathless analysis in the press and academia. Though extraordinary leadership is often the focus (most notable was its iconic cofounder, chairman, and CEO, the late Steve Jobs), there's something more. The internal culture and management principals developed at Apple are different. For starters, Apple is not just focused on product; it's obsessed. Everything, "from strategy to budgets to organizational design and talent management functions," revolves around the product, according to management guru Dr. John Sullivan, who has studied and written about the company for years. Forcing employees to be "all about product" usurps selfish tendencies and "increases coordination, cooperation, and integration between the different functions and teams," says Sullivan. "A product focus increases the feeling of 'we're all in this together' for a single clear purpose: the product."

Apple has not necessarily been the first to invent the things that has made it famous. Expensive computers so large that they filled warehouses already existed when Apple cofounder Steve Wozniak invented the personal computer, but Apple is credited with enabling everyone to have a computer in her or his home office and for making it easy to use. The company has a knack for turning previously existing inventions into products that change the world by bundling and improving innovations plucked from the competitive landscape. From Siri (adapted from the military's CALO, the Cognitive Assistant that Learns and Organizes) to the super-turned-personal computer, Apple doesn't take on a product unless management thinks it can do it better.

Secrecy and Silos

Apple makes ground-breaking, drool-worthy stuff that whips trendsetting techies into a frenzy. The ideal Apple product is intended to be a "pony, not a real horse but instead something so desirable that everyone wants it and considers it 'gorgeous,'" according to Michael Lopp, a former senior engineering manager at Apple—and that puts the pressure on Apple teams. We've read a lot about flat, lattice organizations as of late, which are gaining traction in creative industries like tech especially. Characterized by nebulous, spontaneously forming teams and a lack of traditional management, Apple is not one of these. Apple has managers, and their word is gold; its product and design teams are intentionally organized into small, self-contained silos.

Multiple small teams may be working on the same assignment, without much (or any) knowledge of what peer groups are doing, and may the best team win. The secrecy the company is famous for—which helps to build excitement until the moment a new product hits the market—extends to cross-team communication (or lack thereof, at least in the initial stages). Writes Sullivan, "The level of open collaboration that you might find at other firms like Google is not possible under this process, but neither is early-stage groupthink."

Once work is ready for peer review, ten mock-ups are whittled down to three and then eventually to one. Cross-communication and pollination may now begin. It can be a slow, expensive process, but Sullivan says it is a highly effective one that is unique to Apple.

The outcome must look amazing, and it must be accessible and simple to use, not just for the mainstream user—for *everyone*. Apple teams consider every type of person who might use its product but can't for some reason, because of a disability, for example, and then adapt it so that population can use it.

"We brought the rehabilitation engineers together with product development people," said Alan Brightman, founder of Apple's special education office, "and we told them, 'Take this Apple IIe and put a pencil in your mouth, then put your hands in your pockets and type me a letter.' They all said, 'Well, okay, but first let me turn the power switch on and put a disk in the disk drive.' See? They began to experience some of the difficulties, and they began to appreciate a whole new culture that was never represented in the design room before." Now every product design is graded on a report card according to 64 common obstacles users face.

Simplicity extends to the sales pitch on the retail floor. Front-line retail team members are highly knowledgeable about Apple products—in part because only a handful of Apple products are in circulation at a given time, versus the dozens or more show-cased by less streamlined competitors.

No Career Path Here

Apple motivates its employees in traditional ways—like robust benefits and great salaries—but it also places a special emphasis on stock options, even for its retail folks, which help fuel that "one for all" feeling. Moreover, although there is opportunity for advancement at Apple, don't look to HR for any hand holding. The corporate ladder here is a DIY affair, because Apple believes that "career paths" and automatic advancement, even based on tenure-proven merit, can unintentionally stifle creativity, self-reliance, and learning. "Absent a career path, employees actively seek out information about jobs in other functions and business units. In a company where creativity and innovation are king, you don't want anything reducing your employee's curiosity and the cross-pollination between diverse functions and units," Sullivan writes. The unspoken message is that resting on one's laurels has no place at Apple. Workers must be nimble; once a project has been accomplished, something new and even more impressive better make it to the drawing board. This emphasis on continual innovation and agility keeps employees, and Apple fans and users, ever hungry for the next big thing—which is just how company leaders like it.

For years, Apple has set itself apart as a leader in creativity and innovation—from the first personal computer to the ground-breaking iPod to the first talking virtual assistant. Apple has hammered out success by continually challenging its teams, by sticking to slick and simple, and by altogether staying ahead of the curve. All this has earned it its iconic status and the unabashed love of billions of consumers. If you say to Siri, "I love you, Siri," she'll say, "Oh, I bet you say that to all your Apple products." Which might actually be true.

Case Questions

1. How does Apple utilize innovation for product development?
2. Describe how Apple's corporate ladder inspires continual innovation from employees and how its approach differs from traditional methods of evoking creativity from employees.
3. How does Apple's approach of simplicity and accessibility lead to product innovation?

Sources

Bajarin, Tim. "Six Reasons Apple Is So Successful." *Time.* May 7, 2012. http://techland.time.com/2012/05/07/six-reasons-why-apple-is-successful.

Bosker, Bianca. "Siri Rising: The Inside Story of Siri's Origins—and Why She Could Overshadow the iPhone." *Huffington Post.* January 22, 2013. www.huffingtonpost.com/2013/01/22/siri-do-engine-apple-iphone_n_2499165.html.

Hill, I. "Natural Language versus Computer Language." In Sime, M., and M. Coombs (Eds.). *Designing for Human-Computer Communication,* 55–72 (New York: Academic Press, 1983).

Lewis, Peter H. "A Great Equalizer for the Disabled." *New York Times.* November 6, 1988. www.nytimes.com/1988/11/06/education/a-great-equalizer-for-the-disabled.html.

Lewis, Peter H. "Personal Computers: Putting the Disabled in Touch." *New York Times.* February 20, 1990. www.nytimes.com/1990/02/20/science/personal-computers-putting-disabled-in-touch.html.

McCracken, Harry. "Apple iPhone 4S Review: It's the iPhone 4, Only More So." *Time.* October 15, 2011. http://techland.time.com/2011/10/15/apple-iphone-4s-review-its-the-iphone-4-only-more-so/3/.

Pogue, David. "Apple's AssistiveTouch Helps the Disabled Use a Smartphone." *New York Times.* November 10, 2011. http://nyti.ms/1nGpxJK.

Stern, Joanna. "Meeting Cortana: Microsoft's Sassy Siri Rival." *Wall Street Journal.* April 2, 2014. http://on.wsj.com/1oErOZz.

Sullivan, John. "Talent Management Lessons from Apple . . . A Case Study of the World's Most Valuable Firm." *Drjohnsullivan.com.* October 3, 2011. http://drjohnsullivan.com/talent-management-lessons-from-apple-a-case-study-of-the-worlds-most-valuable-firm-part-4-of-4/.

SELF-ASSESSMENT 9.1

Creative Potential versus Practiced Creativity

Creative potential refers to the creative capacity, skills, and abilities a person possesses. In contrast, practiced creativity is the ability to take opportunities to use creativity skills and abilities. The following assessment will help you to determine both your creative potential and the extent to which you have the opportunity to practice creativity in your work or school situation.

For each statement, circle the number that best describes how you would approach a decision of average importance based on the following scale:

	Strongly Disagree	Disagree	Neither Agree nor Disagree	Agree	Strongly Agree
1. I am good at generating novel and original ideas.	1	2	3	4	5
2. I have the ability to use my creativity to solve problems.	1	2	3	4	5
3. I have a talent for helping to further develop the creative ideas of others.	1	2	3	4	5
4. I am able to find creative ways to solve problems.	1	2	3	4	5
5. I have the talent and skills to do well in my work.	1	2	3	4	5
6. I feel comfortable trying out new ideas.	1	2	3	4	5
7. I have opportunities to use my creative skills and abilities at work or school.	1	2	3	4	5
8. I am invited to submit ideas for improvements in the workplace or in the classroom.	1	2	3	4	5
9. I have the opportunity to participate on team(s) at work or at school.	1	2	3	4	5
10. I have the freedom to decide how my job tasks or school work get done.	1	2	3	4	5
11. My creative abilities are used to my full potential at work or at school.	1	2	3	4	5
12. I have opportunities to put my creative ideas into practice at work or at school.	1	2	3	4	5

Creative Potential

Total for items 1–6 ___________

Practiced Creativity

Total for items 7–12 ___________

Was your score higher for creative potential than for practiced creativity? If so, this gap could indicate that you are not able to fully tap into your creative potential at work or at school.

What are some ways in which you might be able to increase the opportunities to apply your creative potential at work or at school?

SOURCE: Adapted from DiLiello, T. C., Houghton, J. D. "Creative Potential and Practiced Creativity: Identifying Untapped Creativity in Organizations." *Creativity and Innovation Management* 17 (2008): 37–46.

10 Conflict and Negotiation

If you want to bring an end to long-standing conflict, you have to be prepared to compromise.

—Aung San Suu Kyi, Burmese politician

CONFLICT IN TEAMS AND ORGANIZATIONS

10.1 Describe the conflict process and the various types of conflict

Teams and organizations face many challenges and it is inevitable that conflicts will naturally arise. We define **conflict** as a clash between individuals or groups because of different opinions, thought processes, and perceptions.[1] Many types of clashes can occur within organizations and between them and their constituents. For instance, during the past 25 years, US technology company Kodak has come into conflict with the Environmental Protection Agency and with environmental groups as a result of toxic spills in its business park that violate New York state laws. Kodak has paid millions of dollars in fines for these environmental mishaps.[2] As another example, baristas at Starbucks came into conflict with their supervisors who allegedly forced the baristas to share their tips with them. About 120,000 former and current baristas were awarded a total of $105 million between them in compensation following a class action lawsuit against Starbucks.[3]

As a member of an organization you will have opinions that differ at times from those of other teams or individuals. Disagreements and clashes generally cause stress and discomfort, but does this mean all conflict is bad? Not necessarily. There are times when conflict helps teams and organizations be more creative and innovative. One of the most widely publicized business conflicts occurred between Bill Gates, founder of Microsoft, and the late Steve Jobs, founder of Apple. The two moguls took widely differing approaches to developing technology, yet they challenged each other competitively in a positive way that resulted in better and more innovative products.[4] Depending on how it is handled, conflict can have either positive or negative effects on an organization.

LEARNING OBJECTIVES

By the end of this chapter, you will be able to:

- 10.1 Describe the conflict process and the various types of conflict
- 10.2 Identify the five basic conflict management strategies
- 10.3 Outline the bases of trust and predictable outcomes of trust in organizations
- 10.4 Describe the negotiation process
- 10.5 Compare distributive and integrative bargaining approaches

Conflict at Work

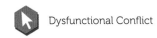

Dysfunctional Conflict

Functional and Dysfunctional Conflict

When conflict is constructive it can help improve work performance, redefine company goals, and encourage people to communicate better. Such **functional conflict** consists of productive and healthy disputes between individuals or groups.[5] For functional conflict to be successful, individuals from opposing sides need to be genuinely interested in finding a resolution to the problem and willing to listen to each other. Providing individuals with a forum to express their opinions often gives rise to critical thinking and helps to generate new ideas and solutions.

In contrast, **dysfunctional conflict** consists of disputes and disagreements that negatively affect individuals and/or teams.[6] This type of conflict often arises from an unwillingness to listen to each other or a reluctance to agree on a resolution or goal. High levels of dysfunctional conflict can lead to absenteeism, turnover, and a substantial drop in work performance, all of which can have a devastating effect on organizational goals and objectives.

Conflict: A clash between individuals or groups in relation to different opinions, thought processes, and perceptions

Functional conflict: A constructive and healthy dispute between individuals or groups

Dysfunctional conflict: A dispute or disagreement that has negative effects on individuals or teams

Master the content.
edge.sagepub.com/neckob

Types of Conflict

The three main types of conflict in organizations are task conflict, relationship conflict, and process conflict.[7]

Task conflict refers to a clash between individuals about the direction, content, or goals of a work assignment. High task conflict can lead to disagreements that may raise negative emotions such as resentment, anger, and aggression. In contrast, low levels of task conflict are believed to have the most positive effect on organizations by stimulating creativity, healthy competition, and critical thinking among the individuals discussing the various ways to approach a task. Another benefit of low-level task conflict is that, if handled appropriately, it allows every viewpoint to be heard and discussed, giving the individuals a sense of recognition and job satisfaction.

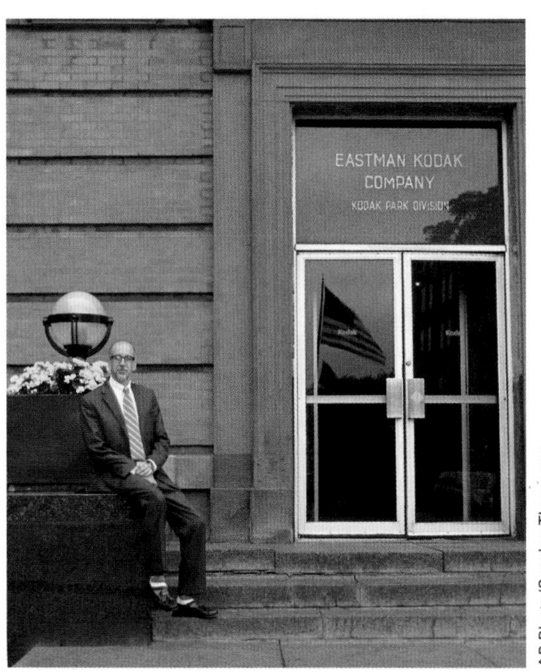

AP Photo/Carolyn Thompson

A business park owner sits outside the former New York offices of Kodak after the company paid millions in fines for violating state environmental laws.

Relationship conflict refers to personality conflicts between two or more individuals in the workplace. This type of conflict can be useful in resolving disputes if the parties are willing to communicate in a constructive and effective way. However, overall, it is considered the most destructive and harmful to organizations because it can give rise to hostility, mistrust, fear, and negativity. Managing relationship conflicts can also be time consuming and take resources away from other goals and priorities. A challenge for organizations today is that workforce diversity brings together a greater number of people from different backgrounds with different personalities, attitudes, and viewpoints, and managers must be vigilant to ensure that workplace relationships remain as harmonious as possible.

Process conflict refers to the clash in viewpoints about how to carry out work. Like task conflict, process conflict can be beneficial to organizations as long as it operates at a low level. When individuals and groups are given the chance to express their thoughts and opinions, they are more likely to generate new ideas regarding the best way to approach and define the process. However, high levels of debate about process can lead to resentment, apathy, and job dissatisfaction.

THE BIG PICTURE: How OB Topics Fit Together

Individual Processes
- Individual Differences
- Emotions and Attitudes
- Perceptions and Learning
- Motivation

Team Processes
- Ethics
- Decision Making
- Creativity and Innovation
- **CONFLICT AND NEGOTIATION**

Organizational Processes
- Culture
- Strategy
- Change and Development
- Structure and Technology

Influence Processes
- Leadership
- Power and Politics
- Communication

Organizational Outcomes
- Individual Performance
- Job Satisfaction
- Team Performance
- Organizational Goals

The Conflict Process

As we have learned, conflicts can have positive or negative outcomes depending on how the situation is managed. The following example illustrates the four different stages of the conflict process: *antecedents of conflict, perceived/felt conflict, manifest conflict,* and *outcomes of conflict.*[8]

Recently you arrive at work at 9:00 a.m. even though company policy states that employees should start work at 8:30 a.m. You haven't communicated the reason for your tardiness to the rest of your team. When you arrive at your desk, you take off your coat, grab a cup of coffee from the kitchen, and turn on your computer. By the time you actually start working it is 9:30 a.m. Without your realizing it, your tendency to arrive later than everyone else is an **antecedent of conflict**. You have set the scene for potential disputes. Antecedents of conflict include lack of communication, incompatible personalities, and collisions in value systems. In this case, your tendency to arrive late is clashing with the rest of the team's value of timeliness.

At 9:35, shortly after you have settled into your workday, one of your coworkers says, "Glad you could join us," which prompts a chuckle from the rest of the team. You perceive that the team has a problem with your tardiness and you feel their disapproval directed toward you. This is the **perceived/felt conflict stage**, during which emotional differences are sensed and felt.

Now you have a choice. Do you address the conflict head-on or do you ignore it? In the **manifest conflict stage** people engage in behaviors that provoke a response. You can either try to resolve the conflict by bringing the matter out into the open, or you can suppress it, which may temporarily solve the problem, but may also leave the situation open to future conflict and escalation.

The final stage is the **outcomes of conflict stage**, which encompasses the consequences of the dispute. Depending on how you and the rest of the team handle the manifest conflict stage, there will be either functional or dysfunctional outcomes. For example, if you choose to address the team in a professional manner and open up the lines of communication by explaining your lateness and pointing out that you stay an hour later than they do on most days to make up for your later arrival at work, then you are more likely to bring about a positive outcome. In contrast, if you decide to angrily retort to the sarcastic comment that when you arrive and leave is none of their business so long as the work gets done, you may make the situation even worse, which will lead to a dysfunctional outcome.

THINKING CRITICALLY

1. Based on the discussion of the differences between functional and dysfunctional conflict, write a series of ground rules that you believe could help individuals and teams resolve conflicts in a functional manner. **[Create]**

2. Why do relationship conflicts (as opposed to task or process conflicts) potentially lead to the most dysfunctional and harmful outcomes? Explain your answer. **[Apply/Analyze]**

3. Consider a disagreement you have recently had with a friend, family member, or colleague. Briefly describe the conflict by breaking it into the four stages of the conflict process (antecedent of conflict stage, perceived/felt conflict stage, manifest conflict stage, outcomes of conflict stage). What might you have done during the manifest conflict stage to lead to a more functional outcome to the conflict? **[Apply/Analyze]**

Task conflict: The clash between individuals in relation to the direction, content, or goal of a certain assignment

Relationship conflict: The clash in personalities between two or more individuals

Process conflict: The clash in viewpoints in relation to how to carry out work

Antecedents of conflict: Factors that set the scene for potential dispute

Perceived/felt conflict stage: The stage at which emotional differences are sensed and felt

Manifest conflict stage: The stage at which people engage in behaviors that provoke a response

Outcomes conflict stage: The stage that describes the consequences of the dispute

CONFLICT MANAGEMENT STRATEGIES

10.2 Identify the five basic conflict management strategies

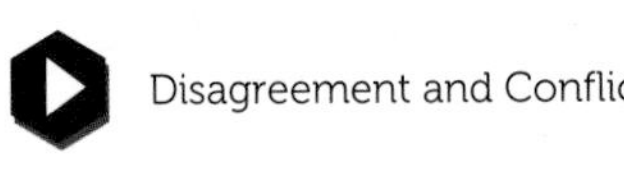

Conflict is inevitable in the workplace. Understanding the five basic conflict-management strategies, however, will help you to manage conflicts so they are productive and don't escalate out of control. The five strategies (see Figure 10.1) are *avoidance, accommodation, competition, compromise,* and *collaboration.*[9]

Let's apply the conflict management strategies to the next installment of the case at the tractor assembly plant.

Back to the Case of Brian Stevens

A year has passed since the innovative rotatable handling arms were developed for the plant and offered for sale to the public. Business is booming and the team is motivated. Brian Stevens is surprised when Head of Sales Shanice Harris, who is responsible for sales orders and the promotion of the handling arms, approaches him one day looking concerned.

"Sales for the handling arms have been going well, but two months ago I was at a trade show and another company, HW Machinery, demonstrated its handling arms, which were almost the same as ours," Shanice explains.

Brian observes that competition is healthy and should be good for business.

"I agree, but HW Machinery is pricing their handling arms much lower than ours—by almost 10 percent," Shanice says. "And it's not because they're lower quality. They're the same high quality as our handling arms. Over the last two months, our sales have started to slow down. To make matters worse, one of our existing customers told me he was considering buying the handling arms for a new plant from HW Machinery instead of us."

"Have you spoken to Hans Wagner about this?" Brian says.

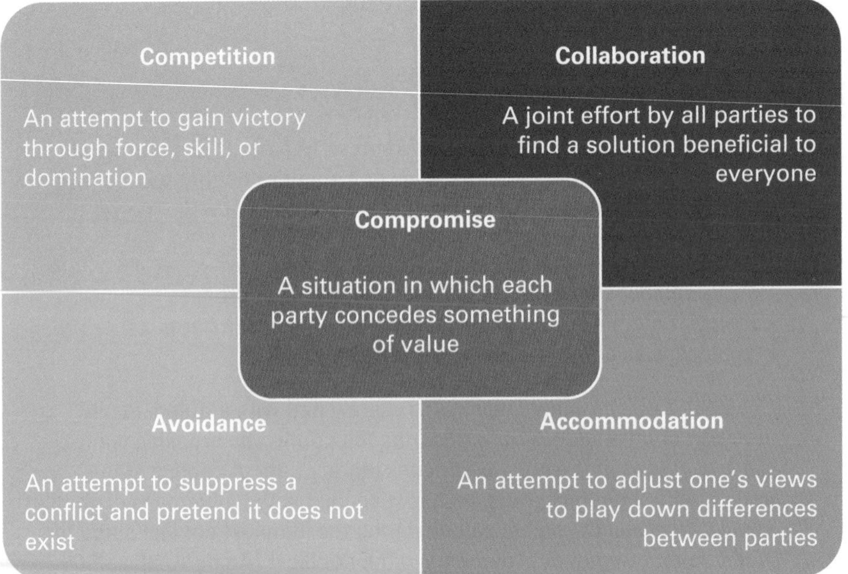

FIGURE 10.1 Conflict Management Strategies

TASK AND RELATIONSHIP CONFLICT

Examining the Evidence

Researchers and practitioners have long asserted that task-related conflict can be beneficial by stimulating creativity and critical thinking in group decision making. However, two recent meta-analyses examining the effects of task-related conflict across multiple studies failed to find support for an overall positive relationship between task conflict and group performance.* These findings led researchers Frank R. C. de Wit and Daan Scheepers of Leiden University and Karen A. Jehn of the Melbourne Business School to delve a little deeper into the relationships between task conflict, relationship conflict, and decision making.^ They found that when relationship conflict was present during task conflict, group members were more likely to rigidly hold onto less than optimal starting positions during group interactions, leading to poor decision outcomes. The findings suggest that task conflict is neither universally good nor universally bad. Instead, its potential benefits in group decision making may depend on whether relationship conflict is also present.

Critical-Thinking Questions

1. **Why is relationship conflict so detrimental to group decision making? Why can task conflict be potentially beneficial?**
2. **What can managers do to facilitate potentially beneficial conflict while minimizing potentially detrimental conflict?**

*De Dreu, Carsten K.W., and Laurie R. Weingart. "Task versus Relationship Conflict, Team Performance, and Team Member Satisfaction: A Meta-analysis." *Journal of Applied Psychology* 88, no. 4 (August 2003): 741–749; de Wit, Frank R. C., Lindred L. Greer, and Karen A. Jehn. "The Paradox of Intragroup Conflict: A Meta-analysis." *Journal of Applied Psychology* 97, no. 2 (March 2012): 360–390.

^De Wit, Frank R. C., Karen A. Jehn, and Daan Scheepers. "Task Conflict, Information Processing, and Decision-Making: The Damaging Effect of Relationship Conflict." *Organizational Behavior and Human Decision Processes* 122, no. 2 (November 2013): 177–189.

"No," Shanice replies. "He noticed the sales decrease and commented on it, but I didn't tell him about the new competitor. I was hoping sales would go back up. I don't think he will react well to this."

Brian can't help but feel that Shanice as head of sales should have tackled the issue head on with Hans rather than avoiding the potential conflict. But what's done is done, and Brian needs to think about his next move. From experience, he knows Hans prefers to be presented with a solution, not a problem.

Brian collaborates with Shanice to come up with an approach to address the decreased sales issue and compete more effectively with HW Machinery. As Shanice and Brian expected, Hans does not take the news of a new competitor well and berates Shanice and Brian for not coming to him sooner.

"Hans, we have an idea to tackle this problem," Brian says.

Hans sighs. "Fine, tell me what you've got."

"One option is to price match HW's price," Brian begins. "It will make us competitive in the market and we can use our existing customer networks to retain and continue to build our business."

"What? No way! I'm not reducing our price just because some two-bit operation has decided to sell their handling arms for less. Forget it!" Hans says.

"What do you suggest we do instead?" Brian asks Hans.

"I say we sit tight and see what happens—these guys might not be in the business for the long haul. We'll give it another two months, and if our sales continue to drop, then we'll take action," Hans says.

Brian doesn't like this short-term solution given Shanice's concerns about losing existing customers to HW Machinery, but he decides to accommodate Hans by agreeing with him for the moment. He looks at Shanice to see what she thinks.

"I think we should drop the price based on what I'm hearing from customers," she says, holding Hans's gaze.

Brian can see Hans getting worked up and interjects once more.

"How about we wait one month, rather than two, to see how the competition is affecting our sales? If sales continue to drop, then we reconvene and come up with another strategy," Brian says. He hopes both sides will agree to compromise on an acceptable, if not ideal, solution.

Shanice agrees immediately. Eventually, and much to Brian's relief, Hans reluctantly agrees to wait only one month.

By the end of the month, sales have dropped dramatically. The plant loses two of its regular handling arms customers to the competition and the situation is serious. Once again, Shanice, Brian, and Hans gather in Hans's office to discuss the issue.

"They want to play hardball? Then bring it on," Hans begins, heatedly. "We're going to undercut them on price and see how they like it!"

"What if they drop their prices too?" asks Shanice. "Then what?"

"We'll have them running scared; they won't be able to afford to compete with us and it will drive them right out of business," Hans retorts.

Brian disagrees with this drastic approach, but he decides to try a different tactic.

"If Shanice is right and the competition drops its price in response, can you give me your assurance that you won't try and undercut them again?" he says. "The last thing we need is a price war. We can't afford to start losing money on every set of handling arms we sell."

"All right, Brian," Hans concedes. "Let's experiment with the first price drop and if that doesn't work, then I'll think of another way. But let me tell you—HW Machinery will not be able to compete with our prices, and when we drive them out of the market, we can put our prices back to where they should be. Trust me—this is going to work."

But Hans is wrong. Two months later HW Machinery drops its prices even lower and the assembly plant loses even more business. Hans breaks his agreement with Brian and, without consulting him, directs Shanice to reduce the price of the handling arms a second time in order to compete. The plant is now engaged in a price war with HW Machinery.

Brian, who has worked hard in previous situations to win Hans's trust and respect, is annoyed that Hans has broken his promise and wonders whether he will ever be able to trust his manager fully. He and Shanice need to persuade Hans to work with them to find a more productive solution to this conflict.

THINKING CRITICALLY

1. Revisit the description of a personal conflict that you described in terms of the four stages in the conflict process in the last section. Describe how you could have approached the conflict using each of the five conflict management strategies (avoidance, accommodation, competition, compromise, and collaboration) and how each strategy would have affected the outcome of your conflict. **[Apply/Analyze]**

2. Of the five conflict management strategies, which do you believe are most likely to occur in a conflict between two unequal parties (a manager and employee, a Board of Directors and its CEO, or a large company and a small supplier). Which do you believe are most likely to occur in a conflict between two equal parties (similarly sized companies, team members, or department heads). Explain your reasoning. **[Apply/Analyze/Evaluate]**

3. Consider Shanice's initial decision to manage conflict through avoidance. What did she avoid by waiting two months to approach Brian with her concerns about control arm sales and discuss the new competitor with Hans? What did she gain? What types of conflict situations are best addressed through avoidance? Explain your answer. **[Apply/Analyze]**

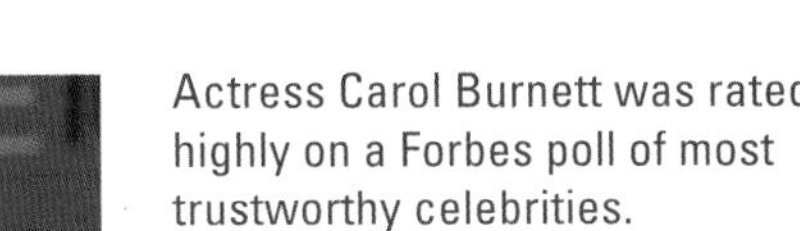

White House photo by Paul Morse

Actress Carol Burnett was rated highly on a Forbes poll of most trustworthy celebrities.

David Shankbone

News anchor Brian Williams's credibility came under scrutiny after revealing that he had exaggerated stories about reporting in Iraq in 2003.

TRUST IN ORGANIZATIONS

10.3 Outline the bases of trust and predictable outcomes of trust in organizations

Trust in Organizations

Trust is a critical factor for organizational performance. For people to successfully work together and build relationships, they need to have a high degree of trust in one another. We define **trust** as dependence on the integrity, ability, honesty, and reliability of someone or something else.[10] In US celebrity culture, Tom Hanks ranks as the most trustworthy celebrity, according to a 2014 poll conducted by *Forbes*. Actor Morgan Freeman and actress and singer Carol Burnett also ranked high on the list.[11] In contrast, other public figures have lost our trust, such as news anchor Brian Williams, who admitted to exaggerating his experiences in Iraq in 2003,[12] and former professional cyclist and seven-time winner of the Tour de France Lance Armstrong, who was stripped of all his titles for using banned performance-enhancing drugs.[13]

Trust: The dependence on the integrity, ability, honesty, and reliability of someone or something else

Types of Trust

How do we know when to trust someone? Say a new team leader has been appointed to your work team. You have never met this person before, yet you are expected to work with him or her every day for the foreseeable future. How do you make up your mind that your team leader is someone you can trust?

Generally, we can form three types of trust: disposition-based trust, cognition-based trust, and affect-based trust (see Figure 10.2).[14]

Disposition-based trust exists when people possess personality traits that encourage them to put their faith in others. For instance, you might be the kind of person who will trust the new team leader unless you are given a reason not to.

In contrast, in *cognition-based trust* people rely on factual information such as someone's past experience and track record as a basis for trust. You might be wary of a new team leader until you recognize that he or she demonstrates the character, integrity, abilities, and benevolence to lead the team.

Finally, *affect-based trust* occurs when people put their faith in others based on feelings and emotions. For example, you are more likely to trust a new team leader if you feel you have made an emotional connection with him or her, such as by finding out you grew up in the same town.

Disposition-based trust	• Derived from possessing personality traits that include a general propensity to trust others
Cognition-based trust	• Derived from relying on factual information as a basis for trust
Affect-based trust	• Derived from putting faith in others based on feelings and emotions

■ FIGURE 10.2 Three Types of Trust

SOURCES: Based on Mayer, Roger C., James H. Davis, and F. David Schoorman. "An Integrative Model of Organizational Trust." *Academy of Management Review* 20, no. 3 (July 1995): 709–734; McAllister, Daniel J. "Affect- and Cognition-Based Trust as Foundations for Interpersonal Cooperation in Organizations." *Academy of Management Journal* 38, no. 1 (February 1995): 24–59.

Outcomes of Trust

When trust is high in the workplace, people tend to work better together and are more focused on their duties. Recent research found that people working in a high-trust environment tend to take more risks, such as initiating new ideas or admitting mistakes, display citizenship behaviors like going the "extra mile" on a work task or project, and exhibit fewer ineffectual or counterproductive behaviors like absenteeism or social loafing.[15]

In contrast, employees working in a low-trust organizational environment are more likely to be distracted from their duties, lack engagement in their tasks, exhibit defensive behaviors, display apathy toward organizational goals, and have higher levels of absenteeism (see Figure 10.3).[16]

Let's return to our case, and explore the issue of trust and how it affects organizational behavior.

Some employees use cognition-based trust, or evidence of someone's qualifications, when deciding to entrust new leaders.

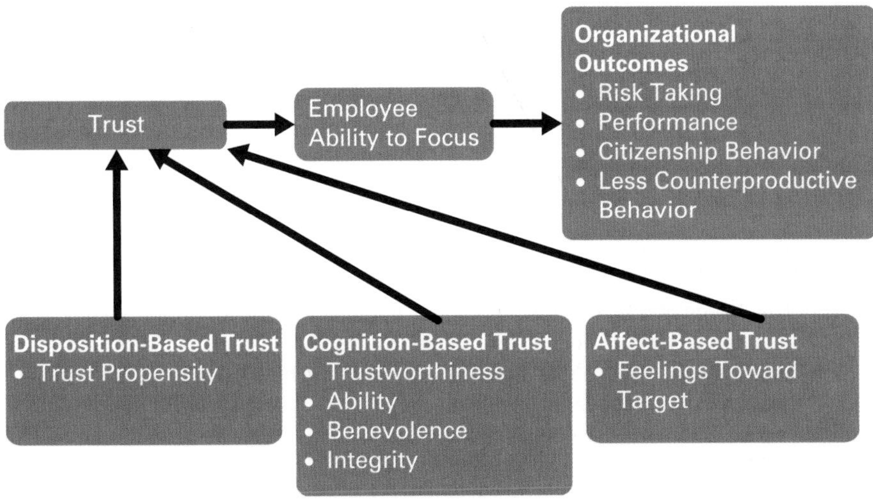

■ FIGURE 10.3 A Model of Trust Within Organizations

It is a week later and Brian is still coming to terms with Hans's rash decision to engage in a price war with HW Machinery despite his promise to consult Brian before taking additional action. Hans's willingness to break his agreement with Brian has put Brian's trust in his boss at an all-time low. Brian is feeling frustrated, powerless, and resentful. Even worse, Hans refuses to discuss the issue further with Brian or Shanice, insisting that his gamble to oust the competition will eventually pay off. Shanice, like Brian, feels that trust has been broken and resents being forced to take part in a sales strategy in which she doesn't believe. She takes two unexplained sick days and has difficulty focusing on other aspects of her job. Her team's stress level rises as they wonder what has happened to their normally optimistic and unflappable boss.

Despite Brian's repeated warnings, Hans continues to retaliate and drop the price of the handling arms every time the competition drops its price. Concerns about the future of the product begin to affect the entire plant. Rumors spread that Hans is considering lay-offs. Worried that their jobs are at risk, two senior members of the assembly team quit and morale decreases even further. Brian feels he can do only so much to reassure plant employees without Hans's support. But then something happens that has the potential to turn the situation around.

One morning, Shanice walks into Brian's office, shoulders slumped.

"I've just seen the month-end financial results," Shanice announces.

Brian groans. "How bad is it?"

"If this price war goes on for much longer, our handling arms business will be forced to shut down," Shanice replies. "And that's not all. Because of the price war, the handling arms are losing market share—fast."

Brian is puzzled. "I thought pricing the products more cheaply would attract a higher volume of buyers. Why have we lost market share?"

"A price war makes consumers suspicious. It calls the quality of the product into question. One potential customer asked me whether the plant is using cheaper materials to warrant the lower price. Customers expect to pay a certain amount for quality, and if a price seems too good to be true, they tend to question it," Shanice explains. "HW Machinery has also lost market share and I imagine is suffering a similar blow to its bottom line."

Brian spends a few moments deep in thought as an idea begins to form. "The way I see it—both parties are in a lose-lose situation," Brian begins. "HW Machinery and our business are quickly losing profit and market share."

"So how do we end this price war?," Shanice asks.

"We find out as much about HW Machinery as we can to see who exactly we are up against and then we negotiate with them," says Brian decisively. Realizing that the plant and HW Machinery have a shared problem makes him feel more optimistic than he has in months that a solution to falling sales and lost market share is possible.

 THINKING CRITICALLY

1. Which type of trust (disposition-based, cognition-based, or affect-based) best describes the way you form relationships with new co-workers? Does a different type of trust best describe how you form new friendships and intimate relationships? If so, explain why this may be the case. **[Apply/Analyze]**

2. Discuss the ways in which the tractor assembly plant reflects the outcomes of a low-trust environment in the case narrative. What steps could Hans take to re-establish trust? **[Apply/Analyze/Evaluate]**

NEGOTIATION AND DISPUTE RESOLUTION

10.4 Describe the negotiation process

We may not realize it, but most of us negotiate on a daily basis in every aspect of our lives, with family members, friends, classmates, roommates and partners, as well as with our coworkers, team leaders, and bosses. We define **negotiation** as the process of reaching an agreement that both parties find acceptable.[17] Since disagreements are common in a range of OB issues, including task allocation, work schedules, and salaries, the art of negotiation is a necessity in life as well as in the workplace.

Let's explore the negotiation process[18] as illustrated by the next installment of our tractor assembly plant case.

Getting Ready to Negotiate

Before any negotiation, it is critical for each party to outline the goals and objectives they would like to achieve. It is also essential for each party to do its homework on its opponent—to consider the other party's position and decision-making power, the length of time it has been in business, and whether it has any other negotiating history.

Thanks to market research, Brian and Shanice discover that HW Machinery is a start-up founded and funded by two entrepreneurs in their early 30s. It is made up of a research and development team of recent engineering graduates, a small manufacturing facility, and two marketing staff. It has been in the manufacturing business for only two years and the handling arms are the company's first product. The company website is impressive and outlines plans for a number of innovations targeted at the aerospace and automotive markets. Brian and Shanice present their market research and Shanice's data on the common loss in market share experienced by both their plant and HW Machinery to Hans.

"I can't believe I've been losing sleep over a company run by kids!" Hans laughs. "I know exactly how we're going to resolve this price war. We're going to buy HW Machinery."

Brian is surprised that Hans changed tactics so quickly, and he asks Hans to elaborate.

Negotiation: The process of reaching an agreement that both parties find acceptable

ALLAN TSANG, *founder, 88 Owls*

OB in the Real World

© Allan Tsang

88 Owls was started in 2007 by Allan Tsang, a business consultant and coach. Its flagship product was a digital platform that connected consultants with businesses requiring specific services. Through the years, Allan has had the chance to work with and learn from some of the best conflict negotiators in the country, and his success in corporate negotiation has helped his company expand its services. Today, 88 Owls focuses on helping companies and executives make better business decisions by teaching them how to use negotiation techniques to formulate and execute their corporate strategies.

"My title is Strategic Ideation Architect because an architect is able to take a vision and create a blueprint and rendering." Allen gets the client to agree on a plan and then communicates the concept to the contractor. He's familiar with the idea all the way from conception to final product and is successful at negotiation through every challenge that comes up in the process.

When leaders understand how to negotiate they can use their behaviors to create the desired outcome in every aspect of business. Allan points out that "conflict is the result of not being able to build agreement between people. Sometimes it comes from the fact that there are different visions. Negotiation is the human effort that brings about agreement between two or more parties with each party having the right to veto or say no."

One client was experiencing high levels of conflict at work but was able to achieve success through negotiation. "I was working with two sales reps, one very strategic and the other focused on execution. The strategy rep was thinking about future obstacles and voicing industry trends. He put a lot of thought into the decisions he was making and the clients he was working with. People sometimes felt like he was full of excuses. Meanwhile the execution sales rep would push through problems, shoot before he would aim, make mistakes and have to correct them later. People sometimes felt like he was aggressive but he closed ten times more sales than the strategic rep. There was a lot of conflict between the two."

Allan worked closely with them to help solve the conflict. What they ended up realizing was that the strategic sales rep "was much better suited for a business development role because he could build long-term relationships and be analytical in his approach to helping clients solve their problems. We put him in the new role and the two started working as a really good team." Allan noted that "negotiation is about helping a client discover and create a new vision which replaces the old one. Then it becomes easy for people to coexist and a lot of the baggage that came before goes away."

Critical-Thinking Questions

1. **How would you analyze the negotiating skills used by Allan Tsang to resolve conflict within the group?**
2. **What kind of negotiating strategies would you use to build relationships in your professional life?**

SOURCE: Allan Tsang, personal interview, September 18, 2013.

"Think about it: they are a start-up enterprise with a strategy to break into the markets that we want to enter, but we lack the staff and the expertise. They are obviously very talented, ambitious entrepreneurs, but our research shows they don't have the facilities or the brand to make their products a reality at the speed they might like," Hans explains.

"And so they join us to benefit from our bigger facilities, larger resources, and more high-profile brand," Brian says, thoughtfully.

"Which means that we benefit from their development expertise and innovations related to new products and new markets," Shanice adds.

"Yep—we join forces to bring new product innovations quickly to the market, thereby increasing profits. Even better, the start-up is self-funded, so we don't need to worry about negotiating with outside investors or shareholders. The decision to sell is solely based on HW Machinery's founders," Hans says, smiling.

"Financially, it makes perfect sense for them—they get a big chunk of cash from us for the acquisition, and they won't have to pay rent on their manufacturing facility any longer, or pay for resources," Shanice adds.

"But what if HW Machinery doesn't want to be acquired?," Brian says.

"We'll have to work out a negotiating strategy that they will find difficult to turn down," Hans replies.

During the next few weeks, Hans, Brian, and Shanice create a strong acquisitions proposal, outlining the reasons why the plant's parent company should buy HW Machinery. Hans is elated when the board and its shareholders agree to the proposed acquisition, allowing Hans to begin negotiation with HW Machinery's founders, CEO Carlos Gonzales and Director of Research and Development Eva Hertzfield.

Hans places a call to Carlos Gonzales stating his company's interest in acquiring HW Machinery. Much to his delight, Gonzales replies that he is open to negotiation and requests a date, time, and location to meet.

"It's an offer they can't refuse," Hans boasts to Brian, after he puts down the phone.

Concerned that Hans's ego is getting in the way of a successful negotiation, Brian steers the discussion toward setting a location for the negotiation. "We'll do it in one of our boardrooms. Let them see what a real business looks like," Hans says, arrogantly.

Brian disagrees. He knows that negotiations should take place on neutral territory to give each party an equal footing. But Hans is adamant that the meeting should take place at the assembly plant.

Shaping Expectations

It is the morning of the negotiation and the founders of HW Machinery walk into the tractor assembly plant boardroom where Hans, Brian, and Shanice are already waiting. Carlos Gonzales and Eva Hertzfield shake hands with the group and everyone sits down at the boardroom table. Brian is taken aback by how young Eva and Carlos look.

Hans clears his throat and shuffles the papers in front of him as a sign to get started, but before he can open the meeting, Eva speaks.

"Let's agree on some ground rules for our negotiation before we get started," she suggests. Hans looks surprised, but Brian and Shanice immediately agree that this is a good way to ensure a smooth negotiation process. Both parties agree that they must talk one at a time, listen to each other, and treat one another with respect. Derogatory language or any other kind of verbal attacks will not be tolerated.

Either party can halt the discussion at any time.

With the ground rules set, the parties begin their negotiation.

Providing Supporting Evidence

In the next stage of the process, all parties take turns explaining their concerns backed up with supporting evidence. Hans begins by clearly stating his objective to buy HW Machinery. With the help of supporting documentation, Hans explains the reasons behind his company's decision as well as the benefits it would bring to both companies.

When Hans has finished, Carlos states his and Eva's objective to sell HW Machinery and also presents supporting documentation, which outlines their vision for the future of their company's products and innovations. Eva discusses control arm improvements she and her team are in the process of implementing.

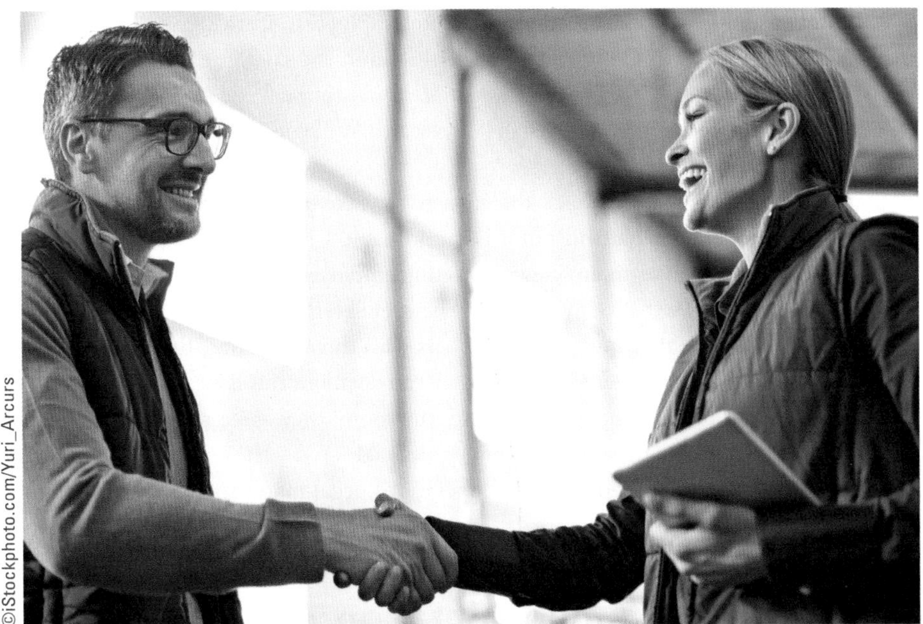
©iStockphoto.com/Yuri_Arcurs

When engaging in negotiations, both parties should outline their goals for the discussion and understand the other party's position.

"We have been working to improve functionality and experimenting with more durable materials. Our product will be a superior version of the ones on the market," Eva explains.

Carlos adds, "And that's not all—we are also in the process of designing new technology to cater to the more specialized needs of the aerospace and automotive markets."

"We have the talent to take over the handling arms market. What we don't have is the resources. If our companies join forces, then we have a larger manufacturing facility and you benefit from our innovations. Together, we can build an unstoppable brand. We believe our business could add significant value to your company in the future. This is why we will need to agree on a fair price for our innovations, research, and expertise," Eva says.

Negotiating the Deal

Brian, Shanice, and Hans exchange glances. Carlos and Eva have certainly come prepared—although they are willing to sell the business, they also intend to drive a hard bargain.

"I can see that you're passionate and committed to your business, and you have presented the benefits of this acquisition very well," Hans begins. "As you pointed out, we have superior facilities, and the resources to get the products to market faster. We also want to strike a fair deal with you."

Hans outlines the acquisition terms agreed to by the board and suggests a price the company would pay for the business that is approximately 25% lower than the highest figure approved by the board.

"We agree that selling the business makes sense, but we have a different figure in mind," Carlos replies.

Brian admires Carlos and Eva's composure. Though they have come into the negotiation prepared to sell their business, they are determined to negotiate the highest price possible.

When Eva suggests an alternative sale price, Brian knows it is not far over Hans's final price as agreed to by the board. The price negotiation goes back and forth for some time until both parties agree on a sale price for the business that is in line with the board's decision. Brian is elated, but keeps his emotions in check.

"Both Eva and I want to be retained as senior employees," Carlos says.

Hans has expected this, and outlines the titles and the salaries each entrepreneur would expect to receive.

"What about our two marketing staff?" Eva asks. "Will you take them on too? They are very talented."

Hans shakes his head. "We lack the capacity to take on any more marketers," he says, firmly. Brian knows that this point is immoveable—the company simply doesn't have the headcount to take on any new marketing employees.

Carlos and Eva leave the room to discuss the overall terms of the sale and the implications of not bringing their two team members with them. Shanice, Brian, and Hans exchange worried glances. There is nothing they can do about this issue.

Fortunately, when Carlos and Eva reenter the room, they agree to Hans's decision not to take on the marketing staff.

Following further discussions around operations, legal matters, and logistics, both parties reach an agreement.

Agreement and Implementation

With the bargaining process complete, the parties move on to the final stage of negotiation—formalizing an agreement and implementing the deal. They spend time clarifying the deal and ensuring that everyone understands the outcome of the negotiations and the specifications of the final agreement. Pending due diligence, the agreement will be formalized in writing and signed by each party by an agreed-upon date.

The parties shake hands and Carlos and Eva leave the boardroom. Brian, Shanice, and Hans are delighted with the outcome. The negotiation has gone much more smoothly than they had anticipated, and they are looking forward to working with two talented new colleagues. News of the acquisition lifts the spirits of plant employees and helps to put their fear and uncertainty to rest. Jacob, the head of the assembly team, is especially happy with the news. "My team came up with an innovative product and now it gets to work with smart engineers to bring out a whole host of new products," he tells Brian. "That is a great motivator for our team."

A year later, thanks to the HW Machinery acquisition, the tractor assembly plant brings out an improved version of the handling arms that overtakes the market. Brian has worked closely with Hans in managing the transition and has become adept at fielding Hans's more erratic decisions. While he will never completely trust his manager, Brian is able to work with him effectively and feels prepared to handle future conflicts and challenges.

Third-Party Dispute Resolution Approaches

Persuasion

In the case of the negotiation just described, both parties managed to resolve their differences and reach an agreement. However, what would have happened if Carlos and Eva, the founders of HW Machinery, were unwilling to be acquired? What if the parties had reached a stalemate in their negotiations or failed to find a mutually beneficial solution to the price war that was harming both their companies? In these instances, it is useful to introduce a neutral third party to help settle disputes. There are three types of third party roles: mediator, arbitrator, and conciliator (see Table 10.1).[19]

Mediator: A neutral third party who attempts to assist parties in a negotiation to find a resolution or come to an agreement using rational arguments and persuasion

A **mediator** is a neutral third party who attempts to assist parties in a negotiation to find a resolution or come to an agreement using rational arguments and persuasion. The chief role of mediators is to get the opposing parties to communicate rather than provide a solution or a decision. A mediator has no right to impose his or her views on the parties.

Mediator	Arbitrator	Conciliator
Reinstates communication between two parties	Issues judgment based on statements from both parties	Persuades opponents to communicate
Offers no opinions or judgment	Judgment is binding for all parties	Offers nonbinding opinion

■ TABLE 10.1 Third-Party Dispute Resolution Approaches

An **arbitrator** is a neutral third party officially assigned to settle a dispute who listens to both sides of the argument as stated by the parties. Unlike a mediator, an arbitrator has the power to issue a judgment, which is final and binding for all parties.

Alternative Dispute Resolution

Finally, a **conciliator** is a neutral third party who is informally assigned to persuade opponents to communicate. The conciliator is allowed to offer an opinion, but unlike that of an arbitrator, this judgment does not carry any legal weight.

Many businesses in conflict choose one or more of these third-party dispute resolution approaches because they can be a useful way to resolve differences and can prevent an issue from escalating.

For example, Major League Baseball teams and players often engage in arbitration to determine a player's salary. The process begins with both the team and the player's agent submitting their "last best" salary offer. Each side then presents their case and a rebuttal to the opposing side's case in a salary hearing to a panel of three arbitrators chosen from a slate of 16 arbitrators determined jointly by major league baseball and the player's association. The panel considers the evidence presented in order to reach a decision on what they consider to be the correct "market salary" for that player. This figure is compared to the two "best final offers," and whichever figure is closest is likely to be selected. For example, suppose that a player's agent submits a best final offer of \$20 million, and the team submits a best final offer of \$15 million. Theoretically, the panel of arbitrators would need to determine whether the player's market value is more or less than \$17.5 million, the midpoint figure. If the arbitrators find the correct price to be higher than the midpoint, they will choose the \$20 million figure requested by the player; if they determine that the player's market value is lower than the midpoint, then they will select the team's offer.[20]

Arbitrator: A neutral third party officially assigned to settle a dispute

Conciliator: A neutral third party who is informally assigned to persuade opponents to communicate

AP Photo/George Nikitin

Major League Baseball players' salary arbitrations are complicated processes where a player's market salary is compared against offers from the player and the team.

1. Explain how the three steps prior to negotiating the deal (getting ready to negotiate, shaping expectations, and providing supporting evidence) can contribute to a successful negotiation. **[Analyze]**
2. Review earlier sections in the chapter regarding conflict. What factors could contribute to a dysfunctional negotiation process and an unsuccessful outcome? **[Apply/Analyze]**
3. Consider the three types of third-party dispute resolution. What types of situations would lend themselves most easily to mediation, to arbitration, or to conciliation? In what circumstances would businesses likely prefer mediation or conciliation over arbitration? **[Analyze/Evaluate]**

BARGAINING APPROACHES

10.5 Compare distributive and integrative bargaining approaches

The ultimate goal of a negotiation should be to provide an agreement that satisfies everyone and leaves all the parties on good terms. But in reality the process is not always straightforward. The reason is that the way people negotiate has an influence on its outcomes. In general, people use two main bargaining strategies: distributive bargaining and integrative bargaining (see Figure 10.4).

Distributive bargaining occurs when two parties both try to claim a "fixed pie" of resources.[21] For example, say you are trying to buy a used car. You know you will need a certain amount of money to fix the car up the way you want it, and for that reason you want a reduction in the price. However, the car salesperson wants the maximum price he can get for the car and tells you to take it or leave it. This is known as a win/lose situation, in which one party only gains and the other one only loses.

Another approach to distributive bargaining is to compromise just for the sake of ending the negotiation. For example, say you and the car salesperson have been haggling for a long time and each of you is getting frustrated. The rep agrees to let you have a small percentage off the price, but you do not feel it is enough. Eventually you both give up something in order to agree on a price, but neither of you is satisfied with the outcome.

In many instances distributive bargaining can be time consuming and inefficient. It can lead to a contest of wills, especially when egos get in the way. It is better suited to short-term bargaining with people you are unlikely to deal with again than to the building of long-term relationships, which require a degree of give and take.

Integrative bargaining occurs when both parties negotiate a win-win solution.[22] It is about enlarging the pie so everyone gets a piece. This type of bargaining applies to businesses that want to build long-term relationships with each other. For example, a clothing manufacturer is looking to negotiate with its fabric supplier to reach a mutually beneficial agreement. The manufacturer wants the supplier to consistently provide it with high-quality fabrics at a fair price within the allotted time frames. The fabric supplier agrees and a formal contract is arranged. In the end, both parties win: the clothing manufacturer has negotiated a long-term contract with the fabric supplier at a fair price, and the fabric supplier is guaranteed a stream of business from the clothing manufacturer. Both parties have achieved the maximum value from the negotiation.

Distributive bargaining: A strategy that involves two parties trying to claim a "fixed pie" of resources

Integrative bargaining: A strategy that involves both parties negotiating a win–win solution

Integrative Bargaining Strategies

There are four basic strategies for integrative bargaining.[23] The best choice will vary depending on the situation. For example, let's say you are preparing to negotiate a salary raise at work and are looking for the best ways to approach the situation.

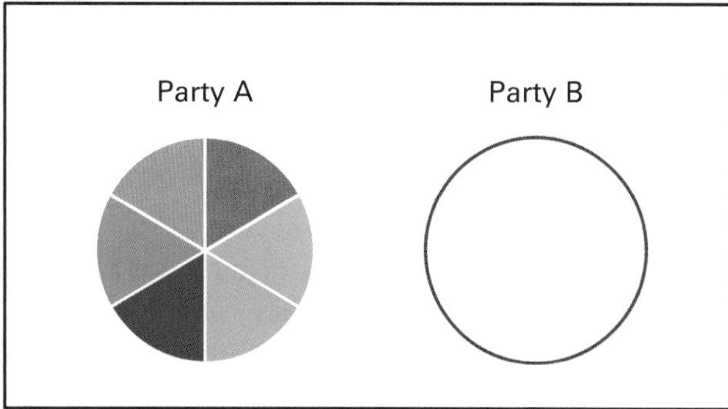

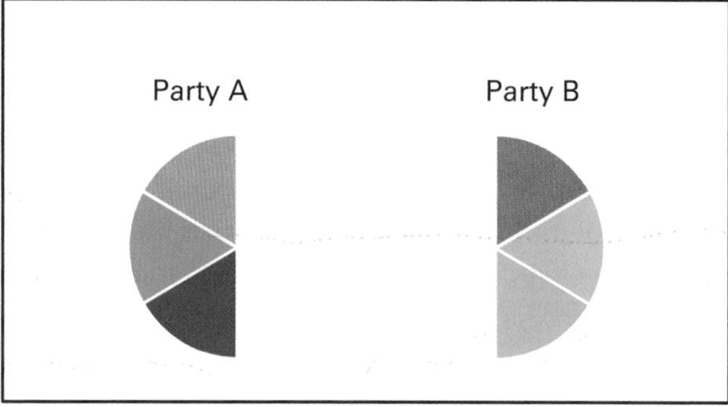

■ FIGURE 10.4 Bargaining Approaches

- Separate the people from the problem

You may not be crazy about your boss, but this shouldn't influence your approach to negotiating a higher salary. In this instance, the focus needs to be on the facts; emotion should never influence your strategy. This is about sitting down with your boss and putting your feelings aside to find a solution that satisfies you both.

- Focus on interests, not positions

When preparing for a negotiation each party must understand its own interests as well as the interests of the other party. Why do you want a raise? And why should your boss give it to you? You may need more money for a mortgage or to pay off your college loans, but frankly this is not of any interest to your boss. From your boss's perspective, a raise is deserved only when the employee promises to deliver more in the future. You need to list all the ways you can benefit the company in the long term.

- Generate a variety of possibilities

It is a mistake to go into a negotiation with only one possible outcome. What if your boss simply says she can't give you a raise? Before the negotiation, consider some other possibilities. What about an increase in benefits, more vacation days, or flexible work options such as a day or two of working from home? When you compile a list of acceptable possibilities, you will probably have a better chance of gaining something out of the negotiation, even if it's not the salary raise that you wanted.[24]

- Insist on some fair standard

Referring your boss to some fair standard other than your opinion, such as a published wage and salary survey, could be helpful. If you succeed in obtaining the salary raise, then ensure that the agreement is formalized. This will give clarity to the negotiations and prevent any misunderstandings further down the line.

Other Negotiating Strategies

It is always wise to have a best possible alternative to a negotiable agreement (**BATNA**), which is the best outcome you could achieve if the negotiation fails and you must follow another course of action.[25] For example, say you want a salary raise of $5,000 per year, but you will accept $3,000 if it is offered. What will you do if you are unable to get the $3,000 raise? Will you settle for your current salary? Will you quit your job and try to find a higher-paying job in another organization? Once you have identified your BATNA, you will be in a better position to figure out your zone of possible agreement (**ZOPA**) (see Figure 10.5), which is the area where two sides in a negotiation may find common ground.[26] For example, say you request your $5,000 salary raise and your boss tells you that the best offer will be $3,500. Since this figure lies within the zone that both parties find acceptable, then it is likely an agreement will be reached.

In this chapter, we have explored the complexities of conflict and negotiation through the experiences of tractor assembly plant manager Brian Stevens and examined the different types of negotiation strategies that can help resolve conflict. In the next chapter, we explore the concept of leadership through the eyes of Langston Burrows, a business graduate who has just been offered a place in the leadership development program (LDP) of a mid-sized regional bank.

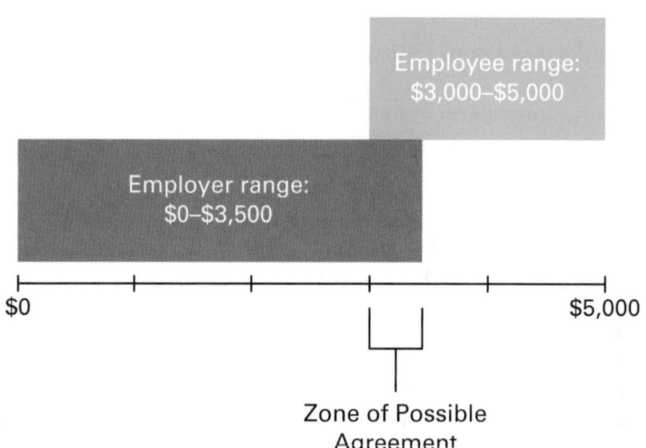

■ FIGURE 10.5 Zone of Possible Agreement

THINKING CRITICALLY

1. Discuss the integrative bargaining strategies used in the case negotiation discussed in the previous section. Which of the four strategies (separate the people from the problem; focus on interests, not positions; generate a variety of possibilities; insist on some fair standard) were used? **[Apply]**
2. What is the primary strategic benefit of entering a negotiation with a clearly defined BATNA (best possible alternative to a negotiable agreement)? What are some possible emotional benefits of having a BATNA in place? **[Analyze/Evaluate]**
3. In what situations might it be useful to let the other party know your BATNA at the beginning of a negotiation? In what situations would it be best to keep that information to yourself? Explain your answer. **[Analyze/Evaluate]**

BATNA: The best possible alternative to a negotiable agreement

ZOPA: The zone of possible agreement, the area where two sides in a negotiation may find common ground

IN REVIEW

Learning Objectives

10.1 Describe the conflict process and the various types of conflict

We define **conflict** as a clash between individuals or groups in relation to different opinions, thought processes, and perceptions. **Functional conflict** consists of constructive and healthy disputes between individuals or groups. In contrast, **dysfunctional conflict** consists of disputes and disagreements that have negative effects on individuals or teams. It often arises from an unwillingness to listen to each other or a reluctance to agree on a resolution or goal.

Task conflict refers to the clash between individuals in relation to the direction, content, or goal of a certain assignment. **Relationship conflict** refers to the clash in personality between two or more individuals. This type of conflict is considered to be the most destructive and harmful to organizations because it can give rise to hostility, mistrust, fear, and negativity. **Process conflict** refers to the clash in viewpoints about how to carry out work. It can be beneficial to organizations as long as it operates at a low level.

The four different stages of the conflict process are antecedents of conflict, perceived/felt conflict, manifest conflict, and outcomes of conflict. **Antecedents of conflict** are the factors that set the scene for potential disputes: lack of communication, incompatible personalities, and collisions in value systems. In the **perceived/felt conflict stage** emotional differences are sensed and felt. The **manifest conflict** stage consists of behaviors that provoke a response. The final stage is the **outcomes of conflict stage,** which describes the consequences of the dispute.

10.2 Identify the five basic conflict management strategies

Avoidance is the attempt to suppress a conflict and pretend it does not really exist. **Accommodation** is one party's attempt to adjust his or her views to play down the differences between the parties. **Competition** is the attempt to gain victory through force, skill or domination. **Compromise** is a situation in which each party concedes something of value. **Collaborating** occurs when all parties work together to find a solution beneficial to everyone.

10.3 Outline the bases of trust and predictable outcomes of trust in organizations

We define **trust** as the dependence on the integrity, ability, honesty, and reliability of someone or something else. Generally, there are three types. People with *disposition-based trust* tend to possess personality traits that encourage them to put their faith in others. In contrast, people with *cognition-based trust* base their faith in others on factual information such as the person's past experience and proven track record. Finally, *affect-based trust* occurs when people put their faith in others based on feelings and emotions.

When trust is high in the workplace, people tend to work better together and are more focused on their duties. They tend to take more risks, display citizenship behaviors, and exhibit fewer ineffectual or counterproductive behaviors.

10.4 Describe the negotiation process

We define **negotiation** as the process of reaching an agreement that both parties find acceptable. Before any negotiation, it is critical that each party get ready to negotiate by outlining the goals and objectives they would like to achieve. The second step is to shape the expectations for the negotiation. Next, both parties take turns in bolstering their demands with supportive evidence. Then the parties bargain back and forth until they both agree upon a deal. This leads to the final stage of the process, known as the agreement and implementation stage. During this stage, the agreement will be formalized in writing.

There are three types of neutral third-party roles in the event of a stalemate. A **mediator** attempts to assist parties to find a resolution using rational arguments and persuasion. A mediator has no right to impose his or her views on the parties. An

arbitrator listens to both sides before issuing a judgment considered final and binding for all parties. Finally, a **conciliator** is informally assigned to persuade opponents to communicate. The conciliator is allowed to offer an opinion but it does not carry any legal weight.

Compare distributive and integrative bargaining approaches

Distributive bargaining occurs when two parties try to claim a "fixed pie" of resources. It is more suitable for short-term bargaining with people you are unlikely to deal with again than for long-term relationships, which require give and take. **Integrative bargaining** occurs when both parties negotiate a win–win solution by enlarging the pie so everyone gets a piece.

KEY TERMS

Antecedents of conflict 241
Arbitrator 253
BATNA 256
Conflict 239
Conciliator 253
Distributive bargaining 254
Dysfunctional conflict 239
Functional conflict 239
Integrative bargaining 254
Manifest conflict stage 241
Mediator 252
Negotiation 248
Outcomes conflict stage 241
Perceived/felt conflict stage 241
Process conflict 240
Relationship conflict 240
Task conflict 240
Trust 245
ZOPA 256

THINKING CRITICALLY ABOUT THE CASE OF BRIAN STEVENS

Consider the five critical-thinking steps in relation to the negotiation process undertaken by Hans, Brian, and Shanice with the founders of HW Machinery, Carlos and Eva.

OBSERVE

What were Brian's concerns about Hans's demeanor going into the negotiation? Were his concerns warranted based on Hans's past behavior? Why or why not?

INTERPRET

What purpose did Eva's request to establish ground rules for communication before proceeding with the negotiation serve? Is it surprising that Eva and Carlos's side of the negotiation made this request rather than Hans, Brian, and Shanice's side? Why or why not?

ANALYZE

The case, out of necessity, provides a streamlined and simplified version of what it takes to negotiate an acquisition. Provide two to three of the talking points Hans could have used to support the initial offer he made for HW Machinery. Provide two to three of the talking points Eva and Carlos could have used to support their higher counter-offer.

EVALUATE

Assess each side's reasons for entering into a negotiation. Do you agree with Hans, Brian, and Shanice's interest in acquiring HW Machinery? Why or why not? Do you agree with Eva and Carlos's reasons for selling their company? Why or why not?

EXPLAIN

Imagine that you are Hans and are leading the negotiation on behalf of your company's Board of Directors and shareholders. What, if anything, would you have done differently during the shaping expectations, providing supporting evidence, and negotiation stages of the negotiation process? Be specific and explain your answer.

EXERCISE 10.1: PREPARING FOR A NEGOTIATION

Consider a possible negotiation situation you might encounter in the near future. It could be as simple as deciding what movie you will see with a friend or as complex as negotiating a job offer with a future employer. Consider the following factors that could help to prepare you for the negotiation.

My Interests

What are my needs, desires, concerns, or fears going into the negotiation?

1. ______________________________

2. ______________________________

3. ______________________________

4. ______________________________

Possible Outcomes

What are some of the possible solutions or agreements that could result from the negotiation?

1. ______
2. ______
3. ______
4. ______

Fair Standards

What are some external standards or precedents other than each person's opinion that could convince us a proposed outcome is fair?

1. ______
2. ______
3. ______
4. ______

The Other Person's Interests

What are the other person's needs, desires, concerns, or fears going into the negotiation?

1. ______
2. ______
3. ______
4. ______

Best Alternatives to an Agreement (BATNA)

What are my best options if I am unable to reach an agreement with the other person?

1. ______
2. ______
3. ______
4. ______

Considering these negotiation dimensions in advance of the actual negotiation should better equip you to reach the best possible outcome in any negotiation situation, ranging from the simple to the complex.

SOURCE: Inspired by ideas presented in Fisher, Roger, and Danny Ertel. *Getting Ready to Negotiate: The Getting To Yes Workbook* (New York: Penguin, 1995).

EXERCISE 10.2: TENSION, CONFLICT, RESOLUTION.

Objectives:

This exercise will help you to be able to better *describe* the conflict process, *describe* the various types of conflict, and *identify* the five basic conflict management strategies.

Instructions:

Step1. Think of a conflict you are currently in (one that you are willing to share with the class), or, if you are not currently in any conflict, one that you have recently been in but were not able to resolve satisfactorily. Write this conflict down in as much detail as possible. (Note, you can give other parties in this description pseudonyms if you want to.) (5 minutes)

Step 2. Find a partner and give each other a brief overview of your conflicts. Choose the conflict that you both agree is the most interesting, and closely related to chapter topics on conflict management. (If one person has chosen an ongoing conflict, and the other person has chosen a past conflict, choose the ongoing conflict.) Both partners should then analyze the conflict for the following elements:

- Determine if the conflict is functional or dysfunctional.
- Determine the type of conflict (task, relationship, or process).
- Describe the conflict development using the four stages of conflict (antecedents of conflict, perceived/felt conflict, manifest conflict, and outcomes of conflict).
- Identify which of the five conflict management strategies were used in the conflict. (10 to 15 minutes)

Step 3. Be prepared to present your analysis to the class or provide details on specific aspects of the analysis when asked by your instructor. (5 minutes)

Reflection Questions:

1. How did analyzing your conflict help you to better understand the reasons for your conflict?
2. How did working through the conflict with someone else help you to understand the conflict more clearly?
3. What new insights did you gain about avoiding dysfunctional conflicts, or better resolving functional conflicts?
4. How could you use this process in future conflicts?
5. As a manager, how could you use this or similar methods to help workers in dealing with a conflict?
6. In what ways would it be beneficial to have all parties in a conflict work through a similar process?

Exercise contributed by Milton R. Mayfield, Professor of Business, Texas A&M International University and Jaqueline R. Mayfield, Professor of Business, Texas A&M International University.

EXERCISE 10.3: TRUST ME, TRUST NO ONE

Objective:

This exercise will help you to better *understand* the bases of trust, and *infer about* the outcomes of trust in organizations.

Instructions:

Step 1. Think about someone in whom you have a high level of trust. Describe that person, and your trust relationship in that person using appropriate terms and concepts from the chapter. Next, think of someone whom you do not trust at all. Also describe that person and your (lack of) trust relationship with that person using chapter terms and concepts. (You may want to use a pseudonym for the people you describe in this exercise.) (5 minutes)

Step 2. Pair with someone with whom you do not typically work with, and read to each other your descriptions. Help each other to improve your descriptions. Specifically, make sure that all points are clear, and that appropriate chapter terms and concepts are applied wherever possible. (10 minutes)

Step 3. As a class, do a poll to rank the most common traits that lead to trust and distrust. (10 to 20 minutes)

Reflection Questions:

1. What were the key differences between the person you trust the most, and the person you trust the least?
2. What were the key differences between the most common characteristics of people that were most and least trusted (from the class generated characteristics)?
3. What are the attitudinal and behavioral results of trusting someone (think especially about such issues as loyalty, doing favors, etc.)?
4. What are the attitudinal and behavioral results of not trusting someone (think especially about such issues as loyalty, doing favors, etc.)?
5. What implications for the workplace do you see from your exercise?
6. What kinds of communication occurred under both scenarios (open, casual, jokes vs formal, careful, less communication)?
7. If you still have regular contact with the person that you do not trust, what forces are keeping you interacting with that person?

Exercise contributed by Milton R. Mayfield, Professor of Business, Texas A&M International University and Jaqueline R. Mayfield, Professor of Business, Texas A&M International University.

CASE STUDY 10.1: PUBLICIZED CONFLICT AT YAHOO

In the Age of Information, many big companies will eventually suffer a publicly aired scandal, but it seems that Yahoo has had more than its share in recent years. To name a few: the public, bitter ousting of CEO Carol Bartz in 2011; the unpopular moves by current CEO Marissa Mayer to halt work-from-home privileges and her decision to rate employees on a bell curve. The most recent commotion came in January 2014 when Mayer ousted Henrique De Castro from his position as COO. De Castro was brought on as her second in command, and he walked out with a much-talked-about $58 million severance—after just 15 months on the job.

De Castro was a former vice president of Google's Partner Business Solutions group, and Mayer, also an ex-Google exec, lured him from Google with a hefty pay bump and more powerful title. His job: to turn around declining ad revenue as Yahoo's de facto top ad man and liaison to marketers on Madison Avenue as the company continued to lose bids to rivals Facebook and Google. There are indications, however, that Mayer did not know quite what she was getting into by hiring De Castro. "Interestingly, despite giving off the impression they did, the pair actually did not work closely at Google, according to dozens of sources there," wrote Kara Swisher in *Re/Code*. "Therefore, Mayer did not seem to grok the many signals that De Castro had a troubled time there near the end of his tenure." Moreover, De Castro's performance reviews by Google peers were mixed; he "was a polarizing figure at Google, where Mayer had hired him from [and] quickly became the same polarizing figure at Yahoo," Swisher added.

As COO with Yahoo, De Castro was charged with nurturing clients, fixing broken relationships with them, and building business. Yet according to Google ex-colleagues quoted by *Business Insider*, De Castro was known as smart and effective but was "not well-liked by people under him" (a sentiment later echoed by his fellow Yahoo-ers). His enemies were many, it seems, and he made a number of incautious public statements—not good characteristics in someone charged with smoothing over troubled relationships. Moreover, he wasn't bringing in the dollars his under-the-gun CEO needed, and pressure was mounting. Within the first couple of months, "he and Mayer had developed a tense relationship that many in meetings with the pair found it hard not to notice," wrote Swisher, quoting a Yahoo insider as saying "They just did not get along and did not hide it at all," adding that "it was really awkward.'" De Castro had also reportedly been fighting for power with Ned Brody, the new sales head, M&A head Jackie Reses, and marketing head Kathy Savitt. "In other words, *everyone* inside the Mayer inner circle."

Although De Castro's performance reviews by Google peers were mixed, his time at Yahoo was decidedly disappointing. He achieved little in terms of boosting ad revenue, and his time was marked by tensions, including with Mayer herself. No top Yahoo-er earned a full bonus given the company's financial troubles that year, but others among the top brass were granted between 83 percent and 92 percent of their target bonuses. De Castro, however, was left out in the cold. Industry watchers began to openly speculate that De Castro was on his way out with his conspicuous absence from the Consumer Electronics Show in early January 2014, where giants like Yahoo typically tout their latest and greatest and court new advertisers. In a company memo announcing De Castro's departure later the same month, Mayer wrote, "Overall, I am confident that the leadership team, our direction, and these changes will enable even more successful execution." Conspicuously absent was any praise for De Castro's brief tenure.

Why did Mayer hire De Castro? According to sources who spoke to *Business Insider*, the reasons were twofold: she believed he was responsible for building Google's advertising business from zero to billions, and she thought he was the driving force behind the brand advertising success of YouTube. Others saw De Castro as having little to do directly with Google's growth, mainly sailing in on the coattails of others and being in the right place at the right time.

Did Mayer's reputation suffer for her decision? Many saw De Castro's departure as a smart and necessary move, but Mayer had hand-selected him and paid him well. Some called for Mayer herself to resign, while others were willing to give her more time in the job to turn the company around. Mayer has taken some responsibility for the mess, saying, ""I think it was the right time for us to go our separate ways. . . . There were issues there that I potentially created, and it was important to me to fix them."

And though Mayer may have made a mistake in hiring De Castro, she's certainly done a lot right in her two years as CEO: she oversaw the acquisition of 37 companies including Tumblr; she launched a tidal wave of new, critically acclaimed products; and she added to Yahoo's brand cachet and credibility by hiring celebrity journalists like Katie Couric and David Pogue, former tech writer for the *New York Times*. On Mayer's watch, Yahoo's stock has more than doubled. Her leadership has not been without controversy, but it hasn't been without achievement, either. As the *Motley Fool* suggested, "Time to move on and focus on what matters: winning back some of Google's industry-leading $14.9 billion in quarterly online revenues, most of which are related to advertising."

"Conflict among team members, in and of itself, is not the enemy," wrote Ilan Mochari in *Inc.* "The enemy is when conflicts become personal. One of the signs of a healthy organization is when members of the top team can openly disagree with each other without their relationships becoming tense." With De Castro and Mayer, that became impossible, and when paired with De Castro's disappointing sales performance, it resulted in one of the most expensive—and embarrassing—executive partings in Silicon Valley history.

Case Questions

1. Explain whether the ousting of former CEO and COO, as well as the employee standards reform, have been functional or dysfunctional conflict for Yahoo.
2. Explain what type of conflict made DeCastro less than suitable for the position of COO at Yahoo.
3. Describe why trust will be an important factor for Yahoo as a company.

Sources

Brugger, Tim. "Yahoo! COO Ouster an Expensive Farewell." *Motley Fool*. January 6, 2014. www.fool.com/investing/general/2014/01/16/yahoo-coo-ouster-an-expensive-learning-experience.aspx.

Carlson, Nicholas. "Did Marissa Mayer Just Make a Horrible Mistake? Several Ex-Googlers Think So." *Business Insider*. October 16, 2012. www.businessinsider.com/yahoo-coo-henrique-de-castro-2012-10#ixzz32xw0Beyu.

Hempel, Jay. "Will Marissa Mayer Save Yahoo?" *Fortune*. May 1, 2014.http://tech.fortune.cnn.com/2014/05/01/will-marissa-mayer-save-yahoo/.

Learmonth, Michael. "Yahoo COO Henrique de Castro Out amid Continued Revenue Declines." *Adage.com*. January 15, 2014. http://adage.com/article/digital/yahoo-coo-henrique-de-castro-amid-revenue-declines/291118/.

Marr, Bernard. "Yahoo in Turmoil: CEO Mayer Fires Her No.2 Henrique De Castro." *LinkedIn.com*. January 16, 2014. www.linkedin.com/today/post/article/20140116205043-64875646-yahoo-in-turmoil-ceo-mayer-fires-her-no-2-henrique-de-castro.

Mochari, Ilan. "The Difficulty of Building a Healthy Top Team." *Inc.* January 16, 2014. www.inc.com/ilan-mochari/yahoo-fires-COO.html.

The Stock Trading Master. "Marissa Mayer Should Be Fired for Hiring Henrique de Castro For $60 Million + $109 Million Golden Parachute." *Guerilla Stock Trading*. January 16, 2014. www.guerillastocktrading.com/stock-market/marissa-mayer-should-be-fired-for-hiring-henrique-de-castro-for-60-million-109-million-golden-parachute/.

Swisher, Kara. "'Dead Man Walking' Walks: COO Henrique De Castro Out at Yahoo." *Re/Code*. January 15, 2014. http://recode.net/2014/01/15/henrique-de-castro-out-at-yahoo/.

Yarow, Jay. "Marissa Mayer's $109 Million Mistake: Why She Hired COO Henrique De Castro in the First Place." *Business Insider*. January 16, 2014. www.businessinsider.com/why-marissa-mayer-hired-henrique-de-castro-2014-1#ixzz32xwSm25R.

SELF-ASSESSMENT 10.1

What Is My Preferred Conflict Management Strategy?

This assessment will help you to determine the extent to which you tend to use the avoiding, accommodating, competing, compromising, or collaborating conflict management styles.

For each statement, circle the number that best describes how you would respond when you have a conflict with another person:

	Not at all Accurate	Somewhat Accurate	A little Accurate	Mostly Accurate	Completely Accurate
1. I usually give in to the other person.	1	2	3	4	5
2. I attempt to identify a middle-of-the-road resolution.	1	2	3	4	5
3. I force my own perspective.	1	2	3	4	5
4. I explore the situation in an effort to find an outcome that satisfies my interests as well as those of the other person.	1	2	3	4	5
5. I generally avoid confronting the other person about our disagreement.	1	2	3	4	5

	Not at all Accurate	Somewhat Accurate	A little Accurate	Mostly Accurate	Completely Accurate
6. I tend to simply agree with the other person.	1	2	3	4	5
7. I stress that we should find a good compromise agreement.	1	2	3	4	5
8. I look for opportunities to gain an advantage.	1	2	3	4	5
9. I try to represent both my interests as well as those of the other person.	1	2	3	4	5
10. I try to avoid disagreements as much as I can.	1	2	3	4	5
11. I do my best to accommodate the other person's wishes if possible.	1	2	3	4	5
12. I suggest that we both budge from our positions in order to reach an agreement.	1	2	3	4	5
13. I strive to get the best possible solution for myself.	1	2	3	4	5
14. I work with the other person to examine both sides of the story in order to find the most mutually beneficial resolution available.	1	2	3	4	5
15. I do my best to make our disagreements seem less important.	1	2	3	4	5
16. I tend to adjust my thinking to the other person's point of view.	1	2	3	4	5
17. I try to facilitate a 50–50 compromise if possible.	1	2	3	4	5
18. I do my best to win at all costs.	1	2	3	4	5
19. I attempt to craft an outcome that meets the other person's interests as well as my own.	1	2	3	4	5
20. I will avoid confronting the other person if at all possible.	1	2	3	4	5

Preference for Accommodating

Total for items 1, 6, 11, and 16 ___________

Preference for Compromising

Total for items 2, 7, 12 and 17 ___________

Preference for Competing

Total for items 3, 8, 13, and 18 ___________

Preference for Collaborating

Total for items 4, 9, 14 and 19 ___________

Preference for Avoiding

Total for items 5, 10, 15 and 20 ___________

1. What was your strongest conflict management strategy (the one with the highest score)?
2. What are some of the strengths and weaknesses of this approach?
3. Under what circumstances might it be beneficial for you to attempt to incorporate more of one of your weaker conflict management strategies?

SOURCE: Adapted from a scale employed by De Dreu, Carsten K. W., Arne Evers, Bianca Beersma, Esther S. Kluwer, and Aukje Nauta. "A Theory-Based Measure of Conflict Management Strategies in the Workplace." *Journal of Organizational Behavior* 22, no. 6 (September 2001): 645–668.

PART 4

LEADERSHIP AND INFLUENCE PROCESSES

11 Leadership Perspectives

Digital Vision/Photodisc/Thinkstock

> *Leadership is hard to define and good leadership even harder. But if you can get people to follow you to the ends of the earth, you are a great leader.*
>
> —Indra Nooyi, CEO, PepsiCo

WHAT IS LEADERSHIP?

11.1 Explain the basic concept of leadership

The search for what makes a good leader has been going on for centuries and, in spite of myriad studies, there are no conclusive answers. Although many definitions exist, for our purposes **leadership** is a process of providing general direction from a position of influence to individuals or groups toward the successful attainment of goals.[1]

The Internet has revolutionized society by giving millions of people a voice and the ability to communicate across cultural and geographical barriers. With enough online resources to access most corners of the world, almost anybody can be a leader, with or without formal authority, given the right skills and a strong initiative. In our global world, effective leaders need to connect and collaborate with people from different types of social groups through global networks in order to be heard.

What makes a great leader? Would you single out presidents and prime ministers, sports coaches, or CEOs as examples of iconic leaders? On what basis do you identify them as leaders? Popularity? Achievement? The way they communicate? Perhaps it's something intangible, like a leader's charisma. Societal norms and media influence have much to do with our perceptions about what makes an effective leader, and sometimes they create a false impression of **leader emergence**, which occurs when someone naturally becomes the leader of a leaderless group.[2] As a result, we can fall prey to stereotypes. For example, it is commonly believed that one of the reasons for the successful leadership of the late Margaret Thatcher, former Prime Minister of the United Kingdom known as the "Iron Lady," was her so-called masculine style, in striking a combative, unyielding tone with political adversaries while supporting conservative free market reforms and the Falklands War. With so many conflicting impressions and opinions of what makes a great leader, it is not surprising that endless studies and research have failed to agree on the actual constituents of leadership.

Despite numerous debates regarding the nature of leadership, there is a general view that today's leaders are most likely to be critical thinkers who lead from a position of influence rather than power, and who use their decision-making, motivational, and communication skills to inspire others with their vision in order to generate results. Researchers have discovered that effective leadership can produce astonishing results in terms of increasing a company's profits, maintaining a successful corporate culture, motivating employees through good times and bad, increasing production levels, connecting with the community, and leading the charge on sustainability.

As an example of effective leadership, refer to the OB in the Real World feature to read about Dave Vogt, manager at Southwest Airlines.

LEARNING OBJECTIVES

By the end of this chapter, you will be able to:

- 11.1 Explain the basic concept of leadership
- 11.2 Distinguish between formal and informal leadership and between leadership and management
- 11.3 Contrast the four basic types of leadership
- 11.4 Describe the trait, behavioral, and contingency leadership perspectives
- 11.5 Compare the inspirational, relational, and follower-centered leadership perspectives
- 11.6 Discuss the power-distributing leadership perspectives of empowering, shared, and self-leadership
- 11.7 Describe the values-based leadership perspectives of authentic, spiritual, servant, and ethical leadership
- 11.8 Discuss leadership across cultures
- 11.9 Identify gender issues in the context of leadership

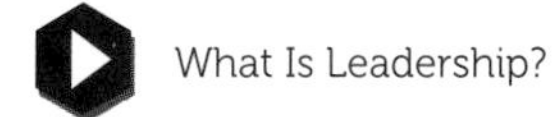
What Is Leadership?

Master the content.
edge.sagepub.com/neckob

SAGE edge™

National Archive and Spaarnestad Photo via Wikimedia Commons

Margaret Thatcher was perceived to have adopted a traditionally masculine style of leadership while acting as prime minister of the United Kingdom.

Leadership: The process of providing general direction, from a position of influence, to individuals or groups toward the successful attainment of goals

Leader emergence: The natural occurrence of someone becoming the leader of a leaderless group

THINKING CRITICALLY

1. Provide two examples of people (alive or dead) whom you consider to be great leaders. What characteristics defined their leadership abilities? **[Apply/Analyze]**

2. Do you agree that adopting a so-called "masculine" style could help make a woman a more effective leader? Why or why not? **[Analyze/Evaluate]**

3. Have you ever had a manager or boss whose leadership disappointed you? If so, explain what made him or her a less than effective leader. If not, describe the most effective manager or boss with whom you have ever worked. What made this person an effective leader? **[Analyze/Evaluate]**

FORMAL AND INFORMAL LEADERSHIP

11.2 Distinguish between formal and informal leadership and between leadership and management

Within most organizations there are two types of leaders: formal and informal.[3] A formal leader is officially designated by the organization, like a CEO who is appointed by the board of directors. For example, Bob Iger has been CEO of the Walt Disney Company since 2005. An informal leader does not receive a title but is perceived by others as a leader. For example, in the nursing profession, nurses with high clinical competencies are often chosen as informal leaders because of their nursing team.[4]

Formal leaders must act in the best interests of the organization and have certain rights and privileges that allow them to reward or discipline employees. Informal leaders do not have official appointments and therefore do not have the same rights as formal leaders, but team members may rely on them to motivate and help them realize their goals. When both formal and informal leaders exist in an organization, it is important for them to share the same vision and ensure the teams are working toward the same goals in order to avoid conflict.

THE BIG PICTURE: How OB Topics Fit Together

DAVE VOGT, *manager, Southwest Airlines*

OB in the Real World

© David Vogt

Dave Vogt is an HR manager at Southwest Airlines who works with employees in the northwestern and northeastern United States. Although other airlines have been struggling, Southwest Airlines has been profitable for the past 40 years. The company prides itself on its dedication to "the triple bottom line of Performance, People, and Planet." As part of its commitment to maintaining a world-class corporate culture, Southwest Airlines places a high level of focus on grooming and developing strong managers and leaders.

"Historically, there was a mentality that the job of a leader was to tell employees what to do and how to do it," says Dave. "It didn't matter how good a leader was, people stuck around because you simply didn't jump from one company to another. As the years have gone by a shift has happened. People want to feel a connection to what they're doing at work. They want to feel connected to their leaders."

When asked what advice he would give to future leaders, Dave replied, "Ask yourself why you want to be a leader. If it's simply to climb the corporate ladder and you're willing to step over people on your way up, then please stay out. Good leaders show humility and vulnerability."

Dave shared the story of his grandfather, Marion, who spent his entire career working for the same phone company. He loved his job and took pride in his work. However, even 30 years after he'd retired from that phone company, Marion still talked about the one manager who didn't believe in him, was condescending, and for two years made him feel he didn't know what he was doing. Marion often reminded Dave how important it was to work at a company where the managers and leaders treated people in a respectful way. It was clear that his ineffective manager's words and actions had deeply hurt Marion and stayed with him for the rest of his life.

Critical-Thinking Questions

1. **As a leader, you can have a lasting impact on the people around you through the choices you make, the things you say, and the way you say them.**
2. **What leaders do you admire and why?**
3. **What kind of leader do you want to be?**

SOURCES: Dave Vogt, personal interview, October 30, 2013; and Southwest Airlines webpage http://southwest.investorroom.com.

Management Versus Leadership

Managers Versus Leaders

Although management and leadership share some similarities, they do not mean the same thing. Both leaders and managers work with people, set goals, and influence others in order to achieve those goals, but several distinctions separate the two functions.

First, leadership has been around far longer than management. History records the strategies employed by military leaders such as Alexander the Great (336–323 BC) and Attila the Hun (406–453 BC). Managers, in contrast, are mainly a product of industrialization in the 20th century, an era when large-scale production and manufacturing demanded the organizational skills necessary to plan, organize, staff, and control the operation. These skills are still highly relevant in the 21st century workplace.

Second, leadership consists of creating a vision, introducing change and movement, and influencing others to achieve goals, while managers maintain the status quo, promote stability, and ensure the smooth running of operations.[5] There is an overlap

Bob Iger was appointed CEO of the Walt Disney Company by a board of directors, making him a formal leader. A nurse working in a hospital may not have been elected or chosen to be a leader, but still embodies the role informally because of his or her competencies and experience.

Josh Hallet (hyku) via Flickr.com; ©iStockphoto.com/IPGGutenbergUKLtd

between managers and leaders, however. For example, if you are a manager running a project and setting goals for your team, then you are leading your team. Similarly, if you are a leader and you are engaged in the daily organization of operations, then you are fulfilling management functions. In each case, both managers and leaders are leading from a position of influence. Therefore, it could be argued that organizations need strong leaders *and* strong managers to be successful.

However, realistically, not all managers are leaders, nor for that matter all leaders managers. For example, managers who put their own interests above those of their employees or who fail to motivate, guide, or positively influence their teams would not be classified as good leaders. Effective managers need to possess some leadership traits in order to optimize the performance of others (see Figure 11.1).

However, although it is useful for leaders to have managerial skills, it is not essential; certainly, it is advantageous for leaders to understand the discipline of management and have a background in the management functions, but it doesn't mean they need to be managers as well as leaders. Their primary strength lies in the ability to influence the behaviors and work of others in order to realize their vision and achieve set goals.

LEADER	BOTH	MANAGER
• Visionary • Sets long-term goals • Inspires followers • Big picture • Role model	• Work with people • Set goals • Influence followers	• Sets short-term goals and expectations • Trains and develops • Promotes stability • Ensures operations run smoothly

■ FIGURE 11.1 Comparison of a Leader and a Manager

THINKING CRITICALLY

1. Do informal leaders have the potential to be as powerful as or more powerful than a formal leader in an organization? Why or why not? **[Analyze/Evaluate]**

2. Do leaders or managers require more training to be successful? Explain your answer. **[Analyze/Evaluate]**

BASIC LEADERSHIP TYPES

11.3 Contrast the four basic types of leadership

Four distinct types of leadership behavior, originally proposed by Charles C. Manz and Henry P. Sims Jr., and since refined by other leadership theorists, are directive leadership, transactional leadership, visionary leadership, and empowering leadership (also known as "superleadership").[6] (See Table 11.1.)

Directive leadership behavior consists of implementing guidelines, providing information about what is expected, setting performance standards, and ensuring that individuals follow rules. Directive leaders are sometimes known as **production-oriented leaders** because they tend to focus more on the technical or task aspects of the job. Directive leaders also tend to rule with an **autocratic style**, making decisions without asking for suggestions from others. They also rely on the power to use their authority to command, reprimand, or intimidate in order to get the desired results from their subordinates.

Transactional leadership assumes employees are motivated by goals and equitable rewards. The transactional leader offers clear and objective goals for followers in order to gain **compliance**, which occurs when the targets of influence readily agree to carry out the leader's requests.

Visionary leadership, often contrasted with transactional leadership, creates visions to motivate, inspire, and stimulate employees. A visionary leader uses charisma to encourage followers to share in the mission and expects them to commit to him or her and work toward the desired goal. Finally, **empowering leadership**, or "SuperLeadership," shifts the focus from the leader to the follower through the idea of self-leadership.[7] Empowering leaders help to develop the individual skills and abilities of their followers, allowing them to utilize these skills, take ownership of their work, and contribute to organizational performance. The idea of "Superleadership" has been defined as the "process of leading others to lead themselves."[8]

Directive Leaders	Transactional Leaders
• Implement guidelines • Provide expectations • Set performance standards • Ensure rules are followed	• Set goals for followers • Motivate with rewards
Visionary Leaders	**Empowering Leaders**
• Create vision to motivate followers • Utilize charisma to gain support • Expect commitment from followers	• Develop followers' skills • Encourage followers to take ownership of their work • Lead others to lead themselves

TABLE 11.1 Four Basic Types of Leaders

Directive leadership: A leadership style characterized by implementing guidelines, managing expectations, setting definite performance standards, and ensuring that individuals follow rules

Production-oriented leader: A leader who tends to focus more on the technical or task aspects of the job

Autocratic style: A leadership style based on making decisions without asking for suggestions from others

Transactional leadership: A behavioral type of leadership that proposes that employees are motivated by goals and equitable rewards

Compliance: The behavior of targets of influence who agree to readily carry out the requests of the leader

Visionary leadership: A behavioral type of leadership that creates visions to motivate, inspire, and stimulate employees

Empowering leadership: A behavioral type of leadership that empowers leaders to help develop the individual skills and abilities of their followers. Also known as "SuperLeadership"

Introducing the Case of Langston Burrows: Leadership Challenges

In the next section, we will meet Langston Burrows, a recent college graduate with a bachelor's degree in business administration (BBA) from a top-50 ranked undergraduate business school, who has been offered a place in the leadership development program (LDP) in a mid-sized regional bank. Let's follow Langston's journey through the different areas of banking as he sets out to fulfill his quest to find his own leadership style.

THINKING CRITICALLY

1. A parent who rewards a child with stickers each time the child performs a desired behavior is enacting which type of leadership (directive, transactional, visionary, empowering)? Explain your answer. **[Understand/Apply]**
2. The expression, "Give a man a fish and he'll eat for a day; teach a man to fish and he'll eat for the rest of his life" is tacitly encouraging which type of leadership? Explain your answer. **[Understand/Apply]**

EARLY LEADERSHIP PERSPECTIVES

11.4 Describe the trait, behavioral, and contingency leadership perspectives

Leadership Theories

As we have learned, there is no set definition or combination of characteristics that describes a good leader. However, in order to support our current understanding of leadership, it is useful to explore the early theories of leadership, each of which focuses on different ways in which a great leader is created. These include trait, behavioral, and contingency theories. Our new OB case focuses on these early leadership perspectives.

Langston Burrows has just completed the first eight weeks of his leadership development program (LDP) training and is looking forward to what's coming next. The first month of training focused on learning about the bank's culture and core values along with the banking industry in general, while the second month was spent learning basic financial concepts and the bank's credit and underwriting standards. The next stage is a one-year rotation in a number of leadership roles throughout the bank.

As Langston waits for his first leadership assignment, he begins to feel a little nervous about putting into practice what he's learned. "What if I don't have what it takes to be an effective leader?" he thinks. "Great leaders from the past were masters at rallying and motivating thousands of followers to do their bidding and made huge strides forward as a result. Maybe someone quiet and easygoing like me isn't going to cut it in this industry!" Langston wonders to what extent he possesses the core traits of an effective leader.

Trait Leadership Perspective

Trait leadership perspective: A theory that explores the relationship between leaders and personal qualities and characteristics and how they differentiate leaders from nonleaders

The **trait leadership perspective** is a theory that explores the relationship between leaders' personal qualities and characteristics and the way their traits differentiate them from nonleaders. In other words, the theory assumes effective leaders are born, not made. Famous leaders such as Ghandi, Churchill, Lincoln, Joan of Arc, and Alexander the Great were studied by early trait theorists, who explored characteristics such as physical appearance, personality, and ability and sought to link them to

Wikimedia Commons

Photos.com/Thinckstock

Early trait theorists studied famous leaders like Winston Churchill and Joan of Arc to determine whether certain characteristics were indicative of strong leadership qualities.

individuals' leadership qualities. However, trait theory has since been widely criticized for its limiting methodology and inaccurate conclusions.[9] Researchers believed that traits in isolation could not predict leadership success.

Despite skepticism about early trait theory, the study of leadership traits has made a bit of a comeback in recent years since researchers have discovered patterns of traits.[10] Modern theorists now believe that leadership characteristics can be nurtured and developed over time, and that leaders must use a combination of these traits effectively to become successful leaders. The following is a list of leadership core traits identified in more recent research studies:[11]

- **Drive.** Leaders are ambitious and motivated and have a natural desire to succeed.
- **Desire to lead.** Leaders are motivated by a keen desire to lead and influence others, and to gain power.
- **Integrity.** Successful leaders are honest, trustworthy, and ethical and maintain behavior consistent with these values.
- **Self-confidence.** Leaders have a high degree of self-confidence in their leadership abilities.
- **Cognitive ability.** Leaders who have a wide range of cognitive skills have the ability to gather, integrate, and process complex information.
- **Knowledge of domain.** Leaders who possess a keen knowledge of their field are better at making decisions, predicting potential problems, and understanding the impact of their actions.
- **Openness to new experiences.** Leaders must be flexible, open to new experiences, and willing to adopt the ideas of others.
- **Extraversion.** Leaders who enjoy engaging with others tend to form relationships that support them in problem solving and in seeking new opportunities.

Although modern trait theory proposes that leadership traits can be nurtured over time, the behavioral leadership perspective focuses on a set of specific behaviors displayed by leaders in any given situation.

Behavioral Leadership Perspective

The **behavioral leadership perspective** proposes that specific behaviors distinguish leaders from nonleaders. During the 1950s, independent researchers at both Ohio State University and University of Michigan conducted studies of leadership behavior (see Table 11.2).

Ohio State University Studies

In the 1940s, researchers at Ohio State University administered a questionnaire to hundreds of people working in the military, business, and educational fields in order to assess leadership styles. The aim was to ascertain how employees perceived the types of leadership behavior exhibited by their superiors. From the results, researchers proposed a two-dimensional view of leadership behavior based on leadership styles they called initiating structure, and consideration.[12] **Initiating structure** is a behavior demonstrated by leaders who define the roles of the employees, set clear guidelines and procedures, and establish distinct patterns of organization and communication. **Consideration** is a behavior demonstrated by leaders who develop mutual trust and respect and actively build interpersonal relationships with their followers.

These two dimensions are similar to the theories proposed by the Michigan studies a few years later.

University of Michigan Studies

In an effort to identify the patterns of leadership behavior, University of Michigan researchers under the general direction of Rensis Likert in the 1950s interviewed leaders from both private and public companies and asked them to complete a questionnaire. The results helped the researchers establish two styles of leadership behavior: *job-centered leadership style*, a behavioral leadership style that emphasizes employee tasks and the methods used to accomplish them, and *employee-centered leadership style*, a behavioral leadership style that emphasizes the personal needs of employees and the development of interpersonal relationships.[13]

Researchers investigated the impact each leadership style had on rates of productivity, staff turnover, job satisfaction, and absenteeism and concluded that because employee-centered leaders had better results in these areas, they were more effective than job-centered leaders. However, there were some inconsistencies within the studies, mainly due to the fact that researchers were skeptical that leaders could possess characteristics from both styles rather than just one, which other theorists thought cast doubt on the results.

The two dimensions of initiating structure and consideration suggested in the Ohio studies are similar to the theories proposed by the Michigan studies. For example, initiating structure is similar to job-centered leadership because both behaviors place an emphasis on assigning tasks and getting the job done, and consideration is comparable to employee-centered leadership, with its focus on employee welfare and development.

Behavioral leadership perspective: The belief that specific behaviors distinguish leaders from nonleaders

Initiating structure: A behavioral leadership style demonstrated by leaders who define the roles of the employees, set clear guidelines and procedures, and establish distinct patterns of organization and communication

Consideration: A behavioral leadership style demonstrated by leaders who develop mutual trust and respect and actively build interpersonal relationships with their followers

The Ohio State Studies	The University of Michigan Studies
1. Initiating structure	1. Job-Centered Leadership Style
2. Consideration	2. Employee-Centered Leadership Style

■ TABLE 11.2 Behavioral Leadership Perspective Studies

SOURCES: Based on Hemphill, J. K., and A. E. Coons, *Leader Behavior: Its Description and Measurement*. Research Monograph No. 88 (Columbus: Ohio State University, Bureau of Business Research, 1957); Likert, Rensis. *New Patterns of Management* (New York: McGraw-Hill, 1961).

Although there are similarities between the Michigan and Ohio State studies, the Ohio State studies offer a more rounded view of leadership behavior by demonstrating that leaders could exhibit characteristics from both dimensions rather than just one.

The Leadership Grid

As an extension of the results published from the Ohio State studies, management researchers Robert R. Blake and Jane S. Mouton designed the **leadership grid**, an approach that plots concern for production on the horizontal axis and concern for people on the vertical axis (Figure 11.2). Each axis is a scale, with 1 representing the least concern and 9 the most. The five leadership styles are country club, produce or perish, impoverished, middle of the road, and team leader.[14]

Leaders who get a low score for production and a high score for people are known as "country club" leaders. This style of leader is more concerned about the well-being of his employees than about production and feels confident that a happy, relaxed workforce is the most productive. However, because of the lack of control and direction, this type of leadership can inhibit productivity.

"Produce or perish" leaders emphasize production over people and lead with an authoritarian rule, using punishment as a motivator. "Impoverished" leaders have very little concern for production *or* for people, which means they are ineffective for the most part. Leaders who are "middle-of-the-road" appear to have achieved the right balance between concern for people and concern for production, but this requires compromise; the problem with compromise is that the needs of both factions are not fully met, resulting in an average performance. Finally, the "team leader" rates production needs and people needs equally highly. According to the Blake-Mouton model, the team leader is the ideal leader, because he or she creates an environment in which teams are motivated and committed to furthering the success of the organization, leading to high production and satisfied employees.

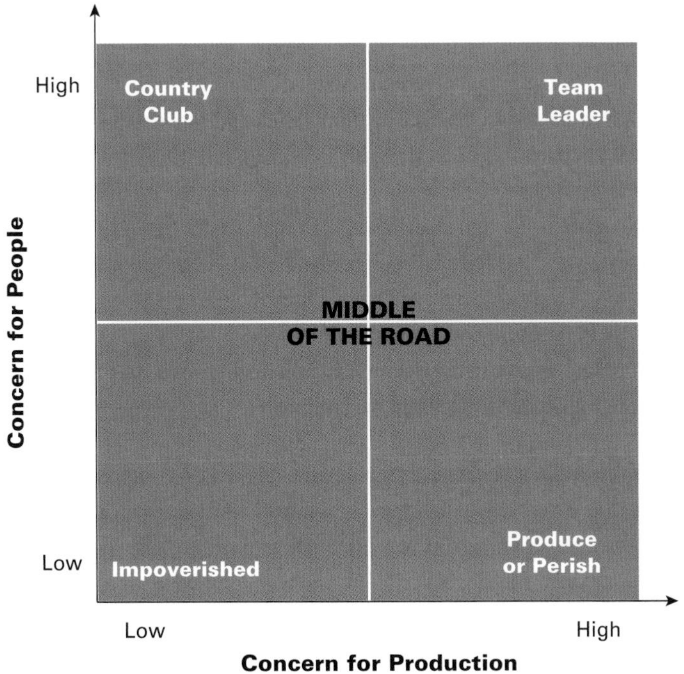

■ FIGURE 11.2 The Blake Mouton Leadership Grid

SOURCE: Adapted from Blake, R. R., and J. S. Mouton, *The Managerial Grid* (Houston, TX: Gulf Publishing, 1964).

Leadership grid: An approach that plots concern for production on the horizontal axis and concern for people on the vertical axis where 1 is the least concern and 9 is the greatest concern

The leadership grid reaffirmed the findings of the Ohio State studies that consideration of employees leads to a higher-performing workforce; however, it also introduced the idea that both people and production should be treated with the highest concern in order for the organization to achieve optimal results.

After completing his training, Langston is assigned to his first three-month leadership rotational position. He will be working in banking operations to learn more about the behind-the-scenes technical aspects of the bank. Ultimately, he will be taking over from one of the managers, Fleur Bernard, who will be going on maternity leave for six weeks. Langston is to shadow her for several weeks during which she will explain the various technical aspects of her job.

After only a week in the operations area, Langston arrives one morning to find the department abuzz with activity. Fleur's baby has arrived a month early and he is expected to step into her job with very little time to prepare. When Langston takes a moment in a quiet corner of the office to absorb this unexpected predicament, he overhears a conversation between the two members of the operations staff, Leila and Miguel.

"He's probably one of those 'fast-tracked' LDP trainees who will eventually move on to bigger and better things," says Miguel. "No doubt he'll be promoted into a management position above us."

"Let's hope he learns fast," Leila replies. "We need all the help we can get now that we're down to only two managers."

Langston wonders what leadership behavior he should adopt for this situation.

Contingency Leadership Perspective

Contingency Approach

The **contingency leadership perspective**, pioneered by Fred E. Fiedler, claimed that the effectiveness of the leader depended on there being an appropriate match between the leader's traits or behaviors and the demands and characteristics of the contingency or situation.[15] Fiedler sought to identify the different types of leadership styles in certain situations and devised a scale called **least preferred coworker (LPC)**, an instrument that evaluates whether a person is task oriented or relationship oriented.

To use the LPC scale, leaders were asked to think of a work situation in which they encountered a person they least enjoyed working with and rate that person's standing based on adjectives such as "friendly" or "unfriendly"; "considerate" or "inconsiderate," and so on (Figure 11.3).

Leaders who gave high scores on the LPC scale were thought to be relationship-motivated, because they tended to describe their least preferred coworker in a positive light. Those who had a more negative view of their coworkers received a low LPC score and were believed to be more task motivated.

In the next stage of this theory, Fiedler set out to prove that leadership style was dependent on the following situational variables:

- **Leader–member relations** describe the degree of confidence, trust, and respect that exist between subordinates and their leaders. Leaders who are well regarded can better influence events and outcomes.
- **Task structure** is the degree to which job assignments are defined. Leaders who provide clear, structured tasks are viewed more favorably.
- **Leader's position power** is the level of power a leader possesses to reward or punish, or promote and demote.

Fiedler's contingency model (Figure 11.4) is designed to predict the effectiveness of leadership styles in certain situations, on a scale from 1 to 8. For example, in instances

Contingency leadership perspective: The view that the effectiveness of the leader relates to the interaction of the leader's traits or behaviors with situational factors

Least preferred coworker (LPC) questionnaire: An instrument that purports to measure whether a person is task oriented or relationship oriented

Leader–member relations: Relationships that reflect the degree of confidence, trust, and respect that exists between subordinates and their leaders

Task structure: The degree to which job assignments are defined

Leader's position power: The level of power a leader possesses to reward or punish, or promote and demote

Unfriendly	1	2	3	4	5	6	7	8	Friendly
Unpleasant	1	2	3	4	5	6	7	8	Pleasant
Rejecting	1	2	3	4	5	6	7	8	Accepting
Tense	1	2	3	4	5	6	7	8	Relaxed
Cold	1	2	3	4	5	6	7	8	Warm
Boring	1	2	3	4	5	6	7	8	Interesting
Backbiting	1	2	3	4	5	6	7	8	Loyal
Uncooperative	1	2	3	4	5	6	7	8	Cooperative
Hostile	1	2	3	4	5	6	7	8	Supportive
Guarded	1	2	3	4	5	6	7	8	Open
Insincere	1	2	3	4	5	6	7	8	Sincere
Unkind	1	2	3	4	5	6	7	8	Kind
Inconsiderate	1	2	3	4	5	6	7	8	Considerate
Untrustworthy	1	2	3	4	5	6	7	8	Trustworthy
Gloomy	1	2	3	4	5	6	7	8	Cheerful
Quarrelsome	1	2	3	4	5	6	7	8	Harmonious

■ FIGURE 11.3 Least-Preferred Coworker Scale

SOURCE: Adapted from Fiedler, F. E., and M. M. Chemers. *Improving Leadership Effectiveness: The Leaders Match Concept* (2nd ed.) (New York: Wiley, 1984).

of high situational control where leader-member relations are good, task structure is low, and the leader has strong position power, the model gives a score of 3, suggesting a low LPC leadership or task-driven style is most effective. Conversely, in instances of low situational control when leader–member relations are poor, task structure is high, and the leader has weak position power, the model assigns a rating of 6, suggesting a high LPC leadership or relationship-driven style is best. Fiedler found that the most favorable situations occurred when leader-member relations, task structure, and position power are all high because then leaders have the most control over the situation.

Although Fiedler's model is useful for matching optimal leadership styles to certain situations, it has been criticized for its lack of flexibility, primarily its assumption that leadership styles cannot be changed. For example, according to the theory, leaders with low LPC ratings (more task driven) in situations where a high LPC approach

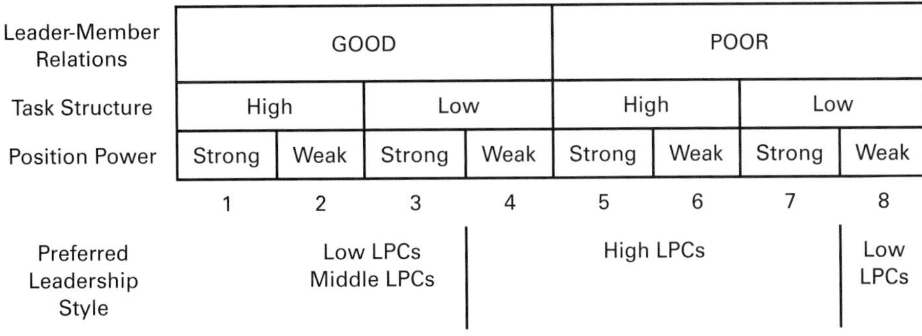

■ FIGURE 11.4 Fiedler's Contingency Model

SOURCE: Adapted from F. E. Fiedler, *A Theory of Leadership Effectiveness* (New York: McGraw-Hill, 1967).

(relationship driven) would be more suitable should be replaced by leaders with a natural flair for building relationships, even though it might be equally effective to encourage the low LPC leaders to adopt a different style or to develop their skills through training or other measures.

According to the Fiedler model, Langston Burrows is facing a situation characterized by a moderate level of situational control, suggesting relationship-oriented leadership will be the most effective.

During the next few weeks, Langston begins to get to know his staff, making a point to find out about their families and interests outside work. He admits that he needs their help to figure out the technical aspects of his role. Gradually, the team comes to like Langston, especially Miguel and Leila, and they help him learn the ropes.

Langston's second rotation has him filling in as manager in one of the bank's smaller branches, which is staffed by four experienced tellers. Langston feels like the new guy all over again. Should he be more task oriented or should he stick with the relationship-oriented approach that served him well in his first leadership role?

Hersey and Blanchard's Situational Leadership Model

Developed in 1969 by Paul Hersey and Ken Blanchard, the **situational leadership model** proposes that leaders should adapt their leadership style based on the types of people they are leading and the requirements of the task.[16] Drawing from the findings of the Ohio State studies, Hersey and Blanchard applied concepts similar to "initiating structure" and "consideration" to the following four main leadership styles:

- **Telling** (S1). Telling is a directive approach in which leaders give clear instructions and guidance to followers, informing them exactly how and when to complete the task. This leadership style works best within environments that have high initiating structure and low consideration, where the completion of the task takes precedence over the relationship with employees. For example, in an emergency people would rather be told what to do in order to deal with the situation as quickly and safely as possible.
- **Selling** (S2). Leaders who adopt the selling style provide support to followers through communicating and "selling" the goals of the task in order to gain commitment. This style is appropriate for issues with high initiating structure and high consideration. For example, a leader of a sales team has to meet regular sales targets but also needs to foster a good relationship with the sales reps in order to motivate them to meet their goals.
- **Participating** (S3). Leaders and followers work together and share in the decision-making responsibilities of the task in the participating style. It works best in situations where there is low initiating structure and high consideration. For example, an employee may have picked up some skills on the job but needs more guidance to complete a task. In this case, the leader will include the follower in decisions and help develop his or her knowledge base.
- **Delegating** (S4). Leaders give most of the responsibility to followers in the delegating style yet still monitor progress. Delegating occurs in instances of low initiating structure and low consideration. For example, when employees are fully functional and skilled to complete a task, there is little need for leadership involvement.

Situational leadership model: A leadership model that proposes leaders should adapt their leadership style based on the types of people they are leading and the requirements of the task

Telling: A leadership behavior characterized by giving clear instructions and guidance to followers, informing them exactly how and when to complete the task

Selling: Leadership behavior characterized by support provided to followers through communication and "selling" them the aims of the task in order to gain commitment

Participating: Leadership behavior in which both leaders and followers work together and share in the decision-making responsibilities of the task

Delegating: The act of giving most of the responsibility to followers while still monitoring progress

Telling and selling are more task-oriented leadership styles, whereas participating and delegating are more focused on the development of team members' ability to work independently to complete the task.

But which leadership style is most appropriate? And how do leaders know which one to use? According to Hersey and Blanchard, the choice of leadership style depends on the willingness and ability of followers, in other words, their level of readiness to get the job done.

The Hersey-Blanchard model expands on previous theories by emphasizing the importance of the readiness or maturity of followers when completing a task. It also allows for greater flexibility in leadership behaviors when it comes to dealing with different types of people in the workforce.

Steve Jennings/Stringer/Getty Images

Elizabeth Holmes, the world's youngest self-made female billionaire and CEO of Theranos, utilizes path-goal theory by encouraging her employees to take leadership positions within the company.

Langston decides to adopt a participating leadership style that is high in relationship behavior and low in task behavior in his new role as branch bank manager. After all, his staff is highly capable and experienced; they know more about running the branch than he does and don't need to be told what to do. Instead, Langston focuses on supportive, relationship-oriented behaviors. He spends time getting to know his staff and makes it clear to them that his primary job as branch manager is to provide them with whatever resources and support they need to do their jobs. The staff warms to him quickly.

House's Path–Goal Theory

Originally developed by Robert House in 1971, **path–goal leadership theory** suggests that leadership effectiveness is the degree to which the leader enhances the performance of followers by guiding them on a defined track toward achieving their goals.[17] Leaders can help followers by clarifying the routes they need to take to achieve their goals, removing obstacles and providing incentives at certain milestones. The level of support and assistance provided to followers depends on the situation, the complexity of the task, and the motivational capabilities of the followers.

House describes how leadership effectiveness is influenced by the interaction among the four main leadership styles:

- **Directive leadership.** Leadership behavior characterized by implementing guidelines, managing expectations, setting definite performance standards, and ensuring that individuals follow rules. This type of leadership is appropriate in the military, where commands are expected to be followed immediately and without question.
- **Supportive leadership.** A type of leadership behavior characterized by friendliness and concern for the welfare of others. For example, a leader might work with followers struggling with a task until they feel empowered enough to carry out the task themselves.
- **Participative leadership.** Leadership behavior that consists of consulting with followers and considering their input in decision making. For example,

Path–goal leadership theory: A theory that proposes that leadership effectiveness depends on the degree to which the leader enhances the performance of followers by guiding them on a defined track towards achieving their goals

Supportive leadership: A leadership behavior characterized by friendliness and concern for the welfare of others

Participative leadership: A leadership style that favors consulting with followers and considering their input in decision making

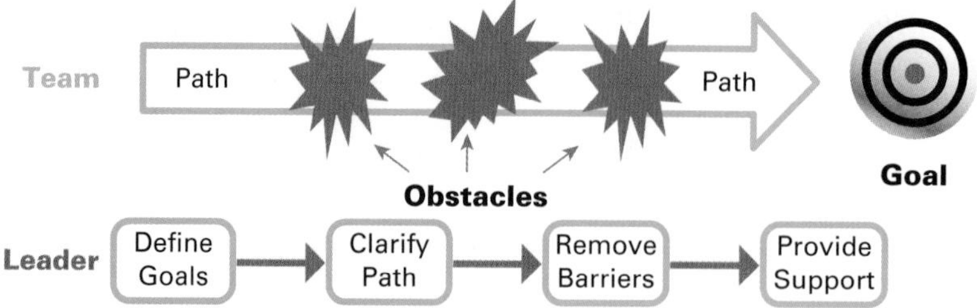

■ FIGURE 11.5 Path–Goal Theory Model

SOURCES: House, R. "Path-Goal Theory of Leadership: Lessons, Legacy, and a Reformulated Theory." *Leadership Quarterly* 7, no. 3 (1996): 323–352; model adapted from Northouse, P. *Leadership: Theory and Practice* (4th ed.) (Thousand Oaks, CA: Sage, 2007): 128.

a marketing leader might gather his or her followers to collect input about the possibility of launching a new product or taking a product off the market.

- **Achievement-oriented leadership.** Leadership behavior characterized by setting challenging goals, improving performance, and assisting in employee training. This style of leadership is often used by football quarterbacks, who are expected to direct the team to perform certain plays at the right time in order to win the game.

According to House, certain styles of leadership may be more suitable in some situations than others in order to influence follower satisfaction, motivation for the task, and acceptance of the leader. There are two main situational contingencies:

- **Subordinate characteristics** such as anxiety, inflexibility, perceived ability, locus of control, and close-mindedness.
- **Task characteristics** outside the follower's control such as team dynamics, authority systems, and task structure.

The theory suggests that leaders can adjust their leadership styles to compensate for employee limitations. For example, a leader may take a supportive approach with a disgruntled employee in an effort to get to the root of the problem and find a resolution.

In contrast to the Fiedler contingency model, the path–goal model states that the four leadership styles are flexible, and that effective leaders can possess and adopt more than one style to help, motivate, and support their employees by removing obstacles on the path to achieving goals (Figure 11.5). Unlike earlier theories, the path–goal model also offers specific suggestions for how leaders can help employees by taking into account relevant contingency factors such as employee characteristics and environmental factors.

Achievement-oriented leadership: Leadership behavior characterized by setting challenging goals, improving performance, and assisting training

Subordinate characteristics: Situational contingencies such as anxiety, inflexibility, perceived ability, locus of control, and close-mindedness

Task characteristics: Situational contingencies outside the follower's control, such as team dynamics, authority systems, and task structure

Substitutes for leadership model: A model that suggests certain characteristics of the situation can constrain the influence of the leader.

Neutralizing: The substitution of leadership attributes that do not affect follower outcomes

Substitutes for Leadership Model

Although path-goal theory focuses on the centrality of the leadership role to employee satisfaction and work performance, the **substitutes for leadership model**[18] proposes that certain characteristics of individuals, the job, and/or the organization can act as substitutes for leadership or neutralize leadership impact altogether. In this context, **neutralizing** means replacing leadership attributes that do not affect followers' outcomes.

A team that is well run, experienced, and organized might substitute for or neutralize the need for a task-oriented leader because the team already knows how to carry out the requirements of their roles. For example, organizations like W. L. Gore, tomato processor Morning Star, and steelmaker Worthington Industries cultivate environments in which teams are largely left to manage themselves.[19]

THINKING CRITICALLY

1. Consider the eight traits identified by the Trait Leadership Perspective: drive, desire to lead, integrity, self-confidence, cognitive ability, knowledge of domain, openness to new experiences, and extraversion. Imagine you are a teacher trying to cultivate leadership qualities in your students. Describe the steps you could take to foster one of the traits in the list. Identify the traits that would be easier to develop. Which traits would be more difficult to develop? Explain your reasoning. **[Analyze/Evaluate]**

2. Which type of leader identified by Blake Mouton's Leadership Grid--country club, produce or perish, impoverished, middle of the road, or team leader—would command the most respect from employees? Explain your answer. **[Analyze/Evaluate]**

3. Use the Least-Preferred Coworker Scale to rank your least preferred coworker or fellow student. Based on the results, do you think you are more relationship-motivated or task-motivated as a leader? Why? **[Apply/Analyze]**

4. Do you agree with Langston's decision to adopt a participating leadership style as new branch bank manager? Could he just as easily have developed a delegating leadership style according to Hersey and Blanchard's Situational Leadership Model? Why or why not? **[Analyze/Evaluate]**

5. Apply House's Path-Goal Theory to Langston's situation as the incoming branch bank manager. Describe the information he would need to gather before determining the best leadership approach in this situation. What are the benefits of applying this model to his situation as opposed to the Situational Leadership Model? **[Analyze/Evaluate]**

CONTEMPORARY LEADERSHIP PERSPECTIVES

11.5 Compare the inspirational, relational, and follower-centered leadership perspectives

Although early leadership perspectives enhanced our understanding of leadership and follower behavior, more recent inspirational and relational leadership perspectives have built on these theories to explain how leaders motivate and build relationships with followers to achieve performance beyond expectations. Popular contemporary perspectives include leader–member exchange (LMX), transformational leadership, and charismatic leadership.

Leader–Member Exchange (LMX) Theory

The **leader–member exchange (LMX) theory**[20] builds on the idea that leaders develop different relationships with different followers. The quality of the relationship determines whether the leader (often subconsciously) places the follower in the "in-group exchange" or the "out-group exchange" (Figure 11.6).

Leader-exchange theory: A theory of leadership that focuses on the relationships between leaders and their group members.

In-group exchange: Interaction that occurs when leaders and followers develop good working relationships based on mutual trust, respect, and a sense of sharing common fates

- **In-group exchange.** Typically, team members who are loyal, trustworthy, and skilled have high-quality relationships with leaders. The leader devotes more attention to this in-group, assigns challenging tasks, and often spends more one-to-one time with members. People in this group are given more opportunities for growth and advancement and often mirror the leader's work ethic and characteristics.

- **Out-group exchange.** People who are perceived to be incompetent, unmotivated, untrustworthy team members have low-quality relationships with their leaders. Leaders tend to assign simple, limited tasks to this group, communicate with them only when necessary, and often withhold opportunities for growth or advancement.

LMX theory demonstrates the dangers of overclassifying individuals. Once an individual is in the out-group and the leader's perception of that person has been sealed, it is almost impossible to change that perception, and often the individual has no recourse but to leave the team or organization. Leaders need to nurture all relationships with their followers to draw out everyone's best efforts and achieve organizational success.

Langston has been assigned to the final rotation in his Leadership Development Training. He is working in the Retail Banking Service Department and reporting to Sonia Valdez, a well-respected Vice President at the bank. While Sonia is professional and welcoming to him, Langston quickly determines that she is very busy and tends to depend upon an in-group of direct reports that have worked with Sonia for many years. Langston concludes that as a new, non-permanent member of Sonia's team he is in the unfortunate position of being in Sonia's out-group. He resolves to work hard to earn the VP's trust and respect with the hope of moving into her in-group. A few days later, he gets his chance. During the weekly staff meeting, Sonia asks for a volunteer to spearhead the rollout of a new customer service program and facilitate the cultural change needed to make it work. Langston sees her looking at the core of her in-group. But before any of them can respond, he says, "I'll do it!"

"Okay, you're on!" Sonia says, surprised. "Show me what you can do."

During the next couple of months Langston works closely with Sonia as he designs and implements the launch of the Quality Banking Guaranteed program. He oversees many of the training sessions and provides each customer service rep with individual attention and coaching. The program is launched and is very successful. Not long after, Sonia takes Langston to lunch.

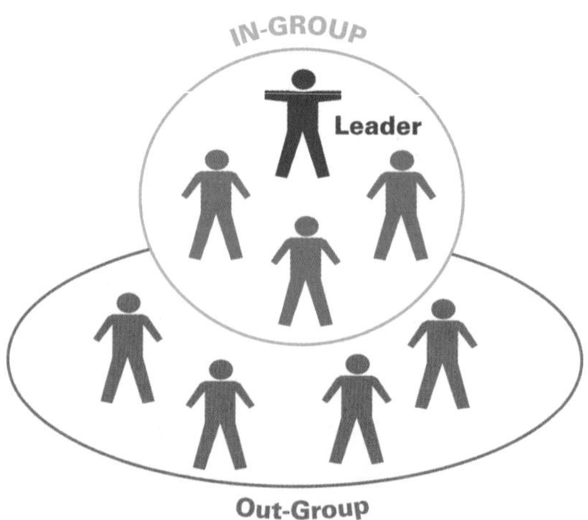

■ FIGURE 11.6 LMX Theory

SOURCE: Gupta, Ashum. "Leader Member Exchange." *Practical Management*. June 6, 2009. http://practical-management.com/pdf/Leadership-Development/Leader-Member-Exchange.pdf?format=phocapdf. Copyright © practical-management.com.

Out-group exchange: Interaction that occurs when leaders and followers fail to create a sense of mutual trust, respect, or common fate

"You really delivered on the Quality Banking Guaranteed program," she says. "I'd like to offer you a permanent position on my staff at the end of your training if you're interested. You'd make a great addition to our team!"

Langston is elated at the prospect of stepping into a full-time position at the bank and tells Sonia that he will be honored to join her team. He is happy to have earned his manager's respect and mentally congratulates himself for moving from out-group to in-group as a result of his performance and hard work.

Transformational Leadership

Transformational leaders inspire their followers to transcend their self-interests for the good of the organization and commit to a shared vision, while also serving as a role model. Transformational leadership is becoming an increasingly popular model for today's leaders. Bill Gates and L.A. Lakers coach Phil Jackson are good examples of transformational leaders who inspire their teams to achieve goals.[21] The four dimensions of transformational leadership are[22]

- **Idealized influence** (also referred to as *charisma*) is behavior that gains the admiration, trust, and respect of followers.
- **Inspirational motivation** promotes commitment to a shared vision of the future.
- **Intellectual stimulation** encourages people to view problems from a different perspective and to think about innovative and alternative ways to address them.
- **Individualized consideration** creates mutual respect or trust and a genuine concern for the needs and desires of others.

In direct opposition to transformational leadership is **laissez-faire leadership**, in which a leader fully delegates responsibility to others.[23] This type of leader has little involvement with followers, almost no control over the task, and little interest in making decisions unless forced into it. Investor Warren Buffett is an example of a laissez-faire leader, who prefers to give his management teams a lot of freedom to make decisions rather than monitoring them to any great degree.[24]

Charismatic Leadership

Transformational leadership theory was inspired by Max Weber's concept of **charismatic leadership**, which is the ability of a leader to use his or her personality or charm to inspire, motivate, and acquire loyalty and commitment from employees.[25]

Charismatic leaders are similar to transformational leaders in that they both use inspirational techniques to energize and motivate their followers. They can certainly use their exceptional leadership skills for good. However, though transformational leaders are focused on the best interests of the individuals and the organization, charismatic leaders may place more emphasis on their own needs and interests[26] and become caught up in their own hype. Leaders who follow their own agendas become inflexible, believe they can do no wrong, and tend to dismiss advice from others if it diverges from their own convictions. Adolf Hitler is an example of a charismatic leader who inspired devotion in others to carry out his own extreme political agenda—to horrifying and tragic results.

In addition, serious repercussions can occur when charismatic leaders become convinced of their own infallibility—their followers may also buy into this belief and perceive such leaders as invincible. The danger is that followers will relate their own personal job satisfaction and the success of the organization directly to the presence of

Idealized influence: Behavior that gains the admiration, trust, and respect of followers, who in turn follow the leader's example with their own actions

Inspirational motivation: Leadership behaviors that promote commitment to a shared vision of the future

Intellectual stimulation: Stimuli that encourage people to think and promote intelligence, logic, and problem solving

Individualized consideration: Leader behavior associated with creating mutual respect or trust and a genuine concern for the needs and desires of others

Laissez-faire leadership: Leadership behavior that fully delegates responsibility to others

Charismatic leadership: The ability of a leader to use his or her personality or charm to inspire, motivate, and acquire loyalty and commitment from employees

LMX AND IMPLICIT LEADERSHIP AND FOLLOWERSHIP PROTOTYPES

Examining the Evidence

Leader–member exchange (LMX) theory suggests that leaders engage in different types of relationships with different followers. Relationships with followers in the leader's "in-group" are characterized by mutual trust, respect, and liking, while relationships with followers in the leader's "out-group" tend to be characterized by more formality and less communication and meaningful interaction. But what factors shape the quality of the relationships between leaders and the followers? There are a number of possible answers to this question, but one compelling possibility makes use of implicit leadership and followership theories. In short, if a follower does not match the leader's prototypic view of how an ideal follower should be, the leader's view of the follower will likely have a negative effect on the quality of the LMX exchange relationship. Similarly, if a leader does not match the follower's implicit leadership prototype, the relationship will likely suffer a negative impact.

Olga Epitropaki and Robin Martin explored this possibility in a longitudinal research study of 439 employees published in the *Journal of Applied Psychology*.[*] They found that the smaller the difference between the prototypic leadership traits followers recognized in their direct supervisors and their own implicit leadership prototypes, the better the quality of the relationship they developed with their leaders. A similar study by Suzanne van Gils, Neils van Quaquebeke, and Daan van Knippenberg published in the *European Journal of Work and Organizational Psychology* concluded that leaders and followers may view the quality of their relationships differently if their implicit leadership theories and implicit followership theories are different.[^] Taken together, these studies suggest that followers' and leaders' perceptions of one another's characteristics relative to their own implicit prototypes may play a key role in determining the quality of LMX relationships and ultimately the job satisfaction, commitment, and well-being of followers.

Critical-Thinking Questions

1. **How can leaders most effectively improve or sustain the quality of their relationships with their followers?**
2. **How can organizations help to enhance the quality of leader-follower relationships?**

*Epitropaki, Olga, and Robin Martin. "From Ideal to Real: A Longitudinal Study of the Role of Implicit Leadership Theories on Leader-Member Exchanges and Employee Outcomes." *Journal of Applied Psychology* 90, no. 4 (July 2005): 659–676.

^van Gils, Suzanne, Niels van Quaquebeke, and Daan van Knippenberg. "The X-factor: On the Relevance of Implicit Leadership and Followership Theories for Leader-Member Exchange Agreement." European Journal of Work and Organizational Psychology 19, no. 3 (June 2010): 333–363.

the leader. In this situation, the departure of a charismatic leader can have a devastating effect on followers. Therefore, the charismatic leader needs to be an appropriate role model for followers.

Follower-Centered Leadership Perspective

Followership: Individuals' capacity to cooperate with leaders

Implicit leadership theories: Hypotheses that explore the extent to which we distinguish leaders and nonleaders based on underlying assumptions, stereotypes, and beliefs

Leadership prototypes: Behaviors that people associate with leadership

Recently, researchers have begun to explore a more follower-centered approach that focuses less on different types of leaders and their behaviors. **Followership** is the capacity of individuals to cooperate with leaders.[27] The theory that studies it stems from cognitive categorization theory, which explores the idea that people tend to label others on the basis of a first impression.[28]

The follower-centered leadership perspective focuses on how followers view leaders and how they view themselves. There are two types of theories in this approach: implicit leadership theories, and implicit followership theories.

According to **implicit leadership theories**, we have a natural tendency to apply traits and attributes to others to determine whether they are leaders. Relevant traits and attributes include charismatic, attractive, intelligent, dedicated, tyrannical, and strong. These traits are called **leadership prototypes** and are behaviors we associate with leadership.[29]

Implicit followership theories are preconceived notions about the types of behaviors that leaders believe characterize followers and nonfollowers.[30] Common prototypes ascribed to good followers included enthusiasm, industriousness, and being a good citizen. Ineffective or nonfollowers are characterized as easily influenced, lacking humility, lacking experience, working slowly, and behaving unprofessionally. Like LMX theory, followership theories show that opinions based on first impressions or very quick judgments can prejudice our views of others and create negativity within groups.

Although transformational and empowering leadership approaches may dominate today's views on leadership, a number of cutting-edge perspectives are quickly gaining ground. Recent theorists have criticized directive leaders for using fear as a motivator, questioned the "carrot-and-stick" methodology of transactional leadership, and argued that transformational leaders may impede independent thinking in followers.

It may be impossible to wrap the constituents of leadership into a neat package. Perhaps, however, we can conclude from the evolution of leadership theories that different situations require different kinds of leaders. Next we focus on emerging leadership perspectives, and how they enhance the skills and improve the effectiveness of 21st century leaders.

THINKING CRITICALLY

1. Who do you think is responsible for employees being placed in the "in-group" or the "out-group"—the leaders or the employees themselves? Explain your answer. **[Analyze/Evaluate]**

2. Which do you think requires leaders to have more confidence in their followers, transformational leadership or laissez-faire leadership? Defend your answer. **[Analyze/Evaluate]**

3. Consider the potential benefits and potential drawbacks of charismatic leadership. In what situations might charismatic leadership be useful to an organization? In what situations could a charismatic leader create problems within an organization? In general, do you believe that charismatic leaders are an asset or a liability? Why? **[Analyze/Evaluate]**

4. The text suggests that different situations require different kinds of leaders. Do you agree with this idea? Why or why not? **[Understand/Apply/Analyze]**

POWER-DISTRIBUTING LEADERSHIP PERSPECTIVES

11.6 Discuss the power-distributing leadership perspectives of empowering, shared, and self-leadership

The concept of '"distributed leadership" has grown in popularity over the past few years and serves as an alternative to those theories that have focused on leadership traits, characteristics, and behaviors. Instead, distributed leadership calls for sharing the power and influence within organizations. Let's return to our narrative to further explore the three main facets of power-distributing leadership: empowering, shared, and self-leadership.

Three months have passed since Sonia asked Langston to join her department at the bank. It is Langston's second day as a full-time employee and Sonia asks him to meet with her to talk about his first assignment. Sonia tells Langston he is to work on a big project with Svetlana Petrova, the head of lending, introducing a new bankwide computer information system and ensuring that tellers, customer service reps, loan

Implicit followership theories: Preconceived notions about the types of behaviors that characterize followers and nonfollowers

officers, and branch managers are up-to-speed on using the new system within three months. Langston assures Sonia he is eager to begin working with Svetlana, but he is actually a little worried. He has observed that Svetlana takes credit for other people's work and it's clear that she is far more polite and professional to coworkers when her superiors are present. To try to get some perspective on working with her, he calls his friend Jonathan Hicks, who has been at the bank for three years and might have helpful advice. Jonathan confirms Langston's impression of Svetlana, and warns Langston to tread carefully when working with her. "No one can ever accuse Svetlana of not playing things smart with the higher ups," notes Jonathan. "Don't trust her, Langston, but provided you make Svetlana look good you shouldn't have any problems with her. Just don't get in the way of her success!" He then goes on to share warm memories of Chuck Branston, the manager who preceded Svetlana in Lending.

"Chuck was an excellent leader and we all enjoyed working for him. He let us give suggestions and make our own decisions, and he was always the first one to get to work and the last to leave. He worked harder than any of us, and that really impressed us, you know? He never criticized us—he just wanted us to be as informed, proficient and knowledgable as possible so we could be more self-reliant," Jonathan goes on. "He was the best boss I've ever had. You always knew where you stood with Chuck. He would fill us in about everything that was going in the company. And he always outlined the company goals for us so we knew where we fit in. When I first started working here he even arranged additional training for me. I really miss Chuck."

"I miss Chuck and I don't even know him!," Langston laughs. He feels inspired by Chuck's *empowering leadership* style and vows to be fair and professional in his dealings with Svetlana. Langston wants to succeed in his new job and Svetlana is someone he may be able to learn from, even if she isn't his first choice as a colleague.

Empowering Leadership

Empowering leadership is the practice of delegating power that motivates employees and inspires them to achieve goals.[31] Bill Gates is a good example of an empowering leader because he encourages employees to share their ideas, innovate new products, processes, and systems, and build on their strengths.[32] Empowering leadership is similar to participative leadership, in which leaders allow their employees to partake in decision-making processes and provide them with the resources and support to carry out their roles. Empowering leaders encourage their employees to act independently and make decisions without the presence of a formal leader. Here are some of the behaviors they use:

Bill Gates demonstrates empowering leadership by encouraging employees to share their ideas, innovate, and build on their strengths.

- **Leading by example.** Empowering leaders inspire their employees by demonstrating a strong commitment to their work. Jonathan tells Langston everyone respected Chuck Branston because of his work ethic.
- **Coaching.** Empowering leaders take active steps to educate and train their employees so they can become more independent. Chuck Branston targeted areas of performance that needed to be improved.

- **Participative decision-making.** Empowering leaders encourage employees to make suggestions and express their ideas. Chuck Branston encouraged the lending staff to take part in the decision-making process.
- **Informing.** Empowering leaders keep their employees up to date with company information and goals. According to Jonathan, Chuck made a point of telling the lending staff the direction the bank was taking and the decisions that were being made at the top.
- **Showing concern.** Empowering leaders take an interest in the well-being of their employees and treat them with respect. For example, Chuck Branston arranged additional training for Jonathan when he was new.

Shared Leadership

Shared Leadership

Shared leadership distributes influence among groups and individuals to achieve organizational or team goals.[33] Rather than being solely responsible for decision making, the leader shares responsibility with the group as members strive to achieve common goals.

Shared leadership is becoming more frequent in patient care and top management teams. For shared leadership to be effective, employees must share the same vision and goals, be provided with the right resources to carry out their tasks, maintain similar levels of knowledge and skills, work in a collaborative environment that fosters trust and cooperation, and be flexible enough to adapt to changing conditions. For example, the Orpheus Chamber Orchestra has performed without a conductor since its founding in 1972; leadership responsibilities are shared among the musicians instead.[34]

Self-Leadership

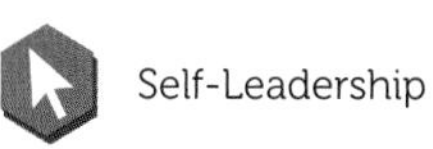

Both empowering and shared leadership facilitate and encourage self-leadership. **Self-leadership** is a process through which people intentionally influence their thinking and behavior to achieve their objectives.[35] In other words, people can deliberately guide themselves toward attaining favorable outcomes. Author and Management Expert Ken Blanchard uses self-leadership techniques to remove constraints, identify points of power, and collaborate with others.[36] There are three main categories of self-leadership strategies.[37]

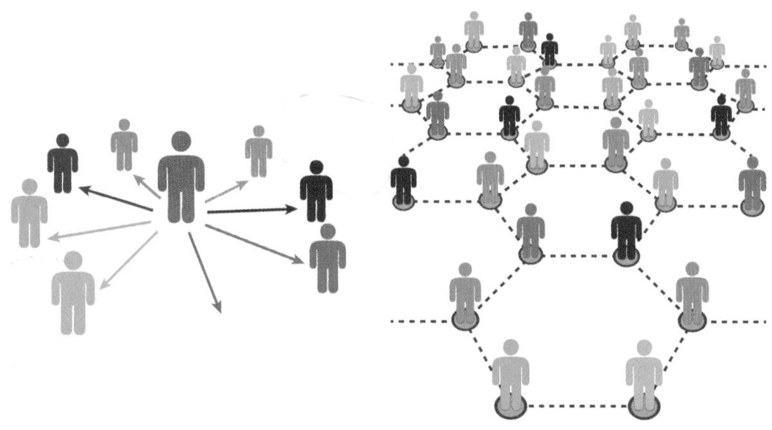

Traditional-Leadership Model **Shared-Leadership Model**

■ FIGURE 11.7 Traditional Leadership Versus Shared Leadership

Shared leadership: A style of leadership that distributes influence among groups and individuals to achieve organizational or team goals

Self-leadership: A process whereby people intentionally influence their thinking and behavior to achieve their objectives

Unlike traditional orchestras, the Orpheus Chamber Orchestra performs without a conductor. This collective responsibility among its members exemplifies shared leadership.

Hiroyuki Ito / Getty Images

Behavior-focused strategies are targeted toward increasing our self-awareness and managing our own conduct. They include self-observation, self-goal setting, self-reward, self-correcting feedback, and self-cueing.[38] Self-observation entails analyzing our own behaviors for the purposes of identifying those that need to be adjusted, enhanced, or eliminated altogether. For example, setting goals that challenge us motivates us to achieve them. Self-reward helps us motivate ourselves and improve performance by mentally praising our own achievements and giving ourselves positive feedback and corrections. Self-cueing strategies, such as writing to-do lists or keeping an efficient record of information, helps to focus our attention on assigned tasks.

Natural reward strategies help us to find pleasure in certain aspects of our roles, leading to an enhanced sense of competence, self-discipline, and application.[39] For example, if you are given a particularly tedious assignment, you could decide to complete the most onerous part of the task first before turning your attention to the more rewarding part. Even external reward strategies can make a difference in the way we work. For example, adding personal touches to your desk can have a calming effect when work becomes frustrating.

Constructive thought pattern strategies focus on the modification of certain key mental processes.[40] That is, the more positive and optimistic our thinking patterns, the better our work performance. Mental imagery is one strategy we can use to shape our thought processes by visualizing the successful attainment of the goal before we begin. This is a common technique among top athletes; for example, Brazilian footballer Ronaldinho uses mental imagery to prepare for a game and to plan his strategy on the pitch.

THINKING CRITICALLY

1. What aspects of Chuck Branston's empowering leadership style strike you as especially useful in generating a positive team environment? Based on the limited information you currently have about Svetlana, what leadership style does she appear to practice? Contrast the effectiveness of these two types of leadership in furthering one's own career and in motivating a team. **[Apply/Analyze]**

2. What challenges might an organization with a shared leadership structure encounter? Discuss at least three potential problems that could arise. **[Analyze/Evaluate]**

Eric Francis/Stringer/Getty Images

Warren Buffett (L) exhibits authentic leadership by surrounding himself with advisers like Charlie Munger (R) who tell him when he is wrong.

3. To what extent do you engage in self-leadership? What techniques have you employed, and how have these techniques helped you succeed at your tasks? **[Apply/Analyze]**

VALUES-BASED LEADERSHIP PERSPECTIVES

11.7 Describe the values-based leadership perspectives of authentic, spiritual, servant, and ethical leadership

Following the economic turbulence over the last few years, there has been a shift from power-based leadership to values-based leadership. Values-based leaders act in concert with a set of principles in order to equip others with the right tools to unleash their potential so that they can act for the greater good.[41] There are four types of values-based leadership: authentic, spiritual, servant, and ethical.

Authentic Leadership

Authentic leadership is a pattern of leadership behavior based on honesty, practicality, and ethicality.[42] Warren Buffett, for instance, empowers his advisors to point out flaws in his reasoning.[43] Support for this type of leadership has been gaining ground as a reaction to the number of corporate scandals and blunders made by high-profile leaders. When authentic leaders find their "true north" or moral compass, they are more focused on empowering their employees, forming meaningful relationships, and fostering an ethical environment.[44] Authentic leadership has been associated with improved job performance, increased job satisfaction, greater trust in the leader/follower relationship, and organizational commitment.[45]

Authentic leadership: A pattern of leadership behavior based on honesty, practicality, and ethicality

Spiritual Leadership

Spiritual leadership is a values-based style of leadership that motivates employees through faith, hope, and vision and encourages positive social emotions such as forgiveness and gratitude.[46] The concept of spirituality is not necessarily connected with religion; rather it is communicated in the workplace through shared values, attitudes, and behaviors.

Spiritual leadership: A values-based style of leadership that motivates employees through faith, hope, and vision and encourages positive social emotions such has forgiveness and gratitude

Richard Murphy's legacy of servant leadership lives on in successful programs like the Harlem Children's Zone in New York, providing services for children and families in need.

Frances Roberts / Alamy Stock Photo

Spiritual leaders use their charisma to unite followers and to encourage them to view their roles as an opportunity for growth and meaningful contribution. Spiritual leadership may be linked to higher organizational commitment and productivity.[47]

Servant Leadership

Servant leadership is a pattern of leadership that places an emphasis on employees and the community rather than on the leader.[48] Servant leaders share their power and tend to "lead from behind," ensuring the team (not the leader) receives recognition for hard work. They are usually empathic, good listeners, perceptive, and committed to growth in the organization and the community. Servant leadership has been connected with high morale, loyalty, and ethics.

Richard Murphy (1944–2013) is a good example of a servant leader. Murphy, at one time New York City's commissioner of youth services, founded the Harlem Children's Zone in New York and created numerous other community learning centers to serve thousands of city students after school hours. He was also the innovator of groundbreaking ideas such as a youth helpline. Uninterested in earning profit or being in the public eye, Murphy was primarily motivated to ensure the well-being of children in disadvantaged areas. Behind the scenes, he championed and supported other leaders and spent his life fighting for social change.[49]

Ethical Leadership

Ethical Leadership

Ethical leadership is a means of influencing others through personal values, morals, and beliefs.[50] By following their own values as well as the organization's values, ethical leaders are role models for ethical conduct. They communicate honestly and openly about the importance of ethical behavior and hold their followers accountable for failing to uphold organizational values, often rewarding those who consistently demonstrate ethical behavior. Typically, they are fair, honest, principled people who excel at making fair, balanced decisions and who practice what they preach. Casey Sheahan, CEO of outdoor-wear company Patagonia, is an example of an ethical leader who works hard to ensure the company not only produces great products but also donates millions of dollars to conservation causes in order to protect the environment.[51]

Servant leadership: A pattern of leadership that places an emphasis on employees and the community rather than on the leader

Ethical leadership: A means of influencing others through personal values, morals, and beliefs

Let's return to our OB case to see how Langston's work with Svetlana has proceeded. Much to Langston's surprise, Svetlana is amendable to his suggestion that he apply the knowledge he gained rolling out the customer service plan when he was a trainee to prepare the proposal for introducing and ensuring proficiency with the new information system. Happy that he will have a chance to prove himself so early in his tenure at the bank, Langston prepares the presentation to introduce the new information system in record time. He presents it to Svetlana and after suggesting some small but useful revisions she commends Langston for his good work, Svetlana then informs him she will deliver the presentation to the bank's managers. Although he would have preferred to present his work himself, Langston recognizes that Svetlana is his superior at the bank and far more experienced than he is in giving presentations. He also remembers Jonathan's warning to learn from Svetlana but not get in her way.

A few days later, as Langston watches her walk the managers through his strategy, he can't help but admire Svetlana's flawless delivery. She is charismatic and charming and has the attention of everyone in the room. The managers are receptive but concerned about how they can get their staff trained by the end of the year when the new system goes into operation.

Svetlana responds, "While I appreciate your concerns, the IT staff will give this project the highest priority. There will also be workshops available for employees who require additional training sessions."

The head of customer service says, "But three months is a very short deadline—we already have other end-of-year deadlines to meet." Langston is surprised to see Svetlana's confident smile falter. Suddenly, he has an idea and jumps to his feet.

"I think I have a way of providing additional training assistance," he announces, with as much confidence as he can muster. "Over the past few weeks, I've become something of an expert in the new computer system and I feel confident I could provide additional support as needed."

Sonia cuts in, saying, "I think this is a great idea. I'm sure everyone here would value your assistance." Langston is elated. Svetlana looks irritated, but she has no choice but to agree with Sonia.

Over the next three months, Langston pays close attention to the range of leadership styles applied in each of the departments where he helps train employees. He is convinced that high rates of job satisfaction and productivity are related to the way the departments are run. By the end of the three months, Langston and the IT staff have managed to train every bank employee on the new computer system without preventing them from performing daily tasks or accomplishing year-end goals. Langston has loved every minute of it—but the training project is over, and he will now be back under the watchful eye of Svetlana. He is determined to make the best of this situation, but how?

THINKING CRITICALLY

1. Consider each of the four types of values-based leaders (authentic, spiritual, servant, and ethical). Is each style equally applicable to all organizations or do certain types lend themselves to particular types of organizations, like nonprofits or religious entities? Defend your answer. **[Analyze/Evaluate]**

2. Which type of values-based leader would you prefer to follow? Why? **[Analyze/Evaluate]**

3. Based on Langston's attitude towards Svetlana and their interactions so far in the chapter, what do you predict will happen when Langston reports to Svetlana directly and has not been tasked with a project by Sonia? To what extent is it up to Langston to ensure his relationship with Svetlana is successful? To what extent is it up to Svetlana to keep Langston motivated and enthusiastic about his work? **[Analyze/Evaluate]**

CROSS-CULTURAL LEADERSHIP

11.8 Discuss leadership across cultures

Cross-cultural leadership is the process of leading across different cultures. Many companies and organizations of all sizes employ people from different cultural backgrounds, have branches in other countries, outsource parts of their business abroad, or use foreign suppliers. For example, General Electric outsources nearly 50 percent of its business overseas, and Walmart has opened stores all over the world, hiring 100,000 employees outside the United States to manage the new stores.[52] For 21st century leaders to lead effectively, they need to be proficient at managing people from different cultural backgrounds.

Project GLOBE (Global Leadership and Organizational Behavior Effectiveness) is the largest research study to date on cross-cultural leadership.[53] Conducted over the course of 11 years, the project surveyed 17,300 managers from 951 organizations, in 62 societal cultures, and relied on about 140 country coinvestigators. It concluded that individuals from different cultures or "societal clusters" associate certain sets of beliefs or preconceived notions with leaders. This is in line with *implicit leadership theory* or ILT, which explains our tendency as individuals to assign personality characteristics, skills, and behaviors to certain leaders. Our personal belief systems (also referred to as prototypes, mental models, and stereotypes) are thus thought to influence the extent to which we accept leaders. The GLOBE project researchers wanted to discover whether societal and organizational culture has a bearing on how people perceive leadership. In short, they tested the same concept as ILT but on a universal level.

The key findings of the GLOBE project centered around six global leadership attributes perceived by business people worldwide to either contribute to or inhibit leadership; these are known as *culturally endorsed leadership theory* or CLT.[54]

The six dimensions of the CLT leadership profiles (see Table 11.3) are[55]

- **Charismatic/Value-based.** This dimension captures the leader's capacity to inspire, motivate, and expect high performance outcomes from others. All cultures believed this CLT profile to be a key contributor to outstanding leadership.
- **Team oriented.** Team orientation highlights effective team building and the implementation of a common purpose or goal among team members. Again, all cultures surveyed found this dimension to be a major contributor to outstanding leadership.
- **Participative.** This CLT describes the extent to which managers engage others in making and implementing decisions.
- **Humane oriented.** The leadership dimension that signifies supportive, considerate compassionate and generous leadership was thought to be only a moderate contributor to outstanding leadership across all the cultures.
- **Autonomous.** This CLT describes independent and individualistic leadership. Unlike the other dimensions, autonomous leadership is thought to impede or only slightly facilitate outstanding leadership.
- **Self-protective.** This leadership dimension describes the self-interests of the leader in terms of face saving, safety, and security and is generally reported to inhibit outstanding leadership.

The findings of GLOBE's empirical study (illustrated in Table 11.3) have improved our knowledge of what professionals across 62 societies perceive to be the key contributors to outstanding leadership. This evidence is essential to today's leaders who will be expected to exhibit cross-cultural skills in most aspects of their roles.

Cross-cultural leadership: The process of leading across cultures

	CLT Leadership Dimensions					
Societal Cluster	**Charismatic/ Value-Based**	**Team-Oriented**	**Participative**	**Humane Oriented**	**Autonomous**	**Self-Protective**
Eastern Europe	M	M	L	M	**H**/H	H
Latin America	H	**H**	M	M	**L**	M/H
Latin Europe	M/H	M	M	L	L	M
Confucian Asia	M	M/H	L	M/H	M	H
Nordic Europe	H	M	H	**L**	M	**L**
Anglo	**H**	M	H	H	M	L
Sub-Sahara Africa	M	M	M	H	L	M
Southern Asia	H	M/**H**	L	**H**	M	**H**/H
Germanic Europe	H	M/L	**H**	M	H/**H**	L
Middle East	**L**	L	L	M	M	H/**H**

■ TABLE 11.3 Summary of Comparisons for CLT Leadership Dimensions

SOURCE: Javidan, Mansour, Peter W. Dorfman, Mary Sully De Luque, and Robert J. House. "In the Eye of the Beholder: Cross Cultural Lessons in Leadership from Project GLOBE." *Academy of Management Perspectives* 20, no. 1 (February 2006): 67–90.

NOTE: For letters separated by a /, the first letter indicates rank with respect to the absolute score, second letter with respect to a response bias corrected score.

H = HIGH RANK; M = MEDIUM RANK; L = LOW RANK.

H OR L (BOLD) INDICATES HIGHEST OR LOWEST CLUSTER SCORE FOR A SPECIFIC CLT DIMENSION.

LEADERSHIP AND GENDER

11.9 Identify gender issues in the context of leadership

Gender inequality remains a source of much discussion and debate. Although more women are achieving leadership positions, there is no doubt that in the United States and other countries they are still underrepresented in the higher levels of organizations. For example, while women make up just over 50% of the U.S. population, there are only 13 women among the 200 highest-paid CEOs in the United States and only 27 women CEOs in the Fortune 1000.[57]

Studies suggest that gender inequality in organizations is due to several likely causes.[58]

Leadership style and expectations. Some studies suggest that men and women differ in their overall leadership styles. Men tend to be autocratic while women employ a more transformational style.[59] Given widespread expectations of leaders employing more traditionally masculine styles of leadership, women may be perceived as less suited for leadership positions. In cases where women do embrace more autocratic styles, however, they may be perceived more negatively than a man displaying similar characteristics. More of today's leaders, regardless of gender, are adopting a participative approach to leadership because it is considered to be more effective. This trend may help to accelerate the promotion of more women to leadership positions.

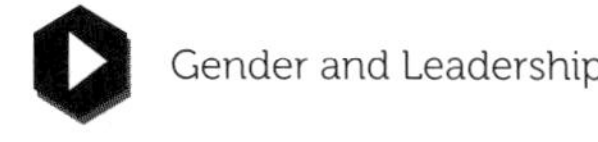

Family and career demands. The burden of balancing domestic and child and elder care responsibilities with work falls heavily on women.[60] In fact, the United States is the only developed country in the world that doesn't guarantee paid maternal leave.

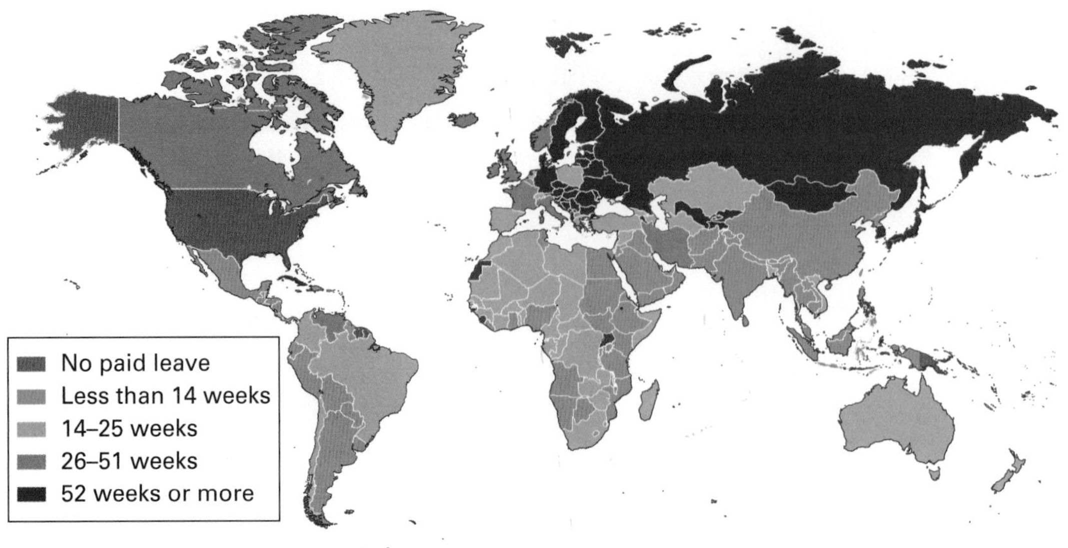

FIGURE 11.8 Maternity Leave Policies Around the World

SOURCE: © 2015 WORLD Policy Analysis Center. Retrieved from http://worldpolicycenter.org/policies/is-paid-leave-available-to-mothers-and-fathers-of-infants.

As Figure 11.8 shows, it shares this policy only with Papua New Guinea, Suriname, and five small Pacific Island nations.[61]

Studies also find that employers may elect not to assign more challenging tasks to women because of assumed domestic responsibilities.[61] Less challenging work assignments generally result in fewer promotions and contribute to the glass ceiling effect discussed in Chapter 2.

Professional networks. Another line of research suggests that women who juggle familial and work duties have less time for socializing with colleagues and building professional networks.[62] When career advancement depends largely on who you know, inability to network can be a drag on advancement. However, even when women devote time to building relationships outside work, they may still face an uphill struggle—many of the most powerful and instrumental organizational networks are composed of men who typically engage in male-bonding activities. Walmart, for example, was sued for gender discrimination because it promoted male-oriented activities such as quail hunting and visiting strip clubs and Hooters restaurants.[63]

Discrimination and stereotypes. Discrimination and stereotypical views of women may provide barriers to advancement.[64] Over the decades, numerous sexual harassment cases have been brought in which women have been passed over for promotion in favor of their male counterparts, and many more instances have gone unreported. In a recent high-profile lawsuit, former employee Ellen Pao sued Silicon Valley venture capital firm Kleiner Perkins Caufield & Byers for gender discrimination and dismissal and lost. Still, the case has raised questions about the treatment of women in the workplace and shone a spotlight on the lack of gender diversity among venture capital firms.[66]

Many people still possess traditional views equating leadership with men rather than women. These views place women in a difficult position: Should they exhibit "male" behaviors (like being tough and task oriented) to get ahead? Or should they embrace the perceived "feminine" behaviors in supporting and encouraging their followers? There is no easy answer to this. We argue that nobody, regardless of gender, should have to conform to any stereotype to carry out a role effectively. Ultimately, it is attitudes and perceptual distortions that need to be altered, not leadership styles.

Organizations can play a big part in challenging these patterns. For example, they can:

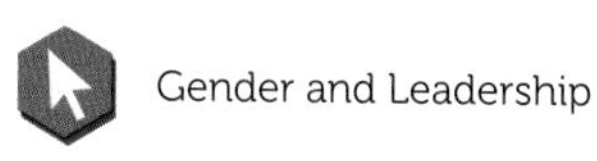

Eliminate prejudice. Organizations can raise awareness of the stereotypes and prejudices toward women leaders through diversity training and workshops. However, managers throughout the organization must also reinforce these lessons. Cultural change begins at the top.

Adjust evaluation process. Many organizations assess employee performance by measuring the number of hours people work rather than by the quality of the work they produce. This tends to skew results, because the employee who works late into the night might not be as productive as the employee who leaves at 5:00 p.m. to pick up the kids from child care. In fact, some employees put in extra-long hours to impress the boss with their commitment or to catch up on work they have neglected to do during the day. Organizations need to assess performance more objectively.

Adopt open-recruitment methods. Organizations need to be transparent in their recruitment by hiring through external agencies and advertising. Internal recruitment should also be as visible as possible to reduce informal processes that can favor male employees over female employees.

Redress the balance. Organizations can make active efforts to recruit and promote women to leadership positions. A higher proportion of women in senior roles will result in less focus on their gender and more on their individual abilities.

Encourage networking. Socializing and network building are key to career advancement. Organizations can provide more opportunities for informal socializing and encourage all employees to participate. They can also establish mentoring programs to help women take advantage of networking opportunities and create new ones.

Provide management opportunities. If organizations do not provide an opportunity for employees to develop the skills and knowledge required for promotion, employees will find it difficult to advance to the next level. They may instead be forced to change companies to find more challenging roles with broader responsibility and better compensation.

Establish family-friendly practices. The high cost of full-time child care can work out to more than an average working salary, leading many working parents to question the point of having one parent work at all. More women are leaving traditional organizations to pursue entrepreneurial ventures or to work for more flexible companies that allow employees to create their own hours. For example, woman-led Geller Law Group believes its employees can still have plenty of family time with their children without giving up their legal careers.[67] However, organizations can encourage both parents to stay in the traditional workforce by providing flextime, job sharing, telecommuting, child care benefits, and on-site child care. Allowing both parents to work more flexible hours helps them balance the vigorous demands of children with a working life.

Encourage men to use family-friendly benefits. Although parental leave and part-time work provide valuable support to mothers, taking advantage of them can also delay career progression. To even the playing field, organizations should encourage men to choose these options if desired, giving more women the opportunity to access managerial roles.

Allow time to achieve. Some organizations expect employees to ascend the career ladder at a rapid pace and ask those who do not keep up—often those with parental responsibilities—to leave. This is not to say employees with children are not capable of performing as well as those without children; they are simply unable to put in the same hours. Firms should capitalize on their initial investment in employees by giving the parents of young children—especially young mothers, who typically bear greater child-care responsibilities—more time to prove themselves and achieve promotion.

Keep the door open. Organizations should stay in touch with high-performing women who leave their roles because of changing personal circumstances. Keeping the lines of communication with former employees open conveys a message that it is still possible to return to work if and when the situation allows.

Although more progress is needed, organizations clearly have a variety of options for fostering a more gender diverse workforce. Achieving more representative numbers of women in leadership positions will encourage nuanced assessments of individual leadership styles.

THINKING CRITICALLY

1. Do you agree with the section's argument that the underrepresentation of women in organizational leadership positions is a problem? Why or why not? **[Evaluate]**
2. Rank the causes of workplace gender discrimination in order of highest impact to lowest impact. Defend your ranking. Do you believe that any causes of gender discrimination are missing from the discussion? **[Analyze/Evaluate]**
3. Rank the proposed solutions to workplace gender discrimination from highest impact to lowest impact. Defend your ranking. **[Analyze/Evaluate]**

Visit **edge.sagepub.com/neckob** to help you accomplish your coursework goals in an easy-to-use learning environment.

- Mobile-friendly **eFlashcards** and **practice quizzes**
- **Video** and **multimedia content**
- A complete online **action plan**
- **Chapter summaries** with **learning objectives**
- EXCLUSIVE! Access to full-text **SAGE journal articles**

SAGE edge™

IN REVIEW

Learning Objectives

11.1 Explain the basic concept of leadership

Leadership is a process of providing general direction, from a position of influence, to individuals or groups toward the successful attainment of goals. Effective leaders today are most likely to be critical thinkers who lead from a position of influence rather than power, and who use their decision-making, motivational, and communication skills to inspire others with their vision in order to generate results.

11.2 Distinguish between formal and informal leadership and between leadership and management

A formal leader such as a CEO is designated by the organization, whereas an informal leader does not have a formal designation but may still be perceived by others as a leader. Leaders create visions, introduce change, and influence others to achieve goals, while managers maintain the status quo, promote stability, and ensure the smooth running of operations.

11.3 Contrast the four basic types of leadership

Directive leadership is characterized by implementing guidelines, providing information on what is expected, setting definite performance standards, and ensuring that individuals follow rules. **Transactional leadership** is a behavioral type of leadership that proposes that employees are motivated by goals and equitable rewards. **Visionary leadership** uses charisma to encourage followers to share in the mission and commit to and work towards the desired goal. **Empowering leadership** shifts the focus from the leader to the follower through the idea of self-leadership.

11.4 Describe the trait, behavioral, and contingency leadership perspectives

The **trait leadership perspective** explores the relationship between leaders and personal qualities and characteristics, and how we differentiate leaders from non leaders. It assumes effective leaders are born, not made. The **behavioral leadership perspective** proposes that specific behaviors distinguish leaders from non leaders. Subsequently, the **contingency leadership perspective** suggests the effectiveness of the leader relates to the interaction of the leader's traits or behaviors and situational factors.

11.5 Compare the inspirational, relational, and follower-centered leadership perspectives

Although early leadership perspectives enhanced our understanding of leadership and follower behavior, inspirational and relational leadership perspectives built on these theories to examine how leaders motivate and build relationships with followers to achieve performance beyond expectations. More recently, there has been a shift from a leadership-centric to a follower-centered approach.

11.6 Discuss the power-distributing leadership perspectives of empowering, shared, and self-leadership

Empowering leadership gives or delegates power to employees that motivates and inspires them to achieve goals. **Shared leadership** distributes influence among groups and individuals to achieve organizational or team goals, or both. **Self-leadership** is a process through which people intentionally influence their thinking and behavior to achieve their objectives, using behavior-focused strategies, natural reward strategies, and constructive thought pattern strategies.

11.7 Describe the values-based leadership perspectives of authentic, spiritual, servant, and ethical leadership

Authentic leadership is a pattern of leadership behavior based on honesty, practicality and ethicality. **Spiritual leadership** is a values-based style of leadership that motivates employees through faith, hope, and vision and encourages positive social emotions such as forgiveness and gratitude. The concept of spirituality is not necessarily connected with religion; rather it is communicated in the workplace through shared values, attitudes, and behaviors. **Servant leadership** emphasizes employees and the community rather than the leader. Servant leaders share their power and are empathic, good listeners, perceptive, and committed to growth in the organization and the community. **Ethical leadership** is the influence of others through personal values, morals, and beliefs.

11.8 Discuss leadership across cultures

Cross-cultural leadership is the process of leading across different cultures. The key findings of the GLOBE project centered around six global leadership attributes: (1) charismatic/value-based, (2) team-oriented, (3) participative, (4) humane oriented, (5) autonomous, and (6) self-protective.

11.9 Identify gender issues in the context of leadership

Although more women are achieving leadership positions, they are still under-represented in higher levels of organizations around the world. Factors that contribute to gender inequality are leadership style, the unequal burden of family and career demands, unequal access to professional networks, discrimination, and stereotypes.

KEY TERMS

Out-group exchange 282
Participating 278
Participative leadership 279
Path–goal leadership theory 279
Production-oriented leader 271
Self-leadership 287
Selling 278
Servant leadership 290
Shared leadership 287
Situational leadership model 278
Spiritual leadership 289
Subordinate characteristics 280
Substitutes for leadership model 280
Supportive leadership 279
Task characteristics 280
Task structure 276
Telling 278
Trait leadership perspective 272
Transactional leadership 271
Visionary leadership 271

THINKING CRITICALLY ABOUT THE CASE OF LANGSTON BURROWS

Put yourself in Langston Burrows' position as a bank trainee and consider the five critical-thinking steps in relation to the types of leadership he exhibits and encounters at the bank.

OBSERVE

Make a list of the leadership behaviors Langston, Sonia, and Svetlana exhibit in the course of the chapter. Make a list, as well, of the behaviors Jonathan Hicks, Langston' s friend, describes in relation to a former manager, Chuck Branston. How does each character treat peers, direct reports, and superiors? Which characters are more autocratic or collaborative in working style? To what extent do they support the company's goals or their own goals?

INTERPRET

At the beginning of the case, Langston worries that he is too quiet and "easygoing" to be an effective leader. To what extent are his reservations appropriate given the core leadership traits identified by research (drive, desire to lead, integrity, self-confidence, cognitive ability, knowledge of a domain, openness to new experiences, extraversion)? Rank Sonia, Svetlana, and Chuck Branston according to each trait. What can Langston learn from each of these three leaders as he develops his own leadership abilities and style?

ANALYZE

Based on the leadership behaviors you listed for the four characters and how you ranked them according to leadership traits, discuss where each of the four characters would fall according to the following leadership approaches:

- The four basic types of leaders (see Table 11.1)
- The Blake Mouton Leadership Grid (see Figure 11.2)
- Hersey and Blanchard's Situational Leadership Model (Telling, Selling, Participating, or Delegating)

To what extent does each approach allow for similar labeling of each character across models?

EVALUATE

Based on your responses above and the discussions of contemporary and power-distributing leadership perspectives, which of the four characters (Langston, Sonia, Svetlana, Chuck) would you be most eager to report to as a new, inexperienced member of a team? Which would you be most eager to report to as an experienced team member with no ambition to move up in the organization? Which would you be most eager to report to as an experienced employee eager for additional challenges and promotions?

EXPLAIN

Describe your own personal leadership style or the style you aspire to attain with more experience. What situations and types of followers would you have the most difficulty managing based on your natural inclinations and approach?

EXERCISE 11.1: THE MISSING WRENCH

It is nighttime and the huge aircraft carrier is headed into the wind. Operations are in full swing, with planes being launched and recovered at the rate of one every 75 seconds. This training exercise is being evaluated and scored by a team of external observers, including the carrier group admiral. The aircraft carrier captain is new to his position, having been in command for only about three weeks. Everyone is aware that the score on this exercise will reflect on his ability to lead the ship.

Eventually, the captain, the admiral, and the other observers retire to their quarters, while the operations continue into the night. There is a special tension among the crew who know how important this operation is to their new captain. Meanwhile, down in the bowels of the ship, a young seaman who is an apprentice mechanic is finishing his shift and checking his tools off on a checklist as he returns them to their cabinet. Suddeny he feels his stomach tighten. He is missing a wrench. He briefly considers forgetting about it and turning in for the night, but then he thinks better of it and informs his chief petty officer. Within minutes, word of the missing wrench has gone up the chain of command and the air boss orders launch operations suspended.

Now you may be wondering, "Why all this fuss about a missing wrench?" But the young seaman had been working on the flight deck earlier in the evening and could have left his wrench there. It could have been sucked into an aircraft engine during launch and would cause a crash. A walkdown of the deck is ordered, in which officers and enlisted men walk shoulder to shoulder down the enormous deck looking for debris, in this case the missing wrench. Because of this delay, the ship's performance on the exercise is ruined.

The next morning, a marine escorts the young seaman to the bridge where he comes to attention before the captain. The captain surveys the young man, takes a deep breath, and says . . .

What should the captain say? What would you say if you were captain?

Consider the following four possible reactions by the captain.

1. You screwed up! I'm going to make an example out of you. You'll stand trial for this.
2. You're paid to do your job, and I expect you to do it right!
3. We must remember our mission! We're here to protect our country. Each one of us must do our job if we are to fulfill our mission!
4. I want to congratulate you for reporting that missing wrench. I know it would have been easy to ignore it, but you faced up to it and you did your duty. You did the right thing. I know you're the kind of person we can count on to make this ship the best in the Navy.

Which of these statements do you think would be appropriate for this situation? Why?

Match each of the statements above with one of the following leadership types by writing the appropriate number in the space provided:

________ **Transformational leadership** creates and communicates a higher-level vision in a charismatic way that elicits an emotional response and commitment from the followers.

________ **Transactional leadership** assumes employees are motivated by goals and equitable rewards.

________ **Empowering leadership** shifts the focus from the leader to the follower through the idea of self-leadership.

________ **Directive leadership** provides specific task-focused directions, giving commands, assigning goals, and providing close supervision and continual follow-up.

In this real-life situation, the captain responded with statement number 4. By the next day, his leadership response was known all over the ship. His crew was now 100 percent commited to their new captain and he had a very successful tour of duty.

Additional Questions for Reflection

What might have happened if the captain had chosen another approach, say statement number 1 (a very traditional leadership reaction in the military)? What would happen the next time someone lost a wrench? Would he or she report it? Is is possible to blend one or more of these approaches? If so, which two might work well together?

SOURCE: This exercise was created based on a story contained in Sims Jr., Henry P., and Charles C. Manz. *Company of Heroes: Unleashing the Power of Self-Leadership* (New York: Wiley, 1996).

EXERCISE 11.2: LEADERSHIP JOLT

Objectives:

This exercise will help you to better explain basic leadership concepts.

Instructions:

While standing in line and talking about your organizational behavior class with some friends at a local coffee house, the person in front of you overhears and asks you a question about leadership. She is the head of a moderate sized, but extremely well connected office supply company and wants to improve the leadership of her managers. She asks you what the most important leadership concept is for making improvements in workplace outcomes, and also says that many other CEOs she knows would be interested in having a presentation on the same subject. She turns around to pay for and pick up her order, so you have a few minutes to collect your thoughts. But you also know that she will not have too long to listen to you idea, and this is your chance to make some very good contacts for your future career.

Step 1. Choose the leadership concept you feel is the most useful for improving workplace outcomes. Write an overview of this concept, what outcomes can be improved by adopting the leadership behavior, and why it is practical to try and model the leadership behavior. (5 minutes)

Step 2. Be prepared to present your description to the class. (1 to 3 minutes)

Reflection Questions:

1. How did framing a description of a leadership concept in terms of a persuasive presentation change your view of the concept?
2. What new insights did you gain from having to make such a succinct overview of the concept?
3. What new ways of applying the concept did you discover through this process?
4. What surprised you most about your classmates´ presentations?

Exercise contributed by Milton R. Mayfield, Professor of Business, Texas A&M International University and Jaqueline R. Mayfield, Professor of Business, Texas A&M International University.

EXERCISE 11.3: THE CHALLENGE OF LEADERSHIP

Objectives:

Successful completion of this exercise will help you to better explain basic leadership concepts, and distinguish between formal and informal leadership.

Instructions:

Step 1. Select a person that you feel is (or was) a leader in an organization, but did not have a formal leadership position. (This person should be someone that you have had personal interactions with.)

Develop an argument about why that person was a leader using chapter concepts and terms. In your description, make sure that you describe the circumstances and environment relevant to this person´s informal leadership role. (5 minutes)

Step 2. Find two other people and select one person to act as a judge. (If no one wants to volunteer, select the person who has had the most recent birthday.) Have each of the contestants present her or his argument for the selected person being an informal leader. If someone selects a person who actually holds a formal leadership role, that person is automatically disqualified. Otherwise, judge the arguments based on how well the argument is supported with chapter concepts.

The judge should award each person 1 point for every argument that is supported by a relevant chapter concept. If no concept is used for support, or if a concept is used incorrectly, then the person has one point deducted from her or his score. After each person has had a chance to present her or his argument, then the judge should tally the scores. Whoever has the highest score wins. In case of a tie, the winner is the person who has the highest proportion of supported arguments to total arguments. (10 to 15 minutes)

Step 3. The judge should be prepared to present the winning person´s argument to the class. (5 minutes)

Reflection Questions:

1. What new insights did you learn about informal leadership?
2. Did you notice any recurring circumstances that lead to someone becoming an informal leader?
3. What were the aspects of informal leadership that surprised you?

Exercise contributed by Milton R. Mayfield, Professor of Business, Texas A&M International University and Jaqueline R. Mayfield, Professor of Business, Texas A&M International University.

CASE STUDY 11.1: LEADERSHIP AT CAMPBELL SOUP COMPANY

When Douglas Conant took the helm as CEO of Campbell Soup Company in 2001, the iconic American brand was in hot water. The family-owned giant founded in 1869 suffered from slowing sales, and it was losing its leadership position in its hallmark product category: soup. Conant stepped into a shareholder's nightmare: the company's share price had sunk from a high of $60 in 1998 to $30, layoffs were ongoing, and morale was abysmal. Yet under his leadership, the company experienced a remarkable turnaround. Conant sold off business units that didn't make sense (like Godiva Chocolatier) and updated Campbell's existing offerings to make them more palatable to changing consumer tastes. He improved Campbell's diversity and inclusion practices and made Campbell's a great place to work again. The result: sales, earnings, and market share rose nearly every year with Conant in the driver's seat. "I can walk away proud of what we've done and excited about the future," Conant said upon his departure.

Conant talked often of the idea of "winning" on two fronts: in the workplace and in the market. And Denise Morrison, his successor and longtime protégé, has continued his winning streak. Before Campbell's, Morrison had built a reputation at companies such as Procter & Gamble, PepsiCo, Nestlé, and Nabisco; she followed her mentor from Nabisco in 2003. Before replacing him as CEO, she had worked closely with Conant as Campbell's president of North American soup, sauces, and beverages. (Some of Campbell's most important products, along with its ubiquitous Campbell's Soup, include Pepperidge Farm, V8 juices, and Prego spaghetti sauce.)

Despite Morrison's experience, sales had softened slightly around the time she took over as CEO; Campbell's needed to continue to innovate in a rapidly changing, highly competitive market. For a company nearing its 141st birthday, that wasn't the easiest thing to achieve. "The first thing I did," says Morrison, "was add the value of courage to our core values. And in doing that, I encouraged people to take bolder moves and bigger risks—all with the highest integrity—but to think outside the box, to push it a little bit harder and further—always putting the consumer first. But not being afraid to fail and make mistakes; that was a very symbolic, and a very aspirational value for us."

Morrison also recognized that the consensus-building atmosphere Conant had encouraged—which had been important for rebuilding the bruised morale of the recent past—was not conducive to speed or necessary for the nimble, innovative company Morrison envisioned. She had to "stress the importance of driving decision making. We were a culture that spent a lot of time driving alignment, which meant we were talking to each other—and it slowed us down. And some decision making requires alignment, and some doesn't. And so, making that determination and figuring out who has the decision . . . We trained all of our leaders on how to do that. And now we get in the room, we make decisions, and we go."

Morrison made sure to set the tone of her leadership early on by modeling the behavior she wanted her employees to adopt. "You can't expect your organization to behave a certain way that you're not willing to behave." When the company made acquisitions, she was front and center. "I spend a lot of time with the innovation teams, calling out the importance of what I call the 'bold moves, innovation, international expansion, package fresh, and availability.'"

In February 2014, Morrison unveiled the fruits of her labor: a bold strategy that promised to deliver more than $1 billion in sales. The plan included expanding Campbell's line of convenient Skillet and Slow Cooker Sauces, debuting Campbell's Oven Sauces, and extending the company's line of premium soups with products like Slow Kettle, Gourmet Bisques, and the Go! line. The hope was to woo younger shoppers along with the more affluent.

Morrison had also overseen Campbell's 2012 acquisition of Bolthouse Farms and announced that Campbell's would be offering Bolthouse's all-natural smoothies at new locations such as convenience stores, drugstores, and schools. Bolthouse helps Campbell tap into the consumer demand for fresh and healthy options, as does Campbell's own venerable juice product, V8. Bolthouse Farms salad dressings and juices would also be entering the market, Morrison announced.

Campbell's is aiming at new international markets. Asia and Latin America are key targets, and the company's acquisition of the Danish snack maker Kelsen Group expanded its presence in China and Hong Kong, which generates almost 40 percent of Kelsen sales.

It's no piece of cake being in the food and beverage business these days. As Morrison put it, a "seismic social change" has disrupted the industry: from changing demographics to explosive growth in packaged fresh food and e-commerce to emerging channels like clubs and dollar stores, the consumer landscape is in continual shift. Consumers want more choices, too; they are more demanding and knowledgeable about their options, and they're voting with their pocketbooks. "These factors are affecting all food companies," Morrison said. "It is not easy today for any company to keep its balance and sense of direction." Morrison's secret sauce? "Those who understand and embrace change can succeed."

Case Questions

1. Describe the type of leader Douglas Conant was when he became CEO of Campbell Soup Company.
2. Describe the type of empowering leadership perspective Denise Morrison used as CEO of Campbell Soup Company.
3. How did Denise Morrison utilize spiritual leadership when she wanted to see employees take bigger risks?

Sources

Marcus, Bonnie. "Campbell Soup CEO Denise Morrison Stirs the Pot to Create Cultural Change" April 25, 2014. www.forbes.com/sites/bonniemarcus/2014/04/25/campbell-soup-ceo-denise-morrison-stirs-the-pot-to-create-cultural-change/.

Skidmore, Sarah. "Campbell CEO Douglas Conant to Step Down in July," *Boston.com*. September 28, 2010. www.boston.com/business/articles/2010/09/28/campbell_ceo_douglas_conant_to_step_down_in_july/.

Stephens, Robert. "Why Campbell Soup Could Be a Winner Rain or Shine." *Motley Fool*. May 15, 2014. www.fool.com/investing/general/2014/05/15/why-campbell-soup-could-be-a-winner-come-rain-or-s.aspx.

Watrous, Monica. "Campbell Counting on 'Four Bold Moves.'" *Food Business News*. February 20, 2014. www.foodbusinessnews.net/articles/news_home/Business_News/2014/02/Campbell_counting_on_four_bold.aspx?ID={2FFDDCFD-E897-4EAD-9838-12764EC594CF}.

SELF-ASSESSMENT 11.1

Leadership Type Preference

For each statement, check the circle that best describes your actions when leading others based on the following scale:

	Not at all Accurate	Somewhat Accurate	A little Accurate	Mostly Accurate	Completely Accurate
1. I give followers instructions about how to do their jobs.	O	O	O	O	O
2. When followers perform well, I recommend that they be rewarded.	O	O	O	O	O
3. I provide my followers with a clear vision of where we are going.	O	O	O	O	O
4. I advise followers to solve problems without always seeking my approval.	O	O	O	O	O
5. I establish performance goals for my followers.	O	O	O	O	O
6. I provide special recognition for follower performance that is especially good.	O	O	O	O	O
7. I inspire followers to strive for achievements they normally would not pursue.	O	O	O	O	O
8. I provide followers the opportunity to take initiative on their own.	O	O	O	O	O
9. I am often critical of my followers' work.	O	O	O	O	O
10. I work with my followers to establish performance goals and associated rewards.	O	O	O	O	O

	Not at all Accurate	Somewhat Accurate	A little Accurate	Mostly Accurate	Completely Accurate
11. I am driven by higher purposes or ideals.	O	O	O	O	O
12. I encourage my followers to find their own favorite ways to get their work done.	O	O	O	O	O

Scoring

Directive leadership (add items 1, 5, 9 and write your score in the blank) ___________

Characterized by implementing guidelines, providing information on what is expected, setting definite performance standards, and ensuring that individuals follow rules

Transactional leadership (add items 2, 6, 10 and write your score in the blank) ___________

Proposes that employees are motivated by goals and equitable reward

Offers clear and objective goals for the followers in order to gain compliance

Visionary leadership (add items 3, 7, 11 and write your score in the blank) ___________

Creates visions to motivate, inspire, and stimulate employees using charisma to encourage followers to share a mission resulting in commitment toward a desired goal

Empowering leadership (add items 4, 8, 12 and write your score in the blank) ___________

Helps to develop the individual skills and abilities of followers so that they may utilize these skills to take ownership of their work in order to contribute to organizational performance

What was your strongest leadership type? What are the advantages and disadvantages of this type of leadership?

What was your weakest leadership type? What are the advantages and disadvantages of this type of leadership?

Digital Vision/Photodisc/Thinkstock

12 Influence, Power, Politics

©iStockphoto.com/Izabela Habur

> *The most common way people give up their power is by thinking they don't have any.*
>
> —Alice Walker, American author and activist

POWER: DEFINITION AND OVERVIEW

12.1 Discuss the concept of power and its relationship to leadership

The concept of **power**, the capacity to influence the actions of others, is inextricably linked with leadership.[1] Leaders have power for different reasons. In organizations, some leaders may be perceived as powerful by their followers because of their ability to give raises or bonuses, assign important tasks, or hire and fire. The power of other types of leaders may lie in their professional or technical expertise, or they may have personal qualities that inspire admiration in their followers. Being aware of why you are influenced by someone else helps you recognize your own power, decide whether you want to accept the way the power is being used, and build on your own leadership skills to learn how to be a positive influence in your organization.

However, there are different ways in which leaders can use their influence. For example, in Chapter 11, we learned about the power that authoritarian leaders wield over their followers to force compliance. But we also learned about transactional, transformational, and charismatic leaders, who are just as influential but instead obtain results by initiating shared goals, building meaningful relationships, and gaining the respect and esteem of others.

Indeed, recent psychological research has suggested that coercive power is a less effective method for gaining power, and that *social intelligence*, or our ability to negotiate, resolve conflicts, and understand the goals of others as well as group norms is the key to moving up in hierarchies.[2] Drawing from this theory, "leaders that treat their subordinates with respect, share power, and generate a sense of camaraderie and trust are considered more just and fair."[3] We might conclude that depending on their psychological make-up, different types of leaders may exert their power to influence in different ways, which can lead to positive or negative outcomes.

THINKING CRITICALLY

1. Discuss the relationship of power to leadership. What types of power can formal leaders exert? What types of power can informal leaders exert? **[Apply/Analyze]**
2. Consider the idea that social intelligence is more likely to lead to power than coercive power. Why might that be the case? Under what circumstances and in what areas might coercive power still prove more effective? **[Analyze/Evaluate]**

LEARNING OBJECTIVES

By the end of this chapter, you will be able to:

- 12.1 Discuss the concept of power and its relationship to leadership
- 12.2 Identify the various sources of power
- 12.3 Describe tactics for influencing others
- 12.4 Outline the results of the various influence tactics
- 12.5 Identify the causes and possible consequences of organizational politics

Power and Influence

Power: The capacity to influence the actions of others

Master the content.
edge.sagepub.com/neckob

BASIC SOURCES OF POWER

12.2 Identify the various sources of power

To truly understand the concept of power, we need to explore the underlying sources of power. There are two: organizational power and personal power.[4]

Organizational Power	Personal Power
Legitimate Power	Expert Power
Reward Power	Referent Power
Coercive Power	

■ FIGURE 12.1 Sources of Power

Organizational Power

Organizations are political structures that operate in a system for distributing power and authority among individuals and teams. Depending on how it is used, power can lead to either positive or negative outcomes in an organization.

There are three main aspects of power within organizations:

- **Legitimate power** is the leader's officially sanctioned authority to ask others to do things. For example, an organization such as the military that operates within a hierarchical structure places managers in a position of legitimate power. This means that by virtue of their organizational position managers have the formal authority or power to give orders and approve or deny employee requests.
- **Reward power** is use of incentives to influence the actions of others. For example, a manager may inspire employees by promising salary raises, bonuses, promotions, and so on. For example, Lord Wolfson, CEO of clothing company Next gave his entire annual bonus of $3.6 million to his employees as a reward for their commitment and hard work.[5]

Legitimate power: The degree to which a person has the right to ask others to do things that are considered within the scope of their authority

Reward power: The extent to which someone uses incentives to influence the actions of others

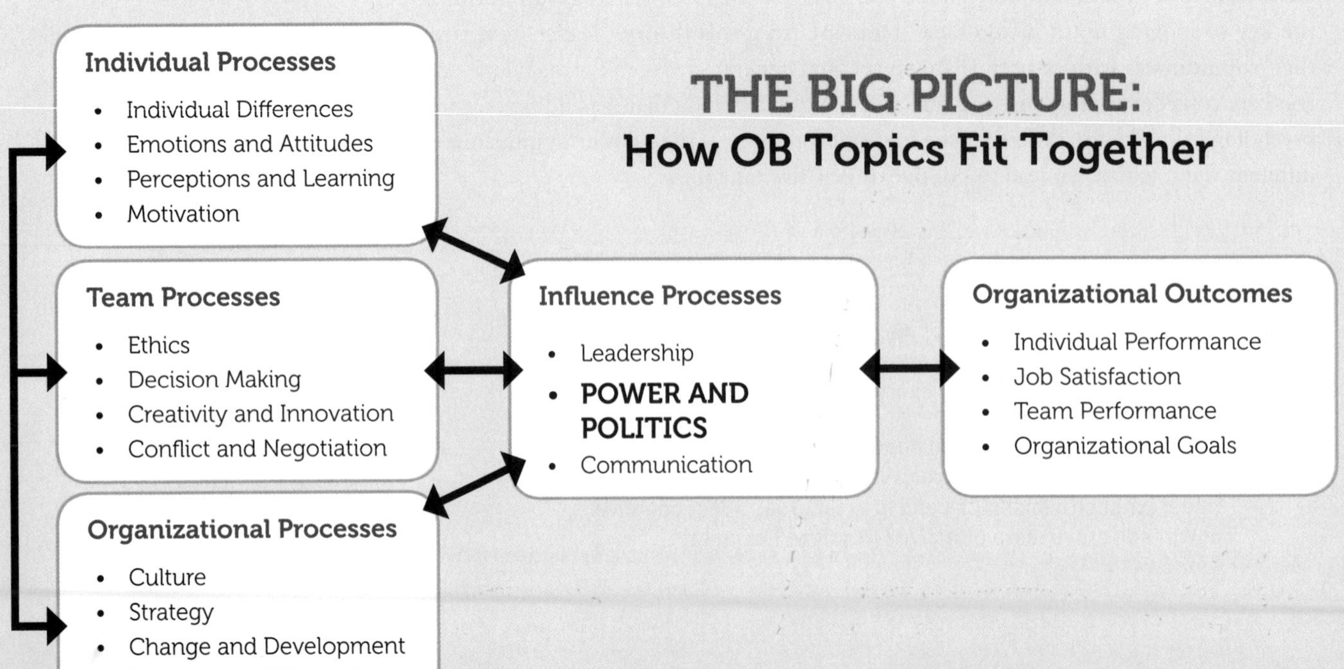

- When used appropriately, reward power can motivate, but if rewards are used unethically or distributed based on favoritism, they can lead to demoralization and apathy.
- **Coercive power** is the means by which a person controls the behavior of others through punishments, threats, or sanctions. For example, a manager might have the power to fire or punish employees if they are perceived as violating the organization's policies and norms. In today's organizations, coercive power is perceived by many leaders as a negative power and is usually used as a last resort.

Rex Features via AP Images

Lord Wolfson, CEO of clothing company Next, used reward power by giving his entire bonus to his employees to reward and reinforce their hard work.

Coercive Power

Personal Power

Personal power comes from within the individual and is independent of the position he or she holds in an organization. Personality and specialist knowledge in a certain area can be useful tools of personal power and influence. There are two main types of personal power:

- **Expert power** is the ability to influence the behavior of others through the possession of knowledge or expertise on which others depend. For example, a team working on a project will look to their leader for guidance if he or she is the one with the knowledge and experience necessary for the task to be done.
- **Referent power** is the influence a leader gains over others when they desire to identify and be associated with him or her. For example, people will naturally gravitate toward a leader who comes across as fair, approachable, and adept at handling certain situations.

Back to the Case of Langston Burrows

When we first met Langston Burrows in Chapter 11, he had just begun a leadership training program in a regional bank. Langston overcame many leadership challenges in his training assignments while acquiring on-the-job-experience that helped him determine his leadership style. After successfully completing his third and final leadership training assignment, he was offered a permanent position in the retail banking services department, working directly for Sonia Valdez, a Vice President at the bank and head of the department. In this capacity he volunteered to manage an employee training program for the bank's new computer system and brought it to a successful conclusion, despite a somewhat rocky relationship with his senior colleague Svetlana Petrova, the head of lending. Let's follow Langston as he takes on his next assignment.

A week into the new year, Langston arrives at Sonia's office for a meeting to discuss his new duties now that the computer training program is complete. Svetlana is already talking with Sonia.

"Langston—good to see you! Please take a seat," says Sonia. "For your next assignment you will be working with Svetlana on our loan exceptions side of retailing banking." Langston nods but doesn't have a clue what loan exceptions are.

As if sensing his uncertainty, Sonia smiles and says, "No need to worry, Langston. I'll explain exactly what you need to do, and you'll have Svetlana as a resource. She'll provide you with all the information and support you need."

Langston is relieved. He admits to Sonia and Svetlana that he has no *expert power* in this assignment and is happy to learn as much as he can. Next, Sonia describes the assignment in detail: Langston is to work with Svetlana on getting loan exceptions, which are problems with existing loans on the banks' books, down by 15 percent across

Coercive power: A strategy by which a person controls the behavior of others through punishments, threats, or sanctions

Expert power: The ability to influence the behavior of others through the amount of knowledge or expertise possessed by an individual on which others depend

Referent power: The degree to which a leader can influence others through their desire to identify and be associated with them

the entire Retail Banking Services division within the next 30 days. He must work with Svetlana to identify the number and nature of the exceptions and then make the rounds to the bank's various retail branches to appeal directly to the lending officers and encourage them to actively reduce their loan exceptions.

"Svetlana, do you have any information to share with Langston that will help him out on this assignment?" Sonia asks.

"Here is a list of all the loan officers in the bank," Svetlana says, handing Langston a sheet of paper. "Most of them have a number of loan exceptions on their books. I need you to match the number of exceptions per officer and then start your visits. There are at least 20 names, so it's a good idea to get started as quickly as possible and speak with each of them over the next two weeks, which will leave an additional two weeks for them to complete their work," Svetlana adds.

Langston regards this assignment as a challenging one and wonders how he should approach it. According to Sonia, loan officers are unlikely to be enthused at the prospect of drilling through their old loan data to clear up existing problems. Langston also lacks the formal authority or *legitimate power* to tell them what to do. He can't rely on *reward power* to influence the lending officers because he is in no position to offer them financial incentives or otherwise. However, Langston comforts himself with the fact he has some *referent power*, judging by the positive response to his final rotational assignment. Since then, a number of employees have approached him for training tips and advice. Yet, the bank lenders don't know him at all, so Langston decides he must find ways to build relationships with them and persuade them to cooperate in this project.

As he and Svetlana are leaving the meeting he decides to stop her. "I'm not entirely sure how to convey the message to the lending officers to clean up their loan exceptions, and I was just wondering how you would handle it."

"That's easy," Svetlana replies. "Just tell them to do what you say or Sonia will fire them. Go get 'em, Langston."

"She seems to be a fan of using *coercive power* in these situations," Langston thinks to himself as he watches Svetlana walk away.

THINKING CRITICALLY

1. Rank the three types of organizational power (legitimate, reward, coercive) and the two types of personal power (expert, referent) in order of most to least likely to yield effective long-term results from employees. Defend your ranking. **[Analyze/Evaluate]**
2. What types of organizational and personal power can Sonia call upon when accomplishing tasks? **[Apply/Analyze]**
3. If Langston had asked Sonia for advice on persuading the loan officers rather than Svetlana, what do you think Sonia would have suggested? **[Evaluate/Create]**

USING POWER: TACTICS FOR INFLUENCING OTHERS

12.3 Describe tactics for influencing others

Langston makes up his mind to put every ounce of effort into bringing the loan exceptions down to prove his worth to Svetlana and Sonia. He needs to choose the most effective influence tactics to persuade the lenders to work with him.

He recalls from an organizational behavior class that he took in college that there are eleven primary tactics for influencing others:[6]

Rational appeals: The use of logic, reason, and evidence to convince another person that cooperation in a task is worthwhile.

Inspirational appeals: The use of emotions to rouse enthusiasm for the task by appealing to the values and ideals of others.

Upward appeals: The argument that the task has been requested by higher management, or a request to higher management to assist in gaining cooperation.

Personal appeals: A request to cooperate on the basis of friendship or as a personal favor.

Consultation: The offer of participation or consultation in the decision-making process.

Exchange: The promise of rewards to persuade another person to cooperate.

Coalition building: Reference to the support of others as a reason for someone to agree to a request.

Ingratiation: An effort to win favor and the good graces of others before making a request.

Silent authority: A passive tactic that relies on unspoken but acknowledged power.

Information control: Withholding key information to influence outcomes.

Assertiveness: The use of demands or threats to persuade someone to carry out a task.

Given his low power situation, Langston chooses ingratiation as his first form of influence. Maybe the loan officers will take pity on him for being so new and inexperienced!

When Langston walks into the first branch on his list to visit, he introduces himself to Trudy, the loan officer.

"Hello, Trudy. My name is Langston Burrows. I'm fresh off the Leadership Development Program and I really need your help!," he says.

Trudy laughs. "Take a seat, Langston. I know what it's like to be new!," she says kindly. "Now, what can I do for you?"

Langston outlines his assignment and brings her through the loan exceptions that have been matched against her name. Trudy listens carefully.

"Thank you for bringing this problem to my attention. I've been so busy that I've dropped the ball on historical data. These exceptions will take no time at all to resolve. I'll make sure I get to it this week," she says.

Langston thanks her for her time and leaves the branch with a spring in his step. "My influence tactic worked!," he thinks delightedly. "That was easier than I thought."

Langston's next call is one he's looking forward to making. The loan officer at this branch is Jonathan Hicks, the friend he consulted about Svetlana's leadership style. Jonathan greets him warmly, and they spend the next few minutes catching up. Finally, Langston tells Jonathan the reason for his visit and shows him the number of loan exceptions Jonathan needs to address.

"You're not the worst offender," Langston tells him, jokingly. "But it would help if you would sort these out!"

Jonathan groans. "Buddy, I don't have time to sift through old data. I'm up to my neck trying to generate new loans, not focus on these dinosaurs," he says.

Langston decides to apply the *personal appeals* approach to see whether he can influence his old friend to complete the task.

"Hey, I get it! It's not a pleasant job, but at the end of the day it has to be done. I'm still new here, and I need to succeed with this assignment. We go back a long way—could you please help me out, please?" Langston coaxes.

Sources of Power

Rational appeals: The use of logic, reason, and evidence to convince another person that cooperation in a task is worthwhile

Inspirational appeals: The use of emotions to raise enthusiasm for the task by appealing to the values and ideals of others

Upward appeals: The argument that the task has been requested by higher management, or a request to higher management to assist in gaining cooperation

Personal appeals: Requests to cooperate on the basis of friendship or as a personal favor

Consultation: The offer of participation or consultation in the decision-making process

Exchange: The promise of rewards to persuade another person to co-operate

Coalition building: Gathering the support of others as a reason for another person to agree to a request

Ingratiation: A strategy of winning favor and putting oneself in the good graces of others before making a request

Silent authority: an influencing tactic that relies on unspoken but acknowledged power

Information control: a hard influencing tactic in which key information is withheld in order to manipulate outcomes

Assertiveness: The use of demands or threats to persuade someone to carry out a task

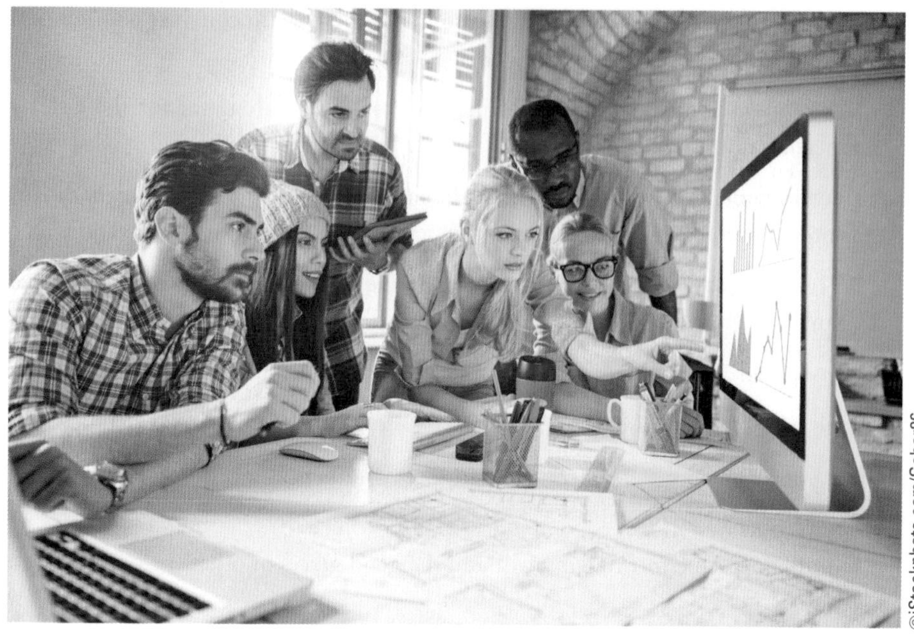
©iStockphoto.com/Geber86

Influencing employees by explaining how their efforts contribute to a greater good is an example of an inspritational appeal.

Jonathan smiles. "Oh all right, but only because you're my friend," he sighs. "The next lunch is on you!"

"Thanks Jonathan!" Langston shakes his hand and they arrange to meet for lunch the next week.

Langston spends the rest of the day visiting three more loan officers. To his surprise, he finds himself using a variety of different influencing tactics. For example, one of the loan officers, Arabella, tells him how stressed out she is at the prospect of cleaning up loan exceptions when she has so much other work to do. Langston feels this is a good time to use the *inspirational appeals* approach, and he describes the vision Sonia has shared with him: reducing the level of loan exceptions will make the bank less exposed to risk. He then tells Arabella how important her efforts and conscientiousness are to the bank. He even finishes with "I know you can do this!" In the end, Arabella agrees, reluctantly, to make time to focus on the exceptions.

In his final two visits of the day Langston draws on *upward appeals* to persuade one loan officer who is skeptical about his authority to make such a request. When Langston mentions that the Vice President of Retail Banking Services, Sonia Valdez, has personally assigned him to this task, the loan officer immediately agrees to address his loan exceptions. Langston also employs the *consultation* tactic with another officer who expresses interest in refining the loan exceptions process. In the end, the loan officer agrees to devote some time to working his way down his list of exceptions.

Langston spends the rest of the week visiting loan officers and making progress through the list of twenty loan officers. The following week, he ends his Thursday with a visit to Judd Siegel, who works in a branch across town. On his way there, Langston reflects on the many tactics he has used successfully in his meetings so far. He concludes that different situations require different influence tactics.

Judd is a senior lending officer. Despite an impressive record for generating new loans, he is also one of the worst offenders for loan exceptions. Langston decides to open with the ingratiation approach and see where it takes him.

"Hi Judd, I'm Langston Burrows. I'm fresh off the Leadership Development Program and I need your help!," he says.

"I have someone coming in for a meeting in two minutes," Judd barks. "What do you want?"

Langston outlines the reasons for his visit, pointing out the high volume of loan exceptions under Judd's name.

"And your point is?" Judd says, looking impatient.

Langston switches to the *rational appeals* approach. "Well, each loan exception exposes the bank to more risk. That's why we need to reduce the levels as soon as possible."

Judd laughs. "Langston, I've been in the lending business for over 15 years. I know it inside out. Do you know what's more important than closing loan exceptions? Generating new loans. And do you know who's the most successful at doing that?"

"You."

"Damn straight. So if you want me to continue to bring in new loans for the bank, don't waste my time telling me to spend precious hours going through old data!"

Langston is getting frustrated. How is he supposed to persuade Judd to do anything? He tries an *appeal to authority.*

"I understand you're very busy, Judd, and very successful at what you do, but this request has come straight from the top. Sonia Valdez has authorized this task with the support of the rest of higher management. I need to report all the findings to Svetlana Petrova. It's out of my hands."

"Is that so?" Judd says, looking at his watch and yawning. "Well, in that case, you can tell Svetlana I would like to talk to her."

Langston is starting to feel annoyed. He doesn't want to allow Judd to go over his head to Svetlana. She will assume he can't handle the situation. Although Langston knows he has no authority to promise any sort of incentives, he opts for the *exchange* tactic.

"I believe the loan officers who comply with this request will be well rewarded," he says.

Judd laughs derisively. "You've only been working here a few months and you look like you're my nephew's age; who do you think you are, making promises like that?"

Langston has had enough. Maybe Svetlana is right: it's time to get coercive.

"Look, Judd, you do your job and get those loan exceptions sorted out, or I'll make sure there are repercussions," Langston says.

Judd looks too surprised to speak. Langston turns and walks out of the office. He has never used the *assertiveness* tactic in any aspect of his life before, and he isn't comfortable with the outcome of the meeting at all.

THINKING CRITICALLY

1. Which influence tactics are more likely to be used by people wielding each type of organizational power (legitimate, reward, coercive)? Which are more likely to be used by people wielding each type of personal power (expert, referent)? Explain your reasoning. **[Apply/Analyze]**

2. To what extent should the type of power you have in an organization affect the influencing tactics you use? Defend your answer. **[Analyze/Evaluate]**

3. Did Langston make a mistake in employing the assertiveness tactic with Judd? Why or why not? **[Evaluate]**

CONSEQUENCES OF INFLUENCE TACTICS

12.4 Outline the results of the various influence tactics

In the previous section, we explored how Langston Burrows used a variety of influence tactics in an effort to complete his assignment. When employed successfully, influence

Compliance is the lowest level of commitment an employee can make as a result of influence tactics. However, compliance is just the right level of commitment an employee needs to make for simple tasks like making photocopies.

©iStockphoto.com/RealDealPhoto

Influence Tactics

tactics can motivate employees, help managers obtain support and resources, and instigate effort, commitment, and cooperation. One of the best ways of choosing the right influence tactic is to understand how people react to different forms of influence. We can explore the effectiveness of an influence tactic by looking at three different possible outcomes: commitment, compliance, and resistance.[7]

Commitment occurs when people are enthusiastic and fully in agreement with an action or decision and are motivated to put in the extra effort to successfully reach a goal. This is the best reaction to an influence tactic.

Compliance occurs when people are indifferent to a task and make only the minimal effort necessary to complete a goal. Although this reaction is not ideal for tasks that require more commitment, compliance has its place, especially when it comes to simple requests. For example, a manager telling an employee to do a routine, monotonous task like scanning a stack of documents may not receive an enthusiastic response, but the task will ultimately get done. In this scenario, compliance may be considered a successful outcome.

Resistance takes place when people oppose the influencer's request by refusing to do it or arguing against carrying out the task. This is the worst reaction to an influence tactic, and it also causes bad feeling and distrust.

In general, people tend to react better to "soft" rather than "hard" tactics. Soft tactics are more likely to result in commitment and are a frequent choice of leaders with personal sources of power such as expert and referent power. In contrast, hard tactics are more likely to generate compliance or resistance, and they are used by leaders with position power such as legitimate, reward, and coercive power.

It's helpful to know which soft influence tactics are the most effective in a given situation and why. For example, people with more knowledge and expertise tend to achieve better results through rational appeals because they have the necessary factual and logical evidence to support their requests. The success of ingratiation, inspirational appeals, or personal appeals largely depends on the sincerity of the person making the request. False behavior displayed by leaders tends to cause their staff to lose respect. Similarly, exchange and consultation as soft influence tactics must be meant sincerely to achieve the desired reaction.

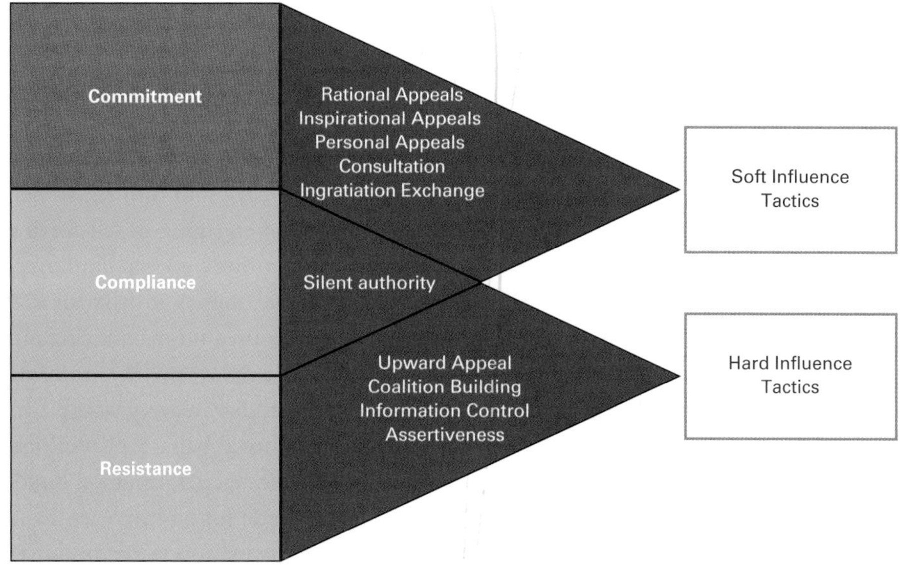

■ FIGURE 12.2 Consequences of Influence Tactics

SOURCE: Based on Falbe, Cecilia M., and Gary Yukl. "Consequences for Managers of Using Single Influence Tactics and Combinations of Tactics." Academy of Management Journal 35, no. 3 (August 1992): 638–652.

Hard and Soft Influence Tactics

What about hard tactics? People with strong legitimate power usually have more success using silent authority to have their requests fulfilled. For example, a CEO of an organization might expect subordinates to immediately carry out his requests even if they might not necessarily agree.

The choice of the most suitable influence tactic depends on personal, organizational, and cultural values. For example, people with an inclination toward power may prefer to use assertiveness to get their demands met, whereas those who prefer to toe the line may seek support from others higher up in the organization through upward appeals. At an organizational level, people in companies with a competitive culture are more likely to build coalitions to protest or debate an issue, or they may deliberately control information to manipulate; both these tactics can generate resistance, and ultimately damage future relationships.

Influence tactics also vary across different cultures. Though extensive studies have been carried out to identify which cultures use certain influence tactics more commonly than others, the results are mixed at best. Some studies suggest information control is more common in Hong Kong than in the United States,[8] while others propose that coalition building is more effective in the United States and Switzerland than in China.[9] Despite these studies, knowledge gaps still exist, and further research is necessary to explain the cultural variations and effectiveness of influence tactics.

THINKING CRITICALLY

1. List at least five sorts of business tasks where commitment would be far better than compliance. List at least five sorts of business tasks where compliance is acceptable and would not damage organizational goals or working relationships. **[Apply/Analyze]**

2. To what extent does an effective leader need to be able to employ both soft and hard influence tactics? Under what circumstances are soft tactics more likely to be effective? Under what circumstances are hard tactics more likely to be effective? **[Analyze/Evaluate]**

ORGANIZATIONAL POLITICS

12.5 Identify the causes and possible consequences of organizational politics

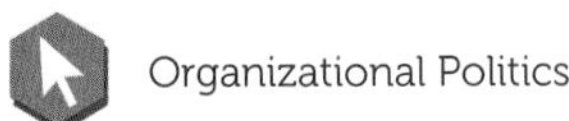
Organizational Politics

The word *politics* often elicits more negative than positive connotations. Popular culture generally portrays politicians as underhanded, power hungry, and ruthless in their ambition to make it to the top. Yet all people are capable of engaging in self-serving behavior. Politics exist wherever there is conflict and competition between employees in the scramble up the career ladder. We define **organizational politics** as behavior that is not formally sanctioned by the organization and that is focused on maximizing our self-interest, often at the expense of the organization or other employees.[10] Whether you choose to engage in it or avoid it, organizational politics is a reality in every workplace.

How do people behave when they are engaging in political behaviors? Political behaviors include ingratiation, self-promotion, strong influence tactics, coalition building, the forging of connections with powerful allies, taking credit for positive events and the success of others, and the circumvention of legitimate channels to secure resources that would otherwise be unattainable.[11] You may notice that some of these terms appeared in section 12.3; political behaviors are indeed closely aligned with tactical influence. People who "play the game" seek to influence others to get ahead, whether it's for their own interests or for the best interests of the organization.

Why is organizational politics an inevitable part of working life? There are two main factors at play: organizational factors and individual factors.[12]

Organizational Factors

Organizational politics: Behavior that is not formally sanctioned by the organization and that is focused on maximizing our self-interest, often at the expense of the organization or other employees

People are more likely to engage in political behavior in organizations where resources such as monetary rewards or promotions are limited. In today's uncertain economy, many companies have implemented austerity measures and cut back on overhead, often by conducting layoffs. For example, US multinational technology company Cisco has laid off thousands of employees since 2012.[13] These cost-cutting steps can fuel political behavior as employees compete for dwindling resources and rewards. "Zero-sum rewards," programs that compensate only one or a few team members at the expense

©iStockphoto.com/Jason Doiy

When Cisco started laying off large numbers of employees in 2012, their remaining workforce started competing for the positions and opportunities that remained. This is an example of how organizational factors can influence political behavior.

ORGANIZATIONAL POLITICS: Nourishing or Suppressing Positive Behavioral Outcomes?

Examining the Evidence

Research suggests that organizational politics often results in negative outcomes for organizations. But in certain situations it may have positive outcomes. Researchers Hsin-Hua Hsiung, Chia-Wu Lin, and Chi-Sheng Lin of National Dong Hwa University in Taiwan found that perceptions of organizational politics may both nourish and suppress positive organizational outcomes such as organizational citizenship behaviors. On the one hand, perceptions of politics among employees can lead to lower job satisfaction and consequently lower levels of organizational citizenship behaviors. On the other hand, that same perception may increase organizational citizenship behaviors through increased careerism, which consists of efforts to pursue career advancement in nonperformance-based ways. Employees with a high careerist orientation will be more likely to pursue their career goals through impression management and interpersonal manipulations. They may therefore engage in more extra-role behaviors, which are positive behaviors not explicitly included in a person's defined role in the organization, in an effort to advance their careers. This paradoxical finding suggests that employees may experience a psychological dilemma in which organizational politics simultaneously results in dissatisfaction, fewer organizational citizenship behaviors, and intentions to disengage, *and* in more efforts to counter a perceived lack of fair and rational performance evaluations that employees fear may put them at a disadvantage relative to their peers who are playing the political game.

Critical-Thinking Questions

1. **How can managers most effectively leverage the nourishing effects of organizational politics?**
2. **What are the potential drawbacks of facilitating organizational citizenship behaviors through organizational politics?**

SOURCE: Hsiung, Hsin-Hua, Chia-Wu Lin, and Chi-Sheng Lin. "Nourishing or Suppressing? The Contradictory Influences of Perception of Organizational Politics on Organizational Citizenship Behaviour." Journal of Occupational and Organizational Psychology 85, no. 2 (June 2012): 258–276.

of the others, can have negative consequences for those who do not receive anything, creating bad feeling and driving unhealthy competition. Similarly, organizations going through periods of organizational change tend to have more politically centered workforces. For example, rumors of layoffs may encourage some employees to use political tactics to ensure that their jobs are secure.

An organization's environment or culture is a good indicator of the extent of politics that exists in it. For example, in organizations that fail to implement formal rules, that tolerate a lack of trust between employees and management, or that put employees under serious pressure to perform, competition and politics prevail.

Individual Factors

Even if your organization is highly political, the extent to which you engage in political behavior depends on your personality. For example, you may be someone who has a strong desire for power and operates with a high internal locus of control (the belief that you can control outcomes). Or you could be a high self-monitor, someone who is more sensitive to social cues, can relate well to others, and inspires trust and confidence. Finally, you might have a Machiavellian personality and be willing to manipulate others and use power to advance your own self-interests.

Let's return to our case and follow how Langston Burrows' use of assertiveness with Judd Siegel leads to his first encounter with organizational politics.

Langston drives away from Judd Siegel's bank branch and starts to worry. What if Siegel complains about him to Sonia? She and Svetlana might accuse him of mishandling the situation and offending one of the bank's most senior employees. Should he go to Svetlana and tell her what happened? It's almost 5 and Langston decides to call it a day, instead. He doesn't really trust Svetlana and reasons she's unlikely to be sympathetic or or give him any helpful advice.

By the next morning, Langston has convinced himself that the meeting with Judd Siegel was no big deal. Siegel didn't take him seriously during the meeting, so Langston reasons he wouldn't have bothered telling anyone about Langston's promise of repercussions if Judd didn't focus on addressing the loan exceptions.

Langston has three more loan officers to speak with and then he's done with this particular task except for following up where needed. He arrives at work confident about his three remaining visits because, he reasons, nothing can be as bad as his meeting with Judd Siegel. However, the next loan officer, Shauna, reacts badly.

"Why is Svetlana sending you along as well? I already told her I'd work on reducing the exceptions under my name. I don't appreciate being hassled like this!"

Langston doesn't know what's going on, but he intends to find out immediately. He apologizes to the frazzled Shauna for any confusion and leaves the branch. Once outside, he calls Svetlana's office number on his cell but no one answers. He leaves a message asking Svetlana to return his call as soon as possible.

At the next branch, the same thing happens. According to another agitated loan officer, Svetlana contacted him at home and told him in no uncertain terms that he must reduce his loan exceptions within the next two weeks.

Langston apologizes and leaves the branch office. He tries Svetlana's office number again but there is still no answer. Langston looks at the final name on the list and wonders what to do. No doubt, Svetlana has paid this loan officer a visit as well. Still, he needs to be sure all the officers on his list are contacted, Langston makes his way to the final branch and diplomatically asks the loan officer whether Svetlana has shared the information about reducing loan exceptions. Sure enough, Svetlana has already paid a visit. Feeling disheartened and concerned, he heads back to the office. An e-mail from Svetlana with the subject header "2:00 Meeting Today" is waiting for him. The meeting will take place in Sonia's office.

Langston arrives at Sonia's office a few minutes early, hoping to speak with Sonia alone, but Svetlana is there before him.

Sonia begins. "Langston, I'll get to the point. Judd Siegel called Svetlana and claims you threatened him and behaved in a very unprofessional manner. Is this true?"

"I did tell him there would be repercussions if he didn't reduce the loan exceptions, but I don't think. . .," Langston begins, but Svetlana interjects.

"Langston, Judd Siegel is one of our most valued and productive employees—you can't go around treating him or any of our colleagues like that!," she says. "Sonia, as I was just starting to share with you, because of Judd's complaint, I decided it was best for the bank for me to focus on completing this task. Langston has spent a lot of time asking me for advice and given all his questions and need for handholding I've been worried that this challenge was more than he was ready to handle. Judd's complaint caused me to worry that Langston wasn't being sufficiently persuasive or diplomatic so I took steps to ensure we achieve our goal."

Langston is outraged by the unfairness of Svetlana's account, but he makes a conscious effort to keep calm so he can tell Sonia his side of the story. He explains how defensive Judd was from the beginning and the difficulty he had persuading Judd to take the project seriously.

"I admit I lost my patience," he says. "But at the same time, Judd was rude to me from the second I walked in the door."

To his annoyance, Svetlana laughs. "Oh, that's just Judd. He's a prickly character. You just need to know how to handle him!"

Sonia nods in agreement, but to Langston's relief, she adds, "But it doesn't give Judd the right to give you a hard time, Langston. I'll be having a word with him, too."

Svetlana shoots Sonia a look but doesn't say anything. Langston guesses she isn't pleased that Sonia is backing him up. He starts to tell Sonia he has successfully persuaded most of the loan officers on the list to work on their loan exceptions, only to be interrupted by Svetlana, who asserts, once again, that she has been advising and supporting Langston throughout the project and needed to step in to ensure success.

Sonia appears to have heard enough and calls the meeting to a close saying, "Langston, I want to thank you for your part in the assignment. It's unfortunate that Judd has complained, but I know there are two sides to the story."

Langston apologizes for his behavior during the meeting with Judd. Then Sonia thanks Svetlana for mentoring Langston and prioritizing the project, especially when she has so many other duties to attend to. Svetlana smiles graciously.

After the meeting, Langston follows Svetlana out. "I just want to know two things," he says. "First, why didn't you talk to me first about the complaint? And second, why did you take all the credit for my work?"

To his surprise, Svetlana doesn't seem the least bit self-conscious about answering his questions. "I'm up for a promotion. Any complaint against one of my staff is a threat to my success and I took the credit because it makes me look good," she replies. "You want some advice? If you want to do well in this organization, you need to play the game, Langston. I can be your ticket up or I can be your ticket out. It's your choice."

Svetlana is engaging in organizational politics. She aligns herself with the right people, takes credit for the work of others, and uses Machiavellian means to advance her own self-interests—in this case, her chance at a promotion. Svetlana is an example of an "immoral user" of political power, someone who ingratiates him- or herself with senior management and seeks to undermine anyone who poses a threat to his or her reputation.[14] So far, the political game has worked for Svetlana, but what about the effects of her behavior on Langston and the rest of the lending team?

Possible Outcomes of Political Behavior

Political Skill

The vast majority of research evidence suggests that organizational politics has negative effects, including increased strain and stress, higher organizational turnover, decreased job satisfaction and performance, lower morale, and reduced organizational commitment.[15] From the OB Story, you may suspect this is always the case. However, politics can be used for positive means when people possess **political skill,** the ability to understand and influence others for the good of the organization.[16] In other words, when people hold the interests of the organization above their own interests, provide high levels of feedback to colleagues and direct reports, and maintain good working relationships to achieve results, then organizational politics can have positive results. The OB in the Real World feature takes a look at how CEO A. Curtis Monk of the Community Idea Stations manages organizational politics in his company.

When Svetlana tells Langston he needs to "play the game," she has a point. Politics will be prevalent in most organizations you join. If you are aiming for a promotion, you will need to network with the right people and take on high-profile projects in order to increase your **visibility,** which is others' awareness of your presence in an organization.[17] Ultimately, your rewards, bonuses, and promotional prospects depend on the relationships you have with others. You don't need to behave in an underhanded way to stand out, but with so much competition in the workplace there is nothing wrong with ensuring that your hard work is acknowledged and fairly rewarded. Of course, you

Political skill: The ability to understand and influence others for the good of the organization

Visibility: The awareness of others regarding your presence in an organization

A. CURTIS MONK, CEO, Community Idea Stations

OB in the Real World

© Curtis Monk

The Community Idea Stations form the largest locally owned and operated radio and TV station company in central Virginia. Every week its three public TV stations and radio station reach more than 300,000 people with nationally acclaimed, innovative PBS and NPR programing. The company breaks its community impact into five different categories: Children's Education, News & Public Affairs, Science & Discovery, History & Heritage, Arts & Culture.

Curtis Monk has been with Community Idea Stations since 1999 and has been president and CEO since 2006. He believes a company needs five fundamental ingredients to be successful. First, employees must be willing to do the best they can. "They don't have to be perfect," says Curtis. "The request is that everyone can look in the mirror and say that they gave it their best shot." Second, they have to be willing to work as a team. "We can't worry about who is getting credit. Every job in this company is important and if we work together to make things happen we will make this company successful." Third is to make good use of communication. "E-mail is nice for setting up meetings and conveying information but a disaster for having difficult conversations. I ask my employees to remember that it's easier to solve problems if they're looking each other in the eyes." Fourth, employees must treat others like you'd treat a friend. "When we view others as friends we tend to see them as good people. When they do something wrong or approach us with a challenge we're more likely to receive their request positively." Finally, "we need to have fun. We spend a lot of time at work and we should enjoy being here."

"Power and politics tend to get in the way when a company has a pyramid that points upward to the head guy," says Curtis. "The farther you move up the pyramid, the more you're jockeying for a position and the less you're worrying about the company. People become more obsessed with how they can be successful within the corporate structure and worry less about being a good teammate."

Curtis points to the infamous "water cooler conversations" that often happen within companies when employees are disgruntled and huddle together to complain. "These conversations are deadly because they foster the development of cliques, silos, and tension which will hinder productivity and ruin the fabric of a corporation. Management has to have open dialogue with employees and be honest and transparent. They have to ask employees to be honest in return. This knowledge is power."

With 48 full-time employees the Community Idea Stations is a small company, but Curtis works hard to eliminate politics and power by continuously reinforcing his five fundamental concepts. He gets to know his people by walking around, talking to them, and learning about both their personal and professional lives. He talks openly with HR about the challenges employees are facing and works to remove roadblocks they're facing. He also makes sure employees get out of the office and have fun together. They can frequently be found playing putt-putt golf, bowling, or going to the movies.

Critical-Thinking Questions

1. **How would you describe Curtis Monk's approach to reducing the negative effects of politics and power in a group?**
2. **What do you think of Curtis Monk's criticism of water cooler moments?**

SOURCE: Curtis Monk, personal interview, August 28, 2013.

can choose to stay out of politics altogether, but this may mean getting passed over for promotions simply because the people responsible for promotional decisions and rewards are unaware of your skills, talents, and contributions.

So far, we have explored the role of power and politics and how it influences relationships in organizations. In the next chapter, we will illustrate the importance of effective communication on organizational behavior.

THINKING CRITICALLY

1. Do you agree with the statement that organizational politics is a reality in every workplace? Why or why not? **[Analyze/Evaluate]**

2. To what extent are small, innovative start-ups more or less likely to be characterized by organizational politics and political behavior than large, well-established multinationals? How does the size of a company affect the extent of organizational politics? **[Analyze/Evaluate]**

3. Discuss the ways in which Sonia exhibits political skill. **[Analyze/Evaluate]**

IN REVIEW

Learning Objectives

12.1 Discuss the concept of power and its relationship to leadership

The concept of **power,** which is the capacity to influence the actions of others, is inextricably linked with leadership. Recent psychological research has suggested that coercive power is a myth, and that true power lies in social intelligence or our ability to negotiate, resolve conflicts, and understand the goals of others. Depending on their psychological make-up, different types of leaders may exert their power to influence in different ways, which can lead to positive or negative outcomes.

12.2 Identify the various sources of power

Organizational power can be broken into three main aspects: legitimate power, reward power, and coercive power. Legitimate power is the right to ask others to do things within the scope of the leader's authority. Reward power is the use of incentives to influence the actions of others. Coercive power controls the behavior of others through punishments, threats, or sanctions.

Personal power can be broken into two main types: expert power and referent power. Expert power is the ability to influence the behavior of others through the possession of knowledge or expertise on which they depend. Referent power is influence over others based on their desire to identify and be associated with the leader.

12.3 Describe tactics for influencing others

There are several different types of tactics we can use to influence others:

- **Rational appeals**: The use of logic, reason, and evidence to convince another person that cooperation in a task is worthwhile

- **Inspirational appeals**: The use of emotions to rouse enthusiasm for the task by appealing to the values and ideals of others
- **Upward appeals**: The argument that the task has been requested by higher management, or a request to higher management to assist in gaining cooperation
- **Personal appeals**: Requests to cooperate on the basis of friendship or as a personal favor
- **Consultation:** The offer of participation or consultation in the decision-making process
- **Exchange:** The promise of rewards to persuade another person to cooperate
- **Coalition building:** Reference to the support of others as a reason for someone to agree to a request
- **Ingratiation:** An effort to win favor and the good graces of others before making a request
- **Silent authority:** a passive tactic that relies on unspoken but acknowledged power.
- **Information control**: withholding key information to influence outcomes.
- **Assertiveness:** The use of demands or threats to persuade someone to carry out a task

12.4 Outline the results of the various influence tactics

The three basic outcomes of influence tactics are commitment, compliance, and resistance. *Commitment* occurs when people are enthusiastic and fully in agreement with an action or decision and are motivated to put in the extra effort to successfully reach a goal. *Compliance* occurs when people are indifferent to a task and make only the minimal effort necessary to complete a goal. *Resistance* takes place when people oppose the influencer's request by refusing to carry out a task or arguing against carrying out a task.

12.5 Identify the causes and possible consequences of organizational politics

Organizational politics is behavior that is not formally sanctioned by the organization and that is focused on maximizing our self-interest, often at the expense of the organization or other employees. They include ingratiation, self-promotion, strong influence tactics, coalition building, connections with powerful allies, the taking of credit for positive events and the success of others, and the circumvention of legitimate channels to secure resources that would be otherwise unattainable.

People are more likely to engage in political behavior in organizations in which resources such as monetary rewards or promotions are limited. Similarly, organizations going through periods of organizational change tend to have a more politically centered workforce.

The vast majority of research evidence suggests negative effects of organizational politics, including increased strain and stress, higher organizational turnover, decreased job satisfaction and performance, lower morale, and reduced organizational commitment. However, politics can be used for positive means when people possess **political skill,** the ability to understand and influence others for the good of the organization, and hold the interests of the organization above their own interests, provide high levels of feedback to employees, and maintain good working relationships to achieve results.

KEY TERMS

Assertiveness 309
Coalition building 309
Coercive power 307
Consultation 309
Exchange 309
Expert power 307
Information control 309
Ingratiation 309
Inspirational appeals 309
Legitimate power 306
Organizational politics 314
Personal appeals 309
Political skill 317
Power 305
Rational appeals 309
Referent power 307
Reward power 306
Silent authority 309
Upward appeals 309
Visibility 317

THINKING CRITICALLY ABOUT THE CASE OF LANGSTON BURROWS

Put yourself in Langston Burrows' position and consider the five critical-thinking steps in relation to organizational politics, political behavior, and accomplishing the loan exception reduction project.

OBSERVE

List the objections Langston encounters as he speaks with each loan officer. Then list the influencing tactics Langston chooses to use to overcome each loan officer's objection(s). To what extent does personality play a role both in the objections given and the tactics Langston chooses to use? Explain your answer.

INTERPRET

Interpret the meeting with Langston from Judd Siegel's perspective. How does he view Langston, Langston's request, and Langston's behavior? To what extent is Judd's reaction to Langston logical and acceptable? Where does Judd's behavior cross a professional line? Is it fair to suggest that Langston's desire to accomplish the project independently undermines the success of his meeting with Judd? Why or why not?

ANALYZE

What steps could Langston have taken to more effectively accomplish the goal of getting Judd to reduce the loan exceptions on his books? Explain your response.

EVALUATE

Evaluate Langston's decisions after he uses coercive power to try to gain Judd Siegel's compliance in addressing loan exceptions. What does he miss in reasoning that Judd won't complain about his behavior to Svetlana and Sonia? What steps should he have taken to resolve the situation?

EXPLAIN

Put yourself in Langston's position and discuss how you would have tackled the loan exception reduction project. What advice would you have sought and from whom? What could you have done to ensure you received credit for your work on the project? How could you have reduced the conflict with Judd Siegel?

EXERCISE 12.1: DOLLAR POWER EXERCISE

You must bring a dollar to class and be willing to risk it. If you do not wish to risk losing a dollar, you may opt out and be an observer. Participants should divide into groups of five.

Part 1

Within your group, discuss the sources of power—legitimate, reward, coercive, expert, and referent—and then come to cons-esus on a rank ordering of the five from the most to the least important source.

Part 2

Line up according to the amount of influence each group member had in establishing the power sources ranking in Part 1. Again use group consensus to arrive at an order of influence ranging from 1 (the most influential) to 5 (the least influential). Reposition yourselves and discuss the lineup until you are satisfied that it is the best possible rank order.

Your professor will give you a card or a sticker on which you should write the number of your place in the lineup, with the most influential person writing 1 on the card, the second most influential writing a 2, and so forth. Display your number throughout the remainder of the exercise.

Part 3

Each group member should place his or her dollar in a pile in the center of the group. You will now decide how to divide up the money according to the following rules:

- Your goal is to influence the group decision in order to win as much money for yourself as you can. You may use any personal influence strategies you like, including coalition building, rational appeals, personal appeals, and so on unless specifically prohibited (see following).
- At least two people in each group will receive no money. The money can be divided among the remaining group members in any proportion decided upon: one member can receive it all, or it can be equally or unequally divided among two or three members.
- The money allocation decision must be determined by means of a vote. Your instructor will tell you how many votes each group member has.
- The voting procedure is determined by the group members. For example, you may decide to have only one voting round, placing your votes for the person(s) you want to receive money, or several rounds of voting for the person you want to receive the money until only two or three people are left.
- Do not vote too quickly, wait until all group members have expressed their thoughts and have indicated they are ready to vote.
- Group members are not permitted to (1) use chance procedures such as drawing straws or flipping coins, (2) give their votes to another person and not participate in the decision, (3) agree to return everyone's original dollar after the exercise, or (4) agree to buy everyone something with the money after class. In other words, at least two people in each group must not get money back in any way, and it is not possible to opt out of the decision-making process.
- If the group cannot decide on the money allocation within a 15-minute time limit, the instructor gets all the money.

Part 4

Individually write down the answers to the following questions:

1. What were your feelings as your participated in this exercise?
2. From what power bases did you draw?
3. What influence strategies did you utilize?

Part 5

Discuss your answers with the rest of your group. Provide feedback to one another regarding the effectiveness of individual strategies and discuss why some people were more successful than others. Share what you learned about yourself in terms of your feelings and your approach to using power in conflict situations.

SOURCE: Adapted from Hunsaker, P., and J. Hunsaker. "Personal Power Strategies: An Experiential Exercise." *Developments in Business Simulation and Experiential Exercises* 14 (1987): 100–101.

EXERCISE 12.2: I HAVE THE POWER

Objectives:

This exercise will help you to be able to better *discuss* the concept of power and *identify* various sources of power.

Instructions:

Step 1. Think of an organization of which you are a member. For each power type (legitimate, reward, coercive, expert, and referent), describe why you do or do not have that particular power. Since power is an exchange process and differs in various relationships, you may also need to specify with who (or what group of people) you have that power. (5 minutes)

Step 2. Find a partner (ideally someone who you do not work with on a regular basis), and prepare a list of similarities and differences in your influence relationships. (10 minutes)

Step 3. Choose a spokesperson for your pair and be prepared to discuss your comparison with the class. (1 to 3 minutes)

Reflection Questions:

1. How would you expect your power bases to change in a different organization?
2. How do you expect your power bases to change after you graduate from your program?
3. What power bases do you prefer to use? How could you improve those power bases?
4. What power bases would you expect to transfer between organizations and positions?

Exercise contributed by Milton R. Mayfield, Professor of Business, Texas A&M International University and Jaqueline R. Mayfield, Professor of Business, Texas A&M International University.

EXERCISE 12.3: GIVE ME A LEVER

Objectives:

This exercise will help you to *identify* sources of power in an organization, *describe* influence tactics, and *outline* the expected results of different influence tactics.

Instructions:

Step 1. Think of and identify a current situation where you would like to persuade someone to do something for you. (And choose a situation that you are willing to share with other people in the class.) Write up the situation in as much detail as possible – including your desired outcome(s). (5 to 10 minutes)

Step 2. Form a triad (a group of three people). If possible, try to form a triad with people you do not work with on a regular basis. Everyone should pass their own write-up to the person to their right after writing her or his name on the paper.

Then take the situation you have been given, and on the same sheet of paper write an influence tactic plan to help that person achieve her or his desired outcome(s). Be sure to use appropriate chapter terms and concepts in developing and describing your plan. Write your name on the paper, and pass the description to the person on your right. (5 to 10 minutes)

Step 3. Examine the influence tactic plan you have been given, and evaluate it in terms of how likely you think the plan is to succeed. Be sure to note the overall difficulty of achieving the desired goals using any tactic. Your analysis should be framed using chapter terms and concepts.

Return the plan to the person who originally wrote the description. (5 to 10 minutes)

Step 4. Be prepared to give a brief overview of the situation, the plan, the plan's evaluation, if you are planning to implement the plan, and why or why not you are planning to implement the plan. (5 minutes)

Reflection Questions:

1. What insights did you gain about chapter concepts from having to implement and evaluate an influence tactic plan?
2. How did having to develop an influence plan help you to better understand systematic methods for generating influence and persuading people?
3. How did evaluating such a plan help you to better understand the strengths and weaknesses of influence methods?
4. How could you utilize such systematic influence plans in your career?

Exercise contributed by Milton R. Mayfield, Professor of Business, Texas A&M International University and Jaqueline R. Mayfield, Professor of Business, Texas A&M International University.

CASE STUDY 12.1: MONSANTO COMPANY

Depending on whom you talk to, Monsanto Company, the chemical and agricultural biotechnology multinational based in Creve Coeur, Missouri, is either the "devil incarnate" or the answer to some of humanity's most vexing problems. Do a quick Google search and you'll find a wide array of opinion in articles with titles ranging from "Monsanto Named 2013's 'Most Evil Corporation in New Poll" and "Monsanto Connected to At Least 200,000 Suicides in India throughout Past Decade" to "One of *CR* magazine's 100 Best Corporate Citizens for 2014" (CR stands for Corporate Responsibility). One thing is for sure: Monsanto is a powerful force on the world stage, with more than 22,000 employees, $14.87 billion in annual sales, and heavy political clout in the United States and beyond.

And it's everywhere. "Like Intel's dominance in the chip market, almost every soybean in America has Monsanto inside," wrote Scott Tong on *Marketplace.org*. Soybeans are the second-largest US crop after corn—they cover nearly a quarter of the country's farmland—and Monsanto is responsible for planting and harvesting about 90 percent of the nation's crop. The animals that produce our milk, eggs, meat, leather, gelatin, and wool feed on soybean meal. About 60 percent of the vegetable fats found in processed *human* food are soy based, too.

Monsanto's agricultural dominance can be traced in part to 1983, when it became a pioneer by genetically modifying a plant cell to become hardier. This was part of a wider GMO movement that for some "constitutes a massive experiment on the planet, with potentially devastating effects on human health and the global environment," as columnist Adam Kapp wrote in 2002. But that innovation, among others, has helped Monsanto produce soybeans cheaply and reliably to feed a growing global population.

Monsanto is also an innovator in pesticides, among other chemicals and technologies. Founded in 1901, over the years the company has led breakthrough research on catalytic asymmetric hydrogenation and light-emitting diodes (LEDs) and produced the insecticide DDT, PCBs, Agent Orange, and bovine growth hormone. Borrowing from biotechnology's and the pharmaceutical industry's playbooks (its founder was a pharmacist), Monsanto spends millions on R&D and biological patents, making much of its money back (and then some) on its patents' reuse. Today, the company is both revered and reviled for its influence in the soybean trade and for the production of Roundup, a powerful pesticide the company insists is safe. Its introduction of the herbicide Roundup-ready Soybeans—meaning farmers can spray their fields to keep away the pests while theoretically keeping their Monsanto soybeans safe—unleashed even louder protests from environmentalists and the organic- and small-farmer movements in 2000 that continues today.

Why all the fuss? The world's population is growing at an unprecedented rate, and determining how to feed everyone is essential to our survival—which Monsanto claims is one of its core goals. But detractors say that GMO crops are nutritionally inferior and hazardous to humans and the environment. Scientists mostly agree that genetic engineering is also leading to the growth of "super" weeds and pests that withstand not only Roundup but any pesticide.

Author Bret Frazer, on *The Northern Light.org,* explains why Monsanto is not just "bad" but *"evil"*: "Monsanto . . . epitomizes the undermining of democracy. Monsanto is an example of revolving door politics." He points out that Supreme Court Justice Clarence Thomas worked as a Monsanto attorney in the 1970s. In 2001, Thomas wrote the majority opinion for *J.E.M. Ag Supply, Inc. v. Pioneer Hi-Bred International, Inc.*, which found that "newly developed plant breeds are patentable," allowing GMO producers like Monsanto to make billions from generations of seeds and sue those farmers who did not abide by strict patent-protecting policies. Linda Fisher, Monsanto vice president from 1995 to 2000, was made deputy administrator of the EPA (Environmental Protection Agency) in 2001. Michael Taylor was once employed by a law firm that lobbied for FDA approval of Monsanto's artificial growth hormone. President Barack Obama reappointed him deputy commissioner of the FDA (Food and Drug Administration) in 2009. In "Why Is Monsanto Evil, but DuPont Isn't?," Stephen D. Simpson of *The Motley Fool* reports that when corporate lobbying "Monsanto does indeed spend millions . . . around $5 million or $6 million a year by most reports." But it is certainly not the first major corporation whose executives have made the transition to the federal payroll.

But perhaps the most ire has been raised by Monsanto's use of litigation to protect its patented crops and its perceived unfair influence within the very government that regulates its industry.

Monsanto has sued farmers, claiming they used its patented seeds without permission (sometimes the seeds in question were several generations removed from the original patented seeds). In 2013, a case taken all the way to the Supreme Court was resolved in favor of Monsanto when Indiana farmer Vernon Hugh Bowman was ordered to pay the company $84,000 for patent infringement.

But thanks in part to grassroots, social media-fueled movements, the legislative tide may turn against Monsanto. In 2014, Vermont passed a bill that mandates the labeling of GMO foods—so consumers can choose to eliminate GMO foods from their grocery carts—and other states may soon follow suit. It doesn't take effect until July 2016, and lawsuits from the agriculture industry are expected to follow.

Simpson sees Monsanto's business practices as par for the course. "Every crop science company works to protect its intellectual property, every crop science company looks to get a good price for its technology, and every crop science company opens its wallet to attempt to sway public and governmental opinion to their side—just as companies in technology, healthcare, banking and virtually every other industry do, and have done for decades."

Whatever argument about Monsanto's behavior sways you, it's clear the company won't be leaving the headlines—or our dinner tables—any time soon. As activists protest more loudly and Vermont and others heed their call, perhaps consumers will have greater purchasing power than ever before.

Case Questions

1. Describe how Monsanto became so powerful in the chemical and agricultural biotechnology industry.
2. Describe how Monsanto uses organizational power.
3. What sort of power do environmentalists and other activists hold in their fight against Monsanto's policies? Where does it come from? How can they best use or increase their power?
4. Describe Monsanto as an example of revolving door politics and the way it gives the company additional organizational power.

Sources

Adams, Mike. "Monsanto Voted Most Evil Corporation of the Year by NaturalNews Readers." *NaturalNews.com.* January 10, 2011. www.naturalnews.com/030967_Monsanto_evil.html##ixzz31WiamJFP.

Bunge, Jacob. "For Weed Control, Farmers Widen Their Arsenal of Herbicides." *Wall Street Journal.* April 25, 2014. http://online.wsj.com/news/articles/SB100014240527023038478045794816417173 50038.

Chatsko, Maxx. "Is Monsanto Company Wrong about Pest Resistance?" *Motley Fool.* April 18, 2014. www.fool.com/investing/general/2014/04/18/is-monsanto-company-wrong-about-pest-resistance.aspx.

Huff, Ethan A. "Monsanto Connected to At Least 200,000 Suicides in India throughout Past Decade." *Naturalnews.com.* January 4, 2011. www.naturalnews.com/030913_Monsanto_suicides.html#.

Kresser, Chris. "Are GMOs Safe?" *Chriskresser.com.* n.d. chriskresser.com/are-gmos-safe.

Liptak, Adam. "Supreme Court Supports Monsanto in Seed-Replication Case." *New York Times.* May 13, 2013. http://www.nytimes.com/2013/05/14/business/monsanto-victorious-in-genetic-seed-case.html?_r=0.

"Monsanto Named as a Top Company for Diversity." *Monsanto.com.* April 24, 2014. news.monsanto.com/press-release/recognition/monsanto%C2%A0named%C2%A0as%C2%A0a%C2%A0top-company%C2%A0-diversity.

Philpott, Tom. "Chicken Nuggets, with a Side of Respiratory Distress." *Motherjones.com.* April 30, 2014. www.motherjones.com/tom-philpott/2014/04/superweeds-arent-only-trouble-gmo-s.

Sheets, Connor Adams. "Monsanto Named 2013's 'Most Evil Corporation' in New Poll." *International Business Times.* June 10, 2013. www.ibtimes.com/monsanto-named-2013s-most-evil-corporation-new-poll-1300217.

Simpson, Stephen D. "Why Is Monsanto Evil, but DuPont Isn't?" *Investopedia.com.* June 19, 2013. www.investopedia.com/articles/investing/061913/why-monsanto-evil-dupont-isnt.asp.

Smith, Jeffrey. "Monsanto Voted World's Most Evil Corp Year after Year for Good Reasons." *RT.com.* October 11, 2013. rt.com/op-edge/monsanto-technique-ruins-evolution-016.

Tong, Scott. "Monsanto: The Behemoth That Controls 90 Percent of Soybean Production." *Marketplace.org* May 13, 2013. www.marketplace.org/topics/sustainability/monsanto-behemoth-controls-90-percent-soybean-production.

"USDA Creates New Government Certification for GMO-Free." *New York Times.* May 14, 2015. www.nytimes.com/aponline/2015/05/14/us/politics/ap-us-genetically-modified-foods-labeling.html?_r=0.

SELF-ASSESSMENT 12.1

How Political Is My Organization?

Consider an organization in which you are a member. This could be an organization for which you work, a fraternity or sorority or other campus organization, a social or community organization, or the like.

For each statement, circle the number that best describes your organization on the following scale:

	Not at all Accurate	Somewhat Accurate	A Little Accurate	Mostly Accurate	Completely Accurate
1. The most successful people in my organization are fairly adept at the art of ingratiation.	1	2	3	4	5
2. The people who get ahead in my organization are very good at self-promotion.	1	2	3	4	5
3. Strong influence tactics must be used in order to accomplish objectives in my organization.	1	2	3	4	5
4. Building coalitions tends to be very important for success in my organization.	1	2	3	4	5
5. The people who are most successful in my organization tend to have connections with powerful allies.	1	2	3	4	5
6. Successful members of my organization do not hesitate in taking credit for positive events and/or the success of others.	1	2	3	4	5
7. Circumventing legitimate channels to secure resources that would be otherwise unattainable is a fairly common practice for success in my organization.	1	2	3	4	5
8. People seem to enjoy the political process in my organization.	1	2	3	4	5

Scoring

Add the numbers circled and write your score in the blank ____________.

Interpretation

32 and above = Your organization is highly political. It will take a significant amount of political skill and political behavior to be successful in this organization.

24-31 = Your organization is moderately political. High levels of political skill and savvy may be helpful in certain situations.

23 and below = Your organization is not very political. High levels of political skill and behaviors are not needed to be successful and may even be detrimental to success in certain situations.

13 Effective Communication

©iStockphoto.com/AzmanL

My belief is that communication is the best way to create strong relationships.

—Jada Pinkett Smith, American actress

THE ROLE OF EFFECTIVE COMMUNICATION IN INFLUENCING OTHERS

LEARNING OBJECTIVES

By the end of this chapter, you will be able to:

- 13.1 Describe the basic model of communication
- 13.2 Compare the types of communication channels
- 13.3 Identify key barriers to effective communication
- 13.4 Describe types of communication networks within organizations
- 13.5 Discuss the elements of effective cross-cultural communication

13.1 Describe the basic model of communication

In an increasingly connected world, communication is more important than ever in the workplace. Today's organizations have no choice but to adapt quickly to the rise of new technologies and social networking tools in order to keep up with the competition and stay in touch with the needs of their customer bases. We define **communication** as the act of transmitting thoughts, processes, and ideas through a variety of channels.[1] Efficient communication leads to better functioning of organizations, which benefits both employees and customers.

Inside the organization, effective communication must take place within and among peer groups and between different hierarchical levels. One of the most important roles of a manager is to encourage and nurture a collaborative working environment by effectively communicating with teams to ensure that tasks are accomplished and organizational goals achieved. Take a look at how the moving company, Moveline, implements effective communication in the OB in the Real World feature.

 The Communication Process

 Shannon-Weaver Communication Model

In 1947, mathematician Claude E. Shannon created a communication model that was later developed further by Warren Weaver. The Shannon-Weaver model (see Figure 13.1) is the cornerstone of communication models and is still in use today.[2]

The Shannon-Weaver model assumes that communication relies on two main components: the *sender* of the message, also known as the source, and the *receiver* of the message. When the sender transmits a message through a communication channel—the route the message travels along—the content of the message is encoded into its intended meaning through different formats such as written, oral, or electronic; the

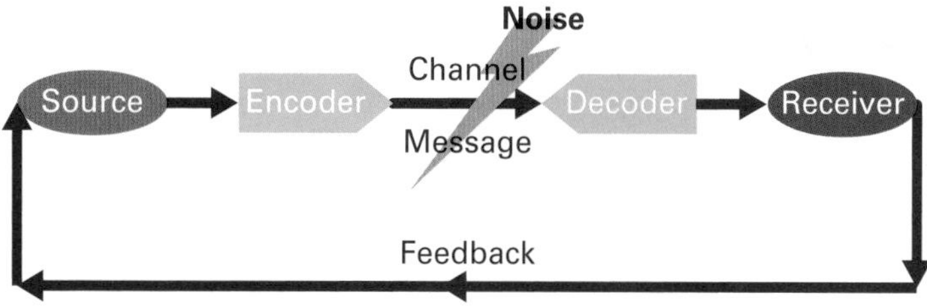

■ FIGURE 13.1 Shannon-Weaver Communications Model

SOURCE: Adapted from Shannon, C. E., & Weaver, W. *The Mathematical Theory of Communication* (Urbana: University of Illinois Press, 1949).

Communication: The act of transmitting thoughts, processes, and ideas through a variety of channels

receiver then decodes or interprets the message into a perceived meaning. The receiver provides feedback or a response to the sender to confirm the message has been received and its meaning understood.

Although this sounds like a fairly simple process, disturbances known as *noise* often occur. Background noise such as people talking loudly, construction work, or telephones ringing can all interfere with our ability to communicate effectively. Noise in the context of the Shannon-Weaver Model does not necessarily refer to sound, however; noise refers to interference that can muddy a message between the sender and receiver. In this context, noise might refer to complex or difficult language or cultural differences that distort meaning. It is essential for sender and receiver to clear their communication channels of any noise that may disrupt the meaning of the message.

THINKING CRITICALLY

1. To what extent have technological advances (smartphones, laptops, tablet devices) made it easier to communicate effectively in organizations? To what extent have these advances made miscommunications more likely? Explain your answers. **[Analyze/Evaluate]**

2. Consider the Shannon-Weaver Communications Model. At what junctures in the model can miscommunications occur? To what extent is noise or some other factor to blame for miscommunication? **[Analyze/Evaluate]**

TYPES OF COMMUNICATION CHANNELS

13.2 Compare the types of communication channels

As recently as 30 years ago, only a handful of communication channels were available to us. But thanks to the rapid rise of technology, we now have myriad ways to send and receive messages (Figure 13.2). Let's explore the different types of communication channels we use in daily life.

Oral communication: The ability to give and exchange information, ideas, and processes verbally, either one on one or as a group

Oral communication is the exchange of information, ideas, and processes verbally, either one on one or as a group. In the workplace, we regularly communicate orally through

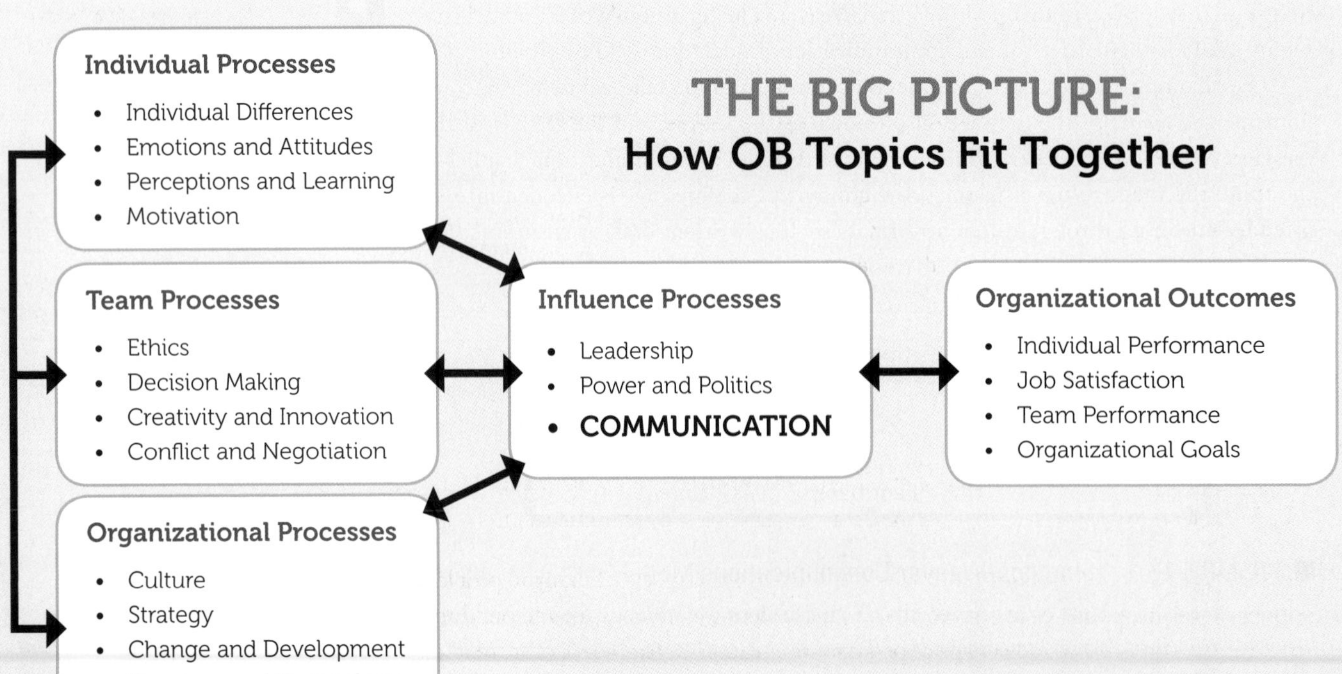

KELLY EIDSON, *manager, Moveline*

OB in the Real World

© Kelly Eidson

Moveline makes life a little easier for people who are moving with its suite of software tools, including a mobile app that allows clients to give a moving expert a tour of their home via video chat or a brief film. After reviewing the footage, Moveline provides customers with an estimate and a price comparison from the best moving companies in town. Customers can book their move online and will receive stellar customer service from their designated Moveline Move captains, who provide support throughout the process. Moveline was founded in 2011 in Blacksburg, Virginia. The company grew quickly, and now has 23 full-time employees headquartered in Las Vegas.

Cofounder Kelly Eidson knows firsthand the importance of strong communication strategies within an organization. "Particularly with start-ups, which are usually made up of people who are either sacrificing high-paying jobs or are walking away from a big job, employees want to be part of building something bigger. The way we are able to recruit those types of employees is by involving them in the vision of the company.

"What starts out as something that's easy to achieve when you have four or five people sitting in a room together all day becomes harder when you have people across locations, from different backgrounds, and who have different styles. With growth comes more stuff to communicate about—more teams, more projects, more initiatives going on at once. As the company grows and you add more people to the team, communication becomes more important than it was in the beginning. You have to keep everyone in the loop or they will begin to feel like they've lost what was special about being part of a start-up. It becomes more of a challenge but it also becomes more important to do it right," says Kelly.

"As a leader," she adds, "you have two options: you can be the one delivering the message or you can let your employees deliver their version of the message. It's better to be transparent about things and own the reality up-front than for people to think that they aren't getting the full story or that they are being shielded from the truth.

"No one wants to share bad news because it's not fun to deliver it. However, when leaders don't share bad news immediately, people often assume you were hiding something. Being transparent is an important part of the corporate communication strategy at Moveline. When companies are really good at communicating it means that people who are working in the business every day can stay focused on what they're doing because they don't have to worry about keeping up with rumors. When people get the information as soon as it's available they don't have to try to hunt it down." Kelly believes that "when companies are really good at communicating, employees feel like they are trusted and they have more incentive to stay involved as the company grows and changes."

Critical-Thinking Question

1. **How would you communicate bad news to a group? Explain your choice.**

SOURCE: Kelly Eidson, personal interview, December 2, 2013.

telephone conversations, presentations, meetings, and conferences. For instance, the United States president's State of the Union address is an example of oral communication

Advantages and disadvantages of oral communication. Talking to people in person or on the phone or in a video chat is an excellent way to network and build relationships. Another major advantage of oral communication is that messages are sent and

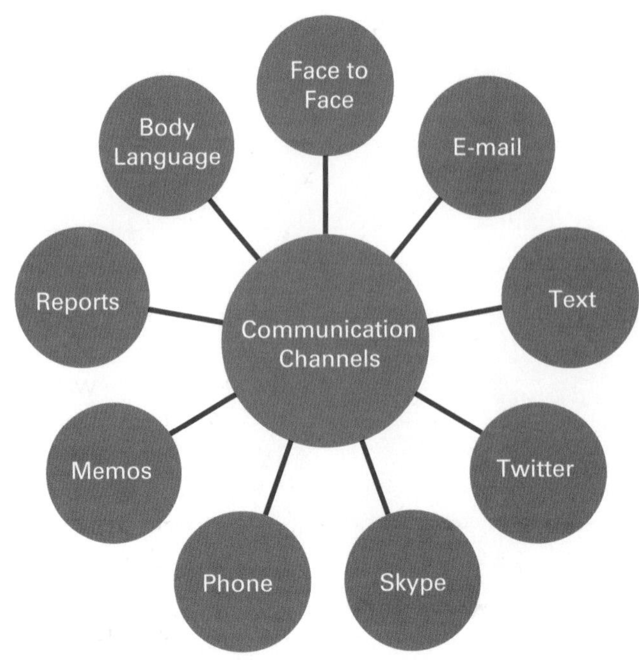

■ FIGURE 13.2 Communication Channels

SOURCE: Neck, C. *Management* (Hoboken, NJ: Wiley, 2013): 379.

received almost instantaneously, and feedback is given just as fast, so misunderstandings can be quickly cleared up. However, sometimes the informal nature of oral communication means that messages or parts of messages are forgotten or misunderstood later.

Written communication makes use of the written word in the form of reports, memos, and letters to communicate messages. Notice of acceptance to college or a formal job offer is usually delivered in a written letter.

Written communication: Messages communicated through the written word, such as e-mails, reports, memos, letters, and other channels

Advantages and disadvantages of written communication. Senders can review written messages before sending and record and archive them if necessary. However, unless the receiver provides feedback, the sender will not always know whether the message has reached its destination or has been interpreted correctly.

The State of the Union is one example of oral communication, when the President of the United States gives a speech to the country about the status of the country and its government.

Chuck Kennedy (Executive Office of the President of the United States)

Electronic communication is the transmission of messages through e-mail, Skype, videoconferencing, blogs, fax, instant messaging, texting, and social networking (Twitter, LinkedIn, Facebook, YouTube, Pinterest, Instagram, and more). Many companies and social activist groups use "hashtag campaigns" to quickly and broadly disperse information and start conversations around certain topics, events, and products.

Electronic Communication

Advantages and disadvantages of electronic communication. There is no better way of instantly reaching a large audience across a global network than through forms of electronic communication. However, electronic communication can be hindered by technical problems, privacy breaches, and misinterpretation. Written electronic communication can be an especially poor channel for delivering negative news because it does not provide an adequate means for expressing emotion.

Nonverbal communication is the transmission of wordless cues between people. Examples of nonverbal cues include facial expression, eye gaze, gestures, tone of voice, the way we walk, stand, dress, and position ourselves.[3] From the way we shake hands to the color of the clothing we wear, nonverbal details show others who we are and influence the way we are perceived. Nonverbal communication occurs in popular sitcoms like *The Big Bang Theory*, as in many sitcoms, the characters often engage in different facial expressions and gestures to convey thoughts and emotions.

Advantages and disadvantages of nonverbal communication. Nonverbal communication can be an important way of interacting with others because it allows for transmission of subtle messages through eye contact, vocal tone, and posture. However, because we are usually unaware of the nonverbal messages we are sending, we are at risk of unintentionally conveying the wrong message, which, in turn, may give the wrong impression. There can also be confusion and discrepancies between the nonverbal cues we convey and the words we are saying. For example, you might tell your professor you are happy to stay after class and take on an extra assignment, but defensive body language such as folded arms, downcast eyes, and legs crossed away from your professor will suggest otherwise.

With so many communication channels to choose from, how do we choose the most appropriate one for certain situations? One way is to weigh **channel richness**, the degree to which a channel allows us to easily communicate and understand information

Electronic communication: The ability to transmit messages through e-mail, Skype, videoconferencing, blogs, fax, instant messaging, texting, and social networking

Nonverbal communication: The transmission of wordless cues between people

Channel richness: The capacity to communicate and understand information between people and organizations

AF archive / Alamy Stock Photo

Characters on CBS's The Big Bang Theory often convey their thoughts and emotions through nonverbal communication such as facial expressions and body language.

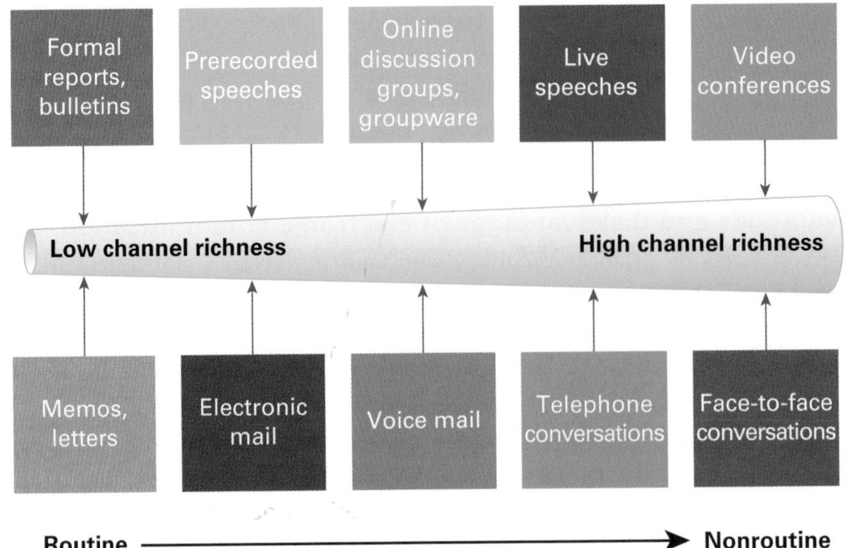

■ FIGURE 13.3 Channel Richness

SOURCE: Based on Lengel, R. H., and D. L. Daft. "The Selection of Communication Media as an Executive Skill." ***Academy of Management Executive*** (August 1988): 225–232; Daft, D. L., and R. H. Lengel. "Organizational Information Requirements, Media Richness, and Structural Design." ***Managerial Science*** (May 1996): 554–572. Reproduced from R. L. Daft and R. A. Noe. ***Organizational Behavior*** (Fort Worth, TX: Harcourt, 2001), 311. (c) 2007 Prentice Hall Inc. All rights reserved.

sent between people and organizations (Figure 13.3.). Face-to-face communication during meetings or videoconferencing is thought to be the richest form of communication. It allows for immediate feedback, the understanding of verbal and nonverbal cues, and opportunities for building relationships.

The second-richest channel is the phone. During phone conversations we are able to listen to verbal cues, detect levels of emotion, and pick up on nonverbal cues such as tone of voice. Despite their popularity, e-mails, text messages, blogs, memos, e-bulletins and so on are considered to be at the lower end of channel richness, especially when the information becomes sensitive or complex. By far the most effective way of resolving a situation or dealing with a difficult issue is to call a face-to-face meeting or pick up the phone.

THINKING CRITICALLY

1. Make a list of all the channels of communication you use on a regular basis. Do you ever choose your communication channel based on the content of your message? Why or why not? **[Understand/Apply]**

2. Discuss a misunderstanding you have had with a friend or work colleague and how you went about clearing up the misunderstanding. Did the channel of communication that you chose to convey the message contribute to the misunderstanding? Did you correct the misunderstanding using the same channel of communication you used or switch to a different channel to address the misunderstanding? Explain your answer. **[Analyze/Evaluate]**

3. Review the list of channels of communication that you use on a regular basis compiled for Question 1 and label them as low in channel richness or high in channel richness. Based on the text discussion, are you inclined to begin using channels higher in communication richness? Why or why not? **[Apply/Analyze]**

BARRIERS TO COMMUNICATION

Identify key barriers to effective communication

Back to the Case of Langston Burrows

In Chapters 11 and 12, we explored the career progression of Langston Burrows. We read about his experiences with the graduate leadership development program and the decision of Sonia Valdez, Vice President of the Retain Banking Service Department, to hire Langston. In Chapter 12, Langston learned about organizational politics working on a project with the highly ambitious and calculating Svetlana Petrova, who took credit for his work. Now that the project is finished, Langston is reporting to Svetlana full time.

A month has passed since the loan exceptions reduction project ended, and Langston is feeling frustrated. He decides to speak directly with Svetlana about the low-level work she has insisted on giving him since she took credit for his work on the loan exceptions project for Sonia. Langston politely requests a meeting and after a number of last-minute postponements by Svetlana has an opportunity to ask her to assign him more challenging tasks in a face-to-face meeting. Svetlana tells Langston that he needs to remember his junior place at the bank and notes that she doubts she will ever consider him a dependable asset to her team. She remarks that it's clear he isn't cut out for banking and asks him if he'd like her to refer him to HR to discuss his options for employment elsewhere. Rather than replying in an unprofessional manner, Langston turns on his heel and walks out of Svetlana's office feeling upset and angry. Seconds later, she slams her door.

Later that morning, Langston is called to Sonia Valdez's office. Sonia greets him politely and gets straight to the point.

"Svetlana tells me you are very unhappy in your role in lending and wish to resign from the bank," Sonia says. "Langston, this comes as a surprise. I'm very disappointed you want to leave the bank. You have excelled here, especially in your role in the computer training project."

Langston can't believe what he is hearing. Svetlana has manipulated their conversation and miscommunicated the message to Sonia to try and get him out of the organization.

"Sonia, I did not tell Svetlana I wanted to resign," Langston says through gritted teeth. "I simply asked whether she would assign me more challenging tasks, because I can do much more than she's allowing me to do."

"I can see you're upset. It appears as though there has been a major miscommunication here," Sonia says. "According to Svetlana, you resigned because you were becoming overwhelmed with work. From what you are telling me, this is clearly not the case. Could you fill me in on exactly what you and Svetlana discussed this morning? I'll talk to her and find out what led to this breakdown in communication."

Langston nods. "Sonia, I absolutely do not want to resign, but I want to be honest with you. I don't feel challenged by my current duties, and Svetlana, for whatever reason, has decided to avoid giving me more complex tasks. Are there any other, more challenging roles for me in lending?"

"I'm afraid it is up to Svetlana to assign the projects in the lending department," Sonia says. "However, I'm happy to learn that you haven't resigned and will discuss the matter with her and see what we can come up with. We don't want to lose you."

Langston gives her a smile, thanks her for her support, and returns to his desk.

As Langston's experience shows, communication can be challenging—especially when you are working with a colleague like Svetlana who is willing to distort communication to gain personal advantage. We are required to communicate throughout our daily lives at work and in our personal lives. Because communication is central to our relationships with others, it is essential that we understand the barriers that can hamper our ability to communicate successfully and learn how to overcome them.[4] Here are some of the barriers most often encountered at work.

- **Filtering.** When someone screens and then manipulates a message from a sender before passing it on to the intended receiver, that person has filtered the message. For example, Svetlana deliberately misinterprets Langston's request for more challenging tasks and passes the message to Sonia that he is unhappy and wants to resign from the bank.
- **Emotions.** Our emotions have an effect on the way we communicate. When we are happy and relaxed, we are more likely to accept constructive criticism in a positive way and convey our messages succinctly and accurately. However, when we are stressed or angry, we might snap at others or feel attacked or defensive when someone tries to offer advice. It is essential that we are aware of our emotions and keep them in check before they spiral out of control. For example, Langston is aware of his heightened emotional state when he is talking to Sonia and takes a moment to calm down before continuing the conversation. He also walks out of Svetlana's office rather than responding to her in an angry or unprofessional manner.
- **Information overload.** At times, we can become overwhelmed by the wealth of information surrounding us. This can lead us to make hasty decisions or lose our ability to prioritize. Being able to prioritize our workload helps us to make better decisions and prevents us from getting overloaded by information.
- **Differing perceptions.** Sometimes the way we interpret situations clashes with the perceptions of others, leading to confusion and misconception. We can overcome this communication barrier by challenging our own assumptions about other people and situations and by seeking advice from others to clarify our perceptions. Proper training for employees in organizations helps to align perceptions. In an ongoing effort to be fair-minded as a manager, Sonia notes the perceptual differences between Langston and Svetlana and promises Langston she will talk to Svetlana to help clear up the misunderstanding.

Filtering: The process of screening and then manipulating a message from a sender before passing it on to the intended receiver

Emotions: A state of feeling that affects the way we communicate

Information overload: Exposure to an overwhelming amount of information

Differing perceptions: The way in which our interpretations of situations clashes with the perceptions of others.

Active Listening

The Greek philosopher Epictetus once said, "We have two ears and one mouth so we should listen twice as much as we speak." This quote references one of the biggest obstacles to successful communication: poor listening. Within organizations, failure to listen properly can lead to misunderstandings that can damage personal and work relationships. Ineffective listening also comes at a high price—it is estimated that millions of

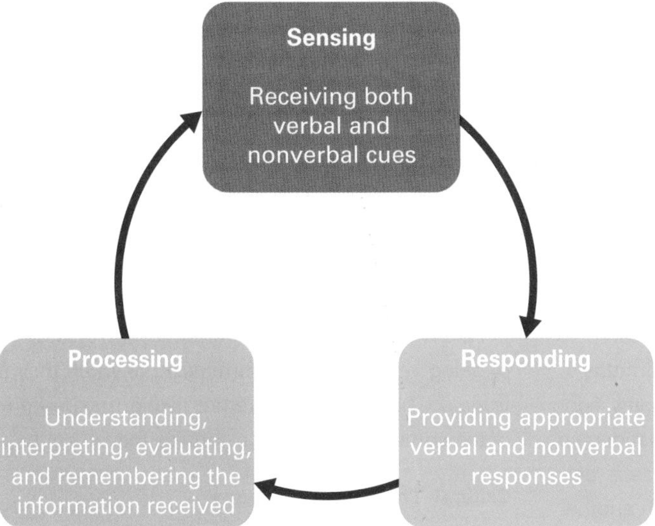

■ FIGURE 13.4 The Active Listening Process

SOURCE: Based on Comer, Lucette B., and Tanya Drollinger. "Active Empathetic Listening and Selling Success: A Conceptual Framework." *Journal of Personal Selling and Sales Management* 19, no. 1 (Winter 1999): 15–29.

dollars are wasted every year due to the time it takes to repeat information, correct misunderstandings, and make up for loss of productivity.[5]

A way to overcome poor listening is through **active listening**, which consists of concentrating on the true meaning of what others are saying.[6] It is an essential skill for employees in the workplace because it allows the receiver to hear and understand the message and reassures the speaker that the message has been heard in the same terms in which it is delivered. Good active listeners remove all distractions so they can concentrate on what is being said, show a real interest in the message the speaker is trying to deliver, and provide appropriate responses to the speaker at suitable times. For example, in our OB case, Sonia demonstrates active listening by waiting until Langston has finished, identifying and understanding his emotional state, and providing feedback on his desire to move departments.

There are three main components to active listening: processing, sensing, and responding (see Figure 13.4).[7]

Processing involves actively understanding and remembering what is being said as well as making an effort to empathize with the speaker's feelings and thoughts and the situation at hand. Active listening also requires looking for nonverbal cues such eye contact or lack thereof, poor posture (slouching, sitting upright and tense), and tone of voice (sarcastic, angry, confident) to really understand the entire message.

Sensing involves paying attention to the signals sent from the speaker. The listener avoids forming an opinion or interrupting the speaker until he or she has finished and consciously remains attentive to what the speaker is saying.

Finally, **responding** is the way active listeners provide feedback to the speaker ("I see what you mean") and clarify the message by repeating some of the key points at appropriate breaks ("So, you're saying that . . . ").

As we have illustrated, communication between individuals can be complex and is often the cause of conflicts and misunderstandings. In the next section, we explore how the different directions of communication affects the functioning of organizations.

Active listening: The act of concentrating on the true meaning of what others are saying

Processing: The act of understanding and remembering what is being said as well as making an effort to empathize with the speaker's feelings and thoughts and the situation at hand.

Sensing: The way listeners pay attention to the signals sent from the speaker

Responding: The way active listeners provide feedback to the speaker

COMMUNICATION APPREHENSION

Examining the Evidence

The ability to communicate effectively is a critical competency for employees in today's workplaces. Researchers Brian D. Blume of the University of Michigan and Timothy T. Baldwin and Katherine C. Ryan of Indiana University conducted a study in which they examined the relationship between communication apprehension, defined as a person's level of fear or anxiety in communicating with another person, and several key outcomes. Their results suggest that communication apprehension is negatively related to willingness to undertake leadership opportunities, and adaptability to new situations. These authors note two important points relative to overcoming communication apprehension. First, individuals should heighten their awareness of their communication apprehension so they can more effectively self-monitor and confront their anxieties. Second, individuals should understand that communication apprehension is not synonymous with poor communication skills. Indeed, some people with high levels of communication anxiety are capable of being very effective communicators when they are forced to do so, but they likely are not taking maximum advantage of the communication opportunities they encounter.

Critical-Thinking Questions

1. **Why is communication apprehension an important problem for managers to consider?**
2. **What actions can managers take to help themselves or their employees overcome communication apprehension?**

SOURCE: Blume, Brian D., Timothy T. Baldwin, and Katherine C. Ryan. "Communication Apprehension: A Barrier to Students' Leadership, Adaptability, and Multicultural Appreciation." *Academy of Management Learning and Education* 12, no. 2 (June 2013): 158–172.

THINKING CRITICALLY

1. Review the barriers to communication (filtering, emotions, information overload, differing perceptions). Provide at least one strategy for counteracting or overcoming each one of these barriers. **[Create]**
2. Active listening is described as the best solution for poor listening skills and Sonia is provided as an example of an adept active listener. In what, if any, situations can you imagine Svetlana being an adept active listener? Defend your answer. **[Analyze/Evaluate]**
3. Review the three active listening steps (processing, sensing, responding). Given the text description of these steps, what obstacles to active listening will channels of communication low in information richness present? Explain your answer. **[Apply/Analyze/Evaluate]**

COMMUNICATING IN ORGANIZATIONS

13.4 Describe types of communication networks within organizations

The flow of communication in an organization can move in three main directions depending on how an organization is structured.[8] (See Figure 13.5.)

Downward communication: Messages sent from the upper levels of the organizational hierarchy to the lower levels

Downward communication sends messages from the upper levels of the organizational hierarchy to the lower levels. For example, in hierarchical organizations like the military, there is a tendency to use downward communication. One of the major functions of downward communication is to maintain discipline and employee compliance through positive influence. When downward communication is successful, it is totally

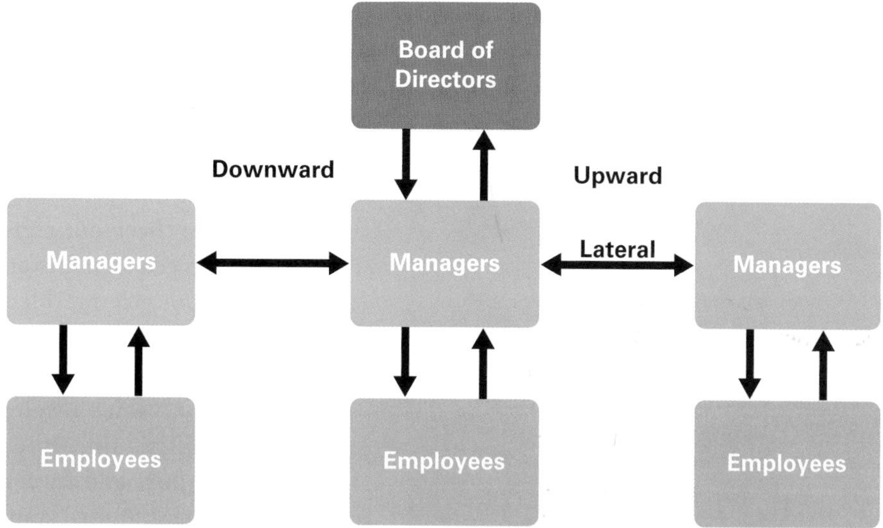

■ FIGURE 13.5 Three Directions of Communication in Organizations

SOURCE: Based on Lunenburg, Fred C. "Formal Communication Channels: Upward, Downward, Horizontal, and External." *Focus on Colleges, Universities, and Schools* 4, no. 1 (2010). www.nationalforum.com/Electronic%20Journal%20Volumes/Lunenburg,%20Fred%20C,%20Formal%20Comm%20Channels%20FOCUS%20V4%20N1%202010.pdf.

transparent. This means that lower-level employees consistently receive clear messages and feedback from their superiors regarding organizational performance, strategies, developments, and goals. Sharing information down the levels provides employees with a sense of involvement and minimizes doubt and insecurity about how the company is performing. However, when downward communication goes wrong and messages fail to be transmitted effectively down the chain of command, it can cause confusion, distrust, and anxiety among the rest of the workforce.

Upward communication sends messages from the lower levels of the organizational hierarchy to the higher levels. Some organizations value feedback, suggestions, and advice from lower-level employees who are "on the ground" and may be closer to knowing the needs of the customer. For example, employees at US restaurant Chick-fil-A came up with Frosted Lemonade, a combination of fresh-squeezed lemonade and ice cream. The drink has caught on with customers as a snack option that's lighter than a full milkshake.[9] These employees are also encouraged to share any problems or thoughts they have about the organization and their roles and provide recommendations for improvement. If lower-level employees do not effectively communicate with their superiors and instead withhold or filter information, this can leave those at the higher levels ignorant of what is really going on in the organization.

Lateral communication sends messages between and among similar hierarchical levels across organizations. Lateral communication can be an effective way for people from different departments to communicate the information they need quickly and accurately. Organizations that foster a collaborative environment encourage lateral communication between their employees. For example, collaborative organizations like IDEO use lateral communication to gather ideas from employees across several disciplines in order to generate creative solutions.[10] Although lateral communication supports teamwork and helps build morale, it requires managerial control to minimize potential interpersonal conflict that may arise as a result of many participants collaborating at once.

Let's take a look at the communication network operated by Trader Joe's.

Thriving US food retailer Trader Joe's owes much of its success to its communication process. When employees join Trader Joe's they participate in a training program that teaches them management, leadership, and communication skills.

Upward communication: Messages sent from the lower levels of the organizational hierarchy to the higher levels

Lateral communication: Messages sent between and among the same hierarchical levels across organizations

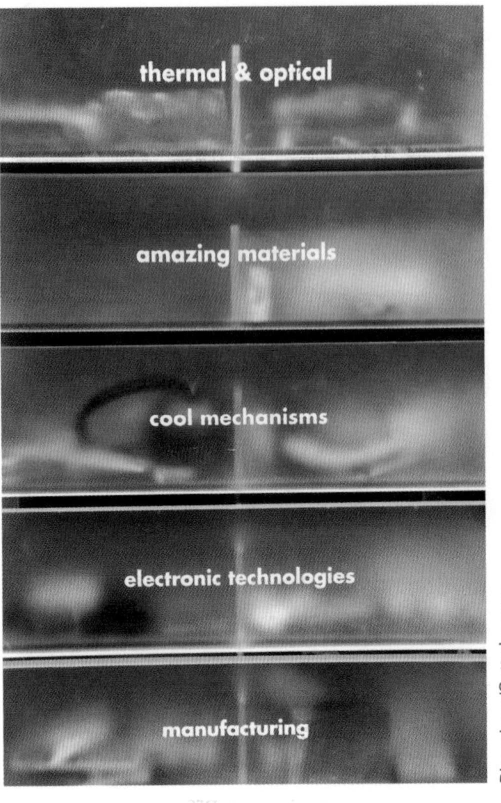

Bloomberg/Getty Images

Design and consulting firm IDEO uses lateral communication by placing filing cabinets throughout their offices that all employees can explore and fill with things they want to share.

The retailer operates a hierarchy in which employees work in a collaborative environment and multitask regardless of their job descriptions. For example, store managers sweep the floor or operate the check-out register when the need arises. Every employee, from vice president to store clerk, is encouraged to contribute ideas about how the store is run, which inspires loyalty and a genuine interest in the business and its customers. Frequent feedback and communication from managers and supervisors means that employees are kept informed about their tasks and duties and how they fit into the goals of the organization. By fostering a strong upward and downward communication chain, Trader Joe's has succeeded in building a successful enterprise equipped with a high-performing, loyal, and committed workforce.[11]

Network Communication

Regardless of the direction of the flow of communication within organizations, most messages are sent through two main communication networks: formal and informal.[12] **Formal networks** transmit the messages established and approved by the organizational hierarchy. Usually, formal networks are imposed by the chain of command, which sends official messages such as policies and procedures to the rest of the staff. For example, when a CEO needs to tell employees about a new company policy, management sends the information in the form of an e-mail. In contrast, **informal networks** handle the unofficial sharing of information between employees and across company

Formal networks: The transmission of messages established and approved by the organizational hierarchy

Informal networks: A casual form of sharing information between employees across company divisions

AP Photo/Daily Herald, Bob Chwedyk

Trader Joe's employees at all levels are encouraged to contribute thoughts and ideas about how the store is run.

Teachers share stories and tips with each other as part of an informal network of communication.

divisions. Informal networks can help employees communicate freely with one another, build relationships, exchange opinions, and share grievances. For instance, informal networks allow minimum wage workers to share their grievances about low pay, teachers to share classroom management strategies, and students to rate their professors and study for a major exam.

One of the main forms of informal networks is the **grapevine,** the unofficial line of communication between individuals or groups.[13] Grapevines are a useful method of communicating messages quickly and efficiently in person, more than e-mails, blogs, or through other technological tools. They can bring about a sense of unity among the employees who meet and share information. However, they are more common where management keeps employees in the dark about what is going on in the organization. Indeed, much of what is said on the grapevine can be inaccurate and is usually based on rumor. As some employees have discovered, missteps on modern-day grapevines like blogs can lead to termination. For example, former Google employee Mark Jen was fired for criticizing his employer through his blog, and a Delta Airlines flight attendant was fired for posting suggestive pictures of herself in uniform on her blog.[14]

Grapevine

Grapevines also give rise to **gossip chains,** communication networks in which one individual creates and spreads untrue or inaccurate information to others through the organization.[15] Each person who hears the gossip has the choice to keep it confidential or to pass it on. For example, one employee might spread gossip to others to discredit an unpopular supervisor. In contrast, a **cluster chain** consists of a group of people who broadcast information only within their group.[16] In both gossip chains and cluster chains, the information moves very quickly and can be damaging to an organization regardless of management's confirming or denying the rumors. Successful organizations actively control rumors and gossip through effective, honest, and consistent communication.[17]

Grapevine: An unofficial line of communication between individuals or groups

Gossip chains: A type of communication that occurs when one individual creates and spreads untrue or inaccurate information through the organization

Cluster chain: A type of communication that occurs when a group of people broadcast information within a larger group

While Langston trusts and respects Sonia, he knows that continuing to report to Svetlana is no longer an option given her dishonesty. Langston needs advice about his position at the bank and starts reaching out to his network immediately. Later that day, he sits down with Saoirse O'Donnell who reports to Sonia and leads Customer Services at the bank. Langston briefly explains that he is not being challenged in lending and that he believes he could better serve the bank's needs in another department.

"So you'd like to leave lending for another role within the bank, is that correct?," she asks.

Langston nods.

"I understand your predicament, Langston, but how can I help you?"

Langston takes a deep breath. "Saoirse, when I reported to you in customer services during my time in the Leadership Development Program, I felt challenged and learned a great deal. I love working with people, and at the time you told me that my skills were an asset to your department. In short, I am hoping you might have a role for me in your area," Langston says.

Saoirse looks at him thoughtfully and replies, "Langston, I think you did an amazing job when you were with us, and I was especially impressed with the training skills you demonstrated during the new computer system initiative, but unless someone leaves there are no positions available in customer services right now. I have an idea that might appeal to you, though. This information isn't official yet, so I trust you'll keep it to yourself."

Langston is intrigued. "Of course!," he responds.

"I'm leaving customer services," Saoirse announces.

Langston didn't see this coming. Saoirse has been in customer services for more than 15 years and is thought of highly at the bank.

Saoirse smiles at Langston's reaction, and adds, "I'm not leaving the bank, just the department." She explains that the bank is setting up a private banking division that will provide personal banking and financial services to high-net-worth individuals. Sonia has chosen Saoirse to set up and lead this new area. Initially it will be staffed by a small team of six individuals from the customer services and human resources departments.

"Congratulations!," Langston says.

"Langston, I need good people with excellent interpersonal and communication skills to attract affluent individuals to our bank," Saoirse says, earnestly. "That means connecting with private banking profile customers within our community such as doctors, dentists, lawyers, and professors by attending professional functions, charity events, presentations, and anywhere else these sort of professionals may be present."

Langston is getting excited. This is his kind of job!

"The role isn't about giving these wealthy people a hard sell," Saoirse warns. "The way we want to attract customers is through professional, friendly exchange, which ideally will result in a meeting. This is all about building relationships, Langston, and I know you can do that."

"Saoirse, this all sounds fantastic! I would love to work for you and be part of the private banking division," Langston says.

Saoirse smiles. "That's good news, Langston. It would be great to have you on my team. I'll speak with Sonia later today and let you know when you can share the news with Svetlana."

As he makes his way happily back to his desk, Langston is surprised that so many of the lending staff greet and smile at him. One employee even gives him a high-five. When his friend Loan Officer Jonathan Hicks calls Langston an hour later, he finds out the reason for his sudden popularity.

"Hey Langston! I heard through the grapevine that you gave Svetlana a piece of your mind. You're my hero!" Jonathan laughs. "Rumor has it you slammed out of Svetlana's office and charged back to your desk like a man on a mission!"

"That's not true!" Langston replies.

"Really?" Jonathan says. "Well in that case, why were you dragged into Sonia's office afterward? She must have told you off for behaving disrespectfully toward Svetlana. But don't worry, the lending department is on your side."

On his way home from work that night, Langston thinks about his predicament. He feels uncomfortable being the target of office gossip, yet if people want to make assumptions about his meeting with Svetlana, they will talk about it whether he likes it or not. His main worry is that the rumors will get back to Saoirse and negatively affect her opinion of him. By morning he has decided to speak with Saoirse directly about the rumors.

When he gets to the office, Langston calls Saoirse, explains the rumor that is going around and how little truth there is to it.

Saoirse responds, "I make it a point never to listen to rumors, but I appreciate you explaining your side to me. Personally, I feel I am a good judge of character, and I think that behaving in such a way would be out of character for you, am I right?"

"Absolutely," Langston says. "And let me reassure you that I will always be professional and courteous to all members of staff and potential clients in my new role."

"I believe you will, Langston. I have Sonia's approval to offer you a job with my team and she told me it was fine for you to let Svetlana know that you'll be leaving lending next month," Saoirse says and ends the call.

Langston writes a polite e-mail message to Svetlana with a cc to Sonia and Saoirse, informing her that he has accepted Saoirse's offer to move to the private banking division. Using this formal communication channel and bringing both Sonia and Saoirse into the conversation prevents Svetlana from manipulating his words. When Sonia calls Langston into her office later that afternoon, he is not surprised to see Svetlana sitting there too.

"I wanted to congratulate you in person, Langston. I'm delighted you've found a new role within the bank with Saoirse. Both Svetlana and I congratulate you. You'll be a real asset to the private banking team," Sonia says.

"Congratulations, Langston!" Svetlana adds, cordial as always when one of her superiors is present.

On his final day in lending, Langston reflects on his experiences at the bank. Although he has experienced plenty of ups and downs, he is proud of his ability to overcome obstacles and the technical and communication skills he has learned. He fully intends to put these skills into practice in his new role in private banking and looks forward to gaining additional managerial and leadership experience.

THINKING CRITICALLY

1. Would you prefer to work in an organization that depends on downward communication, upward communication, lateral communication, or some combination of the three? Explain your reasoning. **[Evaluate]**
2. Are informal networks necessary in a healthy organization? Why or why not? **[Evaluate]**
3. What lessons about combatting office gossip and the grapevine can you draw from Langston's decision to speak to Saoirse directly? Should Langston have directly confronted Svetlana about her miscommunication to Sonia? Why or why not? **[Analyze/Evaluate]**

CROSS-CULTURAL COMMUNICATION

13.5 Discuss the elements of effective cross-cultural communication

The success of global organizations depends on the quality of cross-cultural communication, and without the necessary preparation, it can be a minefield. Cultural

misunderstandings are all too common. When is kissing a business associate appropriate? Or bowing to a colleague? When is it of the utmost importance to arrive on time for a business meeting? When it comes to advertising, it is imperative that the message not get lost in translation through cultural error. For example, KFC's "Finger-Lickin' Good" was interpreted as "Eat your fingers off" in China; Swedish vacuum maker's ad campaign for Electrolux centered on the slogan, "Nothing sucks like an Electrolux," which understandably failed to appeal to many US consumers; and Braniff Airlines advertised its leather seats with the slogan "Fly in leather," which was translated in Mexico as "Fly naked"—not what the airline intended to convey.

To avoid these costly blunders, many organizations encourage their employees to learn a second language and carry out extensive research to increase their understanding of other cultures. In answer to the questions mentioned, by the way, it is appropriate in France to greet business associates with a kiss on the cheek; bowing is a traditional form of greeting in East Asia; and punctuality is essential when attending meetings in the United Kingdom, Germany, and Switzerland, among others.

One of the major barriers to cross-cultural communication is **ethnocentrism**, the tendency to believe your culture or ethnicity is superior to everyone else's.[18] For example, members of Western cultures might judge negatively people from other cultures in which it is customary to use the hands to eat rather than use utensils, or they might belittle other cultures for their passive or formal nature. Figure 13.6 shows a map of the world.

Ethnocentrism: The tendency to believe that your culture or ethnicity is superior to everyone else's

Why does this map appear "wrong" to many people? Because it is shown from a different perspective than what one normally sees on a map. The famed Uruguayan artist Joaquin Torres-Garcia painted South America in this way in his painting *América invertida* to contrast the South with the North, where an ethnocentric perspective lead many in the so-called dominant northern hemisphere to look down on their southern neighbors. For those in the South, however, including Torres-Garcia, that view is simply upside-down.[19]

■ FIGURE 13.6 "Southside Up" Global Map

Source: Anna Versluis/ SAGE

Low-Context Versus High-Context Cultures

The role of language has a major influence on culture and vice versa. In the United States it is common to use sports references in a business environment. "He's a team player," "You're way off base," and "She threw me a curve" are all popular phrases that are familiar in the United States but might be confusing to people from other cultures. Anthropologist Edward T. Hall studied the variety of ways different cultures use language and divided cultures into two main groups on that basis: low-context and high-context.[20]

Low-context cultures depend more on explicit messages conveyed through the spoken or written word. Most English-speaking and Germanic countries have a fast, direct, logical, efficient, "What you say is what you mean" communication style. In business environments in these countries there is less emphasis on interpersonal relationships and more on the individual.

In contrast, in **high-context cultures**, most messages are conveyed through body language, nonverbal cues, and the circumstances in which the communication is taking place. According to Hall, many Middle Eastern and Asian cultures fall into this category. The Japanese, for example, have an indirect, intuitive, unemotional, contemplative, and passive style of negotiation. In short, what you say is not necessarily what you mean. High-context cultures value silence as a way of absorbing information and getting a sense of the people they are communicating with.

Over the years, there have been many well-documented clashes between low-context and high-context cultures. For example, President George H. W. Bush and Chrysler's Lee Iacocca are said to have violated Japanese etiquette during a 1992 trade meeting by making direct demands on Japanese leaders.[21] Some commentators believe this approach damaged the relationship between the two countries for a period of time.

Low-context cultures: Cultures that depend on explicit messages conveyed through the spoken or written word

High-context cultures: Cultures in which meaning is conveyed through body language, nonverbal cues, and the circumstances in which the communication is taking place

Social Context

Communication also depends on the social setting. We tend to use different vocabulary depending on the situation or the person we are talking to, and our response to these social contexts differs by culture. For example, you are unlikely to greet your professor the same way you would your baseball teammate or fellow student.

AP Photo/Dennis Cook

President George H. W. Bush visited Japan in 1992 to meet with Prime Minister Kiichi Miyazawa. Some speculate that the direct demands President Bush made of Japanese leaders were perceived as violating Japanese business ethics.

The way people from different cultures use language can provide a richer understanding of their society. For example, the Japanese base their linguistic styles on status and choose from three different styles to express the appropriate level of social respect: basic speech, average speech, or elegant speech. Novice speakers of Japanese might inadvertently offend someone to whom they are speaking if they mistakenly choose the incorrect linguistic style.[22]

Gender differences can be reflected in language and can, in turn, affect communication. In some areas of the West Indies, for example, women and men use different words to refer to the same thing.

Other Complicating Factors

Several other factors can further complicate our communication with members of other cultures.[23]

Slang and Idioms

Slang is informal language applied in a particular context or group. Although it is not usually appropriate in business communication, slang is often used in daily life. For example, in the United Kingdom and Ireland, "knackered" means "exhausted," while in the United States the slang phrase "in a New York minute" means to do something very fast.

An *idiom* is a word or group of words used to convey a meaning other than its literal one. For example, US businesspeople sometimes use expressions such as "dead in the water" for a project or action that has stalled. Even native English-speakers communicating with people from other English-speaking countries may encounter difficulties with idioms. For example, in a business setting, the US expression, "Table it" means not to discuss a matter further, whereas in the United Kingdom, it means to bring the matter to the table for discussion.

Euphemisms

Most languages include *euphemisms*, vague or general words used in place of those considered to be too blunt or harsh. Popular business euphemisms include "giving (someone) his or her marching orders" instead of firing the person; "under the table" to describe an illegal or concealed transaction; and "pushing the envelope," which means going beyond the limits of performance. Without understanding euphemisms and the social context in which to use them, businesspeople have difficulty appreciating and successfully integrating into different cultures.

Proverbs

Proverbs or wise sayings are common to many different cultures. Common proverbs used in a US business environment include: "A fool and his money are soon parted," "Too many cooks spoil the broth," and "Better late than never." Once again, it is essential to understand the way different societies use proverbs and how they are applied to behavior.

Verbal Dueling

Certain cultural subgroups engage in *verbal dueling*, a form of competitive communication in which the participants exchange insults until one "wins." Although verbal dueling is generally associated with male adolescents (African American adolescents in the United States verbally duel in a game called "The Dozens," and Turkish adolescents play a similar game), verbal battles also take place among political leaders and in a number of societies where exchanging insults is regarded as a better way of diffusing conflict than using weapons.[24] When you are interacting with other cultures, it is useful to become aware of different forms of verbal dueling to truly understand the nature of cross-cultural communication.

AP Photo/Jason R. Henske

Late night talk show host Conan O'Brien utilized humor when giving a memorable commencement speech at Dartmouth College in 2011.

Humor

Most cultures value humor, but what is perceived to be funny in one culture can easily fall flat in another because some jokes are inappropriate for the audience or get lost in translation. While it is common for a British or US businessperson to begin a speech or a presentation with some light humor or an anecdote, that is not the case in Asia where humor is less pervasive in formal business settings. When presenting to people from different cultures, it is essential to know the audience and avoid jokes that could be perceived as inappropriate—or not to joke at all if that is the better course. Television host and comedian Conan O'Brien was praised for his humorous commencement speech to students in Dartmouth College.[25]

Conversational Taboos

Regardless of the participants' cultural background, a degree of small talk usually takes place before the beginning of a meeting, especially when people are meeting for the first time. US businesspeople tend to talk about the weather or sports and avoid taboo or contentious subjects such as religion, politics, and personal matters. Members of other cultures are accustomed to openly discussing religion and politics or asking personal questions in a business setting. What qualifies as taboo varies from culture to culture, so it is vital to know what to expect before the initial meeting.

Overcoming Difficulties in Cross-Cultural Communication

With so many potential obstacles to avoid, communicating with different cultures can seem a daunting prospect. The more knowledge and understanding we have, the smoother and more successful the communication will be. With this in mind, what can we do to reduce misunderstandings and misinterpretations?

- Do your homework and make sure you are familiar with the language and customs of different cultures.
- Never make assumptions; it is better to believe there are differences until similarities have been established.

- Be an active listener and summarize points to confirm you understand what the other party has said.
- Make an effort to be supportive, encouraging, and empathic, particularly toward those interacting in an English-speaking nation for whom English is a second language.
- Avoid slang, jargon, and euphemisms; they often cause confusion.

In this chapter we have explored communication in organizations and its importance across different cultures. In the next chapter, we explore the topic of culture as it relates to organizations and its impact on organizational behavior.

THINKING CRITICALLY

1. List at least three strategies or steps advertisers introducing a product in a new country should take to ensure that their marketing message isn't culturally misconstrued. **[Evaluate/Create]**
2. What difficulties are business people from low-context cultures likely to encounter when doing business in high-context cultures? **[Understand/Apply]**
3. Assume that you are a product manager based in North America and will be collaborating with a team of software engineers based in India. Describe the steps you would take to prepare to work effectively with your new colleagues. **[Create]**

IN REVIEW

Learning Objectives

13.1 Describe the basic model of communication

Communication is the act of transmitting thoughts, processes, and ideas through a variety of channels The Shannon-Weaver Model of communication is based on two components: the sender of the message, known as the *source*, and the receiver of the message. The sender encodes and then transmits a message through a communication channel where it is decoded by the receiver. The receiver must then provide feedback or a response to the sender to confirm that the message has been received and its meaning understood. Disturbances in the communications process are called *noise*.

13.2 Compare the types of communication channels

Oral communication is the verbal exchange of information, ideas, and processes one on one or as a group. **Written communication** makes use of the written word through reports, memos, letters, and other channels. **Electronic communication** transmits messages through e-mail, Skype, videoconferencing, blogs, fax, instant messaging, texting, and social networking. **Nonverbal communication** is the transmission of wordless cues through posture, facial expression, gestures, tone of voice, and so on.

13.3 Identify key barriers to effective communication

Filtering is screening and manipulating a message from a sender before passing it on to the receiver. Our *emotions* have an effect on the way we communicate. The wealth of information surrounding us can lead us to make hasty decisions or prioritize poorly because of *information overload*. Because of *differing perceptions,* the ways we interpret situations can clash with the perceptions of others, leading to confusion and misconception. We can overcome this communication barrier by challenging our own assumptions about other people and situations for accuracy and by seeking advice from others to clarify our perceptions.

13.4 Describe types of communication networks within organizations

Downward communication sends messages from the upper levels of the organizational hierarchy to the lower levels, and **upward communication** sends messages from the lower levels of the organizational hierarchy to the higher levels. **Lateral communication** flows between and among similar hierarchical levels across organizations. **Formal networks** transmit messages established and approved by the organizational hierarchy. In contrast, **informal networks** are a means of unofficially sharing of information between employees across company divisions.

13.5 Discuss the elements of effective cross-cultural communication

Strategies for effective cross-cultural communication include doing your homework and making sure you know the language and customs of different cultures, never making assumptions, believing there are cultural differences until otherwise established, being an active listener and summarizing points to confirm you understand what the other party has said, being supportive and empathic toward those for whom English is a second language and avoiding slang, jargon, and euphemisms.

KEY TERMS

Active listening 335
Channel richness 331
Cluster chain 339
Communication 327
Differing perceptions 334
Downward communication 336
Electronic communication 331
Emotions 334
Ethnocentrism 342
Filtering 334
Formal networks 338
Gossip chains 339
Grapevine 339
High-context cultures 343
Informal networks 338
Information overload 334
Lateral communication 337
Low-context cultures 343
Nonverbal communication 331
Oral communication 328
Processing 335
Responding 335
Sensing 335
Upward communication 337
Written communication 330

THINKING CRITICALLY ABOUT THE CASE OF LANGSTON BURROWS

Put yourself in Langston Burrows' position at the bank and consider the five critical-thinking steps in relation to his dealings with Svetlana, Sonia, and Saoirse.

OBSERVE

How would you describe the communication styles of Langston, Svetlana, Sonia, and Saoirse? Which characters' styles are most alike? Which are most different? Provide support for your responses.

INTERPRET

Why does Sonia choose to speak with Langston individually after Svetlana tells her Langston has resigned from the bank? Why does Sonia choose to speak with Svetlana separately after her meeting with Langston? Do you agree with her decision in both cases? Why or why not?

ANALYZE

If Langston had failed to secure a new job with Saoirse, what would have been logical next steps for him to take? Is it possible that the grapevine's assumption that he had told off Svetlana could have helped him secure another position outside her sphere of influence? Why or why not?

EVALUATE

What communication missteps will Langston need to avoid when he starts his new job? If he encounters any new colleagues similar to Svetlana, what communication channels and strategies could help him to prevent misunderstandings and political snafus?

EXPLAIN

Assume you are Saoirse. What questions, if any, would you ask Sonia about her experiences in dealing with Langston? Would you speak with Svetlana about Langston? Why or why not?

EXERCISE 13.1: OVERCOMING BARRIERS TO EFFECTIVE COMMUNICATION

Step 1. Identifying Your Barriers List two recent situations in which you experienced one or more of the barriers to communication described in the chapter (filtering, emotions, poor listening, information overload, differing perceptions).

Step 2. Analyzing Your Barriers Next, explain in detail how these barriers disrupted the communication process in each situation.

Step 3. Overcoming Your Barriers Finally, list some specific ways that you could overcome or avoid these barriers to communication in similar situations in the future.

EXERCISE 13.2: THERE´S AN APP FOR THAT

Objectives:

Identify key barriers to effective communication.

Discuss the elements of effective cross-cultural communication.

Instructions:

Step 1. Write down as many barriers to intercultural communication as you can think of. (1 to 3 minutes)

Step 2. Find a partner and combine lists. Then, for as many barriers as possible, write down one communication or information technology that can help overcome each barrier. (5 to 10 minutes)

Step 3. Each pair should find another pair and form a quad. These quads should combine lists, and reconcile any differences. Then they should examine the combined list and look for areas where information or communication technology *cannot* help to overcome intercultural communication barriers. (5 to 10 minutes)

Step 4. Choose a spokesperson for your quad and be prepared to discuss your list when called upon by your instructor. (3 to 5 minutes)

Reflection Questions:

1. In what ways do you think using information or communication technologies could actually hurt intercultural communications?
2. What was the most interesting technology use you heard?
3. Were there any overall trends in technology use that you heard from the exercise?
4. Are there any ways that you have personally used information or communication technologies to overcome intercultural communication barriers? If so, which were most effective?

Exercise contributed by Milton R. Mayfield, Professor of Business, Texas A&M International University and Jaqueline R. Mayfield, Professor of Business, Texas A&M International University.

EXERCISE 13.3: CHANNEL CROSS-TALK

Objectives:

This exercise will help you to better *compare* different communication channels and *identify* barriers to effective communication.

Instructions:

Step 1. Find a partner and complete the following tasks:

A) Choose one person to go first (the person with the least recent birthday). This person is designated the *Caller* for this exercise, and the other person is designated the *Namer*.

B) The Caller has 10 seconds to name a communication method. If the Caller cannot name a communication method, then that person is eliminated. For later rounds, the Caller can also be eliminated for naming a communication method twice.

C) The Namer then has to categorize the type of channel, and name one potential communication barrier using chapter concepts. This task also has to be accomplished in 10 seconds.

D) The Namer´s categorization or barrier can be challenged by the Namer. If there is a challenge, check in the chapter to see if categorization and barrier were correctly identified. If the type of channel or barrier is wrong, then the Namer is eliminated.

E) If neither person is eliminated, then switch roles and repeat the steps until someone is eliminated.

(1 to 5 minutes)

Step 2. If you win the exchange, find another winner and continue the process. If you did not win, then you can act as an observer or judge for the remaining pairs. Continue this process until only one person is left. (1 to 5 minutes)

Reflection Questions:

1. What new insights did you gain about communication channels and barriers?
2. In which role did you have the most trouble?
3. Where did other people seem to struggle most?

Exercise contributed by Milton R. Mayfield, Professor of Business, Texas A&M International University and Jaqueline R. Mayfield, Professor of Business, Texas A&M International University.

CASE STUDY 13.1: 3M

With more than $30 billion in annual sales, 88,000 employees, and more than 55,000 products from adhesives to medical device parts to car care products, 3M has been a leader in innovation for over a century. Innovation is, after all, its slogan. How does the company sustain its pioneering attitude? The answer lies in great communication. As it has done with its evolving products, 3M continues to think of new ways to communicate with its employees.

In 2006, 3M executives felt that innovation and efficiency were slowing down, and they needed to do something about it. George W. Buckley had recently become CEO. He and the executive team outlined a strategy to engage employees that they believed would lead to positive effects in creativity and efficiency and, in turn, allow management to set more ambitious market-share goals.

Several areas that needed attention were identified by talent VP Sandra Tokach. Communication needed to be improved throughout; this included fostering collaboration and teaching leaders how to both supervise and develop people. Improved communication also entailed ensuring that employees found meaning in their work, that the work supported the market-focused mission, and that people understood their pay and benefits.

The team realized that implementing a lot of change at once is difficult and can unsettle employees. To combat this, they built upon existing approaches meant to foster innovation and communicated while changes were taking place. Two main initiatives that went hand in hand. First, leaders and employees needed to be educated about work factors that mattered to them, from company mission to pay. Next, open communication, a cornerstone of the company, was to remain front and center to preserve trust as a part of all interactions and relationships within the business.

Education of supervisors was implemented that aimed to give them the necessary skills to "Develop, Teach and Engage Others." A series of short videos, each about 10 minutes in length, was created to demonstrate the relevant aspects of these proficiencies and to teach supervisors how to bring more authenticity to their communication methods and use a coaching perspective to develop their employees. The training focused on defining employee engagement as the leader's responsibility.

An emerging leaders program encouraged leaders to teach other employees by serving as a mentor, sponsor, and champion. As leaders help their employees achieve, those same employees develop leadership skills and help the next generation of workers. The emerging leaders program encouraged collaboration and candid conversation, behaviors that made their way back into the company culture.

Training emphasized the need for a leader to be open, honest, and available. Leaders were given guides on how to ask the right questions and listen to their employees when discussing their work. This inspired more understanding among colleagues as leaders began to understand each employee's different needs and wants.

Engagement extended to raising awareness of the role of everyone in society, not just at 3M. The company's three components of commitment are taking care of the environment, taking care of others, and taking care of yourself. Methods were put into place to communicate the importance of each of these aspects and train employees about how to articulate them to others.

All supervisors were trained to explain how pay is determined. 3M realized that the combination of rank-and-file layoffs and bloated executive bonuses at other companies sent a bad message to employees. Instead of treating pay as secret, the company made discussing it part of its open communication system, knowing that more understanding leads to more trust and stronger perceptions of fairness.

Many new systems for opening channels of communication were put into place. Several relied on modern technology, such as the online brainstorming tool InnovationLive. Blogs, wikis, and an internal social networking site have also been introduced. Other new methods didn't rely on technology at all. "Random lunches" are voluntary monthly meetings in which people sign up and get randomly assigned to have lunch with three other people. This helps employees get to know people across different divisions and work areas and has proved very popular within the company. All these techniques improved both communication and innovation.

3M has never been satisfied with the status quo. By continually examining and improving internal communication, the company provides work environments conducive to pursuing opportunities. This is what creates the innovative mind-set 3M is famous for.

Case Questions

1. Explain why 3M attributes so much of its success to open communication.
2. Describe how 3M has utilized electronic communication.
3. Identify the direction of communication in 3M.

Sources

Govindarajan, Vijay, and Srikanth Srinivas. "The Innovation Mindset in Action: 3M Corporation," *Harvard Business Review.* August 6, 2013. http://blogs.hbr.org/2013/08/the-innovation-mindset-in-acti-3.

McCauley, Cynthia D., and Morgan W. McCall Jr. *Using Experience to Develop Leadership Talent: How Organizations Leverage On-the-Job Development* (San Francisco: Jossey-Bass, 2014).

Oakes, Kevin, and Pat Galagan. *The Executive Guide to Integrated Talent Management* (Alexandria, VA: American Society for Training and Development; 2011).

SHRM Staff. "3M: In the Company We Trust." *Society of Human Resource Management.* August 8, 2011. www.weknownext.com/workforce/3m-in-the-company-we-trust.

SELF-ASSESSMENT 13.1

Listening Skills Self-Assessment

For each statement, circle the number that best describes you based on the following scale:

	Not at all Accurate	Somewhat Accurate	A Little Accurate	Mostly Accurate	Completely Accurate
1. I give people my full attention and maintain eye contact when they are speaking.	1	2	3	4	5
2. I maintain an attentive posture and respond with nonverbal cues to show that I am listening.	1	2	3	4	5
3. I appreciate hearing other people's perspectives.	1	2	3	4	5
4. I try to keep an open mind when I am listening.	1	2	3	4	5
5. I can effectively identify other people's emotions when speaking with them.	1	2	3	4	5
6. I can tell when someone is withholding information or not telling me the truth.	1	2	3	4	5
7. I have good comprehension and recall of what is communicated to me.	1	2	3	4	5
8. I ask for more information or ask follow-up questions as needed.	1	2	3	4	5
9. I try to be patient and understanding when listening to people who are upset.	1	2	3	4	5
10. I make others comfortable in sharing their feelings with me.	1	2	3	4	5
11. I carefully evaluate the information that is shared with me.	1	2	3	4	5
12. I let people know what I think of their message, even if I disagree with them.	1	2	3	4	5

Scoring

Add the numbers circled: ______________

Interpretation

48 and above = You have outstanding listening skills that help you overcome communication barriers to be an effective communicator.

25–47 = You have moderate listening skills. You could improve some key aspects of your listening capabilities to become a more effective communicator.

24 and below = You need to make some substantial improvements in your listening skills in order to effectively communicate with others.

SOURCE: Adapted from Zabava Ford, Wendy S., Andrew D. Wolvin, and Sungeun Chung. "Students' Self-Perceived Listening Competencies in the Basic Speech Communication Course." *International Journal of Listening* 14 (May 2000): 1.

© iStockphoto.com/Izabela Habur

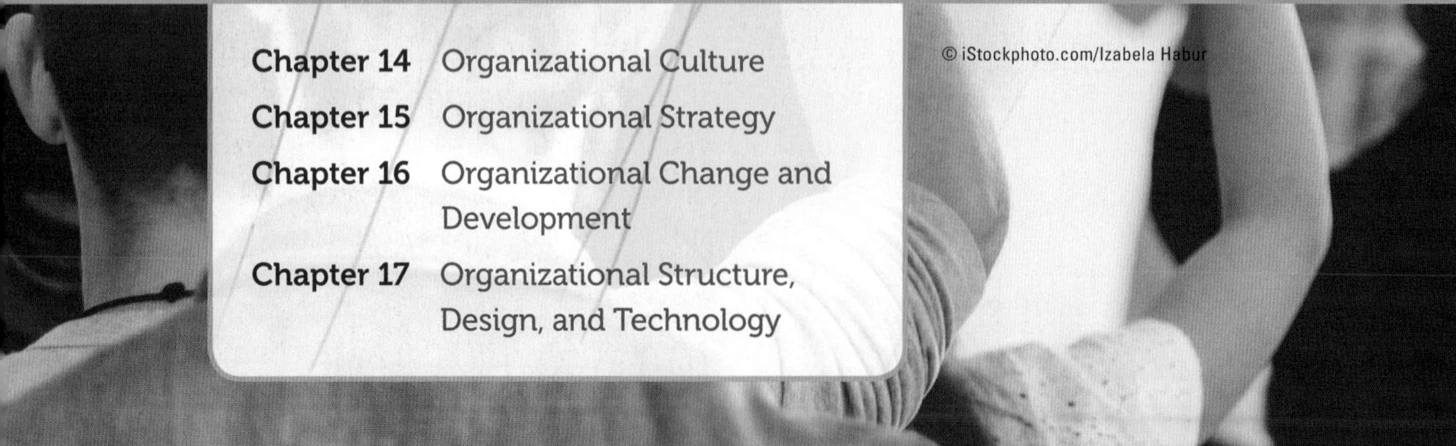

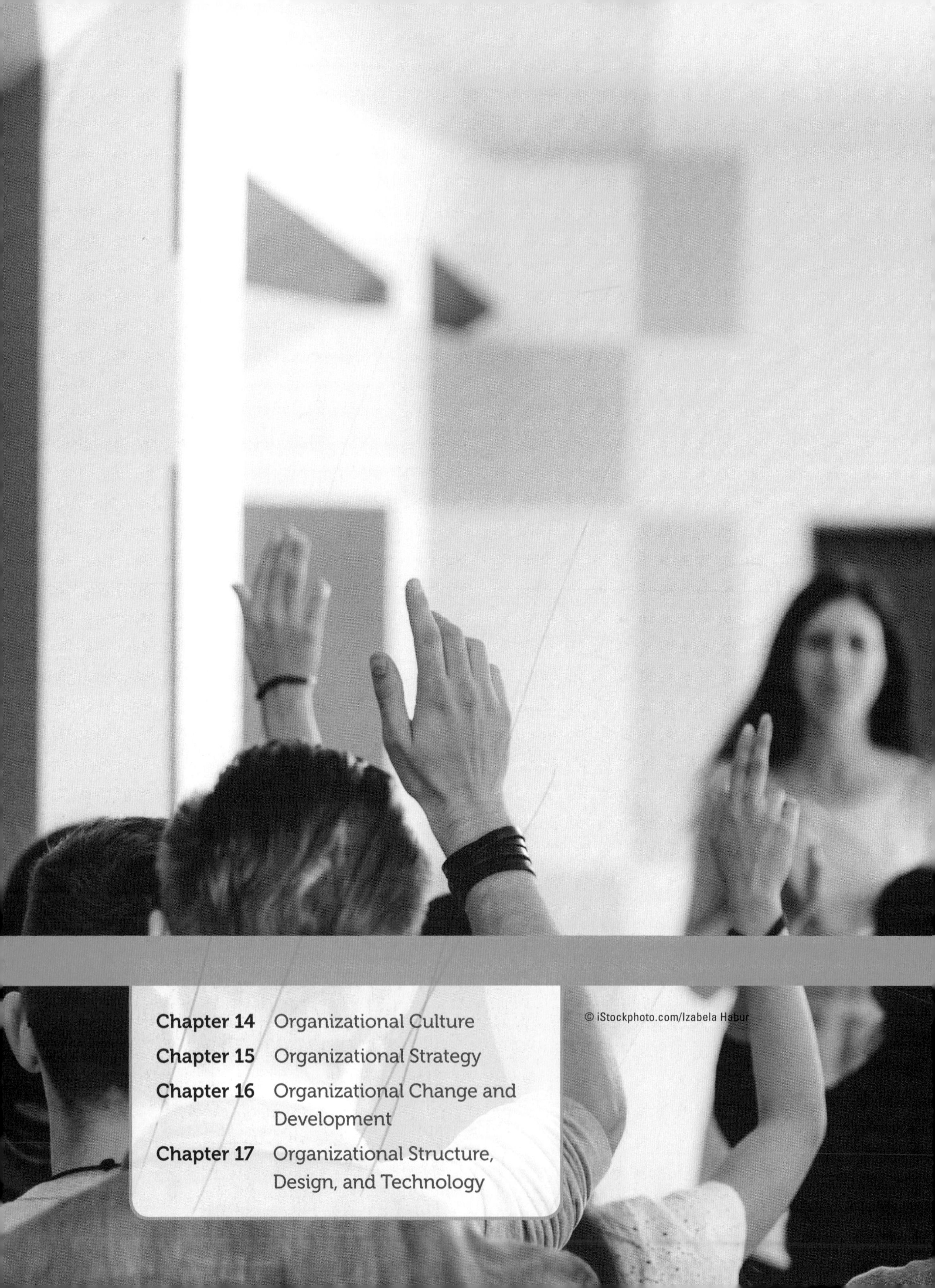

PART 5

ORGANIZATIONAL CONTEXT

14 Organizational Culture

©iStockphoto.com/Geber86

Train people well enough so they can leave, treat them well enough so they don't want to.

—*Sir Richard Branson, founder of Virgin Group*

CHARACTERISTICS OF ORGANIZATIONAL CULTURE

14.1 Describe the basic characteristics of organizational culture

The culture of an organization often influences its degree of success or failure. We define **organizational culture** as a pattern of shared norms, rules, values, and beliefs that guide the attitudes and behaviors of its employees.[1] People are the most important asset to an organization, and the behavioral side of a culture is as important as, if not more important than, the financial side. As we will see, a company that neglects its internal culture is likely to suffer economically.

On a more personal level, the type of organizational culture also affects an employee's chance of fitting in and doing well. So how do you know which kind of culture is best for you? Some corporate cultures encourage long hours with few breaks, while others are more relaxed and informal. This is why doing your research on different organizations before you join one is essential. Finding out how employees rate their companies can be a good way of determining whether an organization is the right one for you. Take the 2014 Employees' Choice Awards conducted by online jobs and career community Glassdoor, for instance. Social networking companies Twitter and LinkedIn were ranked second and third, respectively, on the list of top 50 best companies to work for in the United States. Twitter employees

LEARNING OBJECTIVES

By the end of this chapter, you will be able to:

14.1 Describe the basic characteristics of organizational culture

14.2 Discuss the various artifacts of organizational culture

14.3 Identify the functions of organizational culture

14.4 Compare various types of organizational cultures

14.5 Contrast differing approaches for shaping organizational culture

Organizational culture: A pattern of shared norms, rules, values, and beliefs that guide the attitudes and behaviors of its employees

Ole Spata/dpa/Corbis

Twitter employees enjoy a range of perks, including an on-site cafeteria with a wide selection of dining options.

Master the content.
edge.sagepub.com/neckob

credited consistent communication from the top, great perks (gym membership, yoga classes, laundry service, catered breakfasts and lunch, to name a few), a fun work environment, and a culture of openness and trust as some of the best reasons to work at the micro-blogging giant.[2]

LinkedIn employees also praised their company for the perks, great work/life balance, and support from top management.[3] Perhaps this is the organizational culture of the future—one that supports career progression, provides challenging work plus unusual perks, and incorporates healthy doses of the fun factor.

Take a look at how Marisa Keegan, CEO of Culture Fanatics, views the importance of organizational culture in the OB in the Real World feature.

Components of Culture

Organizational culture can be subtle, with some of its components hidden beneath the surface. As illustrated in Figure 14.1, there are two main components of culture: observable and unobservable.

Observable culture refers to the components of culture that we can see in an organization. For example, personal appearances and dress codes, processes and structures, behaviors and attitudes, and *artifacts* of the culture like awards, myths, and stories[4] (described in more detail following) are all observable parts of organizational culture.

Unobservable culture consists of the components that lie beneath the surface of an organization, such as company values and assumptions.[5] For instance, multinational food manufacturing company Kellogg integrates the passion, integrity, commitment and humility within its organizational culture.[6] The components of unobservable culture are often demonstrated in employee behaviors and attitudes. In some cases, the assumptions and values that make up unobservable culture can become so ingrained in employees' mindsets that their perspectives and behaviors become difficult to change.

Observable culture: The components of culture that can be seen in an organization

Unobservable culture: The components that lie beneath the surface of an organization, such as company values and assumptions

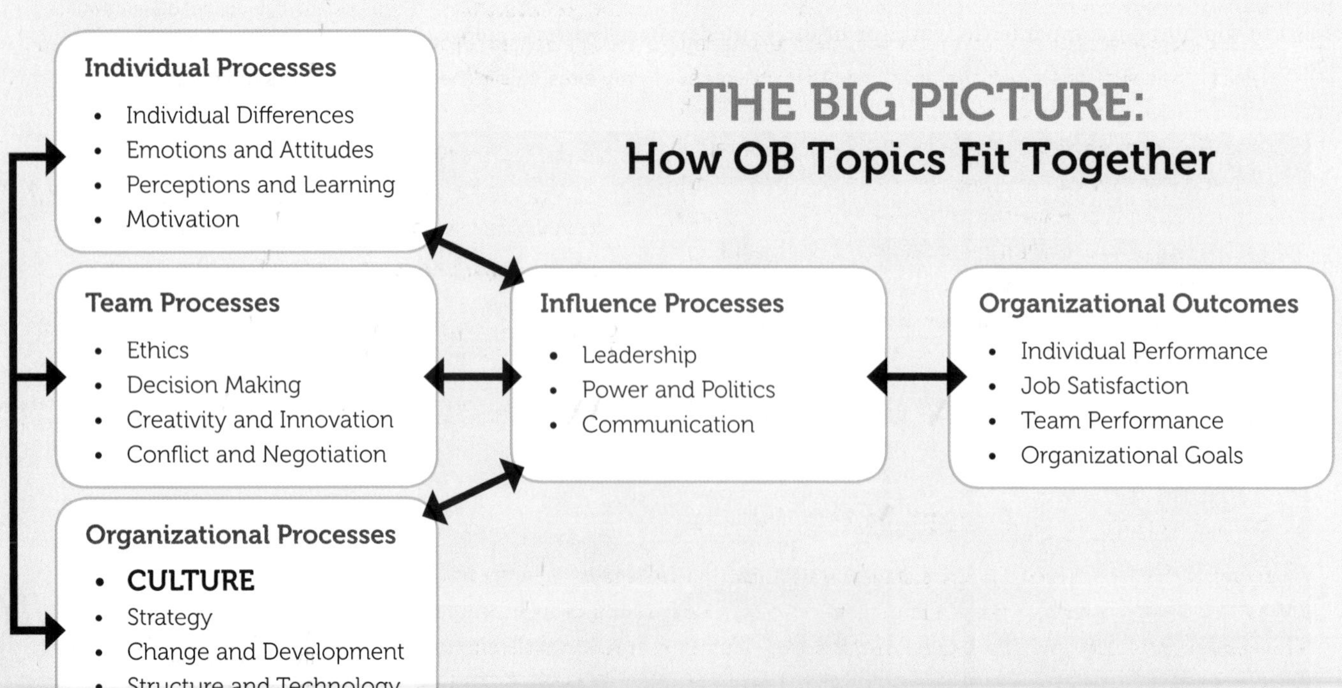

MARISA KEEGAN, CEO, Culture Fanatics

OB in the Real World

© Marisa Keegan

Marisa Keegan is the author of the book *Culture: More Than Jeans and Margarita Machines.* She has worked in culture and employee engagement roles for two nationally recognized "Great Places to Work," founded the networking group Culture Fanatics, and is a blogger, speaker, and consultant on all things culture and engagement.

"The leaders in the best places to work in the country wake up every single morning with one thing in mind: their people. But they don't only think about their people in terms of the generic buckets of productivity, management skills, or ways to get them to work longer and harder. They think about their people as the most important resource they have when it comes to understanding the obstacles the company is facing. They acknowledge that their front-line employees often know more about the company's successes and failures than the people at the top because they're the ones interacting with the customers.

"Too many leaders say, 'If I keep my employees happy my customers will be happy' and try to back that statement up by throwing a company party or putting beer in the fridge. They're missing the point. Keeping employees happy is about giving them a voice, seeking out their feedback and frustrations, and acting on that feedback. The leaders inside companies that have nailed culture seek employee feedback and work every day to do something positive with it.

"When I was the Culture Maven at Rackspace, a nationally recognized 'Best Place to Work,' the senior leadership team focused on building culture and engagement by giving employees a voice. Besides holding one-on-one off-site meetings with employees, encouraging active participation in every department, and attending all company functions, they were huge advocates of the employee engagement surveys that went out twice a year, encouraging everyone to participate and answer honestly.

"It's not the survey that's important, though. It's that you do something with the information. At Rackspace we delivered the high-level results and feedback to the entire company in an all-hands meeting. Then we broke up by departments and delivered segmented feedback, including how effective the manager was at keeping engagement levels high. Employees were encouraged to help us come up with solutions to challenges in areas where their group was scoring low. Then managers received one-on-one coaching to learn how to continue to assess engagement throughout the next six months.

"This process goes one step deeper. When you ask employees for feedback you'd better be ready to make some changes based on that feedback or employees are going to lose faith and soon enough they'll stop telling you their pain points. At Rackspace, the last question on every engagement survey was, "Have you seen changes based on the feedback you gave during your last engagement survey?" Every time I received the survey feedback the first thing I wanted to know was the results for this question. In my eyes, this is the one that matters the most."

Critical-Thinking Questions

1. **How would you describe Marisa's Keegan's approach to building a successful organizational culture?**
2. **What would your ideal workplace culture be like?**

SOURCE: Guest written by Marisa Keegan, author of *Culture: More Than Jeans and Margarita Machines.*

The Competing Values Framework

One popular way of approaching the study of organization culture is the **competing values framework**, which provides a means to identify, measure, and change culture.[7] This model highlights two main value dimensions: the first dimension differentiates *flexibility* and *discretion* from *stability* and *control.* This means that some organizations

Competing values framework: A procedure that provides a way to identify, measure, and change organizational culture

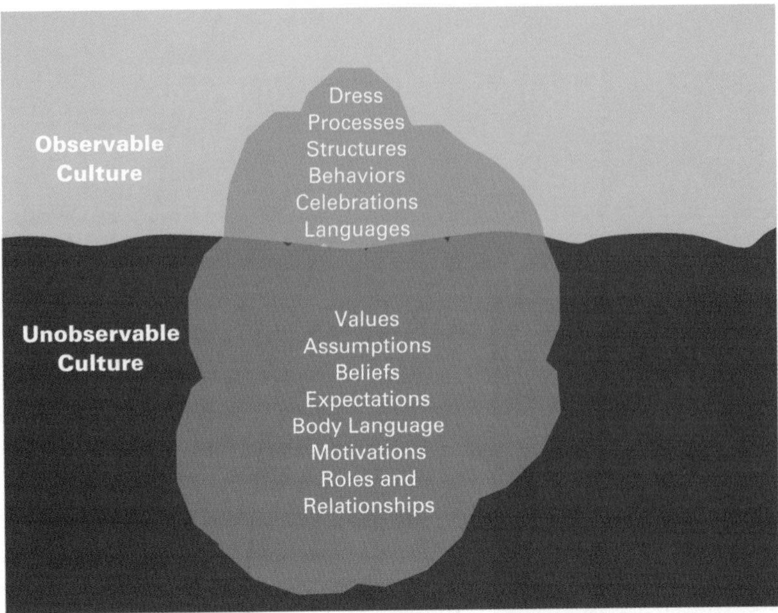

■ FIGURE 14.1 The Cultural Iceberg: Components of Organizational Culture

SOURCE: Based on Hall, Edward T. *Beyond Culture* (Oxford: Anchor, 1976).

benefit from a more adaptable, flexible culture whereas others might thrive on a more stable and mechanical culture. The second dimension differentiates *internal focus* and *integration* from an *external focus* in the workplace. In other words, some organizations are effective if they focus on the internal culture, for example ensuring that employees share the same values, integrate well, and work harmoniously, while other organizations focus on building successful relationships outside the organization such as with suppliers, customers, and clients to make themselves more competitive. Whole Foods Market is an example of a company that has developed strong relationships with a wide range of suppliers.[8] These two dimensions combined result in four different types of culture: clan, hierarchy, adhocracy, and market (see Figure 14.2).

The *clan* culture falls under the flexibility and internal focus dimension. Typically, clan cultures are welcoming places where employees openly share and form strong personal relationships. Leaders tend to be perceived as mentors and coaches who focus

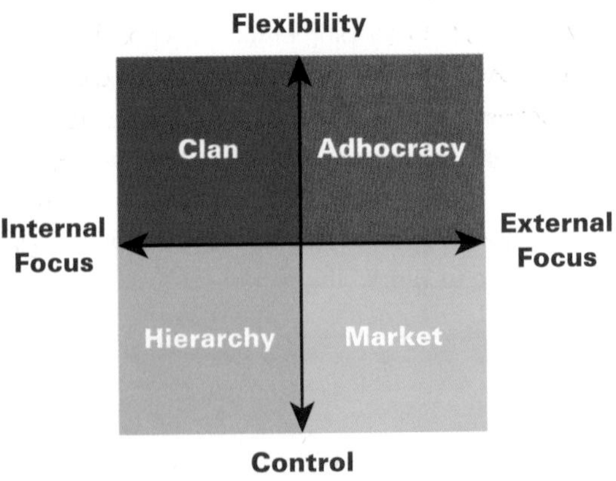

■ FIGURE 14.2 Competing Values Framework

SOURCE: Based on Quinn, Robert E., and John Rohrbaugh. "A Spatial Model of Effectiveness Criteria: Towards a Competing Values Approach to Organizational Analysis." *Management Science* 29, no. 3 (March 1983): 363–377.

Portland Press Herald/Getty Images

Tom Chappell, founder of Tom's of Maine, fosters a company culture that feels more like a family. This is an example of clan culture.

Company Culture

on bringing out the best in each of their employees. The clan culture also furnishes a collaborative environment in which loyalty and commitment are high. Organizations with a clan culture primarily gauge their success against the performance and satisfaction of their employees. Tom's of Maine is a good example of the clan culture. Tom Chappell founded his company, which produces all-natural toothpastes, soaps, and related hygiene products, on the basis of developing strong relationships with a number of stakeholders including employees, customers, suppliers, the community, and the environment. Like many clan cultures, Tom's of Maine, is essentially an "extended family" with Tom serving as the mentor or parental figure.[9]

The *hierarchy* culture exhibits a combination of stability and an internal focus. Unlike organizations adopting the clan culture, hierarchical organizations like the military can be formal and structured places where employees are primarily guided by processes, rules, and procedures. Hierarchical cultures are run via a formal chain of command populated by leaders who use their positions to manage their employees and to emphasize the importance of efficiency, productivity, and organization in the day-to-day running of operations. Organizations that are too rigid and bureaucratic, however, tend not to react well to change.

Like the hierarchy culture, the *market* culture is also positioned under the control and stability dimension but places more emphasis on interactions conducted outside the organization with a view to increasing company competitiveness. Leaders tend to be driven and goal oriented and to gauge success on the basis of market performance. Because this is a results-driven culture, there can sometimes be unhealthy competition between employees. Amazon is an example of a market culture that pressures its employees to perform in a demanding work environment in order to get the results it needs to beat the competition.[10]

The *adhocracy* culture focuses on flexibility and discretion with an external emphasis. These organizations are fast moving and the quickest to adapt to changing markets. Leaders tend to be entrepreneurs and risk takers who encourage their employees to experiment and generate innovative ideas. Success is measured by company growth and the production of unique, cutting-edge, and innovative products and services. Apple demonstrates its adhocracy culture by encouraging its employees to innovate and experiment at a fast rate to keep up with market change.[11]

Although most organizations have elements of all four of these cultural types, some emphasize one type over another. For example, a small family-run business might exhibit

Amazon uses a market culture to justify demanding work schedules, keeping their eyes on the competition.

Rex Features via AP Images

characteristics of a clan culture; an investment bank with a strong emphasis on the bottom line may operate as a hierarchy; a results-driven company such as a call center that makes hundreds of sales every day is characterized by elements of a market culture; and start-ups and high-tech firms often have an adhocracy culture.

Though most organizations require different elements from each of the four cultures to operate effectively, none of the elements should be taken to extremes. For example, an organization that is too bureaucratic tends to stifle creativity and can be slow to react to change. Similarly, organizations that are rigidly results driven can damage relationships between competing employees. In the current business environment we find a focus on clan and adhocracy cultures, with an emphasis on strong relationships based on mutual respect built inside and outside the workplace, and in the most successful organizations an environment that nurtures creativity and innovation.[12]

Dominant Culture, Subculture, Counterculture

Every cultural group has its distinctions. The **dominant culture** is the set of core values shared by the bulk of organizational employees.[13] So, for instance, travel website Tripadvisor places importance on donating to charity and giving back to the community, and members of the dominant culture are expected to do community work such as painting schools.[14] In addition to this dominant culture, **subcultures** may spring up, which are groups in an organization that share different values from those held by the majority (Figure 14.3).[15] For example, the Department of Defense consists of different branches such as the Army, Marines, and the Navy. Overall, the dominant culture pervades, but each individual branch has its own subculture made up of unique characteristics. However, it is more common for subcultures to arise in companies where there is no dominant culture, or in the merger of two companies, each of which has a different culture.

An extreme type of subculture whose values strongly differ from those of the larger organization is a **counterculture**.[16] Such groups openly reject the company's values, embrace change, and challenge the status quo. It might seem that these "rebel" groups would be bad for an organization, but a counterculture can also produce positive results. It can instigate a revolution that brings about much-needed change, and contribute valuable perspectives

Dominant culture: Set of core values shared by the majority of organizational employees

Subcultures: Groups in an organization who share different values to those held by the majority

Counterculture: Values that differ strongly from those of the larger organization

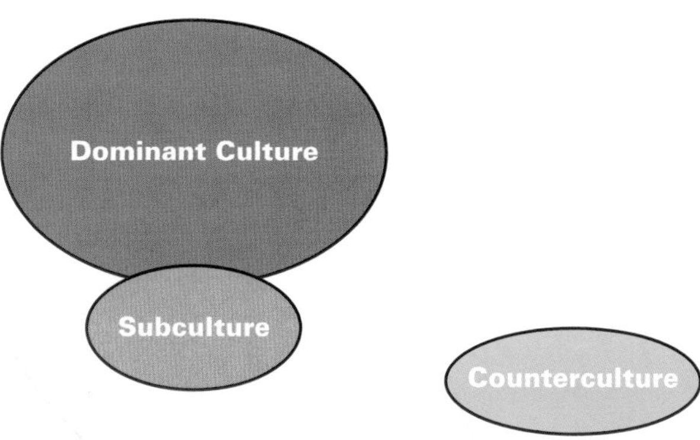

■ FIGURE 14.3 The Relationship Among Dominant Culture, Subculture, and Counterculture

and creative ideas. For example, John DeLorean, division head at General Motors in the 1970s, took steps to create a counterculture that was in direct opposition to GM's corporate culture. The GM culture at that time was based on hierarchy, bureaucracy, and conformity; employees were expected to defer to seniority and be conservative in their choice of work clothes and office decoration. DeLorean sought to change all this by rallying a group of followers to reject the bureaucratic decision making and conformity, dressing in modern styles and redecorating their offices in bright colors. Although GM tolerated DeLorean's counterculture for a while, when he left to start the DeLorean Motor Company (producer of the famous DeLorean DMC-12, featured in Hollywood's blockbuster *Back to the Future* series), the counterculture he left behind fell apart.[17]

Strong and Weak Cultures

When the majority of employees are aligned with the values of an organization, the organization has a strong culture; there is less need for detailed policies and procedures because the rules are accepted and understood.[18] Successful furniture retailer Ikea is an organization with a strong company culture. Ikea prides itself on its limited bureaucracy and its emphasis on cooperation, respect, and teamwork among its employees.[19]

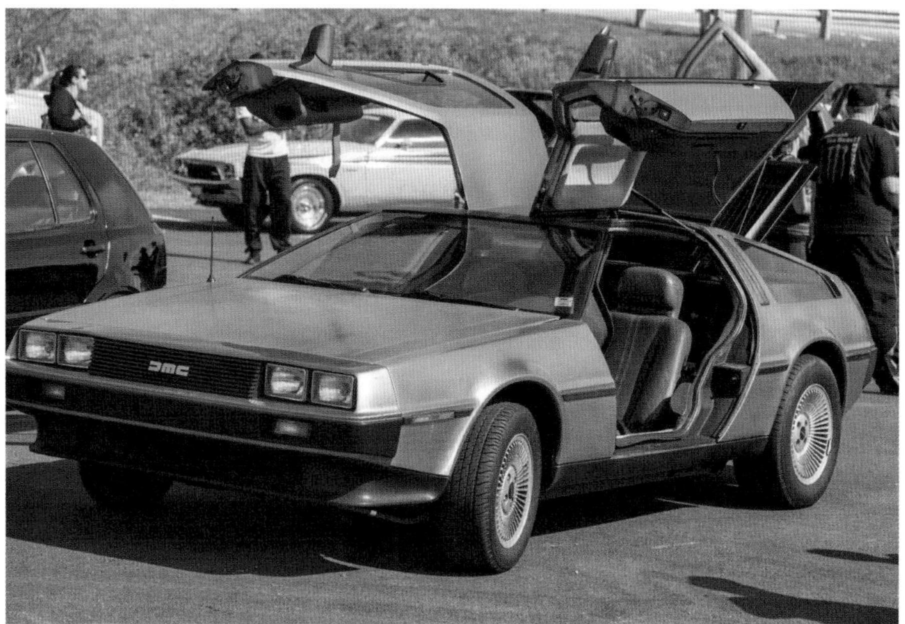

John DeLorean's forward-thinking style ran counter to GM's bureaucratic corporate culture. He eventually left GM to start his own company and created one of the most iconic cars of all time.

After a number of White House lawn security breaches in 2015, an independent investigation into the culture of the Secret Service showed that the organization needed new cultural leadership.

AP Photo/Susan Walsh, File

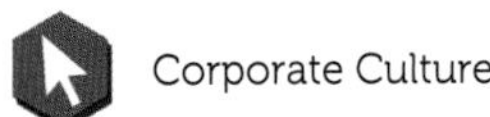

In contrast, an organization with a weak culture is one whose core values are not embraced or shared by its employees. This occurs mainly because the core values are not defined or communicated well, which can lead to inconsistent behavior among employees, which in turn can lead to bad service. For example, following a number of security breaches at the White House, an independent culture investigation has shown that the culture of the US Secret Service, largely based on organizational tradition and personal relationships, needs to achieve a culture change through new leadership.[20]

Although strong organizational cultures are valuable for nurturing a sense of unity and providing direction, they usually take a long time to develop and can be difficult to adapt in a rapidly changing environment. In addition, employees can become conditioned to think the same way as their peers and become reluctant to share different views—a phenomenon known as **groupthink**.[21] Too much groupthink in an organization can lead to stifled creativity and lack of innovation.

THINKING CRITICALLY

1. Review Marisa Keegan's description of the feedback process at Rackspace. Why is it important for company leaders to seek employee feedback about their successes and challenges, and what should leaders do with the feedback they obtain? **[Apply/Analyze]**
2. What factors might contribute to the success of Tom's of Maine as a clan culture? Why do these factors affect the company's ability to thrive? **[Understand/Apply]**
3. Why might a hierarchy culture be comparatively ineffective in dealing with change? **[Apply/Analyze]**
4. Under what circumstances might a counterculture be most likely to arise within a company, and why? **[Analyze/Evaluate]**

ARTIFACTS OF ORGANIZATIONAL CULTURE

14.2 Discuss the various artifacts of organizational culture

Groupthink: A phenomenon whereby employees can become conditioned to think the same way as their peers and become reluctant to share different views

The artifacts or identifiable elements of an organization provide members and outsiders with a better understanding of its culture.[22] The following discussion considers the case of Pioneering Health, a fictional health services company run by Yolande Turner, and illustrates the different types of cultural artifacts present in organizations.

Introducing the Case of Yolande Turner: Pioneering Health Goes International

Pioneering Health is a small organization based outside Chicago and consisting of 300 people. Headed by founder and CEO Yolande Turner, a former pharmaceutical product line manager, the company sells disease management strategies to other health care providers, associations, and corporations that offer health insurance. By gathering population data, carrying out predictive modelling, and applying the latest scientific evidence, Pioneering Health advises companies on how to maintain the health of their employees. Thanks to its innovative approach to health and well-being, Pioneering Health has created a business model that saves clients' health care costs, improves their business performance, and, most important, helps clients' employees maintain healthy lifestyles.

Stories

Stories and Culture

Pioneering Health is a lively place to work populated by plenty of cultural artifacts. Newcomers to the company are often told **stories**, narratives based on real organizational experiences that have become embellished over time and illustrate core cultural values. One of the most popular stories is about senior manager Marcella Delgado. Marcella joined Pioneering Health after her college graduation as a data and statistical health analyst. Concerned about rising obesity levels in the United States, she went beyond the requirements of her role and discovered a tiny pocket of the population in which obesity rates were lower than anywhere else in the country. She was able to analyze the reasons for her remarkable discovery and create a framework based on the results to help others living and coping with obesity. Marcella's story is only one of many inspirational accounts of employees at Pioneering Health and illustrates what they can achieve given the company's desire for employees to take the initiative and be innovative and forward thinking.

The Pioneering Heath office also contains a number of **symbols**, which are objects that express meaning about a culture. The staff dress casually, which gives the impression to any outsider that Pioneering Health is a relaxed placed to work. Employees are also known as "colleagues" or "pioneers," and apart from the positions of CEO Yolande Turner and a few top management staff, there is very little hierarchy in the organization. The fact that the company has few organizational levels is a symbol of its empowering culture.

The culture is also supported by **rituals**, formalized actions, and planned routines. For example, every Monday at 9:00 a.m., the entire staff gathers in a large hall for a question-and-answer and feedback session with the CEO. Senior managers also offer an open-door policy that gives all 300 employees the opportunity for one-to-one conversations with management at any time.

Throughout the year, Pioneering Health also observes **ceremonies**, events that reinforce the relationship between employees and the organization. For example, there is the annual awarding of the coveted "Pioneer of the Year Award," which recognizes and rewards outstanding work. And newcomers or visitors might pick up on some of the **organizational language** that uses certain words or metaphors and expressions

Stories: Narratives based on real organizational experiences that have become embellished over time and illustrate core cultural values

Symbols: Objects that provide meaning about a culture

Rituals: Formalized actions and planned routines

Ceremonies: Events that reinforce the relationship between employees and the organization

Organizational language: Words or metaphors and expressions specific to an organization such as "Go Pioneers!" that the staff regularly uses to motivate each other. Overall, Pioneering Health is a fun, happy place to work, with a culture that cultivates independent and innovative thinking, provides meaningful feedback, and emphasizes personal responsibility.

THINKING CRITICALLY

1. What is the value of Pioneering Health's practice of telling stories to new employees? Who do you think would make the most effective storytellers—company leaders or employees of a similar stature? **[Analyze/Evaluate]**
2. What are three examples of symbols a company could use to demonstrate it cultivates a culture of employee satisfaction? **[Apply/Analyze]**
3. Based on the Pioneering Health case and your own experiences, what types of ceremonies might work best to motivate employees, and why? **[Apply/Analyze]**

FUNCTIONS OF ORGANIZATIONAL CULTURE

14.3 Identify the functions of organizational culture

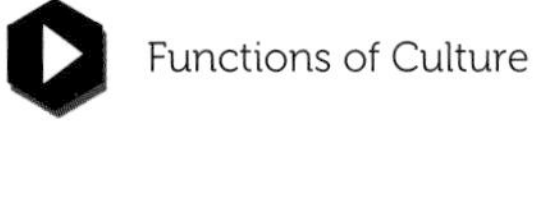

Functions of Culture

Two major functions of organizational culture imperative to an organization's survival are external adaptation and internal integration.[23] **External adaptation** is the way an organization reacts to outside influences. To achieve external adaptation to its environment, the organization must arrive at some basic shared assumptions about its mission and strategy, about the goals, tasks, and methods the organization needs to achieve, and about ways of managing both success and failure.[24] **Internal integration**, in contrast, is the process of creating a shared identity among employees by adopting a common language, group boundaries, an accepted distribution of power and status, and norms of trust, rewards, and punishment.[25] In the following section, we investigate how Yolande and the Pioneering Health team manage these two functions within their organization.

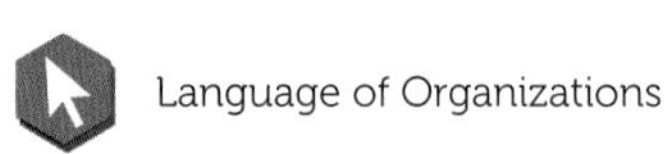

Language of Organizations

External Adaptation

Recently a competitor that focuses on health and well-being has entered Pioneering Health's market. Rather than view the new rival as a threat, Yolande and her core team see it as an opportunity. They sit down to reinforce the mission of the company, prioritize how to respond to the competition, and make sure everyone at the company knows how to contribute to the goals designed for success.

By devising clever ways to remind existing and prospective clients of the outstanding service they receive through Pioneering Health, the organization tries to increase its business in the face of new competition. The staff meticulously informs clients of the latest research in well-being. They make additional visits to their members and follow up on all queries and feedback in a timely manner. Up to now, these personal touches have ensured that Pioneering Health stays ahead of the competition. But its new competitor continues to capture more market share and begins to target the same types of companies as Pioneering Health. When a number of existing Pioneering Health clients move to the competition, the Pioneer staff feels they have failed in their mission

External adaptation: A pattern of basic assumptions shared between employees of the goals, tasks, and methods that need to be achieved, together with ways of managing success and failure

Internal integration: A shared identity with agreed-upon methods of working together to reinforce what makes their company special. However, although Yolande agrees the customer service drive has not been a complete success, she tells the staff that they must use this opportunity to think about other ways Pioneering Health can differentiate itself from the competition.

One of the senior staff members suggests that it could be a good time to expand the company internationally. This would help Pioneering Health capture more market share as well as create a differentiator, because no other well-being company in the United States has an international presence. Yolande has been thinking along the same lines. The expansion is a risk and will take time to implement, but she knows that with a supportive, hardworking team behind her, the company can succeed.

Internal Integration

Every company, regardless of size, needs a degree of internal integration to succeed. Internal integration allows teams to communicate effectively, develop friendships and norms, and define acceptable and unacceptable behaviors.

Thanks to the open communication and sharing culture at Pioneering Health, the staff feels like they belong to a very big family and have built strong relationships with each other as a result. Though the international expansion will require a great deal of change and adjustment, Yolande is confident that the staff has the talent, knowledge, and experience to support it.

Potential Dysfunctions of Culture

What happens when cultures become a liability rather than an asset? There are at least three situations in which organizational culture can become dysfunctional and create hindrances: during organizational change, under organizational diversity, and during mergers and acquisitions.

Change hindrances are cultural obstacles that impede progress and make it difficult for the organization to adapt to different situations.[26] Examples of change hindrances are ineffective communication with employees, unclear processes and procedures, disorganized leadership, failure to involve employees, and inadequate resources. For managers to effectively implement change, such as introducing a new system or restructuring a team, they need to minimize resistance by communicating clear objectives, engaging their employees in decision making, equipping them with the necessary resources to support the change, and keeping them fully informed about how and why the change is taking place.

Diversity hindrances are cultural obstacles that limit the range of employee demographics in organizations.[27] As we explored in Chapter 2, diversity can span a wide range of areas, including age/generation, race/ethnicity, gender, and ability. Many of today's organizations cultivate a diverse workforce because of the benefits diversity can bring.

However, despite the trend toward creating more diverse workplaces, managers at many organizations must still overcome cultural and other obstacles to achieve this ideal. Organizations with strong cultures tend to select the same types of employees because they are perceived to best fit the culture. Software company Apache, for example, scores low on workplace diversity because it has no women or minorities on the board.[28] Organizations that continue to hire the same types of people limit the level of diversity in their organization, which often leads to inequality.[29] For example, the pay

Change hindrances: Obstacles that impede progress and make it difficult for the organization to adapt to different situations

Diversity hindrances: Obstacles that limit the range of employees in organizations

inequity between men and women in the workplace has been well documented, as has the lack of minorities in senior positions.[30] Organizations that work hard to overcome diversity hindrances and recognize the value of differences are more likely to have a rich, varied, and productive workforce.

Mergers and acquisitions hindrances are cultural obstacles that make it difficult for two organizations to join together.[31] Mismatched cultures can lead to a "culture clash" that can have a devastating impact on the success of the merger.[32] For example, the proposed $35 billion merger of US-based advertising giant Omnicom and its French counterpart Publicis fell through because of internal culture clashes and executive power struggles.[33]

An organization that encourages innovation through informal interaction may not blend well with one that follows more formal processes and procedures. To break down these cultural barriers, managers in both organizations need to adopt cultural initiatives, which include promoting open communication with and among employees, providing a forum for questions and concerns, and engaging employees in major decisions.

THINKING CRITICALLY

1. Pioneering Health appears to be losing its competitive edge. Explain how Yolande invokes internal integration as well as external adaptation to improve her company's competitiveness. **[Apply/Analyze]**
2. Why is it necessary or desirable for employees to understand how and why a company change is taking place? To what extent do you think this best practice is actually followed in the real world? **[Understand/Apply/Analyze]**
3. How would a company with a strong culture, and an accompanying tendency to hire the same type of employees, best go about overcoming its diversity hindrances? **[Evaluate/Create]**

TYPES OF ORGANIZATIONAL CULTURES

14.4 Compare various types of organizational cultures

Earlier in this chapter, we explored the different types of organizational cultures, namely the adhocracy, clan, hierarchy, and market cultures, through the competing values framework. As we see next, however, many more types of culture exist in the workplace (see Figure 14.4).

Positive Organizational Culture

Organizations with positive organizational cultures focus on supporting employees' strengths, increasing morale, and providing rewards for good work.[34] In this type of culture, employees are active in decision making and kept informed of the organization's vision and direction. They tend to be productive, engaged, and committed to the company. Pioneering Health, the narrative case in this chapter, is an excellent example of positive organizational culture. Employees are treated as colleagues, there is a focus on teamwork, and a weekly meeting offers the opportunity for staff to give feedback and ask questions.

Mergers and acquisition hindrances: Obstacles that make it difficult for two organizations to join together

Culture	Attributes
Positive Organizational Culture	• Employees' strengths supported • High morale • Good work is rewarded
Communal Culture	• Employees think alike • Employees share knowledge • Have clear focus on goals • Goals achieved as a team
Fragmented Culture	• Little socializing • Work as individuals
Mercenary Culture	• Employees measured by level of performance and productivity • High commitment expected • Financial goals are top priority • Little socializing
Networked Culture	• High degree of trust • Employees communicate openly and share information • Mostly work independently, but come together to share ideas • Highly creative
Ethical Culture	• Managers act as ethical role models • Ethical standards communicated clearly • Employees trained to behave ethically
Spiritual Culture	• Focus on tasks that contribute to the good of society • Prioritizes caring, compassion, and support over profit

■ FIGURE 14.4 Organizational Cultures

Communal Culture

Organizations that nurture a communal culture environment are home to employees who tend to think alike, are happy to share knowledge, and have a clear focus on the direction of the task.[35] They are sociable and responsive and work well together to achieve goals. Southwest Airlines has created a communal culture that encourages staff to work together by pitching in and helping out where necessary.[36]

Fragmented Culture

Fragmented culture is found in companies where employees tend to keep to themselves, avoid socializing, and work as individuals rather than as part of a team.[37] For example, computer programmers often spend long periods of time working alone, which may cause distance and disconnection from the rest of the group.

Mercenary Culture

As the name suggests, mercenary cultures exist in organizations where making money is the top priority.[38] Employees are measured by their levels of performance and productivity and are expected to have a high commitment to achieving organizational goals. Because the culture is task driven, they do not tend to socialize, which can sometimes result in an unfriendly working environment. Disgraced organization Enron is an example of a mercenary company that became ruthless in its quest to dominate new markets through a "win at all costs" attitude.[39]

Networked Cultures

Networked cultures are characterized by a high degree of trust between employees and a willingness to communicate and share information.[40] Employees may work independently of each other, but they come together on an informal basis to swap and exchange ideas. Highly creative organizations such as Google, Apple, and Pixar, in which people are encouraged to think differently, tend to have networked cultures.

Ethical Culture

Ethical Culture

Because of well-documented ethical scandals during the past few years, many organizations are focused on creating more ethical cultures.[41] This means managers need to be role models themselves, communicate ethical standards, and train employees to behave in an ethical manner. To reinforce this type of culture, employees should be rewarded for ethical behavior and punished for unethical behavior. An example of an organization with a strong ethical culture is science-based company 3M (profiled in the Chapter 13 case study), which has been recognized by the Ethisphere Institute as the most ethical company in the world because of its strong commitment to the community and its corporate citizenship.[42]

Spiritual Culture

Spiritual Culture

Spiritual culture focuses on opportunities for employees to grow in the workplace by carrying out meaningful tasks that contribute to the good of society as a whole.[43] Organizations with a spiritual culture prioritize caring, compassion, and support for others over profit. There has been some debate over the effectiveness of spiritual organizations, with supporters believing that workplace spirituality enhances the value of the organization, and critics questioning the legitimacy of this type of culture as well as its effectiveness in terms of profit and financial success.[44]

Many organizations strive to build an organizational culture that promotes respect and trust for others, loyalty and commitment to the company, and positivity and creativity. Yet achieving a desired organizational culture does not happen overnight; indeed, building culture is a slowly evolving process shaped over time.

THINKING CRITICALLY

1. Of the types of organizational cultures discussed in this section, which would you most like to work within? Which would you least like to work within? Explain your answer. **[Understand/Apply]**
2. Do you think that promoting a communal culture is compatible with promoting company diversity? Why or why not? **[Analyze/Evaluate]**
3. If employees don't mind or actually enjoy working in a fragmented culture, should company leaders encourage the continuation of this type of culture? Why or why not? **[Analyze/Evaluate]**
4. What would be an effective way to reward employees for ethical behavior and to punish them for unethical behavior? **[Evaluate/Create]**
5. Why do critics call into question the legitimacy of spiritual culture? In what types of organizations and industries might spiritual culture be more productive and effective than more common culture types? **[Analyze/Evaluate]**

ORGANIZATIONAL CULTURE AND FIRM PERFORMANCE

Examining the Evidence

Organizational culture emerged in the 1970s and 1980s as a concept popularized by practitioner-focused books such as Tom Peters's and Robert Waterman's *In Search of Excellence* and Edgar Schein's *Organizational Culture and Leadership*. Two basic premises developed from these and other similar writings. The first is that organizational culture is derived primarily from the personalities, values, and behaviors of the founders and top executives of organizations. The second premise is that organizational culture is a key determinant of an organization's performance.

More than 40 years later, these fundamental assumptions about organizational culture remain largely in place, yet as researchers Charles A. O'Reilly III of Stanford University, David F. Caldwell of Santa Clara University, and Jennifer A. Chatman and Bernadette Doerr of University of California, Berkeley, point out, empirical evidence supporting them is fragmented and inconclusive. These researchers conducted a comprehensive study of 60 firms in the United States and 44 firms in Ireland to examine these basic assumptions of organizational culture. Their findings provide support for the hypotheses that CEO personality is related to certain types of organizational cultures and that culture is related to firm performance. More specifically, CEOs who are high in openness to experience are more likely to be associated with cultures that emphasize adaptability, CEOs who are high in conscientiousness tend to have more detail-oriented cultures, and CEOs who are low in agreeableness are more likely to have cultures that are results oriented. Their results further show that more adaptable and detail-oriented cultures tend to have higher financial performance outcomes.

Critical-Thinking Questions

1. **Why do you think CEO personality and organizational culture affect firm performance? What are the implications for organizations?**
2. **Based on this evidence, what specific actions can organizational decision makers take to enhance firm performance?**

SOURCE: O'Reilly, Charles A., David F. Caldwell, Jennifer A. Chatman, and Bernadette Doerr. "The Promise and Problems of Organizational Culture: CEO Personality, Culture, and Firm Performance." Group and Organization Management 39, no. 6 (December 2014): 595–625.

SHAPING ORGANIZATIONAL CULTURE

14.5 Contrast differing approaches for shaping organizational culture

Organizational culture can be difficult to change. Unlike many other management functions, shaping organizational culture requires changing mind-sets. In short, it is an emotional process rather than a rational or analytical one, and as we have learned, dealing with emotions in the workplace can be tricky.

Consultancy firm Booz & Co. has outlined a concept called "the critical few" that presents managers with ways to implement effective change within the organizational culture.[45] First, organizations need to define a few *critical behaviors* that managers would like their employees to embody—for example, hire only people who energize others, or make sure employees provide excellent customer service. Once these critical behaviors have been identified, they can be strengthened and nurtured through training until they become a natural part of the company ethos.

Second, focus on a few *cultural traits* that have an emotional effect on employees. What makes employees take pride in their work? What kinds of traits motivate them—loyalty, commitment, trust? Once these traits have been identified, managers can promote them with the goal of encouraging every employee to embrace them.

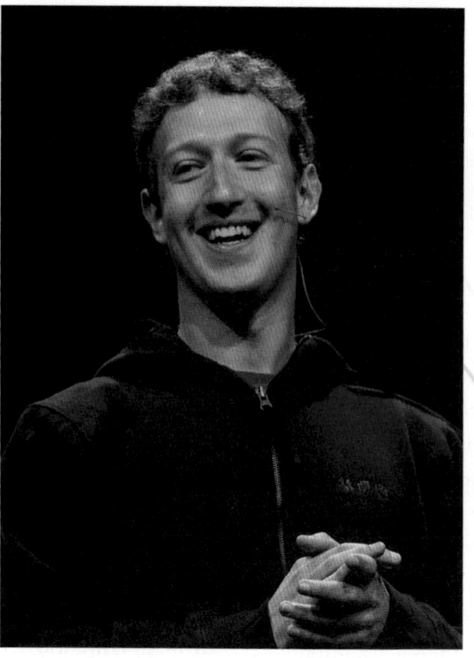

Mark Zuckerberg's values and behaviors are embraced by Facebook employees, who are encouraged to follow their passions and take action.

©iStockphoto.com/EdStock

Finally, managers need to identify the *informal leaders* in the organization. These leaders can exist at every level. They are well liked, trusted, and respected and have a natural way of influencing the behavior of others. Managers need to get these informal leaders motivated to help champion changes and get buy-in from others.

However, change starts at the top, and one of the most important catalysts for change is the behavior of top management.

Influence of Founders and Top Management

Successful organizations tend to be led by top managers who embody certain beliefs, values, and assumptions, thereby influencing employees to do the same.[46] Facebook CEO Mark Zuckerberg is a good example of a leader whose behaviors and values have been embraced by the Facebook staff and have become the core of the company's mission. Facebook employees are given the freedom to work on projects they are most interested in and are encouraged to take action and contribute ideas.[47]

Selection Practices

Managers working in organizations with a certain culture tend to select candidates whose personalities and attitudes best match that culture and values.[48] This match is called **person–organization fit**. Research has shown that hiring for organizational fit can be beneficial for both the organization and the employee. Employees who feel that they "fit in" tend to have low levels of absenteeism, are likely to feel stressed about their day-to-day tasks, and experience higher levels of job satisfaction, performance, and productivity.

Socialization Methods

New hires are integrated into the company's corporate culture through **socialization**, the process through which an organization communicates its values to new employees.[49] For example, when you were hired for your current or most recent job, training probably happened as part of your socialization process. There are three main forms of socialization: context, content, and social dynamics.[50]

Context

Socialization depends on the *context* in which the information is imparted. For example, organizations can choose to socialize new hires through an informal or formal process, and on an individual or collective basis. During an informal process, new hires are put to work immediately so they can learn the company's values through on-the-job-training. For example, US software company Intuit introduces new employees to the company before they even begin their first day of work, with a welcome e-mail, a portal that provides answers for new hires, and a video from the CEO, who shares his

Person–organization fit: The degree of compatibility between job candidates and organizations

Socialization: The process through which an organization communicates its values to new employees

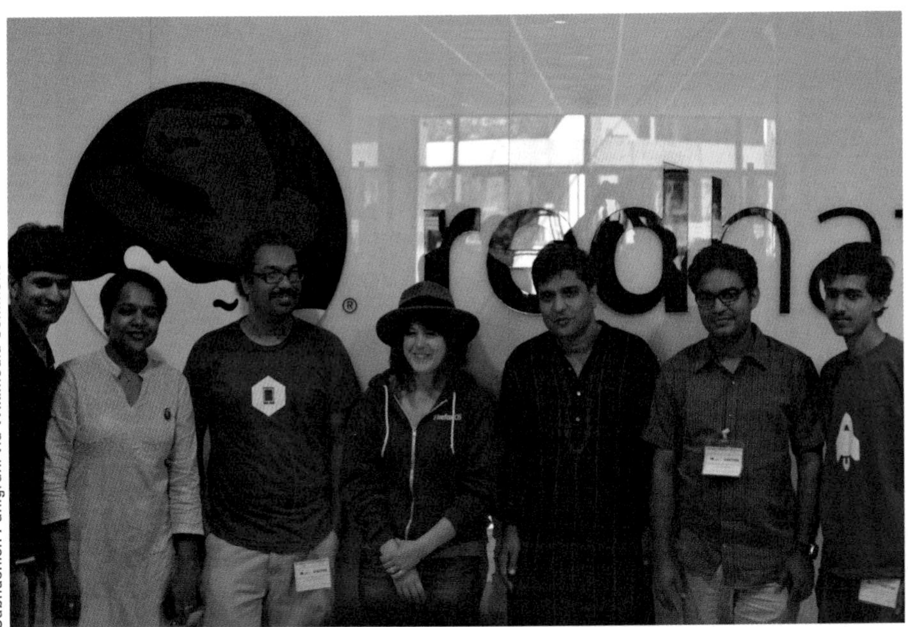

Subhashish Panigrahi via Wikimedia Commons

New Red Hat employees receive special group training and are each given a red fedora to show that they are now part of the team.

experiences at Intuit.[51] However, most organizations advocate a more formal approach, including a ceremonial induction or orientation program that introduces new hires to the specifics of the culture and helps build a sense of cohesiveness and identity.

Content

Organizations often provide new hires with *content,* which is information regarding the activities and tasks they may be expected to carry out, and the time each activity should take to complete. This gives new hires a sense of career direction and provides them with an understanding about what they are expected to do and why they are doing it.

Social Dynamics

Socialization also depends on the nature of *social dynamics* that take place once an employee has been hired. Some organizations assign new hires to specific employees who act as role models or mentors. Technology giant Red Hat shows its new employees that it cares by taking them on a group training program at its Raleigh headquarters, introducing them to a range of employee ambassadors and equipping each of them with his or her own signature red Fedora.[52] However, in many cases, new hires do not receive formal social support from team members. Left to their own devices, they are forced to figure out the dynamics by themselves, which can result in uncertainty and confusion.

Organizations with successful socialization strategies are more likely to have a positive organizational culture and perform better as a result.

Feldman's Model of Organizational Socialization

Researcher Daniel Feldman identified three phases of organizational socialization experienced by an employee before and after entering an organization.[53] These three phases are anticipatory socialization, encounter phase, and change and acquisition phase. (See Figure 14.5.)

Anticipatory Socialization

Anticipatory socialization takes place before the individual joins the organization. This can happen in several ways. For example, the individual may have talked to current

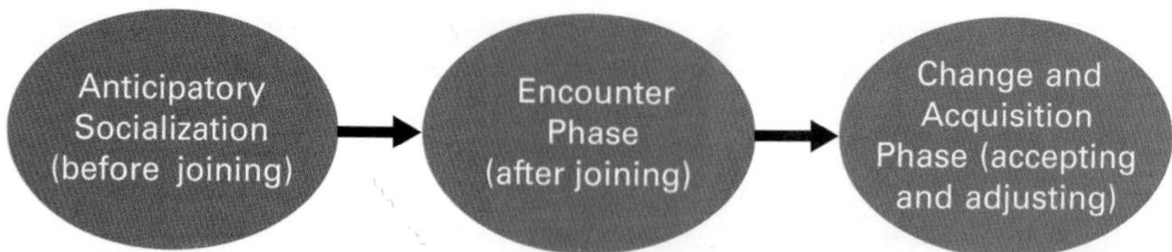

■ FIGURE 14.5 Feldman's Three Stages of Organizational Socialization

SOURCE: Based on Feldman, Daniel Charles. "A Contingency Theory of Socialization." *Administrative Science Quarterly* 21, no. 3 (September 1976): 433–452.

employees to get their opinions about what they like and dislike about the organization, or he or she may have researched the company online to get a better sense of the working environment.

Encounter Phase

The encounter phase begins when the individual signs an employment contract and learns more about what the organization is really like. During this phase, the organization may use a number of socializing techniques to help the new employee become better acquainted with the working environment, such as introductions to key members of the organization, classroom or online training, or written guidelines about the company.

Change and Acquisition Phase

When socialization is successful, the employee will have a clear understanding of his or her role and will have learned how to confidently carry out new tasks and skills. This is also the period when new employees adjust to group values and norms and come to understand where they fit into the team dynamic.

Yolande Turner and the top management team at Pioneering Health have worked hard to shape the culture by building trust and leading by example. Employees are treated like accountable adults who want to take responsibility for their work processes and do good work. New employees are carefully selected using the *person–organization fit* practice, which has helped maintain the company's relaxed but hardworking culture. After joining Pioneering Health, new employees are provided thorough training and are assigned mentors to guide them through their tasks and activities. Senior hires in managerial positions benefit from socialization because it helps them better understand how to manage the Pioneering staff.

However, Pioneering Health is about to encounter the biggest challenge since its inception. The decision to take the company international is undoubtedly an ambitious one, but Yolande Turner is determined to achieve her vision. In the next chapter, we explore how Yolande and her Pioneering team go about creating a strategic plan to expand the organization internationally.

THINKING CRITICALLY

1. If change starts at the top, why is it important to identify the informal leaders of a company and motivate them to support company change? **[Analyze/Evaluate]**

2. Provide examples of the beliefs, values and assumptions held by Yolande Turner at Pioneering Health. How might Yolande's beliefs and values as the CEO of an organization with a positive culture compare to the CEO of an

organization with a mercenary culture? How would socialization methods for new employees at an organization with a mercenary culture differ from the process described at Pioneering Health? **[Understand/Apply/Analyze]**

3. How would you rank the three main forms of employee socialization (context, content, and social dynamics) in order of importance to a new employee, and why? **[Analyze/Evaluate]**

4. What do you consider the most effective way for a new employee to benefit from anticipatory socialization? Explain your answer. **[Analyze/Evaluate]**

IN REVIEW

Learning Objectives

14.1 Describe the basic characteristics of organizational culture

Organizational culture is a pattern of shared norms, rules, values, and beliefs that guide the attitudes and behaviors of its employees. Observable culture refers to the components that can be seen in an organization such as dress, structures, behaviors, and artifacts. **Unobservable culture** consists of the components that lie beneath the surface, such as company values and assumptions.

14.2 Discuss the various artifacts of organizational culture

Symbols are objects that provide meaning about a culture. **Rituals** are formalized actions and planned routines. **Ceremonies** are events that reinforce the relationship between employees and the organization. **Organizational language** consists of certain words or metaphors, and expressions the staff use regularly.

14.3 Identify the functions of organizational culture

External adaptation is a shared understanding of the goals, tasks, and methods that need to be achieved, together with ways of managing success and failure. Every company, regardless of how big or small, needs a degree of **internal integration**, which creates a shared identity with agreed-upon methods of working together.

14.4 Compare various types of organizational cultures

Organizations with a *positive organizational culture* focus on building on employee strengths, increasing morale, and providing rewards for good work. Employees in a *communal culture* tend to think alike, are happy to share knowledge, and have a clear focus on the direction of the task. Organizations with a *fragmented culture* have employees who tend to keep to themselves, avoid socializing, and work as individuals rather than part of a team. As the name suggests, *mercenary cultures* exist in organizations where making money is the top priority. Employees are measured by their levels of performance and productivity and expected to have a high commitment towards achieving organizational goals. In *networked cultures* there is a high degree of trust between employees and a willingness to communicate and share information. In an *ethical culture* managers need to be role models themselves, communicate ethical standards, and train employees to behave in an ethical manner. Organizations with a *spiritual culture* focus on the opportunities for employees to grow in the workplace by carrying out meaningful tasks that contribute to the good of society as a whole.

14.5 Contrast differing approaches for shaping organizational culture

Managers working in organizations with a certain culture tend to select candidates whose personalities and attitudes best match that culture and values. This match is called **person–organization fit**. New hires are integrated into the company's corporate culture through a process of **socialization**, which is a way an organization communicates its values to employees.

KEY TERMS

Change hindrances 365
Ceremonies 363
Competing values framework 357
Counterculture 360
Diversity hindrances 365
Dominant culture 360
External adaptation 364
Groupthink 362
Internal integration 364
Mergers and acquisition hindrances 366
Observable culture 356
Organizational culture 355
Organizational language 363
Person–organization fit 370
Rituals 363
Socialization 370
Stories 363
Subcultures 360
Symbols 363
Unobservable culture 356

THINKING CRITICALLY ABOUT THE CASE OF YOLANDE TURNER AND PIONEERING HEALTH

Put yourself in Yolande Turner's position as the CEO of Pioneering Health and consider the five critical-thinking steps in relation to the decision to take the company international.

OBSERVE

What observable aspects of culture exist at Pioneering Health? How do these aspects affect company productivity and employee satisfaction? How would you evaluate the current level of company productivity and employee satisfaction?

INTERPRET

What sort of culture does Pioneering Health espouse—a clan, hierarchy, adhocracy, or market culture? What specific factors about the way Pioneering Health does business allow you to identify the culture as such?

ANALYZE

To what extent does Pioneering Health's unique culture depend on factors that might change if the company expands internationally? List these key factors and analyze the ways an international expansion is likely to affect them.

EVALUATE

What aspects of Pioneering Health's culture are likely to help it to succeed with its international expansion? Discuss at least one aspect of company culture that could complicate the decision to expand.

EXPLAIN

Is an international expansion a wise choice, culturally speaking, for Pioneering Health? Explain your answer.

EXERCISE 14.1: THAT'S THE WAY WE DO THINGS AROUND HERE!

Consider an organization with which you are very familiar. Ideally, it is one for which you have worked, volunteered, or otherwise served as a member.

Observable Aspects of Culture

If an outsider were to come into your organization, what would he or she see? What would appear striking and characteristic of your organization?

1. List some specific structures and processes, behaviors, and dress and personal appearance factors an outsider might find striking.

2. What cultural artifacts (stories, rituals, symbols, language) are especially representative of your organization's underlying culture?

Unobservable Aspects of Culture

What aspects of the culture would be less visible to an outside observer? What values, norms, and assumptions are hidden beneath the surface?

1. List the core values, the primary or dominant values that are accepted throughout your organization.

____

____

____

____

2. What are the basic underlying assumptions of your organization, the taken-for-granted beliefs and philosophies that are so ingrained that members act on them in a given situation without questioning the validity of their own actions?

____

____

____

____

Categorizing Your Culture

1. Which type of culture does your organization most resemble according to the competing values framework (clan, adhocracy, hierarchy, market)?

____

____

____

____

2. Perhaps your organization's culture more closely resembles one of the other types of cultures discussed in the chapter (positive, communal, fragmented, mercenary, networked, ethical, spiritual).

____

____

____

____

3. Or possibly you would categorize your organization's culture in terms different from any of the following categories described:

____

____

____

____

Thinking Critically About Your Culture

1. What aspects of your organization's culture have enabled it to be successful?

____

____

____

____

2. What aspects of your organization's culture have constrained or inhibited it from succeeding?

____

____

____

____

EXERCISE 14.2: CULTURAL ARTIFACTS

Objectives:

Completing this exercise will help you to better *describe* basic characteristics of an organizational culture, and *discuss* the artifacts of an organizational culture.

Instructions:

Step 1. Find a partner (ideally someone you do not work with on a regular basis), and write down a list of as many cultural artifacts on your university's campus as you can. (5 minutes)

Step 2. Each pair should find another pair to form a quad and combine lists. Group similar artifacts together, and write down what each artifact group represents about your university's culture – especially about what types of activities and successes are most valued by the university. If there is time, write a brief discussion about what aspects of your university's culture is *not* represented by cultural artifacts. (10 minutes)

Step 3. Choose a spokesperson from your quad and be prepared to discuss your observations if called on by the instructor. (5 minutes)

Reflection Questions:

1. How did the artifacts observed by your pair differ from the artifacts listed by the pair you joined to form a quad?
2. In what new ways do you view the cultural characteristics on campus after this exercise?
3. How do you think differently about the influence of artifacts after completing this exercise?
4. How could an organization consciously choose and place artifacts to reinforce, shape, or even alter a culture?

Exercise contributed by Milton R. Mayfield, Professor of Business, Texas A&M International University and Jaqueline R. Mayfield, Professor of Business, Texas A&M International University.

EXERCISE 14.3: YOU GOT LUCKY

Objectives:

1. Describe the basic characteristics of organizational culture.
2. Contrast differing approaches for shaping organizational culture.

Background:

Upon completing your university degree, you have been hired as a store manager for Clover Supermarkets, and can expect to be promoted to a district manager for McQueen Foods (the corporate owner of Clover Supermarkets) in 6 to 18 months if you can show success at Clover. McQueen Foods is a large grocery store chain that has been buying out smaller grocery store chains such as Clover Supermarkets over the past few years. During college, you had worked at a McQueen store and worked your way up to shift manager. You know that McQueen prides itself on caring for its employees and providing excellent customer service while still selling groceries at competitive prices.

You have been managing one of the last free standing Clover Supermarkets for about a month, and you have noticed a big difference between the cultures of McQueen and Clover stores. While all of the Clover employees are polite, none of them seem to have any special drive to provide the extra customer service that McQueen is known for. When customers call, they can be left on hold for long periods of time, and it is very difficult for customers to find help with locating items when they are in the store. Many customers have to bag their own groceries, and it is rare that there is someone who can help customers carry their groceries out to the car. In addition, when workers are asked questions about products, they will rarely be able to answer such questions. And while the store does have a system in place to add new items based on customer requests, such items rarely appear on store shelves.

You are convinced that this lack of customer service has hurt Clover´s performance, and that it needs to be changed. Such a change will also help bring the Clover culture in line with the McQueen culture. You are aware of the difficulty in changing any culture, and that if you want to align the Clover culture with the McQueen culture, then you cannot change the service aspect by hurting the respect for company employees or by making prices non-competitive.

However, you also see this change as a career opportunity for you. If you can successfully change the Clover culture, and provide a blueprint for similar changes at the other stores that McQueen has recently acquired, this accomplishment will greatly help your career progression at McQueen Foods.

To help generate ideas for this change, you have invited other new McQueen store managers that you met in your training program to discuss possibilities.

Instructions:

Step 1. Form into groups of 5 to 7 members and develop an outline for the cultural change. The plan must include a clear description of the current culture, a vision for the desired future culture, and methods for changing the current culture to match the future culture. Because of the difficulty in changing cultures, you will want to list multiple methods for changing the key cultural aspects. Also, sequence the cultural change steps as necessary, and list where expected resistance to change can come from. Describe what approaches you might take to overcome these roadblocks. (15 to 30 minutes)

Step 2. Be prepared to present your change plan to the class. (5 to 10 minutes)

Reflection Questions:

1. What insights did you gain from thinking of organizational cultures from a change perspective?
2. What disagreements arose about cultural diagnosis in your team?
3. What cultural change ideas were the most difficult for your team to develop?
4. How did the constraints of maintaining worker support and competitive prices make the cultural change more challenging?

Exercise contributed by Milton R. Mayfield, Professor of Business, Texas A&M International University and Jaqueline R. Mayfield, Professor of Business, Texas A&M International University.

CASE STUDY 14.1: ZAPPOS.COM

A mind-boggling array of shoes and merchandise, free return policy, and extraordinary customer service helped Zappos reach $1 billion in sales in its eighth year of operation—making it one of the most successful Internet retailers in history and culminating in its purchase by Amazon for nearly $1 billion in 2009. But it's the quirky HR policies and emphasis on happiness and human connection that have earned Zappos thousands of loyal customers and a regular presence on lists of the "Best Places to Work."

Zappos got its start in 1999 when founder Nick Swinmurn pitched the idea of selling shoes online to venture capitalists Tony Hsieh and Alfred Lin. While Hsieh admits he had his doubts, shortly after the launch he jumped on the opportunity to become co-CEO and began developing his "dream corporate culture" and people-centered management style not long after.

Hsieh had sold his start-up, LinkExchange, to Microsoft for $265 million in 1999. But the reason he agreed to sell wasn't price; it was culture. With a hiring strategy based on skills and expertise only, LinkExchange's culture went from exuberant to downtrodden. Hsieh pledged that he'd never run a company that way again and became intrigued with the idea of creating a corporate culture that was everything his earlier start-up was not. He hit the mark with Zappos, which considers itself a customer service company that happens to sell online merchandise.

Something of a philosopher, Hsieh has used Zappos to test his theories on happiness, which is what he claims the company strives to provide. But Zappos doesn't go about ensuring happiness in the typical way. Its salaries aren't great—they are often below market, in fact, and except for 100 percent paid health care benefits, there are few perks. There are, however, lots of great intangibles: nights out with bosses and coworkers that Hsieh often attends; a nap room; a requirement that managers spend 10 percent to 20 percent of their time "goofing off" with their employees; and an emphasis on fun and "weirdness" that affords the opportunity to express yourself at work and feel empowered while doing it.

There are no limits on the time a call center operator can spend on the phone with a customer, for example (the company made headlines in December 2012 with a record- breaking call that lasted 10½ hours), and no scripts to recite. Employees are empowered to make decisions without consulting higher-ups—like offering refunds, or in one case following up a refund with flowers sent to a customer whose husband died unexpectedly after she had ordered him a pair of shoes. Employees are encouraged to be individuals and treat their customers as such—not just as sales figures. All this contributes to what Hsieh calls the "wow" factor in customer service, which keeps his turnover low and his customers coming back while singing the company's praises to others.

"Our philosophy has been that most of the money we might ordinarily have spent on advertising should be invested in customer service, so that our customers will do the marketing for us through word of mouth," said Hsieh. In the beginning, this was a necessity for the cash-strapped company. Now, it's one of its greatest keys to success.

Of course, extending this much freedom to employees implies risk—and this is why Zappos goes to great lengths to make sure it hires the right employees, those who will fit within and contribute to its carefully crafted culture. Its intensive training comes with a unique twist—at its conclusion, prospective employees are offered $2,000 plus compensation for training hours to quit. It's Hsieh's way of weeding out those who are in it for just the paycheck or the goodies—not the type he wants working for him. "We want people who are passionate about what Zappos is about—service. I don't care if they're passionate about shoes."

In late 2013, Hsieh announced he would eliminate hierarchy and job titles in favor of the "holacracy" model in which all work is done in circles. There are "leads" but no managers; circle members make important decisions while leads simply facilitate. The idea is to eliminate politics and bottlenecks and increase innovation. Time will tell whether Hsieh's radical makeover of Zappos' internal workings will produce the intended results. In the meantime, the business world is watching.

Case Questions

1. What was Tony Hsieh's goal regarding organization culture when he became co-CEO of Zappos?
2. Evaluate how the functions of organizational culture are implemented at Zappos.
3. What type of organizational culture does Zappos have? Explain your answer.

Sources

Bloxham, Eleanor. "Zappos and the Search for a Better Way to Run a Business." *CNNMoney.com*. January 29, 2014. http://management.fortune.cnn.com/2014/01/29/zappos-holacracy/.

Bryant, Adam. "On a Scale of 1 to 10, How Weird Are You?" *New York Times*. January 9, 2010. www.nytimes.com/2010/01/10/business/10corner.html?pagewanted=all&_r=0.

Chafkin, Max. "The Zappos Way of Managing." *Inc.* May 1, 2009; http:// inc.com/magazine/20090501/the-zappos-way-of-managing.html?nav=next_

Gelles, David. "At Zappos, Pushing Shoes and a Vision." *New York Times*. July 17, 2015. www.nytimes.com/2015/07/19/business/at-zappos-selling-shoes-and-a-vision.html.

Hsieh, Tony. "How I Did It: Zappos's CEO on Going to Extremes for Customers." *Harvard Business Review*. July 2010. http://hbr.org/2010/07/how- i-did-it-zapposs-ceo-on-going-to-extremes-for-customers/ar/1.

"Meet Our Monkies." http://about.zappos.com/meet-our-monkeys/tony-hsieh-ceo.

O'Connor, Clare. "Zappos Mogul Tony Hsieh's Latest Bet: High Tech Fashion." *Forbes.com*. January 1, 2014. www.forbes.com/sites/clareoconnor/2014/01/30/zappos-mogul-tony-hsiehs-latest-bet-high-tech-fashion/.

Rich, Motoko. "Why Is This Man Smiling?" *New York Times*. April 8, 2011. www.nytimes.com/2011/04/10/fashion/10HSEIH.html?pagewanted=all&_r=0.

SELF-ASSESSMENT 14.1

What Is My Cultural Preference?

When considering job opportunities, people generally consider factors such as salary and benefits, but seldom consider their fit with the culture of the organization. This assessment will help you to determine your organizational cultural preference using the competing values framework.

For each item, circle the number that best describes how well the words appeal to you using the following scale:

	Not at All Appealing	Somewhat Appealing	A Little Appealing	Very Appealing	Extremely Appealing
1. Strict chain of command	1	2	3	4	5
2. Outward looking	1	2	3	4	5
3. Flexibility	1	2	3	4	5
4. Independence	1	2	3	4	5
5. Respect for position and power	1	2	3	4	5
6. Bargaining and decision making	1	2	3	4	5

(Continued)

(Continued)

	Not at All Appealing	Somewhat Appealing	A Little Appealing	Very Appealing	Extremely Appealing
7. Vision and shared goals	1	2	3	4	5
8. Speed and adaptability	1	2	3	4	5
9. Well-defined policies, processes and procedures	1	2	3	4	5
10. Results oriented	1	2	3	4	5
11. Autonomy	1	2	3	4	5
12. Experimentation	1	2	3	4	5
13. Coordination and organization	1	2	3	4	5
14. Hard-driving competition	1	2	3	4	5
15. Facilitative and supportive	1	2	3	4	5
16. Innovation	1	2	3	4	5

Preference for Hierarchy

Total for items 1, 5, 9, and 13 ____________________

Preference for Market

Total for items 2, 6, 10 and 14 ____________________

Preference for Clan

Total for items 3, 7, 11, and 15 ____________________

Preference for Adhocracy

Total for items 4, 8, 12 and 16 ____________________

What was your strongest organizational culture preference?

What are some examples of observable aspects of culture (structures and processes, behaviors, dress and personal appearance, stories, rituals, symbols) that might help you recognize this type of culture in an organization you may be considering joining?

15 Organizational Strategy

©iStockphoto.com/ViktorCap

To stay ahead, you must have your next idea waiting in the wings.

—Rosabeth Moss Kanter, professor of business, Harvard Business School

ORGANIZATIONAL STRATEGY

LEARNING OBJECTIVES

By the end of this chapter, you will be able to:

15.1 Describe the basic concept of organizational strategy

15.2 Discuss organizational learning as a strategic process

15.3 Explain the phenomenon of globalization along with the opportunities and challenges it poses to organizations

15.4 Identify key ways in which organizations adapt their practices across cultures

15.5 Describe how international assignments can be used for employee development

15.1 Describe the basic concept of organizational strategy

Organizations need to continually evolve to stay ahead of the competition, not only by continually innovating but also by responding to market and customer demands. To successfully achieve its long-term goals, an organization needs to choose an optimal **organizational strategy**, an overarching plan of action to guide top-level managers in creating, evaluating, and implementing decisions and objectives that lead to success.[1] A big part of organizational strategy is tactical and operational planning.

While organizational strategy focuses on the future vision of the business, **tactical planning** lays out the short-term actions and plans to implement the strategy. For example, a commercial auction organization might have a long-term goal to provide its customers with the facility to bid for properties online against other bidders rather than bidding in person or over the phone. To build interest in the scheme as soon as possible, the company could use tactics such as gauging customer opinion through surveys or registering customers to try the auction website before it goes live.

Operational planning aligns the strategic plan with the day-to-day tasks required in the running of the organization. The operational plan outlines the strategies and tasks to be undertaken, describes who is responsible for each task, states when these tasks must be completed, and discusses the amount of financial resources needed to achieve the task.

To be successful, an organizational strategy must be supported by every part of the organization. The actions of every group and individual influence its implementation and outcome. An organizational strategy also needs to evolve over time to address where the organization is now and where it would like to be—in many cases, strategy is largely driven by the needs of the organization's customers. For example, fast-food giant McDonald's has been under pressure from customers and consumer advocates to provide healthy alternatives for kids in its Happy Meal boxes. In response, the company designed a strategy to satisfy these demands by introducing yogurt as an option. Yet the innovation doesn't stop there; McDonald's also created an animated Happy Meal box to promote healthy eating and is considering including whole fruit in the boxes in the future.[2]

More companies are basing their strategies on the way they are viewed by their customers. For example, companies like Prime Therapeutics, Safelite Glass, and Aruba Networks gather feedback from their customers to include in their strategic plans, which are then designed and tailored to meet their customer's needs—with a great deal of success.[3] Prime Therapeutics bases its strategy on studies that prove positive customer experiences build loyalty and long-term relationships.[4]

Organizational strategy: The process of creating, evaluating, and implementing decisions and objectives to achieve long-term competitive success

Tactical planning: The short-term actions and plans to implement the strategy

Operational planning: The process of aligning the strategic plan to the day-to-day tasks required in the running of the organization

Master the content.
edge.sagepub.com/neckob

SAGE edge™

Explore how Ryan Hagan, manager of FoxGuard Solutions, views the importance of strategy in his organization in the OB in the Real World feature.

Back to the Case of Yolande Turner and Pioneering Health

In Chapter 14, we were introduced to Yolande Turner, founder of Pioneering Health, which provides disease management and wellness strategies to private health companies throughout the United States. We now return to our story to analyze the way in which Yolande Turner and her senior team design and plan a strategy to expand the business internationally.

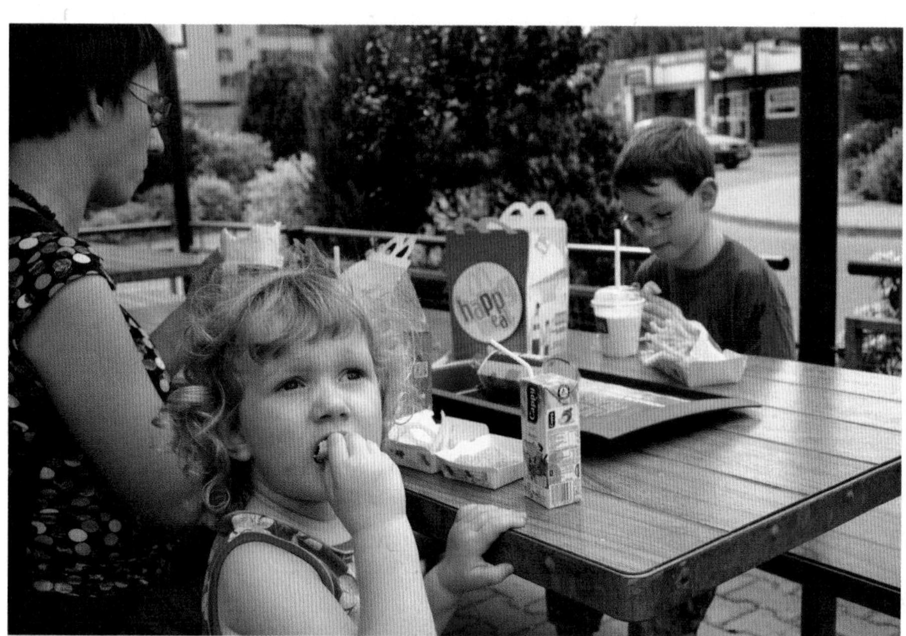

McDonald's responded to customers' requests for healthier food options by including yogurt, juice, and fruit in their Happy Meals.

© iStockphoto.com/Madzia71

THE BIG PICTURE: How OB Topics Fit Together

Individual Processes

- Individual Differences
- Emotions and Attitudes
- Perceptions and Learning
- Motivation

Team Processes

- Ethics
- Decision Making
- Creativity and Innovation
- Conflict and Negotiation

Organizational Processes

- Culture
- **STRATEGY**
- Change and Development
- Structure and Technology

Influence Processes

- Leadership
- Power and Politics
- Communication

Organizational Outcomes

- Individual Performance
- Job Satisfaction
- Team Performance
- Organizational Goals

RYAN HAGAN, *manager, FoxGuard Solutions*

OB in the Real World

FoxGuard Solutions helps power generation facilities comply with required technology security standards. It began providing cybersecurity a few years ago as the wholly owned subsidiary of a computer hardware company called CCS-Inc., but FoxGuard's services were so successful that the two brands merged, took the FoxGuard name, and shifted their focus to cybersecurity and hardware technology.

Ryan Hagan is director of IT and software development at FoxGuard Solutions. He says, "Strategy is important to our business because it helps us establish vision and direction. Without direction that's been set at a higher level it's very easy for employees to focus on work that quickly becomes irrelevant to their industry." Ryan notes that a company that's not looking far enough ahead may not see disruptions like new technology, legislation, or trade agreements coming or plan for them. "The disruption can send the company into a death spiral because managers weren't prepared to act quickly, adapt, and change in order to survive in the changing business landscape."

FoxGuard, in contrast, works hard to keep an eye on industry trends and shapes its strategy accordingly. Years ago the leadership team started meeting once a month to look at both industry and internal data and understand trends that would help them shape their business strategy. The goal was, and still is, to move the company in the right direction based on the data. Several years ago, for instance, CCS saw a trend in cybersecurity and created the FoxGuard division. When FoxGuard began posting significantly higher profit margins than the other side of the business and the CCS division was being squeezed on price because of competitors' offerings, the company's managers made changes that are helping the company not only survive, but thrive. Ryan says, "If our company hadn't been strategic we could have easily become replaceable and our customer base would have left us in favor of another company who could do the same job for cheaper. Instead we made some moves and have become experts in an emerging field."

Critical-Thinking Questions

1. **How would you describe Ryan's approach to strategy?**
2. **What sort of strategies have you devised in your life to reach a goal?**

SOURCES: Ryan Hagan, personal interview, January 14, 2014. www.foxguardsolutions.com/company/history.

Strategic Planning Process

Now that Yolande has the support of the staff to take the company international, she gathers her senior team together to begin the **strategic planning** process, which focuses on the company's desired future and sets defined goals and objectives to translate the vision into reality.

The team consists of Vice President and Chief Financial Officer (CFO) Alfonso Sanchez, who is responsible for risk management and compliance; Chief Commercial Office Zane Kovac, responsible for sales and marketing; Chief Legal Officer Saara Yemen, who is in charge of legal and contracting functions; Chief Health Officer Marcella Delgado, who analyzes the latest scientific research; and HR Manager Imani Clarke.

Levels of Strategy

Typically, managers focus on three main levels of strategy during the strategic planning process: organizational, divisional, and functional.[5] (See Figure 15.1.)

Strategic planning: The process through which a focus on the desired future sets out defined goals and objectives to translate the vision into reality

Yolande begins by focusing on the current *organizational strategy* at Pioneering Health.

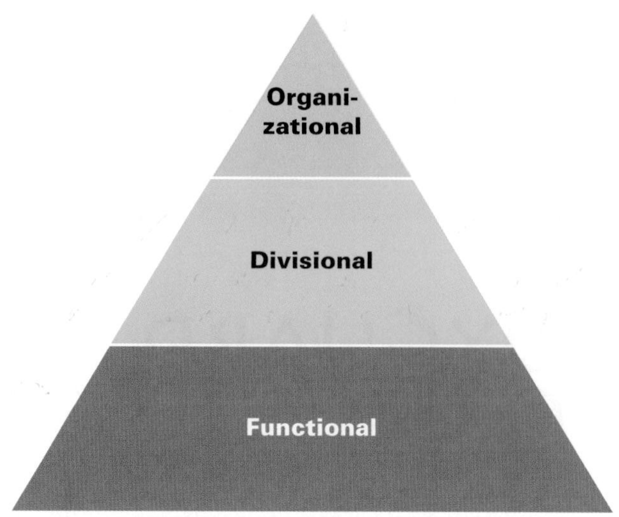

FIGURE 15.1 Levels of Strategy

"We need a strategic plan for our proposed international expansion. I would like to kick-start the process by looking at our current organization and our strategy. In short, what kind of business are we?," Yolande asks.

"We are a health and well-being company and we provide disease management strategies that not only improve the lives of others but save our clients' money," Zane responds.

"We are also a people-focused business," Marcella adds. "Our priority is to promote health and well-being to as many people as possible."

"Now our challenge is to figure out how we can help promote healthy living to people all over the world," Yolande says.

"We need to make sure that our vision is consistent with the international expansion and that we are expanding for the right reasons," Alfonso adds. "If we succeed, we will become more profitable, but our financial success must not be at the sacrifice of our own values."

"Well said," Yolande says with a smile. "We need to hold on to our vision if we are going to maintain the original values of Pioneering Health."

Next, Yolande concentrates on **divisional strategy**, which focuses on how the different departments of the organization comply with the company's vision.

"We need to think about how the different divisions within Pioneering Health are in line with our mission to expand the company. I want to make sure they are supportive of our plan," Yolande says.

"From a human resources standpoint, the welfare of our colleagues is paramount," Imani says. "It will be interesting to hear from the senior managers here about how they think the teams will react to the change."

Zane responds, "The sales and marketing team are passionate about the goal of promoting good health and well-being, and welcome the news of the expansion."

"I can say the same for the health data analysts," Marcella adds. "They are excited about the expansion."

"I don't want to be negative," Alfonso adds, "but the accounting team can be a little inflexible about change. I need to sit down and talk them through the reasons for the expansion, the impact on them, and so on."

"Absolutely," Yolande nods. "Every colleague will receive a full explanation of why we are expanding and will be given ample opportunity to ask questions on a one-to-one basis."

When the team has finished discussing the divisional strategy, Yolande moves on to **functional strategy**, which is a set of rules determining how each department will implement the strategic plan.

Divisional strategy: A plan that focuses on how the different departments of the organization comply with the company's vision

Functional strategy: A set of rules determining how each department will implement the strategic plan

"Once we have defined our global expansion strategy, every colleague in the organization will be equipped with a clear set of guidelines to help implement the initiative," Yolande says. "Now comes the tricky part," she says, smiling. "Team, what's the plan to expand globally?"

Competitive Advantage and Strategy Types

To help develop the strategic plan, the senior team looks at the degree of competitive advantage Pioneering Health holds over its competition and analyzes the types of strategies the organization could adopt to achieve global expansion.[6]

"Team, as you all know, we have quite a few competitors domestically," Yolande says. "Indeed, one particular competitor recently poached two of our best clients. We viewed that situation as a sign to step up our game by providing the best service possible for our customers as well as remaining competitive on price. But we need to do more."

"Like expanding the business," Imani says.

"Exactly. Thanks to extensive market research, we know there are plenty of opportunities for expansion outside the United States—Europe in particular. None of our competitors has ventured into Europe yet. If we succeed, we could achieve real competitive advantage."

Yolande pauses to direct the team's attention toward the whiteboard in the room where she has written *types of strategies*.

Types of Strategies

Organizations generally select one of five strategies: first mover, reactor, analyzer, defender, and prospector.[7] When Pioneering Health entered the market, it was considered a **first mover**, an organization that wins competitive advantage by being the first to establish itself in a particular market. Pioneering Health was the first company of its kind to offer disease management and wellness strategies to health care providers and corporations.

"While I am very proud of our first-mover status," Yolande says, "we need to think about the type of strategy that will define us in the future and will maintain our competitive advantage in the global health industry."

The team discusses the **defender strategy**, in which organizations focus on stability and efficiency of their internal operations to protect their market from new competitors.

"I don't think this strategy accurately defines Pioneering Health," Alfonso says. "I think the focus is too narrow—we are more outward looking than this type of strategy suggests."

Yolande and the rest of the team agree, and they move on to discuss the next type on the list. In the **analyzer strategy**, organizations try to maintain current products and services with a limited amount of innovation.

"This doesn't sound like us either," Zane says. "We need to go beyond merely maintaining our current business model—we need to evolve and cater to new markets."

Marcella joins in. "I agree with Zane—we need to stay ahead of the competition," she says.

Next the team discusses the **reactor strategy**, in which an organization simply responds to environmental threats and opportunities rather than following a defined plan.

"In my mind, this is not a good description of the Pioneering Health approach, either," Yolande says. "Yes, we react to threats and opportunities, but we are also leaders in this industry. We need to set the trend and be forward thinking."

"If we sit back and wait for changes to happen, Pioneering Health will not thrive. We are pioneers after all—the first ones in breaking new ground," Marcella says.

First mover: An organization that wins competitive advantage by being the first to establish itself in a particular market

Defender strategy: The means by which organizations focus on stability and efficiency of their internal operations to protect their market from new competitors

Analyzer strategy: The means by which organizations try to maintain current products and services with a limited amount of innovation

Reactor strategy: A means through which organizations respond to environmental threats and opportunities rather than following a defined plan

The final strategy is **prospector strategy**, in which organizations focus on innovation, creativity, and flexibility and take high risks in order to accelerate growth and gain competitive advantage.

"I think this one is far more relevant," Zane says. "For me, this sums up what we are trying to achieve. To be the forerunners in the health management industry we need to take risks and be innovative. We are the ones creating change to which other competitors must respond."

Yolande smiles and says, "I think this is the perfect definition of what we're trying to achieve with our global expansion."

Strategy

The journey is just beginning. Yolande knows she and the team need as much information as possible before attempting to expand into new markets.

THINKING CRITICALLY

1. Explain the difference between organizational strategy and tactical planning. How does operational planning support tactical planning? **[Understand/Apply]**
2. What steps must a company take before it establishes a functional strategy? Why? **[Understand/Apply]**
3. Consider the five strategy types: first mover, reactor, analyzer, defender, and prospector. Why do company leaders at Pioneering Health see themselves as prospectors rather than first movers in relation to their expansion plans? How will selecting a strategy type inform their organizational strategy? **[Apply/Analyze/Evaluate]**

ORGANIZATIONAL LEARNING AS A STRATEGIC PROCESS

15.2 Discuss organizational learning as a strategic process

Organizational Learning

Continuous learning is essential to organizational strategy, because it helps organizations and their people adapt to rapid change. A **learning organization** is one that facilitates the acquisition, distribution, and retention of knowledge to enable it to react to change.[8] Learning organizations are people focused and provide the opportunity for employees at all levels to learn through formal or on-the-job training or both; for example, teams in a learning organization would be brought together to write a mission statement or invited to engage in regular training sessions. Employees are made to feel part of the organization's overall performance and are encouraged to share their ideas, knowledge, and insights in order to effect improvement and change.

One of the early pioneers of a learning organization is Johnsonville Foods, a sausage manufacturer based in Wisconsin that gives financial awards to employees for learning activity, provides a staff resource center, and offers job shadowing to support the learning process.[9]

Acquiring Knowledge

Yolande's knowledge acquisition skills are one of the main reasons for the success of Pioneering Health. When Yolande left her job as a pharmaceutical product line manager to start Pioneering Health 15 years ago, she made it a priority to learn everything there was to know about starting a successful business from the practices of others—a process called **mimicry**.[10] By applying what she learned from the experts, she was able to build her own business model that provided workable solutions to problems, supported decision making, and defined processes and guidelines for employees or "colleagues."

Prospector strategy: A means through which organizations focus on innovation, creativity, and flexibility and take high risks to accelerate growth and gain competitive advantage

Learning organization: An organization that facilitates the acquisition, distribution, and retention of knowledge to enable it to react to change

Mimicry: The process of learning from the successful practices of others

Indeed, Yolande adopted the practice of calling her employees colleagues from another firm whose business model she admired. She also took management courses, learned about the successes and failures of other organizations, and gained insight into pitfalls to avoid. This process is known as **vicarious learning**, or observing and retaining the lessons gained from the experiences of others.[11]

Over the years, Yolande has continuously acquired knowledge through **scanning**, which is seeking solutions from consultants, competitors, and other successful firms, and through **grafting**, which is a process of hiring experts who bring their knowledge to the firm.[12] In fact, whenever Pioneering Health develops a relationship with a new client in a different location, Yolande brings in people and resources to share their knowledge.

Each senior team member at Pioneering Health also has a wealth of expert knowledge and a proven track record in his or her particular field.

Distributing Knowledge

As soon as Yolande gathers knowledge, she ensures that it is distributed to the people who need it most. For example, the information she receives from attending health forums, industry events, and webinars is passed on to Marcella and the data and statistical health analysts. The team thoroughly researches this information, and if enough scientific evidence supports the findings of the experts, the information is applied to the company's relevant disease management strategies.

Retaining Knowledge

Yolande recognizes the importance of knowledge retention and has created tools and techniques to capture information. The staff are encouraged and rewarded for sharing information. Company procedures and documents are carefully maintained and archived on an accessible database, and a job rotation program ensures that each member of staff acquires a baseline knowledge about each department in the organization. Since the decision was made to expand internationally, Yolande has carried out extensive research with an emphasis on knowledge acquisition in global locations.

THINKING CRITICALLY ABOUT THE SECTION

1. Other than those examples provided in the chapter, what are three things you could do as the leader of a company to facilitate its identity as a learning organization? **[Evaluate/Create]**
2. Imagine you are just starting a new business. Which method of acquiring knowledge (mimicry, vicarious learning, scanning, or grafting) would you find most valuable at this stage, and why? **[Apply/Analyze]**
3. If you were in charge of retaining knowledge for a company, what tools and procedures would you put in place to ensure optimal knowledge retention, and why? **[Evaluate/Create]**

GLOBALIZATION

15.3 Explain the phenomenon of globalization along with the opportunities and challenges it poses to organizations

Yolande and the Pioneering Health team agree that it's a good time to expand the company, but it is really necessary? After all, the company is considered a leader in the health management industry domestically. Why would it or any other company decide

Vicarious learning: A process of learning by watching the actions or behaviors of another person

Scanning: The search for solutions from outside consultants, competitors, and other successful firms

Grafting: A process of hiring experts to bring their knowledge to a firm

US companies expand internationally and can appear in some places you might not expect, like this Pizza Hut located outside of Cairo within view of the Great Pyramids.

Gary Cook / Alamy Stock Photo

Globalization

to expand? The answer is **globalization**, which is the integration of economy, trade, and finance on an international scale.[13] Globalization has been on the increase in the United States since the 1980s. It has enhanced the flow of trade and investment among countries, increased the degree of communication among countries and nationalities, and taken political activity from a national to a global level through the efforts of the European Union (EU) and the International Monetary Fund (IMF). The advent of the Internet and other communication technologies means that most businesses, large and small, can participate in the international marketplace with little additional expense.

The reality for Pioneering Health is that if it does not venture into new markets soon, its competitors will, and Yolande believes that the company cannot afford to be left behind. But as all organizations that choose to expand discover, there are both opportunities and challenges in expanding internationally.

Opportunities and Challenges

Many organizations realize major advantages in going global. For example, there is an opportunity for economic growth; going global makes it easier for their goods and services to flow across borders; and new opportunities arise to invest in developing and emerging-economy countries. Many US companies have reaped the benefits of going global. For example, undergarment manufacturer Spanx originally started as a small operation in Atlanta but has since grown into a global brand, and the products are now available in 55 countries all over the world.[14] Similarly, since going global over 30 years ago, submarine sandwich franchise Subway has grown to 40,000 locations worldwide, surpassing McDonald's 35,000 global locations. Subway's global strategy is to expand to 100,000 locations by 2030.[15]

Free trade between countries is on the rise, with larger markets making reduced prices and higher profits possible at the same time. Organizations that set up in different locations have the advantage of learning and gaining knowledge about different cultures and their business practices. US companies can pop up in the most unexpected places; for example, there is a McDonald's in the Negev Desert in Israel and a Pizza Hut in the Valley of Kings in Egypt.[16]

Globalization: The integration of economy, trade, and finance on an international scale

Global expansion also has its challenges. Countries can become more dependent on other countries for certain goods and services, and in the event of political unrest and war, these resources may become limited. Furthermore, organizations with offices in turbulent countries are at risk of *nationalization,* the process by which the government takes over private business assets while paying little or no compensation to the owners themselves. In short, when certain countries are going through periods of unrest, the government can change the rules at any time, which leads to greater risk and uncertainty. The debate over whether South Africa's mining industry should be nationalized has been going on for some time. Although some South African union leaders believe nationalization could lead to more revenue for the country, the ruling party in government believes it is a threat to investment from other countries. The tensions surrounding this issue have magnified into strikes and labor violence.[17]

There is also a degree of economic risk in the inevitable rise and fall of interest and exchange rates. A drop in foreign currency can be expensive for a firm because it reduces earnings and makes investing in growth more difficult. Managing different cultures and workforces can be a major challenge, too, particularly if the offices are separated by thousands of miles and a number of time zones. Organizations that create thoughtful strategies to maintain diversity and deal with the logistics of working with international partners have a far better chance of survival.

When the Pioneering Team returns from lunch, they focus on the next topic on the agenda: the location of the first Pioneering Health business in Europe.

"Okay team, let's brainstorm!," Yolande says. "As you know, I've carried out a good deal of research, but I would like to hear your ideas regarding the location of our first European office."

"Since it's our first exploration into new markets, I think we need to choose a location where there will be as little risk as possible," Alfonso says.

"I agree with Alfonso," Saara says. "I'd rather not take unnecessary risks with our first international business. It's all new territory for us and we need to tread carefully. Let's not complicate matters right now."

"What would make the expansion go more smoothly?," Imani asks.

"I think an English-speaking country would help with communication," Zane says.

"I agree—and maybe a culture that is somewhat similar to ours," Alfonso suggests.

"Also, a country experiencing political and economic stability would mean less risk," adds Saara.

"We also need to consider the different health issues experienced by the population in these countries so we can be sure we have the expertise to promote health and well-being," Marcella says.

"My thoughts exactly," Yolande says. "In light of this discussion, what are the potential locations for Pioneering Health?"

"England or Ireland," Alfonso says.

"I agree! Both countries meet all our requirements so far," Imani says. "They are both English speaking, culturally similar to the United States, and economically and politically stable. I think they're viable options!"

Zane and Marcella also agree.

Yolande responds, "Team, I had the same thoughts as you, which is why I carried out extensive research into the possibility of setting up in England or Ireland, but in the past few days, I've run into a major stumbling block."

"Did the different health care systems pose a problem? They're very different from ours in the United States," Saara says.

"How so?," Zane asks.

"In the United States, our clients subscribe to many different types of private health plans and service providers, but in England and Ireland the health system is different. For instance, in England, there is a dominant government health care system governed by the Department of Health called the National Health Service [NHS], which provides health care to every legal resident of the UK. Instead of dealing with private health companies, we would be dealing with a publicly funded system," Saara explains.

She then turns to Yolande and says, "Is the unique health care the problem?"

"On the contrary, I was excited about devising a new business model to align our services with the UK," Yolande sighs. "We could have partnered with the NHS, which would have given us access to every single hospital and health institution in the country. Think of the number of people we could have reached using our disease management strategies! I had even started to build relationships with the NHS administrators over the phone, and they seemed genuinely enthusiastic about the prospect of working with us."

"What happened?," Marcella asks.

"The economic recession," Yolande says. "The NHS was forced to lay off thousands of staff members, as well as all their outside consultants, which means there's no chance of our partnering with them."

"Any chance of the situation improving soon?," Imani asks.

"I think a few years down road we might be able to access the UK market, but not right now," Yolande responds.

"That leaves Ireland," Zane says.

"Actually, Ireland is out of the picture too," Yolande replies. "Ireland is suffering the brunt of the economic recession and the country is experiencing a lot of turmoil."

"If England and Ireland aren't options right now, what other possibilities do we have?," Alfonso asks.

"This is what we need to figure out," Yolande says. "I need your help to find a suitable location that includes the criteria we discussed. Talk to your contacts, talk to your teams, talk to as many people as possible. The more knowledge we have the better. I'll be doing the same. We will reconvene in a week's time and discuss our findings," she finishes, and the meeting ends. Senior members of the staff go back to their desks determined to come up with a viable location for the first Pioneering Health office in Europe.

THINKING CRITICALLY

1. Discuss the ways in which the Internet, smartphones, and other communication technologies make the day-to-day running of global companies more efficient. **[Analyze/Evaluate]**
2. Why is choosing a country that is culturally similar to the United States particularly important for Pioneering Health, as opposed to a different type of company? **[Analyze/Evaluate]**
3. When thinking about international expansion, is it more important for Pioneering Health to choose countries that share a common language and/or culture or countries that are experiencing political and economic stability? Explain your answer. **[Analyze/Evaluate]**

ADAPTING ORGANIZATIONAL PRACTICES ACROSS CULTURES

15.4 Identify key ways in which organizations adapt their practices across cultures

One of the main criteria for a successful global expansion is an understanding of different organizational cultures, something the Pioneering Health team will need to take into consideration when deciding on the location of their first international office.

One of the most valuable studies in measuring culture was conducted by Dutch sociologist Geert Hofstede. Hofstede identified five ways of measuring culture based on research analyzing the interactions between people from different cultures all over the world. Known as Hofstede's dimensions, these five measures, each of which is shown as a continuum in Figure 15.2, have been used by organizations to improve understanding and cooperation between cultures.[18]

Hofstede's Dimensions

The **individualist–collectivist** dimension focuses on the degree to which citizens in a given culture believe they have the right to live their lives as they see fit, choose their own values, and act on their own judgment. This dimension is usually high in individualist cultures like the United States. In collectivist cultures such as Thailand people are more likely to value the welfare of the group over that of any particular individual, and suspend personal values and judgment for the sake of the "greater good." **Power distance** expresses the extent to which people in different societies accept the way power is distributed. People in countries with *high power distance* such as Mexico and Singapore are more likely to accept the idea of hierarchy and depend on those with power to make the decisions. At the organizational level, high power distance is most common in hierarchical structures where there is very little interaction between lower- and higher-level employees. In *low power distance* countries such as the United States and Sweden, in contrast, people tend to prefer consultation with others and strive to ensure the distribution of power is equalized as fairly as possible.

Hofstede's Cultural Dimensions

Uncertainty avoidance measures the degree to which people are able to deal with the unexpected and how they cope with uncertainty in unstructured environments. As Figure 15.2 shows, Italy and Mexico have cultures that emphasize more predictable structures, while the United States and Singapore emphasize variable environments. In countries with a competitive culture, such as Austria and China, employees generally tend to display more assertive, striving, merit-oriented personality traits. In contrast, countries with cooperative cultures such as Chile and Bulgaria tend to take a more compassionate, tolerant, and caring approach. Hofstede used the terms "masculine" and "feminine" to denote the competitive vs. cooperative continuum in his work, but the authors consider this nomenclature outdated. Cultures that lean toward **long-term orientation** measure values such as perseverance, respect for tradition, and thrift against

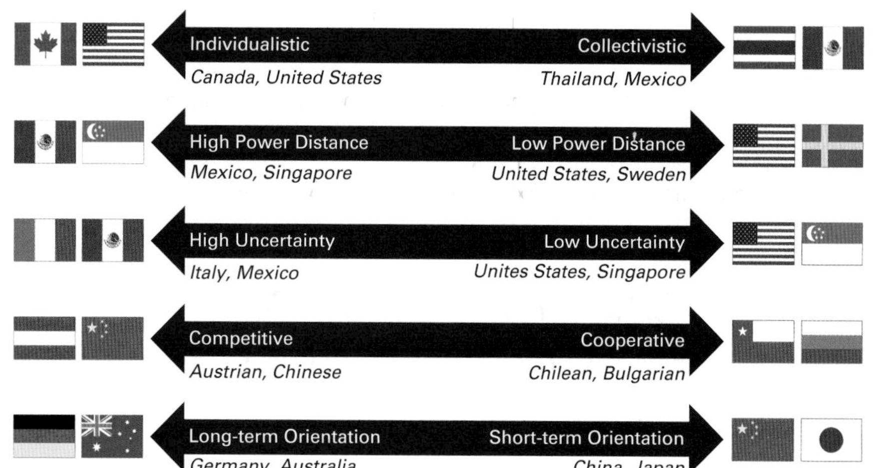

FIGURE 15.2 Hofstede's Dimensions

SOURCE: Neck, C. (2013). *Management* (Hoboken, NJ: Wiley): 122.

Individualist–collectivist: The degree to which employees believe they have the right to live their lives as they see fit, choose their own values, and act on their own judgment

Power distance: The extent to which people in different societies accept the way power is distributed.

Uncertainty avoidance: the degree to which people are able to deal with the unexpected and how they cope with uncertainty in unstructured environments

Long-term orientation: The measurement of values such as perseverance, respect for tradition, and thrift

Singaporeans are more suited to dealing with a variable environment. This cultural characteristic is reflected in their unique and modern skyline.

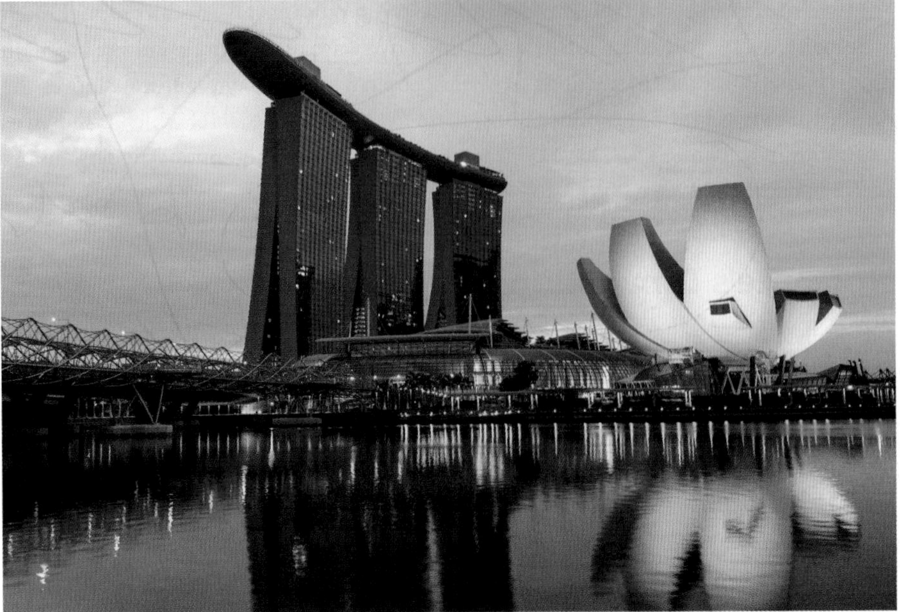

iStockphoto.com/Vincent_St_Thomas

short-term orientation values such as meeting social obligations and avoiding embarrassment or shame.

Hofstede has been criticized for using surveys to measure cultural differences, and overgeneralizing national populations on the basis of the limited size of the model, in that there weren't enough respondents to the questionnaires to draw the conclusions that Hofstede had made. Hofstede has responded to these criticisms by defending his use of surveys, noting that the results closely correlated with other data that represented whole national populations.[19]

Although Hofstede's cultural dimensions provide a useful guideline for organizations considering branching out into new territories, every organization is different and will need to take its own particular traits into consideration. At the same time, an understanding of Hofstede's cultural dimensions may help management in one culture determine how best to launch a business in another culture and support new employees.

Global Integration Versus Local Responsiveness

International companies face challenges in two major areas when they operate in foreign countries: global integration and local responsiveness.[20] This means they often have to strike a balance between following their own global strategies—determining how their products are made and marketed and how employees are treated—and meeting the legal, financial, employment, and other requirements of their host government. Firms may have to change or tailor their operations to remain in compliance with those requirements. As a result, they have to consider how much they should either standardize or localize their practices.

Standardization is the degree to which employees are expected to follow the same rules and policies everywhere.[21] For example, in a manufacturing plant, teams might follow best practices that are applied globally, such as adhering to certain protocols for safety reasons and ensure operations go smoothly. When introducing a new product under a global standardized process, teams may perform *upstream functions* such as identifying the market need, devising strategies, and brainstorming ways to bring the product to market. These functions take place behind the scenes and are invisible to the customer.

Localization, in contrast, is the process of adapting certain functions to accommodate the language, culture, or governing laws of a different country.[22] In the case of a

Short-term orientation: The measurement of values such as meeting social obligations and avoiding embarrassment or shame

Standardization: The degree to which employees are expected to follow the same rules and policies everywhere

Localization: The process of adapting certain functions to accommodate the language, culture, or governing laws of a country

Companies that expand overseas should take care to understand how their brand will be perceived in a foreign culture. For example, when KFC first expanded to China in the 1980's, their slogan "Finger-Lickin' Good" was mistranslated to "Eat Your Fingers Off!"

new product, teams working in a foreign country might step in to manage the *downstream functions* that focus on sales and marketing of the product after the launch. These functions are centered on improving the flow of the product to the customer.

An organization that successfully localizes its product pays attention to the unique cultural customs of each country in which it operates. For example, marketing a violent video game to emphasize its action and realistic "kills" might be a more successful strategy in competitive cultures than in more cooperative cultures. Certain advertising slogans may connect with some cultures but be lost in translation with others. In short, organizations need to know their audience in order to avoid product or advertising blunders.

Leadership Across Different Cultures

Leadership Across Cultures

In Chapter 13, we looked at cross-cultural leadership and the challenges of managing people from different cultural backgrounds. Studies have found that participative management and empowering leadership are particularly effective in Western culture because they provide employees with decision power and the information they need to use that power in the best way.[23] In their home countries, Western firms that adopt this approach, like Pioneering Health, often perform better than other firms. However, care must be taken when implementing this approach in different cultures. A participative management style may fail in high power distance cultures.[24]

Let's return to our narrative to analyze and apply the points just described.

When the Pioneering Health team reconvenes the following week, there is an element of anticipation in the room. Each member hopes that by the end of the meeting the first international location for a Pioneering Health office will be chosen. Having greeted the team, Yolande asks each member to provide the name of the country they consider to be the most viable option.

Alfonso is the first to speak. He feels that an English-speaking country is best and suggests that it might be worth waiting for the economic crises in the United Kingdom and Ireland to be resolved before venturing into international waters. Saara agrees with Alfonso.

It is Zane's turn next. "I disagree with Alfonso," he says. "I don't think we can afford to wait for the countries of our choice to recover. That might take years. If we don't move now, our competitors will get there first. I've been doing a lot of research and I think Germany is the country where we should open our first international office."

"I agree with Zane that we can't afford to wait," Marcella says. "Apart from not being outdone by our competitors, we can help people worldwide with our health management strategies and we need to do it as soon as possible. I think Spain is the best location."

Imani is the last to join the discussion. "I also identified Germany as the best location," she says.

Yolande thanks everybody for their feedback and then shares her opinion.

"Alfonso, I hear what you're saying about the crises in England and Ireland. Things might be different in a year's time—who knows? But I think waiting for that to happen is a greater risk. As Zane says, our competitors could pass us in the meantime, and we can't afford to let that happen," she says.

Next, Yolande addresses Imani and Zane. "It's interesting that both of you have identified Germany as a good location. What are your reasons?" Yolande asks.

Imani answers first. "I started with the language situation. Over half the German population speak English, especially in the main cities such as Frankfurt, Munich, and Berlin. We can also recruit locals who speak both English and German, which should help us with the language barrier," Imani says.

"What about German culture and its impact on how they do business?" Saara asks, leaning forward. "Isn't it a little more conservative than in the United States?"

"Sure," Imani replies. "We would have to be careful in terms of our leadership strategies. In our organization we take an empowering and participative approach, but in Germany processes tend to be standardized and managers are more autocratic and directive. This may make it more difficult for them to adapt to our type of management style. We would need to implement training programs to help them adjust."

"What about Germany's health care system?" Alfonso asks.

"It's similar to England's National Health System in that it's a publicly funded operation," Zane replies. "However, a larger percentage of Germans tend to opt out of the state system in favor of private health insurance. This gives us the opportunity to partner with more private companies than we might be able to do in another country."

"From my analysis, Germany's population suffers from many of the same chronic illnesses affecting those of us in the U.S, including obesity. As experts in the field, we should be able to make a difference there," Marcella adds.

Yolande nods. "I have also been looking into Germany. It certainly meets most of our original criteria," Yolande says. "It has the benefit of being one of the most politically and economically stable countries in Europe. Although it is not entirely an English-speaking country, I think we can cope with the language barrier. As Marcella says, we certainly have the tools to address concerns about rising obesity levels." Yolande turns to Marcella. "Earlier in the meeting, you suggested Spain as a viable location. Can you explain why?"

"After hearing the information about Germany, I can see that focusing on Spain might throw up a couple of red flags," Marcella says. "English isn't as widely spoken in Spain, and the country isn't economically stable at the moment. I guess my decision was based on emotion. The Spanish government has significantly cut spending on health care, excluding a large part of the Spanish population from basic treatment. It's a country on the verge of a health crisis and I want us to go in there and help by sharing our expert health knowledge with the authorities," she finishes.

Yolande nods. "I understand, Marcella, but I hope you know it would be risky for us to open our first location in Spain when the country is in such turmoil. However, I wouldn't rule it out in the future. After all, the plan is for Pioneering Health to have a worldwide presence."

Marcella brightens. "I'm glad Spain is still an option, but agree that for now it's best to focus on one country at a time. I think Germany sounds like a good place to start," she says.

"I agree," Yolande says. "Saara and Alfonso, I know you both wanted to wait out the situation in England and Ireland, but what are your thoughts on Germany?"

"I would have to become better acquainted with their legal system to see what's involved in setting up a branch of a company there, but I think it's a possibility," Saara says.

"I'd need to assess the financial risk, but Germany has an efficient and well-established financial infrastructure that provides a solid basis for companies like ours. I think Germany has potential," Alfonso says.

"OK team. Let's pursue the idea of Germany as our first international location," Yolande says. "Great work, pioneers!"

THINKING CRITICALLY

1. Do different cultures experience high power or low power distance in business as a reflection of their mode of political governance? Explain your answer. **[Analyze/Evaluate]**

2. What are two types of industries that would particularly benefit from standardization? What are two types of industries that would particularly benefit from localization? Why? **[Analyze/Evaluate]**

3. Imani points out that Pioneering Health takes an empowering and participative approach to leadership, while in Germany processes tend to be "standardized and managers are more autocratic and directive." She says that they would need to "implement training programs to help them adjust." Do you agree that this approach, as opposed to adapting the company's management style in Germany to reflect German culture, is best? Why or why not? **[Analyze/Evaluate]**

INTERNATIONAL ASSIGNMENTS AND CAREER DEVELOPMENT

15.5 Describe how international assignments can be used for employee development

Following Alfonso and Saara's legal and financial due diligence, the team gets the go-ahead to set up an office in Germany with the business center of Frankfurt as the city of choice.

Yolande and the team create an organizational strategy and a new business model to align with German corporate culture. Imani is responsible for designing the training programs to help the German staff adapt to the management style at Pioneering Health, finding recruitment agencies to aid the hiring process and office space in Frankfurt to rent. Alfonso and Saara are in charge of learning the local banking and tax systems as well as choosing legal and financial representation. Zane has been busy making calls to administrators at private German health care companies and building relationships with them, and Marcella has been carrying out extensive research into the health issues in Germany and putting together strategies to address these concerns.

Yolande makes several trips to Germany to cement relationships with private health care companies, explaining how Pioneering Health can save them money by helping people manage their illnesses. In particular, Yolande pitches what has been one of the company's most successful disease management strategies in the United States: proactive telephonic management of obesity and other chronic illnesses, which has the dual benefit of providing regular health care from health experts over the phone and reducing the number of hospital admissions. Yolande makes a passionate case for implementing the same initiative and cost savings in Germany and manages to seal contracts with two private German health care companies.

Once the contracts have been signed, Yolande applies for a resident's permit, which will make her an **expatriate** in Germany, an employee who lives and works in a foreign country on a temporary basis.[25] She wants to oversee the setting up of the new German operation and be the direct point of contact for their new German clients. However, Yolande knows she cannot do everything on her own, so she chooses HR manager Imani to join her in Germany for the first couple of months to assist in the hiring process and help her navigate any cultural obstacles.

Yolande views Imani as one of her high-potential employees or **HIPOs**, employees who are flexible, committed, and motivated.[26] Such employees are often chosen to work on international assignments as part of their career development. Over the past couple of years, Imani has advanced from assistant manager to head of HR. Yolande and the rest of the Pioneering Health team have tremendous respect for her and she is well liked. Yolande has no doubt Imani will do an excellent job on the training and recruitment side in Germany.

Culture Shock and Cultural Adaptation

Culture Shock

Although international assignments sound like exciting prospects, they can have downsides. Many people underestimate the difficulty of moving to a different country as an expatriate and experiencing **culture shock**, a feeling of nervousness, doubt, and confusion arising from being in a foreign and unfamiliar environment.[27]

If you ever have the opportunity to work on a long-term foreign assignment, avoid culture shock by doing your homework. Research the culture and the language, talk to people who have been in that country to get their advice and feedback, and make sure the job you will be doing is clear from the very beginning. Many employees have accepted assignments overseas only to find the role or the culture (or both) to be nothing like they envisioned. Ideally, organizations should offer support and provide cultural knowledge and language training if necessary to prepare their employees for an overseas experience.[28]

Stages of Cultural Adaptation

Typically, there are five stages of cultural adaptation.[29] (See Figure 15.3.) The first is the *honeymoon* stage that takes place soon after arrival in the new country. Everything is exciting and novel and there is an immediate impulse to explore and soak up the new culture. However, after a few weeks, the *disintegration* stage sets in; the gloss starts to wear off, and feelings of nervousness and insecurity may appear. It might be difficult to communicate with the residents, the food might seem strange, business and social etiquette might be a struggle, and the local laws may seem confusing. For example, in Singapore you can incur a heavy fine for drinking any kind of liquid on public transportation, including water; in Germany putting your hands in your pockets while you are talking to someone is considered rude; and in India saying the word "no" during a business meeting is frowned upon (people say "possibly" or "we'll see" instead).

The third stage is *reintegration*, which typically occurs after a few months in the foreign location. At this stage, you probably have reached an understanding about how the business and social cultures operate and have accepted the factors that seemed strange in the beginning. You may still have mixed feelings about living and working in the society,

Expatriate: An employee who lives and works in a foreign country on a temporary basis

HIPOs: High-potential employees who are flexible, committed, and motivated

Culture shock: Feelings of nervousness, doubt, and confusion arising from being in a foreign environment

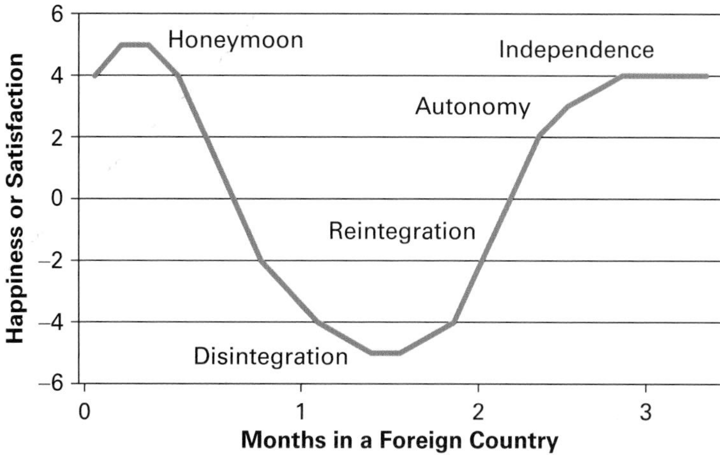

FIGURE 15.3 Stages of Cultural Adaptation

SOURCE: Adapted from Winkelman, Michael. "Cultural Shock and Adaptation." *Journal of Counseling and Development* 73, no. 2 (November 1994): 121-126.

but you are starting to adjust. During the *autonomy* stage you are more confident about knowing how to function in your new environment, you know how to interact with people and where to socialize, and you have a clearer understanding of business practices. In short, you are beginning to settle in.

This leads to the *independence* stage, in which you understand how the culture operates, feel confident that you can handle most situations, and value the culture for its differences from as well as its similarities to your own.

Expatriate Failure

Global firms hope that most employees who are sent on foreign assignments, particularly expatriates who might be expected to last for a couple of years or more, will reach the independence stage. However, expatriates sometimes return home early for a variety of reasons. There are several reasons why expatriates fail to complete the duration of their stay in a different country.[30] The most common is family stress.[31] Although the employee is experiencing a novel and exciting environment and making new friends at work, the spouse, who may have left a job or career behind at home, may be lonely and struggling to adjust to the new culture, which can put an enormous amount of pressure on a relationship.

Another factor is that foreign assignments often come with a higher degree of responsibility, which some people find overwhelming. Managing people from different cultures can be frustrating and perplexing, especially if the expatriate is not familiar with local customs. If an expatriate is unable to fulfill the requirements of his or her role or does not possess the emotional maturity to handle additional responsibility, then the organization itself may choose to terminate the assignment.

Finally, another reason for expatriate failure is inability to adjust to cultural or language differences, which often occurs because of poor advance preparation. This can lead to severe homesickness and an early return home.

Benefits and Costs of International Assignments

Are expatriate assignments worth the cost and extra effort to the employee, the family, and the firm? In some companies, a person's career development depends on his or her taking international assignments. For example, an employee working in a US

EXPATRIATE FAILURE RATES

Examining the Evidence

Books and articles on expatriates have typically referred to very high expatriate failure rates—as high as 25–40 percent in developed countries and 70 percent in developing countries. However, Professor Anne-Wil Harzing of the University of Melbourne has taken a closer look at the existing data and has found such claims to be somewhat distorted and exaggerated.* Through her analyses, Professor Harzing shows how inappropriate referencing and mis-citations have helped to create and entrench an inaccurate myth of high expatriate failure rates.^ Her examination of the empirical evidence suggests that expatriate failure rates could be considered rather low, especially in European and Japanese companies, where the majority of firms report failure rates at less than 5 percent.* These findings do not suggest that expatriate failures are unimportant or that they do not have real financial and human resource implications for multinational companies. Instead, Professor Harzing suggests that a more in-depth understanding of expatriate failure based on our general knowledge of organizational turnover and performance management may be needed.#

Critical-Thinking Questions

1. **Why do you think expatriate failure rates have been exaggerated in books and articles on expatriate management?**
2. **If expatriate failure rates are not as high as previously thought, should managers of expatriates still be concerned about expatriate failure? Why or why not?**

*Harzing, Anne-Wil K. "The Persistent Myth of High Expatriate Failure Rates." *International Journal of Human Resource Management* 6, no. 2 (May 1995): 457–474.

^Harzing, Anne-Wil. "Are Our Referencing Errors Undermining Our Scholarship and Credibility? The Case of Expatriate Failure Rates." *Journal of Organizational Behavior* 23, no. 1 (February 2002): 127–148.

#Harzing, Anne-Wil, and Christensen Claus. "Expatriate Failure: Time to Abandon the Concept?" *Career Development International* 9, no. 7 (July 2004): 616–626.

investment bank in New York with branches located globally can gain great experience and make valuable new contacts in one of the firm's international offices. However, "out of sight, out of mind" can also operate. In other words, sometimes expatriates can return home to find they have been overlooked for career opportunities or promotions while away. To combat this issue, employees working abroad must manage their careers by staying in touch with their mentors and remaining in close contact with their biggest work champions back at headquarters, either through modern technology such as Skype, face-to-face when returning to the main office on scheduled trips, or both.[32]

It has been two months since Yolande and Imani arrived in Germany to set up the new Pioneering Health office, and they are slowly adjusting to life in Germany. Yolande has been struggling with the new language. Though most Germans speak English, she has found it difficult to communicate with some of her local contacts who understand only a limited amount of English. She is determined to learn enough German to assimilate into the culture.

Imani is finding it easier to learn German but is struggling with German social etiquette, especially the practice of using a knife and fork to eat sandwiches and fruit. In spite of these minor hiccups, the two colleagues are settling in well. The office in Frankfurt has been set up, and they have recruited 15 new employees in the fields of administration, accounting, sales, marketing, and HR; each has an excellent command of the English language. Among the staff are four fully qualified nurses who will be

©iStockphoto.com/video1

In order to preserve their role in the company and keep up with the company's culture, expatriates should make an effort to communicate frequently with mentors and colleagues in the home office.

providing expert advice over the phone to patients with chronic health problems. The first Pioneering Health international office is officially open for business.

In the next chapter, we explore the challenges Yolande and Imani face during their efforts to implement organizational change.

THINKING CRITICALLY

1. What factors should Yolande, as the CEO of Pioneering Health, take most into account when deciding which U.S. employee to relocate to Germany? Based on the discussion of culture shock and the stages of cultural adaptation, are there particular company roles that should be allocated to local German employees only? **[Analyze/Evaluate]**
2. List at least two steps Yolande can take to help ensure Imani is successful and comfortable as an expatriate in Germany. How will these steps aid Imani's cultural adaptation? **[Apply/Analyze]**

IN REVIEW

Learning Objectives

15.1 Describe the basic concept of organizational strategy

To successfully achieve long-term goals, organizations need to place a clear focus on **organizational strategy**, the process of creating, evaluating, and implementing decisions and objectives to achieve long-term competitive success. **Tactical planning** lays out the short-term actions and plans to implement the strategy. **Operational planning** aligns the strategic plan with the day-to-day tasks required in the running of the organization. A **first mover** is an organization that wins competitive advantage by being the first to establish itself in a particular market. A firm that chooses the **defender strategy** concentrates on stability and efficiency in its internal operations to protect its market from new competitors. An **analyzer strategy** tries to maintain current products and services with a limited amount of innovation. With the **reactor strategy** an organization simply responds to environmental threats and opportunities rather than following a defined plan. The **prospector** strategy seeks innovation, creativity, and flexibility and favors taking high risks to accelerate growth and gain competitive advantage.

15.2 Discuss organizational learning as a strategic process

A **learning organization** facilitates the acquisition, distribution, and retention of knowledge to enable it to react to change. **Mimicry** is the process of learning from the successful practices of others. **Scanning** seeks solutions from outside consultants, competitors, and other successful firms, and **grafting** means hiring experts to bring their knowledge to the firm.

15.3 Explain the phenomenon of globalization along with the opportunities and challenges it poses to organizations

Globalization is the integration of economy, trade, and finance on an international scale. Advantages of going global include the possibility of economic growth, the ease of transporting goods and services across borders, and the opportunity to invest in developing and emerging-economy countries. However, global companies can become more dependent on suppliers in other countries for certain goods and services—in the event of political unrest and war, these resources may become limited. There is also a degree of economic risk due to the inevitable rise and fall of interest and exchange rates. A drop in foreign currency can be expensive for a firm as it reduces earnings and capital investment.

15.4 Identify key ways in which organizations adapt their practices across cultures

Standardization is the degree to which all employees are expected to follow the same rules and policies. **Localization** is the process of adapting certain functions to accommodate the language, culture, or governing laws of a country.

15.5 Describe how international assignments can be used for employee development

The first stage of cultural adaptation is the *honeymoon* stage in which everything seems exciting and new and there is an immediate impulse to explore and soak up the new culture. After a few weeks, the *disintegration* stage sets in; the gloss starts to wear off, and feelings of nervousness and insecurity set in. In *reintegration* the expatriate reaches an understanding about how the business and social cultures operate and accepts the factors that may have seemed strange in the beginning. During the *autonomy* stage he or she knows how to function in the new environment and has a clearer understanding of business practices. This leads on to the *independence* stage of complete understanding about how the culture operates, enough confidence to handle most situations, and appreciation of the culture for its differences as well as its similarities.

KEY TERMS

THINKING CRITICALLY ABOUT THE CASE OF YOLANDE TURNER AND PIONEERING HEALTH

Put yourself in Yolande Turner's position as the CEO of Pioneering Health and consider the five critical-thinking steps in relation to the decision to expand the company's operations to Germany.

OBSERVE

What cultural, economic and political factors do you observe about Germany that make it an attractive choice for international company expansion? What cultural, economic, or political factors might pose a challenge to expanding Pioneering Health there?

INTERPRET

How do these factors set Germany apart from the potential competitors the Pioneering Health team considers: England, Ireland, and Spain?

ANALYZE

Yolande completes several tasks to prepare Pioneering Health for its transition into Germany. Provide your own analysis of how well each of these tasks has worked to position Pioneering Health as a notable presence in the German marketplace.

EVALUATE

Evaluate which cultural, economic, and political factors are most important to address as Pioneering Health begins its expansion into Germany.

EXPLAIN

Devise specific strategies to deal with each of the factors you identified above, and explain why each of these strategies is an effective means of addressing these factors.

EXERCISE 15.1: SECURING A COMPETITIVE ADVANTAGE THROUGH ORGANIZATIONAL BEHAVIOR

Organizations seek to gain a competitive advantage based on characteristics that distinguish them from competitors and provide an advantage in the marketplace. Efforts to gain a competitive advantage do not happen in isolation from the behavior of individuals in the organization. On the contrary, most strategic processes depend on individuals taking action, making decisions, providing leadership, and generally engaging in a variety of behaviors. This exercise will help you to consider how various aspects of organizational behavior may help an organization to develop and maintain a competitive advantage.

Consider an organization with which you are very familiar. Ideally, it is an organization for which you have worked, volunteered, or otherwise served as a member. With this organization and its people in mind, consider the following questions:

1. Consider the motivational concepts, theories, and practices outlined in Chapters 5 and 6. List some specific ways in which the motivation of organizational members may help to the organization to develop and maintain a competitive advantage.

____

____

____

____

2. Consider the principles of decision making and ethics presented in Chapter 8. List some specific ways in which the decision making and ethical behavior of organizational members may help the organization to develop and maintain a competitive advantage:

____

____

____

____

3. Consider the concepts of creativity and innovation presented in Chapter 9. List some specific ways in which the creative and innovative behavior of organizational members may help the organization to develop and maintain a competitive advantage:

____

____

____

____

4. Consider the leadership theories and concepts presented in Chapters 11–13. List some specific ways in which the leadership behavior of organizational members may help the organization to develop and maintain a competitive advantage:

____

____

____

____

EXERCISE 15.2: I'M GOING TO LEARN ME SOME STRATEGY

Objectives:

Completing this exercise will help you to *discuss* organizational learning practices as a strategic process, and *explain* globalization and the opportunities and challenges that it presents to organizations.

Instructions:

This exercise will help you to think about how organizations with different strategies implement divergent organizational learning practices. You will be examining these learning practices in the context of globalization, and entering markets in new cultures. The exercise consists of 4 steps.

Step 1. Determine which strategic type you will be using based on the day of the month you were born.

1st to the 7th: *first mover*

8th to 15th: *analyzer*

16th to 23rd: *defender*

24th to 31st: *prospector*

Step 2. How would you expect an organization of your targeted strategic type to *acquire, distribute,* and *retain knowledge* when entering into a market in a new culture? Write a brief overview for each of the three stages along with support for why you believe an organization with your strategic type would operate in the manner you describe. Be sure to use chapter concepts where appropriate. (5 minutes)

Step 3. Find a partner using the following method:

First movers pair with defenders

Analyzers pair with prospectors

Once you have paired with an appropriate partner, compare your descriptions for similarities and differences. (10 minutes)

Step 4. Each existing pair should find another pair that completes the strategic types. (A first mover–defender pair should find an analyzer–prospector pair). Again, compare the expected knowledge acquisition methods for similarities and differences. Be prepared to present your findings to the class. (10 minutes)

Reflection Questions:

1. What insights did you gain about how organizational strategy can influence knowledge acquisition?
2. How could knowledge acquisition methods reinforce an organizations' strategy?
3. What external environmental factors could make a knowledge acquisition process more or less effective for a given strategic type?
4. What internal environmental factors could make a knowledge acquisition process more or less effective for a given strategic type?
5. What were the most surprising points that you learned from the exercise?

Exercise contributed by Milton R. Mayfield, Professor of Business, Texas A&M International University and Jaqueline R. Mayfield, Professor of Business, Texas A&M International University.

EXERCISE 15.3: STRATEGY U.

Objectives:

1. Describe the basic concept of organizational strategy.
2. Explain the phenomenon of globalization along with the opportunities and challenges it poses to organizations.

Instructions:

For this exercise, you will need to form into a group of five to seven people. Once you have formed this team, develop a strategy outline for how your business school could enter into an overseas online program. (If your college already has such a program, then select a nation that your college has not yet targeted.) You do not have to create a detailed expansion strategy, but you should develop a general framework for the expansion and be sure to note all of the major strategic points that need to be considered (even if you do not have full information on each point). Write down your framework and be prepared to give a 5 to 10 minute presentation to the class. Be sure to use all appropriate chapter concepts, but pay special attention to the concepts listed in the *Organizational Strategy, Globalization,* and *Adapting Organizational Practices Across Cultures* chapter sections. (10 to 20 minutes)

Reflection Questions:

1. What new insights did you gain about strategic implementation?
2. What information gaps would you need to fill in order to develop a complete strategic framework? How will you fill them?
3. What trade-off considerations would you need to evaluate in developing a full plan?
4. How well would such an international expansion fit with your college's current strengths and competencies?

Exercise contributed by Milton R. Mayfield, Professor of Business, Texas A&M International University and Jaqueline R. Mayfield, Professor of Business, Texas A&M International University.

CASE STUDY 15.1: BURBERRY: PAIRING TRADITION WITH INNOVATION

When Angela Ahrendts took the helm as CEO of Burberry in July 2006, the ancient luxury goods company was struggling. Despite a burgeoning global luxury market, the brand, founded in 1856 in Hampshire, England, was growing at a sluggish 2 percent a year. Competitor brands were far outpacing Burberry in profits: Louis Vuitton Moët Hennessy had nearly 12 times Burberry's revenue, and Pinault-Printemps-Redoute (now Kering) was pulling in more than 16 times.

Eight years later, American-born Ahrendts has turned the company around; her revitalization of Burberry even earned her the title of honorary Dame of the British Empire, and during her reign made her the top-paid CEO (beating out male and female peers alike) in all of Britain. By identifying why sales were sluggish and then making sweeping changes to the company's organization, Ahrendts dramatically increased the company's returns. Her clear vision and execution catapulted Burberry back into the circle of esteemed luxury brands.

How had an iconic brand like Burberry gotten itself into such a predicament? Although the problems were multifaceted, the short answer is inefficient organization. The challenges within the organizational structure resulted in a lack of a clear, long-term vision. Burberry and its employees had simply lost focus.

Ahrendts saw trouble at the very first planning meeting with Burberry's top executives. Despite the typical British weather, none of the managers was wearing the company's signature item: the Burberry trench coat. "If our top people aren't buying our products, despite the great discount they could get, how could we expect customers to pay full price for them?," she wondered.

Burberry had long been organized as though it was a department store. Each category of men's and women's categories had its own leader. That may seem to make sense, but there was little integration. This led to the heads of the various categories making decisions that were good for them but detrimental to the business as a whole. The problem extended all the way down to salespeople, who were focused on moving easy-sell items like shirts instead of higher-priced items that affected the bottom line. They did not have the resources to enable them to convince customers that items like the classic trench were a great purchase.

At the time Ahrendts took over, Burberry had 23 licenses worldwide. Issuing so many licenses with little direction had resulted in too many offerings, from pet outfits to kilts. Sales of signature outerwear made up just 20 percent of Burberry's business. The trademarked check pattern had been coopted by the knock-off industry and had morphed into a distinctly "unluxury" identity. The brand had become more and more ubiquitous, but that's not necessarily a good thing in the luxury market. The company was trying for mass appeal. As Ahrendts put it, Burberry had "something for everybody, but not much of it exclusive or compelling."

Ahrendts took charge to restructure Burberry around an improved brand image. She accomplished this in three main steps. First, she created a clear long-term vision. Next, she made sure it was understood by everyone. Finally, she fully engaged people from top to bottom: top executives, salespeople, customers, and everyone in between.

Her vision began with remembering Burberry's core: outerwear and its famous trench coats. Ahrendts realized that much of the disconnection between departments occurred because of organization, and that affected sales. She appointed designer, Christopher Bailey, as Burberry's "brand czar." His eyes would see every piece of merchandise to be sold anywhere in the world. This gave the brand significantly more unity; Bailey polished Burberry into a "luxury brand with a very British sensibility." Ahrendts found that appointing a brand czar had an effect on customers, saying, "The purer our message, the more compelling it is to consumers." Along similar lines, heads of other practical areas were appointed, including corporate resources, planning, and supply chain. The goal was to keep the best interests of the brand at the forefront of every employee's mind.

The restructuring continued with the goal of injecting more authenticity into the brand. Thirty-five product categories were eliminated. They did away with the entire Hong Kong design team, brought US designers to the UK, and closed factories in New Jersey and Wales. These decisions were not without controversy: Ahrendts was made to testify in front of Parliament regarding the closure of the Welsh factory. However, streamlining in certain areas was paired with investment in others. Burberry's Castleford facility in Yorkshire has since doubled its employee population. The facility has been around since near the founding of the company over 150 years ago. Doing more work in house instead of outsourcing to far-flung locations resulted in more cohesive processes—and brand.

Burberry also began strategically expanding is retail presence and sharpening its customer base. The company looked into cities in which at least two competitors had stores but Burberry did not. They also capitalized on so-called "underpenetrated" markets, including Baku, Azerbaijan; Nashville, Tennessee; Poznan, Poland; and many others. These budding markets have fueled an incredible growth for the business. In the space of six years, Burberry opened 132 new stores. While expanding, the company also trained its sales associates with a new education program so that they could better communicate with customers. Finally, Burberry shifted its customer focus from "everyone, everywhere" to what they saw as an overlooked contingent: millennials. The Burberry team created a mass of captivating digital content and sought to engage customers through storytelling via the latest platforms. As a result, Burberry's Facebook page has several times the number of fans of other luxury brands, among other social media triumphs. Embracing digital and social media gave Burberry an edge, because most rivals were slower to take advantage of such marketing opportunities.

The results of Ahrendts's reorganization speak for themselves. Burberry has since tripled its stock price and has a market capitalization approaching $10 billion. The company was named the fourth-fastest growing brand globally in 2011 and the fastest-growing luxury brand in 2012. Burberry catapulted back to success in its industry by realizing that the classic and the fresh are not mutually exclusive, just as its founder had known so many years before. She knew that tradition could serve as a catalyst rather than a detriment to innovation, and others are paying attention. Apple recently courted Ahrendts to head up its retail division with a signing bonus that could be worth as much as $68 million, making her the highest paid female executive at a public U.S company.

Case Questions

1. Define organizational strategy and why it was so important in the Burberry case study.
2. Discuss what type of organizational learning strategy Burberry used.
3. Explain how Burberry became a first mover to millennials in the digital market.

Sources

Ahrendts, Angela. "Burberry's CEO on Turning an Aging British Icon into a Global Luxury Brand." *Harvard Business* Review. January-February 2013. http://hbr.org/2013/01/burberrys-ceo-on-turning-an-aging-british-icon-into-a-global-luxury-brand/ar/pr.

Forbes, Moira. "Burberry CEO Proves Tradition Doesn't Prevent Innovation." *Forbes*. March 9, 2012. www.forbes.com/sites/moiraforbes/2012/03/09/burberry-ceo-proves-tradition-doesnt-prevent-innovation/.

Golson, Jordan. "New Retail SVP Angela Ahrendts Receives Signing Bonus Worth $68 Million." *Macrumors.com* May 5, 2014. www.macrumors.com/2014/05/05/angela-ahrendts-signing-bonus/.

Kotter, John. "Burberry's Secrets to Successful Brand Reinvention." *Forbes.* February 26, 2013. www.forbes.com/sites/johnkotter/2013/02/26/burberrys-secrets-to-successful-brand-reinvention/.

Mayo, Benjamin. "Apple SVP Angela Ahrendts Becomes 'Dame of the British Empire' Today, Leaves Burberry as Early as This Month." *9to5Mac.* April 7, 2014. http://9to5mac.com/2014/04/07/apple-svp-angela-ahrendts-becomes-dame-of-the-british-empire-today-leaves-burberry-as-early-as-this-month/.

No author. "Checked Growth: How Burberry's Angela Ahrendts Is Steering the Company through a Volatile Economy." *Knowledge@Wharton.* November 20, 2008. http://knowledge.wharton.upenn.edu/article/checked-growth-how-burberrys-angela-ahrendts-is-steering-the-company-through-a-volatile-economy/.

Petroff, Alanna. "Top Paid CEO in U.K. is an American Woman." *CNN Money.* June 11, 2013. http://money.cnn.com/2013/06/11/news/companies/burberry-pay-ceo/.

SELF-ASSESSMENT 15.1

How Culturally Adaptable Am I?

Consider a country's culture with which you are familiar. Ideally, this will be a culture that you have visited in the past, if only for a short period of time.

For each statement, please indicate how much difficulty you would anticipate experiencing in visiting your target culture based on the following scale:

	Very Difficult	Quite Difficult	A Little Difficult	Somewhat Difficult	Not at All Difficult
1. Developing friendships	1	2	3	4	5
2. Finding food that I like	1	2	3	4	5
3. Communicating with people	1	2	3	4	5
4. Dealing with people engaging in behaviors that make me uncomfortable	1	2	3	4	5
5. Interacting with others in social gatherings	1	2	3	4	5
6. Using transportation and finding my way around	1	2	3	4	5
7. Locating and purchasing the things I will need	1	2	3	4	5
8. Adjusting to the weather and the climate	1	2	3	4	5
9. Understanding cultural and political differences	1	2	3	4	5
10. Dealing with regulations and people in authority	1	2	3	4	5
11. Dealing with bad service or rude treatment	1	2	3	4	5
12. Adjusting to the general pace and feel of the culture	1	2	3	4	5

Scoring

Add the numbers circled: ____________

Interpretation

48 and above = You have a high level of cultural adaptability. You would likely enjoy and be very successful living and working in another culture for an extended period of time.

25–47 = You have a moderate level of cultural adaptability. You would likely enjoy visiting another culture for a short period of time, but you might experience some discomfort and difficulties in visiting another culture for an extended period of time.

24 and below = You have a low level of cultural adaptability. You would probably not enjoy and would not be successful in visiting or working in another culture for an extended period of time.

SOURCES: Adapted from Ward, Colleen, and Antony Kennedy. "The Measurement of Sociocultural Adaptation." *International Journal of Intercultural Relations* 23, no. 4 (August 1999): 659-677; Searle, Wendy, and Colleen Ward. "The Prediction of Psychological and Sociocultural Adjustment during cross-Cultural Transitions." *International Journal of Intercultural Relations* 14, no. 4 (1990): 449-464.

16 Organizational Change and Development

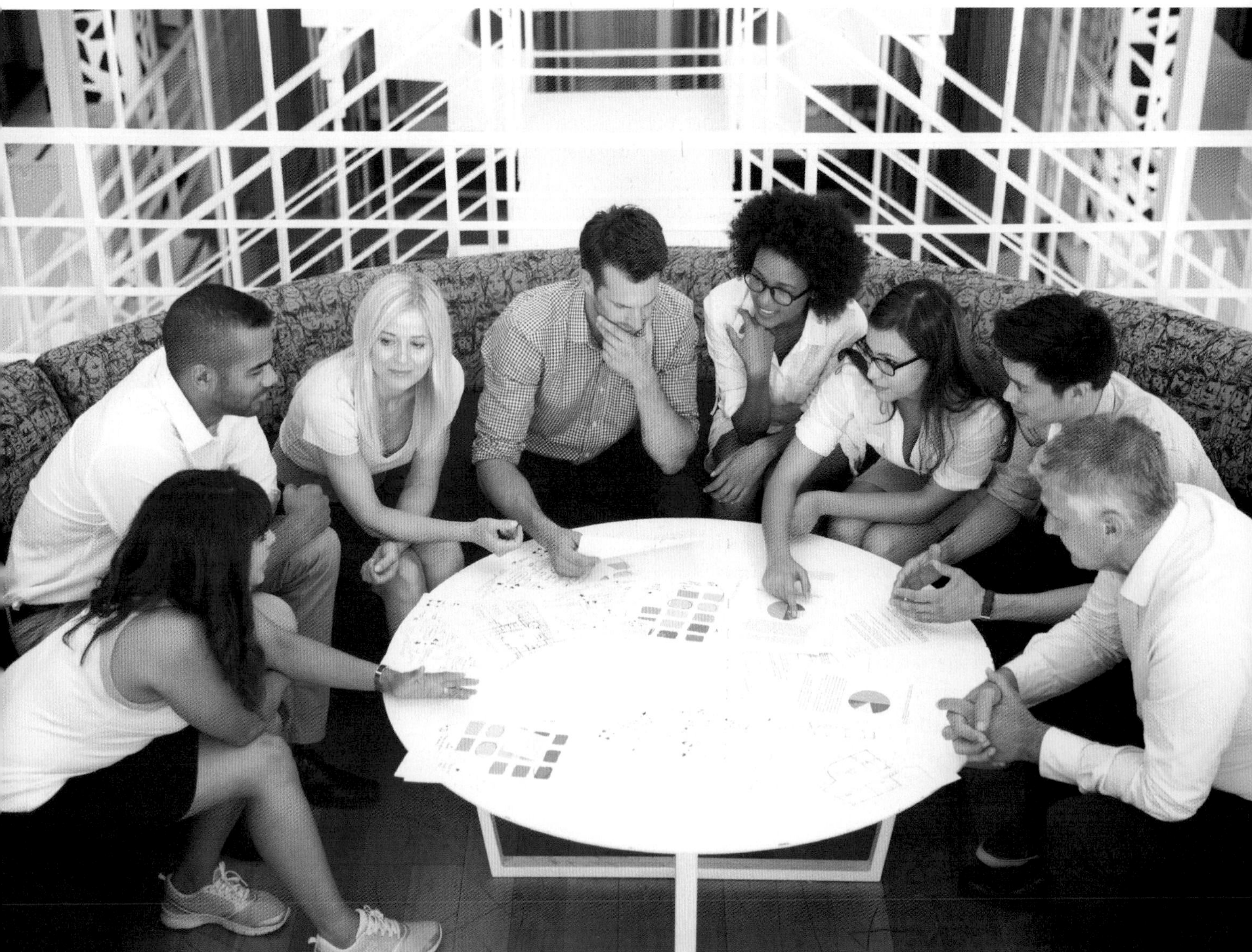

©iStockphoto.com/monkeybusinessimages

If you don't like something, change it. If you can't change it, change your attitude.

—Maya Angelou, American author

THE CHANGE PROCESS

16.1 Compare and contrast various conceptualizations of the change process

Organizations must be both agile and adaptive to deal with the pressure of continual change. It's not easy to implement change inside an organization, however, and successful change requires careful planning, hard work, cooperation, and excellent communication. Change management has been around for more than 50 years, yet studies show that 60-70 percent of organizational change projects fail, despite huge investments in training and education to support them. What are the reasons for these failures? One theory proposes that too many organizations hire outside consultants or experts to design the change projects rather than assigning the responsibility to the managers inside the organization. This means that managers do not get the opportunity to fully embrace the changes, and it weakens their ability to implement the changes effectively.[1]

A 2014 investigation found examples of harassment, racism, bullying, and homophobia and a culture of intolerance in the Miami Dolphins football team's locker room. This scandal dominated the headlines, inciting cries for change. Although some commentators believe hazing, a form of bullying, is "tough love" and inevitable in the sport, others beg to differ. Chicago Bears coach Marc Trestman and quarterback Jay Cutler have openly condemned hazing. They believe in fostering a more ethical environment in the locker room, where the players feel safe, treat each other with respect, and have an opportunity to grow. Although no change in locker room culture will happen overnight, both parties believe instilling a focus on ethics is a step in the right direction.[2]

However, in many cases, change does work if it is approached in the right manner. Take the huge IT systems changes at California State University (CSU), for example. Thousands of employees, staff, and students across 23 campuses had to learn how to use the new systems. In order to manage this enormous change, CSU clearly defined IT employees' roles, assigned responsibility, and explained the function of the system. This clear and frequent communication meant that everyone was able to understand what was expected of them when they proceeded with the implementation.[3]

Take a look at how Shane Kost, president of Chicago Food Plant Food Tours and Food Tour Pros, implemented change in his organization to stay ahead of the competition in the OB in the Real World feature.

LEARNING OBJECTIVES

By the end of this chapter, you will be able to:

16.1 Compare and contrast various conceptualizations of the change process

16.2 Identify the forces for change in organizations

16.3 Describe where resistance to change comes from and how to reduce it

16.4 Describe the concept of organizational development in organizations

16.5 Identify types of OD change interventions

Organizational Change

Back to the Case of Yolande Turner and Pioneering Health

In Chapter 15, we explored how Yolande Turner and the senior team at Pioneering Health used the strategic process to locate their first overseas office in Frankfurt, Germany, recruited 15 German members to the

Master the content.
edge.sagepub.com/neckob
SAGE edge™

staff, and were slowly adjusting to German culture. In this chapter, we follow the next stage in Yolande and Imani's journey as they set out to implement organizational change and development.

The DADA Syndrome

Before the office in Frankfurt officially opens for business, Yolande holds a three-day group training course designed by Imani for the new staff. The goals of the training are to prepare employees for their new roles in the company, acquaint them with the spirit of Pioneering Health, help them bond as a team, and share the benefits of a participative management style. After the first day of training, Imani has identified two main areas she thinks may cause conflict.

Chicago Bears quarterback Jay Cutler, along with head coach Marc Trestman, spoke out against hazing new team members and instead promoted a culture of respect in the locker room.

Mjglasgow via Wikimedia Commons

THE BIG PICTURE: How OB Topics Fit Together

Individual Processes
- Individual Differences
- Emotions and Attitudes
- Perceptions and Learning
- Motivation

Team Processes
- Ethics
- Decision Making
- Creativity and Innovation
- Conflict and Negotiation

Organizational Processes
- Culture
- Strategy
- **CHANGE AND DEVELOPMENT**
- Structure and Technology

Influence Processes
- Leadership
- Power and Politics
- Communication

Organizational Outcomes
- Individual Performance
- Job Satisfaction
- Team Performance
- Organizational Goals

SHANE KOST, *president of Chicago Food Planet Food Tours, and Food Tour Pros*

OB in the Real World

© Shane Kost

Years ago, while on a bike tour in Germany, Shane Kost realized his tour guide was having a great time. It seemed like he was getting paid to have fun. The realization that there was a way to make money while doing something that didn't feel like work was life changing for this young entrepreneur. Shane wanted to create a business that didn't feel like *work*, and he knew the key was to open a business that connected three of the things he loved: food, travel, and people.

Chicago Food Planet Food Tours gave culinary tours of Chicago to 600 people in 2006, the first year it was open for business. Today, more than 17,000 people participate in its tours every year. As Shane's business began to grow, people around the world began asking him how they could replicate his success in other cities. It was from these inquiries that his second company, Food Tour Pros, was born. Food Tour Pros is a training program that educates entrepreneurs interested in establishing food tours in their cities on the crucial aspects of running this business. To date, more than 250 people from 20 different countries have taken the classes and are running food tour businesses around the world.

"I'm calling 2014 the season of change for Chicago Food Planet Food Tours," said Shane. "Five years ago I was having to explain to people what a food tour was. I would tell them that it's a two- to three-hour guided tour that highlights local foods and food artisans, that it's a chance to learn how the local neighborhoods have influenced the food, and how the food has influenced the neighborhoods. It's also a chance for people to taste authentic iconic foods like deep dish pizza, Chicago-style hot dogs, and Italian beef sandwiches."

But appetites are changing. Shane noted that "nearly 26 million Americans are choosing their travel destination based solely on the food they can experience at that location. People now know what food tours are and they are actively seeking them out. It's great for our business, but it means we're seeing more competition. In order to thrive, we have to be creative and we have to be strategic."

Shane encourages his team to compete with themselves and be the best they can be rather than spending their time focusing on what's happening externally, such as beating their competition.

When Shane models this behavior himself, his employees tend to follow. He also encourages them to look at what the consumer wants and changing their offerings to fit the demand. A major result of the "compete with ourselves" mentality was a new price structure that enabled the company to offer less expensive, shorter tours that still had a high standard of quality but would appeal to those on a budget. For example, the original tours ranged from $45 to $60, ran about three hours, and visited between five and eight restaurants. Now one of the choices costs $30 to $35 dollars, is two hours long, and includes stops at five or six restaurants.

"Once you create a product, solution, or service, you can't continue to sell it the same way forever because the industry will be going through its own changes and you have to keep up. By being creative and strategic we realized that you can't always go up the value chain to make more money. Sometimes you have to go down because there's a lot of money to be made there too."

Critical-Thinking Questions

1. **How would you explain Shane's attitude toward organizational change?**
2. **Would you approach change in the same way? Why or why not?**

SOURCE: Shane Kost, personal interview, March 28, 2014.

Overworked and undervalued nurses may suffer from burnout. The position is one of high turnover in certain cultures due to poor working conditions.

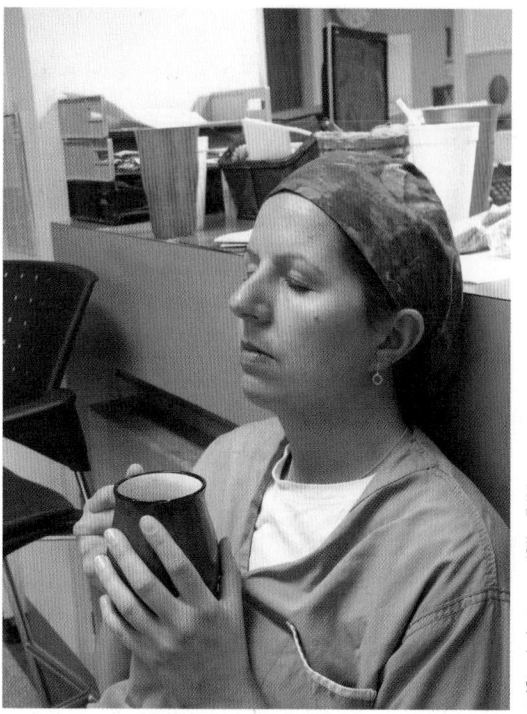

©iStockphoto.com/OliveEdith

The first is the negative perception of nurses in Germany. Nurses are considered on a par with janitors and similar support staff and are not encouraged to communicate with hospital management regarding quality of care or changes to improve care. They are not given many opportunities for advancement, receive very few benefits, and work long hours with little flexibility. Because of their low status, they are often the targets of verbal abuse by patients and higher-level hospital staff. Many nurses suffer burnout from the stress, the struggle to survive on low salaries, and the long hours, and turnover is high.

The nurses Imani has hired have excellent references and qualifications, but their behavior during the training process has her doubting their ability to accept change. They seem uncomfortable and withdrawn during the role play training, as if they are not used to communicating empathically with their patients. They speak only when spoken to, rarely offer feedback, and tend to sit separately from the rest of the group. The rest of the staff barely acknowledges their presence. Imani is worried that the negative perception of the nurses, as well as the nurses' own lack of confidence, will affect the team's ability to bond. With such a small staff, she knows it is imperative that they work well together.

In their new roles the nurses will need to communicate skillfully with patients, be sympathetic to their needs, and provide comfort when necessary. Since their work until now has been centered on carrying out practical tasks for their patients, Imani is worried they won't be able to adopt an approachable manner over the phone.

The second issue that worries Imani is the autocratic and authoritarian approach used by the two senior managers: Niklas the accounting manager, and Petra the sales and marketing manager. Although Niklas and Petra are polite and civil to Imani during the training, she has noticed that they are curt with the junior members of staff. Although Imani is aware that authoritarian leadership style is common in Germany, she knows it won't work in a collaborative organization like Pioneering Health, which prides itself on its participative management style and emphasis on empowerment. She needs to make sure employees in the German office embrace this style, and that the office reflects it as much as possible.

But she needs to tread carefully in addressing both her concerns; otherwise she runs the risk of inciting the **DADA syndrome**, experienced by individuals faced with unwanted change. The syndrome consists of four stages: denial, anger, depression, and finally acceptance.[4] During the denial stage, people deliberately ignore the change; in the anger stage, they begin to express rage about the change; in the depression stage, they often experience low emotional states and lack of motivation; and finally, in the acceptance stage, they begin to come around to the idea of the change and try and make the best of it. In worst-case scenarios, people will leave an organization if they are unable to accept the changes being implemented.

DADA syndrome: Four stages—denial, anger, depression, and acceptance—experienced by individuals when they are faced with unwanted change

Lewin's Basic Change Model

On the second day of training, Imani draws from Lewin's basic change model to help facilitate the change process. Kurt Lewin was a German American psychologist who developed a three-stage model of planned change that explained how to initiate, manage, and stabilize the change process. The three stages are known as *unfreezing*, *transforming*, and *refreezing*.[5]

Unfreezing

Unfreezing requires explaining the rationale for change, breaking down the status quo, challenging existing beliefs, and understanding how starting on a new path is essential for the company's survival. This is the most difficult and stressful part of the change process, because challenging deeply held beliefs about the way things are done can provoke strong reactions from people.

On day two of the training, Imani reiterates the ethos of Pioneering Health and its participative working culture. Although some members seem interested in this approach, she meets resistance from Niklas and Petra, who continue to question the practice of including the junior staff members and the nurses in their decisions. Although Imani tries to explain the reasoning behind the approach, the senior managers simply shrug and shake their heads. They refuse to be "unfrozen."

Transforming

After the unfreezing stage comes the **transforming** stage, in which people begin to make peace with their doubts and uncertainties and embrace the new direction of the company. However, transformation does not happen overnight. Managers need to give employees time to adjust to change and ensure they are communicating with them consistently and effectively. They need to reinforce their vision for change by providing evidence such as research, documentation, and success stories of other companies that have implemented similar changes. Employees who are still struggling with the changes must be offered more support through training and additional resources when necessary.

During the third and final day of training, Imani relays success stories about Pioneering Health. She talks about how the company was founded, how many people the company has helped in the US, and major accomplishments over the years. She describes the techniques they use, based on the latest research, to help people with chronic illnesses live life to the fullest. Imani describes the mission and vision for the Frankfurt branch, telling the team about Pioneering Health's intention to help as many people as possible worldwide. By the time she has finished, she can tell she has captured the imagination of most of the team. But Niklas and Petra have folded arms and skeptical expressions. She fears it will take more than a three-day training session to transform their thinking.

Refreezing

When employees appear to have embraced the change, managers use refreezing to reinforce the new approach and help people internalize the changes. This is done by creating reward systems, tracking behaviors, and setting up continuous training to further enhance skills. During this stage it is very important for managers to promote a sense of stability and consistency in order for the changes to be fully incorporated into daily working life.

Transforming: The process that occurs when people begin to make peace with their doubts and uncertainties and begin to embrace the new direction of the company

When the training is over, Imani hopes she has managed to convince most of the employees that the changes are for the best. However, she knows she needs to continually reinforce these changes through further training, and rewards for a job well done.

Lewin's Force Field Analysis

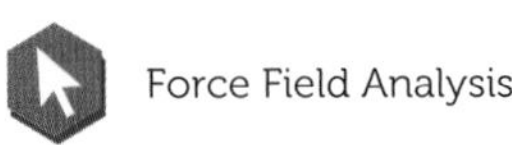

Before implementing any changes, organizations need to assess the validity of the change. Force field analysis (see Figure 16.1) is a useful decision-making technique that helps to assess the reasons for and against making certain changes.[6] The drivers for change must be stronger than the restraining forces in order for the change to work.

Imani sits down with Yolande to relay her feedback from the training program and to share some of her concerns. Yolande says, "I agree we need to address the perception of the nurses in the office and build their confidence when dealing with patients over the phone. We also need to alter this autocratic management style into a more participative one, but that won't happen overnight."

"I think we need to analyze what it will mean to implement these changes so we can prepare for any consequences," Imani replies.

Yolande and Imani spend the next hour going through Lewin's force field analysis to assess the impact of the planned changes. They ask themselves a number of questions, including, What is the benefit of the change? Who is against the change and why? What are the risks of making the change? What are the costs involved?

They agree there are huge benefits to making these changes. If the perception of the nurses changes inside the office, then everyone will work better as a team. Similarly, if the nurses feel valued they will gain confidence, which will help them better assist patients over the phone. Similarly, if the managers can alter their brusque autocratic manner to a more empowering style, team members will feel more included and invested in the vision of their new company.

Then they focus on the employees who are finding it most difficult to accept the changes.

"Niklas and Petra seem to be fighting me every step of the way," says Imani. "Although their experience is outstanding, I worry they'll put obstacles in the way of change."

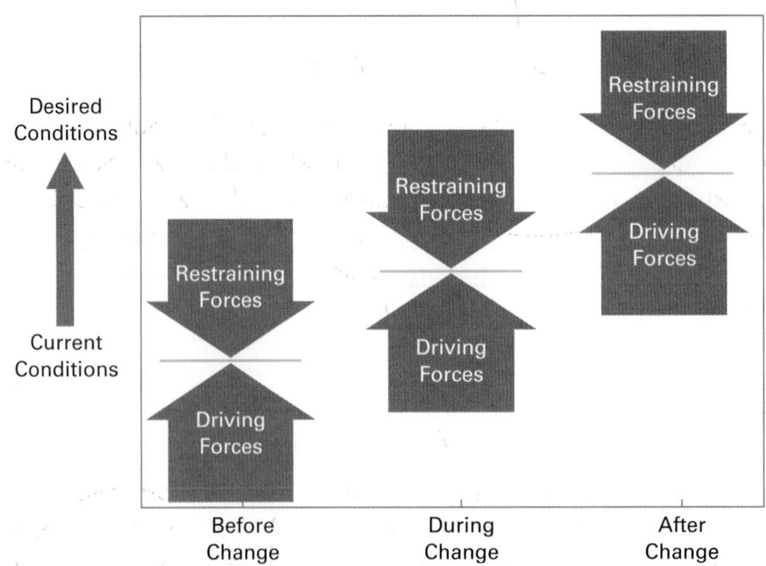

FIGURE 16.1 Lewin's Force Field Analysis Model

Yolande nods thoughtfully. "Okay, let's see how they perform on the job when the office opens for business next week. If they're still behaving in an autocratic manner, we'll have to meet with them to discuss the situation."

Next, Yolande and Imani go over the risks in making the changes. "If the nurses feel too uncomfortable about communicating with patients, or the managers continue to resist the changes, we might lose key staff members," Imani says.

"We need to make sure that doesn't happen," Yolande says. "Staff members walking out when the business is only just up and running is not only bad for morale, it will be costly for us."

Finally, they discuss cost. "What will it cost us to implement these changes?," Imani asks.

"I think the question is, What will it cost if we *don't* make them," Yolande replies. "The most important thing is for us to create a close-knit team that shares the same values and vision. We need everyone on board if we are going to make this company work here in Germany."

THINKING CRITICALLY

1. Discuss the pros and cons of hiring outside consultants to design change projects. The section mentions that failing to assign this responsibility to managers inside an organization prevents managers from fully embracing changes and weakens their ability to implement them, but what other obstacles to change acceptance and implementation might outside consultants create in an organization? **[Apply/Analyze]**

2. Imani explains the reasoning behind Pioneering Health's collaborative work environment, but Niklas and Petra shrug and shake their heads. Describe another approach Imani could take to encourage these senior managers to be "unfrozen." Why might this approach work better than the one Imani has chosen? **[Evaluate/Create]**

3. List possible reasons why Niklas and Petra are skeptical of the collaborative organizational culture at Pioneering Health. Do you think their attitudes can be overcome? Why or why not? **[Analyze/Evaluate]**

FORCES FOR CHANGE

16.2 Identify the forces for change in organizations

Every day, employees are affected by a range of internal and external forces as they try to perform their roles in organizations. Managers who promote an awareness of these forces and make an effort to counteract them have a better chance of creating a more productive and loyal workforce. This means organizations need to adapt to **external forces**, which are outside influences such as competitors' actions and customers' changing preferences, and to **internal forces**, which are inside influences such as company culture and employee diversity.[7]

External Forces for Change

Organizations cannot function in a vacuum—they need to be aware of and respond to events and trends in the outside world. Some examples of these external forces are customers' demographic characteristics, technological advancements, customer and market changes, and social and political pressures. Let's consider each.

External forces: Outside influences for change

Internal forces: Inside influences for change

Companies like Banana Republic have begun featuring same-sex couples in their advertisements, including TV personality Nate Berkus and husband Jeremiah Brent.

David X Prutting/BF Anyc/NEWSCOM

Demographic Characteristics

Organizations need to adapt to demographic changes such as aging and increasingly diversified customer populations. To deal with these changes, many organizations have tailored their marketing strategies to appeal to a variety of different consumers and to ensure fair treatment for people regardless of age, religion, sexual orientation, gender, or race and ethnicity. For example, brands from the United Colors of Benetton to Banana Republic to Expedia have run ad campaigns featuring interracial or gay couples.

Technological Advancements

The rapid rise of and continuous innovation in computer and wireless technology means that organizations must move equally fast to compete. Many organizations now use social networks to market their products, build awareness of their brands, and connect more fully with their consumers. For instance, outdoor activity equipment provider Giantnerd includes a range of radio buttons on its website encouraging visitors to follow the company on social networks. Customers who click the "Like" button on Facebook are given access to exclusive offers and deals. Since adding these buttons to its site, Giantnerd has seen a 50 percent increase in sales.[8]

Customer and Market Changes

Social media has given customers a platform for sharing their opinions in ways that companies have never had to deal with before. Negative feedback from customers that has the potential to reach countless others online can immediately influence sales, and it can also enhance or damage the organization's reputation in the long term. For example, customer comments on review sites like Tripadvisor and Yelp can help or hurt hotels, tourist attractions, and restaurants. Another force for change is changing customer demands, which put pressure on organizations to stay ahead of the competition. Organizations that listen to their customers and keep up with the evolving market landscape are more likely to succeed than those who don't.[9]

Social and Political Pressures

Social values are changing. Consumers are interested in buying environmentally safe products that have been manufactured in an ethical manner, and many organizations have adapted their practices to cater to these values. For example, major restaurant chain Chipotle has eliminated the use of genetically modified ingredients (GMOs); Whole Foods has committed to labeling any products containing GMOs by 2018; and Walmart is expanding its range of organic foods that are also free of GMOs.[10]

Organizations can also be subject to political pressures, and organizations must often comply with new regulations or adapt to existing ones. For example, new regulations regarding the sale and manufacture of e-cigarettes have been proposed, and all European Union (EU) member states will be expected to abide by the new directive, which is set to be implemented in 2016.[11]

Internal Forces for Change

Although it is essential that organizations respond to external forces, it is just as important to look inside the organization at the internal forces at play. Issues such as low job satisfaction can influence productivity and cause conflict or strikes. Organizations must address internal problems as soon as they arise and strive to build a positive working environment based on mutual respect, teamwork, and collaboration.[12] Management changes, organizational restructuring, and intrapreneurship are some examples of the internal forces that affect organizations.

Management Change

New CEOs or executive management can have a significant impact on an organization's culture and strategy. For example, when Trace Devanny joined health care IT solutions provider Trizetto as CEO in 2010, he changed the laid-back company culture to motivate people to listen to customers and act on their feedback, and to always put the customer first. These changes helped the company to become more customer and solution focused.[13]

Organizational Restructuring

Organizational Restructuring

There may be instances when organizations need to change their organizational structure in order to adapt to new strategies, new product lines, or global expansion. For example, out-of-home media agency Kinetic, headquartered in New York, has announced its plans to restructure its organization to further expand into Europe.[14] Changing structures means disruption for employees. Communication and training are essential during a reorganization to ensure that employees understand the reasons for the change and the implications it will have for their daily duties.

Intrapreneurship

Intrapreneurship

Many organizations foster a spirit of intrapreneurship in their employees by encouraging them to come up with new ideas and new ways of doing things. When an employee suggests something innovative, the organization must consider the best way of implementing the idea, which may mean allocating more resources, putting more people to work on the initiative, or coming up with different branding in the case of a new product. American manufacturing company W. L. Gore encourages intrapreneurship by giving employees 10 percent of their working days to develop new ideas. Employee Dave Myers discovered that one of the company's products used for push-pull cables could be used to coat guitar strings for more comfortable strumming. W. L. Gore launched the guitar strings under the brand ELIXIR Strings, and they have become the front-runner in the acoustic guitar string market.[15]

Although organizations must be aware of both external and internal forces for change, they must also be able to manage resistance to change and understand how to reduce it. We look at this challenge next.

Paul Stewart / Alamy Stock Photo

Dave Myers of W.L. Gore discovered that products and processes the company was already engaging in could be used to produce guitar strings. This bout of intrapreneurship lead to the company launching a new brand, ELIXIR Strings.

THINKING CRITICALLY

1. Consider the recent move on the part of food manufacturers to remove trans fats from processed foods such as margarine and vegetable shortening. What external force or forces for change (demographic characteristics, technological advancements, customer and market changes, social and political pressures) do you think caused this to occur? Explain and defend your answer. **[Apply/Analyze]**

2. Of the various forces for internal change (management change, organizational restructuring, and intrapreneurship), which do you think has the greatest potential for employee empowerment? Explain and defend your answer. **[Analyze/Evaluate]**

RESISTANCE TO CHANGE

16.3 Describe where resistance to change comes from and how to reduce it

One of the main obstacles to implementing organizational changes is **resistance to change**, people's unwillingness to accept or support modifications in the workplace.[16] When people resist change it can affect their productivity, performance, and relationships. Let's explore some of the individual and organizational sources of resistance, identified in Figure 16.2, through our Pioneering Health case.

Individual Sources of Resistance to Change

It is the first day of business in the new Frankfurt office and Yolande calls a meeting with the staff. She gives them a speech she hopes will motivate them, explaining that they are about to embark on an exciting venture that will change people's lives for the better. Yolande emphasizes her open-door policy and adds that she will be available to listen to anyone who has any questions, concerns, or feedback. "You are the first European Pioneers. Go Pioneers!," she finishes. Some of the nurses smile at her cautiously, but Niklas and Petra seem unaffected by the speech. Although Yolande is

Resistance to change: The unwillingness to accept or support modifications in the workplace

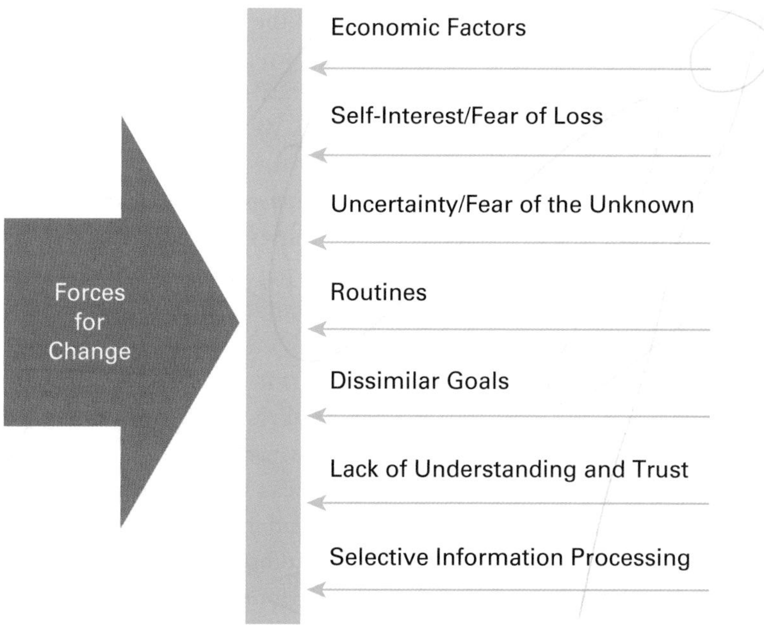

FIGURE 16.2 Sources of Resistance to Change

disappointed, she hopes that in time the staff will feel as passionate and committed to the business as she does.

It is not long before Yolande receives the first visitor to her office. It is Birgit, one of the nurses, who knocks timidly on the door. Yolande greets her warmly and invites her to sit down.

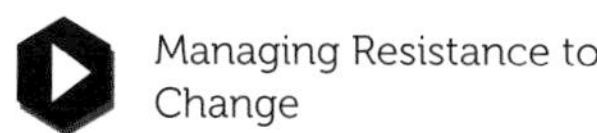

"What's on your mind, Birgit?," Yolande asks.

Birgit shifts uncomfortably. "The other nurses and I are worried about how the patients will react to us when they call looking for help," she explains. "We are afraid they will not listen to us."

Yolande has a sudden realization. She had been concentrating on how the nurses have been treated by the other staff members and their own lack of confidence, but she hadn't accounted for how patients might perceive them.

"Birgit, I am sorry I haven't spoken to you and the other nurses about this matter before. You are right—some patients may not want to speak to a nurse, but I'm counting on the fact that some of them will, especially when they realize the helpful service you can provide. If you or the other nurses get any callers who don't feel you are qualified to help, please transfer them to Imani or me. We will explain that each nurse on our staff is a fully qualified health care professional who has been trained and is positioned to help them with their needs."

Birgit thanks Yolande but still looks worried. "The nurses and I—we have never been in this position before. We don't know what to expect. It is a lot of change to accept," she says.

Yolande recognizes that Birgit and the other nurses are feeling various forms of resistance to change, such as *fear of the unknown, insecurity,* and *habit*. The nurses are out of their comfort zone, feel unsure about their ability to perform, and are wary of breaking their routine to embrace new challenges. Yolande knows she must reassure and support them in order for them to commit to the changes ahead.

"Birgit, change can be hard and I understand that, but your work here will give you an opportunity to put all your experience and education to use helping a broad range of people who need it," Yolande says, passionately.

"I worry people will not respect us," she says. Yolande thinks that Birgit is using *selective information processing* as a way of resisting change. Although Yolande has explained to Birgit that she will support her and the other nurses if they encounter a difficult patient, Birgit is still clinging on to her own perceptions about how nurses are treated. Before Yolande can respond, Birgit adds, "We are concerned that if we cannot perform in these new roles that we will lose our jobs. We are excited about the opportunity, Yolande, but we are worried about financial risks—we cannot afford to be out of work."

Yolande realizes that Birgit is worried about *economic factors* that may arise from her new role. Once again, she explains that all the nurses will receive her full support and that she will be there for them every step of the way. "You don't have to worry about losing your jobs—all I want from you is your commitment and your determination to help our clients," Yolande finishes.

Imani, for her part, has been observing the way in which senior managers Petra and Niklas interact with the other staff and doesn't like what she sees. Both the managers are abrupt with team members and often make sarcastic remarks. Another thing that frustrates Imani is the managers' tendency to speak German whenever she walks by. Based on her limited knowledge of the language and their body language it appears that they are making derogatory remarks about the company, the management, and their coworkers. Knowing the senior managers' behavior will affect motivation and bring down morale, Imani suggests to Yolande that they schedule a meeting with Petra and Niklas to address their attitude and behavior to date.

"Petra, Niklas, I wanted to meet with you today to address any concerns you may have about the direction our company is taking," Yolande begins. "Of course, for our vision to work, it is absolutely essential that we have everyone on board."

"We do have concerns," Niklas says. "We are struggling to accept the participative management style Imani promoted during the training program. We do not understand how you can call your employees 'colleagues' regardless of the position they hold. Petra and I share a great deal of experience—we are used to managing teams. That means we are the bosses. We don't expect our decisions to be questioned, and we don't think anyone else needs to share in those decisions—apart from *our* boss, which of course is you, Yolande."

Petra nods. "Niklas is right. In Germany we operate in a very different way compared to how things work in the United States. We have a chain of command, and that is the way it has always been," she adds.

Yolande wonders if a problem here is that neither Petra nor Niklas has an individual *predisposition toward change,* which means their personalities will not allow them to readily adapt. Have she and Imani hired the wrong managers?

To make matters worse, Petra and Niklas are judging everything by the *past successes* they have had working in more autocratic environments. After all, if they were so successful in their previous roles, why should they *break their routines?* Yolande begins to wonder whether she can convince these two managers that change is a good thing. She turns to Imani for support.

"You never mentioned that you had an issue with the participative management style during training," Imani says. "What do you have against being known as a colleague?"

"Well, it makes us just like everyone else!," Niklas replies.

Yolande recognizes that the managers are worried about *loss of status* and preserving their own *self-interest* in their roles at Pioneering Health.

"And what's the problem with being on an equal footing with the rest of the staff?," Imani queries further.

"We have worked very hard to achieve our level of senior management," Petra says, clearly angry. "We do not feel our hard work is comparable to that of the junior administrative staff or the nurses for that matter. Our experience and education place us higher in the chain of command. We are here to work, not to engage in social banter."

"We have nothing in common with the junior staff, much less with the nurses. I can't accept their approach to their work—they are too light-hearted about things," Niklas adds.

Yolande is surprised that Niklas is citing *personality conflicts* as a reason for not embracing change given how little he and Petra have interacted with the other staff. "Niklas, we have selected excellent nurses with extensive experience to provide advice and telephonic care to patients in need of help. I believe this warrants a high degree of respect. Similarly, all the staff, including yourselves, have been handpicked specifically for these roles. Whether the member is a junior administrator or a senior manager, each of the 15 members of the staff is an expert in his or her field."

Petra and Niklas seem unimpressed with her arguments, but Yolande continues. "Pioneering Health has a culture of empowerment and participation. Every staff member, regardless of status or position, is included in our decision-making processes. Individuals are encouraged to provide feedback, make suggestions, and come to senior staff like me or Imani with any concerns they may have. Even more important, staff members have positive, collaborative relationships with each other, which makes for a fun, productive environment. This is the model that has made Pioneering Health so successful, and this is the model we need to replicate here in Frankfurt in order to achieve the same degree of success," Yolande finishes.

She waits for a response but Niklas and Petra seem to display a real *lack of understanding* about the benefits of what this change in management style could entail. Then Yolande has sinking thought: perhaps she is the problem.

She wonders if she has failed to legitimate the change sufficiently to achieve buy-in from the two managers. She can tell by Imani's expression that she is also at a loss. Yolande wraps up the meeting by asking Niklas and Petra to think about what she and Imani have shared with them. They plan to reconvene the following week.

Organizational Sources of Resistance to Change

In addition to individual sources of resistance to change, organizational factors may prove to be barriers. For example, many organizations are based on stability—people are recruited because they fit in with the organizational culture and are then socialized to behave in certain ways through training, rules, processes, and procedures. However, this uniformity can lead to *structural inertia,* which makes an organization slow to change after having followed the same rules and procedures for many years.

Organizations can also fall prey to *limited focus of change,* which arises when only a small number of departments apply the change rather than the whole organization. Confusion often results because the change is not being fully enforced. Another organizational source of resistance to change is *group inertia*. This means that even if individuals agree with the change, they may be constrained by group norms—a situation that often occurs in unions.[17] Groups may also feel that organizational changes are a *threat to expertise*. For example, a data analysis department may feel threatened when a computer program is brought in to perform many of the data functions. The group may resist learning the program for fear it will render their roles obsolete. Furthermore, the group may not want to entertain *decisions that disrupt cultural traditions or group relationships,* which means they will cling to the familiar way of doing things.

Finally, an organization can experience *threat to established power relationships,* particularly when it is undergoing a reorganization. Companies moving from an autocratic structure to a participative or self-managed one are likely to experience opposition from middle managers who may feel their source of power is being threatened. This is the case at Pioneering Health, as we illustrate further in the next section.

ORGANIZATIONAL CHANGE

Examining the Evidence

Organizational behavior scholars have traditionally viewed organizational change in a one-sided way, approaching it from the perspective of the change agents—the individual or organizations attempting to make the change. This perspective assumes that change agents are attempting to take the correct or appropriate actions, while those resisting change are acting in unreasonable and irrational ways in creating obstacles and barriers to change. Recently, however, Jeffrey D. Ford of the Ohio State University, Laurie W. Ford of Critical Path Consultants, and Angelo D'Amelio of the Vanto Group have taken a second look at organizational change in an effort to show the other side of the change story—from the perspective of the change recipients. These authors suggest that perceived "resistance to change" may actually be the change agents' bias more than any real resistance. And change agents themselves may contribute to these "resistant" behaviors through their own actions, communications, mismanagement, and incompetence—including breaching agreements and failing to maintain trust. In their reinterpretation of the change resistance process, the study authors point out that resistance, rather than being bad and dysfunctional, should be viewed as a natural reaction by change recipients that could contribute positively to the change process by helping to activate discussions and communication, engage people in the change process, and ultimately strengthen commitment to the change.

Critical-Thinking Questions

1. **Why is resistance to change not necessarily bad?**
2. **Given the study's reinterpretation of change resistance, should change agents attempt to overcome resistance to change? Why or why not?**

SOURCE: Ford, Jeffrey D., Laurie W. Ford, and Angelo D'Amelio. "Resistance to Change:The Rest of the Story." *Academy of Management Review* 33, no. 2 (April 2008): 362–377.

Reducing Resistance to Change

Yolande and Imani meet the following day to figure out how to resolve the issues with Birgit and the rest of the nurses, as well as with senior managers, Petra and Niklas. They begin by going through the various methods organizations commonly use to deal with resistance to change.[18]

Education and Communication

One of the most common approaches to addressing resistance to change is education and communication. It is best to teach people about the change before it takes place and ensure the message is communicated clearly and effectively.

When California State University implemented a major IT system change at its main campus, which would affect 23 other satellite campuses and thousands of staff and students, it combated any resistance to change by clearly communicating to employees what needed to be done, who was responsible for the changes, and how far they could make the changes themselves in each of their designated areas. Articulating responsibilities so concisely reduced confusion and encouraged everyone involved to get on board with the new system and to accept a new way of doing things.[19]

Yolande and Imani study this point and agree that from their conversations with Birgit and the two senior managers it is clear that all need further education about the vision and management style of Pioneering Health. Although it will be time consuming, Imani decides to set aside two days to provide additional training to the nurses and the managers as a group. For the nurses, she will focus on role play to boost their confidence on the phone with patients, reinforce the message that they are valued employees with a wealth of experience, and restate that they will have full management support if they have any problems with patients or colleagues.

With the managers, Imani will reiterate the benefits of participative and empowerment management and explain how it encourages teamwork and collaboration. She also intends to address the way the managers perceive their fellow colleagues and teach them skills that may help them adjust their attitudes, behavior, and management approaches.

Participation

When employees are involved in the change, they are more likely to support it rather than resist it. For example, when Wisconsin sausage company Johnsonville Sausages changed its management style, one of the ways it encouraged employee participation was by assigning the tasting of its sausages to production employees—a task previously done by managers. The production employees became responsible for detecting problems and suggesting improvements, which improved results and morale on the rest of the production line. This level of participation meant that employees were more productive and more engaged in their duties.[20]

Yolande and Imani decide to encourage employee participation by allowing employees to give feedback through one-on-one and small-group meetings and by providing opportunities to give suggestions and ideas through online forums. Yolande also wants to reemphasize the company's open-door policy, which she hopes will motivate employees to bring any ideas or concerns to management.

Negotiation

The negotiation method is generally useful when the employees resisting the change feel they have something to lose. Through negotiation, managers can offer them an improved compensation package or other incentives in exchange for agreeing to

Involving employees in organizational changes will make them more invested and more likely to support them.

implement the changes. However, this approach can be expensive and might encourage others to seek the same treatment.

Yolande and Imani both agree that this is not the approach they should take when dealing with the nurses and the senior managers. After all, the business has barely been in operation for a month and the staff has yet to prove themselves. They quickly reject this option and move on to the next method.

Manipulation

In certain circumstances, corporate management may use manipulation to encourage their employees to accept changes. For example, an influential figure of seniority might be drafted into the change process, not necessarily to play an active role, but to give endorsement to the change and convince the rest of the staff that the change is a good idea. However, if employees suspect they are being manipulated, it can lead to even more disruption.

Again, Yolande and Imani do not believe the manipulation method applies to their situation. Besides, both are advocates of honesty and truthfulness in regards to organizational matters at Pioneering Health.

Coercion

Coercion is most commonly used in a crisis when leaders need everyone on board with the changes and right away. However, although threatening job losses or providing poor performance evaluations might work in the short term, it usually leaves employees bitter and ultimately less committed to the changes.

Making threats and using force are simply not Yolande's or Imani's style. When they have finished going through all the methods, they draft a training program for the managers, making sure it hits on the exact points that need to be addressed. They hope that by the end of the program each of the resisting parties will have made some headway toward accepting the changes.

THINKING CRITICALLY

1. Think about Yolande's interaction with Birgit, who is worried that patients won't respect her input. Do you approve or disapprove of the way Yolande deals with the nurse's perceptions about the situation? Explain your answer. **[Apply/Analyze]**

2. Think about Yolande's interaction with Niklas and Petra. How well do you think she handles Niklas and Petra's concerns? What might she do differently to more effectively take their cultural perspectives into account? **[Evaluate/Create]**

3. Imani intends to teach the managers skills that may help them adjust their attitude, behavior, and management approach towards colleagues. What are two concrete examples of skills she might teach them, and how would these help? **[Evaluate/Create]**

4. Of the various methods of addressing resistance to change (education and communication, participation, negotiation, manipulation and coercion), are there any that you feel should never be used by effective managers? Explain your answer. **[Analyze/Evaluate]**

ORGANIZATIONAL DEVELOPMENT

16.4 Describe the concept of organizational development in organizations

Change and Organizational Development

To cope with internal and external changes, many organizations use **organizational development (OD)**, a planned system that uses behavioral science knowledge to increase an organization's efficiency and effectiveness.[21] OD researchers and practitioners observe the culture, strategy, and climate of an organization and try to answer questions such as How do employees communicate? What are their cultural norms, attitudes, and beliefs? How are problems resolved? What is the mood or personality of an organization? Once they have identified these factors, they can begin to work out how to influence the employees' behavior. When faced with increasing competition, management at global telecommunications company Vodafone realized the need to change the culture in order to survive in a challenging market. The current culture was too focused on "blame"—employees failed to take accountability and played political games, which hindered collaboration. To address the lack of cohesiveness in the organization, Vodafone implemented several cultural initiatives, such as introducing new systems that shared information across divisions to encourage cross-functional learning, team-building programs, and leadership coaching programs for top managers to help them set employee goals and delegate to their teams more effectively. As a result of these initiatives, the teams began to work together better and feel more confident about their decision making. A new trust developed between managers and teams, giving rise to new cultural values.[22]

Researchers tend to follow three basic steps in an OD model: diagnosis, interventions, and progress monitoring (see Figure 16.3).[23] First they seek to *diagnose* the problem and bring any issues to the surface so they can be resolved. The most common diagnostic techniques are employee surveys (such as job satisfaction surveys), questionnaires, and interviews.

Once this feedback has been collated, *interventions* can be used that are designed to address the underlying problems. For example, OD specialists may recommend team-building exercises, additional training, or role restructuring for employees who appear to be experiencing job dissatisfaction

Finally, OD specialists *monitor* the effects of the intervention after it has been implemented in order to gauge its effectiveness. Often they ask the employees to complete the same survey post-implementation. This helps identify the change objectives that have

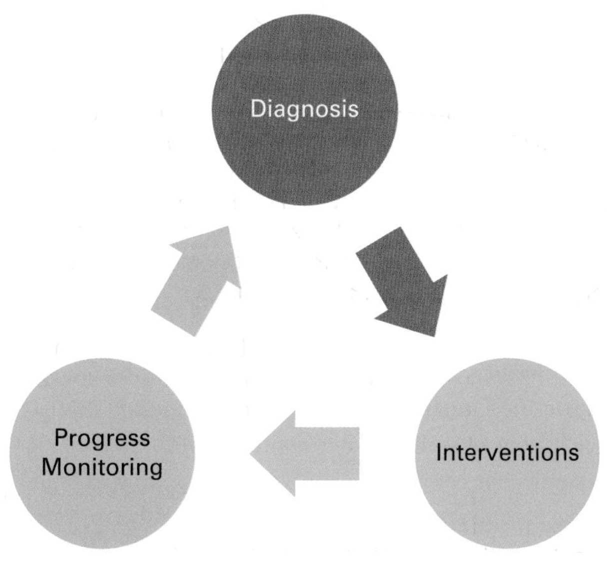

FIGURE 16.3 Organizational Development Techniques

Organizational development (OD): A deliberately planned system that uses behavioral science knowledge to increase the efficiency and effectiveness of an organization

and have not been met. When goals have not been reached, the OD specialists analyze the situation, try to determine why they failed, and introduce modifications to the process. In the following section, we take a more in-depth view of the types of OD interventions adopted in organizations.

THINKING CRITICALLY

1. Based on the description of the steps in the organizational development (OD) model, identify the stage at which Imani and Yolande find themselves in the Frankfurt office of Pioneering Health. Are they at the diagnosis, intervention, or progress monitoring stage? Defend your answer. **[Apply/Analyze]**

2. Generate a list of tools that an OD researcher could use at each stage of the OD model to diagnose problems, intervene, and monitor progress. **[Apply/Analyze]**

TYPES OF OD CHANGE INTERVENTIONS

16.5 Identify types of OD change interventions

OD interventions are plans consisting of specific steps to address problems and create solutions in order to implement change in some facet of an organization, with the overall goal of improving the entire organization. Five different types of change interventions are commonly used in organizations: structural interventions, task-technology interventions, sociotechnical systems design, quality of worklife interventions, and people-focused interventions.[24] Let's explore how these interventions work.

Structural Interventions

Structural interventions focus on job design, tasks, and division of labor. Typically, structural intervention is carried out in three different ways: changing rewards systems, changing the culture, and reorganizing the structure itself.[25]

The millennial generation has forced more and more companies to adjust the way employees are rewarded. As a Gallup survey shows, 82 percent of today's employees would rather receive praise and recognition for their work, which is perceived as more meaningful and motivational, instead of a traditional gold watch. Companies like Gilt, Facebook, Mozilla, and Zendesk integrate praise and recognition into daily work life with real-time continuous feedback through a range of technology applications (such as an electronic note) to boost performance.[26]

Another type of intervention employed in organizations is *changing the culture*. For example, when health care organization Aetna merged with U.S. Healthcare, a major culture clash took place, which forced Aetna to make some changes in its company culture. Over time, Aetna employees went from being risk averse, conservative, and distrustful of outsiders to employees who felt excited, motivated, and proud to work for their company. The change was a result of higher management taking the time to listen to the employees of all levels, to understand their perspectives and seek their views on how to implement changes. Gradually, the Aetna employees became more supportive of the changes and became a more united workforce as a result.[27]

Finally, organizations may choose to *change the structure* of the organization in order to improve communication, problem-solving, and goal-setting techniques. For example, companies like Zappos and adventure travel company G Adventures advocate flat, more open organizational structures as a means of engaging employees, reaching goals, and staying competitive.[28]

©iStockphoto.com/laflor

A new generation in the workforce responds more positively to praise as motivation, encouraging many companies to integrate praise into their day-to-day operations.

Task-Technology Interventions

Task-technology intervention focuses on changing the tasks people perform or the technological processes they use to carry out their roles in order to enhance productivity and increase job satisfaction.[29] For example, in order to find ways to engage employees and enhance communication, HR tech company Wagepoint built a collaboration app called Play, which is a fun way for employees to assign goals and tasks to each other.[30]

Sociotechnical Systems Redesign

In organizational development, **sociotechnical systems** consist of the interaction between human behavior and technical systems.[31] The concept of the sociotechnical system was established to improve the relationship between people and machines to increase organizational effectiveness and efficiency. For example, car manufacturer Volvo was one of the first pioneers of sociotechnical systems redesign. It ended its mechanistic approach—in which people worked separately on a production line, specializing in one task—by creating a sociotechnical system in which a group of highly skilled employees worked together to assemble the cars using a collection of parts. As a result, people no longer felt like they were "machines" and became more motivated, productive, and effective.[32]

Thus, if a company is introducing a new technical system, its managers need to consider the people who will be learning and using it. Unlike technology, people are not mechanistic and cannot be "programmed" in the same way. However, many organizations treat the technical system and the users as two separate entities. This is why the organizational change team and the technical team need to communicate regularly throughout the process of redesigning their sociotechnical system to ensure that the new system meets both organizational and human needs. Studies have shown that organizations like Volvo that focus on improving both technical and human systems have a better chance of adapting and responding to change.[33]

Sociotechnical systems: The interaction between human behavior and technical systems

Quality of Worklife Interventions

Quality of worklife (QWL): The relationship between the employees and the workplace

Another type of OD intervention is **quality of worklife (QWL)**, which alters the relationship between the employees and the workplace.[34] QWL efforts focus on improving employee satisfaction with pay, compensation, job security, responsibilities, performance, work/life balance, health, and career opportunities. For example, Colgate-Palmolive nurture a QWL intervention by providing flexible work hours, telecommuting, and back-up child care centers close by to support parents working from home.[35]

People-Focused Interventions

Finally, organizations can use different types of people-focused interventions during times of change. **Sensitivity training** is a type of program designed to raise awareness of group dynamics and any existing prejudices toward others.[36] Typically, the members of an organization are encouraged to participate in group discussions, exercises, and role plays. They are also invited to share their perspectives and to raise any issues that concern them about dealing with different groups. Then they are shown productive ways to alleviate tensions without causing conflict. Recently, there has been a demand for sensitivity training for police officers following the 2014 shooting of black Missouri teen, Michael Brown, by police officers.[37]

We've seen that organizations sometimes use *survey feedback* to assess the level of job satisfaction in the workplace and take steps to reduce any problems that may hinder success. **Process consultation** is another form of intervention, which attempts to increase groups' awareness or understanding of their behaviors in the workplace.[38] Usually, an outside observer such as a trainer will study the way groups interact with each other and then provide feedback to members in the hope of making them more aware of their attitudes and behaviors and to develop practical solutions to identified problems.

Most organizations use *team-building* exercises to help improve the relationship between groups of employees.[39] These exercises might include physical challenges such as obstacle courses or rowing, or weekend retreats designed to bond employees and teams by giving them a place away from the office to spend time together in informal activities. Team building is also a fundamental part of **intergroup development**, which is finding ways to change the attitudes, perceptions, and stereotypes that employees may have of each other.[40] Part of this approach is to gather different groups together, listen to their perspectives on others, and seek to resolve these views through exercises and discussion.

During Pioneering Health's two-day management training course, Imani uses intervention techniques to try and resolve the conflicts within the group. First she starts with some sensitivity training to address the negative way in which the group members perceive each other. Imani begins by encouraging the nurses to share their past personal experiences as nurses and discuss both their most gratifying moments and their most challenging moments caring for patients and interacting with medical staff. After a few of the nurses recount stories of mistreatment by hospital staff and patients, Imani is surprised and gratified to see Petra listening intently. Imani hopes this is a breakthrough for Petra that will inspire her to behave more respectfully to the nurses.

After the nurses share their personal stories, the group begins a series of role-plays to get the nurses more used to supporting patients on the phone. The nurses quickly gain confidence and Niklas even volunteers to take the part of a difficult patient during one role play. He embraces the role and begins making jokes that the nurses find hilarious.

By the end of the two days, Imani senses a bond forming among the group. During the coffee breaks, Petra and Niklas are chatting with the nurses instead of sitting by themselves as they had done previously. Imani thinks this is a good start, but she knows she needs to continue monitoring the groups to ensure that they fully embrace the Pioneering Health culture of empowerment.

Sensitivity training: A type of program designed to raise awareness of group dynamics and any existing prejudices toward others

Process consultation: An intervention that involves increasing group awareness and/or understanding

Intergroup development: The process of finding ways to change the attitudes, perceptions, and stereotypes that employees may have of each other

In the next chapter, we explore the final installment of the Pioneering Health case in which Yolande and Imani face the challenge of introducing a new system and organizational structure.

THINKING CRITICALLY

1. What step(s) could Yolande and Imani take within the OD model to diagnose the problems they are currently facing with their employees? What research instruments or actions could help them accomplish this goal? **[Apply/Analyze]**

2. What type(s) of interventions (structural interventions, task-technology interventions, socio-technical systems redesign, quality of worklife interventions, or people-focused interventions) does Imani use to deal with Pioneering Health's current challenges? Do you think she chose the best method of intervention? Why or why not? What other method(s) might she have used effectively? **[Apply/Analyze]**

IN REVIEW

Learning Objectives

16.1 Compare and contrast various conceptualizations of the change process

The **DADA syndrome** experienced by individuals faced with unwanted change consists of four stages: denial, anger, depression, and acceptance. Lewin's basic change model is a three-stage model of planned change that explains how to initiate, manage, and stabilize the change process by *unfreezing, transforming,* and *refreezing.* Lewin's force field analysis model is a decision-making technique that helps assess the reasons for and against making certain changes.

16.2 Identify the forces for change in organizations

For organizations to succeed they need to adapt to **external forces,** or outside influences such as customers' demographic characteristics, technological advancements, customer and market changes, and social and political pressures, and **internal forces,** or inside influences such as management changes, organizational restructuring, and intrapreneurship.

16.3 Describe where resistance to change comes from and how to reduce it

Some individual sources of **resistance to change** are *fear of the unknown, insecurity,* and *habit.* Organizational sources include *structural inertia, limited focus of change, group inertia, threat to expertise,* and *threat to established power relationships.*

One of the most common ways to address resistance to change is education and communication before the change takes place. Other methods include participation, negotiation, manipulation, and coercion.

16.4 Describe the concept of organizational development in organizations

Organizational development (OD) is a planned system that uses behavioral science knowledge to increase the efficiency and effectiveness of an organization. OD researchers tend to follow three basic steps in an OD model: diagnosis, interventions, and progress monitoring.

16.5 Identify types of OD change interventions

Structural intervention is carried out in three different ways: changing rewards systems; changing the culture; and reorganizing the structure itself. **Task-technology interventions** restructure tasks, redesign roles, or reconfigure sociotechnical systems. **Sociotechnical systems** redesign improves the interaction between human behavior and technical systems. The concept of the sociotechnical system was established to improve the relationship between people and machines to increase organizational effectiveness and efficiency.

Quality of worklife (QWL) interventions focus on employee satisfaction with pay, compensation, job security, responsibilities, performance, work/life balance, health, and career opportunities. Finally, organizations can use different types of **people-focused interventions** during times of change.

KEY TERMS

THINKING CRITICALLY ABOUT THE CASE OF YOLANDE TURNER AND PIONEERING HEALTH

Consider the five critical-thinking steps in relation to using organizational development strategies to reduce Yolande Turner's new German employees' resistance to change.

OBSERVE

Observe the behavior of the new employees at Pioneering Health's Frankfurt office to identify points of potential conflict with Pioneering Health's culture. Whose behavior is concerning in this regard, what are they doing that concerns you, and why are you concerned?

INTERPRET

What does the behavior of the German employees tell you about their cultural norms, attitudes, beliefs, and assumptions? How do these differ from Yolande and Imani's, and how significant are these differences?

ANALYZE

Provide an analysis of what changes need to occur in order to reduce the potential conflicts identified above. Elaborate on how making these changes will have a positive effect on the Pioneering Health team in Frankfurt.

EVALUATE

Identify the various sources of resistance to change at Pioneering Health's Frankfurt ofice. Which type(s) of change intervention would work best to overcome this resistance to change? Why?

EXPLAIN

Explain the specific steps you can take to implement the change intervention(s) identified above, and elaborate on how these steps can help you achieve your desired changes at Pioneering Health.

EXERCISE 16.1: OVERCOMING RESISTANCE TO CHANGE

Consider an organization with which you are very familiar. Ideally, it is an organization for which you have worked, volunteered, or otherwise served as a member. Now consider a specific change that would be beneficial to the organization, whether it's a change in processes, structure, compensation, management approach, or other. For instance, perhaps you volunteer with an organization in which there seemed to be too many managers and not enough people doing the hands-on work, or perhaps you've worked in an office with a cumbersome way of clocking employees' hours for accumulating vacation days. With this specific change in mind, answer the following questions:

1. What are some of the forces driving change? Consider forces that are both internal and external to the organization. List some of the primary forces for change here:

___

___

___

2. Now consider some of the sources of resistance to change. Consider both the individual and organizational sources of resistance. List the primary sources of resistance here:

___

___

___

3. Finally, think about some ways to overcome the resistance to change in this situation. Being as specific as possible, list some of the primary ways for reducing the resistance to change: ______________________________ ______________________________ ______________________________

EXERCISE 16.2: SEE THE CHANGE YOU WANT TO BE

Objectives:

This exercise will help you to better *compare and contrast* different change process conceptualizations.

Instructions:

Step 1. Select a personal change you would like to make. (Please select a change that you are willing to share with the class.) Describe how you could make your selected change using terms and concepts from one of the change processes described in the book. What would the results of the change look like? What would the benefits be from such a change? Who would benefit from these changes? (5 minutes)

Step 2. Find a partner who selected a different change process than the one you selected. Restate your partner's desired change scenario using the process you originally selected. (10 minutes)

Step 3. Be prepared to present your partner's desired change scenario using her or his original description and how you restated her or his description and plan. (1 to 3 minutes)

Reflection Questions:

1. What new insights did you gain about change processes from using them to describe personal change goals?
2. How did having your change goals restated help you to better understand your goals and the change processes?
3. How did an emphasis on outcomes and benefits affect your change description?
4. What was the most surprising thing you learned from this exercise about the change process?

Exercise contributed by Milton R. Mayfield, Professor of Business, Texas A&M International University and Jaqueline R. Mayfield, Professor of Business, Texas A&M International University.

EXERCISE 16.3: ROAD TO CHANGE AND DEVELOPMENT

Objectives:

This exercise gives you practice in *identifying* organizational change forces, and *describing* change resistance and methods for reducing this change resistance.

Instructions:

Background – It is five years in the future and you are working for your state's department of transportation. You have been placed on a task force to provide a smooth transition to automating highway and road maintenance tasks. This change is expected to take two years to implement, and is expected to enable the department to increase efficiency and reduce costs for many maintenance tasks. It is projected that through a combination of retraining and normal workforce attrition, the department can keep 80 percent of the existing workforce and see a 20 percent reduction in its operational budget. As an alternative, 100 percent of the workforce can be retained, but operational savings will be only 10 percent. All cost reductions will be beneficial, but there are political forces that are pushing for the maximum savings possible. In addition, there is a high level of cohesion and solidarity among the road maintenance workers, and they see these potential changes as threats to their and their colleagues jobs.

For the initial meeting of your task force, you will need to identify the forces that are promoting change, and the forces that will resist the change. In identifying these elements, be sure to discuss both the technical and non-technical issues related to change, and discuss methods for reducing change resistance. You should concentrate your discussion on concepts from this chapter, but you will also need to bring in relevant concepts from other chapters when developing your plan. You should include both change methods (80 percent and 100 percent worker retention) in your discussion.

You will also find it useful to start with identifying and specifying the desirable future state of your organization.

To develop this plan, you should form into teams of five to seven people. Once you have formed a team, take 20 to 30 minutes to develop the plan and be prepared to have a team spokerperson present your plan in a 5 to 10 minute presentation.

Reflection Questions:

1. How did the change plans differ under the two scenarios?
2. What elements remained consistent between the two scenarios?
3. What disputes about the change plans arose in your team?
4. What were the easiest change elements to identify and decide upon?
5. How would you expect the change resistance elements to differ if the change time period was substantially longer or shorter?

Exercise contributed by Milton R. Mayfield, Professor of Business, Texas A&M International University and Jaqueline R. Mayfield, Professor of Business, Texas A&M International University.

CASE STUDY 16.1: MILLENNIALS IN THE WORKPLACE

Welcome to the millennial-centered workplace. At Euro-RSCG, a public relations firm, about 80 millennials (members of the generation born in the 1980s and 1990s) can be found wearing flip-flops, displaying tattoos, indulging in a rooftop happy hour, and using Facebook during work hours. The firm provides time off for volunteer work, and employees leave early on Fridays during the summer. Google offers a free juice bar, a yoga and Pilates room, and even reimbursement for a personal trainer. Chesapeake Energy boasts a 72,000-square-foot on-site gym for employees and encourages employees to partake in smoking cessation programs.

Millennials, or generation Y, are a demanding bunch. "I have a girlfriend. I have family. I have friends. And these are all things that are very important, because we work to live and not the other way around," said Greg Housset, a millennial employee of Euro-RSCG. In the age of social media, millennials are hyperconnected, have little patience for traditional hierarchy, and expect to find opportunities to connect in the workplace. According to MTV's "No Collar Workers" survey, 80 percent of millennials want regular feedback from their managers, and 75 percent said what they really want are mentors. Millennials tend to be motivated to work in a job that is meaningful, not just lucrative—where their ideas count and they can put their creativity to work.

In the same study, a total of 81 percent of surveyed millennials think they should have flexible work hours and make their own schedules; 70 percent said that they needed to have personal time off while on the job; and 79 percent thought they should be allowed to wear jeans to work. Many would like the option to work in the convenience of their homes, using technologies like Skype to telecommute when needed.

It can be trying for baby boomers (who are often the signers of millennials' paychecks) to entertain some of this generation's philosophies about the workplace. Especially during a time when unemployment and underemployment is high for teens and 20-somethings, a prevailing reaction among older employers seems to be, "Beggars can't be choosers, right?" But like it or not, millennials are, in fact, the future. There are about 80 million millennials and 76 million baby boomers in the United States today. About half of those millennials are already in the workplace, and millions more follow each year. By 2025, three of every four workers will be millennials.

"They're the new marketplace," said Marian Salzman, CEO of Euro-RSCG, who began her career in the 1980s. But she knows she must adapt her company culture to the new kids in town in order to thrive. "[Millennials] are the new brains. They come with all the new social media tools and tricks already embedded in them as natives."

She later added, speaking to her fellow baby boomers, "You're not the smartest person in the room anymore. You may be the most experienced. You may be the wisest. You're not the smartest."

Salzman is learning to employ generation Y's strengths to benefit the firm. She accomplishes this by listening to, and in many cases accommodating, their wishes. Other employers are now being advised on how to better manage millennials in the workplace. A few key tips for those managing the new generation: facilitate mentoring to allow for more cross-generational interaction, offer different working options like telecommuting or working off-site, and accommodate different learning styles. Keep employees engaged with educational and training opportunities and create recognition programs. Accommodate personal employee needs, and don't confuse generational traits with character flaws.

And most of all, provide the more democratic, transparent, and collaborative working environment that is fast becoming the norm of the modern workplace, thanks in part to millennial influence.

Case Questions

1. Discuss how millennials have been both and external and internal force of change for organizations.
2. Discuss structural changes and how organizations having to make these to better suit millennials.
3. Recognize why baby boomers may be resistant to all of these changes being made in the modern workplace.

Sources

Chernoff, Allan. "How One CEO Bends the Rules to Get the Most out of Millennials." *CNN.com*. July 21, 2011. www.cnn.com/2011/US/07/21/millennials.managing/index.html.

Editorial Staff. "How Millennials Are Transforming the Workplace." *The Week*. August 24, 2012. http://theweek.com/article/index/232375/how-millennials-are-transforming-the-workplace.

"How to Manage Different Generations." *Wall Street Journal*. n.d. http://guides.wsj.com/management/managing-your-people/how-to-manage-different-generations/.

Kiisel, Ty. "GimmeGimmeGimme—Millenials in the Workplace." *Forbes*. May 16, 2012. www.forbes.com/sites/tykiisel/2012/05/16/gimme-gimme-gimme-millennials-in-the-workplace/.

Matchar, Emily. "How Those Spoiled Millennials Will Make the Workplace Better for Everyone." *Washington Post*. August 16, 2008. http://articles. washingtonpost.com/2012-08-16/opinions/35490487_1_boomerang- kids-modern-workplace-privileged-kids.

Schwabel, Dan. "Millenials vs. Baby Boomers: Who Would You Rather Hire?" *Time*. March 29, 2012. http://business.time.com/2012/03/29/millennials-vs-baby-boomers-who-would-you-rather-hire/.

Seaoms, Kate. "13 Companies That Offer Amazing Perks." *Newser*. January 30, 2011. www.newser.com/story/110603/13-companies-that-offer-amazing-perks.html.

SELF-ASSESSMENT 16.1

How Resistant Am I to Change?

For each statement, circle the number that best describes you based on the following scale:

	Not at All Accurate	Somewhat Accurate	A Little Accurate	Mostly Accurate	Completely Accurate
1. I tend to consider change to be a bad thing.	1	2	3	4	5
2. I prefer daily routine over new and unexpected events.	1	2	3	4	5
3. I would rather be bored than surprised.	1	2	3	4	5
4. When plans change, I tend to get stressed.	1	2	3	4	5
5. If I were told that there would be a major change in how things are done at school or at work, I would probably feel tense about it.	1	2	3	4	5
6. I really dislike changing my plans.	1	2	3	4	5
7. If one of my professors changed the grading criteria in a class, I would feel uncomfortable even if I thought I would do just as well with no additional effort.	1	2	3	4	5
8. I tend to avoid changes despite knowing that they will probably be for the best.	1	2	3	4	5
9. When others pressure me to make changes, I tend to resist even if I think the changes will benefit me.	1	2	3	4	5
10. I tend to avoid changes, even if I know they will be beneficial for me.	1	2	3	4	5
11. I seldom change my mind.	1	2	3	4	5
12. I tend to maintain the same opinions and viewpoints over time.	1	2	3	4	5

Scoring

Add the numbers circled: ____________

Interpretation

48 and above = You are highly resistant to change. You prefer set routines and predictability. Even changes that may benefit you may appear threatening.

25–47 = You have moderate level of resistance to change. Although you are comfortable with established routines, you are occasionally open new approaches and changes of plans.

24 and below = You have a low level of change resistance. You are open to new ways of doing things and actively seek ways to break established routines.

SOURCE: Adapted from Oreg, Shaul. "Resistance to Change: Developing an Individual Differences Measure." *Journal of Applied Psychology* 88, no. 4 (August 2003): 680–693.

17 Organizational Structure, Design, and Technology

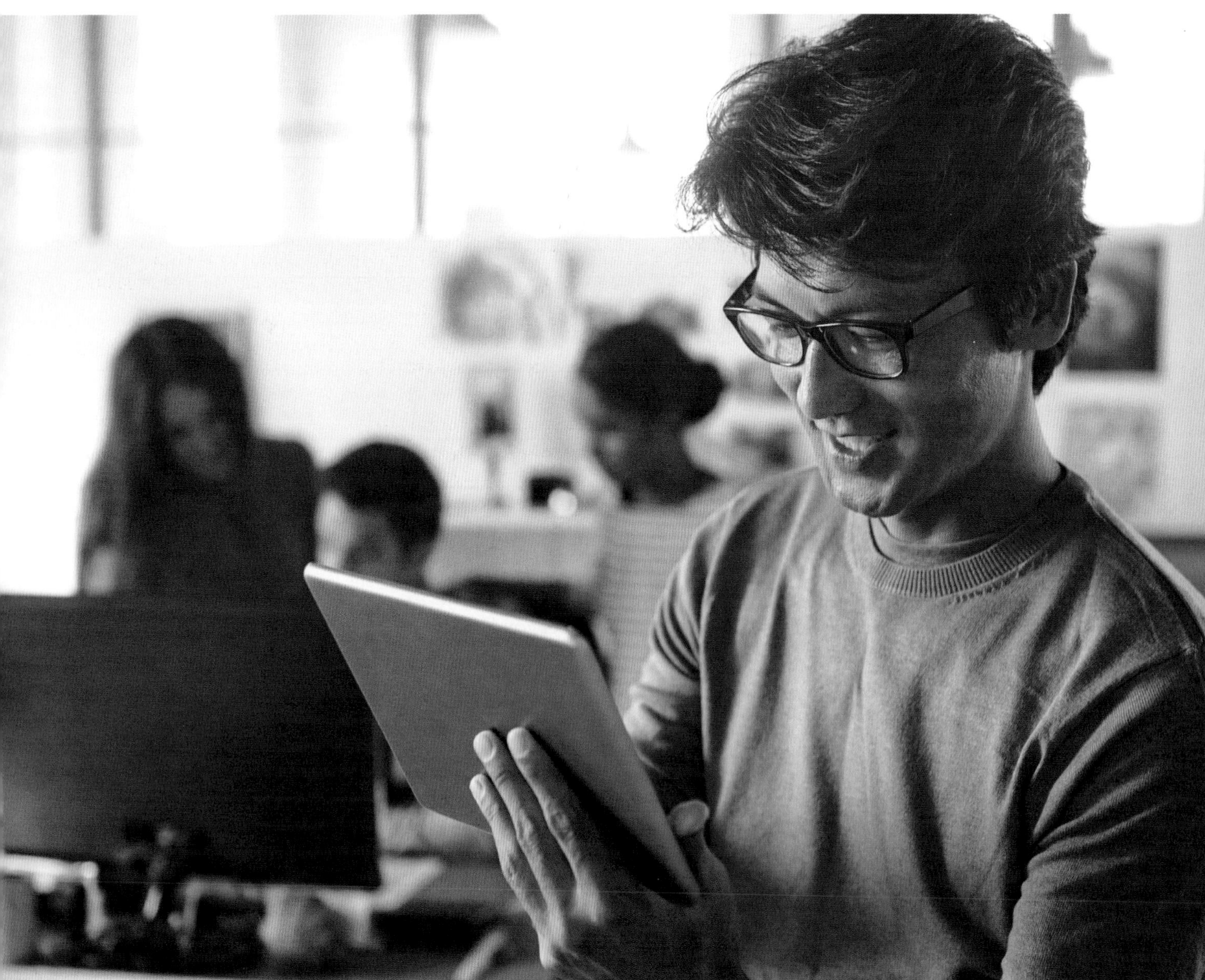

Every company has two organizational structures: The formal one is written on the charts; the other is the everyday relationship of the men and women in the organization.

—Harold S. Geneen, American businessman

ORGANIZATIONAL STRUCTURE

17.1 Describe how organizational structure helps shape behavior in organizations

In the preceding three chapters, we have focused on organizational culture, organizational strategy, and organizational change. Although these factors form the building blocks of an organization, none of them would be fully functional without the support of an underlying structure. For instance, implementing a strategy requires installing and empowering people at the right levels of authority; and reacting to change is possible only when the organization's structure reflects its business goals and objectives. We define **organizational structure** as the framework of work roles and functions that helps shape and support employee behavior.[1] There are many different ways to organize work. For instance, Toyota's global corporate structure is organized around the geographical regions it serves, which include Japan, North America, Latin America, Europe, and Asia,[2] while General Mills' US retail operations are structured into divisions based on five product areas: baking, cereal, meals, snacks, and yogurt.[3] On a smaller scale, think of a superstore like a Walmart or Target organized into departments like pharmacy, grocery, house wares, outdoor, and clothing.

Lines of reporting that define who reports to whom are also examples of organizational structure. Workers can report to a shift supervisor who reports to a manager, as at McDonald's; they can function as a team that manages itself, as at W. L. Gore;[4] or they can simultaneously report to multiple managers in different areas of the firm, as at Vodafone.[5] We take a closer look at all these structures later in the chapter.

For now, note that the structure of an organization has a significant influence on the behavior of its employees. It groups and separates people geographically, hierarchically, or both; it builds and limits relationships by setting up lines of reporting and teams; and it defines employees' responsibilities by outlining their areas of influence and accountability. Many types of organizational structures are possible, and the most successful choices of structure are made with knowledge of the way each structure shapes behavior, including work performance and, to a degree, working relationships. Organizations can undertake rapid reorganizations to make themselves more competitive and adaptable to change. Examples include the division of HP into two separate companies[6] and the splitting of payments system PayPal from eBay.[7]

To create the best working culture, it is essential to understand how organizational structure influences employee behavior. Take a look at how organizational structure has influenced employee behavior at the digital services agency Modea in the OB in the Real World feature.

LEARNING OBJECTIVES

By the end of this chapter, you will be able to:

17.1 Describe how organizational structure helps shape behavior in organizations

17.2 Define basic organizing concepts such as division of labor, chain of command, and span of control

17.3 Identify the types of organizational structures

17.4 Describe the organizational design process and its connection to organizational behavior

17.5 Explain how technology can be integrated into organizational structure and design

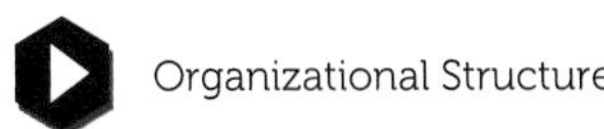

Organizational structure: A framework of work roles that helps shape and support employee behavior

Large stores that sell a wide range of products like Target organize their stores by department to help customers find what they need.

Peter J. Romano II via Wikimedia Commons

Master the content.
edge.sagepub.com/neckob

SAGE edge™

Back to the Case of Yolande Turner and Pioneering Health

Over the course of the past three chapters, we have followed Yolande Turner, founder of Pioneering Health, on her mission to expand the organization outside the United States. The first global office in Frankfurt, Germany, has been staffed with 15 German employees, and Yolande and her colleague Imani have weathered a number of staff challenges since the office opened.

Accustomed to a more autocratic style of management, marketing manager Petra and accounting manager Niklas have struggled to accept the participative management style of Pioneering Health. In addition, Birgit and the other German nurses, who are responsible for providing patient

THE BIG PICTURE: How OB Topics Fit Together

Individual Processes
- Individual Differences
- Emotions and Attitudes
- Perceptions and Learning
- Motivation

Team Processes
- Ethics
- Decision Making
- Creativity and Innovation
- Conflict and Negotiation

Organizational Processes
- Culture
- Strategy
- Change and Development
- **STRUCTURE AND TECHNOLOGY**

Influence Processes
- Leadership
- Power and Politics
- Communication

Organizational Outcomes
- Individual Performance
- Job Satisfaction
- Team Performance
- Organizational Goals

care over the phone, have faced challenges given their concerns about not being taken seriously by patients and colleagues. However, thanks to some intensive additional training by HR manager Imani, the dissenting groups seem to have come together. A year later, Yolande announces that because

SHANNON WRIGHT, *manager, Modea*

OB in the Real World

© Shannon Wright

Modea is a digital services agency that focuses on solving problems for its clients by offering business and product solutions and design customization. Modea helps companies improve their technology so they can become more productive. It creates new and better websites for clients and writes software to help them make better use of smartphones to improve customer service. Some of its recent clients are Chiquita, HTC, Hasbro, Mizuno, and Verizon. Modea has been recognized by *Ad Age* as an advertising agency with a unique culture.

Since Shannon joined Modea in 2009, the company has doubled in size. She is the director of production services and manages the team that focuses on support care products. "Structure and design are important," says Shannon, "because as soon as we have a new product going into production it requires us to scale our infrastructure. The same is true when a new client comes on board and we need to scale the entire organization."

Shannon notes that having a strong structure and company design provides the flexibility and agility she needs to ramp up and down based on production needs.

Her advice to leaders and managers is to gain an understanding of what the longer-term picture is so they can keep their eye on the main goal. She adds that is also important to reassess when necessary. "What do you want your team, department, or company to look like in five years? When you're building your company you need to build it with enough flexibility to change as the market changes and as your people change."

Shannon notes that some companies focus so much on the structure and design of their product they fail to recognize the importance of establishing a deliberative structure and design for the operations side of the business, such as performance appraisals, hiring processes and procedures, and feedback systems. "It is much harder to scale a business when the operational processes aren't in place early on."

When Modea was going through a growth spurt, management noticed that the culture was beginning to change. Employees weren't spending time together as much as they had in the past, and because of all the new hires there were times when it wasn't clear who in the office was a client and who was a colleague. Modea's managers wanted to restore the focus on employees and the corporate culture, so they worked together to come up with a solution. They decided to build a system that would allow employees to get to know each other better and ended up rolling out Who Dot, a digital platform that allows employees to interact with one another online. Think of it as a corporate Facebook account that showcases the personalities of employees and the company. Each employee has a page that includes a quirky picture, a Mad Libs description of who he or she is, and a badge system that highlights his or her likes, dislikes, and interests. Employees can navigate through pages to find colleagues or they can click on the badges to find out who else in the company has the same interests. The purpose of the platform is to bring employees together in order to increase productivity, collaboration, camaraderie, and teamwork, and it was possible only because the leaders at Modea were invested in the structure and design of their people strategy.

Critical-Thinking Questions

1. **How does Shannon support her employees through the structure and design process?**
2. **In what way do you think Shannon evaluated the Modea culture in order to encourage teamwork, collaboration, and camaraderie in a group project?**

SOURCE: Shannon Wright, personal interview, January 13, 2014.

of the growth of the Frankfurt branch, a new organizational structure needs to be put in place. Will the team accept the changes ahead?

Before we continue the rest of the Pioneering Health case, let's explore some basic organizing concepts as a foundation for organizational structure and design.

THINKING CRITICALLY

1. Create a list of the daily aspects of a worker's life that organizational structure can affect. Using your list, explain why organizational structure exerts such a significant influence over the behavior of employees. **[Understand/Apply]**

2. Provide at least three reasons why the rapid expansion at Modea caused corporate culture to change. Defend your answer. **[Apply/Analyze]**

BASIC ORGANIZING CONCEPTS

17.2 Define basic organizing concepts such as division of labor, chain of command, and span of control

An organization's structure affects how successfully it can coordinate and accomplish its work activities. (Think about why elementary and high schools organize their students by age rather than by height, for instance.) Several different organizing concepts, such as how specialized a given job is and how many people report to an individual manager, describe the kinds of choices an organization's top managers must make in choosing the most appropriate structure. Let's look at these.

Specialization and Division of Labor

Work specialization, also known as **division of labor**, is the degree to which jobs are divided into specific tasks.[8] When work is specialized, employees who work in a certain department carry out only the tasks that relate to their roles. For example, at a restaurant there might be someone greeting the customers, another person showing them to their table, someone taking their orders, and another person bussing the tables, but

Division of labor: The degree to which certain jobs are divided into specific tasks

A hostess at a restaurant performs different skills from a server or a chef. These specializations allow each employee to be more skilled and efficient at their designated jobs.

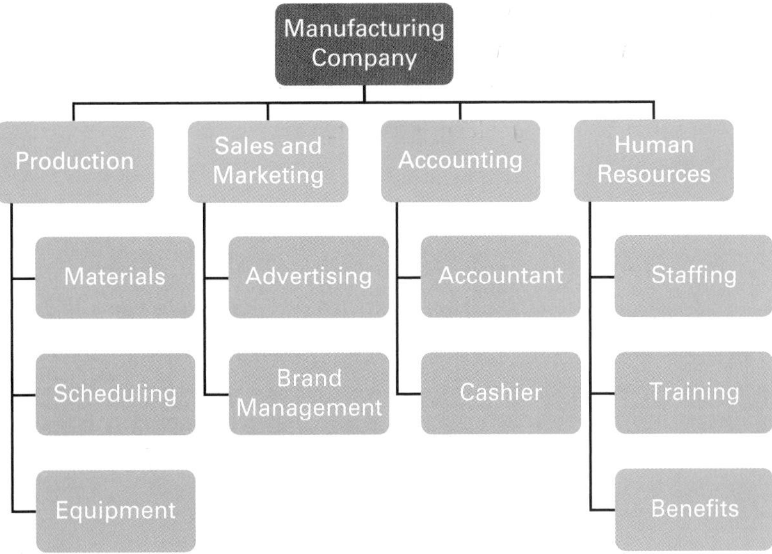

FIGURE 17.1 Example of Departmentalization Structure

all the employees would not perform all these tasks to accomplish the job of feeding customers. The advantages of specialization may include increased efficiency and more accurate production as workers become more skilled in a particular task.

However, many organizations are moving away from specialization because too much of it—as when employees repeatedly perform the same few tasks—can lead to bored employees with narrow skill sets. Instead, many companies are widening the scope of their employees' roles and creating environments in which employees can rotate among tasks to broaden their skill base. This was the case in our Waterfront Grill case (Chapter 6), when assistant restaurant manager Katie O'Donnell redesigned the division of labor in place at the restaurant in order to implement job rotation and job enlargement as a way of engaging and motivating the jaded restaurant staff.

Departmentalization

Departmentalization is a process of grouping people with related job duties, skills, and experiences into the same area within the overall organizational structure.[9] Many mid-sized and larger companies structure their organizations in this way. For example, a manufacturing plant may be divided into production, sales and marketing, accounting, and human resources with very little crossover between the departments (see Figure 17.1).

As you may remember, the tractor assembly plant featured in Chapters 7 through 10 was departmentalized, with very clear divisions between the areas. The successful development and design of the new product (the rotatable handling arms) came about only when workers from different departments began to work together as a team.

Chain of Command

Some organizations devise a **chain of command**, a flow of authority and power from the highest to the lowest levels of the organization (see Figure 17.2).[10] As we have explored during the course of this book, many organizations such as Campbell Soup and Microsoft are advocating a more inclusive and participative approach, rather than a strict chain of command such as in the military, as a way to meet organizational goals and objectives.

In the West Texas Regional Theatre Company case in Chapters 2–4, Abigail Swenson held all the power until circumstances forced her to seek support from

Departmentalization: A process of grouping people with related job duties, skills, and experiences into different areas within the overall organizational structure

Chain of command: The flow of authority and power from the highest to the lowest levels of the organization

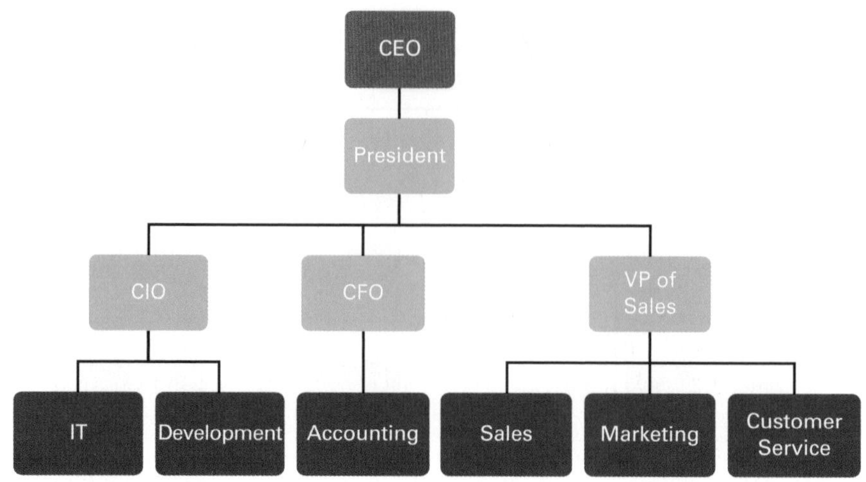

■ FIGURE 17.2 Example of Chain of Command

the rest of the theatre staff. Similarly, in the tractor assembly plant case, company president Hans Wagner operated a strict chain of command and didn't take kindly to his decisions being questioned. In both scenarios, the organization ended up taking a more participative approach to management. In the Pioneering Health case in Chapters 14–17, the chain of command is more participative—an approach that has proved difficult for Petra and Niklas to embrace in Pioneering Health's Frankfurt office.

Span of Control

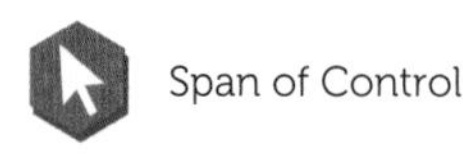

When organizations expand by hiring more people, the number of direct reports to a given manager usually increases, giving that manager a wider **span of control**.[11] For example, in Chapter 5, when Katie O'Donnell is promoted from server to assistant manager of the Waterfront Grill, she is given responsibility for a large number of staff members, which gives her a wider span of control. Some of the advantages for both employees and managers of a wide span of control are better communication and collaboration as more employees are included in the decision-making process, and higher morale as employees are given more responsibility and less supervision. Some of the disadvantages are that managers may lose control over what employees are doing, and they can become overloaded with work.

Companies like Google, Apple, and Facebook prefer a wider span because it encourages the sharing of ideas and communication,[12] although in an organization like U.S. Steel we historically find a narrower span of control, applied in an effort to exert more control over workers.[13]

Centralization and Decentralization

Decision making can be either centralized or decentralized.[14] In a centralized organizational structure, such as McDonald's or Burger King, senior management makes all the major decisions, whereas in a decentralized organization like UK department stores John Lewis and Debenhams, employees at lower levels are given the power to make decisions and solve problems without seeking approval from senior management.[15] Again, many organizations are seeking to move toward a decentralized approach because the evidence suggests that empowered employees are a key factor of organizational success.[16]

Span of control: The number of direct reports to a given manager following an expansion

CENTRALIZATION VERSUS DECENTRALIZATION

Does Organizational Structure Matter?

Examining the Evidence

Given the trend toward employee empowerment and flexible organizations that can adjust rapidly to changes in the competitive environment, in recent years many organizations have moved in the direction of decentralized organizational structures. But, depending on the situation, can centralized structures be more effective for accomplishing work tasks? That's the question investigated by researchers John D. McCluskey of Rochester Institute of Technology, Jeffrey M. Cancino of Texas State University-San Marcos, and Marie Skubak Tillyer and Rob Tillyer of the University of Texas-San Antonio in a recent study of the organizational structure of detectives in the San Antonio Police Department. On one hand, a community policing model suggests that decentralized detective units that patrol the streets could develop closer ties with the communities they serve and see better processes and outcomes. On the other hand, the centralization of resources, staff, and decision making could help coordinate information processing when following up leads and provide more rationality and objectivity. The percentage of robberies cleared (solved) by an arrest increased after a reorganization from a decentralized to centralized organizational structure in the San Antonio robbery detectives' department. Interviews with detectives suggested that changes in the collection and use of information, cooperation among detectives, and police–prosecutor interface all improved as a result of the reorganization. These findings suggest that centralized organizational structures remain beneficial in certain situations.

Critical-Thinking Questions

1. **What other types of organizations may benefit from centralized structures? Would their employees differ from those in the San Antonio Police Department? How?**
2. **What are the dangers of generalizing or applying the results of this study to other organizations?**

SOURCE: McCluskey, John D., Jeffrey M. Cancino, Marie Skubak Tillyer, and Rob Tillyer. "Does Organizational Structure Matter? Investigation Centralization, Case Clearances, and Robberies." *Police Quarterly* 17, no. 3 (September 2014): 250–275.

Mechanistic and Organic Models

The **mechanistic model** is a formalized structure based on centralization and departmentalization.[17] There is a definite chain of command, employees tend to work separately rather than collaborating, and there is very little communication between

Mechanistic model: A formalized structure based on centralization and departmentalization

Rob LaRosa via Wikimedia Commons

McDonald's operates with a centralized organizational structure, with decisions and standards being handed down to individual stores from the corporate office.

The Motor Vehicle Bureau is a bureaucratic structure with centralized authority and specialized routine tasks.

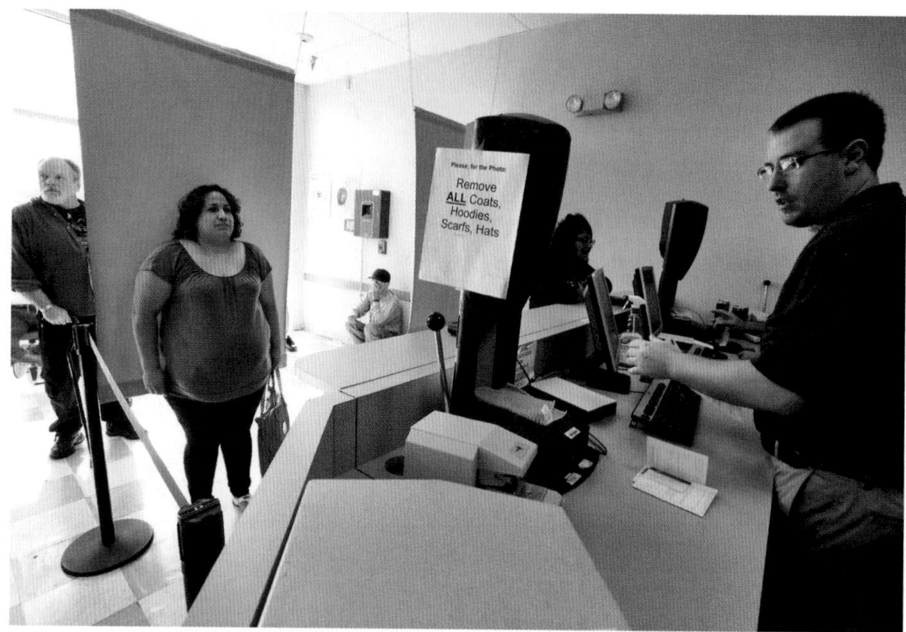

AP Photo/Brennan Linsley

lower-level employees and upper-level management. This sort of model is predominant in manufacturing, where everyone is assigned specific tasks and expected to follow certain rules and procedures. Although the mechanistic structure is relatively easy to implement, it can be difficult to adapt it to rapid change.

The **organic model** is a less formalized structure based on decentralization and cross-functional teams.[18] Decision making is participative and distributed throughout the organization. Communication is open and frequent, and employees are more likely to accept and adapt to change.

Formalization and Bureaucracy

Formalization is the degree to which rules and procedures are standardized in an organization.[19] McDonald's is an example of an organization whose employees are expected to follow strict guidelines. Although there are some benefits to having strict rules, such as less confusion about how and why things are done, employees may become frustrated at the lack of opportunity to exercise their own judgment. Today's organizations tend to follow a less formalized structure to manage employee behavior.

Bureaucracy is characterized by formalized rules and regulation, specialized routine tasks, division of labor, and centralized authority.[20] Bureaucratic structures, such as the IRS or the Motor Vehicle Bureau, tend to follow a chain of command with decision making and power firmly at the top.

You may remember that in Chapter 16 Niklas and Petra struggled to accept a participative management style at Pioneering Health because they have been used to working in bureaucratic, formalized, mechanistic, centralized, departmentalized organizations that have a strong chain of command. Until now, every employee at the companies for which they have worked was expected to follow orders and not question decisions. Although Niklas and Petra are both very good at carrying out the tasks associated with their roles, they do not communicate well with the other members of staff, find it difficult to accept change, and refuse to invite feedback or include the other team members in their decisions. They may seem to be stubborn in their refusal to accept change, but their work history and culture provide a clear reason for their behavior. Although they come from a different type of organization and approach to management, it doesn't mean that they will never be able to accept change; it will just take more time.

Organic model: A less formalized structure based on decentralization and cross-functional teams

Formalization: The degree to which rules and procedures are standardized in an organization

Bureaucracy: An organizational style characterized by formalized rules and regulation, specialized routine tasks, division of labor, and centralized authority

THINKING CRITICALLY

1. List at least two types of industries that could benefit from specialization. Defend your list. **[Apply/Analyze]**

2. Describe the ways in which an inclusive and participatory organizational structure could help companies meet goals and objectives more effectively than a strict chain of command like the one organizing the military. **[Analyze/Evaluate]**

3. Put yourself in the role of CEO at a growing technology company. What techniques could you use to mitigate the potential disadvantages of a wider span of control within your organization? Explain how each technique could help to mitigate potential drawbacks. **[Evaluate/Create]**

4. Do you think it would be easier to run a company with a high level of formalization and bureaucracy or a low level of formalization and bureaucracy? Explain your answer. **[Analyze/Evaluate]**

TYPES OF ORGANIZATIONAL STRUCTURES

17.3 Identify the types of organizational structures

A year has passed since Yolande and her senior team decided to expand Pioneering Health into the German health care market, and business is booming. It hasn't been a smooth journey, but thanks to frequent team-building exercises and additional training, employees are working together toward the achievement of organizational goals. Yolande feels the company has turned a corner: the culture is becoming more participative, the staff more respectful and considerate of each other, and the nurses have become more confident when dealing with patients. Yolande is delighted everyone has embraced the changes she and HR manager Imani have implemented.

Yet there are more changes ahead for the German team. Yolande has decided it is time for her to return to the head office in Chicago. She has been traveling between Frankfurt and Chicago for months now, and though she is very pleased with the way the Chicago office has been run in her absence, she thinks she should spend most of her time in the head office overseeing operations. Imani has decided to stay in Germany. She will become president of the Frankfurt branch, an arrangement that benefits both of them. Yolande is delighted she is leaving the office in the hands of a trusted, loyal, and committed manager, and Imani is excited with her new promotion as well as the opportunity to live in Germany—a country she has grown to love. But before Yolande can return to the Chicago office, one more issue needs to be addressed: the rapid growth of business flowing into Pioneering Health.

Over the past few months, business has really taken off. Thanks to Petra and her marketing team, three additional health care plans with hundreds of patients on their books have signed up with Pioneering Health. The phone has been ringing off the hook, nurses have been struggling to keep up with the demand for advice, and the rest of the staff has begun drowning in paperwork. As a result, the team has been working longer hours and is beginning to experience burnout.

Yolande and Imani recognize the need to recruit more people to meet the demand, so they consult with the existing staff, analyzing their current roles and workloads, to find out how many people they need to hire. They calculate that the Frankfurt office needs to hire an additional 50 staff members in the areas of administration, research

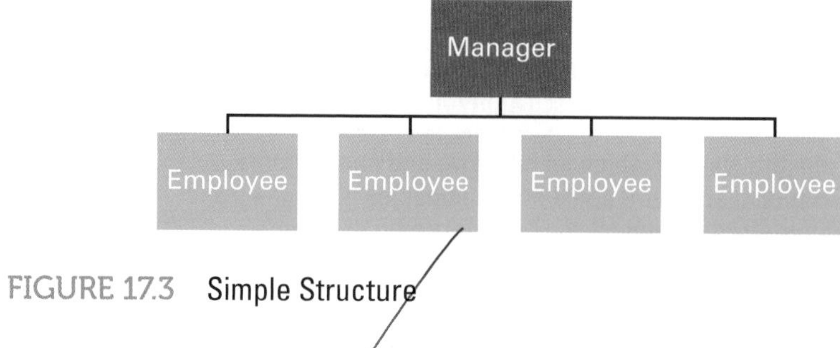

FIGURE 17.3 Simple Structure

and health care, human resources, marketing, technology, and accounting, bringing the new total to 75. To accommodate and make the best use of this increase in staff, the German branch of Pioneering Health will need a new organizational structure. Yolande and Imani have sketched an outline of the structure they feel would best suit the growing organization, but for it to work, they will need buy-in from the rest of the staff prior to implementation.

Pioneering Health has offices in several US locations, each of which is decentralized and autonomous, operating in the same way as a franchise. The German office is the newest and the smallest office and operates independently from the other Pioneering Health offices. Yolande and Imani organize a staff meeting to take the team through the structural changes planned for the German office. Yolande begins the meeting with a PowerPoint presentation that outlines the different types of organizational structures.

She explains that typically there are four main types of organizational structures: simple structures, functional structures, divisional structures, and matrix structures.[21]

Simple structures (see Figure 17.3) are more common in small organizations where is there is one central authority figure, usually a business owner, who tends to make the decisions. For example, the owner of a small clothing store might have to manage a cashier and salespeople. Because there are no layers of management, decisions can be made and implemented quickly. However, this structure has its drawbacks. The business owner may become overloaded with work or may be reluctant to delegate when necessary, which could slow down the progress of the organization.

Functional structures group employees according to the tasks they perform for the organization, such as marketing, finance, and human resources. Here employees are managed by means of clear levels of authority. In general, this structure works well for smaller organizations, but there is a risk of lack of communication between the departments because of their tendency to work separately from each other. Yolande shows that the Frankfurt branch of Pioneering Health operates partly as a functional structure (Figure 17.4).

The **divisional structure**—sometimes called *multidivisional structure*—groups employees by products and services, by geographic regions, or by customers.

Simple structures: Organizational structures, common in small organizations where is there is one central authority figure, usually a business owner, who tends to make decisions

Functional structures: Organizational structures that group employees according to the tasks they perform for the organization

Divisional structure: (sometimes called *multidivisional structure*) An organizational structure that groups employees by products and services, geographic regions, or customers

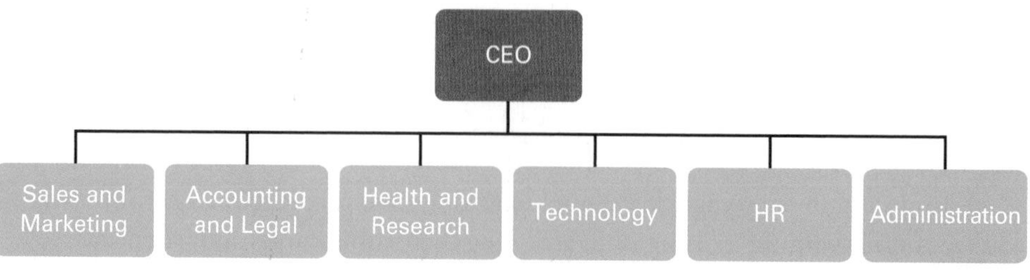

FIGURE 17.4 Current Pioneering Health Frankfurt Organizational Structure

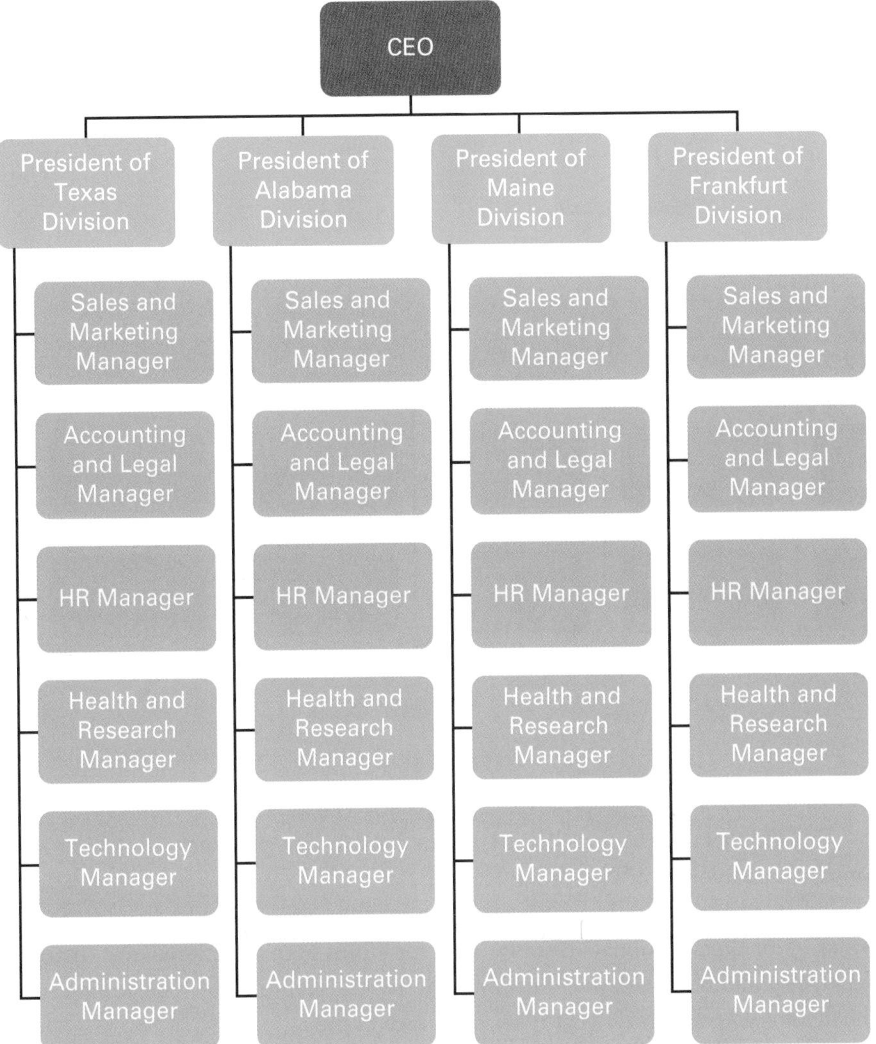

■ FIGURE 17.5 Pioneering Health Domestic and Global Divisions

Although divisional structures are ideally placed to meet external demands, divisions that are performing similar tasks—in different locations, for example—may be at risk of duplicating their work. They may also compete for shared resources. As Yolande explains, Pioneering Health has a number of different branches domestically and one office globally, so it also reflects elements of a divisional structure. Figure 17.5 provides a basic snapshot of how both domestic and global locations are organized at Pioneering Health. Each president has managers for accounting, marketing, and human resources reporting to him or her.

"Why can't we keep the functional model we have now?," Niklas asks.

"We don't feel that it's going to work when 50 more people join the staff," Imani responds. "Our current structure works now because there are only 25 of us. We have ample opportunities to communicate, which we think has been working out great for everyone. However, in a functional environment, there is a temptation for people to break off into different groups and work separately from each other, and that is not what we want to happen when we're fully staffed."

"The idea is that we want everyone to continue communicating with each other regardless of the departments they work in," Yolande adds. "That's how teams bond, how ideas spark, and how strategies are built. Communication is the key to Pioneering Health's success."

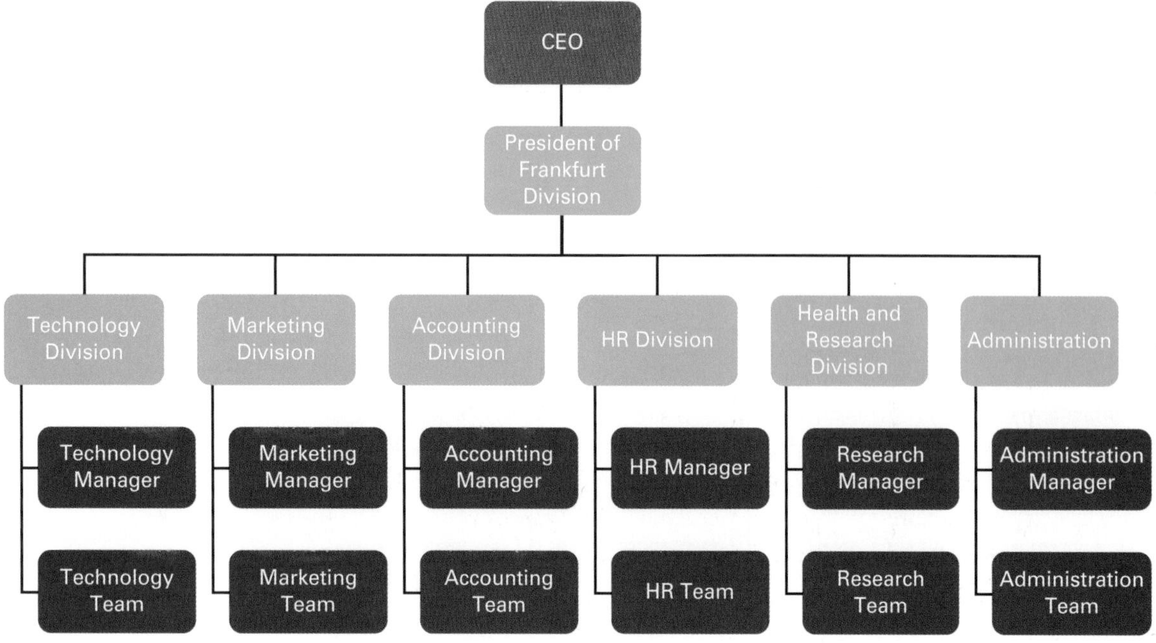

■ FIGURE 17.6 Matrix Structure

"What plan are you proposing to implement?" Petra asks.

Yolande clicks to the next PowerPoint to demonstrate the proposed new structure for the German office of Pioneering Health.

Yolande has proposed a **matrix structure** for Pioneering Health's Frankfurt office, which is an organizational structure that combines both functional and divisional departmentalization, with dual lines of authority (see Figure 17.6). The group looks at the figure trying to absorb what it means to each of them.

"Yolande, you're obviously the CEO, but who will be the president?" Petra asks.

"I will," Imani responds.

There is a buzz in the room at the announcement, and when the chatter has died down, Niklas says, "I have another question about the chart. It appears the departments will become divisions. Does that mean there will be a head of each division?"

"Yes," Yolande responds. "You will head up your division and you will also be supported by a new accounting manager who will also manage the team. The same goes for you, Petra."

"So that means Petra and I will be in charge of the new managers in our respective departments plus the team themselves?," Niklas asks.

"That's right," Yolande responds. "You will be responsible for overseeing the entire accounting division, and you will be reporting directly to Imani." Niklas sits back, looking pleased.

"What do you think, Petra?," Imani asks, noticing that Petra has been looking thoughtful. "Is this okay with you?"

"I guess so," Petra says, slowly. "It's just that I used to report directly to Yolande but now it seems as though I have to go through Imani to reach Yolande. That seems like an inconvenient arrangement to me."

"You will be reporting to Imani, and I have absolute faith in her ability to run this operation. However, if you ever feel the need to get in touch with me directly for whatever reason, just give me a call. I will always be there to help you with whatever you need," Yolande replies.

"Or I guess I could just walk into your office instead!," Petra says.

Matrix structure: An organizational structure that combines both functional and divisional departmentalization together with dual lines of authority

Yolande and Imani exchange looks.

"Well, I was going to make the announcement at the end of the meeting," Yolande says, "but I'm going to be largely based in the Chicago office." Yolande waits until the team quiets down before continuing. "I will be making frequent visits to the Frankfurt office, but Imani will head up this operation and report to me. The rest of the staff will report to Imani," Yolande says. "I may not be in the Frankfurt office every day, but as I said, I'm always available to you and anyone else on the team," she says.

Relieved that the major announcements have been made, Yolande asks the group whether they have any more questions about the new structure.

"I'm a little confused with the chart," says Fredrick, a member of the marketing team. "At the moment my manager is Petra, but now you're bringing in a new boss to whom I also have to report?"

"Yes, Fredrick," Imani responds. "The company is expanding and is likely to get even larger. We need dual management to make sure our operations run smoothly and ensure that the teams function to the best of their ability. That means you will have a manager who will be a new hire, and Petra, the division manager, to report to."

"I think I understand the matrix concept, but I'm struggling to visualize how it would work in practice," Fredrick replies. "You don't think it will create power struggles given that there will be two leaders per department?"

"I understand your concerns, Fredrick," Yolande says, "but we have carried out a lot of research and we hope to put the matrix structure in place for all the Pioneering Health offices. Admittedly, power struggles are a concern, but we believe that if the teams are managed appropriately and team members are given enough resources and support to do their jobs, we can limit or prevent those types of conflicts. This is why communication is so important—the more we communicate the less likely we are to clash with others. Any more questions?"

Birgit says, "I'm struggling to understand where the nurses fit in to the overall structure."

Yolande explains, "The nurses and the research team have been combined into the 'health and research' division to further cement the lines of communication. This means the researchers will be on hand to provide you with the latest information about a variety of health conditions, which will enable you to give the most up-to-date advice to your patients over the phone."

"I see there is going to be a new HR team," Petra interjects.

Imani nods. "Yes, because my role has changed, I will no longer be able to carry out my daily HR tasks, so a new HR manager and team will be recruited."

"I'm a little worried about the new staff fitting into the Pioneering Health culture. What if they don't understand our policy on equality for every employee?," Birgit asks.

"Don't worry, Birgit, each new recruit will receive extensive induction training as well as on-the-job training. We will endeavor to cultivate the same culture of respect and collaboration that has served us so well to date. Nothing less will be tolerated. I also expect all of you to be welcoming and to include the new staff in all the team-bonding activities and social outings. We won't be a small team of pioneers anymore, but there's nothing to say we can't be one big happy group of pioneers!" The group responds with laughter and smiles.

Yolande says, "What we're trying to do here with the matrix structure is to create an environment that encourages collaboration and open communication. Although the teams have been divided into distinct divisions and functions, everyone should continue to talk to each other and share information. The aim is to blend the different skills of each department so we can work closely together to come up with solutions that keep us at the forefront of health management."

"The most important thing is that we get your buy-in on the new organizational structure," Imani adds. "Without your support as a group, the new structure will not work."

THINKING CRITICALLY

1. What specific qualities make Pioneering Health a functional structure? What qualities make it a divisional structure? **[Understand/Apply]**
2. When Fredrick suggests that power struggles might result from having two leaders per department, Yolande responds that if teams are managed appropriately and team members have enough resources and support, power struggles will be limited. Do you agree with Yolande's assessment? Why or why not? To what extent will hiring decisions impact Pioneering Health's ability to embrace a matrix structure? **[Apply/Analyze]**
3. In what ways will a matrix structure encourage collaboration and communication within Pioneering Health more than a functional structure or a divisional structure? Explain your reasoning. **[Analyze/Evaluate]**

ORGANIZATIONAL DESIGN

17.4 Describe the organizational design process and its connection to organizational behavior

How do organizations choose the right structure for their firms? Most companies, large or small, will go through a period of **organizational design**, which is the process of creating or changing the structure of an organization to integrate people, information, and technology.[22] The choice of structure depends on the organization's size, strategy, and environment. As we learned in the preceding section, smaller organizations tend to use basic designs such as simple or functional structures. However, when these companies grow, their design often becomes more complex.[23]

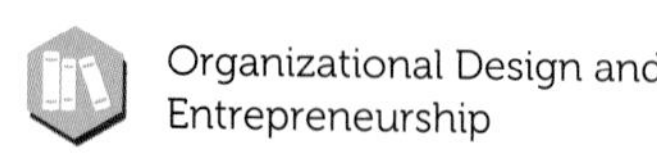

For example, for the first time in more than a decade, Garland ISD, Dallas County's (Texas) second-largest school district, has redesigned its organizational structure. New hires and dedicated senior management will oversee student services, human resources, technology, administration, facilities, and curriculum and instruction. There is a renewed focus on specific departments, with seven area directors appointed to help support the transition from the elementary and middle schools' curriculum, all centered on the district's seven high schools. In addition, Superintendent Bob Morrisson committed to visiting each of the 71 campuses in the district in order to gather teachers' feedback and concerns and to build trust among the faculty and staff. It is hoped that the new structural design will cut through the layers of administration and stimulate an environment of collaboration, communication, and trust.[24]

The organizational design process includes six key steps: understanding the business climate, setting the scene, gathering data, transforming the design, implementing the design, and evaluating the design (Figure 17.7).[25] Let's take a closer look at each of these.

The organizational design process often arises from a changing *business climate*. In most cases, businesses will redesign their structures as a result of an expanding market, new competitors, globalization, or other industry changes.

Organizational design: The process of creating or changing a structure of an organization to integrate people, information, and technology

When the need for change has been recognized and the structure has been chosen, a design team often works together to *set the scene* by establishing the rationale behind the decision and drafting a rough plan for change. Then the *data gathering* process begins. During this stage, the team assesses the existing structure and looks for ways to mold it

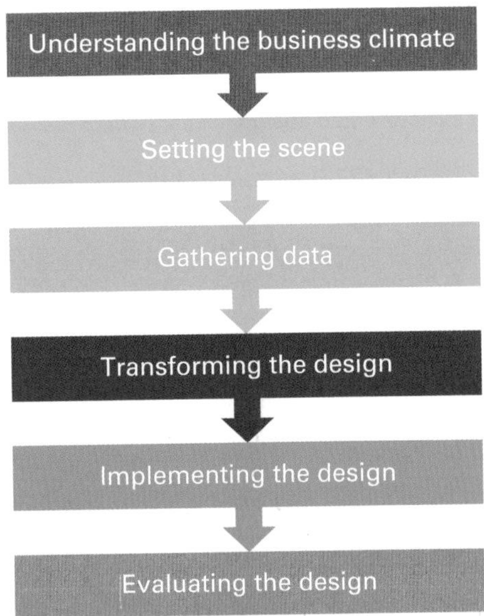

■ FIGURE 17.7 Organizational Design Process

SOURCE: Based on Beakey, Diane, Kathleen Wells Webster, and Jackie Rubin. "Organizational Design and Implementation." *Graziadio Business Review* 10, no. 4 (2007). https://gbr.pepperdine.edu/2010/08/organizational-design-and-implementation/.

into the new design. This includes focusing on employees' roles and performance, the way they communicate with each other, and their willingness to adjust to change.

Once the design team is confident the new structure is feasible, the *design transformation* stage begins. During this stage, the team drafts an image of the new organizational structure that outlines the interconnections among different roles and departments. Following this process, the design is put into action based on the pattern of the structure. This might mean employees adjusting to new reporting lines, a change in their roles, or communications with different divisions. Post implementation, it is vital to have a *design evaluation* process to ensure the new structure is functioning well. This requires assessing the performance of employees and their level of satisfaction with the new structure. A revised or newly created organizational design can have an enormous impact on employee behavior. Some employees might thrive on the change, but others may struggle to accept new responsibilities or different reporting lines. During this period, additional training is imperative for those employees who struggle to accept the structure. The design team must also be open to making changes to the plan based on levels of performance and feedback.

One of the most important elements of the organizational design process is the integration of technology. In the next section, we explore how organizations incorporate technology into their design processes and its influence on employee behavior.

THINKING CRITICALLY

1. Discuss the changing business climate to which Pioneering Health needs to adjust. What pitfalls may the Frankfurt office encounter as it staffs up? What difficulties is it likely to need to address as it transforms into a matrix structure? **[Analyze/Evaluate]**

2. Describe at least three procedures or techniques you would you use as a company leader to carry out the design evaluation process after a restructuring. Explain the benefit of each procedure or technique. **[Evaluate, Create]**

INTEGRATING TECHNOLOGY

17.5 Explain how technology can be integrated into organizational structure and design

It has been six months since Yolande announced the new organizational matrix structure to the team in Germany. Since then, much has changed. Yolande has moved back to the Chicago office; 50 new employees have been recruited for the Frankfurt office; and Imani has rented a second floor of the building where their office is located to accommodate the new staff. Imani has been working closely with the heads of each division to ensure all is going as smoothly as possible. So far, it appears the new matrix design is working well. Niklas and Petra, in particular, are enjoying their roles as divisional heads. Imani had been concerned that the additional power and responsibility would cause them to revert to their autocratic ways, but the two managers are communicating well with their direct reports and respecting the Pioneering Health culture. The new recruits are beginning to settle in, thanks to extensive training, team-bonding activities, and plenty of one-to-one time with divisional heads and with Imani, who makes it a priority to address any concerns they may have.

There have been a few hiccups. Fredrick, key member of the marketing team, has struggled to accept the idea of reporting to a new manager. When pressed, he confesses to Imani that he feels that he should have been promoted to manager. When Imani explains that he is not experienced enough, he becomes upset and threatens to resign. Although Imani values Frederick as a staff member, she refuses to give in to his demands and says there will be promotional opportunities when he has gained more experience. Fredrick's dissatisfaction spreads to two other key members of marketing and they resign along with Fredrick three months into Imani's tenure as president of the Frankfurt office.

Imani is unhappy to lose valuable employees, but puts the incident behind her and moves on to the next big change on her list: integrating new technology into the new design structure at Pioneering Health.

Technology and Organizational Design

Technology is a vital part of any organization's day-to-day operations and needs to be woven into the very fabric of organizational design. We define **technology** as the development of scientific knowledge as applied to machinery and devices.[26] There are two main types of technology in the workplace: operations technology and information technology.

Operations technology is the combination of processes, knowledge, and techniques that creates product or service value for an organization.[27] For example, a car assembly line consists of a number of operational components that must work in sequence for the end product to be successfully manufactured.

Information technology (IT) is a set of tools, processes, systems, and data communications based on microelectronic technology designed to disseminate information and provide support to individuals in an organization.[28] Ten years ago, the perception of IT was very different. Organizations had a dedicated IT department to troubleshoot system issues and provide technical support. Today the role of IT goes beyond merely repairing machine glitches. The introduction of the Web and the rise of social media, as well as the rapid launch and expansion of communication devices such as smartphones and tablets, have made IT an essential part of operations that not only provides critical support but also enhances business performance. For example, Cisco has launched a Social Media Listening Center that monitors thousands of mentions of Cisco across Facebook, Twitter, LinkedIn, and YouTube, as well as on its own blogs and forums. By monitoring customer queries and complaints, Cisco employees have been able to

Technology: The development of scientific knowledge as applied to machinery and devices

Operations technology: The combination of processes, knowledge and techniques that creates product or service value for an organization

Information technology (IT): A set of tools, processes, systems, and data communications based on microelectronic technology, designed to disseminate information to provide support to individuals in an organization

©iStockphoto.com/RicAguiar

A car assembly line shows how operations technology—processes, knowledge, and techniques—comes together to create a final product.

respond more quickly to problems and customer concerns. As a result of using social media, Cisco has saved on the cost of marketing and customer service and also seen an increase in staff productivity.[29]

Sociotechnical Systems

In Chapter 16, we learned about sociotechnical systems that describe the relationship between human behavior and technical systems.[30] Researchers have shown that organizations that focus on both the technical side and the human side have a better chance of success. In the next section, drawing on sociotechnical theory, we explore Imani's plan to introduce a new IT system to Pioneering Health.

Designing Technology

The health and research teams at Pioneering Health are the principle drivers for their new system. The rise in patient calls has been growing to such an extent that the current patient care telephonic process no longer works as well. At present, patients call the Pioneering Health number for help with particular illnesses, and the nurses advise them using their own expertise together with the evidence gathered by the research team. However, as the business expands, so do the volume of callers and the variety of health problems. The nurses are finding that some of these health problems are outside the scope of their expertise and are struggling to provide the necessary advice. When they are unable to advise the patient, they get the patient's number and promise to call back within 30 minutes. During this period, the nurses consult with the research team to find the best advice to give the caller. Armed with this new information, they call the patient to share the information.

Although this system worked when Pioneering Health in Germany was a smaller operation, it is no longer sufficient. The nurses are stressed because they are unable to meet all their patients' needs, the researchers are under pressure to come up with solutions to a large number of health problems within a short time, and the patients are frustrated at having to wait for the nurses to call them back. Imani arranges a meeting with the technology team, the nurses, and the research team to discuss the design of a new system.

First, the nurses and the research team describe their concerns to the technology team. The technology team asks detailed questions and sketches a rough plan of the problem until everyone agrees on the points that need to be addressed. More discussions follow over a series of meetings until all parties agree on a solution. The outcome of these sessions is a new IT interface embedded in the company's technology platform. When a patient calls, the nurses enter the details of the health issue into a database that has been uploaded with all the research information carried out by the research team to date. The database then returns the information to the nurses in real time. In short, the exchange of information now drives the consultation process.

Once the nurses have been trained to use it, the new system benefits everyone. The researchers can focus on their core roles of information gathering without being under time pressure from the nurses, the nurses are comforted by the extra support they receive from the system and the ability to help patients in a timely manner, and the patients are pleased to be given expert advice in real time. Thanks to Imani's plan to bring the users and technology teams together, a new system has been created that satisfies all parties while enhancing business performance.

Over the course of this textbook we have explored many different facets of organizational behavior supported by the latest theory and research, media, firsthand accounts, and fictional cases. At the core of organizational behavior is an understanding and tolerance of others. As you have learned through our fictional characters, people can be unpredictable, withdrawn, manipulative, enthusiastic, motivated, and thoughtful. Although our characters work in very different industries (the arts, dining, banking, manufacturing, and health management) they all have one thing in common: the desire to work in a fair and respectful organizational environment.

Regardless of the industry you work in, it is people who are the backbone of a successful organization. Knowing how to manage your own behavior as well as the behavior of others lies at the heart of your future career success.

THINKING CRITICALLY

1. Describe the ways in which operations technology and information technology interact to foster greater efficiency and communication within an organization. **[Understand/Apply]**
2. Do you think Imani should have done more to keep Frederick from resigning? If so, what should she have done? If not, why not? **[Analyze/Evaluate]**
3. How would monitoring social media sites allow Cisco to save money on marketing and customer service? Explain your answer. **[Analyze/Evaluate]**
4. When the nursing and research staff at Pioneering Health becomes stressed due to the growth of their workload, why wouldn't it be preferable to simply hire more nurses and researchers, rather than implement a new IT system? **[Analyze/Evaluate]**

IN REVIEW

Learning Objectives

Describe how organizational structure helps shape behavior in organizations

Organizational structure is a framework of work roles that helps shape and support employee behavior. The structure of an organization has significant influence over the behavior of its employees. It groups and separates people geographically, hierarchically, or both; it builds and limits relationships by setting up lines of reporting and teams; and it defines employees' responsibilities by outlining their area of influence and accountability.

17.2

Define basic organizing concepts such as division of labor, chain of command, and span of control

Work specialization or the **division of labor** is the degree to which jobs are divided into specific tasks. **Departmentalization** is a process of grouping people with related job duties, skills, and experiences into the same areas. Some organizations follow a **chain of command**, the flow of authority and power from the highest to the lowest levels. The more direct reports under a manager, the wider the organization's **span of control**. In a centralized structure, senior management makes decisions; in a decentralized organization, employees in the lower levels are given the power to make decisions and solve problems without seeking approval from senior management. The **mechanistic** model is a formalized structure based on centralization and departmentalization. The **organic model** is a less formalized structure based on decentralization and cross-functional teams; decision making is participative and distributed throughout the organization. **Formalization** is the degree to which rules and procedures are standardized in an organization. **Bureaucracy** is characterized by formalized rules and regulation, specialized routine tasks, division of labor, and centralized authority.

Identify the types of organizational structures

In **simple structures** one central authority figure, usually a business owner, tends to make decisions. **Functional structures** group employees according to the tasks they perform for the organization. **Divisional structures** (sometimes called *multidivisional structures*) group employees by products and services, geographic regions, or customers. **Matrix structures** combine functional and divisional departmentalization, with dual lines of authority.

Describe the organizational design process and its connection to organizational behavior

Organizational design is the process of creating or changing a structure of an organization to integrate people, information, and technology. The steps in process are: understanding the business climate, setting the scene, gathering data, and transforming, implementing, and evaluating the design.

Explain how technology can be integrated into organizational structure and design

Technology is the development of scientific knowledge as applied to machinery and devices. **Operations technology** is the combination of processes, knowledge, and techniques that creates product or service value for an organization. **Information technology** is a set of tools, processes, systems, and data communications based on microelectronic technology designed to disseminate information to provide support to individuals in an organization.

KEY TERMS

Bureaucracy 440
Chain of command 437
Departmentalization 437
Division of labor 436
Divisional structure 442
Formalization 440
Functional structures 442
Information technology 448
Matrix structure 444
Mechanistic model 439
Operations technology 448
Organic model 440
Organizational design 446
Organizational structure 433
Simple structures 442
Span of control 438
Technology 448

THINKING CRITICALLY ABOUT THE CASE OF YOLANDE TURNER AND PIONEERING HEALTH

Put yourself in Yolande Turner's position as the CEO of Pioneering Health and consider the five critical-thinking steps in relation to the decision to restructure the company.

OBSERVE

What is the current business climate for Pioneering Health's Frankfurt office, and how is it changing? What is the current organizational structure of the company, and how well is that structure operating in the face of the changing business climate?

INTERPRET

How is the company going to have to change, structurally speaking, to accommodate the business climate? Why are these changes necessary?

ANALYZE

What, in your opinion, is the most effective new organizational structure for Pioneering Health, and why? Which employee roles and responsibilities have to change, and how will they change?

EVALUATE

What are the potential advantages of the new organizational structure? What are some potential disadvantages and/or sources of conflict? Discuss the ways that operational and information technology could fit into the planned reorganization of Pioneering Health.

EXPLAIN

As the CEO of Pioneering Health, what specific steps will you take to reduce sources of conflict related to the redesign of the organization's structure among your employees? Discuss the benefits of each step you choose to take.

EXERCISE 17.1: CREATE AN ORGANIZATIONAL STRUCTURE

Instructions

1. Working by yourself or in a team, choose one of the following organizations (your instructor may assign one to you or your team) and create an organizational structure including spans of control. You may be as traditional or creative in your approach as you like.
   a. Airline
   b. Local fast-food restaurant
   c. National hotel chain
   d. Professional football franchise
   e. Local lawn-care company
   f. College or university
   g. Movie production company
2. Briefly describe your structure and why you chose it.
3. Is your structure more centralized or decentralized? Why?
4. Does your structure have a narrow or wide span or control? Why?
5. Is your structure more organic or more mechanistic? Why?

EXERCISE 17.2: THIS WAY AND THAT WAY

Objectives:

This exercise will help you to better *define* basic organizing concepts, *distinguish* between different organizational structures, and *explain* how technology can be integrated into organizational structure and design.

Instructions:

For this exercise, you will be creating a list of ways in which modern communication and information technologies can be used in developing organizational structure and design. This exercise consists of four steps.

Step 1. Assign yourself to the Violets or the Purples. You are a Violet if your birth date falls on an odd day, and a Purple if it falls on an even day. (1 minute)

Step 2. Form into groups of five to seven students. Each group should consist only of Violets or Purples. (2 minutes)

Step 3. The outcome of this step is the same for both types of groups, but the methods will be different. For both types of groups, create a list of different organizational structures, and basic organizing concepts. Provide a brief overview for these concepts. Then, specific to each concept, write down how information or communication technology can be integrated into the business process/structure to improve an organization´s performance. (10 minutes)

For Violet groups, complete these tasks using a division of labor process.

For purple groups, complete these tasks using an interactive labor process.

Step 4. Be prepared to present your findings and experiences to the class. (1 to 3 minutes)

Reflection Questions:

1. What insights did you gain about integrating technology to improve organizational designs?
2. How might you think your task would have been easier if your team used the other development process?
3. How would it have been more difficult?

Exercise contributed by Milton R. Mayfield, Professor of Business, Texas A&M International University and Jaqueline R. Mayfield, Professor of Business, Texas A&M International University.

EXERCISE 17.3: A CHANGE OF VIEW

Objectives:

Successful completion of this exercise will help you to better *describe* how organizational structure shapes organizational behaviors, *distinguish* between different types of organizational structures, and *describe* the connection between the organizational design process and organizational behaviors.

Background:

You have been a manager at Marée Rouge Cosmetics International for five years now. When you first began at Marée Rouge, there was a marked lack of communication between the product development and marketing departments, and a good bit of distrust or actual hostility between members of these departments. Why these problems existed was not clear, and often even people in long standing feuds seemed to have forgotten the original causes of these disputes. While these conflicts did not prohibit professional working relationships, it was obvious that they were hurting the overall operational effectiveness of two departments that needed to work closely together.

About three years ago, Marée Rouge leased a new building, and was able to house the two departments on the same floor while also giving all areas greater office space. (In the old building, the departments had been housed on separate floors.) Largely due to the greater physical interactions between the departments, you have seen a marked improvement in the communications and work relationships between departmental members. Now there is a strong working relationship between the two areas, and this relationship has lead to faster product development and deployment as well as the initiation of several innovative (and strong selling) new products.

However, partly due to this improved firm performance and revenues, Marée Rouge has increased its workforce and needs to find new office space. Currently, the company is looking at a small office park location where each of the major areas can be housed in separate facilities. The office park is beautiful, is located more centrally to most workers' homes, will be far more comfortable than the existing location, and provides easy access to major suppliers and customers. However, you worry that physically separating the two divisions will destroy their current strong working relationship and may even lead to the same problems that existed before between the divisions.

While you know that the move has already been decided on by top management, you feel sure that they will be willing to listen to well thought out suggestions for maintaining the good relationship between the divisions. In order to develop such relationships, you have asked some of your colleagues to help you draft an overview of the situation and suggested methods for avoiding problems.

Instructions:

Step 1. Form into teams of five to seven students. Draft a presentation for the upper management of Marée Rougue Cosmetics about this issue. In developing this presentation, you will need to detail your desired goals for the move, what potential problems you see the new physical location creating, and suggestions for preventing (or reducing) these potential problems. Use all appropriate chapter concepts in developing this presentation. Also, due to the nature of the link between organizational design and organizational behavior, you should draw upon appropriate concepts from other chapters for your answer as well. (20 to 30 minutes)

Step 2. Be prepared to choose a team spokesperson to give your presentation to the class if called upon by your instructor. (5 to 10 minutes)

Reflection Questions:

1. What new links did you see between organizational design and organizational behavior?
2. What organizational behavior principles could be used to overcome problems with a given organizational design?
3. What organizational design principles could be used to improve organizational behavior problems?
4. Could communication technology be used to help overcome the expected organizational design problems? Why or why not?

Exercise contributed by Milton R. Mayfield, Professor of Business, Texas A&M International University and Jaqueline R. Mayfield, Professor of Business, Texas A&M International University.

CASE STUDY 17.1: VALVE CORPORATION

Gabe Newell was a founder and is the CEO of Valve Corporation, a Bellevue, Washington–based video game maker founded by former Microsoft employees Newell and Mike Harrington—or that's what it says on paper somewhere, anyway. Not surprising, given the loose, fluid structure (or lack thereof) at Valve, Greg Coomer, a designer and artist who was one of the first employees, said of Newell, "I think he's technically the CEO, but it's funny that I'm not even sure of that."

That's because Valve Corporation is not exactly, well, the archetypal vision of a "corporate" environment. Valve doesn't use formal titles, except in the hiring process so as to not scare away prospective applicants who might find the titleless work environment a bit peculiar. Here, desks move on wheels so that employees can relocate anywhere in the office and form work groups at a moment's notice. Employees don't have strict job duties; they fill in where they think they can contribute the most. Valve has no formal bosses, pay is often determined by peers, and employees create their own schedules and workdays.

Valve personifies the trend of recent years to flatten out hierarchies within companies, reducing the role of middle management where information and processes can get clogged, enabling, in theory, a freer flow of communication and increased productivity. "When you're an entertainment company that's spent the last decade going out of its way to recruit the most intelligent, innovative, talented people on Earth, telling them to sit at a desk and do what they're told obliterates 99 percent of their value," states the now-famous employee handbook, which generated buzz in 2012 when it was leaked online. "This company is yours to steer. Toward opportunities and away from risks."

Valve developed Steam, an online service that is basically the iTunes of the video gaming world. Though some say its plans are overambitious, the 300-employee company is competing with Google to develop wearable computing—like video games played through goggles or glasses where you might see a zombie coming out of your own bathroom at home. Even competitors acknowledge that Valve is on the cutting edge of the industry. Valve is responsible for Half-Life—a game that has received numerous "Game of the Year" awards and is still widely regarded as influential among its peers; Half-Life 2, Left 4 Dead, and Counterstrike are among wildly popular and industry-shaping games.

In other flat (also called "lattice") organizations, lines of communication flow directly from one person to the other with no intermediary; there is no fixed or assigned authority; natural leadership is identified by those who follow; and objectives are set by the same employees who have to realize them. In many flat organizations, including Valve, associates decide how much they think their peers should be paid but are never allowed to vote on their own salaries. Teams at Valve decide together whether a team member isn't working out. "We don't have any management, and nobody 'reports to' anybody else," states Valve's employee handbook. Valve said it was rare that anyone chose to leave the company, and when someone did, it was often for something like a sick parent needing help.

There are challenges to the flat approach—like lack of accountability. Though the environment can trigger creativity and collaboration, some still leave for more traditional companies that are more structured and organized. Retaining highly motivated individuals is critical for effectiveness within a flat organization. Discipline and motivation need to be off the chart, but unfortunately, the types of employees that a flat organization requires in order to thrive represent a small segment of the workforce. This type of structure does not work for everyone. Other challenges include talent management, appraising and motivating employees, and enforcing any policy the company might have. There is often a lack of standardization to ensure that salaries and benefits are competitive, internally and externally. Working in a flat organization may feel disorganized and chaotic, which, depending on the employee, can either be a great source of inspiration or great frustration.

"I think of it as being a lot like evolution—messy, with lots of inefficiencies that normal companies don't have—but producing remarkable results, things that would never have seen the light of day under normal hierarchical management," said Michael Abrash, an engineer at Valve. "Almost by definition, it's a great place for the right sort of creative people to work."

Case Questions

1. Would you describe Valve Corporation as a flat organization? Why? Does such a structure seem to be effective for Valve?
2. Describe the potential downsides of a flat or lattice organization. Do you think these consequences outweigh the positives at Valve?
3. Think of Valve as a future employer of your services and skills. Would your personality fit the flat structure of Valve? Why or why not?

Sources

Ramblings in Valve Time. Blog. http://blogs.valvesoftware.com/abrash/valve-how-i-got-here-what-its-like-and-what-im-doing-2/.

Silverman, Rachel Emma. "Who's the Boss? There Isn't One." *Wall Street Journal*. June 19, 2012. http://online.wsj.com/article/SB10001424052702303379204577474953586383604.html.

Wingfield, Nick. "Game Player without a Rule Book." *New York Times*. September 12, 2012. www.nytimes.com/2012/09/09/technology/valve-a-video-game-maker-with-few-rules.html?pagewanted=all&_r=0.

SELF-ASSESSMENT 17.1

Would You Fit in an Organic or a Mechanistic Environment?

For each of the following paired statements, circle the letter next to the statement that best describes you:

1. a. I prefer organizations in which employees work separately and specialize on a single task.
   b. I prefer organizations in which employees work together and coordinate tasks.
2. a. I prefer organizations in which the authority hierarchy is well defined.
   b. I prefer organizations in which people from across the organization work together in teams and task forces.
3. a. I prefer organizations in which decision making is centralized at the top of the organizational structure.
   b. I prefer organizations in which decision making is delegated to the lower levels of the organizational structure.
4. a. I prefer organizations in which there are extensive rules, standards, and procedures.
   b. I prefer organizations in which work processes are informal and unpredictable.
5. a. I prefer organizations in which there is a lot of formal written communication.
   b. I prefer organizations in which there is a lot of informal face-to-face communication.
6. a. I prefer organizations in which there are fixed duties.
   b. I prefer organizations in which there are adaptable duties.
7. a. I prefer organizations in which there are rigid hierarchical relationships.
   b. I prefer organizations in which there is both vertical and horizontal collaboration.

Scoring

Preference for Mechanistic Organizations

Add the total number of a's circled and write that number in the blank. ____________________

Mechanistic organizations tend to have a traditional centralized hierarchical bureaucratic organizational structure. Mechanistic organizations are often found in industries in which there is little change and little competition.

Preference for Organic Organizations

Add up the total number of b's circled above write that number in the blank. ____________________

Organic organizations tend to have nontraditional decentralized organizational structures. Organic organizations are often found in industries characterized by high growth, rapid change, and fierce competition.

GLOSSARY

A

Ability diversity. The representation of people with different levels of mental and physical abilities within an organization

Achievement-oriented leadership. Leadership behavior characterized by setting challenging goals, improving performance, and assisting training

Acquired needs theory. Theory that suggests three main categories of needs: need for achievement, need for affiliation, and need for power

Active listening. The act of concentrating on the true meaning of what others are saying

Adjourning. The stage when individuals either leave the team or have no reason to be in further contact with their teammates

Affects. The range of feelings in form of emotions and moods that people experience

Age diversity. People of all different ages included within the workplace

Analyzer strategy. The means by which organizations try to maintain current products and services with a limited amount of innovation

Anchoring and adjustment heuristic. A process whereby people base their decisions on the first piece of information they are given without taking other probabilities into account

Antecedents of conflict. Factors that set the scene for potential dispute

Anthropology. The study of people and their activities in relation to societal, environmental, and cultural influences

Arbitrator. A neutral third party officially assigned to settle a dispute

Assertiveness. The use of demands or threats to persuade someone to carry out a task

Attitude. A learned tendency to consistently respond positively or negatively to people or events

Attribution theory. A theory that holds that people look for two causes to explain the behavior of others: internal attributions, which are personal characteristics of others, and external attributions, which are situational factors

Authentic leadership. A pattern of leadership behavior based on honesty, practicality, and ethicality

Autocratic style. A leadership style based on making decisions without asking for suggestions from others

Availability heuristic. A rule of thumb for making judgments on examples and events that immediately spring to mind

Awareness of others. The way we are aware (or unaware) of the feelings, behaviors, personalities, likes, and dislikes in other people

B

BATNA. The best possible alternative to a negotiable agreement

Behavioral goals (proximal goals). Short-term goals

Behavioral leadership perspective. The belief that specific behaviors distinguish leaders from nonleaders

Big Five Model. Five basic dimensions of personality to include neuroticism and frequently used to evaluate and assess people in the workplace

Bonus pay. A pay plan that rewards employees for recent performance rather than historical performance

Bounded rationality. The idea that we are restricted by a variety of constraints when making decisions

Brainstorming. The process of generating creative, spontaneous ideas from all members of a group without any criticism or judgment

Bureaucracy. An organizational style characterized by formalized rules and regulation, specialized routine tasks, division of labor, and centralized authority

C

Ceremonies. Events that reinforce the relationship between employees and the organization

Chain of command. The flow of authority and power from the highest to the lowest levels of the organization

Change hindrances. Obstacles that impede progress and make it difficult for the organization to adapt to different situations

Channel richness. The capacity to communicate and understand information between people and organizations

Charismatic leadership. The ability of a leader to use his or her personality or charm to inspire, motivate, and acquire loyalty and commitment from employees

Classical conditioning. A conditioning concept developed by Russian physiologist Ivan Pavlov that suggests that learning can be accomplished through the use of stimuli

Cluster chain. A type of communication that occurs when a group of people broadcast information within a larger group

Coalition building. Gathering the support of others as a reason for another person to agree to a request

Coercive power. A strategy by which a person controls the behavior of others through punishments, threats, or sanctions

Cognitive dissonance. The inconsistency between a person's beliefs, attitudes or behaviors

Cohesion. The degree to which team members connect with each other

Common-information bias. The inclination to overemphasize information held by the majority of group members while failing to consider other perspectives held by the minority

Communication. The act of transmitting thoughts, processes, and ideas through a variety of channels

Competence. The ability to perform work tasks successfully

Competing values framework. A procedure that provides a way to identify, measure, and change organizational culture

Competitive advantage. The edge that gives organizations a more beneficial position than their competitors and allows them to generate more profits and retain more customers

Complete rationality. The assumption that we take in to account every single criterion or possible alternative to make a decision

Compliance. The behavior of targets of influence who agree to readily carry out the requests of the leader

Compressed workweeks. A work arrangement that gives employees the benefit of an extra day off by allowing them to work their usual number of hours in fewer days per pay period

Conceptual skill. The capacity to see the organization as a whole and understand how each part relates to each other and how it fits into its overall environment

Conciliator. A neutral third party who is informally assigned to persuade opponents to communicate

Confirmation bias. The tendency to seek out information that fuels our preexisting views and to discount information that conflicts with our worldview

Conflict. A clash between individuals or groups in relation to different opinions, thought processes, and perceptions

Consideration. A behavioral leadership style demonstrated by leaders who develop mutual trust and respect and actively build interpersonal relationships with their followers

Consultation. The offer of participation or consultation in the decision-making process

Content theories. Theories that explain why people have different needs at different times and how these needs motivate behavior, such as Maslow's hierarchy of needs, Alderfer's ERG theory, McClelland's need theory, and Herzberg's two-factor theory

Contingency leadership perspective. The view that the effectiveness of the leader relates to the interaction of the leader's traits or behaviors with situational factors

Contingency thinking. The approach that describes actions as dependent on the nature of the situation; one size does not fit all

Continuous reinforcement. A reinforcement schedule in which a reward occurs after each instance of a behavior or set of behaviors

Contrast effect. An effect that takes place when people rank something higher or lower than they should as a result of exposure to recent events or situations

Coping. The effort to manage, reduce, or minimize stressors

Correlation. A reciprocal relationship between two or more factors

Counterculture. Values that differ strongly from those of the larger organization

Counterproductive work behaviors. Voluntary behaviors that purposefully disrupt or harm the organization

Creative potential. The skills and capacity to generate ideas

Creativity. The generation of meaningful ideas by individuals or teams

Critical thinking. The ability to use intelligence, knowledge, and skills to question and carefully explore situations and arrive at thoughtful conclusions based on evidence and reason

Cross-cultural leadership. The process of leading across cultures

Cross-functiaonal team. A group of workers from different units with various areas of expertise, assembled to address certain issues

Culture shock. Feelings of nervousness, doubt, and confusion arising from being in a foreign environment

D

DADA syndrome. Four stages—denial, anger, depression, and acceptance—experienced by individuals when they are faced with unwanted change

Decentralization. The distribution of power across all levels of the organization

Decision making. The action or process of identifying a strategy to resolve problems

Deep acting. Efforts to change your actual emotions to better match the required emotions of the situation

Deep-level diversity. Differences in verbal and nonverbal behaviors that are not as easily perceived because they lie below the surface, such as differences in attitudes, values, beliefs, and personality

Defender strategy. The means by which organizations focus on stability and efficiency of their internal operations to protect their market from new competitors

Delegating. The act of giving most of the responsibility to followers while still monitoring progress

Delphi technique. A method of decision making in which information is gathered from a group of respondents within their area of expertise

Departmentalization. A process of grouping people with related job duties, skills, and experiences into different areas within the overall organizational structure

Dependent variable. Factor affected by independent variables

Differing perceptions. The way in which our interpretations of situations clashes with the perceptions of others.

Directive leadership. A leadership style characterized by implementing guidelines, managing expectations, setting definite performance standards, and ensuring that individuals follow rules

Display rules. Basic norms that govern which emotions should be displayed and which should be suppressed

Distress. High levels of stressors that have destructive and negative effects on effort and performance

Distributive bargaining. A strategy that involves two parties trying to claim a "fixed pie" of resources

Distributive justice. The degree to which people think outcomes are fair

Diversity hindrances. Obstacles that limit the range of employees in organizations

Division of labor. The degree to which certain jobs are divided into specific tasks

Divisional strategy. A plan that focuses on how the different departments of the organization comply with the company's vision

Divisional structure (*sometimes called multidivisional structure*). An organizational structure that groups employees by products and services, geographic regions, or customers

Dominant culture. Set of core values shared by the majority of organizational employees

Downward communication. Messages sent from the upper levels of the organizational hierarchy to the lower levels

Dysfunctional conflict. A dispute or disagreement that has negative effects on individuals or teams

E

Ease-of-recall bias. The propensity to over-rely on information recollected from memory when making a decision

Electronic communication. The ability to transmit messages through e-mail, Skype, videoconferencing, blogs, fax, instant messaging, texting, and social networking

Emotional contagion. A phenomenon in which emotions which are experienced by few people of a work group are spread to the others

Emotional dissonance. A discrepancy between the emotions a person displays and the emotions he or she actually feels

Emotional intelligence. The ability to understand emotions in oneself and others in order to effectively manage one's own behaviors and relationships with others

Emotional labor. The process of managing one's feelings to present positive emotions even when they are contrary to one's actual feelings

Emotional regulation. A set of processes through which people influence their own emotions and the ways in which they experience and express them

Emotional stability. The extent to which we can remain calm and composed

Emotion-focused coping. An effort to try to change a person's emotional reaction to a stressor by using positive language and distracting techniques

Emotions. Intense feelings directed at a specific object or person

Employee engagement. A connection with the organization and passion for one's job

Employee stock ownership plans (ESOPs). Plans in which employees purchase stock, often at below market price as a part of their benefits

Empowering leadership. A behavioral type of leadership that empowers leaders to help develop the individual skills and abilities of their followers. Also known as "SuperLeadership"

Equity theory. Theory that holds that motivation is based on our perception of fairness in comparison with others

ERG theory. Theory that suggests that people are motivated by three categories of needs arranged in the form of a hierarchy

Escalation of commitment. The increased commitment to a decision despite negative information

Ethical dilemma. A conflict between two or more morally unpleasant alternatives

Ethical leadership. A means of influencing others through personal values, morals, and beliefs

Ethics. Moral principles that guide our behavior

Ethnicity. Sociological factors such as nationality, culture, language, and ancestry

Ethnocentrism. The tendency to believe that your culture or ethnicity is superior to everyone else's

Eustress. Moderate levels of stressors that have constructive and positive effects on effort and performance

Evidence-based management. The practice of using research-based facts to make decisions

Exchange. The promise of rewards to persuade another person to co-operate

Expatriate. An employee who lives and works in a foreign country on a temporary basis

Expectancy theory. Theory that holds that people will choose certain behaviors over others with the expectation of a certain outcome

Expectancy. The probability that the amount of work effort invested by an individual will result in a high level of performance

Expert power. The ability to influence the behavior of others through the amount of knowledge or expertise possessed by an individual on which others depend

Exploitative innovation. The enhancement and reuse of existing products and processes

Exploratory innovation. Risk taking, radical thinking, and experimentation

External adaptation. A pattern of basic assumptions shared between employees of the goals, tasks, and methods that need to be achieved, together with ways of managing success and failure

External forces. Outside influences for change

External locus of control. The extent to which people believe their performance is the product of circumstances which are beyond their immediate control

Extinction. A reinforcement contingency in which a behavior is followed by the absence of any consequence, thereby reducing the likelihood that the behavior will be repeated in the same or similar situations

Extrinsic rewards. External awards to employees such as salary, bonuses, and paid vacations

F

Filtering. The process of screening and then manipulating a message from a sender before passing it on to the intended receiver

First mover. An organization that wins competitive advantage by being the first to establish itself in a particular market

Flextime. Flexible working hours in which employees customize their own work hours within limits established by management

Followership. Individuals' capacity to cooperate with leaders

Formal networks. The transmission of messages established and approved by the organizational hierarchy

Formalization. The degree to which rules and procedures are standardized in an organization

Forming. A process whereby team members meet for the first time, get to know each other, and try to understand where they fit in to the team structure

Framing error. The tendency to highlight certain aspects of a situation depending on whether they are positive or negative to solve a problem while ignoring other aspects

Free agents. Independent workers that supply organizations with short-term talent for projects or time-bound objectives

Functional conflict. A constructive and healthy dispute between individuals or groups

Functional strategy. A set of rules determining how each department will implement the strategic plan

Functional structures. Organizational structures that group employees according to the tasks they perform for the organization

Fundamental attribution error. The tendency to underestimate the influence of external factors and overestimate the impact of internal factors when making judgments about the behavior of others

G

Gain sharing. A system whereby managers agree to share the benefits of cost savings with staff in return for their contribution to the company's performance

Gender diversity. The way different genders are treated in the workplace

Glass ceiling. An invisible barrier that limits one's ability to progress to more senior positions

Globalization. The integration of economy, trade, and finance on an international scale

Goal-setting theory. Theory that suggests that human performance is directed by conscious goals and intentions

Gossip chains. A type of communication that occurs when one individual creates and spreads untrue or inaccurate information through the organization

Grafting. A process of hiring experts to bring their knowledge to a firm

Grapevine. An unofficial line of communication between individuals or groups

Group. Three or more people who work independently to attain organizational goals

Groupthink. A psychological phenomenon in which people in a cohesive group go along with the group consensus rather than offering their own opinions

H

Halo effect. A perception problem through which we form a positive or negative bias of an individual based on our overall impressions of that person

Heuristics. Shortcuts or "rules of thumb" that allow us to make judgments and decisions quickly and efficiently

Hierarchy of needs theory. Maslow's theory that suggests people are motivated by their desire to satisfy specific needs, and that needs are arranged in a hierarchy with physiological needs at the bottom and self-actualization needs at the top

High-context cultures. Cultures in which meaning is conveyed through body language, nonverbal cues, and the circumstances in which the communication is taking place

High-involvement management. The way managers empower employees to make decisions, provide them with extensive training and the opportunities to increase their knowledge base, share important information, and provide incentive compensation

Hindsight bias. The tendency to overestimate the ability to predict an outcome of an event

HIPOs. High-potential employees who are flexible, committed, and motivated

Human capital inimitability. The degree to which the skills and talents of employees can be emulated by other organizations

Human capital rareness. The skills and talents of an organization's people that are unique in the industry

Human capital value. The way employees work toward the strategic goals of an organization to achieve competitive advantage

Human capital. People's skills, knowledge, experience, and general attributes

Human skills. The ability to relate to other people

Hygiene factors. Sources of job satisfaction such as salary, status, and security

Hypothesis. A statement that specifies the relationships between the two variables

I

Idealized influence. Behavior that gains the admiration, trust, and respect of followers, who in turn follow the leader's example with their own actions

Impact. The feeling of making a difference

Implicit followership theories. Preconceived notions about the types of behaviors that characterize followers and nonfollowers

Implicit leadership theories. Hypotheses that explore the extent to which we distinguish leaders and nonleaders based on underlying assumptions, stereotypes, and beliefs

Impression management. The process by which we attempt to influence the perceptions others may have of us

Independent variables. Factors that remain unchanged

Individual differences. The degree to which people exhibit behavioral similarities and differences

Individualist–collectivist. The degree to which employees believe they have the right to live their lives as they see fit, choose their own values, and act on their own judgment

Individualized consideration. Leader behavior associated with creating mutual respect or trust and a genuine concern for the needs and desires of others

Informal networks. A casual form of sharing information between employees across company divisions

Information control. a hard influencing tactic in which key information is withheld in order to manipulate outcomes

Information overload. Exposure to an overwhelming amount of information

Information technology (IT). A set of tools, processes, systems, and data communications based on microelectronic technology, designed to disseminate information to provide support to individuals in an organization

Ingratiation. A strategy of winning favor and putting oneself in the good graces of others before making a request

In-group exchange. Interaction that occurs when leaders and followers develop good working relationships based on mutual trust, respect, and a sense of sharing common fates

Initiating structure. A behavioral leadership style demonstrated by leaders who define the roles of the employees, set clear guidelines and procedures, and establish distinct patterns of organization and communication

Innovation. The creation and development of a new product or service

Inspirational appeals. The use of emotions to raise enthusiasm for the task by appealing to the values and ideals of others

Inspirational motivation. Leadership behaviors that promote commitment to a shared vision of the future

Instrumentality. The probability that good performance will lead to various work outcomes.

Integrative bargaining. A strategy that involves both parties negotiating a win–win solution

Intellectual stimulation. Stimuli that encourage people to think and promote intelligence, logic, and problem solving

Interdependence. The extent to which team members rely on each other to complete their work tasks

Intergroup development. The process of finding ways to change the attitudes, perceptions, and stereotypes that employees may have of each other

Intermittent reinforcement. Reinforcement schedule in which a reward does not occur after each instance of a behavior or set of behaviors

Internal forces. Inside influences for change

Internal integration. A shared identity with agreed-upon methods of working together

Internal locus of control. The degree to which people believe they control the events and consequences which affect their lives

Intrinsic motivation. The performance of tasks for our own innate satisfaction

Intuition. An unconscious process of making decisions based on imagination and possibilities

J

Job characteristics model. Five core dimensions of jobs: skill variety, task identity, task significance, autonomy, and feedback

Job content–based pay. A salary paid based on the evaluation of a job's worth

Job design. A method of setting duties and responsibilities of a job with the intention of improving productivity and performance

Job enlargement. An increase in the range of tasks and duties associated with a job

Job enrichment. An increase in the scope of a job to make it more complex, interesting, stimulating, and satisfying for employees

Job rotation. A process of periodically moving staff employees from one job to another

Job satisfaction. The degree to which an individual feels positive or negative about a job

Job sharing. An employment option in which one full-time job is divided among two or more people according to predetermined hours

Justice approach. A way to base decisions on the basis of the fairness

L

Lack of participation error. The inclination to exclude certain people from the decision-making process

Laissez-faire leadership. Leadership behavior that fully delegates responsibility to others

Lateral communication. Messages sent between and among the same hierarchical levels across organizations

Leader emergence. The natural occurrence of someone becoming the leader of a leaderless group

Leader-exchange theory. A theory of leadership that focuses on the relationships between leaders and their group members.

Leader–member relations. Relationships that reflect the degree of confidence, trust, and respect that exists between subordinates and their leaders

Leader's position power. The level of power a leader possesses to reward or punish, or promote and demote

Leadership grid. An approach that plots concern for production on the horizontal axis and concern for people on the vertical axis where 1 is the least concern and 9 is the greatest concern

Leadership prototypes. Behaviors that people associate with leadership

Leadership. The process of providing general direction, from a position of influence, to individuals or groups toward the successful attainment of goals

Learning organization. An organization that facilitates the acquisition, distribution, and retention of knowledge to enable it to react to change

Learning. An ongoing process through which individuals adjust their behavior based on experience

Least preferred coworker (LPC) questionnaire. An instrument that purports to measure whether a person is task oriented or relationship oriented

Legitimate power. The degree to which a person has the right to ask others to do things that are considered within the scope of their authority

Localization. The process of adapting certain functions to accommodate the language, culture, or governing laws of a country

Locus of control. The extent to which people feel they have influence over events

Long-term orientation. The measurement of values such as perseverance, respect for tradition, and thrift

Low-context cultures. Cultures that depend on explicit messages conveyed through the spoken or written word

M

Machiavellianism. A philosophy that describes people who manipulate others and use unethical practices for personal gain

Manifest conflict stage. The stage at which people engage in behaviors that provoke a response

Matrix structure. An organizational structure that combines both functional and divisional departmentalization together with dual lines of authority

Meaningfulness. The value of work tasks in line with a person's own self-concepts and ideals

Mechanistic model. A formalized structure based on centralization and departmentalization

Mediator. A neutral third party who attempts to assist parties in a negotiation to find a resolution or come to an agreement using rational arguments and persuasion

Mergers and acquisition hindrances. Obstacles that make it difficult for two organizations to join together

Merit pay. A pay plan consisting of a pay rise which is linked directly to performance

Mimicry. The process of learning from the successful practices of others

Model. A simplified snapshot of reality

Moods. Generalized positive or negative feelings of mind

Motivation. Forces from within individuals that stimulate and drive them to achieve goals

Motivators. Sources of job satisfaction such as achievement, recognition, and responsibility

N

Need for achievement. Need to perform well against a standard of excellence

Need for affiliation. Need to be liked and to stay on good terms with most other people

Need for competence. The motivation derived from stretching and exercising our capabilities

Need for power. Desire to influence people and events

Need for self-determination. The state of motivation and control gained through making efforts that are not reliant on any external influences

Negative affect. A mood dimension that consists of emotions such as nervousness, stress, and anxiety at the high end and relaxation, tranquility, and poises the low end.

Negative reinforcement. A reinforcement contingency through which behaviors are followed by the removal of previously experienced negative consequences, resulting in the likelihood that the behavior will occur again in the same or similar situations

Negotiation. The process of reaching an agreement that both parties find acceptable

Neuroticism. A personality trait that involves being tense, moody, irritable, and temperamental

Neutralizing. The substitution of leadership attributes that do not affect follower outcomes

Nominal group technique. A structured way for team members to generate ideas and identify solutions in which each member is asked the same question in relation to a work issue and requested

GLOSSARY

to write as many answers as possible. Answers are read aloud and voted upon

Non-programmed decisions. New or nonroutine problems for which there are no proven answers

Nonverbal communication. The transmission of wordless cues between people

Norming. The process by which team members resolve the conflict and begin to work well together and become more cohesive

Norms. The informal rules of a team's behavior that govern the team

O

Observable culture. The components of culture that can be seen in an organization

Open systems theory. The assumption that organizations are systems that interact with their environments to obtain resources or inputs and transform them into outputs returned to the environment for consumption

Operant conditioning. The process of forming associations between learning and behavior by controlling its consequences

Operational planning. The process of aligning the strategic plan to the day-to-day tasks required in the running of the organization

Operations technology. The combination of processes, knowledge and techniques that creates product or service value for an organization

Oral communication. The ability to give and exchange information, ideas, and processes verbally, either one on one or as a group

Organic model. A less formalized structure based on decentralization and cross-functional teams

Organization structural innovation. The introduction or modification of work assignments, authority relationships, and communication and reward systems within an organization

Organization. A structured arrangement of people working together to accomplish specific goals

Organizational behavior modification. The use of behavioral techniques to reinforce positive work behavior and discourage unhelpful work behavior.

Organizational behavior. A field of study focused on understanding, explaining, and improving attitudes of individuals and groups in organizations

Organizational citizenship behavior. Discretionary and voluntary behavior that is not a part of the employee's specific role requirements and is not formally rewarded

Organizational cultural lag. The deficit in organizations that fail to keep up with new emerging innovations

Organizational culture. A pattern of shared norms, rules, values, and beliefs that guide the attitudes and behaviors of its employees

Organizational design. The process of creating or changing a structure of an organization to integrate people, information, and technology

Organizational development (OD). A deliberately planned system that uses behavioral science knowledge to increase the efficiency and effectiveness of an organization

Organizational justice. The perception of fairness in workplace practices

Organizational language. Words or metaphors and expressions specific to an organization

Organizational politics. Behavior that is not formally sanctioned by the organization and that is focused on maximizing our self-interest, often at the expense of the organization or other employees

Organizational strategy. The process of creating, evaluating, and implementing decisions and objectives to achieve long-term competitive success

Organizational structure. A framework of work roles that helps shape and support employee behavior

Outcomes conflict stage. The stage that describes the consequences of the dispute

Out-group exchange. Interaction that occurs when leaders and followers fail to create a sense of mutual trust, respect, or common fate

P

Participating. Leadership behavior in which both leaders and followers work together and share in the decision-making responsibilities of the task

Participative leadership. A leadership style that favors consulting with followers and considering their input in decision making

Part-time workers. (similar to *free agents*). Independent workers who supply organizations with part-time talent for projects or time-bound objectives

Path–goal leadership theory. A theory that proposes that leadership effectiveness depends on the degree to which the leader enhances the performance of followers by guiding them on a defined track towards achieving their goals

People innovation. Changes in the beliefs and behaviors of individuals working in an organization

Perceived inequity. The sense of feeling under-rewarded or over-rewarded in comparison with others

Perceived/felt conflict stage. The stage at which emotional differences are sensed and felt

Perception. The process by which we receive and interpret information from our environment

Performance goals (distal). Long-term goals set into the future

Performance-based pay. A financial incentive awarded to employees for meeting certain goals or objectives

Performing. The way in which a team is invested towards achieving its goals and operates as a unit

Personal appeals. Requests to cooperate on the basis of friendship or as a personal favor

Personal conception traits. The degree to which individuals relate to and think about their social and physical environment and their personal beliefs regarding a range of issues

Personality traits. Characteristics that describe our thoughts, feelings, and behaviors

Personality. A stable and unique pattern of traits, characteristics, and resulting behaviors that gives an individual his or her identity

Person–organization fit. The degree of compatibility between job candidates and organizations

Piece rate. A pay plan in which workers are paid a fixed sum for each unit of production completed

Political science. The study of the behavior of individuals and groups within a political environment

Political skill. The ability to understand and influence others for the good of the organization

Pooled interdependence. An organizational model in which each team member produces a piece of work independently of the other members

Positive affect. A mood dimension that consists of emotions such as excitement, self-assurance, and cheerfulness at the high end and boredom, sluggishness, and tiredness at the low end

Positive organizational behavior. The strengths, virtues, vitality, and resilience of individuals and organizations

Positive reinforcement. A reinforcement contingency through which behaviors followed by positive consequences, are more likely to occur again in the same or similar situations

Power distance. The extent to which people in different societies accept the way power is distributed.

Power. The capacity to influence the actions of others

Practiced creativity. The ability to seize opportunities to apply creative skills in the workplace

Primacy effect. A perception problem through which an individual assesses a person quickly on the basis of the first information encountered.

Proactive personality. The tendency for individuals to take the initiative to change their circumstances

Problem-focused coping. A type of coping that aims at reducing or eliminating stressors by attempting to understand the problem and seeking practical ways in which to resolve it

Problem-solving team. A group of workers coming together for a set amount of time to discuss specific issues

Procedural justice. The degree to which people perceive the implementation of company policies and procedures to be fair

Process conflict. The clash in viewpoints in relation to how to carry out work

Process consultation. An intervention that involves increasing group awareness and/or understanding

Process gains. Factors that contribute to team effectiveness

Process innovation. The introduction of new or improved operational and work methods

Process losses. Factors that detract from team effectiveness

Process theories. Theories that describe the cognitive processes through which needs are translated into behavior, such as equity theory, expectancy theory, and goal-setting theory

Processing. The act of understanding and remembering what is being said as well as making an effort to empathize with the speaker's feelings and thoughts and the situation at hand.

Product innovation. The development of new or improved goods or services that are sold to meet customer needs

Production-oriented leader. A leader who tends to focus more on the technical or task aspects of the job

Productive forgetting. The ability to abandon a solution that isn't working in favor of a new one

Profit sharing. Sharing profits with employees of an organization by the owners

Programmed decisions. Automatic responses to routine and recurring situations

Projecting. A process through which people ascribe their own personal attributes onto others

Projection bias. The inclination to believe other people think, feel, and act the same way we do

Prospector strategy. A means through which organizations focus on innovation, creativity, and flexibility and take high risks to accelerate growth and gain competitive advantage

Psychological empowerment. The extent to which employees feel a sense of personal fulfillment and intent when carrying out tasks, together with a belief that their work contributes to some larger purpose

Psychology. The scientific study of the human mind that seeks to measure and explain behavioral characteristics

Punishment. A reinforcement contingency that discourages undesirable behavior by administering unpleasant consequences

Q

Quality of worklife (QWL). The relationship between the employees and the workplace

R

Race. Identifying biological factors such as skin, hair, or eye color

Randomness error. The tendency for people to believe they can predict the outcome of chance events based on false information or superstition

Rational appeals. The use of logic, reason, and evidence to convince another person that cooperation in a task is worthwhile

Reactor strategy. A means through which organizations respond to environmental threats and opportunities rather than following a defined plan

Recency effect. A perception problem through which we use the most recent information available to assess a person

Reciprocal interdependence. An organizational model in which team members work closely together on a piece of work, consulting with each other, providing each other with advice, and exchanging information

Referent power. The degree to which a leader can influence others through their desire to identify and be associated with them

Reinforcement theory. A theory that states that behavior is a function of its consequences and is determined exclusively by environmental factors such as external stimuli and other reinforcers

Reinforcement. The application of consequences to establish patterns of behavior

Relationship conflict. The clash in personalities between two or more individuals

Representativeness heuristic. A shortcut that bases a decision on our existing mental prototype and similar stereotypes

Resistance to change. The unwillingness to accept or support modifications in the workplace

Responding. The way active listeners provide feedback to the speaker

Reward power. The extent to which someone uses incentives to influence the actions of others

Rights approach. A decision-making method based on using moral principles that least infringe on the entitlements of others

Risk-taking propensity. The tendency to engage in behaviors that might have positive or negative outcomes

Rituals. Formalized actions and planned routines

S

Satisficing decisions. Solutions that aim for acceptable results rather than for the best or optimal ones

Scanning. The search for solutions from outside consultants, competitors, and other successful firms

Scientific management. Early 20th century theory introduced by Frederick Taylor and his colleagues that analyzes workflow through systematic observation or reasoning

Selective attention. The tendency to selectively focus on aspects of situations that are most aligned with our own interests, values, and attitudes

Self-awareness. Being aware of our own feelings, behaviors, personalities, likes, and dislikes

Self-concept. The beliefs we have about who we are and how we feel about ourselves

Self-determination. The understanding of skills, knowledge, and strengths that enable a person to make choices and initiate work tasks

Self-efficacy. The belief we have in our ability to succeed in a specific task or situation

Self-esteem. The beliefs we have about our own worth following the self-evaluation process

Self-fulfilling prophecy. The way a person behaves based on pre-existing expectations about another person or situation so as to create an outcome that is aligned with those expectations

Self-leadership. A process whereby people intentionally influence their thinking and behavior to achieve their objectives

Self-managing team. A group of workers who manage their daily duties under little to no supervision

Self-monitoring. Adjusting our behavior to accommodate different situations

Self-regulation. A process whereby people set goals, creating a discrepancy between the desired state and the current state

Self-serving bias. The tendency for individuals to attribute their own successes to internal factors and put the blame for failures on external factors

Selling. Leadership behavior characterized by support provided to followers through communication and "selling" them the aims of the task in order to gain commitment

Seniority-based pay. Guaranteed wages and salary increases based on the amount of time the employee has spent with the organization

Sensing. The way listeners pay attention to the signals sent from the speaker

Sensitivity training. A type of program designed to raise awareness of group dynamics and any existing prejudices toward others

Sequential interdependence. An organizational model in which one team member completes a piece of work and passes it on to the next member for their input, similar to an assembly line

Servant leadership. A pattern of leadership that places an emphasis on employees and the community rather than on the leader

Sexual orientation. A person's sexual identity and the gender(s) to which she or he is attracted

Shared leadership. A style of leadership that distributes influence among groups and individuals to achieve organizational or team goals

Short-term orientation. The measurement of values such as meeting social obligations and avoiding embarrassment or shame

Silent authority. an influencing tactic that relies on unspoken but acknowledged power

Simple structures. Organizational structures, common in small organizations where is there is one central authority figure, usually a business owner, who tends to make decisions

Situational leadership model. A leadership model that proposes leaders should adapt their leadership style based on the types of people they are leading and the requirements of the task

Skill-based pay. A system of pay that rewards employees for the acquisition and the development of new skills that lead to enhanced work performance

Social cognitive theory. A theory that proposes that learning takes place through the observation, imitation, and the modeling of others within a social context

Social facilitation. The tendency for individuals to perform tasks better when they are in the presence of others

Social loafing. A phenomenon wherein people put forth less effort when they work in teams than when they work alone

Social psychology. The social science that blends concepts from sociology and psychology and focuses on how people influence each other in a social setting

Socialization. The process through which an organization communicates its values to new employees

Sociology. The study of the behavior of groups and how they relate to each other in a social setting

Sociotechnical systems. The interaction between human behavior and technical systems

Span of control. The number of direct reports to a given manager following an expansion

Spiritual leadership. A values-based style of leadership that motivates employees through faith, hope, and vision and encourages positive social emotions such has forgiveness and gratitude

Standardization. The degree to which employees are expected to follow the same rules and policies everywhere

Stereotypes. An individual's fixed beliefs about the characteristics of a particular group

Stories. Narratives based on real organizational experiences that have become embellished over time and illustrate core cultural values

Storming. A phase during which, after a period of time, tension may arise between members and different personalities might clash, leading to tension and conflict in the team

Strategic OB approach. The idea that people are the key to productivity, competitive edge, and financial success

Strategic planning. The process through which a focus on the desired future sets out defined goals and objectives to translate the vision into reality

Stressors. Environmental stimuli that place demands on individuals

Subcultures. Groups in an organization who share different values to those held by the majority

Subordinate characteristics. Situational contingencies such as anxiety, inflexibility, perceived ability, locus of control, and close-mindedness

Substitutes for leadership model. A model that suggests certain characteristics of the situation can constrain the influence of the leader.

Sunk cost bias. The decision to continue an investment based on past investments of time, effort, and/or money

Supportive leadership. A leadership behavior characterized by friendliness and concern for the welfare of others

Surface acting. A person suppresses their true feelings while displaying the organizationally desirable ones

Surface-level diversity. Easily perceived differences between people, such as age/generation, race/ethnicity, gender, and ability

Symbols. Objects that provide meaning about a culture

Synergy. The concept that the total amount of work produced by a team is greater than the amount of work produced by individual members working independently

T

Tactical planning. The short-term actions and plans to implement the strategy

Task characteristics. Situational contingencies outside the follower's control, such as team dynamics, authority systems, and task structure

Task conflict. The clash between individuals in relation to the direction, content, or goal of a certain assignment

Task structure. The degree to which job assignments are defined

Team. A group of people brought together to use their individual skills on a common project or goal

Technical skill. The aptitude to perform and apply specialized tasks

Technology. The development of scientific knowledge as applied to machinery and devices

Telecommuting. Working from home or from a remote location on a computer or other advanced telecommunications that are linked to the office

Telling. A leadership behavior characterized by giving clear instructions and guidance to followers, informing them exactly how and when to complete the task

Theory. A set of principles intended to explain behavioral phenomena in organizations

Three-component model of creativity. A model proposing that individual creativity relies on domain-relevant skills and expertise, creativity-relevant processes, and intrinsic task motivation

Trait leadership perspective. A theory that explores the relationship between leaders and personal qualities and characteristics and how they differentiate leaders from nonleaders

Transactional leadership. A behavioral type of leadership that proposes that employees are motivated by goals and equitable rewards

Transforming. The process that occurs when people begin to make peace with their doubts and uncertainties and begin to embrace the new direction of the company External forces. Outside influences for change

Triadic reciprocal model of behavior. A model that shows human functioning shaped by three factors that are reciprocally related: reinforcement, cognitive processes, and behavior

Trust. The dependence on the integrity, ability, honesty, and reliability of someone or something else

Two-factor theory (*motivation-hygiene theory or dual theory*). The impact of motivational influences on job satisfaction

Type A orientation. The way people are characterized as competitive, impatient, aggressive, and achievement oriented

Type B orientation. The way people are characterized as relaxed, easygoing, patient, and noncompetitive

U

Uncertainty avoidance. the degree to which people are able to deal with the unexpected and how they cope with uncertainty in unstructured environments

Unobservable culture. The components that lie beneath the surface of an organization, such as company values and assumptions

Upward appeals. The argument that the task has been requested by higher management, or a request to higher management to assist in gaining cooperation

Upward communication. Messages sent from the lower levels of the organizational hierarchy to the higher levels

Utilitarian approach. Action that results in the greater good for the majority of people

V

Valence. The value individuals place on work outcomes

Value chain. The sequence of activities carried out by organizations to create valued goods and services to consumers

Vicarious learning. A process of learning by watching the actions or behaviors of another person

Virtual teams. Groups of individuals from different locations work together through e-mail, video conferencing, instant messaging, and other electronic media

Visibility. The awareness of others regarding your presence in an organization

Visionary leadership. A behavioral type of leadership that creates visions to motivate, inspire, and stimulate employees

W

Wellness program. A personal or organizational effort to promote health and wellbeing through providing access to services like medical screenings, weight management, health advice, and exercise programs

Workplace diversity. The degree to which an organization represents different cultures

Written communication. Messages communicated through the written word, such as e-mails, reports, memos, letters, and other channels

Z

ZOPA. The zone of possible agreement, the area where two sides in a negotiation may find common ground

Chapter 1

1. For an overview of the field of organizational behavior see: Thompson, Leigh, and Jo-Ellen Pozner. "Organizational Behavior." In *Social Psychology: Handbook of Basic Principles* (2nd ed.), 913–939 (New York: Guilford, 2007); Greenberg, Jerald. *Organizational Behavior: The State of the Science* (2nd ed.) (Mahwah, NJ: Erlbaum, 2003).
2. Fayol, Henri. *Industrial and General Administration* (Paris: Dunod, 1916).
3. Katz, Robert L. "Skills of an Effective Administrator." *Harvard Business Review* 34, no. 2 (March 1956): 127; Cai, Houqing. "Management Development: A Principles Framework and Critical Skills Approach." *Human Systems Management* 33, no. 4 (September 2014): 207–212.
4. Ibid.
5. Ibid.
6. Salovey, Peter, and John D. Mayer. "Emotional Intelligence." *Imagination, Cognition and Personality* 9, no. 3 (1989): 185–211; Stough, Con, Donald H. Saklofske, and James D. A. Parker. "A Brief Analysis of 20 Years of Emotional Intelligence: An Introduction to Assessing Emotional Intelligence: Theory, Research, and Applications." In *Assessing Emotional Intelligence: Theory, Research, and Applications*, 3–8 (New York: Springer Science + Business Media, 2009).
7. Katz, "Skills of an Effective Administrator; Cai, "Management Development."
8. Crook, T. Russell, Samuel Y. Todd, James G. Combs, David J. Woehr, and David J. Ketchen Jr. "Does Human Capital Matter? A Meta-analysis of the Relationship between Human Capital and firm Performance." *Journal of Applied Psychology* 96, no. 3 (May 2011): 443–456; Wright, Patrick M., Russell Coff, and Thomas P. Moliterno, "Strategic Human Capital: Crossing the Great Divide." *Journal of Management* 40, no. 2 (February 2014): 353–370.
9. Hatch, Nile W., and Jeffrey H. Dyer. "Human Capital and Learning as a Source of Sustainable Competitive Advantage." *Strategic Management* 25, no. 12 (December 2004): 1155–1178; Lawler, Edward E. III. "Make Human Capital a Source of Competitive Advantage." *Organizational Dynamics* 38, no. 1 (January 2009): 1–7; Campbell, Benjamin A., Russell Coff, and David Kryscynski. "Rethinking Sustained Competitive Advantage from Human Capital." *Academy of Management Review* 37, no. 3 (July 2012): 376–395.
10. Hatch and Dyer, "Human Capital and Learning"; Lawler, "Make Human Capital a Source of Competitive Advantage"; Campbell et al., "Rethinking Sustained Competitive Advantage from Human Capital."
11. See for example, Dunn, Dana S., Jane S. Halonen, and Randolph A. Smith. *Teaching Critical Thinking in Psychology: A Handbook of Best Practices* (n.p.: Wiley-Blackwell, 2008); Stanovich, Keith E., and Paula J. Stanovich. "A Framework for Critical Thinking, Rational Thinking, and Intelligence." In *Innovations in Educational Psychology: Perspectives on Learning, Teaching, and Human Development,* 195–237 (New York: Springer, 2010).
12. See for example, Lennon, Chauncy. "Lack of Skilled Workers Threatens Economic Growth." *U.S. News & World Report,* October 30, 2014. www.usnews.com/news/stem-solutions/articles/2014/10/30/lack-of-skilled-workers-threatens-economic-growth-in-stem-fields.
13. Casserly, Meghan. "The 10 Skills That Will Get You Hired in 2013." Forbes.com. December 10, 2012. www.forbes.com/sites/meghancasserly/2012/12/10/the-10-skills-that-will-get-you-a-job-in-2013/.
14. Conference Board, Are They Really Ready to Work? Employers' Perspectives on the Basic Knowledge and Applied Skills of New Entrants to the 21st-Century U.S. Workforce. Study conducted by The Conference Board, Partnership for 21st-Century Skills, Corporate Voices for Working Families, and the Society for Human Resource Management, 2006.
15. B. Hagemann and J. M. Chartrand. 2009 Trends in Executive Development: A Benchmark Report. Technical report (Oklahoma City: Executive Development Associates, 2009).
16. Deniz S. Ones, and Stephan Dilchert. "How Special Are Executives? How Special Should Executive Selection Be? Observations and Recommendations." *Industrial and Organizational Psychology* 2, no. 2 (June 2009): 163–170.
17. Casserly, "10 Skills."
18. Kuncel, Nathan R., and Sarah A. Hezlett. "Fact and Fiction in Cognitive Ability Testing for Admissions and Hiring Decisions." *Current Directions in Psychological Science* 19, no. 6 (December 2010): 339–345.
19. Wolfe, Alexandra. "Weekend Confidential: Daniel Ek." *Wall Street Journal,* June 21, 2013. http://online.wsj.com/news/articles/SB10001424127887323566804578553691334279504.
20. For an overview of the scientific method and theory testing in the behavioral sciences see: Marczyk, Geoffrey, David DeMatteo, and David Festinger. *Essentials of Research Design and Methodology* (Hoboken, NJ: Wiley, 2005).
21. Rousseau, Denise M. (Ed.). *The Oxford Handbook of Evidence-Based* Management (New York: Oxford University Press, 2012).
22. Emery, Merrelyn. "Refutation of Kira and van Eijnatten's Critique of the Emery's Open Systems Theory." *Systems Research and Behavioral Science* 27, no. 6 (November 2010): 697–712; Rosen, Ned A. "Open Systems Theory in an Organizational Sub-System: A Field Experiment." *Organizational Behavior and Human Performance* 5, no. 3 (1970): 245–265.
23. Gertner, Moryosseff Iris. "The Value Chain and Value Creation." *Advances in Management* 6, no. 10 (October 2013): 1–4; Champion, David. "Mastering the Value Chain." *Harvard Business Review* 79, no. 6 (June 2001): 108–115.
24. Jonsen, Karsten, et al. "The Tragedy of the Uncommons: Reframing Workforce Diversity." *Human Relations* 66, no. 2 (February 2013): 271–294; Sreedhar, Uma. "Workforce Diversity and HR Challenges." *Advances in Management* 4, no. 10 (October 2011): 33–36.
25. "PepsiCo to No Longer Call Naked Juices 'Natural.'" *USA Today,* July 26, 2013. www.usatoday.com/story/money/business/2013/07/26/pepsi-co-naked-juice-not-natural/2589717/.
26. Mutnick, Ally. "New Business School Aims to Build Moral Corporate Leaders." *USA Today,* June 5, 2013. www.usatoday.com/story/news/nation/2013/06/04/catholic-university-business-school/2389499/.
27. See for example, Thompson and Pozner, *Organizational Behavior.*
28. Van Wyden, Genevieve, "Examples of Great Teamwork." *Houston Chronicle.* http://smallbusiness.chron.com/examples-great-teamwork-12607.html.
29. Frenz, Roslyn, "Google's Organizational Structure." http://www.ehow.co.uk/about_6692920_google_s-organizational-structure.htm.
30. Campbell Quick, James, Cary L. Cooper, Philip C. Gibbs, Laura M. Little, and Debra L. Nelson. "Positive Organizational Behavior at Work." In *International Review of Industrial and Organizational Psychology* 2010 (Vol. 25), 253–291 (n.p.: Wiley-Blackwell, 2010); Luthans, Fred, and Bruce J. Avolio. "The 'Point' of Positive Organizational Behavior." *Journal of Organizational Behavior* 30, no. 2 (February 2009): 291–307.
31. Zatzick, Christopher D., and Roderick D. Iverson. "High-Involvement Management and Workforce Reduction: Competitive Advantage or Disadvantage?" *Academy of Management Journal* 49, no. 5 (October 2006): 999–1015; Wood, Stephen, Marc Van Veldhoven, Marcel Croon, and Lilian M. de Menezes. "Enriched Job Design, High Involvement Management and Organizational Performance: The Mediating Roles of Job Satisfaction and Well-Being." *Human Relations* 65, no. 4 (April 2012): 419–445.
32. Steiner Sports. "Healthy Discrimination." June 3, 2013. http://brandonsteiner.com/blog/healthy-discrimination/.
33. Ibid.
34. Ibid.

Chapter 2

1. For a recent review of diversity research see: Plaut, Victoria C., Sapna Cheryan, and Flannery G. Stevens, "New Frontiers in Diversity Research: Conceptions of Diversity and Their Theoretical and Practical Implications." In *APA Handbook of Personality and Social Psychology, Volume 1: Attitudes and Social Cognition*, 593–619 (Washington, DC: American Psychological Association, 2015).
2. Lu, Chia-Mei, Shyh-Jer Chen, Pei-Chi Huang, and Jui-Ching Chien, "Effect of Diversity on Human Resource Management and Organizational Performance." *Journal of Business Research* 68, no. 4 (April 2015): 857–861; Peretz, Hilla, Ariel Levi, and Yitzhak Fried, "Organizational Diversity Programs across Cultures: Effects on Absenteeism, Turnover, Performance and Innovation." *International Journal of Human Resource Management* 26, no. 6 (March 2015). 875–903; *Global Diversity and Inclusion: Fostering Innovation through a Diverse Workforce* (New York: Forbes/Insights).
3. www.diversityinc.com/the-diversityinc-top-50-companies-for-diversity-2015/
4. Broughton, Ashley. "Minorities Expected to Be Majority in 2050." *CNN*. August 13, 2008. http://edition.cnn.com/2008/US/08/13/census.minorities/.
5. Harrison, David A., Kenneth H. Price, Joanne H. Gavin, and Anna T. Florey. "Time, Teams, and Task Performance: Changing Effects of Surface- and Deep-Level Diversity on Group Functioning." *Academy of Management Journal* 45, no. 5 (October 2002): 1029–1045.
6. Bieling, Gisela I., and Florian Dorozalla. "Making the Most of Age Diversity: How Age Diversity Climate Contributes to Employee Performance." *Academy of Management Annual Meeting Proceedings* (January 2014): 1308–1314; Stone, Dianna L., and Lois E. Tetrick. "Understanding and Facilitating Age Diversity in Organizations." *Journal of Managerial Psychology* 28, no. 7–8 (2013): 725–728.
7. Byars-Winston, Angela, Nadya Fouad, and Yao Wen. "Race/Ethnicity and Sex in U.S. Occupations, 1970–2010: Implications for Research, Practice, and Policy." *Journal of Vocational Behavior* 87, (April 2015): 54–70; Humes, Karen, and Howard Hogan. "Do Current Race and Ethnicity Concepts Reflect a Changing America?" In *Race and Social Problems: Restructuring Inequality*, 15–38 (New York: Springer Science + Business Media, 2015).
8. See for example: Roh, Hyuntak, and Eugene Kim. "The Business Case for Gender Diversity: Examining the Role of Human Resource Management Investments." *Human Resource Management* (June 22, 2015): 000–000: *PsycINFO*, EBSCO*host*; Muzio, Daniel, and Jennifer Tomlinson. "Editorial: Researching Gender, Inclusion and Diversity in Contemporary Professions and Professional Organizations." *Gender, Work and Organization* 19, no. 5 (September 2012): 455–466.
9. See for example: Wilson, Eleanor. "Diversity, Culture and the Glass Ceiling." *Journal of Cultural Diversity* 21, no. 3 (Fall 2014): 83–89.
10. Mandel, Hadas, and Moshe Semyonov. "Gender Pay Gap and Employment Sector: Sources of Earnings Disparities in the United States, 1970–2010." *Demography* 51, no. 5 (October 2014): 1597–1618.
11. Details of the survey results can be found at www.harrisinteractive.com/NewsRoom/HarrisPolls/tabid/447/ctl/ReadCustom%20Default/mid/1508/ArticleId/1514/Default.aspx.
12. www.census.gov/newsroom/releases/archives/miscellaneous/cb12-134.html.
13. Dobbin, Frank, Alexandra Kalev, and Erin Kelly. "Diversity Management in Corporate America." *Contexts* 6, no. 4 (2007): 21–27.
14. For an overview of individual differences research, see Chamorro-Premuzic, Tomas, Sophie von Stumm, and Adrian Furnham. *The Wiley-Blackwell Handbook of Individual Differences* (New York: Wiley-Blackwell, 2011).
15. Carver, Charles S. "Self-Awareness." In *Handbook of Self and Identity* (2nd ed.), 50–68 (New York: Guilford, 2012); Church, Allan H. "Managerial Self-Awareness in High-Performing Individuals in Organizations." *Journal of Applied Psychology* 82, no. 2 (April 1997): 281–292.
16. Figurski, Thomas J., "Self-Awareness and Other-Awareness: The Use of Perspective in Everyday Life." In *Self and Identity: Psychosocial Perspectives*, 197–210 (Oxford: Wiley, 1987); Reddy, Vasudevi. "Experiencing Others: A Second-Person Approach to Other-Awareness." In *Social Life and Social Knowledge: Toward a Process Account of Development*, 123–144 (New York: Taylor & Francis / Erlbaum, 2008).
17. Berndt, Thomas J., and Leah Burgy. "Social Self-Concept." In *Handbook of Self-Concept: Developmental, Social, and Clinical Considerations*, 171–209 (Oxford: Wiley, 1996); Vancouver, Jeffrey B., and E. Casey Tischner. "The Effect of Feedback Sign on Task Performance Depends on Self-Concept Discrepancies." *Journal of Applied Psychology* 89, no. 6 (December 2004): 1092–1098.
18. Donnellan, M. Brent, Kali H. Trzesniewski, and Richard W. Robins. "Self-Esteem: Enduring Issues and Controversies." In *The Wiley-Blackwell Handbook of Individual Differences*, 718–746 (New York: Wiley-Blackwell, 2011); Vermout, Riël, Daan van Knippenberg, Barbara van Knippenberg, and Eric Blaauw. "Self-Esteem and Outcome Fairness: Differential Importance of Procedural and Outcome Considerations." *Journal of Applied Psychology* 86, no. 4 (August 2001): 621–628.
19. Bandura, Albert. *Self-Efficacy: The Exercise of Control*. New York: W H Freeman/Times Books/Henry Holt, 1997); Bandura, Albert. "On the Functional Properties of Perceived Self-Efficacy Revisited." *Journal of Management* 38, no. 1 (January 2012): 9–44.
20. For an overview or personality theory and research, see Cervone, Daniel, and Lawrence A. Pervin, *Personality: Theory and Research* (12th ed.) (New York: Wiley, 2013).
21. Costa, Paul T. Jr., and Robert R. McCrae. "Trait Theories of Personality." In *Advanced Personality*, 103–121 (New York: Plenum, 1998); Harkness, Allan R. "Theory and Measurement of Personality Traits." In *Oxford Handbook of Personality Assessment*, 150–162 (New York: Oxford University Press, 2009).
22. See for example, Quenk, Naomi L. *Essentials of Myers-Briggs Type Indicator® Assessment* (2nd ed.) (Hoboken, NJ: Wiley, 2009).
23. McCaulley, Mary H. "The Myers-Briggs Type Indicator: A Measure for Individuals and Groups." *Measurement and Evaluation in Counseling and Development* 22, no. 4 (January 1990): 181–195.
24. Mi-Ran, Kim, and Han Su-Jeong. "Relationships between the Myers-Briggs Type Indicator Personality Profiling, Academic Performance and Student Satisfaction in Nursing Students." *International Journal of Bio-Science & Bio-Technology* 6, no. 6 (December 2014): 1–11; Leonard, Dorothy, and Susan Straus. "Identifying How We Think: The Myers-Briggs Type Indicator and the Herrmann Brain Dominance Instrument." *Harvard Business Review* 75, no. 4 (July 1997): 114–115; McCaulley, "The Myers-Briggs Type Indicator."
25. For additional details see www.myersbriggs.org/my-mbti-personality-type/my-mbti-results/how-frequent-is-my-type.htm.
26. Barrick, Murray R., and Michael K. Mount. "The Big Five Personality Dimensions and Job Performance: A Meta-Analysis." *Personnel Psychology* 44, no. 1 (Spring 1991): 1–26; John, Oliver P., and Sanjay Srivastava. "The Big Five Trait Taxonomy: History, Measurement, and Theoretical Perspectives." In *Handbook of Personality: Theory and Research* (2nd ed.), 102–138 (New York: Guilford, 1999).
27. Deloitte. *CFO Insights: The Power of Business Chemistry*. www.deloitte.com/view/en_US/us/Services/additional-services/chief-financial-officer/cfo-insights/ae6743f2b7886310VgnVCM2000001b56f00aRCRD.htm.

28. McDonald, Roy, Vincent J. Tempone, and William L. Simmons, "Locus of control as a Personality and Situational Variable." *Perceptual and Motor Skills* 27, no. 1 (1968): 135–141; Rotter, Julian B., and Ray C. Mulry, "Internal versus External Control of Reinforcement and Decision Time." *Journal of Personality and Social Psychology* 2, no. 4 (October 1965): 598–604.
29. Christie, Richard, and Geis, Florence L. *Studies in Machiavellianism* (New York: Academic Press, 1970); Bagozzi, Richard P., Willem J. M. I. Verbeke, Roeland C. Dietvorst, Frank D. Belschak, Wouter E. van den Berg, and Wim J. R. Rietdijk. "Theory of Mind and Empathic Explanations of Machiavellianism: A Neuroscience Perspective." *Journal of Management* 39, no. 7 (November 2013): 1760–1798.
30. Snyder, Mark. "Self-Monitoring of Expressive Behavior." *Journal of Personality and Social Psychology* 30, no. 4 (October 1974): 526–537; Fuglestad, Paul T., and Mark Snyder. "Self-Monitoring." In *Handbook of Individual Differences in Social Behavior*, 574–591 (New York: Guilford, 2009); Oh, In-Sue, Steven D. Charlier, Michael K. Mount, and Christopher M. Berry. "The Two Faces of High Self-Monitors: Chameleonic Moderating Effects of Self-Monitoring on the Relationships between Personality Traits and Counterproductive Work Behaviors." *Journal of Organizational Behavior* 35, no. 1 (January 2014): 92–111.
31. Bateman, Thomas S., and J. Michael Crant. "The Proactive Component of Organizational Behavior: A Measure and Correlates." *Journal of Organizational Behavior* 14, no. 2 (March 1993): 103–118; Li, Wen-Dong, Doris Fay, Michael Frese, Peter D. Harms, and Xiang Yu Gao. "Reciprocal Relationship between Proactive Personality and Work Characteristics: A Latent Change Score Approach." *Journal of Applied Psychology* (March 17, 2014): 000–000.
32. Ganster, Daniel C., John Schaubroeck, Wesley E. Sime, and Bronston T. Mayes. "The Nomological Validity of the Type A Personality among Employed Adults." *Journal of Applied Psychology* 76, no. 1 (February 1991): 143–168; Billing, Tejinder K., and Pamela Steverson. "Moderating Role of Type-A Personality on Stress-Outcome Relationships." *Management Decision* 51, no. 9 (November 2013): 1893–1904.
33. Cummings, L. L., and G. W. Mize. "Risk Taking Propensity and Cognitive Set." *Journal of Social Psychology* 79, no. 2 (1969): 277–278; Taylor, Ronald N., and Marvin D. Dunnette. "Influence of Dogmatism, Risk-Taking Propensity, and Intelligence on Decision-Making Strategies for a Sample of Industrial Managers." *Journal of Applied Psychology* 59, no. 4 (August 1974): 420–423; Gardiner, Elliroma, and Chris J. Jackson. "Workplace Mavericks: How Personality and Risk-Taking Propensity Predicts Maverickism." *British Journal of Psychology* 103, no. 4 (November 2012): 497–519.
34. Casselman, Ben. "Risk-Averse Culture Infects U.S. Workers, Entrepreneurs." *Wall Street Journal*, June 2, 2013. http://online .wsj.com/article/SB10001424127887324031404578481162903760052.html.
35. Tugend, Alina. "Too Many Choices: A Problem That Can Paralyze." *New York Times*. February 26, 2010. www.nytimes .com/2010/02/27/your-money/27shortcuts .html?_r=1.

Chapter 3

1. Augustine, Adam A., and Randy J. Larsen. "Personality, Affect, and Affect Regulation." In *APA Handbook of Personality and Social Psychology, Volume 4: Personality Processes and Individual Differences*, 147–165 (Washington, DC: American Psychological Association, 2015); George, Jennifer M. "Trait and State Affect." In *Individual Differences and Behavior in Organizations,* edited by Kevin R. Murphy, 145 (San Francisco: Jossey-Bass, 1996).
2. Charles, Susan T., and Jennifer W. Robinette. "Emotion and Emotion Regulation." In *APA Handbook of Clinical Geropsychology, Vol. 1: History and Status of the Field and Perspectives on Aging*, 235–258 (Washington, DC: American Psychological Association, 2015); Frijda, Nico H. "Moods, Emotion Episodes, and Emotions." In *Handbook of Emotions*, 381–403 (New York: Guilford, 1993).
3. Ong, Anthony D., and Alex J. Zautra. "Intraindividual Variability in Mood and Mood Regulation in Adulthood." In *Handbook of Intraindividual Variability across the Life Span*, 198–215 (New York: Routledge/Taylor & Francis Group, 2015); Guterman, Yossi, Inbal Kleifeld, and Rachel Vegmister. "Just Think! Mood Regulation Effects of Cognitive Activity." In *Emotional Intelligence: Current Evidence from Psychophysiological, Educational and Organizational Perspectives*, 57–70 (Hauppauge, NY: Nova Science Publishers, 2015).
4. Silvia, Paul J., and John B. Warburton. "Positive and Negative Affect: Bridging States and Traits." In *Comprehensive Handbook of Personality and Psychopathology, Vol. 1: Personality and Everyday Functioning*, 268–284 (Hoboken, NJ: Wiley, 2006).
5. Gannett, Anita B. "On the Job: Don't Let a Shiny New Position Blind You to Its Realities" *Salt Lake Tribune*. June 1, 2013. www.sltrib.com/sltrib/money/56385863-79/job-says-heath-dan .html.csp.
6. Goudreau, Jenna. "From Crying to Temper Tantrums: How to Manage Emotions at Work." *Forbes.com*. January 9, 2013. www.forbes.com/sites/jennagoudreau/2013/01/09/from-crying-to-temper-tantrums-how-to-manage-emotions-at-work/.
7. Tee, Eugene Y. J. "The Emotional Link: Leadership and the Role of Implict and Explicit Emotional Contagion Processes across Multiple Organizational Levels." *Leadership Quarterly* (June 23, 2015): *PsycINFO*, EBSCO*host*; Hatfield, Elaine, John T. Cacioppo, and Richard L. Rapson. *Emotional contagion* (New York, NY: Cambridge University Press, 1994).
8. Gabriel, Allison S., Michael A. Daniels, James M. Diefendorff, and Gary J. Greguras. "Emotional Labor Actors: A Latent Profile Analysis of Emotional Labor Strategies." *Journal of Applied Psychology* 100, no. 3 (May 2015): 863–879; Ashforth, Blake E., and Ronald H. Humphrey. "Emotional Labor in Service Roles: The Influence of Identity." *Academy of Management Review* 18, no. 1 (January 1993): 88–115; Hochschild, Arlie R. *The Managed Heart: Commercialization of Human Feeling* (Berkeley: University of California Press, 1983).
9. Christoforou, Paraskevi S., and Blake E. Ashforth. "Revisiting the Debate on the Relationship between Display Rules and Performance: Considering the Explicitness of Display Rules." *Journal of Applied Psychology* 100, no. 1 (January 2015): 249–261; Ashforth, Blake E., and Ronald H. Humphrey. "Emotional Labor in Service Roles: The Influence of Identity." *Academy of Management Review* 18, no. 1 (January 1993): 88–115; Rafaeli, Anat, and Robert I. Sutton. "The Expression of Emotion in Organizational Life." *Research in Organizational Behavior* 11 (January 1989): 1–42.
10. Côté, Stéphane. "A Social Interaction Model of the Effects of Emotion Regulation on Work Strain." *Academy of Management Review* 30, no. 3 (July 2005): 509–530; Kenworthy, Jared, Cara Fay, Mark Frame, and Robyn Petree. "A Meta-analytic Review of the Relationship between Emotional Dissonance and Emotional Exhaustion." *Journal of Applied Social Psychology* 44, no. 2 (February 2014): 94–105.
11. Côté. "A Social Interaction Model"; Grandey, Alicia A. "When 'The Show Must Go On': Surface Acting and Deep Acting as Determinants of Emotional Exhaustion and Peer-Rated Service Delivery." *Academy of Management Journal* 46, no. 1 (February 2003): 86–96.
12. Gross, James J., and Ross A. Thompson. "Emotion Regulation: Conceptual Foundations." In *Handbook of Emotion Regulation*, 3–24 (New York: Guilford, 2007).

13. Appleton, Allison A., Eric B. Loucks, Stephen L. Buka, and Laura D. Kubzansky. "Divergent Associations of Antecedent- and Response-Focused Emotion Regulation Strategies with Midlife Cardiovascular Disease Risk." *Annals of Behavioral Medicine* 48, no. 2 (October 2014): 246–255; Gross, James J. "Antecedent- and Response-Focused Emotion Regulation: Divergent Consequences for Experience, Expression, and Physiology." *Journal of Personality and Social Psychology* 74, no. 1 (January 1998): 224–237.
14. Appleton et al. "Divergent Associations of Antecedent- and Response-Focused Emotion Regulation Strategies; Gross. "Antecedent- and response-Focused Emotion Regulation."
15. Salovey, Peter, and John D. Mayer. "Emotional Intelligence." *Imagination, Cognition and Personality* 9, no. 3 (1989): 185–211; Joseph, Dana L., Jing Jin, Daniel A. Newman, and Ernest H. O'Boyle. "Why Does Self-Reported Emotional Intelligence Predict Job Performance? A Meta-Analytic Investigation of Mixed EI." *Journal of Applied Psychology* 100, no. 2 (March 2015): 298–342.
16. Goleman, Daniel. *Emotional Intelligence* (New York: Bantam Books, 1995); Goleman, Daniel, Richard Boyatzis, and Annie McKee. *Primal Leadership: Realizing the Power of Emotional Intelligence* (Boston: Harvard Business School Press, 2002).
17. Thygesen, Kes. "Why Emotional Intelligence Is More Important to Hiring Than You Think." *Fast Company.* April 21, 2014. www.fastcompany.com/3029306/why-you-should-make-emotional-intelligence-the-cornerstone-of-your-hiring-strategy.
18. Molinsky, Andy. "Emotional Intelligence Doesn't Translate across Borders." *Harvard Business Review.* April 20, 2015. https://hbr.org/2015/04/emotional-intelligence-doesnt-translate-across-borders.
19. Nishi, Dennis. "'Soft Skills' Can Help You Get Ahead." *Wall Street Journal.* May 18, 2013. http://online.wsj.com/article/SB1000142412788732471570457848129088822474.html.
20. Goleman. *Emotional Intelligence*; Goleman, Boyatzis, and McKee. *Primal Leadership.*
21. See for example, Harms, P. D., and Marcus Credé. "Remaining Issues in Emotional Intelligence Research: Construct Overlap, Method Artifacts, and Lack of Incremental Validity." *Industrial and Organizational Psychology: Perspectives on Science and Practice* 3, no. 2 (June 2010): 154–158; Murphy, Kevin R. *A Critique of Emotional Intelligence: What Are the Problems and How Can They Be Fixed?* (Mahwah, NJ: Erlbaum, 2006).
22. Baer, Drake. "Emotional Intelligence Predicts Job Success: Do You Have It?" *Fast Company.* December 16, 2013. www.fastcompany.com/3023335/leadership-now/emotional-intelligence-predicts-job-success-do-you-have-it.
23. Allport, G. W. "Attitudes." In *A Handbook of Social Psychology*, 798–844 (Worcester, MA: Clark University Press, 1935); Bem, Daryl J. *Beliefs, Attitudes, and Human Affairs* (Oxford: Brooks/Cole, 1970).
24. Ajzen, Icek, and Martin Fishbein. "The Influence of Attitudes on Behavior." In *The Handbook of Attitudes*, 173–221 (Mahwah, NJ: Erlbaum, 2005); Ajzen, Icek, and Martin Fishbein. "Attitudes and Normative Beliefs as Factors Influencing Behavioral Intentions." *Journal of Personality and Social Psychology* 21, no. 1 (January 1972): 1–9; Ajzen, Icek. "The Theory of Planned Behavior." *Organizational Behavior and Human Decision Processes* 50, no. 2 (December 1991): 179–211.
25. Festinger, Leon. *A Theory of Cognitive Dissonance* (Stanford, CA: Stanford University Press, 1957).
26. Rafferty, Alannah E., and Mark A. Griffin. "Job Satisfaction in Organizational Research." In *The Sage Handbook of Organizational Research Methods*, 196–212 (Thousand Oaks, CA: Sage, 2009).
27. Klein, Howard J., Thomas E. Becker, and John P. Meyer. *Commitment in Organizations: Accumulated Wisdom and New Directions* (New York: Routledge/Taylor & Francis, 2009).
28. Albrecht, Simon L. *Handbook of Employee Engagement: Perspectives, Issues, Research and Practice* (Northampton, MA: Edward Elgar, 2010).
29. Organ, Dennis W. *Organizational Citizenship Behavior: The Good Soldier Syndrome* (Lexington, MA: Lexington Books/D. C. Heath, 1988).
30. Berry, Christopher M., Ariel M. Lelchook, and Malissa A. Clark. "A Meta-analysis of the Interrelationships between Employee Lateness, Absenteeism, and Turnover: Implications for Models of Withdrawal Behavior." *Journal of Organizational Behavior* 33, no. 5 (July 2012): 678–699.
31. Ones, Deniz S., and Stephan Dilchert. "Counterproductive Work Behaviors: Concepts, Measurement, and Nomological Network." In *APA Handbook of Testing and Assessment in Psychology, Vol. 1: Test Theory and Testing and Assessment in Industrial and Organizational Psychology*, 643–659 (Washington, DC: American Psychological Association, 2013).
32. Folkman, Susan, and Richard S. Lazarus. "If It Changes It Must Be a Process: Study of Emotion and Coping during Three Stages of a College Examination." *Journal of Personality and Social Psychology* 48, no. 1 (January 1985): 150–170.
33. For details see www.stress.org/stress-is-killing-you/.
34. Cavanaugh, Marcie A., Wendy R. Boswell, Mark V. Roehling, and John W. Boudreau. "An Empirical Examination of Self-Reported Work Stress among U.S. Managers." *Journal of Applied Psychology* 85, no. 1 (February 2000): 65–74; Lepine, Jeffery A., Nathan P. Podsakoff, and Marcie A. Lepine. "A Meta-Analytic Test of the Challenge Stressor—Hindrance Stressor Framework: An Explanation for Inconsistent Relationships among Stressors and Performance." *Academy of Management Journal* 48, no. 5 (October 2005): 764–775.
35. Nelson, Debra L., and Bret L. Simmons. "Savoring Eustress While Coping with Distress: The Holistic Model of Stress." In *Handbook of Occupational Health Psychology* (2nd ed.), 55–74 (Washington, DC: American Psychological Association, 2011).
36. Ibid.
37. Perrewé, Pamela L., Christopher C. Rosen, and Christina Maslach. "Organizational Politics and Stress: The Development of a Process Model." In *Politics in Organizations: Theory and Research Considerations*, 213–255 (New York: Routledge/Taylor & Francis Group, 2012).
38. Penwell-Waines, Lauren M., Kevin T. Larkin, and Jeffrey L. Goodie. "Coping." In *Biopsychosocial Assessment in Clinical Health Psychology*, 154–170 (New York: Guilford, 2015); Steptoe, Andrew. "Psychological Coping, Individual Differences and Physiological Stress Responses." In *Personality and Stress: Individual Differences in the Stress Process*, 205–233 (Oxford: Wiley, 1991).
39. Penwell-Waines et al. "Coping"; Steptoe. "Psychological Coping."
40. Sung Doo, Kim, Elaine C. Hollensbe, Catherine E. Schwoerer, and Jonathon R. B. Halbesleben. "Dynamics of a Wellness Program: A Conservation of Resources Perspective." *Journal of Occupational Health Psychology* 20, no. 1 (January 2015): 62–71.
41. Berry, Leonard L., Ann M. Mirabito, and William B. Baun. "What's the Hard Return on Employee Wellness Programs?" *Harvard Business Review.* December 2010. https://hbr.org/2010/12/whats-the-hard-return-on-employee-wellness-programs.
42. Ibid.
43. www.totalhrmanagement.com/12-companies-with-seriously-impressive-corporate-wellness-programs.

Chapter 4

1. Weingartern, Gene. "Pearls before Breakfast." *Washington Post,* April 8, 2007. www.washingtonpost.com/wp-dyn/content/article/2007/04/04/AR2007040401721.html.

2. See for example, Coren, Stanley. "Sensation and Perception." In *Handbook of Psychology, Vol. 1: History of Psychology* (2nd ed.), 100–128 (Hoboken, NJ: Wiley, 2013); Pike, Graham, Graham Edgar, and Helen Edgar. "Perception." In *Cognitive Psychology* (2nd ed.), 65–99 (New York: Oxford University Press, 2012).
3. Haden, Jeff. "Why What Kind of Car You Drive Matters." *Inc.* August 10, 2012. www.inc.com/jeff-haden/small-business-owners-does-it-matter-what-you-drive.html.
4. Lewin, Kurt, Fritz Heider, and Grace M. Heider. *Principles of Topological Psychology* (New York: McGraw-Hill, 1936).
5. Silcox, Beth. "Perception Is Everything." *Success.* n.d. www.success.com/article/perception-is-everything.
6. Devos, Thierry. "Stereotypes and Intergroup Attitudes." In *APA Handbook of Multicultural Psychology, Vol. 1: Theory and Research*, 341–360 (Washington, DC: American Psychological Association, 2014).
7. Lamy, Dominique, Andrew B. Leber, and Howard E. Egeth. "Selective Attention." In *Handbook of Psychology, Vol. 4: Experimental Psychology* (2nd ed.), 267–294 (Hoboken, NJ: Wiley, 2013).
8. Dudycha, G. J. "A Note on the 'Halo Effect' in Ratings." *Journal of Social Psychology* 15 (1942): 331–333; Dennis, Ian. "Halo Effects in Grading Student Projects." *Journal of Applied Psychology* 92, no. 4 (July 2007): 1169–1176.
9. Raffel, G. "Two Determinants of the Effect of Primacy." *American Journal of Psychology* 48 (1936): 654–657; Nahari, Galit, and Gershon Ben-Shakhar. "Primacy Effect in Credibility Judgements: The Vulnerability of Verbal Cues to Biased Interpretations." *Applied Cognitive Psychology* 27, no. 2 (March 2013): 247–255.
10. Postman, Leo, and Jerome S. Bruner. "Hypothesis and the Principle of Closure: The Effect of Frequency and Recency." *Journal of Psychology: Interdisciplinary and Applied* 33 (1952): 113–125; Jones, Matt, Bradley C. Love, and W. Todd Maddox. "Recency Effects as a Window to Generalization: Separating Decisional and Perceptual Sequential Effects in Category Learning." *Journal of Experimental Psychology: Learning, Memory, and Cognition* 32, no. 2 (March 2006): 316–332.
11. Preston, M. G. "Contrast Effects and the Psychometric Function." *American Journal of Psychology* 48, (1936): 625–631; Kopelman, M. D. "The Contrast Effect in the Selection Interview." *British Journal of Educational Psychology* 45, no. 3 (November 1975): 333–336; Boillaud, Eric, and Guylaine Molina. "Are Judgments a Form of Data Clustering? Reexamining Contrast Effects with the k-Means Algorithm." *Journal of Experimental Psychology: Human Perception and Performance* 41, no. 2 (April 2015): 415–430.
12. Thomsen, A. "Psychological Projection and the Election: A Simple Class Experiment." *Journal of Psychology: Interdisciplinary and Applied* 11 (1941): 115–117; Morry, Marian M., Mie Kito, and Lindsey Ortiz. "The Attraction–Similarity Model and Dating Couples: Projection, Perceived Similarity, and Psychological Benefits." *Personal Relationships* 18, no. 1 (March 2011): 125–143.
13. Dvir, Taly, Dov Eden, and Michal Lang Banjo. "Self-Fulfilling Prophecy and Gender: Can Women Be Pygmalion and Galatea?" *Journal of Applied Psychology* 80, no. 2 (April 1995): 253–270; Eden, Dov, and Dov Yaakov Zuk. "Seasickness as a Self-Fulfilling Prophecy: Raising Self-Efficacy to Boost Performance at Sea." *Journal of Applied Psychology* 80, no. 5 (October 1995): 628–635; Madon, Stephanie, Jennifer Willard, Max Guyll, and Kyle C. Scherr "Self-fulfilling Prophecies: Mechanisms, Power, and Links to Social Problems." *Social and Personality Psychology Compass* 5, no. 8 (August 2011): 578–590.
14. Bourdage, Joshua S., Jocelyn Wiltshire, and Kibeom Lee. "Personality and Workplace Impression Management: Correlates and Implications." *Journal of Applied Psychology* 100, no. 2 (March 2015): 537–546; Kacmar, K. Michele, John E. Delery, and Gerald R. Ferris. "Differential Effectiveness of Applicant Impression Management Tactics on Employment Interview Decisions." *Journal of Applied Social Psychology* 22, no. 16 (August 1992): 1250–1272; Kacmar, K. Michele, and Dawn S. Carlson. "Effectiveness of Impression Management Tactics across Human Resource Situations." *Journal of Applied Social Psychology* 29, no. 6 (June 1999): 1293–1315.
15. Malle, Bertram F. "Attribution Theories: How People Make Sense of Behavior." In *Theories in Social Psychology*, 72–95 (n.p.: Wiley-Blackwell, 2011); Martinko, Mark J., Scott C. Douglas, and Paul Harvey. "Attribution Theory in Industrial and Organizational Psychology: A Review." In *International Review of Industrial and Organizational Psychology 2006* (Vol. 21), 127–187 (Hoboken, NJ: Wiley, 2006).
16. Harvey, Paul, Kristen Madison, Mark Martinko, T. Russell Crook, and Tamara A. Crook. "Attribution Theory in the Organizational Sciences: The Road Traveled and the Path Ahead." *Academy of Management Perspectives* 28, no. 2 (May 2014): 128–146; Mehlman, Rick C., and C. R. Snyder. "Excuse Theory: A Test of the Self-Protective Role of Attributions." *Journal of Personality and Social Psychology* 49, no. 4 (October 1985): 994–1001.
17. Harvey, John H., and Richard P. McGlynn. "Matching Words to Phenomena: The Case of the Fundamental Attribution Error." *Journal of Personality and Social Psychology* 43, no. 2 (August 1982): 345–346; Ross, Lee D., Teresa M. Amabile, and Julia L. Steinmetz. "Social Roles, Social Control, and Biases in Social-Perception Processes." *Journal of Personality and Social Psychology* 35, no. 7 (July 1977): 485–494; Moran, Joseph M., Eshin Jolly, and Jason P. Mitchell. "Spontaneous Mentalizing Predicts the Fundamental Attribution Error." *Journal of Cognitive Neuroscience* 26, no. 3 (March 2014): 569–576.
18. Larson Jr., James R. "Evidence for a Self-Serving Bias in the Attribution of Causality." *Journal of Personality* 45, no. 3 (September 1977): 430–441; Arkin, Robert M., et al. "Self-Presentation, Self-Monitoring, and the Self-Serving Bias in Causal Attribution." *Personality and Social Psychology Bulletin* 5, no. 1 (January 1979): 73–76; Sanjuán, Pilar, and Alejandro Magallares. "Coping Strategies as Mediating Variables between Self-Serving Attributional Bias and Subjective Well-Being." *Journal of Happiness Studies* 15, no. 2 (April 2014): 443–453.
19. See for example, Allport, Floyd H. "Perception and Theories of Learning: The Behavior Theory Approach." In *Theories of Perception and the Concept of Structure: A Review and Critical Analysis with an Introduction to a Dynamic-Structural Theory of Behavior*, 437–466 (Hoboken, NJ: Wiley, 1955).
20. Robson, David. "Old Schooled: You Never Stop Learning Like a Child." *Neuroscience.* May 26, 2013. http://neurosciencestuff.tumblr.com/post/51428289471/old-schooled-you-never-stop-learning-like-a-child?utm_source=Dan+Pink%27s+Newsletter&utm_campaign=f2973b957c-august_newsletter&utm_medium=email&utm_term=0_4d8277f97a-f2973b957c-306048817.
21. Clark, Robert E. "The Classical Origins of Pavlov's Conditioning." *Integrative Physiological and Behavioral Science* 39, no. 4 (October 2004): 279–294.
22. Davey, Graham, and Chris Cullen. *Human Operant Conditioning and Behavior Modification* (Oxford: Wiley, 1988).
23. Thorndike, E. L. "The Law of Effect." *American Journal of Psychology* 39, (1927): 212–222.
24. Skinner, B. F. "The Effect on the Amount of Conditioning of an Interval of Time before Reinforcement." *Journal of General Psychology* 14, (1936): 279–295; Scriven, Michael, James J. Gallagher, Allen D. Calvin, Charles Hanley, James V. McConnell, and F. J. McGuigan. "An Overview of Stimulus-Response Reinforcement Theory." In *Psychology*, 321–329 (Needham Heights, MA: Allyn & Bacon, 1961).

25. Luthans, Fred, and Mark J. Martinko. "Organizational Behavior Modification: A Way to Bridge the Gap between Academic Research and Real World Application." *Journal of Organizational Behavior Management* 3, no. 3 (1981): 33–50; Stajkovic, Alexander D., and Fred Luthans. "A Meta-analysis of the Effects of Organizational Behavior Modification on Task Performance, 1975–95." *Academy of Management Journal* 40, no. 5 (October 1997): 1122–1149.
26. Caprino, Kathy. "Six Essential Ways to Build a Positive Organization." *Forbes. com.* December 13, 2013. www.forbes .com/sites/kathycaprino/2013/12/13/6-essential-ways-to-build-a-positive-organization/.
27. Wexley, Kenneth N., and Wayne F. Nemeroff. "Effectiveness of Positive Reinforcement and Goal Setting as Methods of Management Development." *Journal of Applied Psychology* 60, no. 4 (August 1975): 446–450; Briefer Freymond, Sabrina, Elodie F. Briefer, Anja Zollinger, Yveline Gindrat-von Allmen, Christa Wyss, and Iris Bachmann. "Behaviour of Horses in a Judgment Bias Test Associated with Positive or Negative Reinforcement." *Applied Animal Behaviour Science* 158 (September 2014): 34–45.
28. McConnell, James V. "Negative Reinforcement and Positive Punishment." *Teaching of Psychology* 17, no. 4 (December 1990): 247–249.
29. Burger, Richard. "The Marvelous Benefits of Positive and Negative Reinforcement." *Selah Independent.* March 11, 2009.
30. McConnell, James V. "Negative Reinforcement and Positive Punishment." *Teaching of Psychology* 17, no. 4 (December 1990): 247–249; Hockenhull, Jo, and Emma Creighton. "Training Horses: Positive Reinforcement, Positive Punishment, and Ridden Behavior Problems." *Journal of Veterinary Behavior: Clinical Applications and Research* 8, no. 4 (July 2013): 245–252.
31. Ibid.
32. Angelloz, Robert E. "The Practical Application of Behavior Management Principles and Strategies to Everyday Living." *Psychology: A Journal of Human Behavior* 15, no. 3 (August 1978): 17–21; MacDonald, Jacquelyn M., William H. Ahearn, Diana Parry-Cruwys, Stacie Bancroft, and William V. Dube. "Persistence during Extinction: Examining the Effects of Continuous and Intermittent Reinforcement on Problem Behavior." *Journal of Applied Behavior Analysis* 46, no. 1 (Spring 2013): 333–338.
33. Lundin, Robert W. "Schedules of Reinforcement." In *Personality: An Experimental Approach,* 76–101 (New York: MacMillan, 1961); MacDonald et al. "Persistence during Extinction."
34. Ibid.
35. Crossman, Edward K. "Schedules of Reinforcement." In *Human Behavior in Today's World,* 133–138 (New York, Praeger, 1991); Okouchi, Hiroto. "An Exploration of Remote History Effects in Humans: II. The Effects under Fixed-Interval, Variable-Interval, and Fixed-Ratio Schedules." *Psychological Record* 60, no. 1 (Winter 2010): 27–42.
36. Ibid.
37. Ibid.
38. Ibid.
39. Bandura, Albert. *Social Learning Theory* (Oxford: Prentice-Hall, 1977); Bandura, Albert. "Social Cognitive Theory of Self-Regulation." *Organizational Behavior and Human Decision Processes* 50, no. 2 (December 1991): 248–287; Bandura, Albert. "Social Cognitive Theory." In *Handbook of Theories of Social Psychology* (Vol. 1), 349–373. (Thousand Oaks, CA: Sage, 2012).
40. Reingold, Jennifer. "PepsiCo's CEO Was Right. Now what?" *Fortune.* June 5, 2015. http://fortune.com/2015/06/05/pepsico-ceo-indra-nooyi/.
41. Bandura, Albert. *Self-Efficacy: The Exercise of Control* (New York: W H Freeman/Times Books/Henry Holt & Co, 1997); Bandura, Albert. "The Role of Self-Efficacy in Goal-Based Motivation." In *New Developments in Goal Setting and Task Performance,* 147–157 (New York: Routledge/Taylor & Francis Group, 2013).
42. Ibid.
43. Bandura. "Social Cognitive Theory of Personality"; Hoover, J. Duane, Robert C. Giambatista, and Liuba Y. Belkin. "Eyes On, Hands On: Vicarious Observational Learning as an Enhancement of Direct Experience." *Academy Of Management Learning and Education* 11, no. 4 (December 2012): 591–608.
44. Musolf, DeAnne. "New Year's Resolutions: Tips from Science to Make Them Stick." *San Jose Mercury News.* December 31, 2013. www.mercurynews.com/bay-area-living/ci_24817826/new-years-resolutions-tips-from-science-make-them.
45. Bandura. "Social Cognitive Theory of Personality"; Bandura. "Social Cognitive Theory of Self-Regulation.
46. Bandura, Albert. "Human Agency in social Cognitive Theory." *American Psychologist* 44, no. 9 (September 1989): 1175–1184; Wood, Robert, and Albert Bandura. "Social Cognitive Theory of Organizational Management." *Academy of Management Review* 14, no. 3 (July 1989): 361–384.

Chapter 5

1. Refer to the following for an overview of work motivation theory: Grant, Adam M., and Jihae Shin. "Work Motivation: Directing, Energizing, and Maintaining Effort (and Research)." In Richard M. Ryan (Ed.), *Oxford Handbook of Motivation,* 505–519 (New York: Oxford University Press, 2012): Kanfer, Ruth. "Work Motivation: Advancing Theory and Impact," *Industrial and Organizational Psychology: Perspectives on Science and Practice* 2, no. 1 (March 2009): 118–127; Kanfer, Ruth, Gilad Chen, and Robert D. Pritchard, *Work Motivation: Past, Present, and Future* (New York: Routledge/Taylor & Francis, 2008); Landy, Frank J., and Wendy S. Becker. "Motivation Theory Reconsidered." *Research in Organizational Behavior* 9 (January 1987): 1.
2. Kanfer, Ruth. "Motivation Theory and Industrial and Organizational Psychology." In Marvin D. Dunnette (Ed.), *Handbook of Industrial and Organizational Psychology,* 2nd ed., Vol. 1, 75–130 (Palo Alto, CA: Consulting Psychologists Press).
3. Barbuto, John E. Jr. "Four Classification Schemes of Adult Motivation: Current Views and Measures." *Perceptual and Motor Skills* 102, no. 2 (April 2006): 563–575; Borkowski, Nancy. "Content Theories of Motivation." In *Organizational Behavior in Health Care,* 113–138 (Boston, MA: Jones and Bartlett, 2005); Dachler, H. Peter. "Process Theories of Motivation in Organizations." *Revista Interamericana De Psicología* 12, no. 1 (1978): 81–92.
4. Maslow, A. H. "A Theory of Human Motivation," *Psychological Review* 50, no. 4 (July 1943): 370–396.
5. Wahba, Mahmoud A., and Lawrence G. Bridwell. "Maslow Reconsidered: A Review of Research on the Need. Hierarchy Theory." *Organizational Behavior and Human Performance* 15, no. 2 (April 1976): 212–240; Harrigan, William Joseph, and Michael Lamport Commons. "Replacing Maslow's Needs Hierarchy with an Account Based on Stage and Value." *Behavioral Development Bulletin* 20, no. 1 (April 2015): 24–31.
6. Ibid.
7. Alderfer, Clayton P. "An Empirical Test of a New Theory of Human Needs," *Organizational Behavior and Human Performance* 4, no. 2 (1969): 142–175; Schneider, Benjamin, and Clayton P. Alderfer. "Three Studies of Measures of Need Satisfaction in Organizations." *Administrative Science Quarterly* 18, no. 4 (December 1973): 489–505.
8. Herzberg, F., B. Mausner, and B. Snyderman. *The Motivation to Work,* 2nd ed. (Oxford: Wiley, 1959); Herzberg, Frederick. "One More Time: How Do You Motivate Employees?" *Harvard Business Review* 81, no. 1 (January 2003): 87–96.
9. Ibid.
10. http://www.leadership-central.com/two-factor-theory.html#axzz3YDaoZUtX.
11. King, Nathan. "Clarification and Evaluation of the Two-Factor Theory of Job Satisfaction." *Psychological Bulletin*

74, no. 1 (July 1970): 18–31; Wall, Toby D., and Geoffrey M. Stephenson. "Herzberg's Two-Factor Theory of Job Attitudes: A Critical Evaluation and Some Fresh Evidence." *Industrial Relations Journal* 1, no. 3 (September 1970); Furnham, Adrian, Andreas Eracleous, and Tomas Chamorro-Premuzic. "Personality, Motivation and Job Satisfaction: Hertzberg Meets the Big Five." *Journal of Managerial Psychology* 24, no. 8 (2009): 765–779.

12. McClelland, David C. *The Achieving Society* (New York: Van Nostrand, 1961); McClelland, David C. *Power: The Inner Experience* (New York: Irvington, 1975); Harrell, Adrian M., and Michael J. Stahl. "A Behavioral Decision Theory Approach for Measuring McClelland's Trichotomy of Needs." *Journal of Applied Psychology* 66, no. 2 (April 1981): 242–247; Royle, M. Todd, and Angela T. Hall. "The Relationship between McClelland's Theory of Needs, Feeling Individually Accountable, and Informal Accountability for Others." *International Journal of Management and Marketing Research (IJMMR)* 5, no. 1 (January 2012): 21–42.
13. Greene, Katherine, and Greene, Richard. *The Man behind the Magic: The Story of Walt Disney* (New York: Viking, 1991); Thomas, Bob. *Walt Disney: An American Original* (New York: Hyperion, 1994).
14. http://uk.businessinsider.com/the-top-10-highest-paid-ceos-of-2014-2015-5?r=US&IR=T.
15. Greenblatt, Drew. "A Simple Spreadsheet for Motivation and Versatility," *Inc.*, January 8, 2013, www.inc.com/drew-greenblatt/simple-spreadsheet-for-motivation-and-versatility.html.
16. Haislip, Barbara. "Keep Employees Happy with Creative Perks." *Wall Street Journal*, August 19, 2013.
17. Adams, J. Stacy. "Towards an Understanding of Inequity." *Journal of Abnormal and Social Psychology* 67, no. 5 (November 1963): 422–436; Polk, Denise M, "Evaluating Fairness: Critical Assessment of Equity Theory." In *Theories in Social Psychology* (Chichester, West Sussex, UK: Wiley-Blackwell, 2011), 163–190.
18. Colquitt, Jason A., Donald E. Conlon, Michael J. Wesson, Christopher O. L. H. Porter, and K. Yee Ng, "Justice at the Millennium: A Meta-analytic Review of 25 Years of Organizational Justice Research." *Journal of Applied Psychology* 86, no. 3 (June 2001): 425–445; Greenberg, Jerald, and Jason A. Colquitt. *Handbook of Organizational Justice* (Mahwah, NJ: Erlbaum, 2005); Wang, Hai-jiang, Chang-qin Lu, and Oi-ling Siu. "Job Insecurity and Job Performance: The Moderating Role of Organizational Justice and the Mediating Role of Work Engagement." *Journal of Applied Psychology* 100, no. 4 (July 2015): 1249–1258.
19. Smith, Jacquelyn. "(How to Deal with Favoritism in the Office." *Forbes*. October 26, 2012, pp 1–2.
20. Latham, Gary P., and Edwin A. Locke. "Goal Setting—A Motivational Technique That Works." *Organizational Dynamics* 8, no. 2 (September 1979): 68–80; Locke, Edwin A., and Gary P. Latham, "Building a Practically Useful Theory of Goal Setting and Task Motivation: A 35-Year Odyssey." *American Psychologist* 57, no. 9 (September 2002): 705–717; Locke, Edwin A., and Gary P. Latham. *A Theory of Goal Setting and Task Performance* (Englewood Cliffs, NJ: Prentice Hall, 1990); Kleingeld, Ad, Heleen van Mierlo, and Lidia Arends. "The Effect of Goal Setting on Group Performance: A Meta-Analysis." *Journal of Applied Psychology* 96, no. 6 (November 2011): 1289–1304.
21. Gregory, Jane Brodie, and Paul E. Levy. "How Feedback and Goals Drive Behavior: Control Theory." In *Using Feedback in Organizational Consulting*, 21–30 (Washington, DC: American Psychological Association, 2015); Krenn, Björn, Sabine Würth, and Andreas Hergovich. "The Impact of Feedback on Goal Setting and Task Performance: Testing the Feedback Intervention Theory." *Swiss Journal of Psychology* 72, no. 2 (April 2013): 79–89; Neubert, Mitchell J. "The Value of Feedback and Goal Setting over Goal Setting Alone and Potential Moderators of This Effect: A Meta-analysis." *Human Performance* 11, no. 4 (1998): 321–335.
22. Locke and Latham, 1990; Latham, Gary P., and J. James Baldes, "The 'Practical Significance' of Locke's Theory of Goal Setting." *Journal of Applied Psychology* 60, no. 1 (February 1975): 122–124; Kleingeld et al. "The Effect of Goal Setting on Group Performance."
23. Ibid.
24. Locke, Edwin A., Gary P. Latham, and Miriam Erez. "The Determinants of Goal Commitment." *Academy of Management Review* 13, no. 1 (January 1988): 23–39; Lee, Jean, and Feng Wei. "The Mediating Effect of Psychological Empowerment on the Relationship between Participative Goal Setting and Team Outcomes—A Study in China." *International Journal of Human Resource Management* 22, no. 2 (January 2011): 279–295.
25. Erez, Miriam. "Feedback: A Necessary Condition for the Goal Setting–Performance Relationship." *Journal of Applied Psychology* 62, no. 5 (October 1977): 624–627; Kim, Jay S., and W. C. Hamner. "Effect of Performance Feedback and Goal Setting on Productivity and Satisfaction in an Organizational Setting." *Journal of Applied Psychology* 61, no. 1 (February 1976): 48–57; Wack, Stephanie R., Kimberly A. Crosland, and Raymond G. Miltenberger. "Using Goal Setting and Feedback to Increase Weekly Running Distance." *Journal of Applied Behavior Analysis* 47, no. 1 (Spring 2014): 181–185.
26. Latham, Gary P., and Gerard H. Seijts. "The Effects of Proximal and Distal Goals on Performance on a Moderately Complex Task." *Journal of Organizational Behavior* 20, no. 4 (July 1999): 421–429; Latham, Gary P., and Edwin A. Locke. "New Developments In and Directions For Goal-Setting Research." *European Psychologist* 12, no. 4 (2007): 290–300.
27. Vroom, Victor H. *Work and Motivation* (New York: Wiley, 1964); Matsui, Tamao, and Toshitake Terai. "A Cross-Cultural Study of the Validity of the Expectancy Theory of Work Motivation." *Journal of Applied Psychology* 60, no. 2 (April 1975): 263–265.
28. Adapted from Lunenburg, Fred C. "Expectancy Theory of Motivation: Motivating by Altering Expectations." *International Journal of Management, Business, and Administration* 15, no. 1 (2011): 1–6.

Chapter 6

1. Deci, Edward L. *Intrinsic Motivation* (New York: Plenum, 1975); Hagger, Martin S., Severine Koch, and Nikos L. D. Chatzisarantis. "The Effect of Causality Orientations and Positive Competence-Enhancing Feedback on Intrinsic Motivation: A Test of Additive and Interactive Effects." *Personality and Individual Differences* 72 (January 2015): 107–111.
2. Deci, *Intrinsic Motivation*; Deci, Edward L. "The Effects of Contingent and Noncontingent Rewards and Controls on Intrinsic Motivation." *Organizational Behavior and Human Performance* 8, no. 2 (October 1972): 217–229; Deci, Edward L., and Richard Koestner. "The Undermining Effect Is a Reality After All." *Psychological Bulletin* 125, no. 6 (November 1999): 692; Pritchard, Robert D., Kathleen M. Campbell, and Donald J. Campbell. "Effects of Extrinsic Financial Rewards on Intrinsic Motivation." *Journal of Applied Psychology* 62, no. 1 (February 1977): 9–15; Olafsen, Anja H., Hallgeir Halvari, Jacques Forest, and Edward L. Deci. "Show Them the Money? The Role of Pay, Managerial Need Support, and Justice in a Self-Determination Theory Model of Intrinsic Work Motivation." *Scandinavian Journal of Psychology* (March 24, 2015): *PsycINFO*, EBSCO*host*.
3. Rusbult, Caryl E., Chester A. Insko, and Yuan-Huei W. Lin. "Seniority-Based Reward Allocation in the United States and Taiwan." *Social Psychology Quarterly* 58, no. 1 (March 1995): 13–30; Ogoshi, Yonosuke. "Current Japanese Employment Practices and Industrial Relations: The Transformation of

Permanent Employment and Seniority-Based Wage System." *Asian Business and Management* 5, no. 4 (December 2006): 469–485.

4. Pierson, David A., Karen S. Koziara, and Russel E. Johannesson. "Equal Pay for Jobs of Comparable Worth: A Quantified Job Content Approach." *Public Personnel Management* 12, no. 4 (Winter 1983): 445; Wallace Jr., Marc J., and Charles H. Fay. "Job Evaluation and Comparable Worth: Compensation Theory Bases for Molding Job Worth." *Academy of Management Proceedings* (00650668) (August 1981): 296–300; Patten, Thomas H. Jr. *Fair Pay: The Managerial Challenge of Comparable Job Worth and Job Evaluation* (San Francisco: Jossey-Bass, 1988); Gittleman, Maury, and Brooks Pierce. "Inter-Industry Wage Differentials, Job Content and Unobserved Ability." *Industrial and Labor Relations Review* 64, no. 2 (January 2011): 356–374.
5. Mitra, Atul, Nina Gupta, and Jason D. Shaw. "A Comparative Examination of Traditional and Skill-Based Pay Plans." *Journal of Managerial Psychology* 26, no. 4 (2011): 278–296; Murray, Brian, and Barry Gerhart. "Skill-Based Pay and Skill Seeking." *Human Resource Management Review* 10, no. 3 (2000): 271–287; Lee, Cynthia, Kenneth S. Law, and Philip Bobko. "The Importance of Justice Perceptions on Pay Effectiveness: A Two Year Study of a Skill–Based Pay Plan." *Journal of Management* 25, no. 6 (November 1999): 851.
6. Boachie-Mensah, Francis, and Ophelia Delali Dogbe. "Performance–Based Pay as a Motivational Tool for Achieving Organisational Performance: An Exploratory Case Study." *International Journal of Business and Management* 6, no. 12 (December 2011): 270–285; Van Yperen, Nico W. "The Perceived Profile of Goal Orientation within Firms: Differences between Employees Working for Successful and Unsuccessful Firms Employing Either Performance-Based Pay or Job-Based Pay." *European Journal of Work and Organizational Psychology* 12, no. 3 (September 2003): 229–243.
7. Arthur, Jeffrey B., and Dong-One Kim. "Gainsharing and Knowledge Sharing: The Effects of Labour–Management Co-operation." *International Journal of Human Resource Management* 16, no. 9 (September 2005): 1564–1582; Graham-Moore, Brian E., and Ross, Timothy L. *Gainsharing and Employee Involvement* (Washington, DC: Bureau of National Affairs, 1995).
8. Florkowski, Gary W. "The Organizational Impact of Profit Sharing." *Academy of Management Review* 12, no. 4 (October 1987): 622–636; Magnan, Michel, and Sylvie St-Onge. "The Impact of Profit Sharing on the Performance of Financial Services Firms. *"Journal of Management Studies* 42, no. 4 (June 2005): 761–791.
9. Ettling, Jennifer. "Winning and Losing with ESOPs: The Design of Effective Employee Stock Ownership Plans." *Academy of Management Best Papers Proceedings* (August 1990): 269–273; Park, Sangsoo, and Moon H. Song. "Employee Stock Ownership Plans, Firm Performance, and Monitoring by Outside Blockholders." *FM: The Journal of the Financial Management Association* 24, no. 4 (Winter 1995): 52–65; Bergstein, Warren M., and Wanda Williams. "The Benefits of Employee Stock Ownership Plans." *CPA Journal* 83, no. 4 (April 2013): 54–57.
10. Johns, Gary, Xie Jia Lin, and Fang Yongqing. "Mediating and Moderating Effects in Job Design." *Journal of Management* 18, no. 4 (December 1992): 657; Kempner, T., and Ray Wild. "Job Design and Productivity." *Journal of Management Studies* 10, no. 1 (February 1973): 62–81; Umstot, Denis D., Terence R. Mitchell, and Cecil H. Bell Jr. "Goal Setting and Job Enrichment: An Integrated Approach to Job Design." *Academy of Management Review* 3, no. 4 (October 1978): 867–879; Cullinane, Sarah-Jane, Janine Bosak, Patrick C. Flood, and Evangelia Demerouti. "Job Design under Lean Manufacturing and the Quality of Working Life: A Job Demands and Resources Perspective." *International Journal of Human Resource Management* 25, no. 21 (November 2014): 2996–3015.
11. Chung, Kae H., and Monica F. Ross. "Differences in Motivational Properties between Job Enlargement and Job Enrichment." *Academy of Management Review* 2, no. 1 (January 1977): 113–122; Bishop, Ronald C., and James W. Hill. "Effects of Job Enlargement and Job Change on Contiguous but Nonmanipulated Jobs as a Function of Workers' Status." *Journal of Applied Psychology* 55, no. 3 (June 1971): 175–181; Scott, Richard D. "Job Enlargement: The Key to increasing Job Satisfaction?" *Personnel Journal* 52, no. 4 (April 1973): 313–317; Campion, Michael A., Troy V. Mumford, Frederick P. Morgeson, and Jennifer D. Nahrgang. "Work Redesign: Eight Obstacles and Opportunities." *Human Resource Management* 44, no. 4 (Winter 2005): 367–390.
12. Campion, Michael A., Lisa Cheraskin, and Michael J. Stevens. "Career–Related Antecedents and Outcomes of Job Rotation." *Academy of Management Journal* 37, no. 6 (December 1994): 1518–1542; Gannon, Martin J., and Uri Brainin. "Job Rotation and Employee Tenure among Temporary Workers." *Academy of Management Journal* (March 1971), 142–144.
13. Chung, Kae H., and Monica F. Ross. "Differences in Motivational Properties between Job Enlargement and Job Enrichment." *Academy of Management Review* 2, no. 1 (January 1977): 113–122; Testerman, Michael B. "Job Enrichment: Concepts and Consequences." *Industrial Management* 22, no. 3 (May 1980): 9; Grote, Richard C. "Implementing Job Enrichment." *California Management Review* 15, no. 1 (1972): 16–21.
14. Hackman, J. Richard, and Greg R. Oldham. *Work Redesign* (Reading, MA: Addison–Wesley, 1980); Hackman, J. Richard, and Greg R. Oldham. "Motivation through the Design of Work: Test of a Theory." *Organizational Behavior and Human Performance* 16, no. 2 (August 1976): 250–279.
15. Spreitzer, Gretchen M. "Psychological, Empowerment in the Workplace: Dimensions, Measurement and Validation." *Academy of Management Journal* 38, no. 5 (October 1995): 1442–1465; Spreitzer, Gretchen M., Mark A. Kizilos, and Stephen W. Nason. "A Dimensional Analysis of the Relationship between Psychological Empowerment and Effectiveness, Satisfaction, and Strain." *Journal of Management* 23, no. 5 (December 15, 1997): 679.
16. Ibid.
17. Ibid.
18. Ibid.
19. Ibid.
20. Pink, Daniel H. *Free Agent Nation: The Future of Working for Yourself* (New York: Warner Business Books, 2001); Pfeffer, Jeffrey, "Why Free Agents Don't Feel Free," *Business 2.0* 7, no. 9 (October 2006): 78.
21. Taylor, Kate. "Why Millennials Are Ending the 9 to 5," *Forbes,* August 23, 2013; www.forbes.com/sites/katetaylor/2013/08/23/why-millennials-are-ending-the-9-to-5/.
22. Goudreau, Jenna. "Back to the Stone Age? New Yahoo CEO Marissa Mayer Bans Working from Home," *Forbes.* February 25, 2013; www.forbes.com/sites/jennagoudreau/2013/02/25/back-to-the-stone-age-new-yahoo-ceo-marissa-mayer-bans-working-from-home/.
23. Hicks, William D., and Richard J. Klimoski. "The Impact of Flextime on Employee Attitudes." *Academy of Management Journal* 24, no. 2 (June 1981): 333–341; Denton, D. Keith. "Using Flextime to Create a Competitive Workplace." *Industrial Management* 35, no. 1 (January 1993): 29.
24. Arbon, Chyleen A., Rex L. Facer II, and Lori L. Wadsworth. "Compressed Workweeks—Strategies for Successful Implementation." *Public Personnel Management* 41, no. 3 (Fall 2012): 389–405; Baltes, Boris B., Thomas E. Briggs, Joseph W. Huff, Julie A. Wright, and George A. Neuman. "Flexible and Compressed Workweek Schedules: A Meta–analysis of Their Effects on Work-Related Criteria." *Journal of Applied Psychology* 84, no. 4 (August 1999): 496–513.

25. Christensen, Stephanie Taylor. "Job Sharing: The Devil Is in the Details." *Managing People at Work* no. 363 (June 2012): 3; Hall, Elizabeth M. "Job Sharing: Evidence from New Zealand." *Australian Journal of Management (University Of New South Wales)* 18, no. 1 (June 1993): 63.
26. Golden, Timothy D. "Unraveling Telecommuting and Satisfaction: Towards a Relational View." *Academy of Management Proceedings* (August 2004): F1–F6; Meinert, Dori, "Make Telecommuting Pay Off," *HR Magazine* 56, no. 6 (June 2011): 32–37; Pearlson, Keri E., and Carol S. Saunders. "There's No Place Like Home: Managing Telecommuting Paradoxes." *Academy of Management Executive* 15, no. 2 (May 2001): 117–128.
27. Silverman, Rachel Emma. "House Party: Working and Living at the Office." *Wall Street Journal*, July 20, 2013. http://www.wsj.com/articles/SB10001424127887324170004578638002403132048.

Chapter 7

1. For an overview of teams in organizations, see Kozlowski, Steve W. J., and Bradford S. Bell. "Work Groups and Teams in Organizations." In *Handbook of Psychology*, Vol. 12: *Industrial and Organizational Psychology* (2nd ed.), 412–469 (Hoboken, NJ: Wiley, 2013).
2. Kesling, Ben, and James R. Hagerty. "'Soft Skills' Can Help You Get Ahead." *Wall Street Journal*. April 2, 2013. http://online.wsj.com/news/articles/SB10001424127887323466204578383022434680196?mg=reno64-wsj&url=http%3A%2F%2Fonline.wsj.com%2Farticle%2FSB10001424127887323466204578383022434680196.html.
3. Zábojník, Ján. "Centralized and Decentralized Decision Making in Organizations." *Journal of Labor Economics* 20, no. 1 (January 2002): 1–22.
4. Carr, Austin. "Deep Inside Taco Bell's Doritos Locos Taco." *Fast Company*. May 1, 2013. www.fastcompany.com/3008346/deep-inside-taco-bells-doritos-locos-taco.
5. Katzenbach, Jon R., and Douglas K. Smith. "The Discipline of Teams." *Harvard Business Review* 83, no. 7/8 (July 2005): 162–171; Stewart, Greg L., Charles C. Manz, and Henry P. Sims, *Team Work and Group Dynamics* (New York: Wiley, 1999).
6. Ibid.
7. Kirkman, Bradley L., Benson Rosen, Paul E. Tesluk, and Cristina B. Gibson. "The Impact of Team Empowerment on Virtual Team Performance: The Moderating Role of Face-to-Face Interaction." *Academy of Management Journal* 47, no. 2 (April 2004): 175–192; Malhotra, Arvind, Ann Majchrzak, and Benson Rosen. "Leading Virtual Teams." *Academy of Management Perspectives* 21, no. 1 (February 2007): 60–70; Montoya-Weiss, Mitzi M., Anne P. Massey, and Michael Song. "Getting It Together: Temporal Coordination and Conflict Management in Global Virtual Teams." *Academy of Management Journal* 44, no. 6 (December 2001): 1251–1262; Klitmøller, Anders, Susan Carol Schneider, and Karsten Jonsen. "Speaking of Global Virtual Teams: Language Differences, Social Categorization and Media Choice." *Personnel Review* 44, no. 2 (2015): 270–285.
8. Beyerlein, Michael M., and A. Douglas. Johnson. *Advances in Interdisciplinary Studies of Work Teams: Theories of Self-Managing Work Teams*, Vol. 1. (Stamford, CT: Elsevier Science/JAI Press, 1994); Neck, Christopher P., Mary L. Connerley, and Charles C. Manz. "Toward a Continuum of Self-Managing Team Development." In *Advances in Interdisciplinary Studies of Work Teams*, Vol. 4, 193–216 (Stamford, CT: Elsevier Science/JAI Press, 1997).
9. Colvin, Geoff. "The Art of the Self-Managing Team." *Fortune.com*. December 5, 2012. http://fortune.com/2012/12/05/the-art-of-the-self-managing-team/.
10. Ilgen, Daniel R., Jeffrey A. LePine, and John R. Hollenbeck. "Effective Decision Making in Multinational Teams." In *New Perspectives on International Industrial/Organizational Psychology*, 377–409 (San Francisco: New Lexington Press/Jossey-Bass, 1997); Scott, Jonathan T. "Chapter 10: Managing Teams and Work Groups." In *Concise Handbook of Management: A Practitioner's Approach*, 79–84 (n.p.: 2005).
11. www.ideo.com/work/openideo.
12. Aime, Federico, Stephen Humphrey, D. Scott Derue, and Jeffrey B. Paul. "The Riddle of Heterarchy: Power Transitions in Cross-Functional Teams." *Academy of Management Journal* 57, no. 2 (April 2014): 327–352; Likert, Rensis. "Improving Cost Performance with Cross-Functional Teams." *Management Review* 65, no. 3 (March 1976): 36.
13. www.inc.com/encyclopedia/cross-functional-teams.html.
14. See for example, Hackman, J. R. "The Design of Work Teams." In *Handbook of Organizational Behavior*, edited by J. W. Lorsch, 315–342 (Englewood Cliffs, NJ: Prentice-Hall, 1987); Ilgen, Daniel R., John R. Hollenbeck, Michael Johnson, and Dustin Jundt. "Teams In Organizations: From Input-Process-Output Models to IMOI Models." *Annual Review of Psychology* 56, no. 1 (February 2005): 517–543; McGrath, J. E. *Social Psychology: A Brief Introduction* (New York: Rinehart and Winston, 1964).
15. Stewart et al. *Team Work and Group Dynamics*; Thompson, James D. *Organizations in Action: Social Science Bases of Administrative Theory* (New York: McGraw-Hill, 1967).
16. Daft, Richard L. *Organization Theory and Design* (Boston: Cengage, 2015).
17. Chakravarty, Amiya K. *Supply Chain Transformation: Evolving with Emerging Business Paradigms* (Heidelberg, Germany: Springer, 2014).
18. Daft, *Organization Theory and Design*.
19. Barry, Bruce, and Greg L. Stewart. "Composition, Process, and Performance in Self-Managed Groups: The Role of Personality." *Journal of Applied Psychology* 82, no. 1 (February 1997): 62–78.
20. Peeters, Miranda A. G., Harrie F. J. M. Van Tuijl, Christel G. Rutte, and Isabelle M. M. J. Reymen. "Personality and Team Performance: A Meta-analysis." *European Journal of Personality* 20, no. 5 (August 2006): 377–396.
21. Schneider, Benjamin. "The People Make the Place." *Personnel Psychology* 40, no. 3 (September 1987): 437–453; Schneider, Benjamin, Harold W. Goldstein, and D. Brent Smith. "The ASA Framework: An Update." *Personnel Psychology* 48, no. 4 (Winter 1995): 747–773.
22. Bretz, Robert D. Jr., Ronald A. Ash, and George F. Dreher. "Do People Make the Place? An Examination of the Attraction-Selection-Attrition Hypothesis." *Personnel Psychology* 42, no. 3 (September 1989): 561–581; Ployhart, Robert E., Jeff A. Weekley, and Kathryn Baughman. "The Structure and Function of Human Capital Emergence: A Multilevel Examination of the Attraction-Selection-Attrition Model." *Academy of Management Journal* 49, no. 4 (August 2006): 661–677; Schneider, Benjamin, D. Brent Smith, and Michelle C. Paul. "P–E Fit and the Attraction-Selection-Attrition Model of Organizational Functioning: Introduction and Overview." In *Work Motivation in the Context of a Globalizing Economy*, 231–246 (Mahwah, NJ: Erlbaum, 2001).
23. Bonebright, Denise A. "Forty Years of Storming: A Historical Review of Tuckman's Model of Small Group Development." *Human Resource Development International* 13, no. 1 (February 2010): 111–120; Tuckman, Bruce W. "Developmental Sequence in Small Groups." *Psychological Bulletin* 63, no. 6 (June 1965): 384–399; Tuckman, Bruce W., and Mary Ann C. Jensen. "Stages of Small-Group Development Revisited." *Group and Organization Studies* 2, no. 4 (December 1977): 419–427.
24. Amason, Allen C., and Harry J. Sapienza. "The Effects of Top Management Team Size and Interaction Norms on Cognitive and Affective Conflict." *Journal of Management* 23, no. 4 (1997):

495–516; Celani, Anthony, and Kevin Tasa. "We're All in This Together: Examining Associations between Collectivistic Group Norms, Collective Efficacy, and Team Performance." *Academy of Management Annual Meeting Proceedings* (August 2010): 1–6; Chatman, Jennifer A., and Francis J. Flynn. "The Influence of Demographic Heterogeneity on the Emergence and Consequences of Cooperative Norms in Work Teams." *Academy of Management Journal* 44, no. 5 (October 2001): 956–974; De Jong, Bart A., and Katinka M. Bijlsma-Frankema. "When and How Does Norm-Based Peer Control Affect the Performance of Self-Managing Teams?" *Academy of Management Annual Meeting Proceedings* (August 2009): 1–6; Taggar, Simon, and Robert Ellis. "The Role of Leaders in Shaping Formal Team Norms." *Leadership Quarterly* 18, no. 2 (April 2007): 105–120.

25. Beal, Daniel J., Robin R. Cohen, Michael J. Burke, and Christy L. McLendon. "Cohesion and Performance in Groups: A Meta-analytic Clarification of Construct Relations." *Journal of Applied Psychology* 88, no. 6 (December 2003): 989–1004; Carron, Albert V., Mark A. Eys, and Shauna M. Burke. "Team Cohesion: Nature, Correlates, and Development." In *Social Psychology in Sport*, 91–101 (Champaign, IL: Human Kinetics, 2007).
26. Stagl, Kevin C., C. Shawn Burke, Eduardo Salas, and Linda Pierce. "Team Adaptation: Realizing Team Synergy." In *Understanding Adaptability: A Prerequisite for Effective Performance within Complex Environments*, 117–141 (Amsterdam, Netherlands: Elsevier, 2006); Mumford, Troy V., and Marifran Mattson. "Will Teams Work? How the Nature of Work Drives Synergy in Autonomous Team Designs." *Academy of Management Annual Meeting Proceedings* (August 2009): 1–6.
27. Miner, Frederick C. "Group versus Individual Decision Making: An Investigation of Performance Measures, Decision Strategies, and Process Losses/Gains." *Organizational Behavior and Human Performance* 33, no. 1 (February 1984): 112–124; Steiner, Ivan D. "Models for Inferring Relationships between Group Size and Potential Group Productivity." *Behavioral Science* 11, no. 4 (1966): 273–283.
28. Ibid.
29. Geen, Russell G. "Alternative Conceptions of Social Facilitation." In *Psychology of Group Influence* (2nd ed.), 15–51 (Hillsdale, NJ: Erlbaum, 1989); Williamson, E. G. "Allport's Experiments in 'Social Facilitation.'" *Psychological Monographs* 35, no. 2 (1926): 138–143.
30. For a detailed discussion of groupthink, see Janis, Irving L. "Groupthink." *Psychology Today* 5, no. 6 (November 1971): 43–46, 74–76; Janis, Irving. L. *Victims of Groupthink: A Psychological Study of Foreign-Policy Decisions and Fiascoes* (Boston: Houghton Mifflin, 1972); Janis, Irving. L. *Groupthink: Psychological Studies of Policy Decisions and Fiascoes* (Boston: Houghton Mifflin, 1982).
31. Litchfield, Robert C. "Brainstorming Reconsidered: A Goal-Based View." *Academy of Management Review* 33, no. 3 (July 2008): 649–668; Taylor, Donald W., Paul C. Berry, and Clifford H. Block. "Does Group Participation When Using Brainstorming Facilitate or Inhibit Creative Thinking?" *Administrative Science Quarterly* 3, no. 1 (June 1958): 23–47.
32. Delbecq, Andre L., and Van de Ven Andrew. H. "A Group Process Model for Problem Identification and Program Planning." *Journal of Applied Behavioral Science* no. 7 (July/August, 1971), 466–91; Van de Ven, Andrew H., and Andre L. Delbecq. "The Effectiveness of Nominal, Delphi, and Interacting Group Decision Making Processes." *Academy of Management Journal* 17, no. 4 (December 1974): 605–621.
33. Ibid.

Chapter 8

1. For an overview see Miller, Susan J., David J. Hickson, and David C. Wilson. "Decision-Making in Organizations." In *Handbook of Organization Studies*, 293–312 (Thousand Oaks, CA: Sage, 1996).
2. Simon, Herbert A. *The New Science of Management Decision* (New York: Harper & Brothers, 1960).
3. Hess, Alexander E. M., Vince Calio, and Thomas C. Frohlich. "Companies with the Best (and Worst) Reputations." *24/7 Wall St.* May 1, 2014. http://247wallst.com/special-report/2014/05/01/companies-with-the-best-and-worst-reputations-2/#ixzz3aKRwTf6X.
4. Satariano, Adam. "Apple's $10.5B on Robots to Lasers Shores Up Supply Chain." *Bloomberg Business.* November 13, 2013. www.bloomberg.com/news/articles/2013-11-13/apple-s-10-5b-on-robots-to-lasers-shores-up-supply-chain.
5. Based on Kepner, Charles H., and Benjamin B. Tregoe. *The Rational Manager: A Systematic Approach to Problem Solving and Decision-Making* (New York: McGraw-Hill, 1965).
6. Selten, Reinhard. "What Is Bounded Rationality?" In *Bounded Rationality: The Adaptive Toolbox*, 13–36 (Cambridge, MA: MIT Press, 2001).
7. Ibid.
8. Baumol, William J. "On Rational Satisficing." In *Models of a Man: Essays in Memory of Herbert A. Simon*, 57–66 (Cambridge, MA: MIT Press, 2004); Janis, Irving L., and Leon Mann. "Satisficing." In *The Effective Manager: Perspectives and Illustrations*, 157–159 (Thousand Oaks, CA: Sage, 1996).
9. Strack, Fritz, and Roland Deutsch. "Intuition." In *Social Cognition: The Basis of Human Interaction*, 179–197 (New York: Psychology Press, 2009); Plessner, Henning, and Sabine Czenna. "The Benefits of Intuition." In *Intuition in Judgment and Decision Making*, 251–265 (Mahwah, NJ: Erlbaum, 2008).
10. Dearborn, George Van N. "Intuition." *Psychological Review* 23, no. 6 (November 1916): 465–483; Isenman, Lois. "Understanding Unconscious Intelligence and Intuition: 'Blink' and Beyond." *Perspectives in Biology and Medicine* 56, no. 1 (Winter 2013): 148–166.
11. Isaacson, Walter. "The Genius of Jobs." *New York Times.* October 29, 2011. www.nytimes.com/2011/10/30/opinion/sunday/steve-jobss-genius.html?_r=1&.
12. Gigerenzer, Gerd, Ralph Hertwig, and Thorsten Pachur. *Heuristics: The Foundations of Adaptive Behavior* (New York: Oxford University Press, 2011).
13. Schwarz, Norbert, and Leigh Ann Vaughn. "The Availability Heuristic Revisited: Ease of Recall and Content of Recall as Distinct Sources of Information." In *Heuristics and Biases: The Psychology of Intuitive Judgment*, 103–119 (New York: Cambridge University Press, 2002).
14. Mass, Harold. "The Odds Are 11 Million to 1 That You'll Die in a Plane Crash." *The Week.* July 8, 2013. http://theweek.com/article/index/246552/the-odds-are-11-million-to-1-that-youll-die-in-a-plane-crash.
15. Epley, Nicholas, and Thomas Gilovich. "Putting Adjustment Back in the Anchoring and Adjustment Heuristic." In *Heuristics and Biases*, 139–149.
16. Nilsson, Håkan, Peter Juslin, and Henrik Olsson. "Exemplars in the Mist: The Cognitive Substrate of the Representativeness Heuristic." *Scandinavian Journal of Psychology* 49, no. 3 (June 2008): 201–212.
17. Stasser, Garold, and William Titus. "Effects of Information Load and Percentage of Shared Information on the Dissemination of Unshared Information during Group Discussion." *Journal of Personality and Social Psychology* 53, no. 1 (July 1987): 81–93.
18. Green, David W. "Confirmation Bias, Problem-Solving and Cognitive Models." In *Cognitive Biases*, 553–562 (Oxford: North-Holland, 1990); Lewicka, Maria. "Confirmation Bias: Cognitive Error or Adaptive Strategy of Action Control?" In *Personal Control in Action: Cognitive and Motivational Mechanisms*, 233–258 (New York: Plenum, 1998).

19. Buontempo, Gina, and Joel Brockner. "Emotional Intelligence and the Ease of Recall Judgment Bias: The Mediating Effect of Private Self-Focused Attention." *Journal of Applied Social Psychology* 38, no. 1 (January 2008): 159–172.
20. Hoffrage, Ulrich, Ralph Hertwig, and Gerd Gigerenzer. "Hindsight Bias: A By-Product of Knowledge Updating?" In *Heuristics: The Foundations of Adaptive Behavior*, 223–241 (New York: Oxford University Press, 2011); Hoffrage, Ulrich, and Ralph Hertwig. "Hindsight Bias: A Price Worth Paying for Fast and Frugal Memory." In *Simple Heuristics That Make Us Smart*, 191–208 (New York: Oxford University Press, 1999).
21. Krueger, Joachim I., and Melissa Acevedo. "Social Projection and the Psychology of Choice." In *The Self in Social Judgment*, 17–41 (New York: Psychology Press, 2005).
22. Staw, Barry M. "The Escalation of Commitment: An Update and Appraisal." In *Organizational Decision Making*, 191–215 (New York: Cambridge University Press, 1997).
23. Hsuchi, Ting, and Thomas S. Wallsten. "A Query Theory Account of the Effect of Memory Retrieval on the Sunk Cost Bias." *Psychonomic Bulletin and Review* 18, no. 4 (August 2011): 767–773.
24. Steele-Johnson, Debra, and Zachary T. Kalinoski. "Error Framing Effects on Performance: Cognitive, Motivational, and Affective Pathways." *Journal of Psychology: Interdisciplinary and Applied* 148, no. 1 (January 2014): 93–111.
25. May, Steve. "Ethical Challenges and Dilemmas in Organizations: A Case Study Approach." In *Case Studies in Organizational Communication: Ethical Perspectives and Practices*, 1–18 (Thousand Oaks, CA: Sage, 2006); Mathews, M. Cash. *Strategic Intervention in Organizations: Resolving Ethical Dilemmas*. (Thousand Oaks, CA: Sage, 1988).
26. See, for example, Josephson, Michael S. "Character: Linchpin of Leadership." *Executive Excellence* 16, no. 8 (August 1999): 13.
27. Gustafson, Andrew. "In Defense of a Utilitarian Business Ethic." *Business and Society Review* 118, no. 3 (Fall 2013): 325–360; Schumann, Paul L. "A Moral Principles Framework for Human Resource Management Ethics." *Human Resource Management Review* 11, nos. 1/2 (Summer 2001): 93.
28. Ibid.
29. Ibid.
30. http://josephsoninstitute.org/about.html.
31. Josephson, Michael. "Six Pillars of Character." *Personal Excellence* (October 2007): 4.
32. http://charactercounts.org/overview/faq.html.
33. Ibid.
34. Ibid.
35. Josephson, Michael S., and Wes Hanson. *Making Ethical Decisions*. (Los Angeles, CA: Josephson Institute of Ethics, 1992).

Chapter 9

1. For an overview of creativity in organizations see, Hennessey, Beth A., and Teresa M. Amabile. "Creativity." *Annual Review of Psychology* 61, (2010): 569–598; Amabile, Teresa M., and Julianna Pillemer. "Perspectives on the social psychology of creativity." *Journal of Creative Behavior* 46, no. 1 (March 2012): 3–15.
2. For an overview of innovation in organizations see, Ahlstrom, David. "Innovation and Growth: How Business Contributes to Society." *Academy of Management Perspectives* 24, no. 3 (August 2010): 11–24; Anthony, Scott D. "The Little Black Book of Innovation: How It Works, How to Do It." *Harvard Business School Press Books* (January 2012): 1.
3. Bacon, John U., & Heward, Lyn. *Cirque du Soleil® The spark: Igniting the creative fire that lives within us all* (New York: Doubleday, 2006); Nussbaum, Bruce, Robert Berner, and Diane Brady. "GET CREATIVE!" *Businessweek*. August 2005: 60–68.
4. Ibid.
5. Chapman, Lizette. "How I Built GoPro Extreme Sports Camera." *Wall Street Journal*. June 19, 2013.
6. Amabile, Teresa M. "The Social Psychology of Creativity: A Componential Conceptualization." *Journal of Personality and Social Psychology* 45, no. 2 (August 1983): 357–376; Amabile, Teresa M. "How to Kill Creativity." *Harvard Business Review* 76, no. 5 (September 1998): 76–87.
7. Ibid.
8. Ibid.
9. Ibid.
10. Ibid.
11. DiLiello, Trudy C., and Jeffery D. Houghton. "Creative Potential and Practised Creativity: Identifying Untapped Creativity in Organizations." *Creativity and Innovation Management* 17, no. 1 (March 2008): 37–46.
12. Amabile, Teresa M., Regina Conti, Heather Coon, Jeffrey Lazenby, and Michael Herron. "Assessing the Work Environment for Creativity." *Academy of Management Journal* 39, no. 5 (October 1996): 1154–1184; DiLiello, Trudy C., Jeffery D. Houghton, and David Dawley. "Narrowing the Creativity Gap: The Moderating Effects of Perceived Support for Creativity." *Journal of Psychology: Interdisciplinary and Applied* 145, no. 3 (March 2011): 151–172.
13. Stallard, Michael Lee. "Three Ways Pixar Gains Competitive Advantage from Its Culture." *FOXBusiness*. May 23, 2014. www.foxbusiness.com/business-leaders/2014/05/23/3-ways-pixar-gains-competitive-advantage-from-its-culture/.
14. DiLiello et al., "Narrowing the Creativity Gap."
15. Ibid.
16. Amabile et al., "Assessing the Work Environment for Creativity"; DiLiello et al. "Narrowing the Creativity Gap."
17. Ibid.
18. Ibid.
19. "Innovation Inspiration from Nonprofits." *Inc.* www.inc.com/ss/innovation-inspiration-from-nonprofits#1.
20. Process developed based on Utterback, James M. "The Process of Technological Innovation within the Firm." *Academy of Management Journal* 14, no. 1 (March 1971): 75–88.
21. Inspired by handling arms designed by Atlas Copco. www.atlascopco.com/achieve/themes/innovation/lighttools.aspx.
22. Knight, Kenneth E. "A Descriptive Model of the Intra-firm Innovation Process." *Journal of Business* 40, no. 4 (October 1967): 478–496.
23. Ibid.
24. Ibid.
25. Ibid.
26. Smith, Wendy K., and Michael L. Tushman. "Managing Strategic Contradictions: A Top Management Model for Managing Innovation Streams." *Organization Science* 16, no. 5 (September 2005): 522–536.
27. Ibid.
28. Ogburn, William F. "Cultural Lag as Theory." *Sociology and Social Research* 41, (1957): 167–174.
29. Smith and Tushman, "Managing Strategic Contradictions."

Chapter 10

1. For an overview see Burke, W. Warner. "Conflict in Organizations." In *The Handbook of Conflict Resolution: Theory and Practice* (2nd ed.), 781–804 (Hoboken, NJ: Wiley, 2006); De Dreu, Carsten K. W., and Michele J. Gelfand. *The Psychology of Conflict and Conflict Management in Organizations* (New York: Taylor & Francis Group/ Erlbaum, 2008).
2. Orr, Steve. "Kodak Taking Steps to Hand Off Environmental Concerns." *USA Today*. May 30, 2013. www.usatoday.com/story/money/business/2013/05/30/kodak-taking-steps-to-hand-off-environmental-concerns-/2372503/.
3. Vincent, Roger, and Andrea Chang, "Starbucks Tips Ruling Is Made to Order for Baristas." *LA Times*. March 21, 2008. www.latimes.com/business/la-fi-starbucks21mar21-story.html.
4. Sieczkowski, Cavan. "Steve Jobs and Bill Gates History: The Dueling Wizards."

International Business Times. October 6, 2011. www.ibtimes.com/steve-jobs-bill-gates-history-dueling-wizards-321739.

5. Amason, Allen C. "Distinguishing the Effects of Functional and Dysfunctional Conflict on Strategic Decision Making: Resolving a Paradox for Top Management Teams." *Academy of Management Journal* 39, no. 1 (February 1996): 123–148.
6. Ibid.
7. Jehn, Karen A. "A Qualitative Analysis of Conflict Types and Dimensions in Organizational Groups." *Administrative Science Quarterly* 42, no. 3 (September 1997): 530–557.
8. Pondy, Louis R. "Organizational Conflict: Concepts and Models." *Administrative Science Quarterly* 12, no. 2 (September 1967): 296–320.
9. Kilmann, Ralph H., and Kenneth W. Thomas. "Interpersonal Conflict-Handling Behavior as Reflections of Jungian Personality Dimensions." *Psychological Reports* 37, no. 3, Pt 1 (December 1975): 971–980.
10. For a detailed discussion of the definition of trust, see Mayer, Roger C., James H. Davis, and F. David Schoorman. "An Integrative Model of Organizational Trust." *Academy of Management Review* 20, no. 3 (July 1995): 709–734.
11. Pomerantz, Dorothy. "Tom Hanks Tops Our List of the Most Trustworthy Celebrities." *Forbes.com.* February 12, 2014. www.forbes.com/sites/dorothypomerantz/2014/02/12/tom-hanks-tops-our-list-of-the-most-trustworthy-celebrities/.
12. Jones, Roxanne. "Brian Williams Broke Public Trust." *CNN.com.* February 6, 2015. http://edition.cnn.com/2015/02/05/opinion/jones-brian-williams-controversy/.
13. "Lance Armstrong Fined $10m for Drugs Lies in SCA Promotions Case." *Guardian.* February 16, 2015. www.theguardian.com/sport/2015/feb/16/lance-armstrong-fined-10m-drugs-lies-sca-promotions.
14. Mayer, Roger C., James H. Davis, and F. David Schoorman. "An Integrative Model of Organizational Trust." *Academy of Management Review* 20, no. 3 (July 1995): 709–734; McAllister, Daniel J. "Affect- and Cognition-Based Trust as Foundations for Interpersonal Cooperation in Organizations." *Academy of Management Journal* 38, no. 1 (February 1995): 24–59.
15. Colquitt, Jason A., Brent A. Scott, and Jeffery A. LePine. "Trust, Trustworthiness, and Trust Propensity: A Meta-analytic Test of Their Unique Relationships with Risk Taking and Job Performance." *Journal of Applied Psychology* 92, no. 4 (July 2007): 909–927; Mayer, Roger C., and Mark B. Gavin. "Trust in Management and Performance: Who Minds the Shop While the Employees Watch the Boss?" *Academy of Management Journal* 48, no. 5 (October 2005): 874–888.
16. Ibid.
17. For an overview, see Thompson, Leigh L., Jiunwen Wang, and Brian C. Gunia. "Negotiation." In *Group Processes*, 55–84 (New York: Psychology Press, 2013).
18. The negotiation process explained here is based on information contained in Lewicki, Roy J., Stephen E. Weiss, and David Lewin. "Models of Conflict, Negotiation and Third Party Intervention: A Review and Synthesis." *Journal of Organizational Behavior* 13, no. 3 (May 1992): 209–252.
19. Angoff, Samuel E. "Impartial Opinion and Constructive Criticism of Mediators, Mediation Agencies and Conciliators. *"Labor Law Journal* 12, no. 1 (January 1961): 67; Lewicki et al., "Models of Conflict, Negotiation and Third Party Intervention."
20. Gorman, Thomas. "The Arbitration Process." *Baseball Prospectus.* January 18, 2012. www.baseballprospectus.com/article.php?articleid=15864.
21. Lewicki et al., "Models of Conflict, Negotiation and Third Party Intervention."
22. Ibid.; Fisher, Roger. "Getting to Yes." *Management Review* 71, no. 2 (February 1982): 16–21.
23. Ibid.
24. Hedges, Kristi. "How to Negotiate a Higher Salary." *Forbes Woman.* April 24, 2013. www.forbes.com/sites/work-in-progress/2013/04/24/how-to-negotiate-a-higher-salary/.
25. Fisher, Roger, and William Ury. "What If They Are More Powerful? (Develop Your BATNA—Best Alternative to a Negotiated Agreement)." In *Getting to Yes*, 101–111 (n.p.: 1983).
26. Sebenius, James K. "Negotiation Analysis: A Characterization and Review." In *Negotiation, Decision Making and Conflict Management,* Vols. 1–3, 18–41 (Northampton, MA: Edward Elgar, 2005).

Chapter 11

1. For an overview of leadership research see one or more of the following: Bass, Bernard M. *The Bass Handbook of Leadership: Theory, Research, and Managerial Applications* (4th ed.) (New York: Free Press, 2008); House, Robert J., and Ram N. Aditya. "The Social Scientific Study of Leadership: Quo Vadis?" *Journal of Management* 23, no. 3 (1997 Special Issue 1997): 409; Jago, Arthur G. "Leadership: Perspectives in Theory and Research." *Management Science* 28, no. 3 (March 1982): 315–336.
2. See for example Foti, Roseanne J., and Neil M. A. Hauenstein. "Pattern and Variable Approaches in Leadership Emergence and Effectiveness." *Journal of Applied Psychology* 92, no. 2 (March 2007): 347–355.
3. See, for instance, Neubert, Mitchell J., and Simon Taggar. "Pathways to Informal Leadership: The Moderating Role of Gender on the Relationship of Individual Differences and Team Member Network Centrality to Informal Leadership Emergence." *Leadership Quarterly* 15, no. 2 (April 2004): 175–194.
4. Krueger, Deborah L. "Informal Leaders and Cultural Change." *American Nurse Today.* August 2014. www.americannursetoday.com/informal-leaders-and-cultural-change/.
5. Clemens, John K. "Leaders versus Managers: The Case of Captain Vere." *Journal of Leadership Studies* 1, no. 3 (June 1994): 117–128; Watkins, Michael D. "How Managers Become Leaders." *Harvard Business Review* 90, no. 6 (June 2012): 64–72; Zaleznik, Abraham. "Managers and Leaders: Are They Different?" *Harvard Business Review* 55, no. 3 (May 1977): 67–78.
6. Manz, Charles C., and Henry P. Sims Jr. "SuperLeadership: Beyond the Myth of Heroic Leadership." *Organizational Dynamics* 19, no. 4 (1991): 18–35; Pearce, Craig L., Henry P. Jr. Sims, Jonathan F. Cox, Gail Ball, Eugene Schnell, Ken A. Smith, and Linda Trevino. "Transactors, Transformers and Beyond: A Multi-Method Development of a Theoretical Typology of Leadership." *Journal of Management Development* 22, no. 4 (2003): 273–307.
7. Manz and Sims, "SuperLeadership"; Manz, Charles C., and Henry P. Sims Jr. *The New SuperLeadership: Leading Others to Lead Themselves* (San Francisco: Berrett-Koehler, 2001); Pearce, Craig L., and Henry P. Jr. Sims. "Vertical versus Shared Leadership as Predictors of the Effectiveness of Change Management Teams: An Examination of Aversive, Directive, Transactional, Transformational, and Empowering Leader Behaviors." *Group Dynamics: Theory, Research, and Practice* 6, no. 2 (June 2002): 172–197.
8. Ibid.
9. See, for example, Jenkins, William O. "A Review of Leadership Studies with Particular Reference to Military Problems." *Psychological Bulletin* 44, no. 1 (January 1947): 54–79; Stogdill, Ralph M. "Personal Factors Associated with Leadership: A Survey of the Literature." *Journal of Psychology: Interdisciplinary and Applied* 25 (1948): 35–71.
10. Colbert, Amy E., Timothy A. Judge, Daejeong Choi, and Gang Wang. "Assessing the Trait Theory of Leadership Using Self and Observer Ratings of Personality: The Mediating Role of Contributions to Group Success." *Leadership Quarterly* 23, no. 4 (August 2012): 670–685; Derue, D. Scott, Jennifer D. Nahrgang, Ned Wellman, and Stephen E. Humphrey. "Trait and Behavioral

Theories of Leadership: An Integration and Meta-analytic Test of Their Relative Validity." *Personnel Psychology* 64, no. 1 (2011): 7–52.

11. Kirkpatrick, Shelley A., and Edwin A. Locke. "Leadership: Do Traits Matter?" *Academy of Management Executive* 5, no. 2 (May 1991): 48–60; Zaccaro, Stephen J. "Trait-Based Perspectives of Leadership." *American Psychologist* 62, no. 1 (January 2007): 6–16.
12. Hemphill, J. K., and A. E. Coons. *Leader Behavior: Its Description and Measurement* (Research Monograph No. 88) (Columbus: Ohio State University, Bureau of Business Research, 1957).
13. Cartwright, D. and A. Zander. *Group Dynamics Research and Theory* (Evanston, IL: Row, Peterson, 1960); Katz, D. and R. L. Kahn. "Human Organization and Worker Motivation." *Industrial Productivity* (Madison, WI: Industrial Relations Research Association, 1951); Likert, Rensis. *New Patterns of Management* (New York: McGraw-Hill, 1961).
14. Blake, R. R., and J. S. Mouton, *The Managerial Grid* (Houston, TX: Gulf, 1964).
15. See, for example, Hughes, Richard L., Robert C. Ginnett, and Gordon J. Curphy. "Contingency Theories of Leadership." In *Leading Organizations: Perspectives for a New Era*, 141–157 (Thousand Oaks, CA: Sage, 1998); Fiedler, F. E. "A Contingency Model of Leadership Effectiveness." In *Advances in Experimental Social Psychology,* Vol. 1, edited by L. Berkowitz, 149–190 (New York: Academic Press, 1964); Fiedler, F. E. *A Theory of Leadership Effectiveness* (New York: McGraw-Hill, 1967); Fiedler, F. E., and J. E. Garcia, *New Approaches to Leadership: Cognitive Resources and Organizational Performance* (New York: Wiley, 1987).
16. Hersey, Paul, and Kenneth H. Blanchard *Management of Organizational Behavior: Utilizing Human Resources* (Englewood Cliffs, NJ: Prentice Hall, 1969); Blanchard, Kenneth H., Drea Zigarmi, and Robert B. Nelson. "Situational Leadership® After 25 Years: A Retrospective." *Journal of Leadership Studies* 1, no. 1 (November 1993): 21–36; Luo, Haibin, and Shanshi Liu. "Effect of Situational Leadership and Employee Readiness Match on Organizational Citizenship Behavior in China." *Social Behavior and Personality* 42, no. 10 (2014): 1725–1732.
17. House, Robert J. "A Path Goal Theory of Leader Effectiveness." *Administrative Science Quarterly* 16, no. 3 (September 1971): 321–339; House, Robert J. "Path-Goal Theory of Leadership: Lessons, Legacy, and a Reformulated Theory." *Leadership Quarterly* (Fall 1996): 323; House, Robert J., and Terence R. Mitchell. "Path-Goal Theory of Leadership." In *Leadership: Understanding the Dynamics of Power and Influence in Organizations* (2nd ed.), 241–254.
18. Kerr, Steven, and John M. Jermier. "Substitutes for Leadership: Their Meaning and Measurement." *Organizational Behavior and Human Performance* 22, no. 3 (December 1978): 375–403; Nübold, Annika, Peter M. Muck, and Günter W. Maier. "A New Substitute for Leadership? Followers' State Core Self-Evaluations." *Leadership Quarterly* 24, no. 1 (February 2013): 29–44.
19. Colvin, Geoff. "The Art of the Self-Managing Team." *Fortune,* December 5, 2012. http://fortune.com/2012/12/05/the-art-of-the-self-managing-team/.
20. Dansereau, Fred, George Graen, and William J. Haga. "A Vertical Dyad Linkage Approach to Leadership within Formal Organizations: A Longitudinal Investigation of the Role Making Process." *Organizational Behavior and Human Performance* 13, no. 1 (February 1975): 46–78; Gerstner, Charlotte R., and David V. Day. "Meta-Analytic Review of Leader-Member Exchange Theory: Correlates and Construct Issues." *Journal of Applied Psychology* 82, no. 6 (December 1997): 827–844; Graen, George B., and Mary Uhl-Bien. "Relationship-Based Approach to Leadership: Development of Leader–Member Exchange (LMX) Theory of Leadership over 25 Years: Applying a Multi-level Multi-domain perspective." *Leadership Quarterly* 6, no. 2 (1995): 219–247.
21. Bennett, Kristen. "What Is Meant by Transformational Leadership?" *Houston Chronicle*. http://smallbusiness.chron.com/meant-transformational-leadership-18267.html.
22. Bass, Bernard M. *Leadership and Performance beyond Expectations* (New York: Free Press, 1985); Avolio, Bruce J., and Bernard M. Bass. "Transformational Leadership, Charisma, and Beyond." In *Emerging Leadership Vistas* (Lexington, MA: Lexington Books, 1988): 29–49.
23. Bass, *Leadership and Performance beyond Expectations;* Hinkin, Timothy R., and Chester A. Schriesheim. "An Examination of 'Nonleadership': From Laissez-Faire Leadership to Leader Reward Omission and Punishment Omission." *Journal of Applied Psychology* 93, no. 6 (November 2008): 1234–1248; Moors, Guy. "The Effect of Response Style Bias on the Measurement of Transformational, Transactional, and Laissez-Faire Leadership." *European Journal of Work and Organizational Psychology* 21, no. 2 (April 2012): 271–298.
24. Stern, Gary M. "Why Warren Buffett's Laissez-Faire Management Style Works." *Investor's Business Daily.* www.marshallgoldsmithlibrary.com/cim/articles_print.php?aid=897.
25. Conger, Jay A., and Rabindra N. Kanungo. 1987. "Toward a Behavioral Theory of Charismatic Leadership in Organizational Settings." *Academy of Management Review* 12, no. 4: 637–647; Conger, Jay A. "Charismatic and Transformational Leadership in Organizations: An Insider's Perspective on These Developing Streams of Research." *Leadership Quarterly* 10, no. 2 (Summer 99 1999): 145.
26. Conger, Jay A. "The Dark Side of Leadership." *Organizational Dynamics* 19, no. 2 (September 1990): 44–55; Howell, Jane M. "Two Faces of Charisma: Socialized and Personalized Leadership in Organizations." In *Charismatic Leadership: The Elusive Factor in Organizational Effectiveness* (San Francisco: Jossey-Bass, 1988): 213–236.
27. Carsten, Melissa K., Mary Uhl-Bien, Bradley J. West, Jaime L. Patera, and Rob McGregor. "Exploring Social Constructions of Followership: A qualitative Study." *Leadership Quarterly* 21, no. 3 (June 2010): 543–562.
28. See, for example, Hogg, Michael A. "Social Categorization, Depersonalization, and Group Behavior." In *Self and Social Identity,* 203–231 (Malden, MA: Blackwell, 2004).
29. Foti, Roseanne J., Scott L. Fraser, and Robert G. Lord. "Effect of Leadership Labels and Prototypes on Perceptions of Political Leaders." *Journal of Applied Psychology* 67, no. 3 (June 1982): 326–333.
30. Shondrick, Sara J., and Robert G. Lord. "Implicit Leadership and Followership Theories: Dynamic Structures for Leadership Perceptions, Memory, and Leader–Follower Processes." In *International Review of Industrial and Organizational Psychology 2010,* Vol. 25, 1–33 (n.p.: Wiley-Blackwell, 2010): Sy, Thomas. "What Do You Think of Followers? Examining the Content, Structure, and Consequences of Implicit Followership Theories." *Organizational Behavior and Human Decision Processes* 113, no. 2 (November 2010): 73–84.
31. Arnold, Josh A., Sharon Arad, Jonathan A. Rhoades, and Fritz Drasgow. "The Empowering Leadership Questionnaire: The Construction and Validation of a New Scale for . . . " *Journal of Organizational Behavior* 21, no. 3 (May 2000): 249–269; Vecchio, Robert P., Joseph E. Justin, and Craig L. Pearce. "Empowering Leadership: An Examination of Mediating Mechanisms within a Hierarchical Structure." *Leadership Quarterly* 21, no. 3 (June 2010): 530–542; Zhang, Xiaomeng, and Kathryn M. Bartol. "Linking Empowering Leadership and Employee Creativity: The Influence of Psychological Empowerment, Intrinsic Motivation, and Creative Process Engagement." *Academy*

of Management Journal 53, no. 1 (February 2010): 107–128.

32. www.brighthubpm.com/resource-management/120498-five-real-world-examples-of-successful-leadership/.
33. Drescher, Marcus A., M. Audrey Korsgaard, Isabell M. Welpe, Arnold Picot, and Rolf T. Wigand. "The Dynamics of Shared Leadership: Building Trust and Enhancing Performance." *Journal of Applied Psychology* (April 14, 2014): *PsycARTICLES*, EBSCO*host*; Pearce, Craig L., and Charles C. Manz. "The New Silver Bullets of Leadership: The Importance of Self- and Shared Leadership in Knowledge Work." *Organizational Dynamics* 34, no. 2 (May 2005): 130–140; Pearce, Craig L. "The Future of Leadership: Combining Vertical and Shared Leadership to Transform Knowledge Work." *Academy of Management Executive* 18, no. 1 (February 2004): 47–57.
34. Walker, Laura. "Developing a Workplace Team Where Everyone's a Leader." *EHS Today*. August 9, 2010. http://ehstoday.com/safety/best-practices/developing-workplace-team-everyone-leader-8228.
35. Manz, Charles C. "Self-Leadership: Toward an Expanded Theory of Self-Influence Processes in Organizations." *Academy of Management Review* 11, no. 3 (July 1986): 585–600; Stewart, Greg L., Stephen H. Courtright, and Charles C. Manz. "Self-Leadership: A Multilevel Review." *Journal of Management* 37, no. 1 (January 2011): 185–222; Neck, Christopher P., and Jeffery D. Houghton. "Two Decades of Self-Leadership Theory and Research." *Journal of Managerial Psychology* 21, no. 4 (June 2006): 270–295.
36. Blanchard, Ken. "Three Ways To Be An Effective Self-Leader: You Can't Lead Others If You Can't Lead Yourself, And You Can't Lead Yourself without The Right Tools." *Fast Company*. February 6, 2014. www.fastcompany.com/3026046/leadership-now/3-ways-to-be-an-effective-self-leader.
37. Neck and Houghton, "Two Decades of Self-Leadership Theory and Research."
38. Ibid.
39. Ibid.
40. Ibid.; Neck, Chris P., and Charles C. Manz. "Thought Self-Leadership: The Influence of Self-Talk and Mental Imagery on Performance." *Journal of Organizational Behavior* 13, no. 7 (December 1992): 681–699.
41. McGuire, Jeanne. *The Case for Values Based Leadership: Maximizing People and Profitability* (White paper). Corporate Education Group. www.corpedgroup.com/resources/ml/ValuesBasedLeadership.asp.
42. Gardner, William L., Claudia C. Cogliser, Kelly M. Davis, and Matthew P. Dickens. "Authentic Leadership: A Review of the Literature and Research Agenda." *Leadership Quarterly* 22, no. 6 (December 2011): 1120–1145; Walumbwa, Fred O., Bruce J. Avolio, William L. Gardner, Tara S. Wernsing, and Suzanne J. Peterson. "Authentic Leadership: Development and Validation of a Theory-Based Measure." *Journal of Management* 34, no. 1 (February 2008): 89–126.
43. Zeigler, Maseena. "Five Counterintuitive Habits of Truly Authentic Leaders." *Forbes*. June 22, 2014. www.forbes.com/sites/maseenaziegler/2014/06/22/5-counterintuitive-habits-of-truly-authentic-leaders/.
44. Cashman, Kevin, *Awakening the Leader Within: A Story of Transformation* (Hoboken, NJ: Wiley, 2003); George, Bill. *True North: Discover Your Authentic Leadership* (San Francisco: Jossey-Bass, 2007).
45. Peus, Claudia, Jenny Sarah Wesche, Bernhard Streicher, Susanne Braun, and Dieter Frey. "Authentic Leadership: An Empirical Test of Its Antecedents, Consequences, and Mediating Mechanisms." *Journal of Business Ethics* 107, no. 3 (May 2012): 331–348; Walumbwa et al. "Authentic leadership"; Clapp-Smith, Rachel, Gretchen R. Vogelgesang, and James B. Avey. "Authentic Leadership and Positive Psychological Capital: The Mediating Role of Trust at the Group Level of Analysis." *Journal of Leadership and Organizational Studies* 15, no. 3 (February 2009): 227–240.
46. Fry, Louis W. "Toward a Theory of Spiritual Leadership." *Leadership Quarterly* 14, no. 6 (December 2003): 693–727; Fry, Louis W. "Spiritual Leadership and Faith and Spirituality in the Workplace." In *Handbook of Faith and Spirituality in the Workplace: Emerging Research and Practice*, 697–704 (New York: Springer Science + Business Media, 2013).
47. Fry, Louis W., Sean T. Hannah, Michael Noel, and Fred O. Walumbwa. "Impact of Spiritual Leadership on Unit Performance." *Leadership Quarterly* 22, no. 2 (April 2011): 259–270; Fry, Louis W., Sean T. Hannah, Michael Noel, and Fred O. Walumbwa. "Corrigendum to 'Impact of spiritual leadership on unit performance.' [The Leadership Quarterly. 22 (2011) 259–270]." *Leadership Quarterly* 23, no. 3 (June 2012): 641.
48. Greenleaf, R. K. *The Servant as Leader* (Newton Centre, MA: Robert Greenleaf Center, 1970); Neubert, Mitchell J., K. Michele Kacmar, Dawn S. Carlson, Lawrence B. Chonko, and James A. Roberts. "Regulatory Focus as a Mediator of the Influence of Initiating Structure and Servant Leadership on Employee Behavior." *Journal of Applied Psychology* 93, no. 6 (November 2008): 1220–1233; Walumbwa, Fred O., Chad A. Hartnell, and Adegoke Oke. "Servant Leadership, Procedural Justice Climate, Service Climate, Employee Attitudes, and Organizational Citizenship Behavior: A Cross-Level Investigation." *Journal of Applied Psychology* 95, no. 3 (May 2010): 517–529.
49. Schmitz, Paul. "Richard Murphy: A Powerful Example of Servant Leadership." *Huffington Post*. April 10, 2013. www.huffingtonpost.com/paul-schmitz/true-servant-leadership-f_b_3016044.html; Douglas Martin, "Richard L. Murphy, Who Aided Disadvantaged Youths, Dies at 68." *New York Times*. February 15, 2013. www.nytimes.com/2013/02/17/nyregion/richard-l-murphy-former-nyc-youth-services-commissioner-dies-at-68.html?_r=0.
50. Brown, Michael E., and Linda K. Treviño. "Ethical Leadership: A Review and Future Directions." *Leadership Quarterly* 17, no. 6 (December 2006): 595–616; Brown, Michael E., Linda K. Treviño, and David A. Harrison. "Ethical Leadership: A Social Learning Perspective for Construct Development and Testing." *Organizational Behavior and Human Decision Processes* 97, no. 2 (July 2005): 117–134.
51. www.onlinemba.com/blog/10-most-ethical-ceos-in-corporate-america/.
52. Matthews, Merrill. "Companies 'Outsource' Because That's Where the Sales Are." *Forbes*. July 20, 2012. www.forbes.com/sites/merrillmatthews/2012/07/20/companies-outsource-because-thats-where-the-sales-are/.
53. Chhokar, Jagdeep S., Felix C. Brodbeck, and Robert J. House. *Culture and Leadership across the World: The GLOBE Book of In-Depth Studies of 25 Societies* (Mahwah, NJ: Erlbaum, 2008); Javidan, Masour, Peter W. Dorfman, Mary Sully De Luque, and Robert J. House. "In the Eye of the Beholder: Cross Cultural Lessons in Leadership from Project GLOBE." *Academy of Management Perspectives* 20, no. 1 (February 2006): 67–90.
54. Ibid.
55. Ibid.
56. Winfrey, Graham. "The Highest-Paid Female CEO Is a Transgender Founder (Who Built a Robot Version of Her Wife)." *Inc.* September 8, 2014. www.inc.com/graham-winfrey/the-highest-paid-female-executive-in-the-us-is-a-transgender-ceo.html.
57. Fairchild, Caroline. "Women CEOs in the Fortune 1000: By the Numbers." *Fortune*. July 8, 2014. http://fortune.com/2014/07/08/women-ceos-fortune-500-1000/.
58. For an overview see Eagly, Alice H., and Linda L. Carli. "Women and Men as Leaders." In *The Nature of Leadership*, 279–301 (Thousand Oaks, CA: Sage, 2004).

59. Eagly, Alice H., Mary C. Johannesen-Schmidt, and Marloes L. van Engen. "Transformational, Transactional, and Laissez-Faire Leadership Styles: A Meta-analysis Comparing Women and Men." *Psychological Bulletin* 129, no. 4 (July 2003): 569–591; Eagly, A. H., and B. T. Johnson. "Gender and Leadership Style: A Meta-analysis." *Psychological Bulletin* 108, no. 2 (September 1990): 233.
60. Eagly, Alice H., and Linda L. Carli. "Women and the Labyrinth of Leadership." *Harvard Business Review* 85, no. 9 (September 2007): 63–71.
61. Is paid leave available to mothers and fathers of infants? (2015). Retrieved September 15, 2015, from http://worldpolicycenter.org/policies/is-paid-leave-available-to-mothers-and-fathers-of-infants.
62. Hoobler, Jenny M., Sandy J. Wayne, and Grace Lemmon. "Bosses' Perceptions of Family-Work Conflict and Women's Promotability: Glass Ceiling Effects." *Academy of Management Journal* 52, no. 5 (October 2009): 939–957.
63. Eagly and Carli. "Women and the Labyrinth of Leadership."
64. Ibid.
65. Ibid.
66. Streitfeld, David. "Ellen Pao Loses Silicon Valley Bias Case against Kleiner Perkins." *New York Times*. March 27, 2015. www.nytimes.com/2015/03/28/technology/ellen-pao-kleiner-perkins-case-decision.html?_r=0.
67. Ibid.
68. Scheiber, Noam. "A Woman-Led Law Firm That Lets Partners Be Parents." *New York Times*. May 1 2015. www.nytimes.com/2015/05/03/business/a-woman-led-law-firm-that-lets-partners-be-parents.html.
69. Efrati, Amir, and Rachel Emma Silverman. "Yahoo's Marissa Mayer Hits One-Year Mark." *Wall Street Journal*. July 15, 2013. http://online.wsj.com/article/SB10001424127887323664204578608180731225420.html.
70. Ibid.
71. Carlson, Nicholas. "Marissa Mayer Defends Her Work from Home Ban." *Business Insider*. April 19, 2013. www.businessinsider.com/marissa-mayer-defends-her-work-from-home-ban-2013-4?IR=T.

Chapter 12

1. Hollander, Edwin P., and Lynn R. Offermann. "Power and Leadership in Organizations." In *Contemporary Issues in Leadership* (3rd ed.), 62–86 (Boulder, CO: Westview, 1993).
2. Keltner, Dacher. "The Power Paradox." *Greater Good*. December 1, 2007. http://greatergood.berkeley.edu/article/item/power_paradox.
3. Ibid.
4. French, John R., and Bertram Raven. D. Cartwright, ed. *The Bases of Social Power* (Ann Arbor, MI: Institute for Social Research, 1959); Wood, Jay K. "Fight the Power: Comparing and Evaluating Two Measures of French and Raven's (1959) Bases of Social Power." *Current Research in Social Psychology* 21 (2013): *PsycINFO*, EBSCO*host*.
5. Farnham, Alan. "CEO Gives Away His Bonus to Employees." *ABC News*. April 18, 2013. http://abcnews.go.com/Business/ceo-shares-bonus-employees/story?id=18981639.
6. Yukl, Gary, and Cecilia M. Falbe. "Influence Tactics and Objectives in Upward, Downward, and Lateral Influence Attempts." *Journal of Applied Psychology* 75, no. 2 (April 1990): 132–140; Kipnis, David, Stuart M. Schmidt, and Ian Wilkinson. "Intraorganizational Influence Tactics: Explorations in Getting One's Way." *Journal of Applied Psychology* 65, no. 4 (August 1980): 440–452.
7. Falbe, Cecilia M, and Gary Yukl. "Consequences for Managers of Using Single Influence Tactics and Combinations of Tactics." *Academy of Management Journal* 35, no. 3 (August 1992): 638–652.
8. Ralston, David A., David J. Gustafson, Fanny M. Cheung, and Robert H. Terpstra. "Differences in Managerial Values: A Study of U.S., Hong Kong and PRC Managers." *Journal of International Business Studies* 24, no. 2 (June 1993): 249–275.
9. Yukl, G., P. P. Fu, and R. McDonald. "Cross-Cultural Differences in Perceived Effectiveness of Influence Tactics for Initiating or Resisting Change." *Applied Psychology: An International Review* 52, no. 1 (January 2003): 68–82.
10. Ferris, Gerald R., and Wayne A. Hochwarter. "Organizational Politics." In *APA Handbook of Industrial and Organizational Psychology*, Vol. 3: *Maintaining, Expanding, and Contracting the Organization*, 435–459 (Washington, DC: American Psychological Association, 2011).
11. Ferris, Gerald R., Gail S. Russ, and Patricia M. Fandt. "Politics in Organizations." In *Impression Management in the Organization*, 143–170 (Hillsdale, NJ: Erlbaum, 1989); Munyon, Timothy P., James K. Summers, Katina M. Thompson, and Gerald R. Ferris. "Political Skill and Work Outcomes: A Theoretical Extension, Meta-Analytic Investigation, and Agenda for the Future." *Personnel Psychology* 68, no. 1 (Spring 2015): 143–184.
12. Parker, Christopher P., Robert L. Dipboye, and Stacy L. Jackson. "Perceptions of Organizational Politics: An Investigation of Antecedents and Consequences." *Journal of Management* 21, no. 5 (December 1995): 891–912.
13. Lomax, Alyce. "Cisco Systems, Inc.'s Layoffs Aren't Good News." *Motley Fool*. August 19, 2014. www.fool.com/investing/general/2014/08/19/cisco-systems-incs-layoffs-arent-good-news.aspx.
14. Quimby, Michelann. "Organizational Politics: Using Your Power for Good." *BizNik*. June 6, 2008. http://biznik.com/articles/organizational-politics-using-your-power-for-good.
15. Chang, Chu-Hsiang, Christopher C. Rosen, and Paul E. Levy. "The Relationship between Perceptions of Organizational Politics and Employee Attitudes, Strain, and Behavior: A Meta-analytic Examination." *Academy of Management Journal* 52, no. 4 (August 2009): 779–801; Ferris, Gerald R., Dwight D. Frink, Maria Carmen Galang, Jing Zhou, and Jack L. Howard. "Perceptions of Organizational Politics: Prediction, Stress-Related Implications, and Outcomes." *Human Relations* 49, no. 2 (February 1996): 233–266.
16. Ferris, Gerald R., Darren C. Treadway, Robyn L. Brouer, and Timothy P. Munyon. "Political Skill in the Organizational Sciences." In *Politics in Organizations: Theory and Research Considerations*, 487–528 (New York: Routledge/Taylor & Francis Group, 2012).
17. Warren, Donald I. "Power, Visibility, and Conformity in Formal Organizations." *American Sociological Review* 33, no. 6 (1968): 951–970; Lewis, Patricia, and Ruth Simpson. "Kanter Revisited: Gender, Power and (In)visibility." *International Journal of Management Reviews* 14, no. 2 (June 2012): 141–158.

Chapter 13

1. For an overview, see Hargie, Owen, and Dennis Tourish. *Auditing Organizational Communication: A Handbook of Research, Theory and Practice* (New York: Routledge/Taylor & Francis Group, 2009); Harris, Thomas E., and Mark D. Nelson. *Applied Organizational Communication: Theory and Practice in a Global Environment* (3rd ed.) (New York: Taylor & Francis Group/Erlbaum, 2008); May, Steve, and Dennis K. Mumby, *Engaging Organizational Communication Theory and Research: Multiple Perspective* (Thousand Oaks, CA: Sage, 2005).
2. Berlo, D. K. *The Process of Communication* (New York: Holt, Rinehart, & Winston, 1960); Shannon, C. E., & W. Weaver. *The Mathematical Theory of Communication* (Urbana: University of Illinois Press, 1949).
3. Beattie, Geoffrey. *Visible Thought: The New Psychology of Body Language* (New York: Routledge, 2004); Gifford, Robert. "The Role of Nonverbal Communication

in Interpersonal Relations," In *Handbook of Interpersonal Psychology: Theory, Research, Assessment, and Therapeutic Interventions,* 171–190 (Hoboken, NJ: Wiley, 2011).

4. For a review see Button, Kenneth, and Fabio Rossera. "Barriers to Communication." *Annals of Regional Science* 24, no. 4 (December 1990): 337.
5. See http://innolectinc.com/services-overview/the-cost-of-poor-listening/.
6. See, for example, Weger, Harry Jr, Gina Castle Bell, and Melissa C. Robinson. "The Relative Effectiveness of Active Listening in Initial Interactions." *International Journal of Listening* 28, no. 1 (January 2014): 13–31.
7. Comer, Lucette B., and Tanya Drollinger. "Active Empathetic Listening and Selling Success: A Conceptual Framework." *Journal of Personal Selling and Sales Management* 19, no. 1 (Winter 1999): 15–29; Drollinger, Tanya, Lucette B. Comer, and Patricia T. Warrington. "Development and Validation of the Active Empathetic Listening Scale." *Psychology and Marketing* 23, no. 2 (February 2006): 161–180.
8. Goris, José R., Bobby C. Vaught, and John D. Pettit Jr. "Effects of Communication Direction on Job Performance and Satisfaction: A Moderated Regression Analysis." *Journal of Business Communication* 37, no. 4 (October 2000): 348–368; Lunenburg, Fred C. "Formal Communication Channels: Upward, Downward, Horizontal, and External." *Focus on Colleges, Universities, and Schools* 4, no. 1 (2010): 1–7; Roberts, Karlene H., and Charles A. O'Reilly. "Measuring Organizational Communication." *Journal of Applied Psychology* 59, no. 3 (June 1974): 321–326.
9. "Chick-fil-A Introduces New Frosted Lemonade." *Brand Eating.* March 17, 2015. www.brandeating.com/2015/03/chick-fil-introduces-new-frosted.html.
10. Kelley, Tom, and Jonathan Littman. *The Art of Innovation: Lessons in Creativity from IDEO, America's Leading Design Firm* (New York: Doubleday, 2001).
11. Lewis, Len. "Fostering a Loyal Workforce at Trader Joe's." *Workforce.* June 2, 2005. www.workforce.com/articles/fostering-a-loyal-workforce-at-trader-joe-s.
12. Hartman, Rosanne L., and J. David Johnson. "Formal and Informal Group Communication Structures: An Examination of Their Relationship to Role Ambiguity." *Social Networks* 12, no. 2 (June 1990): 127–151; Langan-Fox, Janice. "Communication in Organizations: Speed, Diversity, Networks, and Influence on Organizational Effectiveness, Human Health, and Relationships." In *Handbook of Industrial, Work and Organizational Psychology.* Vol. 2: *Organizational Psychology*, 188–205 (Thousand Oaks, CA: Sage, 2002).
13. Davis, Keith. "Management Communication and the Grapevine." *Harvard Business Review* 31, no. 5 (September 1953): 43–49; Mishra, Jitendra. "Managing the Grapevine." *Public Personnel Management* 19, no. 2 (Summer 1990): 213; Nicoll, David Cathmoir. "Acknowledge and Use Your Grapevine." *Management Decision* 32, no. 6 (August 1994): 25; Smith, Bob. "Care and Feeding of the Office Grapevine." *Management Review* 85, no. 2 (February 1996): 6.
14. Hansen, Evan. "Google Blogger: 'I Was Terminated.'" *CNET.* February 11, 2005. http://news.cnet.com/Google-blogger-I-was-terminated/2100-1038_3-5572936.html.
15. Davis, Keith, "Management Communication and the Grapevine." *Harvard Business Review* 31, no. 5 (September 1953): 43–49; Foster, Eric K., and Ralph L. Rosnow. "Gossip and Network Relationships." In *Relating Difficulty: The Processes of Constructing and Managing Difficult Interaction*, 161–180 (Mahwah, NJ: Erlbaum, 2006).
16. Ibid.
17. Mishra, "Managing the Grapevine."
18. LeVine, Robert A., and Donald T. Campbell. *Ethnocentrism: Theories of Conflict, Ethnic Attitudes, and Group Behavior* (Oxford: Wiley, 1972).
19. "I have said School of the South; because in reality, our north is the South. There must not be north, for us, except in opposition to our South. Therefore we now turn the map upside down, and then we have a true idea of our position, and not as the rest of the world wishes. The point of America, from now on, forever, insistently points to the South, our north" (Joaquín Torres García, *Constructive Universalism*, Bs. As., *Poseidon*, 1941).
20. Hall, Edward T. *Beyond Culture* (Oxford: Anchor, 1976); Kittler, Markus G., David Rygl, and Alex Mackinnon. "Beyond Culture or Beyond Control? Reviewing the Use of Hall's High-/Low-Context Concept." *International Journal of Cross Cultural Management* 11, no. 1 (April 2011): 63–82.
21. www.kwintessential.co.uk/cultural-services/articles/results-of-poor-cross-cultural-awareness.html.
22. Ferraro, Gary P., and Elizabeth K. Briody. *The Cultural Dimensions of Global Business* (7th ed.) (Upper Saddle River, NJ: Pearson, 2012).
23. Ferraro and Briody, *The Cultural Dimensions of Global Business.*
24. Ibid.
25. Coleman, Dan. "Conan O'Brien Kills It at Dartmouth Graduation." *OpenCulture.com.* June 13, 2011. www.openculture.com/2011/06/conan_obrien_kills_it_at_dartmouth_graduation.html.

Chapter 14

1. For overviews of organizational culture see: Ehrhart, Mark G., Benjamin Schneider, and William H. Macey. *Organizational Climate and Culture: An Introduction to Theory, Research, and Practice* (New York: Routledge/Taylor & Francis Group, 2014); Ostroff, Cheri, Angelo J. Kinicki, and Rabiah S. Muhammad. "Organizational Culture and Climate." In *Handbook of Psychology,* Vol. 12: *Industrial and Organizational Psychology* (2nd ed.), 643–676 (Hoboken, NJ: Wiley, 2013).
2. Smith, Jacquelyn. "The Best Companies to Work for in 2014." *Forbes.* December 11, 2013. www.forbes.com/sites/jacquelynsmith/2013/12/11/the-best-companies-to-work-for-in-2014/.
3. Ibid.
4. Schein, Edgar H. "Organizational Culture." *American Psychologist* 45, no. 2 (February 1990): 109–119.
5. Ibid.
6. For more information see: www.kelloggcompany.com/en_US/our-values.html.
7. Hartnell, Chad A., Amy Yi Ou, and Angelo Kinicki. "Organizational Culture and Organizational Effectiveness: A Meta-analytic Investigation of the Competing Values Framework's Theoretical Suppositions." *Journal of Applied Psychology* 96, no. 4 (July 2011): 677–694; Quinn, Robert E., and John Rohrbaugh. "A Spatial Model of Effectiveness Criteria: Towards a Competing Values Approach to Organizational Analysis." *Management Science* 29, no. 3 (March 1983): 363–377.
8. www.wholefoodsmarket.com/tags/supplier-stories.
9. Tharp, Bruce M. "Four Organizational Culture Types." *Haworth.* Organizational Culture White Paper (2009). http://faculty.mu.edu.sa/public/uploads/1360757023.3588organizational%20cult98.pdf.
10. Simoes, Mariana. "Don't Work for a Tech Company If You Want a Stress-Free Job." *Business Insider.* February 11, 2013. www.businessinsider.com/tech-companies-stressful-places-to-work-2013-1?IR=T.
11. Thompson, Chris. "Social Networking, Organizational Culture, and Recruiting." *Social Media Recruiter.* April 15, 2012. https://thesocialmediarecruiter.wordpress

.com/2012/04/15/social-networking-organizational-culture-and-recruiting/.

12. Hartnell, Ou, and Kinicki. "Organizational Culture and Organizational Effectiveness; Quinn and Rohrbaugh. "A Spatial Model of Effectiveness Criteria."
13. Hofstede, Geert. "Identifying Organizational Subcultures: An Empirical Approach." *Journal of Management Studies* 35, no. 1 (January 1998): 1–12; Martin, Joanne, and Caren Siehl. "Organizational Culture and Counterculture: An Uneasy Symbiosis." *Organizational Dynamics* 12, no. 2 (September 1983): 52–64.
14. "5 Companies That Give Back All Year Long." *Daily Muse.* www.themuse.com/advice/5-companies-that-give-back-all-year-long.
15. Hofstede. "Identifying Organizational Subcultures"; Martin and Siehl. "Organizational Culture and Counterculture."
16. Ibid.
17. Martin and Siehl. "Organizational Culture and Counterculture."
18. Denison, Daniel R. "Bringing Corporate Culture to the Bottom Line." *Organizational Dynamics* 13, no. 2 (September 1984): 5–22; Saffold III, Guy S. "Culture Traits, Strength, and Organizational Performance: Moving Beyond "Strong" Culture." *Academy of Management Review* 13, no. 4 (October 1988): 546–558; Kotter, John P. *Corporate Culture and Performance* (New York: Simon and Schuster, 2008).
19. "Creating and Sustaining a Strong Corporate Culture." *HC Online.* September 12, 2013. www.hcamag.com/hr-news/creating-and-sustaining-a-strong-corporate-culture-179289.aspx.
20. Kuppler, Tim. "The Top 10 Organizational Culture Crises of 2014." *Switch & Shift.* January 12, 2015. http://switchandshift.com/the-top-10-organizational-culture-crises-of-2014.
21. Janis, Irving L. "Groupthink and Group Dynamics: A Social Psychological Analysis of Defective Policy Decisions." *Policy Studies Journal* 2, no. 1 (September 1973): 19–25; Sunstein, Cass R., and Reid Hastie. *Wiser: Getting beyond Groupthink to Make Groups Smarter* (Cambridge, MA: Harvard Business Press, 2014).
22. Schein, Edgar H. "Organizational Culture." *American Psychologist* 45, no. 2 (February 1990): 109–119; Bonavia, Tomas, J. Gabriel Molina, and Joan Boada. "Further Examination of the Organizational Culture Scale of Artifacts." *Psychological Reports* 105, no. 3, Pt 1 (December 2009): 827–834.
23. Schein. "Organizational Culture."
24. Ibid.
25. Ibid.
26. Ibid.
27. Arnold, Pamela, and Terri Kruzan. "Organizational Culture Roadblocks and Shortcuts for Leveraging Diversity: Part 1." *Profiles in Diversity* 14, no. 3 (May 2012): 71. *Business Source Elite*, EBSCO*host*.
28. Adams, Susan. "The Best and Worst Companies for Women and Minorities." *Forbes.* March 7, 2013. www.forbes.com/sites/susanadams/2013/03/07/the-best-and-worst-companies-for-women-and-minorities/.
29. See, for instance, Dwyer, Sean, Orlando C. Richard, and Ken Chadwick. "Gender Diversity in Management and Firm Performance: The Influence of Growth Orientation and Organizational Culture." *Journal of Business Research* 56, no. 12 (December 2003): 1009–1019.
30. See, for example, Covert, Bryce. "The Highest-Paid Female CEOs Still Make Millions Less Than Their Male Counterparts." *Think Progress.* June 9, 2014. http://thinkprogress.org/economy/2014/06/09/3446365/women-ceos-pay-gap/.
31. Schein, "Organizational Culture"; Schraeder, Mike, and Dennis R. Self. "Enhancing the Success of Mergers and Acquisitions: An Organizational Culture Perspective." *Management Decision* 41, no. 5 (2003): 511–522; Horwitz, F. M., K. Anderssen, A. Bezuidenhout, S. Cohen, F. Kirsten, K. Mosoeunyane, N. Smith, K. Thole, and A. van Heerden. "Due Diligence Neglected: Managing Human Resources and Organizational Culture in Mergers and Acquisitions." *South African Journal of Business Management* 33, no. 1 (March 2002): 1.
32. Bligh, Michelle C. "Surviving Post-Merger 'Culture Clash': Can Cultural Leadership Lessen the Casualties?" *Leadership* 2, no. 4 (November 2006): 395–426; Van den Steen, Eric. "Culture Clash: The Costs and Benefits of Homogeneity." *Management Science* 56, no. 10 (October 2010): 1718–1738; Want, Jerry. "When Worlds Collide: Culture Clash." *Journal of Business Strategy* 24, no. 4 (July 2003): 14.
33. Weiss, Geoff. "How Culture Clash Killed a $35 Billion Merger." *Entrepreneur.* May 9, 2014. www.entrepreneur.com/article/233762.
34. Laschinger, Heather K. Spence, Carol A. Wong, Greta G. Cummings, and Ashley L. Grau. "Resonant Leadership and Workplace Empowerment: The Value of Positive Organizational Cultures in Reducing Workplace Incivility." *Nursing Economics* 32, no. 1 (January 2014): 5–44; Rinke, Wolf J. "How to Build a Positive Organizational Culture." *Food Management* 33, no. 11 (November 1998): 17.
35. Goffee, Rob, and Gareth Jones. *The Character of a Corporation* (New York: Harper Collins, 1998).
36. Makovsky, Ken. "Behind the Southwest Airlines Culture." *Forbes.* November 21, 2013. www.forbes.com/sites/kenmakovsky/2013/11/21/behind-the-southwest-airlines-culture/.
37. Goffee and Jones, *The Character of a Corporation.*
38. Ibid.
39. Free, Clinton, Norman Macintosh, and Mitchell Stein. "Management Controls: The Organizational Fraud Triangle of Leadership, Culture and Control in Enron." *Ivey Business* (July/August 2007). http://iveybusinessjournal.com/publication/management-controls-the-organizational-fraud-triangle-of-leadership-culture-and-control-in-enron/.
40. Ibid.
41. Ruiz-Palomino, Pablo, Ricardo Martínez-Cañas, and Joan Fontrodona. "Ethical Culture and Employee Outcomes: The Mediating Role of Person-Organization Fit." *Journal of Business Ethics* 116, no. 1 (August 2013): 173–188; Meinert, Dori. "Creating an Ethical Culture." *HR* 59, no. 4 (April 2014): 22–27.
42. http://news.3m.com/press-release/company/3m-named-worlds-most-ethical-company-second-consecutive-year.
43. Fawcett, Stanley E., James C. Brau, Gary K. Rhoads, David Whitlark, and Amydee M. Fawcett. "Spirituality and Organizational Culture: Cultivating the ABCs of an Inspiring Workplace." *International Journal of Public Administration* 31, no. 4 (March 2008): 420–438.
44. See, for example, Case, Peter, and Jonathan Gosling. "The Spiritual Organization: Critical Reflections on the Instrumentality of Workplace Spirituality." *Journal of Management, Spirituality and Religion* 7, no. 4 (December 2010): 257–282.
45. Schachter, Harvey. "Key Steps to Change Corporate Culture." *Globe and Mail.* March 23, 2014. www.theglobeandmail.com/report-on-business/careers/management/key-steps-to-change-corporate-culture/article17557724/.
46. Schein, E. "The Role of the Founder in Creating Organizational Culture." *Organizational Dynamics* 12, no. 1 (Summer 1983): 13–28; Hambrick, Donald C, and Phyllis A. Mason. "Upper Echelons: The Organization as a Reflection of Its Top Managers." *Academy of Management Review* 9, no. 2 (April 1984): 193–206.
47. Walter, Ekaterina. "How to Lead Like Zuck." *Inc.* May 14, 2014. www.inc.com/ekaterina-walter/as-zuckerberg-turns-30-leadership-lessons.html.

48. O'Reilly III, Charles A., Jennifer Chatman, and David F. Caldwell. "People and Organizational Culture: A Profile Comparison Approach to Assessing Person-Organization Fit." *Academy of Management Journal* 34, no. 3 (September 1991): 487–516; Swider, Brian W., Ryan D. Zimmerman, and Murray R. Barrick. "Searching for the Right Fit: Development of Applicant Person-Organization Fit Perceptions during the Recruitment Process." *Journal of Applied Psychology* 100, no. 3 (2015): 880–893.
49. Kammeyer-Mueller, John, Connie Wanberg, Alex Rubenstein, and Song Zhaoli. "Support, Undermining, and Newcomer Socialization: Fitting In during The First 90 Days." *Academy of Management Journal* 56, no. 4 (August 2013): 1104–1124; Chao, Georgia T., Anne M. O'Leary-Kelly, Samantha Wolf, Howard J. Klein, and Philip D. Gardner. "Organizational Socialization: Its Content and Consequences." *Journal of Applied Psychology* 79, no. 5 (October 1994): 730–743.
50. Ashforth, Blake E., Alan M. Saks, and Raymond T. Lee. "Socialization and Newcomer Adjustment: The Role of Organizational Context." *Human Relations* 51, no. 7 (July 1998): 897–926; Ashforth, Blake E., David M. Sluss, and Spencer H. Harrison. "Socialization in Organizational Contexts." In *International Review of Industrial and Organizational Psychology 2007* (Vol. 22): 1–70 (New York: Wiley, 2007).
51. http://www.intuitatwork2013.com/hiring-and-welcoming.html.
52. Biro, Meghan M. "The Onboarding Experience Matters to Your Future Employees." *Forbes.* June 1, 2014. www.forbes.com/sites/meghanbiro/2014/06/01/the-onboarding-experience-matters-to-your-future-employees/.
53. Feldman, Daniel Charles. "A Contingency Theory of Socialization." *Administrative Science Quarterly* 21, no. 3 (September 1976): 433–452; Feldman, Daniel C. "A Practical Program for Employee Socialization." *Organizational Dynamics* 5, no. 2 (September 1976): 64–80; Baker III, H. Eugene, and Daniel C. Feldman. "Linking Organizational Socialization Tactics with Corporate Human Resource Management Strategies." *Human Resource Management Review* 1, no. 3 (Fall 1991): 193.

Chapter 15

1. For overviews of strategy processes in organizations see Galbraith, Jay R. *Designing Organizations: Strategy, Structure, and Process at the Business Unit and Enterprise Levels* (3rd edition) (San Francisco: Jossey-Bass, 2014); Grant, Robert M. *Contemporary Strategy Analysis* (8th edition) (New York: Wiley, 2013).
2. Horovitz, Bruce. "McDonald's Rolls Out Yogurt Option in Happy Meals." *USA Today.* May 19, 2014. www.usatoday.com/story/money/business/2014/05/19/mcdonalds-yogurt-happy-meals-go-gurt-nutrition/9277709/.
3. Crandell, Christine. "Meet the New Boss and His Take on Your Strategy." *Forbes,* June 1, 2013. www.forbes.com/sites/christinecrandell/2013/06/01/meet-the-new-boss-and-his-take-on-your-strategy/.
4. "Prime Therapeutics' Chief Customer Experience Officer, Ingrid Lindberg, Presents at America's Health Insurance Plans Institute." *PR Newswire.* June 12, 2013. www.prnewswire.com/news-releases/prime-therapeutics-chief-customer-experience-officer-ingrid-lindberg-presents-at-americas-health-insurance-plans-institute-211172391.html.
5. Beard, Donald W., and Gregory G. Dess. "Corporate-Level Strategy, Business-Level Strategy, and Firm Performance." *Academy of Management Journal* 24, no. 4 (December 1981): 663–688; Hofer, Charles W., and Dan. E. Schendel, *Strategy Formulation: Analytical Concepts* (St. Paul, MN: West, 1978).
6. For an overview of the concept of competitive advantage see Barney, Jay. "Firm Resources and Sustained Competitive Advantage." *Journal of Management* 17, no. 1 (March 1991): 99; Barney, Jay B., "Resource-Based Theories of Competitive Advantage: A Ten-Year Retrospective on the Resource-Based View." *Journal of Management* 27, no. 6 (November 2001): 643.
7. Miles, Raymond E., Charles C. Snow, Alan D. Meyer, and Henry J. Coleman, Jr. "Organizational Strategy, Structure, and Process." *Academy of Management Review* 3, no. 3 (July 1978): 546–562; Shortell, Stephen M., and Edward J. Zajac. "Perceptual and Archival Measures of Miles and Snow's Strategic Types: A Comprehensive Assessment of Reliability and Validity." *Academy of Management Journal* 33, no. 4 (December 1990): 817–883.
8. Huber, George P. "Organizational Learning: The Contributing Processes and the Literatures." *Organization Science* 2, no. 1 (February 1991): 88–115; Senge, Peter M. "The Leader's New Work: Building Learning Organizations." *Sloan Management Review* 32, no. 1 (1990): 7–23; Senge, Peter M. *The Fifth Discipline* (New York: Doubleday/Currency, 1990).
9. www.moyak.com/papers/learning-organization-presentation.pdf.
10. Huber, "Organizational Learning."
11. Ibid.
12. Ibid.
13. Ibid.
14. Bhagwati, Jagdish N. *In Defense of Globalization* (New York: Oxford University Press, 2004); Wolf, Martin. *Why Globalization Works* (New Haven, CT: Yale University Press, 2004).
15. www.spanx.com/wholesale-distribution.
16. Lutz, Ashley. "Four Reasons for Subway's Explosive Growth." *Business Insider.* June 9, 2014. www.businessinsider.com/subway-business-strategy-2014-6?IR=T.
17. http://allday.com/post/1035-the-worlds-weirdest-places-to-find-a-burger/pages/3/.
18. Maylie, Devon. "Mining Debate Rattles South Africa." *Wall Street Journal,* May 15, 2013. www.wsj.com/articles/SB10001424127887323309604578430833278491840.
19. Hofstede, Geert. "Culture and Organizations." *International Studies of Management and Organization* 10, no. 4 (1980): 15–41; Hofstede, Geert. "National Cultures in Four Dimensions." *International Studies of Management and Organization* 13, no. 1/2 (Summer 1983): 46–74; Taras, Vas, Bradley L. Kirkman, and Piers Steel. "Examining the Impact of Culture's Consequences: A Three-Decade, Multilevel, Meta-analytic Review of Hofstede's Cultural Value Dimensions." *Journal of Applied Psychology* 95, no. 3 (May 2010): 405–439.
20. McSweeney, Brendan. "Hofstede's Model of National Cultural Differences and Their Consequences: A Triumph of Faith—a Failure of Analysis." *Human Relations* 55, no. 1 (2002): 89–118; Hofstede, Geert. "Dimensions Do Not Exist: A Reply to Brendan McSweeney." *Human Relations* 55, no. 11 (2002): 1355–1361.
21. Bartlett, Christopher A., and Sumantra Ghoshal. *Managing across Borders: The Transnational Solution* (2nd edition) (Boston: Harvard Business School Press, 2002).
22. Evans, Paul, Vladimir Pucik, Jean-Louis Barsoux. *The Global Challenge: Frameworks for International Human Resource Management* (Boston: McGraw-Hill, 2002).
23. Gregory, Ann. "Firm Characteristics and Political Risk Reduction in Overseas Ventures." *Academy of Management Proceedings* (August 1982): 73–77.
24. See, for example, Vecchio, Robert P., Joseph E. Justin, and Craig L. Pearce. "Empowering Leadership: An Examination of Mediating Mechanisms within a hierarchical Structure." *Leadership Quarterly* 21, no. 3 (June 2010): 530–542; Zhang, Xiaomeng, and Kathryn M. Bartol. "Linking Empowering Leadership and Employee Creativity: The Influence of Psychological Empowerment, Intrinsic Motivation, and Creative Process Engagement." *Academy of Management Journal* 53, no. 1 (February 2010): 107–128.

25. Guzzo, Richard A. "The Expatriate Employee." In *Trends in Organizational Behavior,* Vol. 3: 123–137 (Hoboken, NJ: Wiley, 1996); Lee, Yosup, and Laurie Larwood. "The Socialization of Expatriate Managers in Multinational Firms." *Academy of Management Journal* 26, no. 4 (December 1983): 657–665; Tung, Rosalie L. *The New Expatriates: Managing Human Resources Abroad.* (New York: Ballinger/Harper & Row, 1988).
26. Derr, C. Brooklyn, Candace Jones, and Edmund L. Toomey. "Managing High-Potential Employees: Current Practices in Thirty-Three U.S. Corporations." *Human Resource Management* 27, no. 3 (Fall 1988): 273–290; Gelens, Jolyn, Joeri Hofmans, Nicky Dries, and Roland Pepermans. "Talent Management and Organisational Justice: Employee Reactions to High Potential Identification." *Human Resource Management Journal* 24, no. 2 (April 2014): 159–175.
27. Feldman, Daniel C., and Holly B. Tompson. "Entry Shock, Culture Shock: Socializing the New Breed of Global Managers." *Human Resource Management* 31, no. 4 (Winter 1992): 345–362; Ward, Colleen, Stephen Bochner, and Adrian Furnham. *The Psychology of Culture Shock* (2nd ed.). New York: Routledge, 2001.
28. Winkelman, Michael. "Cultural Shock and Adaptation." *Journal of Counseling and Development* 73, no. 2 (November 1994): 121–126.
29. Shaules, Joseph. "Are you struggling with expat culture shock?" *Telegraph,* May 4, 2015. www.telegraph.co.uk/expat/before-you-go/11553062/Are-you-struggling-with-expat-culture-shock.html.
30. Hays, Richard D. "Ascribed Behavioral Determinants of Success-Failure Among U.S. Expatriate Managers." *Journal of International Business Studies* 2, no. 2 (Fall 1971): 40–46; Tung, Rosalie L. "Expatriate Assignments: Enhancing Success and Minimizing Failure." *Academy of Management Executive* 1, no. 2 (May 1987): 117–125; Kataria, Neeraj, and Shweta Sethi. "Making Successful Expatriates in Multinational Corporations." *Asian Journal of Business and Economics* 3, no. 3 (2013): 1–12.
31. Tung, Rosalie L. "Expatriate Assignments: Enhancing Success and Minimizing Failure." *Academy of Management Executive* 1, no. 2 (May 1987): 117–125; Gupta, Ritu, Pratyush Banerjee, and Jighyasu Gaur. "Exploring the Role of the spouse in Expatriate Failure: A Grounded Theory-Based Investigation of Expatriate' Spouse Adjustment Issues from India." *International Journal of Human Resource Management* 23, no. 17 (October 2012): 3559–3577.
32. Driscoll, Ian. "Expat's Dilemma: Out of Sight—and Mind?" *BBC.* October 21, 2014. www.bbc.com/capital/story/20141020-expat-woes-out-of-sight-and-mind.

Chapter 16

1. Ashkenas, Ron. "Change Management Needs to Change: Interaction." *Harvard Business Review.* April 16, 2013. https://hbr.org/2013/04/change-management-needs-to-change/.
2. King, Peter. "Chicago Takes Charge. *Monday Morning Quarterback.* n.d. http://mmqb.si.com/2014/06/09/jay-cutler-marc-trestman-bears-locker-room-dr-z/?eref=sihp.
3. Troyani, Laura. "Three Examples of Organizational Change and Why They Got It Right." *TINYpulse.* December 9, 2014. www.tinyhr.com/blog/3-examples-of-organizational-change-and-why-they-got-it-right.
4. The DADA syndrome is an adaptation of the Kübler-Ross death and dying model to the context of organizational change as outlined in the following sources: Morano, Richard A. "How to Manage Change to Reduce Stress." *Management Review* 66, no. 11 (November 1977): 21; Rashford, Nicholas S., and David Coghan. "Phases and Levels of Organisational Change." In *The Effective Manager: Perspectives and Illustrations*, 119–130 (Thousand Oaks, CA; Maidenhead, BRK, England: Sage, 1996); Zell, Deone. "Organizational Changes as a Process of Death, Dying and Rebirth." *Journal of Applied Behavioral Science* 39, no. 1 (March 2003): 73–96.
5. Lewin, Kurt. "Frontiers in Group Dynamics: Concept, Method and Reality in Social Science: Social Equilibria and Social Change." *Human Relations* 1, (1947): 5–41; Burnes, Bernard. "Kurt Lewin and the Planned Approach to Change: A Re-appraisal." *Journal of Management Studies* 41, no. 6 (September 2004): 977–1002.
6. Lewin, Kurt. *Field Theory in Social Science: Selected Theoretical Papers.* Edited by Dorwin Cartwright (Oxford: Harpers, 1951); Burnes, "Kurt Lewin and the Planned Approach to Change."
7. Taylor, Helen, and Cary L. Cooper. "Organisational Change—Threat or Challenge? The Role of Individual Differences in the Management of Stress." *Journal of Organizational Change Management* 1, no. 1 (January 1988): 68; Maxwell, Paul D. "Resistance to Change and Change Management." In *Organizational Behavior in Health Care,* 379–411. (Boston: Jones and Bartlett, 2005).
8. Gordner, Courtney. "How Small Businesses Should Use Social Media." *SocialStrategy1.* January 23, 2014 www.socialstrategy1.com/how-small-businesses-should-use-social-media/.
9. Huang, Cheng-Kui, Ting-Yi Chang, and Badri Narayanan. "Mining the Change of Customer Behavior in Dynamic Markets." *Information Technology and Management* 16, no. 2 (June 2015): 117–138; "Research, Knowing Customers' Needs Help Avoid Being Surprised by Market Changes." *Marketing News* 8, no. 10 (November 15, 1974): 4.
10. Strom, Stephanie. "Chipotle to Stop Using Genetically Altered Ingredients." *New York Times.* April 26, 2015. www.nytimes.com/2015/04/27/business/chipotle-to-stop-serving-genetically-altered-food.html?_r=1.
11. https://cigelectric.co.uk/e-cig-uk-regulation-2016/.
12. Daniel, Teresa A. "Tools for Building a Positive Employee Relations Environment." *Employment Relations Today* 30, no. 2 (Summer 2003): 51–64; "Positive Employee Relations Key to Defeating Corporate Campaigns." *Management Report for Nonunion Organizations* 33, no. 3 (March 2010): 7–8.
13. Bradt, George. "How TriZetto's CEO Changed Its Culture by Changing Its Attitude." *Forbes.com.* August 29, 2012. www.forbes.com/sites/georgebradt/2012/08/29/how-trizettos-ceo-changed-its-culture-by-changing-its-attitude/.
14. http://kineticww.com/us/kinetic-worldwide-announces-restructure-rapid-expansion/.
15. Kneece, Richard. "10 Inspiring Examples of Successful Intrapreneurship." *Wired.com.* September 17, 2014. http://insights.wired.com/profiles/blogs/10-inspiring-examples-of-successful-intrapreneurship#axzz3eqE2nLJc.
16. Alas, Ruth. "Resistance to Institutional and Organizational Change: An Individual Perspective." In *Change Management and the Human Factor: Advances, Challenges and Contradictions in Organizational Development*, 153–165 (Cham, Switzerland: Springer International, 2015); Kotter, John P., and Leonard A. Schlesinger. "Choosing Strategies for Change." *Harvard Business Review* 57, no. 2 (March 1979): 106–114.
17. Youngblood, Stuart A., Angelo S. DeNisi, Julie L. Molleston, and William H. Mobley. "The Impact of Work Environment, Instrumentality Beliefs, Perceived Labor Union Image, and Subjective Norms on Union Voting Intentions." *Academy of Management Journal* 27, no. 3 (September 1984): 576–590; Mulder, Catherine P. "Unions'

Resistance to Capital and the Potential for Class Transformation." *Rethinking Marxism* 25, no. 1 (January 2013): 114–120.

18. Alas, "Resistance to Institutional and Organizational Change"; Kotter and Schlesinger, "Choosing Strategies for Change."
19. Troyani, "3 Examples of Organizational Change and Why They Got It Right."
20. Stayer, Ralph. "How I Learned to Let My Workers Lead." *Harvard Business Review* (November–December 1990). https://hbr.org/1990/11/how-i-learned-to-let-my-workers-lead.
21. Bartunek, Jean M., and Richard W. Woodman. "Organizational Development." In *The Oxford Handbook of Positive Organizational Scholarship*, 727–736 (New York: Oxford University Press, 2012); Austin, John R., and Jean M. Bartunek. "Theories and Practices of Organizational Development." In *Organization Development: A Jossey-Bass Reader*, 89–128 (San Francisco: Jossey-Bass, 2006).
22. Eaton, John, and Duncan Brown. "Coaching for a Change with Vodafone." *Career Development International* 7, no. 5 (2002): 284–287.
23. For an overview of OD process models see McLean, Gary L. *Organization Development: Principles, Processes, Practices* (San Francisco: Berrett-Koehler, 2006).
24. For reviews of differing types of OD interventions see Friedlander, Frank, and L. Dave Brown. "Organization Development." *Annual Review of Psychology* 25, no. 1 (February 1974): 313: Neuman, George A., Jack E. Edwards, and Nambury S. Raju. "Organizational Development Interventions: A Meta-analysis of Their Effects on Satisfaction and Other Attitudes." *Personnel Psychology* 42, no. 3 (September 1989): 461–489.
25. Margulies, Newton, Penny L. Wright, and Richard W. Scholl. "Organization Development Techniques: Their Impact on Change." *Group and Organization Studies* 2, no. 4 (December 1977): 428–448.
26. Webb, Maynard. "Reinventing Reward Systems for a Happier Office." *Fast Company*. February 6, 2013. www.fastcompany.com/3005519/reinventing-reward-systems-happier-office.
27. Katzenbach, Jon R., Ilona Steffen, and Caroline Kronley. "Cultural Change That Sticks." *Harvard Business Review* 90, no. 7/8 (July 2012): 110–117.
28. Swinscoe, Adrian. "Do You Need to Change Your Organisational Structure to Improve Your Customer Experience?" *Forbes.com*. January 9, 2014. www.forbes.com/sites/adrianswinscoe/2014/01/09/do-you-need-to-change-your-organisational-structure-to-improve-your-customer-experience/.
29. Margulies et al., "Organization Development Techniques."
30. Kolbenschlag, Bill. "Three Things That Can Make Employees More Productive." *Forbes.com*. January 16, 2014. www.forbes.com/sites/unify/2014/01/16/three-things-that-can-make-employees-more-productive/.
31. Emery, Fred. "Characteristics of Socio-Technical Systems." In *The Social Engagement of Social Science: A Tavistock Anthology*, Vol. 2: *The Socio-technical Perspective*, 157–186 (Philadelphia: University of Pennsylvania Press, 1993); Eijnatten, Frans M. van. "Developments in Socio-technical Systems Design (STSD)." In *Handbook of Work and Organizational Psychology*. Vol. 4: *Organizational Psychology* (2nd ed.), 61–88 (Hove, England: Psychology Press/Erlbaum (UK)/Taylor & Francis, 1998).
32. Jenkins, Daniel P., Neville A. Stanton, Paul M. Salmon, and Guy H. Walker. *Command and Control: The Sociotechnical Perspective* (Burlington, VT: Ashgate, 2009: 23).
33. See, for example, Blanck, Paul. "From a 'Rational' Structure to a 'Socio-Technical' System: A Whole-Mind Metaphor for Organizational Change." *ETC: A Review of General Semantics* 51, no. 4 (95 1994): 422–431; Reese, Rick, and John W. Slocum Jr. "Redesigning for Dial Tone: A Socio-Technical Systems Case Study." *Organizational Dynamics* 24, no. 2 (September 1995): 80–90.
34. Hammer, Leslie B., and Kristi L. Zimmerman. "Quality of Work Life." In *APA Handbook of Industrial and Organizational Psychology*. Vol 3: *Maintaining, Expanding, and Contracting the Organization*, 399–431 (Washington, DC: American Psychological Association, 2011).
35. Smith, Jacqueline. "The Best Big Companies for Work-Life Balance." *Forbes.com*. June 3, 2013. www.forbes.com/sites/jacquelynsmith/2013/06/03/the-best-big-companies-for-work-life-balance/.
36. Lomranz, Jacob, Martin Lakin, and Harold Schiffman. "A Three-Valued Typology for Sensitivity Training and Encounter Groups." *Human Relations* 26, no. 3 (June 1973): 339; Nikels, Holly J., Grace Ann Mims, and Matthew J. Mims. "Allies against Hate: A School-Based Diversity Sensitivity Training Experience." *Journal for Specialists in Group Work* 32, no. 2 (June 2007): 126–138.
37. Chumley, Cheryl K. "Black Lawmakers Press Obama to Mandate 'Sensitivity Training' for Police." *Washington Times*. February 11, 2015. www.washingtontimes.com/news/2015/feb/11/black-lawmakers-press-obama-to-mandate-sensitivity/.
38. Jason, Leonard A., Louise Ferone, and Thomas Anderegg. "Evaluating Ecological, Behavioral, and Process Consultation Interventions." *Journal of School Psychology* 17, no. 2 (Summer 1979): 103–115; Lipshitz, Raanan, and John J. Sherwood. "The Effectiveness of Third-Party Processes Consultation as a Function of the Consultant's Prestige and Style of Intervention." *Journal of Applied Behavioral Science* 14, no. 4 (October 1978): 493–509.
39. Dyer, William G., W. Gibb Dyer Jr., and Jeffrey H. Dyer. *Team Building: Proven Strategies for Improving Team Performance* (4th ed.) (San Francisco: Jossey-Bass, 2007); Murrell, Kenneth L., and E. H. Valsan. "A Team-Building Workshop as an OD Intervention in Egypt." *Leadership and Organization Development Journal* 6, no. 2 (1985): 11–16.
40. Randolph, W. Alan, and Barry Z. Posner. "The Effects of an Intergroup Development OD Intervention as Conditioned by the Life Cycle State of Organizations: A Laboratory Experiment." *Group and Organization Studies* 7, no. 3 (September 1982): 335–352; Killen, Melanie, Aline Hitti, and Kelly Lynn Mulvey. "Social Development and Intergroup Relations." In *APA Handbook of Personality and Social Psychology*. Vol. 2: *Group Processes*, 177–201 (Washington, DC: American Psychological Association, 2015).

Chapter 17

1. Gibson, Linda K., Bruce Finnie, and Jeffrey L Stuart. "A Mathematical Model for Exploring the Evolution of Organizational Structure." *International Journal of Organizational Analysis* 23, no. 1 (2015): 21–24; Peiró, José M. "Organizational Structure." In *Advances in Organizational Psychology: An International Review*, 191–206 (Thousand Oaks, CA: Sage, 1987); Bourgeois, L. J. III, Daniel W. McAllister, and Terence R. Mitchell. "The Effects of Different Organizational Environments upon Decisions about Organizational Structure." *Academy of Management Journal* 21, no. 3 (September 1978): 508–514.
2. www.toyota-global.com/company/history_of_toyota/75years/data/automotive_business/sales/activity/north_america/index.html#america.
3. http://www.generalmills.com/en/Company/Businesses/US-retail.
4. Blakeman, Chuck. "Why Self-Managed Teams Are the Future of Business." *Inc.com*. November 25, 2014. www.inc.com/chuck-blakeman/why-self-managed-teams-are-the-future-of-business.html.

5. Rogers, Paul, and Jenny Davis-Peccoud. "Networked Organizations: Making the Matrix Work." *Bain Brief.* December 7, 2011. www.bain.com/publications/articles/decision-insights-12-networked-organizations-making-the-matrix-work.aspx.
6. "Hewlett-Packard to Split Into Two Companies." *BBC News.* October 6, 2014. www.bbc.com/news/business-29501235.
7. "eBay to Split Off PayPal Online Payment Business." *BBC News.* September 30, 2014. www.bbc.com/news/business-29423251.
8. Shepard, Jon M. "Functional Specialization and Work Attitudes." *Industrial Relations* 8, no. 2 (February 1969): 185–194; Jagoda, Agnieszka. "Deskilling as the Dark Side of the Work Specialization." *International Journal of Academic Research* 5, no. 3 (May 2013): 331–334.
9. Nieberding, Amy Owen. "Employee Engagement and Other Bonding Forces in Organizations." *Consulting Psychology Journal: Practice and Research* 66, no. 4 (December 2014): 320–323; Price, James L. "The Impact of Departmentalization on Interoccupational Cooperation." *Human Organization* 27, no. 4 (Winter 1968): 362; Yeh, Dowming, and Jeng Jing-Hwa. "An Empirical Study of the Influence of Departmentalization and Organizational Position on software Maintenance." *Journal of Software Maintenance and Evolution: Research and Practice* 14, no. 1 (January 2002): 65–82.
10. Davis, Stanley M. "Two Models of Organization: Unity of Command Versus Balance of Power." *Sloan Management Review* 16, no. 1 (Fall 1974): 29–40; Fayol, Henri *General and Industrial Management.* Trans. C. Storrs (London: Sir Isaac Pitman & Sons, 1949); Wren, Daniel A., Arthur G. Bedeian, and John D. Breeze. "The Foundations of Henri Fayol's Administrative Theory," *Management Decision* 40, no. 9 (October 2002): 906.
11. Wong, Carol A., Pat Elliott-Miller, Heather Laschinger, Michael Cuddihy, Raquel M. Meyer, Margaret Keatings, Camille Burnett, and Natalie Szudy. "Examining the Relationships between Span of Control and Manager Job and Unit Performance Outcomes." *Journal of Nursing Management* 23, no. 2 (March 2015): 156–168; Entwisle, Doris R., and John Walton. "Observations on the Span of Control." *Administrative Science Quarterly* 5, no. 4 (March 1961): 522–533; Ouchi, William G., and John B. Dowling. "Defining the Span of Control." *Administrative Science Quarterly* 19, no. 3 (September 1974): 357–365; Udell, Jon G. "An Empirical Test of Hypotheses Relating to Span of Control." *Administrative Science Quarterly* 12, no. 3 (December 1967): 420–439; Urwick, Lyndall F. "The Manager's Span of Control." *Harvard Business Review* 34, no. 3 (May 1956): 39–47; Urwick, L. F. "V. A. Graicunas and the Span of Control." *Academy of Management Journal* 17, no. 2 (June 1974): 349–354.
12. See, for example, Lebowitz, Shana. "Apple CEO Tim Cook Now Has 17 Direct Reports—and That's Probably Too Many." *Business Insider.* July 8, 2015. www.businessinsider.com/apple-ceo-tim-cook-has-too-many-direct-reports-2015-7?r=UK&IR=T.
13. Stone, Katherine. "The Origins of Job Structures in the Steel Industry." *Review of Radical Political Economics* 6 (Summer 1974): 61–97.
14. Bayramzadeh, Sara, and Mariam F. Alkazemi. "Centralized vs. Decentralized Nursing Stations: An Evaluation of the Implications of Communication Technologies in Healthcare." *Health Environments Research and Design Journal (HERD) (Vendome Group LLC)* 7, no. 4 (Summer 2014): 62–80; Fayol, *General and Industrial Management*; Wren et al., "The Foundations of Henri Fayol's Administrative Theory"; Zábojník, Ján. "Centralized and Decentralized Decision Making in Organizations." *Journal of Labor Economics* 20, no. 1 (January 2002): 1.
15. www.cimaglobal.com/Documents/Student%20docs/2010%20syllabus%20docs/E1/E1_fmarticle_nov2013.pdf.
16. See, for example, Fong, Kai Hung, and Ed Snape. "Empowering Leadership, Psychological Empowerment and Employee Outcomes: Testing a Multi-level Mediating Model." *British Journal of Management* 26, no. 1 (January 2015): 126–138; Frazier, M. Lance, and Stav Fainshmidt. "Voice Climate, Work Outcomes, and the Mediating Role of Psychological Empowerment: A Multilevel Examination." *Group and Organization Management* 37, no. 6 (December 2012): 691–715.
17. Courtright, John A., Gail T. Fairhurst, and L. Edna Rogers. "Interaction Patterns in Organic and Mechanistic System." *Academy of Management Journal* 32, no. 4 (December 1989): 773–802; Gillen, Dennis J., and Stephen J. Carroll. "Relationship of Managerial Ability to Unit Effectiveness in More Organic Versus More Mechanistic Departments." *Journal of Management Studies* 22, no. 6 (November 1985): 668–676; Zanzi, Alberto. "How Organic Is Your Organization? Determinants of Organic/Mechanistic Tendencies in a Public Accounting Firm." *Journal of Management Studies* 24, no. 2 (March 1987): 125–142; Dust, Scott B., Christian J. Resick, and Mary Bardes Mawritz. "Transformational Leadership, Psychological Empowerment, and the Moderating Role of Mechanistic–Organic Contexts." *Journal of Organizational Behavior* 35, no. 3 (April 2014): 413–433.
18. Ibid.
19. Podsakoff, Philip M., Larry J. Williams, and William D. Todor. "Effects of Organizational Formalization on Alienation among Professionals and Nonprofessionals." *Academy of Management Journal* 29, no. 4 (December 1986): 820–831; Peters, Gangolf. "Organisation as Social Relationship, Formalisation, and Standardisation: A Weberian Approach to Concept Formation." *International Sociology* 3, no. 3 (September 1988): 267–282; Mattes, Jannika. "Formalisation and Flexibilisation in Organisations—Dynamic and Selective Approaches in Corporate Innovation Processes." *European Management Journal* 32, no. 3 (June 2014): 475–486.
20. Toren, Nina. "Bureaucracy and Professionalism: A Reconsideration of Weber's Thesis." *Academy of Management Review* 1, no. 3 (July 1976): 36–46; Walton, Eric J. "The Persistence of Bureaucracy: A Meta-analysis of Weber's Model of Bureaucratic Control." *Organization Studies* 26, no. 4 (April 2005): 569–600; Weiss, Richard M. "Weber on Bureaucracy: Management Consultant or Political Theorist?" *Academy of Management Review* 8, no. 2 (April 1983): 242–248.
21. Concepts presented in the following discussion are taken in part from these sources: Anand, N., and Richard L. Daft "What Is the Right Organization Design?" *Organizational Dynamics* 36, no. 4 (November 2007): 329–344; Duncan, Robert. "What Is the Right Organization Structure? Decision Tree Analysis Provides the Answer" *Organizational Dynamics* 7, no. 3 (Winter 1979): 59–80; Galbraith, Jay R. *Designing Complex Organizations* (Reading, MA: Addison–Wesley, 1973); Galbraith, Jay R. *Organization Design* (Reading, MA: Addison-Wesley, 1977); Galbraith, Jay R. "Matrix Organization Designs." *Business Horizons* 14, no. 1 (February 1971): 29.
22. Hendrick, Hal W. "Organizational Design." In *Handbook of Human Factors*, 470–494 (Oxford: Wiley, 1987); Thompson, James D. *Approaches to Organizational Design* (Pittsburgh, PA: University of Pittsburgh Press, 1966).
23. See, for example, Moch, Michael K. "Structure and Organizational Resource Allocation." *Administrative Science Quarterly* 21, no. 4 (December 1976): 661–674.
24. Leszcynski, Ray. "Garland ISD Touts New Hires, Revised Organizational Structure." *Dallas Morning News.* May 19, 2013. www.dallasnews.com/news/community-news/garland-mesquite/

headlines/20130519-garland-isd-touts-new-hires-revised-organizational-structure.ece.

25. Beakey, Diane, Kathleen Wells Webster, and Jackie Rubin. "Organizational Design and Implementation." *Graziadio Business Review* 10, no. 4 (2007). http://gbr.pepperdine.edu/2010/08/organizational-design-and-implementation/#_edn1.
26. For an overview of technology in organizations, see Mowery, David C. "Technology and Organizations: An Economic/Institutional Analysis." In *Technology and Organizations*, 200–231 (San Francisco: Jossey-Bass, 1990).
27. Cosman, Eric C. "Industrial Control Systems Security: The Owner-Operator's Challenge." *Chemical Engineering* 121, no. 6 (June 2014): 30–35; Hickson, David J., D. S. Pugh, and Diana C. Pheysey. "Operations Technology and Organization Structure: An Empirical Reappraisal." *Administrative Science Quarterly* 14, no. 3 (September 1969): 378–397; Khandwalla, Pradip N. "Mass Output Orientation of Operations Technology and Organizational Structure." *Administrative Science Quarterly* 19, no. 1 (March 1974): 74–97.
28. Dedrick, Jason, Kenneth L. Kraemer, and Eric Shih. "Information Technology and Productivity in Developed and Developing Countries." *Journal of Management Information Systems* 30, no. 1 (Summer 2013): 97–122; Walton, Richard E. *Up and Running: Integrating information Technology and the Organization* (Boston: Harvard Business School Press, 1989).
29. Twentyman, Jessica. "Networking for Networking: How Cisco Uses Social Media Marketing." *Guardian.* October 8, 2013. www.theguardian.com/technology/2013/oct/09/networking-for-networking-how-cisco-uses-social-media-marketing.
30. Wu, Paul Pao-Yen, Clinton Fookes, Jegar Pitchforth, and Kerrie Mengersen. "A framework for Model Integration and Holistic Modelling of Socio-Technical Systems." *Decision Support Systems* 71, (March 2015): 14–27; Maguire, Martin. "Socio-technical Systems and Interaction Design: 21st Century Relevance." *Applied Ergonomics* 45, no. 2, pt A (March 2014): 162–170; Emery, Fred. "Characteristics of Socio-technical Systems." In *The Social Engagement of Social Science: A Tavistock Anthology.* Vol. 2: *The Socio-technical Perspective*, 157–186 (Philadelphia: University of Pennsylvania Press, 1993); Eijnatten, Frans M. van. "Developments in Socio-technical Systems Design (STSD)." In *Handbook of Work and Organizational Psychology.* Vol. 4: *Organizational Psychology* (2nd ed.), 61–88 (Hove, England: Psychology Press/Erlbaum (UK)/Taylor & Francis, 1998).

CHAPTER 1 SELF-TEST

LO 1.1 Explain the basic concept of organizational behavior and its value in organizations

1. Define *organizational behavior.*
2. The three reasons you should have an interest in understanding behavior are so you can explain it, predict it, and change it.
   a. True
   b. False
3. Which of the following is not one of the specific skills necessary to be an effective manager?
   a. Technical
   b. Human
   c. Conceptual
   d. Social

LO 1.2 Describe the key role of managing human capital in creating a sustainable competitive advantage for organizations

4. What are the two main types of resources in organizations?
5. Three main aspects of human capital enhance true competitive advantage: value, genuineness, and inimitability.
   a. True
   b. False

LO 1.3 Identify the major behavioral science disciplines that contribute to OB

6. What are the four contributing disciplines to the OB field?
7. The study of people and their activities in relation to societal, environmental, and cultural influences is known as:
   a. Anthropology
   b. Sociology
   c. Psychology
   d. Theology

LO 1.4 Demonstrate the value of critical thinking in the context of organizational behavior

8. According to the study of more than 400 senior HR professionals, critical thinking is the most important skill for new hires.
   a. True
   b. False
9. What is the first step in the critical-thinking methodology?
   a. Observe
   b. Interpret
   c. Analyze
   d. Evaluate
10. ______________ states that actions must be dependent on the nature of the situation.
   a. Open systems theory
   b. Contingency thinking
   c. Evidence-based management
   d. High-involvement management

LO 1.5 Identify the major challenges and opportunities in the field of OB

11. What are five challenges and opportunities facing organizations today?
12. Define *workforce diversity.*

LO 1.6 Describe the importance of ethical behavior in global organizations

13. Ethics can be defined as:
   a. An obligation to act for the benefit of society at large
   b. The study of the fundamental nature of knowledge, reality, and existence
   c. Moral principles that guide our behavior
   d. The desire to promote the welfare of others
14. An organization is unethical if it violates the basic rights of its employees and ignores health, safety, and environmental standards.
   a. True
   b. False

LO 1.7 Differentiate the three basic levels of analysis at which OB may be examined

15. List the three main levels of analysis within the OB model.
16. Teams are the foundation of organizations.
   a. True
   b. False

LO 1.8 Outline the benefits of positive organizational behavior and high-involvement management

17. Which of the following focuses on the strengths, virtues, vitality, and resilience of individuals and organizations?

a. High-involvement management
b. Evidence-based management
c. Contingency thinking
d. Positive organizational behavior

18. Managers who practice positive organizational behavior value human capital as their most important resource.

a. True
b. False

19. In high-involvement management, who has an input in how work is conducted?

a. Managers
b. Senior-level employees
c. Lower-level associates
d. All the above

CHAPTER 2 SELF-TEST

LO 2.1 Explain the importance of diversity in OB

1. ________________ can be defined as the understanding, acceptance, and recognition of differences between groups of people.
2. Surface-level diversity includes all but which of the following?

a. Age/generation
b. Race/ethnicity
c. Personality
d. Gender

3. Diversity training can help to reduce bias and break down any prejudices or psychological barriers from coworkers who struggle to accept employees whom they perceive as "different."

a. True
b. False

LO 2.2 Discuss why individual differences and are important

4. Define *individual differences*.
5. Self-esteem and self-efficacy are two main factors of self-concept.

a. True
b. False

6. The belief we have about our own worth following the self-evaluation process is known as:

a. Self-awareness
b. Self-concept
c. Self-efficacy
d. Self-esteem

LO 2.3 Contrast the nature and nurture explanations of personality development

7. ____________ ____________ are characteristics that describe our thoughts, feelings, and behaviors.
8. Explain the nature versus nurture debate.
9. What percentage of an individual's personality traits do researchers believe are attributed to nurture?

a. 40
b. 50
c. 60
d. 70

LO 2.4 Describe the Myers-Briggs Type Indicator Types

10. There are _____ different personality types defined by the Myers-Briggs Type Indicator.
11. The majority of the US population is identified as INFJ personality types.

a. True
b. False

LO 2.5 Identify the five personality factors of the Big Five Model.

12. Which of the following is NOT one of the five personality factors in the Big Five Model?

a. Agreeableness
b. Positivity
c. Neuroticism
d. Conscientiousness

13. Being trusting, good natured, tolerant, forgiving, and cooperative describes which of the following Big Five personality factors?

a. Agreeableness
b. Openness to experience
c. Extraversion
d. Neuroticism

14. The Big Five Model differs from the MBTI because the MBTI does not examine an individual's emotional stability.

a. True
b. False

LO 2.6 Differentiate among the most common personality attributes

15. Explain the difference between internal locus of control and external locus of control.
16. Describe a typical individual who has a highly proactive personality.
17. Individuals who are competitive, aggressive, and achievement oriented are characterized as Type ____ orientation.

CHAPTER 3 SELF-TEST

LO 3.1 Describe the basic concept of emotions in the context of organizational behavior

1. Discuss the difference between emotions and moods.
2. Excitement, cheerfulness, and self-assurance are examples of __________ affect emotions.
3. Emotions last longer than moods.
   a. True
   b. False

LO 3.2 Discuss the various roles of emotions in the workplace

4. When employees must display emotions desired by the organization that are contrary to what they are actually feeling, they enact:
   a. Emotional contagion
   b. Emotional labor
   c. Emotional regulation
   d. Emotional intelligence
5. Explain the difference between **surface acting** and **deep acting**.
6. Which of the following is NOT one of the four dimensions of EI?
   a. Relationship Management
   b. Self-Management
   c. Self-Awareness
   d. Self-Control

LO 3.3 Explain the ways in which attitudes influence behavior in organizations

7. List the three main elements that form attitudes.
8. Attitudes, feelings, likes, and dislikes are examples of:
   a. Behavioral intentions
   b. Actual behaviors
   c. Affective evaluation
   d. Cognitive appraisal
9. What causes cognitive dissonance to occur?

LO 3.4 Identify some common workplace attitudes and related outcomes

10. Job satisfaction and job performance are strongly correlated.
    a. True
    b. False
11. Define organizational commitment.
12. Behaviors that purposefully disrupt or harm an organization are called ________________________________.

LO 3.5 Illustrate the ways in which stress can affect behavior in the workplace

13. Name and describe the two main types of stressors.

LO 3.6 Discuss different outcomes of stress and the benefits of wellness programs

14. Eustress involves high levels of stressors that have destructive and negative effects on effort and performance.
    a. True
    b. False
15. _________ coping aims at reducing or eliminating stressors by attempting to understand the problem, and seeking practical ways in which to resolve it.
    a. Emotion-focused
    b. Problem-focused
    c. Distress-focused
    d. Eustress-focused
16. _________ is a personal or organizational effort to promote health and wellbeing.

CHAPTER 4 SELF-TEST

LO 4.1 Describe the basic concept of perception

1. The process by which we receive and interpret information from the environment is known as ____________.
   a. Discrimination
   b. Judging
   c. Perception
   d. Bias
2. What are the three listed factors that can influence and/or distort perception?

LO 4.2 Explain the different types of perceptual distortions

3. Which of the following is a perception problem in which we form a positive or negative bias of an individual based on our overall impressions of that person?
   a. Halo Effect
   b. Selective Attention
   c. Primacy Effect
   d. Stereotyping
4. A facet of impression management is ingratiation.
   a. True
   b. False
5. **Self-fulfilling prophecy** occurs when a person behaves based on pre-existing _______ about another person or situation so as to create an outcome that is aligned with those ______.

LO 4.3 Apply attribution theory to more effectively interpret behavior

6. The three types of determinants of attribution that influence our internal and external attributions are consensus, consistency, and correlation.
   a. True
   b. False
7. The inclination to attribute internal factors to the behavior of others more that external factors is called:
   a. Self-serving bias
   b. Consensus
   c. Distinctiveness
   d. Fundamental attribution error

LO 4.4 Use reinforcement theory to understand learning and modify behavior

8. Ivan Pavlov's experiment in which he trained dogs to salivate at the sound of a bell is associated with which type of behavioral view?
   a. Classical conditioning
   b. Operant conditioning
   c. Reinforcement theory
9. The law of effect is most closely associated with operant conditioning.
   a. True
   b. False
10. The process of forming associations between learning and behavior by controlling its consequences is ______ conditioning.
11. The reinforcement theory is the most fully developed theory of classical conditioning to date.
    a. True
    b. False
12. The two types of reinforcement schedules are _______ reinforcement and _______ reinforcement.

LO 4.5 Apply social cognitive theory to social learning and cognitive processes

13. An individual's personal conviction in our ability to perform certain tasks or behaviors is known as:
    a. Self-regulation
    b. Self-efficacy
    c. Self-servant
    d. Selective perception
14. **Vicarious learning** is a process of learning by watching the actions or behaviors of another person.
    a. True
    b. False
15. Which one of the below is a factor of the Triadic Reciprocal Model of Behavior?
    a. Self-efficacy
    b. Reinforcement
    c. Defensiveness
    d. Perception

CHAPTER 5 SELF-TEST

LO 5.1 Explain the basic motivation process

1. _________ is defined as forces from within individuals that stimulate and drive them to achieve goals.
2. Maslow's hierarchy of needs, McClelland's need theory, goal setting theory, and the ERG theory are all examples of content theories.
   a. True
   b. False
3. Explain the two different types of motivation theories.

LO 5.2 Compare the various needs theories of motivation

4. The pyramid detailing higher-level and lower-level needs that people are motivated to satisfy is known as:
   a. ERG Theory
   b. Maslow's Hierarchy of Needs

c. Two Factor Theory

d. Acquired Needs Theory

5. According to McClelland, the need for _______ is the desire to belong to a group and to be liked.

6. Which of the following aspects of Maslow's need hierarchy is NOT used in any of the other content theory models?

   a. Esteem
   b. Belongingness
   c. Safety
   d. Physiological

7. Money is one of the primary mechanisms used for motivating people in the workplace.

   a. True
   b. False

LO 5.3 Examine equity theory in the context of organizational justice and distinguish among the predictable outcomes of perceived inequity

8. __________ focuses on how people perceive fairness in the workplace.

   a. Perceived inequity
   b. Procedural justice
   c. Equity theory
   d. Organizational justice

9. This theory, introduced by J. Stacey Adams, holds that motivation is based on our perception of fairness in comparison with others:

   a. ERG Theory
   b. Two Factor Theory
   c. Equity Theory
   d. Expectancy Theory

10. The two main aspects of organizational justice are __________ and __________.

LO 5.4 Apply goal setting theory in organizational contexts

11. The goal setting theory is the most dominant motivation theory.

   a. True
   b. False

12. Which of the following is NOT a characteristic of an effective goal?

   a. Concise
   b. Specific
   c. Difficult
   d. Accepted by employees

13. ________ goals are short-term goals that provide employees with frequent feedback about their performance.

LO 5.5 Describe the expectancy theory of motivation and its practical implications. Name and describe the three parts of the expectancy theory

14. The question of "Do I find the outcomes desirable?" relates to the ________ part of the expectancy theory.

CHAPTER 6 SELF-TEST

LO 6.1 Explain the concept of intrinsic motivation and its primary determinants

1. __________ motivation is performing tasks for your own innate satisfaction.

2. The need for competence and the need for self-determination are examples of extrinsic rewards.

   a. True
   b. False

3. Which of the following is an example of intrinsic motivation?

   a. Salary
   b. Competence
   c. Bonuses
   d. Paid vacation

LO 6.2 Differentiate among the various types of extrinsic rewards

4. Which of the following rewards employees for the acquisition and the development of new skills that leads to enhanced work performance?

   a. Seniority-based pay
   b. Job-content based pay
   c. Skill-based pay
   d. Performance-based pay

5. List and describe the three types of individual-level pay.

6. The performance-based plan in which an organization shares profits with employees is known as _________.

LO 6.3 Discuss the various facets of job design

7. ____________ increases the range of tasks and duties associated with a job.
   a. Job enrichment
   b. Job rotation
   c. Job enhancement
   d. Job enlargement
8. Identify the five core dimensions discussed in the job characteristics model.
9. Task identity is the extent to which an employee completes an entire piece of work from start to finish.
   a. True
   b. False

LO 6.4 Discuss psychological empowerment and its components

10. The extent to which employees feel a sense of personal fulfillment and intent when carrying out tasks is known as:
    a. Psychological empowerment
    b. Extrinsic motivation
    c. Task significance
    d. Autonomy
11. A belief in a person's ability to perform work tasks successfully is known as his or her __________.
12. Which of the following is NOT one of the four main beliefs associate with psychological empowerment?
    a. Autonomy
    b. Determination
    c. Ability
    d. Competence

LO 6.5 Evaluate various approaches to nontraditional work schedules

13. Free agents and part-time workers are the same thing.
    a. True
    b. False
14. One full-time job is divided among two or more people according to predetermined hours is known as:
    a. Part-time work
    b. Job sharing
    c. Compressed workweeks
    d. Flextime
15. What is flextime? Give an example.

CHAPTER 7 SELF-TEST

LO 7.1 Distinguish between a team and a group

1. Decentralization is the distribution of ________ across all levels of the organization.
2. Explain the difference between groups and teams.

LO 7.2 Compare the various types of teams in organizations today

3. A group of workers who manage their own daily duties with little to no supervision is called a
   a. Virtual team
   b. Self-managing team
   c. Problem-solving team
   d. Cross-functional team
4. Many global companies now operate in virtual teams, where members from different locations work together through e-mail, video-conferencing, instant messaging, and other electronic media.
   a. True
   b. False
5. A group of workers from different units with various areas of expertise are called a
   a. Virtual team
   b. Self-managing team
   c. Problem-solving team
   d. Cross-functional team

LO 7.3 Apply the model of team effectiveness to evaluate team performance

6. According to the model of team effectiveness, team contextual influences and team composition factors are both factors that influence team processes.
   a. True
   b. False
7. Team size, skills and abilities, personality, and diversity are the components of
   a. Team contextual influences
   b. Team composition factors
   c. Team processes
   d. Team outcomes
8. Explain the three types of interdependence.

LO 7.4 Explain how team processes affect team outcomes

9. The five stages of team development in order are ______; ______; ______; ______; and ______.
10. According to the team development model, this stage is the point when team members resolve conflicts and begin to work well together and become more cohesive:
    a. Norming
    b. Forming
    c. Performing
    d. Storming
11. A team is said to be in ______ when the total amount of work produced is greater than the amount of work produced by an individual working independently.
12. Give an example of a process gain.

LO 7.5 Identify the advantages and disadvantages of different team decision-making approaches

13. Groupthink can be beneficial to the productivity of a group.
    a. True
    b. False
14. Generating creative, spontaneous ideas from all members of a group without any criticism or judgment is known as:
    a. Groupthink
    b. Cohesion
    c. Brainstorming
    d. Forming
15. The Delphi technique of decision making is particularly useful when team members are working from different locations.
    a. True
    b. False

CHAPTER 8 SELF-TEST

LO 8.1 Identify the primary types of decisions managers make to solve problems

1. The two main types of decisions are ______ and ______.
2. Programmed decisions are complex choices in which we have little past experience to draw from.
    a. True
    b. False

LO 8.2 Apply a rational model of decision making to solve problems and make decisions

3. After you have defined the problem, what is the next step in the five-step model of decision making?
    a. Generate multiple alternatives
    b. Choose, implement, and evaluate the best alternative
    c. Identify and weigh decision criteria
    d. Rate alternatives on the basis of decision criteria
4. After choosing and implementing the best decision, you must remember to ______ the decision.

LO 8.3 Identify factors that influence the way we make decisions in the real world

5. When buying a car, customers are most likely to use bounded rationality.
    a. True
    b. False
6. Shortcuts or "rules of thumb" that allow us to make judgments and decisions quickly and effectively are called:
    a. Intuition
    b. Bias
    c. Satisficing
    d. Heuristics
7. Which type of heuristic bases a decision on our existing mental prototype and similar stereotypes?
    a. Availability
    b. Anchoring and adjustment
    c. Representative
8. ______ bias is the tendency to overestimate the ability to predict an outcome of an event.
9. This type of error is the tendency for people to believe they can predict the outcome of events based on false information or superstition.
    a. Randomness
    b. Lack of participation
    c. Framing

LO 8.4 Explain a basis for resolving ethical dilemmas in organizations

10. Ethics are moral principles that manage our ______.
11. The key to being an ethical person or organization is to consistently choose to do the right thing.
    a. True
    b. False

LO 8.5 Contrast various approaches to ethical decision making

12. Which ethical decision-making approach involves making decisions based on moral principles that least infringe on the entitlements of others?
    a. Utilitarian approach
    b. Rights approach
    c. Justice approach
13. Which ethical decision-making approach focuses on taking action that results in the greater good for the majority of the people?
    a. Utilitarian approach
    b. Rights approach
    c. Justice approach
14. Which ethical decision-making approach centers on decisions made on the basis of fairness?
    a. Utilitarian approach
    b. Rights approach
    c. Justice approach
15. List Josephson's Six Pillars of Character.

CHAPTER 9 SELF-TEST

LO 9.1 Discuss the critical nature of creativity and innovation in today's organizations

1. __________ is the creation and development of a new product or service.
2. What is the generation of meaningful ideas by individuals or teams?
    a. Innovation
    b. Creativity
    c. Exploration

LO 9.2 Describe the three-component model of creativity

3. The three components of the three-component model of creativity are domain-relevant skills and expertise, creativity-relevant processes, and intrinsic task motivation.
    a. True
    b. False
4. Even individuals with the highest levels of knowledge still need creative-relevant processes such as personality, a method of thinking, a certain work style, and a knowledge of heuristics to be truly creative.
    a. True
    b. False
5. The statement "Intrinsic is more effective than extrinsic" is best related to:
    a. Expertise
    b. Creative thinking skills
    c. Motivation

LO 9.3 Identify the three types of support for creativity

6. Practiced creativity is the tendency of people to possess the skills and capacity to generate ideas.
    a. True
    b. False
7. Which of the following helps cultivate an environment for creativity?
    a. Organizational support
    b. Supervisory support
    c. Work group support
    d. All the above

LO 9.4 Outline the steps in the innovation process

8. Assessing the feasibility and practicality of ideas is considered the first step of the innovation process.
    a. True
    b. False
9. Identifying any advantages and disadvantages associated with the innovation, exploring costs and value, and setting goals and priorities take place in what step of the innovation process?
    a. Idea generation
    b. Problem solving
    c. Implementation and diffusion
10. Bringing the prototype solution or invention to its first use or market introduction is known as:
    a. Idea generation
    b. Problem solving
    c. Implementation and diffusion

LO 9.5 Distinguish among the various types of innovation in organizations

11. The introduction of new or improved operation and work methods is called
    a. Product innovation
    b. Process innovation
    c. Exploitative innovation
    d. Exploratory innovation

12. The introduction or modification of formal interaction and communication and reward systems is known as ______________ innovation.
13. This type of innovation focuses on the enhancement and reuse of existing products and processes:

    a. Product innovation
    b. Process innovation
    c. Exploratory innovation
    d. Exploitative innovation

14. Explain organizational cultural lag.

Chapter 10 SELF-TEST

LO 10.1 Describe the conflict process and the various types of conflict

1. __________ conflict consists of constructive and healthy disputes between individuals or groups.
2. Which type of conflict refers to the clash in viewpoints about how to carry out work?

    a. Task conflict
    b. Relationship conflict
    c. Process conflict

3. The four stages of the conflict process are _____ of conflict, _____ conflict, ____ conflict, and _____ of conflict.

LO 10.2 Identify the five basic conflict management strategies

4. The attempt of one party in a conflict to adjust his views to play down the differences between both parties is known as:

    a. Avoiding
    b. Accommodating
    c. Compromising
    d. Collaborating

5. Compromising is when all parties involved in a conflict work together to find a solution that is beneficial to everyone.

    a. True
    b. False

6. ________ is the desire to gain victory over the opponent through force, skill, or domination.

LO 10.3 Outline the bases of trust and predictable outcomes of trust in organizations

7. The definition of **trust** is the dependence on the integrity, ability, ______________, and reliability of someone or something else.
8. People with ______________ trust tend to possess the types of personality traits that encourage them to put their faith in others.

    a. disposition-based
    b. cognition-based
    c. affect-based

9. Recent research has found that people working in a high-trust environment tend to take more risks and are less likely to exhibit ineffectual or counterproductive behaviors.

    a. True
    b. False

LO 10.4 Describe the negotiation process

10. The first step in the negotiation process is

    a. Shaping expectations
    b. Providing supporting evidence
    c. Getting ready to negotiate

11. A neutral third party who attempts to assist parties in a negotiation to find a resolution or come to an agreement using rational arguments and persuasion is known as a(n):

    a. Arbitrator
    b. Mediator
    c. Conciliator

LO 10.5 Compare distributive and integrative bargaining approaches

12. __________ bargaining occurs when two parties try to claim a "fixed pie" of resources.
13. In many instances distributive bargaining can be time consuming and inefficient, because it can lead to a contest of wills.

    a. True
    b. False

14. One example of an integrative bargaining strategy is to separate people from the problem.

    a. True
    b. False

CHAPTER 11 SELF-TEST

LO 11.1 Explain the basic concept of leadership

1. __________ is the process of providing general direction, from a position of influence, to individuals or groups toward the successful attainment of goals.

LO 11.2 Distinguish between formal and informal leadership and between leadership and management

2. Explain the difference between formal and informal leaders.
3. ___________ create visions, introduce change, and influence others to achieve goals, while ___________ maintain the status quo, promote stability, and ensure the smooth running of operations.

LO 11.3 Contrast the four basic types of leadership

4. Leadership behavior characterized by implementing guidelines, providing information on what is expected, setting definite performance standards, and ensuring that individuals follow rules is often known as:

   a. Directive leadership

   b. Transactional leadership

   c. Visionary leadership

   d. Empowering leadership

5. Which type of leadership involves creating a vision to motivate, inspire, and stimulate employees?

   a. Directive leadership

   b. Transactional leadership

   c. Visionary leadership

   d. Empowering leadership

6. Transactional leaders help to develop the individual skills and abilities of their followers so that they may utilize these skills to take ownership of their work in order to contribute to organizational performance.

   a. True

   b. False

LO 11.4 Describe the trait, behavioral, and contingency leadership perspectives

7. All of the following are core leadership traits according to modern researchers except:

   a. Self-confidence

   b. Narcissism

   c. Cognitive ability

   d. Integrity

8. According to the Ohio State University studies, which of the following leader behaviors involves the extent to which the leader defines the roles of the employees, sets clear guidelines and procedures, and establishes distinct patterns of organization and communication?

   a. Employee centered

   b. Consideration

   c. Initiating structure

   d. Relationship oriented

9. According to the leadership grid, a leader who is high in concern for people and low in concern for production is exhibiting which of the following leadership styles?

   a. Impoverished

   b. Team leader

   c. Produce or perish

   d. Country club

10. Which of the following is not a situational variable included within Fiedler's contingency model?

    a. Leader-member relations

    b. Follower maturity level

    c. Task structure

    d. Leader's position power

11. According to the Situational Leadership Model, the most appropriate leadership style for a follower at the lowest level of readiness (R1) is:

    a. S1: Telling

    b. S2: Selling

    c. S3: Participating

    d. S4: Delegating

12. List and briefly describe the four primary leadership styles according to the path–goal theory.

LO 11.5 Compare the inspirational, relational, and follower-centered leadership perspectives

13. According to leader-member exchange (LMX) theory, leaders devotes more attention to members of the in-group, assigning more challenging tasks and spending more one-to-one time with them.

    a. True

    b. False

14. Transformational leadership is characterized by which of the following?

    a. Idealized influence

    b. Inspirational motivation

    c. Intellectual stimulation

    d. Individualized consideration

    e. All of the above

15. _______________ explore the extent to which we distinguish leaders and nonleaders based on underlying assumptions, stereotypes, and beliefs.

LO 11.6 Discuss the power-distributing leadership perspectives of empowering, shared, and self-leadership

16. Leading by example, coaching, and participative decision making are behaviors of what type of leadership style?
    a. Empowering leadership
    b. Shared leadership
    c. Self-leadership
17. Empowering leadership is leadership distributed among groups to achieve organizational or team goals, or both.
    a. True
    b. False
18. Describe self-leadership.
19. What are the three main self-leadership strategies?

LO 11.7 Describe the values-based leadership perspectives of authentic, spiritual, servant, and ethical leadership

20. Which type of leadership places an emphasis on employees and the community rather than on oneself?
    a. Authentic
    b. Spiritual
    c. Servant
    d. Ethical
21. ____________ leaders strive to promote transparency, positive development, and greater self-awareness during their interactions with others.
    a. Authentic
    b. Spiritual
    c. Servant
    d. Ethical
22. Spiritual leadership has been linked to higher organizational commitment and productivity.
    a. True
    b. False
23. Which leadership style influences others through personal values, morals, and beliefs?
    a. Authentic
    b. Spiritual
    c. Servant
    d. Ethical

LO 11.8 Discuss leadership across cultures

24. ______________ leadership is the process of leading across different cultures.
25. Which of the following is NOT one of the six global leadership attributes perceived by business people worldwide to either contribute to or inhibit leadership?
    a. Charismatic
    b. Autonomous
    c. Intelligent
    d. Humane oriented
26. How many societies are included in the Project GLOBE study?
27. Which leadership attribute does the Anglo society find least important?
    a. Participative
    b. Self-protective
    c. Autonomous
    d. Team oriented

LO 11.9 Identify gender issues in the context of leadership

28. List three factors that can contribute to gender discrimination in the workplace.
29. Many organizations assess employee performance by the number of hours they work rather than productivity.
    a. True
    b. False

CHAPTER 12 SELF-TEST

LO 12.1 Discuss the concept of power and its relationship to leadership

1. __________ is the capacity to influence the actions of others.
2. Recent psychological research has suggested that coercive power is a less effective method for gaining power, and that true power lies in social intelligence.
    a. True
    b. False

LO 12.2 Identify the various sources of power

3. Two main sources of power are ____________ and ____________.
4. The degree to which a person has the right to ask others to do things that are considered within the scope of their authority is known as what type of organizational power?
    a. Legitimate
    b. Reward
    c. Coercive

5. This type of organizational power is often perceived to be negative and is used only as a last resort:
   a. Legitimate
   b. Reward
   c. Coercive
6. ____________ power is the ability to influence others through their desire to identify and be associated with them.
7. The ability to influence the behavior of others through the amount of knowledge or expertise possessed by an individual in which others depend is known as referent power.
   a. True
   b. False

LO 12.3 Describe tactics for influencing others

8. When a person tries to persuade another person to cooperate on the basis of friendship or by doing her a personal favor, it is known as:
   a. Rational appeal
   b. Inspirational appeal
   c. Upward appeal
   d. Personal appeal
9. ____________ ____________ occurs when a person uses the argument that the task has been requested by higher management or approaches high management directly to ask them to assist in the process of persuading others to cooperate.
   a. Rational appeal
   b. Inspiration appeal
   c. Upward appeal
   d. Personal appeal
10. An **exchange** is a person using the promise of rewards to provide incentive for another person to cooperate.
    a. True
    b. False
11. When a person cites the support of others as a reason for another person to agree to a request it is known as:
    a. Exchange
    b. Assertiveness
    c. Ingratiation
    d. Coalition building

LO 12.4 Outline the results of the various influence tactics

12. Which of the following is NOT one of the three basic outcomes of influence tactics?
    a. Commitment
    b. Reassessment
    c. Compliance
    d. Resistance

LO 12.5 Identify the causes and possible consequences of organizational politics

13. **Organizational politics** is behavior that is not formally sanctioned by the organization and that is focused on maximizing our self-interest, often at the expense of the organization or other employees.
    A. True
    B. False
14. People are more likely to engage in political behavior in organizations in which resources such as monetary rewards or promotions are limited.
    a. True
    b. False
15. Two examples of political behavior are ____ and ____ .
16. Organizational politics can be used for positive means when people possess ____________ ____________, the ability to understand and influence others for the good of the organization.

CHAPTER 13 SELF-TEST

LO 13.1 Describe the basic model of communication

1. _______ is the act of sharing, exchanging, or imparting information and ideas through a variety of channels.
2. The Shannon-Weaver Model of communication is based on two main components: the sender of the message (the source) and the receiver of the message.
   a. True
   b. False
3. Which of the following is NOT an example of **noise** in the communication model?
   a. Jargon
   b. Unknown language
   c. Construction work
   d. All the above are examples

LO 13.2 Compare the types of communication channels

4. Two examples of different communication channels are ___________communication and ___________ communication.
5. What are the advantages and disadvantages of oral communication?
6. ___________ ___________ is the capacity to communicate and understand information between people and organizations.

LO 13.3 Identify key barriers to effective communication

7. When the sender and receiver of a message have differing perceptions, it can result in a barrier to communication.

   a. True

   b. False
8. Which of the following is NOT a barrier to communication?

   a. Filtering

   b. Emotions

   c. Active listening

   d. Differing perceptions

LO 13.4 Describe types of communication networks within organizations

9. **Downward communication** occurs when messages are sent from the ________ levels of the organizational hierarchy to the ________ levels.
10. The transmission of messages established and approved by the organizational hierarchy is known as:

    a. Formal networks

    b. Informal networks
11. A **grapevine** is one of the main types of formal networks.

    a. True

    b. False
12. A ___________ is a group of people that broadcast information within their group.

LO 13.5 Discuss the elements of effective cross-cultural communication

13. **Ethnocentrism** is the tendency to believe your culture or ethnicity is ___________ to everyone else's.
14. Germany has a very **low-context culture**; Japan has a very **high-context culture**.

    a. True

    b. False
15. _____-context cultures leave much of the message unspecified while the rest is conveyed through body language, nonverbal cues, and the circumstances in which the communication is taking place.

CHAPTER 14 SELF-TEST

LO 14.1 Describe the basic characteristics of organizational culture

1. **Organizational culture** is a pattern of shared norms, rules, values, and beliefs that guide the ___________ and ___________of its employees.
2. The type of organizational culture very much predicates the chances of fitting in to an organization.

   a. True

   b. False
3. Which of the following is NOT an example of observable culture?

   a. Behaviors

   b. Structures

   c. Artifacts

   d. Values
4. The hierarchy culture has high flexibility and is externally focused.

   a. True

   b. False

LO 14.2 Discuss the various artifacts of organizational culture

5. ________ are objects that provide meaning about a culture.
6. **Organizational language** is certain words, metaphors, and expressions that the staff regularly use to ________ each other.

LO 14.3 Identify the functions of organizational culture

7. A company's shared understanding of the goals, tasks, and methods that need to be achieved is known as its:

   a. Observable culture

   b. External adaptation

   c. Internal integration

8. The cultural dysfunction that can make it difficult for two organizations to join together due to mismatched cultures resulting in a "culture clash" is
   a. Change hindrance
   b. Diversity hindrance
   c. Mergers and acquisitions hindrance
9. Which cultural dysfunction represents obstacles that limit the range of employees in organizations?
   a. Change hindrance
   b. Diversity hindrance
   c. Mergers and acquisitions hindrance

LO 14.4 Compare various types of organizational cultures

10. A ________ type of culture is typified by companies with employees who tend to keep to themselves, avoid socializing, and work as individuals rather than as part of a team.
11. Managers in the **ethical culture** need to be role models and communicate and train employees on how to behave in an ethical manner.
    a. True
    b. False
12. Which type of organizational culture focuses on building employee strengths, increasing morale, and providing rewards for good work?
    a. Communal
    b. Networked
    c. Mercenary
    d. Positive

LO 14.5 Contrast differing approaches for shaping organizational culture

13. ____________ is a way an organization communicates its values to employees.
14. When socialization is successful, employees have a clear understanding about their role and will have learned how to confidently carry out new tasks and skills.
    a. True
    b. False
15. Which of the following is NOT one of Feldman's three stages of organizational socialization?
    a. Anticipatory socialization
    b. Accommodation
    c. Acclimation
    d. Role management

CHAPTER 15 SELF-TEST

LO 15.1 Describe the basic concept of organizational strategy

1. **Organizational strategy** is the process of creating, evaluating, and implementing ________ and objectives to achieve long-term competitive success.
2. Which of the three levels of strategy focuses on how the different departments of the organization comply with the company's vision?
   a. Organizational
   b. Divisional
   c. Functional
3. When organizations try to maintain current products and services with a limited amount of innovation, they are using a(n) ________ strategy.
4. Which type of strategy describes the process by which organizations focus on stability and efficiency of their internal operations to protect their market from new competitors?
   a. Defender
   b. Analyzer
   c. Reactor
   d. Prospector

LO 15.2 Discuss organizational learning as a strategic process

5. What type of process involves observing and retaining the lessons attained from the experiences of others?
   a. Strategic learning
   b. Grafting
   c. Vicarious learning
   d. Standardization
6. Scanning is a process of hiring experts to bring their knowledge to a firm.
   a. True
   b. False

LO 15.3 Explain the phenomenon of globalization along with the opportunities and challenges it poses to organizations

7. The integration of economy, trade, and finance on an international scale is known as __________.

8. Globalization has been on the increase since the 1980s and has enhanced the flow of trade and investment between countries.

    a. True

    b. False

LO 15.4 Identify key ways in which organizations adapt their practices across cultures

9. A pattern of shared attitudes, values, and behaviors held by members of a particular group of people or society is called a(n) _________.
10. Which of the following is NOT one of Hofstede's five dimensions of measuring culture?

    a. Individualism

    b. Uncertainty

    c. Power distance

    d. Creativity
11. Two countries high in uncertainty avoidance are United States and Singapore.

    a. True

    b. False
12. The process of adapting certain functions to accommodate the language, culture, or governing laws of a country is known as ___________.

    a. Standardization

    b. Globalization

    c. Localization

LO 15.5 Describe how international assignments can be used for employee development

13. An expatriate is an employee who lives and works in a foreign country on a ___________ basis.
14. There are ___________ stages in cultural adaptation.
15. The first stage of cultural adaptation is

    a. Honeymoon

    b. Reintegration

    c. Autonomy

    d. Independence

CHAPTER 16 SELF-TEST

LO 16.1 Compare and contrast various conceptualizations of the change process

1. The four stages of the **DADA syndrome** are denial, anger, depression, and acceptance.

    a. True

    b. False
2. Of the three phases in Lewin's basic change model, in which phase do people start to make peace with their doubts and insecurities?

    a. Unfreezing

    b. Transforming

    c. Refreezing
3. According to Lewin's force field analysis, the drivers for change must be stronger than the restraining forces in order for the change to work.

    a. True

    b. False

LO 16.2 Identify the forces for change in organizations

4. Which of the following is an example of an **internal force** for change?

    a. Demographic characteristics

    b. Social pressures

    c. Technological advancements

    d. Job satisfaction
5. In order for an organization to be successful, it is more important to focus on internal forces for change than **external forces**.

    a. True

    b. False

LO 16.3 Describe where resistance to change comes from and how to reduce it

6. One of the main obstacles to implementing organizational changes is the _____________ to change.
7. Fear of the unknown, insecurity, and habit can be attributed to which source of resistance?

    a. Individual

    b. Organizational

    c. Additional
8. Which one of the following is NOT a source of **resistance to change**?

    a. Lack of understanding

    b. Differing goals

    c. Supporting modifications

    d. Uncertainty

9. ______________ is most commonly used when leaders desperately need everyone on board with the changes.

   a. Manipulation
   b. Participation
   c. Coercion
   d. Negotiation

LO 16.4 Describe the concept of organizational development in organizations

10. To cope with internal and external changes, many organizations use organizational development.

    a. True
    b. False

11. The basic OD model tends to follow three basic steps: __________, ____________, and progress monitoring.

12. **Organizational development (OD)** is a deliberately planned system that uses behavioral science knowledge to increase the _____________ and effectiveness of an organization.

LO 16.5 Identify types of OD change interventions

13. Changing reward systems, changing the culture, and reorganizing the structure itself are examples of what type of intervention?

    a. Task-technology
    b. People-focused
    c. Structural
    d. Sociotechnical

14. __________ training, also known as diversity training, is a type of program designed to improve the communication between groups of different genders, ages, races, religion, or sexual orientation.

15. Finding ways to change the attitudes, perceptions, and stereotypes that employees may have of each other is known as

    a. Process consultation
    b. Sociotechnical systems
    c. Sensitive training
    d. Intergroup development

CHAPTER 17 SELF-TEST

LO 17.1 Describe how organizational structure helps shape behavior in organizations

1. We define **organizational structure** as a framework of work roles that helps shape and support employee _________________.

2. The structure of an organization has a significant influence over the behavior of its employees.

   a. True
   b. False

LO 17.2 Define basic organizing concepts such as division of labor, chain of command, and span of control

3. Work specialization, also known as __________, is the degree to which jobs are divided into specific tasks.

4. The process of grouping people with related job duties, skills, and experiences into the same area within the overall organization structure is known as:

   a. Division of labor
   b. Chain of command
   c. Departmentalization
   d. Centralization

5. In a decentralized structure, organizations rely on the senior management to make decisions.

   a. True
   b. False

6. Which of the following is a formalized structure based on centralization and departmentalization?

   a. Mechanistic
   b. Organic

LO 17.3 Identify the types of organizational structures

7. Small organizations with one central authority figure who tends to make decisions usually use which type of structure?

   a. Matrix
   b. Functional
   c. Simple
   d. Divisional

8. Which type of structure groups employees according to the tasks they perform for the organization?

   a. Matrix
   b. Functional
   c. Simple
   d. Divisional

9. This type of structure is typically used in larger companies that tend to have offices in different geographic areas:

   a. Matrix
   b. Functional

c. Simple

d. Divisional

LO 17.4 Describe the organizational design process and its connection to organizational behavior

10. ______________ ___________ is the process of creating or changing a structure of an organization to integrate people, information, and technology.
11. Which of the following is the first step in the organizational design process?

    a. Setting the scene

    b. Business climate

    c. Data gathering

    d. Design evaluation

12. After gathering the needed data, what is the next step in the organizational design process?

    a. Business climate

    b. Implementing the design

    c. Evaluating the design

    d. Transforming the design

LO 17.5 Explain how technology can be integrated into organizational structure and design

13. The two main types of technology in the workplace are ________technology and _________ technology.
14. Researchers have shown that organizations that focus on both the technical side and the human side have a better chance of success.

    a. True

    b. False

15. _________ technology is the combination of processes, knowledge, and techniques that creates product or service value for an organization.

CHAPTER 1 SELF-TEST ANSWER KEY

1. Organizational behavior is a field of study focused on understanding, explaining, and improving attitudes of individuals and groups in organizations.
2. b: False. The three reasons are so you can explain it, predict it, and change it.
3. d
4. Tangible, intangible
5. b: False. Value, rareness, inimitability
6. Psychology, sociology, anthropology, social psychology
7. a
8. a: True
9. c
10. b
11. Any five of the following: globalization, economic factors, workforce diversity, customer service, people skills, innovation and change, ethics, sustainability
12. Workforce diversity exists when organizations foster working environments that do not discriminate against others regardless of gender, race, ethnicity, age, sexual orientation, and disability.
13. c
14. a: True
15. Individuals, teams, organizations
16. b: False. Individuals are the foundation of organizations
17. b
18. a. True
19. d.

CHAPTER 2 SELF-TEST ANSWER KEY

1. Diversity
2. c
3. a: True
4. Individual differences are an effort to find behavioral similarities and differences.
5. a: True
6. d
7. Personality traits
8. The origins of our personality traits have yet to be fully determined, and the nature versus nurture debate still abounds. Some people believe personality traits are inherited (nature) while others believe that the environment and situational factors (nurture) influence our personalities.
9. c
10. 16
11. b: False. The majority of the US population is the ISTJ personality type.
12. b
13. a
14. a: True
15. **Internal locus of control** is when people believe they are responsible for influencing events; whereas people with **external locus of control** believe outside influences are responsible for their fate.

16. Individuals high in proactive personality look for opportunities to change events and take action to ensure the desired change takes place.
17. a

CHAPTER 3 SELF-TEST ANSWER KEY

1. **Emotions** are intense feelings directed at a specific object or person. Emotions are numerous and intense, but they are usually fleeting, and short-lived. **Moods** are less intense and more generalized feelings not directed at a specific object or person. Moods last longer than emotions, and it can be difficult to identify the source of the negative feelings.
2. Positive
3. b: False. Moods last longer than emotions.
4. b:
5. **Surface acting** occurs when a person suppresses their true feelings while displaying the organizationally desirable ones. **Deep acting** involves efforts to change your actual emotions to better match the required emotions of the situation.
6. d
7. Cognitive appraisal, affective evaluation, behavioral intention
8. c
9. **Cognitive dissonance** occurs when there is inconsistency between a person's beliefs, attitudes or behaviors.
10. a: True.
11. **Organizational commitment** is the loyalty of an individual to the organization.
12. Counterproductive work behaviors (CWBs)
13. *Challenge stressors* are associated with workload, job demands, job complexity, and deadlines and positively related to motivation and performance. *Hindrance stressors* inhibit progress toward objectives. Examples include role ambiguity or conflict, hassles, red tape, and highly political environments. These stressors are negatively related to motivation and performance.
14. b: False. *Distress* involves high levels of stressors that have destructive and negative effects on effort and performance.
15. b: Problem-focused
16. Wellness

CHAPTER 4 SELF-TEST ANSWER KEY

1. c
2. The perceiver, the environment, the focal object
3. a
4. a: True
5. Expectations, expectations
6. b: False. The three types of determinants of attribution that influence our internal and external attributions are *distinctiveness*, consensus, and consistency.
7. d
8. a
9. a: – True
10. Operant
11. b: False. Reinforcement theory is the most fully developed theory of *operant* conditioning to date.
12. continuous, intermittent
13. b
14. a: True
15. b

CHAPTER 5 SELF-TEST ANSWER KEY

1. Motivation
2. b: False. The goal setting theory is an example of a process theory.
3. **Content theories** explain why people have different needs at different times and how these needs motivate behavior. **Process theories** describe the cognitive processes through which needs are translated into behavior.
4. b
5. Affiliation
6. c
7. a: True
8. d
9. c
10. Distributive, Procedural
11. a: True
12. a
13. Behavioral
14. Valence/Rewards

CHAPTER 6 SELF-TEST ANSWER KEY

1. Intrinsic
2. b: False. These are both examples of intrinsic motivation.
3. b
4. c
5. **Piece rate** is a pay plan in which workers are paid a fixed sum for each unit of production completed. **Merit pay** is a pay plan comprising of a pay rise which is linked directly to performance. **Bonus** is a pay plan that rewards employees for recent rather than historical performance.
6. Profit sharing
7. d
8. Skill variety, task identity, task significance, autonomy, and feedback
9. a: True
10. a
11. Competence
12. c
13. b: False. Although the two are similar, **free agents** are independent workers that supply organizations with short-term talent for projects or time-bound objectives and **part-time workers** are independent workers that supply organizations with part-time talent for projects or time-bound objectives.
14. b
15. **Flextime** means flexible working hours where you customize your own work hours within limits established by management. For example, you might work a 7:00 a.m. to 3:00 p.m. or 11:00 a.m. to 7:00 p.m. workday rather than the more traditional 9:00 a.m. to 5:00 p.m.

CHAPTER 7 SELF-TEST ANSWER KEY

1. Power
2. A **group** usually consists of three or more people who work independently to attain organizational goals. **Teams** comprise people who use their complementary skills to collaborate together in a combined joint effort.
3. b
4. a: True
5. d
6. a: True
7. b
8. **Pooled interdependence:** Each team member produces a piece of work independently of the other members. **Sequential interdependence**: One team member completes a piece of work and passes it on to the next member for their input, similar to an assembly line. **Reciprocal interdependence**: Team members work closely together on a piece of work, consulting with each other, providing each other with advice, and exchanging information.
9. Forming, storming, norming, performing, adjourning
10. a
11. Synergy
12. Any of the following answers are acceptable: A sense of shared purpose, plans, and goals; the confidence team members have in their own abilities to achieve objectives; a shared vision of how the work should be carried out; and constructive task-focused conflict that can help teams with their problem solving and decision making.
13. b: False. Groupthink is a major disadvantage to team decision making as the team members are more concerned with preserving harmony in the group than risking opinions that may cause conflict or offense.
14. c
15. a: True

CHAPTER 8 SELF-TEST ANSWER KEY

1. Programmed, non-programmed
2. b: False. **Programmed decisions** are automatic responses to routine and recurring situations.
3. c
4. evaluate
5. a: True
6. d
7. c
8. Hindsight
9. a
10. behavior
11. a: True.
12. b
13. a

14. c
15. Trustworthiness, Respect, Responsibility, Fairness, Caring, Citizenship

CHAPTER 9 SELF-TEST ANSWER KEY

1. Innovation
2. b
3. a: True
4. a: True
5. a
6. b: False. Practiced creativity is how people perceive the opportunities to apply these skills in the workplace.
7. d
8. d: False. This is the second step of the innovation process.
9. b
10. c
11. b
12. organizational structure
13. d
14. The idea that organizations are slow at keeping up with new emerging innovations, which puts them in danger of missing lucrative opportunities.

CHAPTER 10 SELF-TEST ANSWER KEY

1. Functional
2. c
3. antecedents of conflict, perceived/felt conflict, manifest conflict, outcomes of conflict
4. b
5. b: False. Compromising is a situation in which each party in a conflict concedes to give something of value.
6. Competing
7. honesty
8. a
9. a: True
10. c
11. b
12. Distributive
13. a: True
14. a: True

CHAPTER 11 SELF-TEST ANSWER KEY

1. Leadership
2. A formal leader is formally designated by the organization, such as a CEO; whereas an informal leader does not receive the same designation but may still be perceived by others as a leader.
3. Leaders, managers
4. a
5. c
6. b: False. *Empowering* leaders help to develop the individual skills and abilities of their followers so that they may utilize these skills to take ownership of their work in order to contribute to organizational performance.
7. b
8. c
9. d
10. b
11. a
12. Path–goal theory's four primary leadership styles are:
    - *Directive leadership*. This is leadership behavior that is characterized by implementing guidelines, managing expectations, setting definite performance standards, and ensuring that individuals follow rules.
    - *Supportive leadership*. This is a type of leadership behavior that is characterized by friendliness and concern for the welfare of others.
    - *Participative leadership*. This occurs when leaders consult with followers and consider their input in decision making.
    - *Achievement-oriented leadership*. This style of leadership behavior is characterized by setting challenging goals, improving performance, and assisting training.
13. a: True
14. e
15. Implicit leadership theories
16. a
17. b: False. **Shared leadership** occurs when leadership influence is distributed among groups to achieve organizational or team goals, or both.
18. **Self-leadership** is a process whereby people intentionally influence their thinking and behavior to achieve their objectives.

19. Behavior-focused, natural rewards, constructive thought
20. c
21. a
22. a: True
23. d
24. Cross-cultural
25. c
26. 62
27. c
28. Factors that contribute to gender inequality are leadership style, the unequal burden of family and career demands, unequal access to professional networks, discrimination, and stereotypes.
29. a

CHAPTER 12 SELF-TEST ANSWER KEY

1. Power
2. a
3. organizational and personal
4. a
5. c
6. Referent
7. b: False. Expert power is the ability to influence the behavior of others through the amount of knowledge or expertise possessed by an individual on which others depend.
8. d
9. c
10. a: True
11. d
12. b
13. a: True
14. a: True
15. Any of the following answers are acceptable: Ingratiation, self-promotion, strong influence tactics, coalition building, connections with powerful allies, taking credit for positive events and the success of others, and circumventing legitimate channels to secure resources that would be otherwise unattainable.
16. political skill

CHAPTER 13 SELF-TEST ANSWER KEY

1. Communication
2. b: True
3. d
4. Any of the following answers are acceptable: Oral, written, electronic, nonverbal
5. Talking to people in person or on the phone is an excellent way to network and build relationships; however, sometimes the informal nature of oral communication means that messages can get lost or misunderstood unless there is an attempt to record the conversation.
6. Channel richness
7. a: True
8. c
9. Upper, lower
10. a
11. b: False. A grapevine is one of the main forms of informal networks.
12. Cluster chain
13. superior
14. a: True
15. High

CHAPTER 14 SELF-TEST ANSWER KEY

1. attitudes, behaviors
2. a: True
3. d
4. b: False. The hierarchy culture has high control and is internally focused.
5. Symbols
6. motivate
7. b
8. c
9. d
10. fragmented
11. a: True
12. d
13. Socialization
14. a: True
15. c

CHAPTER 15 SELF-TEST ANSWER KEY

1. Decisions
2. b
3. Analyzer
4. a
5. c
6. b: False. Grafting is a process of hiring experts to bring their knowledge to the firm.
7. Globalization
8. a: True
9. Culture
10. d
11. b: False
12. c
13. Temporary
14. Five
15. a

CHAPTER 16 SELF-TEST ANSWER KEY

1. a: True
2. b
3. a: True
4. d
5. b: False. Although it is essential that organizations to respond to internal forces, it is just as important to look inside the organization at the external forces at play.
6. Resistance
7. a
8. c
9. c
10. a: True
11. Diagnosis, interventions
12. Efficiency
13. c
14. Sensitivity
15. d

CHAPTER 17 SELF-TEST ANSWER KEY

1. Behavior
2. a: True
3. Division of labor
4. c
5. b: False. In a decentralized organization, employees in the lower levels are given the power to make decisions and solve problems without seeking approval from senior management
6. a
7. c
8. b
9. d
10. Organizational design
11. b
12. d
13. Operations, Information
14. a: True
15. Operations

NAME INDEX

SUBJECT INDEX

SUBJECT INDEX